Understanding

AS/400® System Operations

Understanding AS/400 System Operations

Mike Dawson

Marge Hohly
IBM Certified Specialist
Cerritos College, Norwalk, CA.

PRESS

First Edition
Third Printing—March 2003

ISBN: 1-58347-015-8

MC Press, LLC
Corporate Offices
125 N. Woodland Trail
Double Oak, TX 75077 USA

Sales Offices
P.O. Box 4300
Big Sandy, TX 75755-4300
877-226-5394
www.MCPressOnline.com

For information on translations or book distributors outside the USA or to arrange bulk-purchase discounts for sales promotions, premiums, or fund-raisers, please contact MC Press, LLC at the above address.

V4R4

To

My daughter, Jeri, and her boys, Branden and Patrick

Mike

To

My parents, Lois and Robert, and my sister, Jeanne

Marge

Acknowledgments

We thank the following reviewers for their many helpful suggestions: Nick Vonada, Pennsylvania College of Technology; and Norman Seaton, El Centro College.

A special thank you goes to Phil Levinson, Jefferson Community College, for providing lab assignment materials. Also, special thanks go to Nora Laredo who helped prepare materials for this book and to members of the Computer and Information Sciences department at Cerritos College for their support.

Mike and Marge

CONTENTS

PREFACE

Understanding AS/400 System Operations is for students learning computer operations and administration on the AS/400 computer system. Offering a unique approach to learning AS/400 operations with extensive end-of-chapter, hands-on labs, self-tests, and review questions, this book prepares you from the ground up to be productive at AS/400 operations—using real-world situations.

The primary goal of this book is to teach you how to perform day-to-day operations on an AS/400 computer system. Operations include IPL, starting and stopping the system, backup and recovery, and system cleanup. Procedures covered are creating and maintaining user environments, device configuration and management, security implementation, work and data management, and TCP/IP configuration. Console operations include jobs, message handling, and working with spooled files and peripheral devices. Electronic Customer Support (ECS) and Program Temporary Fix (PTF) upgrades are introduced. Most topics include a hands-on lab.

Understanding AS/400 System Operations has 20 chapters, four appendices, and a glossary. At the front of the book, the Contents provides a road map from which students can get a quick overview of the concepts presented in each chapter. Each chapter is organized into the following sections:

1. Chapter objectives.
2. Chapter text material explaining AS/400 system operation concepts.
3. Chapter summary.
4. Key terms.
5. Review questions.
6. Self-test questions.
7. Lab assignments.

Chapter objectives are presented on the first page of each chapter to provide a quick overview of important concepts presented in the chapter. The objectives also inform readers what is expected of them and what material is most important.

The chapter text material explains AS/400 system operation concepts and gives examples of how they might be used in a business environment.

A chapter summary gives students an opportunity to review the major concepts presented in each chapter.

Each section of key terms provides an overview of important terms presented in the chapters. The sections provide a quick reference of new terms for students.

Review questions provide students with an opportunity to reinforce the concepts presented in the chapters. These questions may be used in four ways:

- For class discussion at the conclusion of a discussion of the chapter.
- As homework assignments at the conclusion of each chapter.
- As quizzes.
- As class reviews for examinations.

Students are provided with self-test questions to measure their understanding of the system operation concepts presented in the chapters. These questions consist of fill-in-the-blank, true-false, and illustrative system-operations questions.

With most chapters, several practice assignments are provided. These assignments require the use of the concepts presented in the chapter and give students an opportunity to apply their knowledge of skills introduced in the chapter.

The lab assignments supplement the chapter material and provide an opportunity for students to practice the different aspects of the AS/400 operations environment.

IBM Certification Testing

Understanding AS/400 System Operations prepares students for two IBM AS/400 certification exams: Test #052, AS/400 Associate System Operator Certification and Test #053, the AS/400 Professional System Operator.

Objectives of This Book

Upon completion of this book, you should be able to:

- Describe the functions of the operating system.
- Send messages and respond to inquiries.
- Use common CL commands.
- Manage jobs.
- Control work management.

- Describe security problems and solutions.
- Track and manage jobs on the system.
- Manage print functions.
- Identify various device configurations.
- Perform backup, restore, and PTFs.

INSTRUCTOR'S MANUAL

An Instructor's Manual has been prepared by Marge Hohly and has been tested for quality assurance. The manual is available to those colleges that adopt this book. Support materials include overhead transparency masters, a test bank, lab setup instructions, user environment material/definitions, lab submission sheets, and AS/400 objects required for labs.

TO THE READER

This book is appropriate for introductory computer students. Although no previous AS/400 experience is required, we suggest that, before studying AS/400 operations, students have some understanding of basic computer concepts. A course in AS/400 concepts or at least some exposure to the AS/400 computer system is recommended.

If you know another operating system, you might be able to proceed more quickly through the text. We hope you find the approach more conceptual than you might have experienced with other textbooks. Accordingly, we recommend that you read the text in sequence and practice each topic by completing the lab assignments at the end of each chapter. If you have studied a course in AS/400 concepts or at least have some exposure to the AS/400, you could consider skimming the first four to six chapters. However, you should complete the labs to confirm your knowledge of each topic area.

We welcome your comments, criticisms, and suggestions. Please submit suggestions by email at *textbooks@midrangecomputing.com*. Requests for reprint permissions should be addressed to the Permissions Department, Midrange Computing. For product-ordering information, visit our Web site at *www.midrangecomputing.com* or contact:

Wendy Quirk, Account Executive
Midrange Computing
5650 El Camino Real
Carlsbad, CA 92008
Telephone: 1-800-477-5665, ext. 213
email: *wquirk@midrangecomputing.com*

1

BACKGROUND OF THE AS/400

CHAPTER OBJECTIVES

Upon completion of this chapter, you should be able to:

- Describe the history of the AS/400.
- Describe the basic architecture of the AS/400 computer system.
- Describe the various parts of an AS/400 menu screen.
- Explain the purpose of the command line.

AN INTRODUCTION TO THE AS/400 ENVIRONMENT

The AS/400 computer system consists of a family of IBM "midrange" computers based on a single hardware/software architecture. From the beginning, it has represented a milestone in reliability, ease of use, and system integration not found in any other computer system.

The AS/400 is also a linch pin in IBM's System Application Architecture (SAA) connectivity scheme between mainframe, midrange, and personal computers. SAA is a unified approach to software design and interplatform communications. The SAA solution is based on a set of software interfaces, conventions, and protocols that provide a framework for designing and developing applications. Ultimately, the goal of SAA is an environment that is transparent to the user.

THE EVOLUTION OF IBM MIDRANGE COMPUTERS

The evolution of IBM minicomputers, now referred to as *midrange computers*, began with the announcement of the System/3 minicomputer system in June 1969. The System/3, which was the first computer system totally developed at the IBM plant in Rochester, Minnesota, was designed as a punched card-oriented computer system. Because mainframe computers controlled the high-end segment of the market, the System/3 was aimed at low-end commercial users running small-size batch applications.

Although the System/3 seems laughable by today's computer standards, its impact on the computer industry, like other Rochester efforts, cannot be overemphasized. It represented significant advances in the technology of its time. Before the System/3, computer architecture design took place in New York City and New England. All computers followed the same model for hardware design originally developed at MIT.

Rochester is located in cold, southern Minnesota, remote enough that its designers were free to rethink how computers should work. The System/3 was the first, the Adam or Eve, of the IBM midrange line, and it represented two new concepts in computing:

- A small, efficient computer would sell as well as the huge, expensive behemoths that the mainframes had become.
- The single computer model that had been the industry standard was not the only option.

The System/32 was the System/3's offspring. Announced in January 1975, it was still card-based, but it also touted direct keyboard data entry and a screen display that could present up to six rows of text 40 characters long. The System/32 was primarily single-user, although toward the end of its life cycle, IBM offered a model that supported five data-entry terminals simultaneously.

In April 1977, IBM announced the System/34—the first *multiuser minicomputer* system in the world. The system was designed to meet the demand for a low-cost computer system that provided interactive multiuser facilities and managed multiple local and remote workstations, each being up to 5,000 feet away from the computer. The System/34 quickly became the most installed computer system in the world, boasting more installations than the mighty mainframe. IBM began to see that the minicomputer was not going away.

The IBM Rochester facility was never one to rest on its successes, however. While the other midrange computers were enjoying such popularity, IBM began a secret project in 1975. They again threw away all computer architecture models, even their own, and started a new design. This became the System/38 that was announced in 1978. When the first models shipped, it turned out they were very slow. IBM did not want the System/38 to be known for anything negative, so they did the unheard of and pulled the System/38 off the market until performance was achieved. It was not until 1980 that System/38s started to be installed.

This System/38 architectural design represented a divergence from its S/3X predecessors, offering several innovative concepts. One concept was *machine independence*. Prior to this, when a computer company came out with a new processor chip, customers had no choice but to replace their existing hardware with new. This implied converting existing data and programs. So every couple of years, customers had a major replacement and conversion project. The System/38 was designed so that the hardware could be changed at any time in the future with no impact to the customer.

Another concept pioneered in the System/38 was the large amount of built-in functions. For the first time, customers received a computer that already contained a relational database, superior security system, extensive backup/recovery tools, performance, journaling, and other functions. Other concepts unique to the System/38 were an advanced operating system and *object-based architecture*. Object-based architecture is very similar to object-oriented architecture. The difference between them is IBM disabled the object-oriented functions that caused problems. The cost was relatively small, but that is why the machine is referred to as object-based. We will discuss objects more in this chapter but, for now, think about how advanced the System/38 was. It took the rest of the industry until 1990 before the idea of object-orientation even caught on, and then it was years before it found its way into anything commercial. But, starting with the System/38, IBM midrange customers had an object-based architecture.

For its time, the System/38 was fairly pricey for midrange computer customers, so IBM developed the original System/3-based computer line as a low-end offering. In May 1983, while the System/38 was getting all the headlines, IBM announced the System/36, the successor to the System/34. Surprising to IBM, most System/34 customers elected to upgrade to the System/36 rather than the System/38. The migration was much easier and cheaper. System/38 customers tended to be new customers to IBM's midrange computers.

The System/38 was a giant leap in the evolution of computer genealogy, and it had some unforeseen limitations that affected its upward growth. While the System/38 had been touted as hardware independent, it only was to a point. In 1985, IBM started, under code name "Silverlake," development of the successor to the System/38. Silverlake would be the computer that would carry IBM midrange customers into the next millennium and beyond.

In June 1988, IBM announced the first *Application System/400 (AS/400)*, the B-series that began shipping in September 1988. The first AS/400s did not seem as radical a change from the System/38 at first, but customers did notice dramatic speed and capacity improvements immediately. Over the years, speed and capacity increased once a year, at a rate of about 10 percent per year. The advantage was that any IBM AS/400 that was upgraded to the latest release could expect a 10 percent growth in its computing power without having to change equipment. That growth matched typical business growth. The claim, though, that the AS/400 was hardware-independent remained untested until 1995.

One aspect of the original AS/400 computer architecture was that the instruction set that its processor used was complex—the computer was known as a *complex instruction set computer (CISC)*. That meant that a single instruction carried with it as much detail as was needed to execute. The alternative was a reduced instruction set or *reduced instruction set computer (RISC)*.

Actually, there is nothing reduced about a RISC machine; it has as much functionality as a CISC computer. The instruction lengths on a RISC machine are all equal, where the instruction lengths on a CISC machine are variable and can be quite large. A computer designed to process a known instruction length can be many times more efficient than one designed to handle variable length instructions. For instance: When taking a taxi across town; using the CISC method, you would say, "Take me to the airport," and sit back and enjoy the ride. Using the RISC method, you would issue continual instructions, "Turn left at the next light." "Slow down here." "Now turn right." CISC is easier, but RISC may get you where you are going faster and more directly. Besides, with CISC, you need a driver who knows his way around, while with RISC, you can use any driver.

The CISC-to-RISC migration was the biggest undertaking of the AS/400 since its birth. Remember that one of the major promises of the System/38 was hardware independence? Some people in the computer world were critical that System/38 customers were forced to sell their old equipment and purchase a new AS/400. The 38-to-400 change did not show customers true machine independence, but the CISC-to-RISC change did. Changing the processor architecture was an undertaking unparalleled in the history of computers, and it proved AS/400's claim to machine independence. There was more to the change than the instruction set; the new processor was going from a basic 48-byte word (that is bytes, not bits) to 64-byte basic addressing. This was more than a processor upgrade; this was a complete architecture change.

The AS/400's capacity to handle this change without requiring its customers to go through either a program or database conversion proved the AS/400 to be a true hardware-independent computer. Customers only had to replace a board, and in some cases, increase disk capacity and memory slightly; and they had the next generation of AS/400 installed. They did not have to sell one computer and buy another; they did not have to copy programs off and recompile them; and they did not have to take large database files to flat files and reload them on another machine. Except in very unusual circumstances, all AS/400 customers made the migration over a weekend.

The AS/400 was not just basking in glory—IBM renewed it every year with a rich set of new features and functions. It also broadened its market to the point that the AS/400 range of current models went from a low price of $7,000 to somewhere around $2 million. Except for storage and speed differences, every AS/400 is identical in how it executes its programs and operates on the data it supports. Any size business can get into an AS/400 at any level and grow to any level.

While all this was going on, there was a large group of customers fiercely loyal to the System/36 that came out in 1983. Not a database machine, the System/36 still boasted very low cost of ownership, reliability, and ease of use. Even though the System/38 (and the AS/400) could support System/36 customers' applications and the machine's operating system directly, many refused to make the jump to AS/400.

With the continued popularity of and demand for the System/36 in the user community, IBM developed an AS/400-based alternative. It announced the AS/400 Advanced 36 in 1994. Available today for those customers, the Advanced 36 uses state-of-the-art 64-bit RISC technology just like its big brother.

Just to add a few more sprinkles on the AS/400 cake—in 1994, IBM Rochester foresaw the tremendous business potential that the Internet would offer. To meet the growth ahead of the rest, IBM developed a new series of AS/400s known as the Enhanced series, or e-series. This line was formally announced in August 1997. The new Enhanced series offers high performance through models equipped with up to twelve individual processors. For example, the top-of-the-line AS/400 e-server has a twelve-way processor. Multiple processor computers are referred to as n-way.

Every major announcement from IBM breaks new ground. This was the first time IBM offered packages of software and hardware preconfigured and preloaded. With this approach, the customer literally unpacked and plugged in the AS/400, and they had a powerful Internet server.

Collectively, the System/3, System/32, System/34, System/36, and System/38 are known as the System/3X family of midrange computers.

AS/400 ARCHITECTURE

LAYERED DESIGN CONCEPT

The key to the AS/400's uniqueness starts with its architecture. It boasts a layered design concept that is one factor that distinguishes it from traditional computers. This concept isolates machine hardware and system software through a series of horizontal interfaces as shown in Figure 1-1. This layering is the key to the AS/400's machine independence. The layered design allows low-level functions to be replaced by improved technology at any time, yet causes minimal disruption to the high-level software.

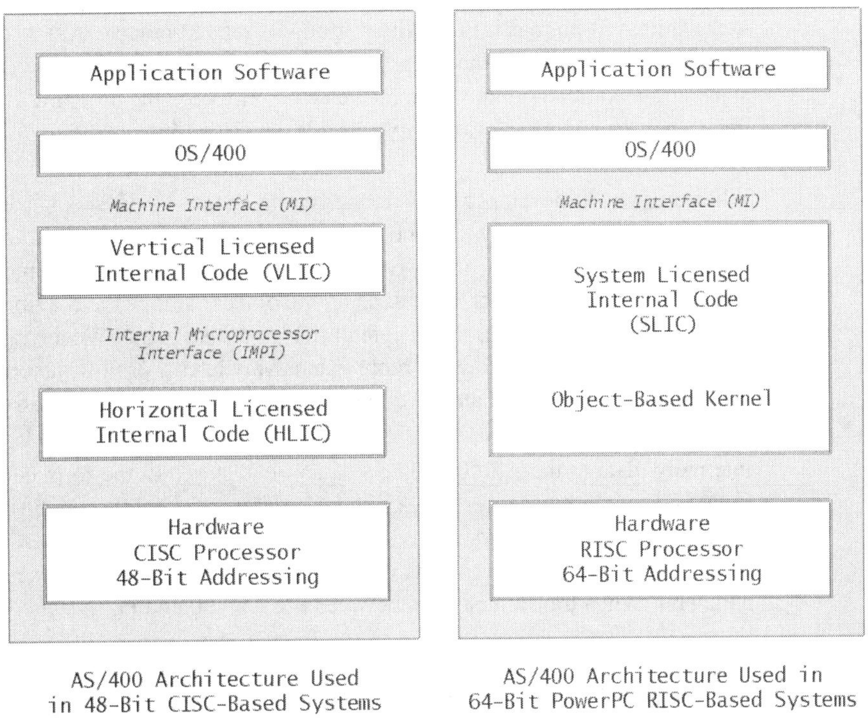

Figure 1-1: AS/400 layered software architecture.

When you refer to items at or near the top (application software) layer, you are at the high level of the architecture. Conversely, the bottom layers are referred to as low-level architecture. LIC means licensed internal code. The vertical licensed internal code (VLIC), horizontal licensed internal code (HLIC), and system licensed internal code (SLIC) layers are collectively referred to as the machine interface (MI). Generally, AS/400 items are referred to as being above or below the MI layer.

In plain language, VLIC translates instructions passed to the MI. It hands the translated instructions to the HLIC that deals directly with the hardware. When IBM was coming out with the RISC architecture, it rewrote millions of lines of the MI layer and, in the process, combined VLIC and HLIC into a single layer, SLIC. By the way, the SLIC layer is written in C++ and makes heavy use of objects. This layer is sometimes referred to as the *kernel* of the machine.

DATA STORAGE AND AS/400 OBJECTS

The AS/400 is an object-based computer, meaning that everything is stored as an object. An object can best be described as an entity that exists on the AS/400 upon which procedures can be performed by the AS/400. There are many types of objects that can be stored on the AS/400. Some of the more common objects discussed in this book include programs, data files (databases), and libraries. Object names consist of the given name concatenated with the object type. For example, a file object (file type *FILE) could be named OBJ1. A program has an object type *PGM associated with it. Because each object name is a concatenation of the name and the type, you could have a file named OBJ1 and a program named OBJ1, and the AS/400 would not get confused—it would know one is a file and one is a program.

This object type and name association is implicit; AS/400 professionals are not often aware of it. More commonly, objects on an AS/400 can be grouped into libraries. A library can be anything the user wants it to be, but it is usually a group of related objects. ARLIB could be the name of the library that contains all the programs and files that make up the Accounts Receivable (AR) application. Another organization may elect to only keep the programs in ARLIB and have another library named ARDATA for the application's database files.

When an AS/400 developer refers to a program or file, he often concatenates the library and file together to identify the object and its location. If the developer wanted the master file named MASTFILE in the ARDATA library, ARDATA/MASTFILE would be entered. Doing this explicitly is optional—many people get by with using the object name without a library qualifier. This works because the AS/400 will assign a default library to that name. We are getting ahead of ourselves, though; we will discuss libraries more extensively later. For now, just remember that objects are implicitly associated with an object type and explicitly or implicitly associated with a library.

Internally, data in the AS/400 objects database is stored in the form called the Extended Binary Coded Decimal Interchange Code (EBCDIC). This is different from the internal form used in PCs, called the American Standard Code for Information Interchange (ASCII). The two forms were defined by separate organizations in the 1950s to represent alphanumeric characters (letters and numbers). When transferring data between the AS/400 and PCs, data conversion must be done.

SINGLE-LEVEL STORAGE

Another distinguishing factor between traditional computer systems and the AS/400 is the AS/400's single-level storage. With single-level storage, the AS/400 makes no distinction between disk storage and main memory and, thus, treats main memory and disk storage as if they are one vast region in main memory. Files stored on disk are treated as addressable memory. Therefore, all disk and main storage appear as one seamless linear address space and the system accesses all data in the same way.

Single-level storage is unique to AS/400s. Other computers first identify the region in memory or disk storage, then the address within the region before attempting to access an object.

Single-level storage addressing means that at a low level, below the MI, a single virtual address space exists. This storage space encompasses both main storage and disk storage and is large enough to contain all data to be stored on the system. Functions operating above this MI see data as objects that are being stored in contiguously addressable locations within the auxiliary storage and main storage.

Although the AS/400 can very quickly locate objects through this addressing scheme, it still makes the distinction of objects in addresses that are executable versus those in addresses that are only for storage. This is because operations cannot be performed on an object that is not in main storage—so the system moves a part or all of the object from auxiliary storage into main storage as it is needed, and moves it back into an auxiliary storage when it is not needed.

An entire object does not have to be in main storage when active; using *virtual storage*, the machine automatically divides a program or storage area into blocks called *pages*. Only the pages that are needed at the time are kept in main storage. When a new page is needed, pages in memory that have not been used in a while are placed in a holding area on the disk to make room for space for pages that will be used. The actual process of moving pieces of programs or data between memory and the Direct Access Storage Device (DASD) is called *paging*. Machines that use paging increase the efficiency of their memory many times and are called virtual computers. Sometimes the memory is referred to as virtual storage. Virtual storage gives the appearance that the system has more than enough main storage for all active jobs at all times.

TYPES OF COMPUTER PROGRAMS

A program is a set of instructions that enables a computer to process data. There are two types of computer programs: system programs that control the overall operations of the computer, and application programs that actually perform tasks required by users. The term used to describe all types of programs is called software.

OPERATING SYSTEM SOFTWARE

All programs run under the control of an operating system. An operating system is itself a series of programs that monitor and control the overall operations of the computer. The programs that comprise the operating system are normally supplied by the manufacturer and are designed to be the interface between the users of the computer system and the lower-level hardware layer.

The AS/400's operating system is called Operating System/400, or OS/400. OS/400 is unique to the AS/400; it does not run on any other computer. In addition, it is a rich operating system, providing many integrated features that form the foundation of the computer system. OS/400 provides a complete, fully integrated set of batch and interactive work management functions that make processing application programs efficient and productive. It controls the execution of programs and provides services such as controlling resources, scheduling jobs, controlling input and output, and managing data. Among these built-in features is its powerful DB2/400 database and support facilities, interactive workstation support, security, software development support, and extendable architecture. In short, OS/400 is a resource manager: it allocates the computer's processor, main storage (memory), I/O devices, and data resources to the various users in the most efficient manner possible. OS/400 also provides the following services: user interfaces, security, work management, message handler, communication support, job control language, object management, database management, spooling support, and Electronic Customer Support (ECS).

One of the most powerful features of the AS/400 is that it is controlled through a single, consistent control language that is supported by the operating system. Regardless of which AS/400 model an organization has, they all use the same operating system. They function in the same way, whether it's an earlier model or the new Enhanced series.

APPLICATION PROGRAMS

The top level of the AS/400 architecture is the application software. It is at this level that software developers develop application programs. An application program operates on input data and converts it to meaningful output information. A computer can process data only as efficiently and effectively as it is programmed. Figure 1-2 diagrams how a computer processes data.

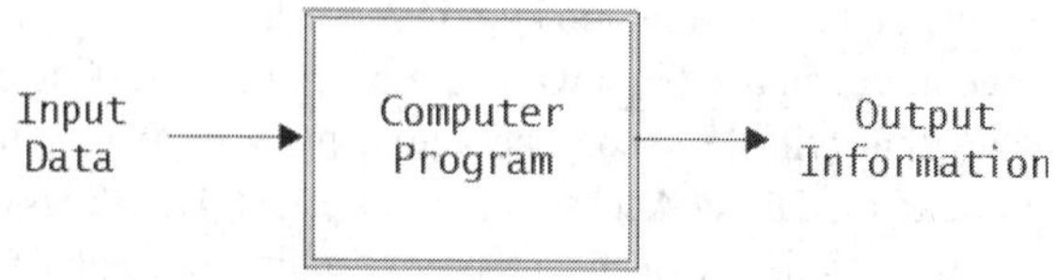

Figure 1-2: The basic flow of computer data.

The set of instructions in an application program is written by a computer professional called a programmer or software developer. Some application programs are designed to obtain a quick solution to a onetime problem; others run periodically on a regularly scheduled basis to provide users with the information they need. An application program to display the average grade for a set of exams entered as incoming data would be an example of a onetime job. An application program to print student transcripts each semester would be an example of a program that would be run periodically or on a regular basis.

A computer program generally computerizes business procedures. A set of related programs forms an application. A set of applications is called an *information system*.

There are two major types of programs on any computer: interactive and batch. Programs that accept input data from a workstation, immediately process that data, and do something with the output (display it back out and/or write it to disk) are *interactive programs*. An example of an interactive program would be an order entry program. As orders are received, they are immediately entered into the computer for processing and shipping. *Batch programs* process large volumes of input at periodic intervals. For these types of batch applications, the data stored in a file is processed from beginning to end. Batch programs typically run when interactive programs are at a minimum—at night and on weekends, for example. Examples of batch programs are daily balance or reconciliation programs, and monthly processing programs.

INTEGRATED LANGUAGE ENVIRONMENT (ILE)

The Integrated Language Environment (ILE) allows software developers to include small, reusable code modules, written in different languages, that call each other from within a single program. The addresses of each module are resolved at compile time rather than dynamically as the program executes, thus speeding the execution process. The result is improved performance since the modules can be written in the appropriate language suitable for each different module.

Modular programming means that instead of writing one large program, applications are developed as separate, smaller units or *modules*. This provides more flexibility in the development process, allows easier integration into third-party software packages, and keeps down maintenance costs.

ACCESSING THE AS/400 COMPUTER SYSTEM

USER PROFILE

Before signing onto the AS/400, every user must obtain a *user ID* and *password*. Normally, a system administrator or security officer creates the user ID (user profile). The user ID uniquely identifies an individual to the AS/400 and is the user's signature.

A password is used in conjunction with the user ID to identify a user to the AS/400. It is a secret name that the user assigns to his or her user ID so that no one else can sign onto the AS/400 using that person's user ID. Unlike the user ID, users should not know one another's passwords. The secret password prevents others from breaking into a person's AS/400 account. Change your password on a regular basis.

THE AS/400 SIGN-ON PROCESS

The sign-on screen shown in Figure 1-3 is used to enter the necessary data into the AS/400 so it can identify a user of the system.

```
                              Sign On
                                   System . . . . . :   BLUE400
                                   Subsystem . . . . :   QINTER
                                   Display . . . . . :   QAPDEV0001

          User . . . . . . . . . . . . . .  __________
          Password . . . . . . . . . . . .
          Program/procedure . . . . . . . .  __________
          Menu . . . . . . . . . . . . . .  __________
          Current library . . . . . . . . .  __________




                                 (C) COPYRIGHT IBM CORP. 1980, 1994.
```

Figure 1-3: An AS/400 sign-on screen.

To sign onto the AS/400, enter your user ID on the line identified as user. Press either the Field Exit key (the right Ctrl key) or Field Advance key (the Tab key) to move the cursor to the password field. Then enter your password on the line identified as Password and press Enter. You should change your password often for security reasons. It is the password that prevents others from stealing your identity and signing onto your unique AS/400 account.

Once you enter the data into the sign-on screen and press Enter, the system verifies that you are an authorized user of the system by checking your user ID name and password. If you are authorized, you are signed onto the AS/400 and an initial screen appears. The initial screen will usually be the AS/400 Main Menu screen, but it can be a screen specified in your user profile.

THE AS/400 SIGN-OFF PROCESS

Once signed onto the AS/400, there are two long lines at the bottom of the screen marked with a separator symbol: ===>. These lines actually make one very long line known as the *command line.* Get to know this line, as most AS/400 commands and menu options are taken by entering something on this line. There are two ways to sign off the AS/400:

1. If you are at a menu screen that has a sign-off option, enter the option number on the command line and press Enter. The AS/400 Main Menu screen contains an option 90 for sign off. To sign off from this menu, enter 90 on the command line and press Enter.

2. If you are at a screen that has a command line at the bottom, enter signoff or *signoff* on the command line and press Enter.

> **Note:**
>
> The OS/400 operating system is not case sensitive when entering commands, so signoff is the same as entering SIGNOFF.

LAB #1: THE BACKGROUND OF THE AS/400

Upon completion of this lab, you should be able to:

- Demonstrate how to sign on and sign off the AS/400 computer system.
- Change your password.
- Navigate the AS/400 menu system.

Before beginning this lab, make sure your workstation (microcomputer) is connected to the AS/400. Since there are many different ways to connect a workstation to the AS/400, we will not discuss the various possibilities here. If you need instructions or help getting to the sign-on screen, ask your instructor for assistance.

NAMING CONVENTIONS FOR THIS LAB

Most organizations establish naming convention rules that must be followed within the user environment. These rules are established to make maintaining the AS/400 easier for operators and system administrators. They normally apply to the creation of user profiles, output queues, libraries, and so on. Since there are certain objects that must be named uniquely (libraries are one example), it is important that you follow the naming rules at your location.

To establish a user environment that follows the naming conventions of your location, Figure L1-1 is provided. Your instructor will provide you with the information needed to complete the table. In this way, you will have preassigned names to use as you establish your environment.

During the lab, every time you encounter one of the identifier names that begin with `user` (`userID`, `userLIB`, `userOUTQ`), substitute user with your assigned name. As you complete the lab assignment, you will create and modify your environment to reflect your specific assigned names.

	Identifier Name: Identified in Commands as:	Your Assigned Name:
Profile (User ID)	USERID	
Library Name	USERLIB	
Output Queue	USEROUTQ	

Figure L1-1: Naming conventions.

SIGNING ON AND OFF THE AS/400 COMPUTER SYSTEM

When a user signs onto the AS/400, a *work session* is started. A work session is considered the time from when a user signs onto the system to the time he or she signs off the system. Before you can establish a work session on the AS/400, you must sign on, or identify yourself, to the computer. The sign-on screen shown in Figure L1-2 is used to enter the necessary data into the AS/400 so it can identify which user is signing onto the system.

AS/400 SIGN ON

As shown in Figure L1-2, the sign-on screen is a specific screen that allows users to identify themselves to the AS/400.

- System information is displayed in the upper-right corner of the screen.
  - What is the system name of the AS/400? ______________________
  - Which subsystem is your interactive job running in? ______________
  - What is the name assigned to the display station? ______________

```
                              Sign On
                                    System . . . . . :   BLUE400
                                    Subsystem . . . . :   QINTER
                                    Display . . . . . :   QPADEV0001

        User . . . . . . . . . . . . . . ___________
        Password . . . . . . . . . . . .
        Program/procedure . . . . . . . . ___________
        Menu . . . . . . . . . . . . . . ___________
        Current library . . . . . . . . . ___________

                              (C) COPYRIGHT IBM CORP. 1980, 1994.
```

Figure L1-2: AS/400 sign-on screen.

The cursor is automatically positioned at the USER field. To begin the sign-on procedure:

- Enter `userID` (user ID for your profile) in the `User` field. Do not press any other keys (i.e., Enter key or Field Exit key) at this time.

Note:

Normally, you would press the Field Exit key or the Tab key next and continue by entering your password. Before we continue, however, let us distinguish between the Enter and Field Exit keys.

With the cursor located at the end of the USER field:

- Press Enter.

You see the sign-on screen similar to Figure L1-3.

```
                                 Sign On
                                        System . . . . . :   BLUE400
                                        Subsystem . . . . :  QINTER
                                        Display . . . . . :  QPADEV0001

                User . . . . . . . . . . . . . . ___________
                Password . . . . . . . . . . . .
                Program/procedure . . . . . . . . ___________
                Menu . . . . . . . . . . . . . . ___________
                Current library . . . . . . . . . ___________

CPF1107 - Password not correct for user profile.
```

Figure L1-3: An AS/400 sign-on screen with invalid password error message.

Notice the error message `CPF1107 - Password not correct for user profile` at the bottom of the screen. This message indicates that the user pressed Enter and sent the data to the AS/400 with an invalid password. Sending the sign-on screen to the AS/400 without entering a password is the same as sending an invalid password.

There are three keys strongly associated with AS/400 screen entry that are often confused. These are:

- Field Exit: Pressing the Exit key advances the cursor to the next available field (top to bottom, left to right). If the cursor is in the middle of the field and there is old data present, the old data will be wiped out. If the field contains data that is to be right-adjusted (like numeric data), pressing this key will perform the adjustment.

- Field Advance (or Tab): The Field Advance key acts like a tab. It advances the cursor to the next available input field (top to bottom, left to right). Adjustments and data-clearing do not take place.
- Enter: When the Enter key is pressed, the screen's current contents are sent to the AS/400. The cursor returns to the top-left field (unless the program positions it on another field). This is the only time screen data goes into the AS/400. Other computers send each keystroke into their hosts; the AS/400 sends a screen at a time and only does so when this key is pressed.

If Enter is pressed from the screen shown in Figure L1-3 instead of the Field Exit key or Field Advance key (Tab key) after entering the user ID, the AS/400 will respond with this error message. The Enter key is pressed only after all of the data required for the screen has been entered.

Remember to press either the Field Exit key or the Field Advance key (Tab key) to move from field to field on the screen. The Enter key should be pressed only when the entire screen needs to be sent to the AS/400.

In this example, Enter was pressed after entering the user ID without entering a password, which is the same as entering an invalid password.

To correct the invalid CPF1107 password error:

- Reenter user ID and press the Field Exit key (or Tab key).

Notice that the cursor exits the USER field and moves to the Password field.

- Enter your password. (Your initial password will be the same as your user ID, and you will be required to change this password when you initially sign on.)

Note:

If you make an error while entering your user ID or password, tab to the beginning of the User field and reenter your user ID. Press the Field Exit key to delete everything from your last character to the end of the line and move to the Password field. Enter your password and press Enter.

Once you enter the data into the sign-on screen and press Enter, the system verifies that you are an authorized user of the system by checking your user ID name and password. If you have entered the correct user ID and password, you are now signed onto the AS/400. Normally, your initial screen either will be the AS/400 Main Menu screen shown in Figure L1-5 or a screen assigned in your user profile by the system administrator. In this case, however, you are signing on for the first time and are being prompted to change your password with the screen in Figure L1-4.

The only time the AS/400 will prompt you to change your password in this manner is if you are signing on for the first time, when your password has expired, or when the security person has marked the password as expired. Usually when the system administrator creates user profiles, he or she will specify that the password must be changed upon signing on for the first time.

CHANGING YOUR INITIAL PASSWORD

When you initially sign onto the AS/400, you will be prompted to change your password. Thus, when you press Enter after entering your user ID and password, Figure L1-4 appears.

```
                              Change Password

 Password last changed . . . . . . . . . . :   99/09/04

 Type choices, press Enter.

   Current password  . . . . . . . . . . . .   userID

   New password  . . . . . . . . . . . . . .   bigblue

   New password (to verify)  . . . . . . . .   bigblue




 F3=Exit          F12=Cancel
```

Figure L1-4: Change Password screen with sample field values.

Your initial password was userID, the same as your user ID. You are going to change the initial password to BIGBLUE. This will be a temporary password. Later in this lab, you will have an opportunity to change the password to a password of your choice.

Remember that you must enter the new password the same both times. You must also press Enter only after all three fields have been entered.

Note:

None of the information shown in bold print in Figure L1-4 will be visible on the screen.

THE AS/400 MAIN MENU SCREEN

Once the AS/400 has verified your user ID and password, the sign-on procedure is complete. The first screen you normally see is the AS/400 Main Menu screen as shown in Figure L1-5. Depending upon your user profile setup and security restrictions, your AS/400 Main Menu screen may contain fewer options.

```
MAIN                          AS/400 Main Menu
                                                          System:   BLUE400
 Select one of the following:

      1. User tasks
      2. Office tasks
      3. General system tasks
      4. Files, libraries, and folders
      5. Programming
      6. Communications
      7. Define or change the system
      8. Problem handling
      9. Display a menu
     10. Information Assistant options
     11. Client Access tasks

     90. Sign off

 Selection or command
 ===> ____________________________________________________________________

 F3=Exit   F4=Prompt   F9=Retrieve   F12=Cancel   F13=Information Assistant
 F23=Set initial menu
 (C) COPYRIGHT IBM CORP. 1980, 1994.
```

Figure L1-5: AS/400 Main Menu screen.

The AS/400 Main Menu screen is quite different from the sign-on screen. Menu screens like the AS/400 Main Menu screen are divided into several elements.

In the upper-left corner of the menu screen is the menu name that has been assigned to the menu. As you can see, Main is used as the menu name for the AS/400 Main Menu screen. This screen name is used to distinguish this menu from other menus. We will see later how this name can be used to quickly jump to a particular menu. The menu title, AS/400 Main Menu, is located in the center of the screen header and describes the purpose of the screen. In the upper-right corner of the screen is the system name, BLUE400 on our system, which should be the same system name shown on the sign-on screen.

In the middle of the screen is the numbered list of menu options. This list identifies which functions can be performed from this menu.

The Selection or command ===> lines are located after the menu options near the bottom of the screen. This is where you key in your selection from the menu. In addition to menu selections, commands can be entered that allow users to control the operations of the system. These commands are part of the operating system's Control Language (CL).

Below the command line, at the bottom of the screen, is a list of function keys that are active for this screen. By active, we mean that only those function keys identified in the function key area can be used with this screen. Pressing a function key not listed will result in the system message `Function key not allowed`.

Below the list of function keys and their descriptions is a message line. In the example, there are no messages and it contains the IBM copyright notice. This message line is the line that the system will use to communicate to the user.

We will examine how menu screens can be used in the next section; but first, let us see how to sign off the AS/400.

SIGNING OFF THE AS/400

We will illustrate the sign-off procedure here so you will have the necessary information about signing off the AS/400 if the need arises before you finish this lab in its entirety.

You can sign off the AS/400 by entering 90 on any menu screen that has the `90 Sign off` option, such as the AS/400 Main Menu screen in Figure L1-6. To sign off:

- Enter 90 on the Selection or command ===> line.
- Press Enter.

Once you press Enter, your work session ends and the system returns you to the AS/400 sign-on screen that was displayed in Figure L1-2.

```
MAIN                             AS/400 Main Menu
                                                            System:   BLUE400
 Select one of the following:

      1. User tasks
      2. Office tasks
      3. General system tasks
      4. Files, libraries, and folders
      5. Programming
      6. Communications
      7. Define or change the system
      8. Problem handling
      9. Display a menu
     10. Information Assistant options
     11. Client Access tasks

     90. Sign off

 Selection or command
 ===> 90
 ____________________________________________________________________________
 F3=Exit   F4=Prompt   F9=Retrieve   F12=Cancel   F13=Information Assistant
 F23=Set initial menu
 (C) COPYRIGHT IBM CORP. 1980, 1994.
```

*Figure L1-6: Entering **90** on the command line to sign off the AS/400.*

You may also sign off the AS/400 by entering the Signoff (SIGNOFF) command on any command line. Figure L1-7 illustrates how to enter the SIGNOFF command on the command line to sign off the AS/400. To use this method:

- Enter `signoff` or `SIGNOFF` on the command line.
- Press Enter.

```
MAIN                           AS/400 Main Menu
                                                             System:   BLUE400
 Select one of the following:

      1. User tasks
      2. Office tasks
      3. General system tasks
      4. Files, libraries, and folders
      5. Programming
      6. Communications
      7. Define or change the system
      8. Problem handling
      9. Display a menu
     10. Information Assistant options
     11. Client Access tasks

     90. Sign off

 Selection or command
 ===> signoff
 
 F3=Exit   F4=Prompt   F9=Retrieve   F12=Cancel   F13=Information Assistant
 F23=Set initial menu
 (C) COPYRIGHT IBM CORP. 1980, 1994.
```

Figure L1-7: Entering `signoff` *on the command line to sign off the AS/400.*

You now know the sign-on and sign-off procedures for the AS/400. Sign back onto the AS/400 now and continue with the lab. If you need help with the sign-on procedure, refer back to the earlier session on signing onto the AS/400. Remember to enter the new password you entered on the Change Password screen. You will not see the changed password as you enter it.

Note:

Although you have signed off the AS/400, you may not have disconnected the PC from the communications line that linked the PC to the AS/400. Since there are different methods used to connect and disconnect a workstation to an AS/400, we will not discuss that aspect here. Your instructor will inform you of the procedures that are necessary at your location to disconnect your PC from the AS/400.

NAVIGATING THE MENUS

Let us consider how menu screens, such as the AS/400 Main Menu screen can be used to perform different AS/400 tasks.

CHANGING YOUR PASSWORD

Since it is important to protect your password and change it often, let us examine how to change your password as a way of learning about menu screens.

Several methods can be used to change your password. In this section, we demonstrate how to change your password through menu navigation. In a future lab, we demonstrate how to change your password using a CL command.

Menus help you get started on a task by providing a list of options from which to choose. Using menus is easier to learn than entering a long string of commands each time you want to perform a task because you do not have to remember any command names.

Examine the options on the AS/400 Main Menu screen and try to determine which selection might be used to change your password. Sometimes the menu descriptions are not clear enough to determine which selection is correct. Guessing at menu selections is allowed and sometimes welcomed as a method of learning new AS/400 concepts. As you progress forward through menu screens, Function key F3 (Exit) and F12 (Cancel) can be used to return to previous screens.

Changing your password is a user function. Therefore, option 1 (User Tasks) is the required option on the AS/400 Main Menu screen to begin the menu navigation that allows you to change your password. To select an option from a menu screen, enter the number corresponding to your menu selection on the command line and press Enter.

To select the User Tasks option from the AS/400 Main Menu screen:

- Enter `1` on the Selection or command ===> line.
- Press Enter.

Figure L1-8 illustrates the User Tasks menu screen. This menu is named User and results from selecting option 1 from the AS/400 Main Menu. Note that the User Tasks menu screen has the same general format as the AS/400 Main Menu screen, although the specific options are different.

```
USER                              User Tasks
                                                       System:   BLUE400
 Select one of the following:

      1. Display or change your job
      2. Display messages
      3. Send a message
      4. Submit a job
      5. Work with your spooled output files
      6. Work with your batch jobs
      7. Display or change your library list
      8. Change your password
      9. Change your user profile

     60. More user task options

     90. Sign off

 Selection or command
 ===> ____________________________________________________________________

 _____________________________________________________________________
 F3=Exit   F4=Prompt   F9=Retrieve   F12=Cancel   F13=Information Assistant
 F16=AS/400 Main menu
```

Figure L1-8: AS/400 User Tasks menu.

The User Tasks menu screen provides a selection of different options relating to user-specific tasks. It is easy to see that option 8 is the option that you are looking for to change your password.

To change your password, on the User Tasks menu screen:

- Enter 8 on the Selection or command line ===>.
- Press Enter.

The Change Password screen shown in Figure L1-9 appears. This screen is referred to as an *entry screen* because it displays fill-in-the-blank fields for the user to enter the necessary parameters for the command. If you wish to return to the User Tasks menu screen without changing your password, press F12 (Cancel) or F3 (Exit).

```
                              Change Password
Password last changed . . . . . . . . . . :   05/15/96

Type choices, press Enter.

  Current password  . . . . . . . . . . . .   __________

  New password  . . . . . . . . . . . . . .   __________

  New password (to verify)  . . . . . . . .   __________







F3=Exit           F12=Cancel
```

Figure L1-9: Change Password screen.

To change your password:

- Enter your current password (`BIGBLUE`) in the `Current password` field.
- Press the Field Exit key (right Ctrl key).

Now you have to decide on a new password. Try to make your password a series of letters and numbers that only you will know. For example, use the first character of each word in a phrase such as "My birthday is May 15," where the password would be MBIM15.

Note:

If you have a password on another system, you might use that. If you have access to several computer systems, it is often a good idea to keep the passwords on them the same. That means changing the passwords of all your systems when one needs changing.

In addition, your new password cannot be the same as your current password. If you try to enter a new password that is the same as your current password, the system will respond with an error message.

- Enter your `new password` in the `New password` field.
- Press the Field Exit key.
- Enter the new password a second time in the `New password (to verify)` field.
- Press Enter to send the data to the AS/400 system.

The system will return to the User Tasks screen and respond with the message `Password changed successfully`.

- Press F3 (Exit) or F12 (Cancel) to return to the AS/400 Main Menu screen.

DETERMINING THE OS/400 VERSION NUMBER

The examples in this book were written on an AS/400 running V4R4 of the OS/400 operating system. To practice the menu system of the AS/400, let's follow a menu path to determine which version of the operating system your system is running.

Note:

Depending on how your user profile is set up, you may not have access to the commands needed to do this next section. If you find this section does not work, skip it and continue with the next section.

To begin the menu navigation for the version number, select the `Define or change the system` option on the AS/400 Main Menu screen:

- Enter 7 on the Selection or command ===> line.
- Press Enter.

This takes you to the Define or Change the System menu screen, called Define, shown in Figure L1-10.

From the Define or Change the System menu screen, select the `Work with licensed programs` option (option 2):

- Enter 2 on the Selection or command ===> line.
- Press Enter.

```
DEFINE                    Define or Change the System
                                                        System:   BLUE400
 Select one of the followin
      1. Configuration
      2. Work with licensed programs
      3. Security
      4. Work with support contact information
      5. System resources
      6. Program temporary fix
      7. IBM product information
      8. Work with system values




 Selection or command
 ===> 2

 F3=Exit   F4=Prompt   F9=Retrieve   F12=Cancel   F13=Information Assistant
 F16=AS/400 Main menu
 (C) COPYRIGHT IBM CORP. 1980, 1994.
```

Figure L1-10: Define or Change the System menu screen.

The Work with Licensed Programs screen, called LICPGM, in Figure L1-11, appears.

```
LICPGM                    Work with Licensed Programs
                                                        System:   BLUE400
 Select one of the following

   Manual Install
      1. Install all

   Licensed Programs
     10. Display installed licensed programs
     11. Install licensed programs
     12. Delete licensed programs
     13. Save licensed programs

   Secondary Languages
     20. Display installed secondary languages
     21. Install secondary languages
     22. Delete secondary languages
                                                                   More...
 Selection or command
 ===> 10

 F3=Exit   F4=Prompt   F9=Retrieve   F12=Cancel   F13=Information Assistant
 F16=AS/400 Main menu
 (C) COPYRIGHT IBM CORP. 1980, 1994.
```

Figure L1-11: Work with Licensed Programs menu screen.

From the Work with Licensed Programs menu screen, select the `Display installed licensed programs` option (option 10):

- Enter 10 on the Selection or command ===> line.
- Press Enter.

It may take several seconds for the system to gather the necessary information about the licensed programs. Be patient. The Display Installed Licensed Programs screen in Figure L1-12 appears.

```
                    Display Installed Licensed Programs
                                                          System:   BLUE400
Licensed  Installed
Program   Status       Description
5769SS1   *COMPATIBLE  OS/400 - Library QGPL
5769SS1   *COMPATIBLE  OS/400 - Library QUSRSYS
5769SS1   *COMPATIBLE  Operating System/400
5769SS1   *COMPATIBLE  OS/400 - Extended Base Support
5769SS1   *COMPATIBLE  OS/400 - Online Information
5769SS1   *COMPATIBLE  OS/400 - Extended Base Directory Support
5769SS1   *COMPATIBLE  OS/400 - Example Tools Library
5769SS1   *COMPATIBLE  OS/400 - AFP Compatibility Fonts
5769SS1   *COMPATIBLE  OS/400 - *PRV CL Compiler Support
5769SS1   *COMPATIBLE  OS/400 - Host Servers
5769SS1   *COMPATIBLE  OS/400 - System Openness Includes
5769SS1   *COMPATIBLE  OS/400 - GDDM
5769SS1   *COMPATIBLE  OS/400 - Ultimedia System Facilities
5769SS1   *COMPATIBLE  OS/400 - Extended NLS Support
                                                                  More...
Press Enter to continue.

F3=Exit   F11=Display release   F12=Cancel   F19=Display trademarks

(C) COPYRIGHT IBM CORP. 1980, 1998.
```

Figure L1-12: Display Installed Licensed Programs screen.

Function key F11 (Display Release) is a toggle key that switches between three options: Display release, Display option, and Display status. Use F11 to display the installed release version number for the currently installed software.

From the Display Installed Licensed Programs screen, press F11 to display the version number of the currently installed software:

- Press F11 on the Display Installed Licensed Programs screen.

The Display Installed Licensed Programs screen changes and the Installed Release column shown in Figure L1-13 appears.

Depending upon the release of OS/400 and software installed, the list of licensed programs on your screen could differ slightly from that shown in Figure L1-13. Make sure your screen shows the licensed program ending in SS1. This is the designation for the operating system.

```
                         Display Installed Licensed Programs
                                                                System:   BLUE400
 Licensed  Installed
 Program   Release      Description
 5769SS1   V4R4M0 L00   OS/400 - Library QGPL
 5769SS1   V4R4M0 L00   OS/400 - Library QUSRSYS
 5769SS1   V4R4M0 L00   Operating System/400
 5769SS1   V4R4M0       OS/400 - Extended Base Support
 5769SS1   V4R4M0       OS/400 - Online Information
 5769SS1   V4R4M0       OS/400 - Extended Base Directory Support
 5769SS1   V4R4M0       OS/400 - Example Tools Library
 5769SS1   V4R4M0       OS/400 - AFP Compatibility Fonts
 5769SS1   V4R4M0       OS/400 - *PRV CL Compiler Support
 5769SS1   V4R4M0       OS/400 - Host Servers
 5769SS1   V4R4M0       OS/400 - System Openness Includes
 5769SS1   V4R4M0       OS/400 - GDDM
 5769SS1   V4R4M0       OS/400 - Ultimedia System Facilities
 5769SS1   V4R4M0       OS/400 - Extended NLS Support
                                                                       More...
 Press Enter to continue.

 F3=Exit   F11=Display option   F12=Cancel   F19=Display trademarks
```

Figure L1-13: Display Installed Licensed Programs screen with Installed Release.

Look under the Installed Release column to find the version number of the OS/400 operating system. This release number will be in the format VxRxMx, where V means Version, R means Release, M means Modification, and x refers to the actual release number. Therefore, the release number of the OS/400 operating system in Figure L1-13 is V4R4M0 (Version 4, Release 4, Modification 0).

- Which version (Installed Release) of the OS/400 operating system is running on your AS/400? ______________________________

- If an AS/400 is running under release V4R4M1, what does V4R4M1 mean?

  ____

Exit the Display Installed Licensed Programs screen and return to the Define or Change the System screen.

- Press F12 (Cancel) twice to return to the Define or Change the System screen.

DETERMINING THE AS/400 MODEL NUMBER

Let us navigate the menu system again to determine the model number of your AS/400. The model number is stored as part of the system values. *System values* are a group of attributes that are used by the system administrator to control the operation and environment of the system.

You need programmer privileges on the AS/400 to work with the Define screen. If you do not have this privilege, skip this section and continue with the next topic.

From the Define or Change the System screen in Figure L1-14, select the `Work with system values` option (option 8):

- Enter 8 on the Selection or command ===> line.
- Press Enter.

```
DEFINE                    Define or Change the System
                                                              System:   BLUE400
 Select one of the following:

      1. Configuration
      2. Work with licensed programs
      3. Security
      4. Work with support contact information
      5. System resources
      6. Program temporary fix
      7. IBM product information
      8. Work with system values







 Selection or command
 ===> 8

 F3=Exit   F4=Prompt   F9=Retrieve   F12=Cancel   F13=Information Assistant
 F16=AS/400 Main menu
 (C) COPYRIGHT IBM CORP. 1980, 1994.
```

Figure L1-14: Selecting option 8 from the Define or Change the System screen.

The Work with System Values screen in Figure L1-15 appears.

The Work with System Values screen is a *list panel* or *work with panel* that contains a list of objects from which the user can perform some type of processing. The information on the screen is arranged in columns, each with a description. At the left of each item is an input field (OPTION) where an option number from the upper part of the display may be entered. These options vary depending on the purpose of the list screen and the user's authority.

In the example, the items listed are system values. The only option available is Display (option 5). The reason that Display is the only option available is that students have limited authority to the system. The system security officer or another user with the proper security would have full authority to change any of the system values.

A list may contain more items than can be displayed on a single screen. When this happens, `More...` appears in the lower-right corner of all but the last list screen, as shown in Figure L1-15. The word `Bottom` appears in the lower-right corner of the last screen when you reach the end of the list. The Page Up and Page Down keys are used to move from one screen to another.

```
                         Work with System Values
                                                      System:   BLUE400
Position to  . . . . . .                Starting characters of system value
Subset by Type . . . . .   *ALL         F4 for list

Type options, press Enter.
  5=Display

        System
Option  Value        Type      Description
        QABNORMSW    *SYSCTL   Previous end of system indicator
        QACGLVL      *MSG      Accounting level
        QACTJOB      *ALC      Initial number of active jobs
        QADLACTJ     *ALC      Additional number of active jobs
        QADLSPLA     *ALC      Spooling control block additional storage
        QADLTOTJ     *ALC      Additional number of total jobs
        QALWOBJRST   *SEC      Allow object restore option
        QALWUSRDMN   *SEC      Allow user domain objects in libraries
                                                                  More...
Command
===>____________________________________________________________________
________________________________________________________________________
F3=Exit   F4=Prompt   F5=Refresh   F9=Retrieve   F11=Display names only
F12=Cancel
```

Figure L1-15: Work with System Values screen.

To determine the AS/400 model number:

- Press the Page Down key until the system value QMODEL appears in the list. The screen should look similar to the Work with System Values screen in Figure L1-16.
- Enter 5 in the `Option` column beside the system value QMODEL.
- Press Enter.

```
                         Work with System Values
                                                      System:   BLUE400
Position to  . . . . . .                Starting characters of system value
Subset by Type . . . . .   *ALL         F4 for list

Type options, press Enter.
  5=Display

        System
Option  Value        Type      Description
  5     QMODEL       *SYSCTL   System model number
  _     QMONTH       *DATTIM   Month of the year
  _     QPFRADJ      *SYSCTL   Performance adjustment
  _     QPRBFTR      *MSG      Problem log filter
  _     QPRBHLDITV   *MSG      Problem log hold interval
  _     QPRTDEV      *SYSCTL   Printer device description
  _     QPRTKEYFMT   *SYSCTL   Print header and/or border information
  _     QPRTTXT      *MSG      Print text
                                                                  More...
Command
===>____________________________________________________________________
________________________________________________________________________
F3=Exit   F4=Prompt   F5=Refresh   F9=Retrieve   F11=Display names only
F12=Cancel
```

Figure L1-16: QMODEL system model shown in Work with System Values screen.

The QMODEL system value in Figure L1-17 appears.

```
Display System Value

 System value . . . . . :   QMODEL
 Description  . . . . . :   System model number


 Model number . . . . . :    S20









 Press Enter to continue.

 F3=Exit   F12=Cancel
```

Figure L1-17: The QMODEL System Value screen.

- What is the model number of your AS/400 system? ____________________

Exit the Display System Value screen and return to the Define or Change the System screen.

- Press F3 (Exit) twice and return to the Define or Change the System screen shown in Figure L1-14.

DETERMINING WHICH COMPILERS ARE INSTALLED

Next, we will investigate which compilers are installed on your system. Compilers are products that turn human-readable source code into machine-readable programs. If the AS/400 Main Menu screen is shown on the screen, the Define or change the system option should be selected. Since we stopped at the Define or Change the System menu screen during our search for the system model number, we can continue from there.

From the Define or Change the System menu screen in Figure L1-14, select the `Work with licensed programs` option (option 2):

- Enter 2 on the Selection or command ===> line.
- Press Enter.

The Work with Licensed Programs menu screen in Figure L1-18 appears.

```
LICPGM                    Work with Licensed Programs
                                                         System:   BLUE400
 Select one of the following:

   Manual Install
      1. Install all

   Licensed Programs
     10. Display installed licensed programs
     11. Install licensed programs
     12. Delete licensed programs
     13. Save licensed programs

   Secondary Languages
     20. Display installed secondary languages
     21. Install secondary languages
     22. Delete secondary languages
                                                                  More...
 Selection or command
 ===> 10

 F3=Exit   F4=Prompt   F9=Retrieve   F12=Cancel   F13=Information Assistant
 F16=AS/400 Main menu
 (C) COPYRIGHT IBM CORP. 1980, 1994.
```

Figure L1-18: Work with Licensed Programs menu screen.

From the Work with Licensed Programs menu screen, select the `Display installed licensed programs` option (option 10):

- Enter 10 on the Selection or command ===> line.
- Press Enter.

The system will take some time before returning. The Display Installed Licensed Programs screen appears with a list of licensed programs that are installed on the system. To find out which compilers are installed:

- Press the Page Down key to search through the installed licensed programs.
- Which compilers are installed on your system? There could be more than one. List one ______ or ______ two.
  ______

Once you have determined which compilers are installed, return to the AS/400 Main Menu screen:

- Press F3 (Exit) twice and return to the AS/400 Main Menu screen.

SIGNING OFF THE AS/400

You have completed this lab assignment. Let us review the two methods that you can use to sign off the AS/400.

If you are at the AS/400 Main Menu screen shown in Figure L1-19:

- Enter 90 on the Selection or command ===> line.
- Press Enter.

If you are at a screen that has a command line, you can enter the SIGNOFF command to sign off the system. Figure L1-19 illustrates the SIGNOFF command entered on the command line, identified as the Selection or command ===> at the bottom of the AS/400 Main Menu screen. To use the SIGNOFF command:

- Enter `SIGNOFF` or `signoff` on the command line.
- Press Enter.

```
MAIN                          AS/400 Main Menu
                                                         System:   BLUE400
 Select one of the following:

      1. User tasks
      2. Office tasks
      3. General system tasks
      4. Files, libraries, and folders
      5. Programming
      6. Communications
      7. Define or change the system
      8. Problem handling
      9. Display a menu
     10. Information Assistant options
     11. Client Access tasks

     90. Sign off

 Selection or command
 ===> signoff

 F3=Exit   F4=Prompt   F9=Retrieve   F12=Cancel   F13=Information Assistant
 F23=Set initial menu
 (C) COPYRIGHT IBM CORP. 1980, 1994.
```

Figure L1-19: Entering the `signoff` *command on the command line to sign off the AS/400.*

You should now have an understanding of how to sign on and off the AS/400 and to navigate the AS/400 menu systems.

END-OF-CHAPTER AIDS

CHAPTER SUMMARY

1. The AS/400 (Application System) evolved from the System/3X family of computers that got its beginning in Rochester, Minnesota, in 1969.

2. The AS/400 is a multiuser, multitasking computer system.

3. The AS/400 architecture:

   a. The layered design concept of the AS/400 isolates machine hardware and system software through a series of horizontal interfaces.

   b. The main advantage of the layered design concept is that upgrades can be made at the low-level functions without any impact on the high-level software.

   c. The machine interface (MI) separates the OS/400 operating system from the hardware.

   d. Approximately 90 to 95 percent of the OS/400 operating system resides above the MI. As a result, the operating system is not affected by hardware changes.

   e. CISC-based systems:

      i. Named for complex instruction set computer.

      ii. The architecture for all older model AS/400s.

   f. RISC-based systems:

      i. Named for reduced instruction set computer.

      ii. IBM's new family of AS/400s.

   g. Everything stored and used by the AS/400 is an object.

   h. The AS/400 uses single-level storage that makes no distinction between disk storage and main memory.

4. The operating system, OS/400, monitors and controls the overall operation of the AS/400.

5. Programs are divided into two types: operating system and application programs.

   a. Application programs perform user tasks.

   b. Operating system programs control and monitor the system.

   c. Programs execute either interactively or in batch.

KEY TERMS

alphanumeric characters
American Standard Code for Information Interchange (ASCII)
application program
Application System/400 (AS/400)
batch programs
command line
complex instruction set computer (CISC)
DB2/400
Direct Access Storage Device (DASD)
Electronic Customer Support (ECS)
entry screen
Extended Binary Coded Decimal Interchange Code (EBCDIC)
function keys
horizontal licensed internal code (HLIC)
kernel
information system
input data
Integrated Language Environment (ILE)
interactive programs
library
licensed internal code (LIC)
list panel
machine independence
machine interface (MI)
menu name
menu options
menu title
message line
midrange computers
modular programming
multiuser minicomputer
n-way
object
object-based architecture
object-based computer
operating system
Operating System/400
OS/400
output information
pages
paging
password
program
programmer
reduced instruction set computer (RISC)
sign-off option
sign-on screen
single-level storage
software
software developers
System Application Architecture (SAA)
system licensed internal code (SLIC)
system name
system values
user ID
vertical licensed internal code (VLIC)
virtual storage
work session
work with panel

CHAPTER SELF-TEST

Self-test questions found throughout the book are designed to help you evaluate your understanding of the topics presented in the chapter. The solutions to these self-test questions are in appendix D.

True-False Questions

___ 1. A library is an object.

___ 2. When the Enter key is pressed, the cursor will move to the next field on the screen.

___ 3. Entering SIGNOFF on a command line is the only method to sign off the AS/400.

___ 4. ASCII is used to represent data in the AS/400.

___ 5. The AS/400 was developed in Rochester, NY.

___ 6. The AS/400 treats all storage as a single large region of memory.

___ 7. The AS/400 evolved from a midrange computer for which the market was the low-end commercial user.

___ 8. The AS/400 demonstrates the concept of hardware independence.

Fill in the Blanks

1. The AS in AS/400 is an abbreviation for ______________ ________________.
2. The AS/400 is a(n) computer system that can interact with many users at a time.
3. The AS/400 is a(n) system able to perform several functions over the same time period.
4. The current AS/400s and OS/400 are based on (CISC/RISC) ______________ architecture.
5. Application programs execute (above/below) __________________________ the machine interface.
6. Data on the AS/400 is stored as (EBCDIC/ASCII)__________________.
7. The ____________ ______________ controls and monitors the overall operation of the computer.

Chapter Review Questions

1. Define the following terms:
   a. Program.
   b. DASD.
   c. Multitasking.
   d. Virtual storage.
   e. Object-based architecture.
   f. Library.
2. Indicate the difference between operating system software and applications software.
3. What is the meaning of the term "object"?
4. The AS/400 is a multiuser, multitasking computer system. Explain.
5. Programs which require human interaction are called (batch/interactive) ___________________ work/jobs.
6. What is the purpose of function keys?
7. What is the purpose of the following function keys:
   a. F1.
   b. F3.
   c. F9.
   d. F12.
8. Describe single-level storage.
9. In order to sign onto an AS/400, you need to have a(n) ______________ and a(n) ____________________.

2

NAVIGATING AROUND THE AS/400

CHAPTER OBJECTIVES

Upon completion of this chapter, you should be able to:

- Describe the user interfaces.
- Describe how to find help on the system.
- Describe how to find support information.
- Explore the menu structure and on-screen help features.
- Describe the various types of screens on the system.
- Describe the assistance levels on the system.

USER INTERFACE

Most users new to the AS/400 system experience a little culture shock when faced with learning a new, fully integrated operating system. Fortunately, the AS/400 supplies a comprehensive user interface that is extremely friendly to the new user, yet can be operated at light speed by the experienced user.

USER INTERFACE COMPONENTS

Menu Interface: A primary part of the user interface is a set of menus that organize users' tasks into specific groups. When users become more experienced, they can work with lists, take a fast path to any menu, or bypass menus to enter commands directly. All of these methods are interchangeable, allowing use of more advanced interface methods without abandoning the simple *menu interface*.

Help Interface: When a user does not understand something on a screen or how to start specific tasks, help is available from any screen through the OS/400 *help interface*. Help can range from information about a screen, an individual field on a screen, a command, or a message.

Command Prompting: Every command on the AS/400 can be prompted. That is, by entering the command name and pressing the F4 key, the command is displayed in an easy-to-use format.

Other AS/400 Display Interfaces: Other than menus, the AS/400 uses several different screens or panels as part of its user interfaces. Among the other interfaces available are the entry and list panels.

User Support: The *Information Center* is a browser-based quick and easy way to find AS/400 technical information in one place. The Information Center contains a collection of technical topics designed for people who need fast, easy access to technical information. This *user support* is available over the Internet at:

```
http://publib.boulder.ibm.com/html/as400/infocenter.html
```

or from a local CD. The Information Center, on the Internet, has three major components: the Information Center, Online Library, and Technical Studio.

InfoSeeker: *InfoSeeker* provides the capability to search online manuals. The user may search for information when not sure how to handle a situation. Note, however, that this feature is not available in V4R4.

National Language Support: *National language support* allows users to interact with the system in the language of their choice and supports multiple languages at the same time. With this support, all menus' help information and messages are displayed in the language specified in each user's profile.

The most important aspect of the user interfaces is the initial ability for a user to operate the AS/400 while still learning. The interfaces hand-hold the new user as he or she moves around the system. The advanced person, on other hand, can aggressively dictate where he or she wants to go on the system. In fact, on the AS/400, the difference between a beginner and an expert is most evident in the person's command of the interfaces.

INTERFACES

SIGN-ON SCREEN

The first interface everyone deals with is the sign-on screen shown in Figure 2-1. This is an example of an *entry panel* interface. This screen is automatically displayed when a user initiates a session with the AS/400, which can be done by powering on a terminal or selecting Client Access from a personal computer workstation.

```
                              Sign On
                                        System . . . . . :   BLUE400
                                        Subsystem . . . . :   QINTER
                                        Display . . . . . :   QPADEV0001

                User . . . . . . . . . . . . . .  ___________
                Password . . . . . . . . . . . .
                Program/procedure . . . . . . . .  ___________
                Menu . . . . . . . . . . . . . .  ___________
                Current library . . . . . . . . .  ___________

                                  (C) COPYRIGHT IBM CORP. 1980, 1994.
```

Figure 2-1: An AS/400 sign-on screen.

The exact screen (or panel) that appears could be slightly different, depending upon how the system is configured and how it is ultimately customized. Some companies customize this screen to incorporate their logo.

The system name, interactive subsystem name, and display station ID are displayed on the sign-on screen. Signing onto the AS/400 is discussed in chapter 1.

THE AS/400 MAIN MENU

The AS/400 Main Menu screen in Figure 2-2 is the first screen most users see after they sign onto the system. The AS/400 Main Menu screen is typical of all AS/400 menu screens.

```
MAIN                          AS/400 Main Menu
                                                      System:   BLUE400
 Select one of the following:

      1. User tasks
      2. Office tasks
      3. General system tasks
      4. Files, libraries, and folders
      5. Programming
      6. Communications
      7. Define or change the system
      8. Problem handling
      9. Display a menu
     10. Information Assistant options
     11. Client Access tasks

     90. Sign off

 Selection or command
 ===>_______________________________________________________________

 F3=Exit   F4=Prompt   F9=Retrieve   F12=Cancel   F13=Information Assistant
 F23=Set initial menu
 (C) COPYRIGHT IBM CORP. 1980, 1994.
```

Figure 2-2: The AS/400 Main Menu screen.

Although there is no hard rule, AS/400 menus tend to have the same components:

The *screen header* is used to identify three attributes to the user:

a. The *menu name* (MAIN) in the upper-left corner is used to distinguish this menu from other menus. Menus are the only types of screens that have names.

b. The *menu title* (AS/400 Main Menu) is located in the center of the top line of the screen and is used to describe the purpose of the screen.

c. The *system name* (BLUE400) in the upper-right corner of the screen names the AS/400 to which the user is attached. AS/400s can have unique names given to them. If no name is given, they are known by their serial number and that will appear in the corner. Users in shops that support multiple AS/400s (most do these days), make it a habit of frequently verifying the system they are working on.

The numbered *list of options* makes up the body of the menu. This list identifies the options by number and provides a description for each option that is available with this menu. Note that the last option is a sign-off option and is identified as selection 90.

The Selection or command line, distinguished by ===>, is where the user keys in his or her selection number from the menu or enters a CL command to be executed. For example, to display office tasks from the menu shown in Figure 2-2, type the number 2 on the command line and press Enter.

Below the Selection or command ===> line is a list of function keys that can be used with the screen. These function keys are referred to as *active function keys* and will differ from display to display. When there are more active function keys than can be shown on the screen, F24 (More Keys) will be active to allow the additional function keys to be displayed.

On the last line of the screen, below the function keys, is a *message line* that is used by the system to communicate to the user. Normally, the message line displays IBM copyright information or is blank. When the AS/400 needs to communicate with the user, a message will be displayed on the message line.

Menus tend to be *nested*, especially from the AS/400 Main Menu screen. This means that any option taken from the main menu will produce another menu. An option from that menu will produce another. This goes on until a level is reached where an option will invoke a command.

Nesting of menus makes it hard to get lost. While options move menus forward, the F12 (Cancel) key will move to the previous menu. The F12 key can be used repeatedly to reverse direction; the AS/400 remembers the sequence that was used and it will back out the same way.

That is a convenient feature; however, after users gain experience on the AS/400, they usually know where they want to go and want to get there more quickly. For those users, OS/400 also supplies a fast path to all of its menus.

The fast path to go directly to a menu is to use the menu name with the GO command. For example, the AS/400 has a message menu named MESSAGE that helps a user work with messages. A user can go directly to the MESSAGE menu by entering:

```
GO MESSAGE
```

on the command line and pressing Enter.

All displays, including menus, define function keys available for that specific display. In applications, some function keys provide for a direct connection to other parts of an application.

Hot-key navigation is not usually the case within OS/400, but it is quite common in large enterprisewide applications. For example, a user in accounts receivable would do most of his work from an AR Main Menu but would occasionally need to verify something in another part of the application, like a product part number. If this function is common enough, his menu may have a function key that quickly links him to the Inventory Main Menu.

THE SYSTEM REQUEST MENU

OS/400 offers a special menu known as the *System Request menu* that provides quick access to as many system-level functions as the user is allowed. Take note that, although you can get to this menu, you cannot do anything that your security (in your user profile) does not allow you to do.

This menu, shown in Figure 2-3, is displayed by pressing `SHIFT (OR ALT) + ESC` (Escape) followed by Enter.

```
System Request
                                                        System:   BIGBLUE

Select one of the following:

     1. Display sign on for alternative job
     2. End previous request
     3. Display current job
     4. Display messages
     5. Send a message
     6. Display system operator messages
     7. Display work station user

    10. Start system request at previous system
    11. Transfer to previous system

    13. Start system request at home system
    14. Transfer to home system

    90.  Sign off
                                                                More...
Selection   ______



F3=Exit   F12=Cancel
(C) COPYRIGHT IBM CORP. 1980, 1998.
```

Figure 2-3: System Request menu.

SYSTEM REQUEST MENU OPTIONS

The options on the System Request menu are listed in Figure 2-4.

Option #1	This option displays a sign-on screen for an alternative job. After signing onto an alternative job, you can then use this option to toggle between your primary and secondary job. (Note: Only one session is active at a time.)
Option #2	This message cancels your previous command (action).
Option #3	This option allows you to display your current job information.
Option #4	This option allows you to display messages that have been sent to you.
Option #5	This option allows you to send a message.
Option #6	This option lets you display a message on the qsysopr (the system operator's) message queue.
Option #7	This option allows you to display information about the jobs running from your workstation.
Options #10, 11, 13, and 14	These options apply to networks of systems and may not be displayed on your system.
Option #90	This option allows you to sign off of the session.

Figure 2-4: System Request menu options.

USER INTERFACE—HELP SUPPORT

The help interface provided with OS/400 allows users to obtain several levels of help. Help can range from information about a whole panel to how the user can complete a specific task when the command is not known. Additionally, help is also provided for messages sent to users by OS/400. (Remember the menu shown in Figure 2-2—its bottom line is reserved for messages.) By simply positioning the cursor on specific areas of the screen and pressing the Help key (F1), help information is instantly displayed. Help can be *contextual help* or *extended help*. Help may also be field-level, which provides detailed help for particular fields. To use this feature, place the cursor on the field and press the F1 (Help) key.

The quality and extent of help on the AS/400 is entirely voluntary—within OS/400, you can count on help being available for most commands. For applications, though, help may or may not be there. When you have a question about something, always try to get help. Remember, position your cursor first, then press the F1 (Help) key.

CONTEXTUAL HELP

Contextual help is the first level of help available about the fields on a screen. By putting the cursor on a specific field or region of the screen and pressing the Help key, users can find information relating to that specific field or region. Often, the ability to find specific information allows users to determine solutions quickly without looking through manuals.

EXTENDED HELP

Extended help is more general than contextual help. Extended help provides information about the task, the prompts on the screen shown, and the functions provided by the function keys. With this help, users can page through all of the topics related to a screen. Pressing the Help key while the cursor is not on a specific field accesses this help.

HELP MESSAGE LEVELS

Sometimes messages are cryptic or ambiguous. Messages have help text associated with them that help clarifies what they mean. In many cases, these help texts also suggest solutions to problems.

The process to view message help is simple. Position the cursor on the message and press F1 (Help). The system will produce an expanded version of the message. If the message is still unclear, use what is known as the *second-level message text* to display even more information.

A second-level text may not exist. To find out if it does, check the function keys listed at the bottom of the screen. If a second-level text exists, it will be associated with a function key. Press this key to bring it up. For most operational problems, second-level message texts' values cannot be overestimated. Get in the habit of looking for the second-level text for any problem that is not instantly familiar.

Even for routine problems, second-level message texts have evolved into a kind of standard. Here is what happens: The operator experiences a problem in a production job that will require a developer's attention. Before the operator calls the developer, he or she should print both levels of message text. The developer will usually want to know exactly what the message says, and this is a professional way to get the information to him.

ASSISTANCE LEVELS

OS/400 is built to be sensitive to the different skill levels of a wide range of customers. People new to the AS/400 do not want to be blown away by technically cryptic screens, and advanced users have no patience for constant hand-holding from the system.

For this reason, OS/400 allows the customer to select the assistance level each user is comfortable with. There are three possible assistance levels:

1. Basic (*BASIC). The basic level is for the inexperienced computer user. The basic assistance level supports some common user and operator tasks through the *Operational Assistant (OA) menu* and does not use computer terminology. This level does not allow for full access to system functions, but rather presents common functions such as printing, working with batch jobs, handling messages, and problem handling.
2. Intermediate (*INTERMED). This intermediate level supports all system tasks and uses computer terminology that information technology professionals are familiar with.
3. Advanced (*ADVANCED). This advanced level supports the same functions as the intermediate assistance level; however, the displays contain as much information as possible by not displaying the allowed function keys and options. It uses most of the same displays as intermediate.

There are three ways to set the assistance levels:

1. Globally, by using the system value QASTLVL (refer to chapter 11, Security and Security System Values, for more information). This sets the default assistance level that the machine will use for everyone, unless otherwise instructed.
2. For each user, by specifying an assistance level in the user's profile. (Refer to chapter 3.)
3. For each job or task, by using the F21 (Select Assistance Level) function key on the CHGJOB command.

While learning to operate the AS/400, it is best to use the intermediate level of help. The screens in this book are at the intermediate level.

USER INTERFACE—INFOSEEKER

OVERVIEW

The AS/400 will be phasing out the use of InfoSeeker in V4R4. InfoSeeker will be replaced with the use of the Information Center, but the concepts will be the same.

InfoSeeker is a product that resides on the AS/400 that allows customers to search for and read the AS/400 manuals on-line. Actually, the AS/400 manuals are so extensive, a complete set would fill a small library, so many people also use them in CD-ROM form (on a shareable network server) or over the Internet. InfoSeeker is the AS/400-based manual reader.

There are so many manuals for the AS/400 that they are grouped into many *bookshelves* of related books. Sometimes one book can be found on multiple bookshelves. By selecting a bookshelf to get started, one can be pretty sure he or she will be presented with all the books related to a subject.

With InfoSeeker, the user can enter, in layman's terms, any word or phrase for which he or she would like information. When the search is complete, a *list display* of index items containing the search words or synonyms is produced. From this list display, the user can select which item to display and/or print.

Because the search is a *fuzzy* search, sometimes sections or books are displayed that have some piece of the search phrase, but not the entire search phrase. Fuzzy matching searches for alternative forms of the search words or phrases.

InfoSeeker provides the following search capabilities:

1. Through bookshelves. Bookshelves organize related online books.

2. Across a set of books for a specific topic.

3. Within a single book for a specific topic.

4. Hypertext linking from one topic to another.

5. Prints or copies a topic or sequence of topics.

Not all users can access InfoSeeker. They must be set up in what is known as the *system distribution directory*. The command to do so is Add Directory Entry (ADDDIRE).

InfoSeeker can be accessed in three ways:

- From most menus, by pressing F13 (Information Assistant).
- From any Help screen, by pressing F11.
- By entering STRINFSKR on the command line and pressing Enter.

The book reader for online manuals can do other things besides search for topics. They can:

1. Copy topics—allows topics to be copied for later reading or editing.
2. Print topics—print topics to read later as reference when using a program or application.
3. Group books in a bookshelf.
4. Create custom *softcopy* books.
5. Link to related information.

LAB #2: NAVIGATING AROUND THE AS/400

Upon completion of this lab, you should be able to:

- Use the online help facility.
- Navigate the AS/400 menu system.
- Describe the user interfaces.
- Describe how to find help on the system.
- Describe how to find support information.
- Explore the menu structure and on-screen help features.
- Describe the various types of screens on the system.
- Describe the assistance levels on the system.

MENU NAVIGATION AND BASIC HELP

Let's start exploring menus with the main menu. To go directly to a menu, you can use the GO command followed by the menu's object name.

- Enter `GO MAIN` on the command line of any screen.
- Press Enter.

The Main Menu is often the first screen a user sees when logging onto the system. At this point, you should spend some time exploring the functions available from this menu. First, explore functions available when you take option 1, `User tasks`.

- Enter `1` on the command line.
- Press Enter.
- What is the menu name of the resulting menu? ______________________

A variety of options are available from the user menu. It is a good practice to keep private message queues clean. Use option 2 from the User Tasks menu (Figure L2-1) to read and delete messages in your message queue. The AS/400 sends and holds messages in a variety of message queues. The topic of *message queues* is explored in chapter 5.

```
USER                                  User Tasks
                                                           System:   BIGBLUE
 Select one of the following:

      1. Display or change your job
      2. Display messages
      3. Send a message
      4. Submit a job
      5. Work with your spooled output files
      6. Work with your batch jobs
      7. Display or change your library list
      8. Change your password
      9. Change your user profile

     60. More user task options

     90. Sign off

 Selection or command
 ===> 2

 F3=Exit   F4=Prompt   F9=Retrieve   F12=Cancel   F13=Information Assistant
 F16=AS/400 Main menu
 (C) COPYRIGHT IBM CORP. 1980, 1998.
```

Figure L2-1: User Tasks menu—selecting option 2.

- Which function key would you use to delete all messages? ________________
- Press the function you selected in the previous question and delete all your messages.

Return directly to the Main Menu. (Do you remember the command? If not, review the beginning of this section.)

- What is the command you used to return to the main menu? ____________________System Request menu

SYSTEM REQUEST MENU

The System Request menu is a special menu that allows a user to quickly access a variety of system-related tasks. To access the System Request menu, use a three-keystroke sequence. This results in Figure L2-2.

- Press and hold the `Shift` key, tap the `Esc` (Escape) key, then release all keys. A blue line will appear at the bottom of the screen. *Note*: This is often shown as Shift-Escape.
- Press Enter.

```
System Request
                                                          System:   BIGBLUE
 Select one of the following:

      1. Display sign on for alternative job
      2. End previous request
      3. Display current job
      4. Display messages
      5. Send a message
      6. Display system operator messages
      7. Display work station user

     10. Start system request at previous system
     11. Transfer to previous system

     13. Start system request at home system
     14. Transfer to home system
                                                                   More...
 Selection _1


 F3=Exit   F12=Cancel
 (C) COPYRIGHT IBM CORP. 1980, 1998.
```

Figure L2-2: System Request menu.

From the System Request menu, you can sign onto an alternate job, end a command previously entered, display messages in your message queue, display the messages in the operator message queue, and many other functions. Now sign onto an alternate session.

- Enter `1` on the command line.
- Press Enter. The sign-on screen appears. Follow the normal procedure to sign onto the AS/400 again.

You now have two sessions. You can go back and forth between these two sessions by pressing the Shift-Escape followed by pressing Enter. This brings up the System Request menu again. You then select option 1 again, and you are back to the previous session. As you become more familiar with this menu and remember the number of the option, you can shorten the process. The shortened process is the Shift-Escape key sequence followed by the option.

Now that you have two sessions, it is important to realize that only one of these sessions is active at a time.

FORMS OF HELP

The amount of help available on the AS/400 is one of its strengths. If you are unsure of a particular screen field, you can use contextual help. This portion of the lab uses the Work with All Spooled Files *list screen*. Before proceeding, make sure there are printouts in your out queue. A simple way to produce printouts is a screen print.

- Press and hold the `Ctrl` key, tap the `Scroll Lock` key.

The following message will appear:

```
Print operation complete to the default printer device file.
```

Now proceed to the Work with All Spooled Files list screen.

- Enter `WRKSPLF` on the command line.
- Press Enter. The Work with All Spooled Files screen in Figure L2-3 appears.

```
                          Work with All Spooled Files

 Type options, press Enter.
   1=Send    2=Change    3=Hold    4=Delete    5=Display    6=Release    7=Messages
   8=Attributes          9=Work with printing status

                                     Device or                        Total      Cur
 Opt  File          User             Queue          User Data   Sts   Pages     Page   Copy
      QSYSPRT       OPR0001          OPROUTQ                    RDY       1                1
      QSYSPRT       OPR0001          OPROUTQ                    MSGW      1                1




                                                                                      Bottom
 Parameters for options 1, 2, 3 or command
 ===> ____________________________________________________________________________
 F3=Exit    F10=View 3    F11=View 2    F12=Cancel    F22=Printers    F24=More keys
```

Figure L2-3: The Work with All Spooled Files screen showing an example of a list display.

The screen shown in Figure L2-3 is an example of a list display or *list panel*. The screen can be divided into three distinct parts:

1. Top portion—the available options are displayed. The option number is placed to the left of a spool file.
2. Center portion—displays a *list* of files available to be printed from the queue. This is a list of printouts (files) stored in out queues.
3. Bottom portion—the command line and function keys are displayed.

Notice the MSGW status on one print file shown in Figure L2-3.

- Move the cursor right to the `Status` (Sts) column.
- Press F1 (Help) key.
- A Help window will appear.
- Press the Page Down key until you find the MSGW status.
- What does MSGW mean? ________________________________
- Press F2 (Extended Help).
- Scroll through the available information.
- How is extended help different from contextual help? ______________
  ____
- Press F12 (Cancel) twice to return to the Work with All Spooled Files screen.

Explore other locations on this screen and notice the different information that is produced with contextual help at different locations on the screen. To further explore this list display screen, do the following:

- Enter `5` (Display) on the `Option` line to the left of one of your printouts.
- Press Enter and view the printout on the screen.
- Press Enter to return to the Work with All Spooled Files screen.
- Enter `4` (Delete) on the `Option` line before you printout.
- Press Enter.
- Press Enter again to confirm that you want to delete this file.
- Enter the command to return to the AS/400 Main Menu screen.

THE INFORMATION ASSISTANT OPTIONS (INFO) MENU

From the main menu, take option 10 (Information Assistant Options) as shown in Figure L2-4.

```
INFO                    Information Assistant Options
                                                        System:   BIGBLUE
 To select one of the following, type its number below and press Enter:

      1. Where do I look for information?
      2. How can I comment on information?

     10. What's new this release?

     20. Start InfoSeeker (BookManager)
     21. Start online education

     23. Work with problems
     24. Start search index




 Type a menu option below
     _____


 F1=Help   F3=Exit   F9=Command line   F12=Cancel
 (C) COPYRIGHT IBM CORP. 1980, 1998.
```

Figure L2-4: The Information Assistant Options menu.

By now, you should notice some consistency among the screens.

- Choose option `10` (Where do I look for Information?).
- Press Enter.
- Move the cursor to the highlighted words, `Online Information, on the Internet.`
- Press Enter.
- List two of the Internet addresses provided.

  ____

  ____

INTERNET FOLLOW-UP

For this section, you are going to work in a two-window environment. One window will contain your AS/400 session; the second window, your Internet session. Use your windows skills to reduce or minimize the size of your AS/400 session window.

- Using windows techniques, *reduce* or *minimize* the AS/400 session.
- On your desktop, locate your *Internet browser*. (You may use either Netscape or Internet Explorer.)
- Double-click on your browser to open a second session/window.
- In the *Location* window of the browser, the first of the Internet addresses you found in the previous section.
- What is the title of one of the articles on that page? ______________________
____
____
- Return to your AS/400 window.
- Press F12 until you are back at the Info menu (Information Assistant Options).
- Enter 1 on the Info menu.
- Press Enter. The screen in Figure L2-5 appears.
- Press F12 until you return to the AS/400 main menu screen.

MORE: INFORMATION ASSISTANT OPTIONS (INFO) MENU

```
Help                    Where Do I Look for Information?

     AS/400* information comes in many different forms.  For more
     information about any of these, move your cursor to the topic and
     press Enter:
      o  Online Books (AS/400 Softcopy Library)
                What is Softcopy?
              > How Do I Read Softcopy Books?
                How the Library is Organized (New Softcopy Bookshelves)
                Using the Information Directory
      o  AS/400 Printed Manuals (AS/400 System Library)
                Getting Started
                Books for the OS/400 LP
                Other Documentation (Redbooks and Related Information)
      o  Online Information
                Online Information on the Internet
                Online Help Information
                Online Tools and Examples (QUSRTOOL Library)
                Online Education
                Handling System Problems
                                                                  More...
 F3=Exit help   F10=Move to top   F12=Cancel   F13=Information Assistant
 F14=Print help
```

Figure L2-5: The Where Do I Look for Information? menu screen points to sources of information.

USER INTERFACE—INFOSEEKER

InfoSeeker is not available in all versions of the operating system. If you are using V4R4, skip this section on InfoSeeker.

InfoSeeker is a product that allows you to search for and read the AS/400 manuals on-line. The collection of manuals is so large that they have been organized into bookshelves. The bookshelves are organized by topics. You will find most of the books (manuals) you will need to research a given topic. You can use any of the three methods you learned in the previous section. One of the easiest ways is to select the InfoSeeker option from the Info menu.

- Enter `GO INFO` on the command line.
- Press Enter.
- Enter 20 on the command line.
- Press Enter.
- Enter 1 next to the bookshelf shown in Figure L2-6.
- Press Enter.

```
                                  InfoSeeker

Type options, press Enter.
  1=Open    2=Search    4=Remove from view    8=Display description
  9=Put in shelf

Opt     Description
1__    (S) OS/400 V4R1 Commonly Used Books Bookshelf







                                                               Bottom
F3=Exit     F5=Refresh    F6=Change list    F11=Display data    F12=Cancel
F13=Sort    F14=Clear markers
(C) COPYRIGHT IBM CORP. 1980, 1998.
```

Figure L2-6: Initial InfoSeeker screen.

Now that you have opened the Commonly Used Books Bookshelf, search for information.

SEARCHING FOR INFORMATION

InfoSeeker has powerful searching functions. Information can be searched for using the list of bookshelves, from a list of books, or while reading an individual book. In this exercise, you are to find information about one of the following topics:

— Working with and printing a spool file.
— Saving files while active.

Refer to the screen shown in Figure L2-7.

```
Bookshelf-OS/400 V4R1 Commonly Used Books Bookshelf

 Type options, press Enter.
   1=Open   2=Search   4=Remove from shelf   8=Display description
   9=Put in shelf

 Opt Description
 __* AS/400 System Operation V3R6
 __  System Upgrade Road Map (RISC to RISC) V4R1
 __  Getting Your AS/400 Working for You V4R1
 __  AS/400 Basic System Operation, Administration, and Problem Handling V4
 __  OS/400 InfoSeeker - Getting Started V4R1
 __  OS/400 InfoSeeker Use V4R1
 __  AS/400 Publications Reference V4R1
 __  Security - Basic V4R1
 __  Security - Reference V4R1
 __* OS/400 Backup and Recovery, V4R1
 __  OS/400 Work Management V4R1
 __  OS/400 Communications Configuration V4R1
 __  Programming Reference Summary V4R1
                                                              More...
 F3=Exit    F5=Refresh   F6=Search all   F11=Display data   F12=Cancel
 F13=Sort   F14=Clear markers
```

Figure L2-7: V4R1 Commonly Used Books Bookshelf.

When performing searches using InfoSeeker, phrase the search string in English. It is not necessary to use commands unless looking for information on a particular command.

- Enter 2 (Search) next to either `AS/400 System Operation V3R6` or `OS/400 Backup and Recovery`, V4R1, depending on the topic of your search.
- Press Enter.
- Leave the search type 1 (Fuzzy).
- Enter `search string`.
- Press Enter.

Because the search was a fuzzy search, it returns a list of sections or books that contains a piece of the search phrase, not always the entire search phrase. Select the plus sign (+) to the left of a topic to view the line that best matches the search criteria.

A plus sign to the left of a heading indicates that lower-level headings are available for displaying. To expand the heading under a topic, place the cursor on the plus sign next to the heading and press Enter; the screen in Figure L2-8 will appear.

If no search results are found, `No search match found` message will be displayed. If a long search string was used, a match may occur at a bookshelf level but not at a book level; bookshelf searches are more general. If the search phrase is more general, the search has a better chance of finding matches.

```
Search Results- Saving files while active
                                                         Lines 1 to 15 of 56
  To view topic, tab to topic heading, press Enter.
  To expand or compress lines, tab to + or -, press Enter.

    + 6.2.3  Journaling with the Save-While-Active Function
    + 1.2.2.3  Complex Save Strategy
    + 2.6.1  Overview of the Save-While-Active Function
    + 2.6.2  Backup and Recovery Strategy Considerations
    + 2.6.2.1  Save-While-Active Restrictions
    + 2.6.5.2  Recommended Save Procedures
    + 2.6.6.2  Save-While-Active Timestamp Processing
    + 2.6.6.3  Save-While-Active Commitment Control Processing
    + 2.6.2.3  Storage Considerations
    + 2.6.2.1.1  Object Locking Considerations
    + 2.6.2.2  Performance Considerations
    + 2.6.5.1  Considerations for Restore Recovery Procedures
    + 2.6.6.1  Checkpoint Processing
    + 2.6    Chapter 9.  Save-While-Active Function
    + 2.6.6  How the Save-While-Active Function Works
                                                               More...
 F3=Exit      F5=Show topics only   F6=Show first matches   F11=Go to
 F12=Cancel   F13=Show all matches for a topic   F24=More keys
```

Figure L2-8: Search results.

After reviewing the results of your search, determine if these results have produced the information sought.

- Press Tab to move to the most appropriate hypertext link found.
- Move the cursor to the plus sign (+).
- Press Enter.
- Press Tab to move to the main topic number.
- Press Enter.

Read through the information and determine if the information adequately meets the search string criteria. If it does not, return to the above steps and explore other search results.

When you find what you are looking for, print a copy of the material. Remember that when you select an item to print, it will not go to the printer directly. The printout will go to a printout queue. The printout is referred to as a *spooled file*.

- Press F13 (Services).
- Enter 3 (Print topics).
- Press Enter.
- Press F3 (Exit) twice.
- Leave the reply 3 (`Exit without closing bookmark`).

- Press Enter.
- Press F3 (Exit).
- Leave the response Y (Close the bookshelf).
- Press Enter.
- Press F3 (Exit).
- Leave the response Y (Exit InfoSeeker).
- Press Enter.
- Press F3 (Exit).

At this point, you have a copy of the InfoSeeker information in your spool file. To get a printed copy of that file, follow these instructions. (Assume that you are using an AS/400 system printer named PRT01. If printing is done differently at your site, see your instructor for instructions.)

- Enter WRKSPLF on the command line.
- Press Enter.
- Enter 2 (Change) next to the QPBKIPRTF file. See Figure L2-9.
- Press Enter.

```
                          Work with All Spooled Files

Type options, press Enter.
  1=Send   2=Change   3=Hold   4=Delete   5=Display   6=Release   7=Messages
  8=Attributes        9=Work with printing status

                                 Device or                       Total      Cur
Opt  File         User           Queue        User Data   Sts    Pages      Page  Copy
___  QSYSPRT      OPR0001        OPROUTQ                  RDY        1               1
___  QSYSPRT      OPR0001        OPROUTQ                  RDY        1               1
___  QSYSPRT      OPR0001        OPROUTQ                  RDY        1               1
___  QSYSPRT      OPR0001        OPROUTQ                  RDY        1               1
 2   QPBKIPRTF    OPR0001        OPROUTQ                  RDY        3               1



                                                                              Bottom
Parameters for options 1, 2, 3 or command
===> ______________________________________________________________________________
F3=Exit   F10=View 3   F11=View 2   F12=Cancel   F22=Printers   F24=More keys
```

Figure L2-9: Selecting a file to print from the Work with All Spooled Files screen.

- Enter PRT01 for the name of the printer.
- Press Enter.
- Retrieve the printout from the printer.
- Label the printout #1 and attach it your lab submission form.

USER SUPPORT: THE INFORMATION CENTER

The Information Center is IBM's newest method of finding technical information related to the AS/400. It provides three areas of information: Information Center, Technical Studio, and Online Library. The Information Center is available in two forms: CD-ROM and the Internet. It is a rich and up-to-date source of information.

Access the Information Center from the AS/400 home page:

```
http://www.as400.ibm.com
```

or from the AS/400 Information Entry Page—Information Center at:

```
http://publib.boulder.ibm.com/html/as400/infocenter.html
```

The Information Center is shown in Figure L2-10.

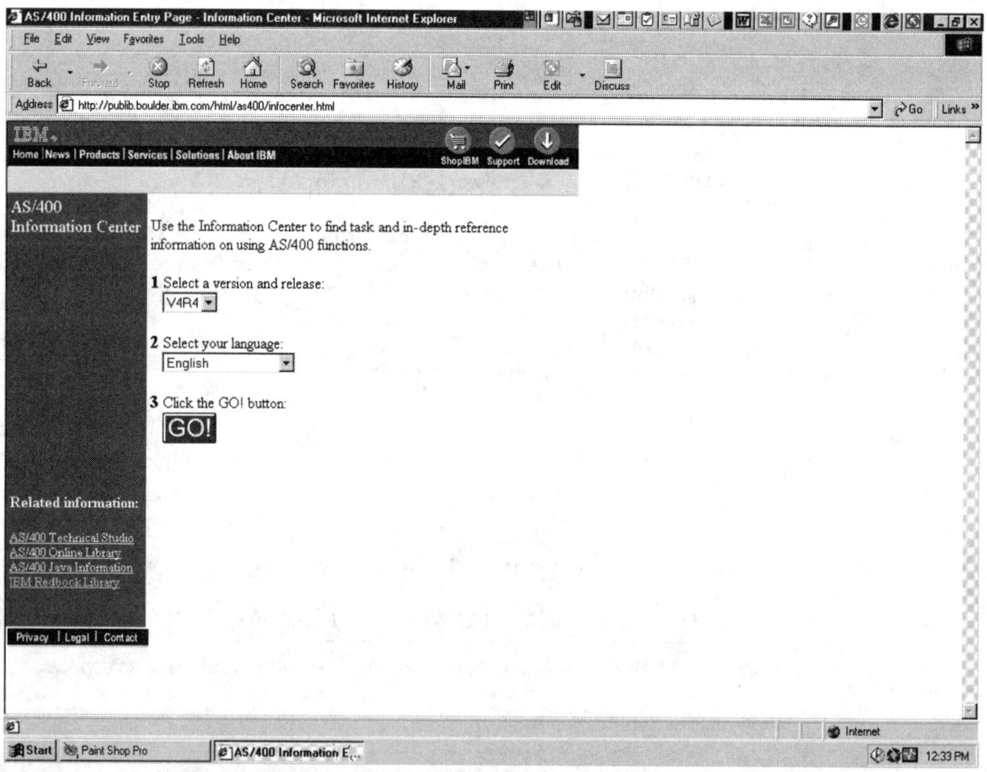

Figure L2-10: Entry page for the Information Center, Internet version.

To access and explore the Information Center, you need the CD-ROM version on the PC or access to the Internet. To start from the Internet, use one of the two URLs above. This section of the lab uses the main site.

- Open an `Internet browser`.
- Enter
  `http://publib.boulder.ibm.com/html/as400/infocenter.html`
  in the location box on your Internet browser.
- Press Enter.
- Single-click on the `GO` link.
- Identify three topics of information available from the Information Center.
  ____
  ____
  ____
- Spend some time exploring the resources available.
- Click on the browser's `Back` button until you return to the initial Information Center screen.

The Technical Studio provides users with workshops, tools, and technical information to expand the strategic use of AS/400.

- Click on the `Technical Studio`.
- Click on the `GO` link.
- Identify three topics of information available in the Technical Studio.
  ____
  ____
  ____
- Spend some time exploring the resources available.
- Click on the browser's `Back` button until you return to the initial Information Center screen.

The manuals that were shipped with your AS/400 are now available on-line through the `Online Library` link of the Information Center.

- Click on the `Online Library` topic.
- Click on the `GO` link.
- Click on the `Latest Release of the Operating System` link.
- Click on the `Category bookshelf for V4R4` (or release of choice).
- Click on `Search or View all V4R4 books in English`.
- Click on the `Search books` button.

- Enter one of the following search topics in the view.
  - Save while active.
  - Start a printwriter.
  - Clear a message queue.
  - Work and print a spool file.
- Go through the links to pages from manuals until you find the information.
- Print the page you found.
- Label the printout #2 and attach it to your lab submission form.

Now that you are familiar with the Information Center, it is time to apply the knowledge.

- What is the latest release of the operating system? ____________________
- Exit the browser.

END-OF-CHAPTER AIDS

CHAPTER SUMMARY

1. The AS/400 provides the user with a series of user-friendly interfaces to facilitate its user.
2. The user interfaces consist of the following types:
   a. Menu.
   b. Help.
   c. Entry panel.
   d. List panel.
   e. Information.
   f. InfoSeeker.
   g. Information Center.
3. Help support on the AS/400 provides various levels of help.
4. The position of your cursor on a screen determines what help topics you are provided, and is known as contextual help.
5. The AS/400 provides three different *assistance levels*. These provide a different support environment based on the user's skill level.
6. Information support is provided through InfoSeeker and the Information Center. InfoSeeker provides text-based versions of the manuals available on-line. The newer Information Center provides more than the manuals available over the Internet. The Information Center is the new support and will be replacing InfoSeeker after V4R4.

KEY TERMS

active function keys
assistance levels
bookshelves
contextual help
entry panel
extended help
fuzzy
help
help interface
hot-key navigation
Information Assistant
Information Center
InfoSeeker
list
list display
list of options
list panel
list screen
location box
menu interface
menu name
message line
message queues
national language support
nested
Operational Assistant (OA) menu
screen header
second-level message text
softcopy books
system distribution directory
system name
System Request Menu
user support

CHAPTER SELF-TEST

The solutions to these self-test questions are in appendix D.

True-False Questions

___ 1. The word GO followed by a menu name entered from the command line will take you directly to that menu.

___ 2. The F11 function key takes you to an entry screen allowing you to control or limit the actions of a command.

___ 3. F1 functions as the Help key.

___ 4. Contextual help is when the cursor position determines what help topic will be displayed.

___ 5. For ease of use, most systems set the default assistance level to "basic."

___ 6. InfoSeeker provides a graphic version of the manuals on-line.

___ 7. The most up-to-date versions of the manuals are available on the Internet.

Fill in the Blanks

1. The _______ function key toggles back and forth between keywords and choices/values screen format.

2. The sign-on screen is an example of a(n) ___________ screen.

3. The Information Center is an example of a ______________ interface.

4. To cancel the actions of an incorrectly issued command, you would reference the _____________ menu.

5. ______________________ allows you to access and read AS/400 manuals on- line.

6. When you receive a system-supplied message and want more information, you would _______________________________________.

Chapter Review Questions

1. Define the following terms:
   a. Assistance level.
   b. Extended help.
   c. Contextual help.
   d. Object program.

2. Identify an example of each of the following display interfaces.
   a. Menu.
   b. Entry panel.
   c. List panel.

3. Indicate the difference between extended help and contextual help.

4. When would you use the following assistance levels?
   a. Basic.
   b. Intermediate.
   c. Advanced.

5. Give an example of:
   a. First-level message text.
   b. Second-level message text.

6. Identify the areas of information provided in the Information Center.

3

OS/400 Command Structure and Control Language

Chapter Objectives

Upon completion of this chapter, you should be able to:

- Describe Control Language (CL).
- Describe the syntax of an OS/400 command.
- Describe the structure of command names.
- Explain what parameters are.
- Explain what keywords and positional parameters are.
- Demonstrate how to enter and run CL commands using keyword and positional parameters.
- Explain the difference between required parameters and optional parameters.
- Demonstrate free-form entry and command prompting of CL commands.
- Demonstrate how to enter commands using Command Entry Screen (QCMD).

CONTROL LANGUAGE: THE ULTIMATE INTERFACE

We have discussed user interfaces before. Any tool that makes it easier to communicate with the computer is a user interface. Menus are user interfaces. Data entry screens are also interfaces. Screens and menus on slick GUI screens are as much interfaces as those on "green" (textual) screens.

Underneath it all lies the AS/400 *Control Language*, usually referred to as *CL*. CL statements are actually AS/400 *commands*. When a user makes a menu selection, that selection really invokes one or more CL statements to make the computer perform the selected function. Even IBM-supplied menus that make life easy for users invoke CL commands under their covers.

Menus are nice interfaces while learning the AS/400 or when doing unfamiliar activities, but the AS/400 is quick to master, and most operators soon want to enter CL commands directly.

The AS/400's Main Menu (and many other AS/400 menus) has a line across the bottom of the screen that is called a *command line*. Menu selections, as well as commands, are entered on this line. This command line is set off with the phrase:

```
Selection or command ===>
```

to its left.

What are referred to as *CL commands* actually have two parts: the *command name* and its *parameters*.

Several CL commands can be grouped together into a special program called a *CL Program,* or *CLP* for short, to do very complex system tasks automatically. Because a CLP needs to do tasks unique to a program, like controlling logic and storing local variables, the set of CL commands includes some that can only be used within CLPs, and others that can be used individually on a command line or in a CLP. This chapter will focus on only those nonprogram CL commands.

CONTROL LANGUAGE (CL) COMMAND NAMES

All CL commands are derived from a common syntax. *Syntax* refers to the rules that must be followed when constructing a CL command. Any violation of these rules is considered a syntax error. The system informs the developer of these errors when the command is run. Do not let this discussion of system errors scare you. Once you understand the syntax, you can quickly find your way around any AS/400.

The command name identifies the function to be performed when the command is run. It is limited to a maximum of ten characters and is a concatenation of several abbreviated words. Just like English, these words can be nouns, verbs, or adjectives. These abbreviations are not cryptic; they relate to the word they are replacing, and they are applied consistently across the system. Once you learn an abbreviation, its meaning will be the same every time you encounter it.

A few simple abbreviations are used for all nouns, verbs, and adjectives. These abbreviations are concatenated to create meaningful command names. As you learn the abbreviations and command name construction, you will soon be sticking them together to make your own guesses at command names.

For example, consider the CRTLIB command shown below. This command will create (CRT) a library (LIB). It consists of the verb CRT and the noun LIB.

```
CRTLIB
|  \
|   └─▶ Noun (object of the action) "Library"
|
└─▶Verb (action) "Create"
```

Figure 3-1 lists examples of several other action CL abbreviations. Figure 3-2 lists examples of some CL noun abbreviations.

Verb or Action	CL Abbreviation
Add	ADD
Change	CHG
Clear	CLR
Create	CRT
Copy	CPY
Delete	DLT
Display	DSP
Hold	HLD
Release	RLS
Remove	RMV
Restore	RST
Retrieve	RTV
Save	SAV
Send	SND
Submit	SBM
Work with	WRK

Figure 3-1: Examples of the verb (action) portion of CL commands.

Noun	CL Abbreviation
Configuration	CFG
Command	CMD
Description	D
Entry	E
File	F
Job	JOB
Library	LIB
List	L
Member	MBR
Message	MSG
Object	OBJ
Queue	Q
Source	SRC
Spool	SPL
Subsystem	SBS
System	SYS

Figure 3-2: Examples of the noun (subject) portion of CL commands.

An example of a CL command that also uses an adjective is the CHGCURLIB (Change Current Library) command:

```
CHGCURLIB
|  \  \
|   \  └─▶ Noun (object of the action) "Library"
|    \
|     └─▶ Adjective (qualifier) "Current"
|
└─▶ Verb (action) "Change"
```

Some adjectives also only have a single letter. The adjectives, "physical" and "logical," are abbreviated to P and L respectively and are often used to qualify the noun file that is abbreviated F.

When a command contains PF or LF after the verb, it will take some action on a *physical file* or a *logical file*. Here are some common CL commands and what they mean:

CRTLIB (Create Library)
CPYF (Copy File)
WRKSPLF (Work with All Spooled Files)
CRTSRCPF (Create Source Physical File)

As in most cases, there are exceptions to the rules for creating a command name. Interestingly, the most used command, CALL, consists entirely of a verb that has four letters and is not abbreviated. Figure 3-3 lists some additional common command abbreviations.

Abbreviation	Meaning
ACT	Active
BRK	Break
CUR	Current
EDT	Edit
PRF	Profile
PRT	Printer
STR	Start
WRK	Work with

Figure 3-3: Additional common CL command name abbreviations.

CONTROL LANGUAGE (CL) COMMAND PARAMETERS

CL command names can be followed by parameters. Some commands do not have parameters; others have many. IBM knows no one is going to memorize all parameters for all commands, so it gives us a powerful command aid. There is no name for this aid, but the process of entering commands this way is called *prompting* the command. To illustrate a sample command and its parameters, we will prompt it to show this concept.

For this example, we will create a library. Assume you have already figured out that the command to use is Create Library (CRTLIB), but you do not know anything about how to use it. On the command line, enter the command CRTLIB and press the F4 key to prompt it. You will get a screen that looks similar to the one shown in Figure 3-4.

```
                          Create Library (CRTLIB)

 Type choices, press Enter.

 Library . . . . . . . . . . .   __________     Name
 Library type  . . . . . . . .   *PROD          *PROD, *TEST
 Text 'description'  . . . . .   *BLANK


                                                                    Bottom
 F3=Exit   F4=Prompt   F5=Refresh   F10=Additional parameters   F12=Cancel
 F13=How to use this display        F24=More keys
```

Figure 3-4: Create Library command screen.

As you can see, you do not have to know anything about a command other than its name, and prompting will walk you through the rest.

Here is a tour of the prompted view: There is a parameter, LIBRARY, on the left that is followed by dots to a blank line where the library name to create (or display or change or whatever the verb is) can be entered. If there is any doubt about what to do next, there is a brief description of what the system is looking for to the right of that line—in this case, the name of the library. These are called *values*.

The next parameter is LIBRARY TYPE. Notice that the letters *PROD are already in place in its entry line. This is referred to as a *default value*. Default parameters' values are most often predefined *special values* that begin with an asterisk (*). If necessary, the cursor can be placed on this value to change it. This parameter is a little different from the first one, though, because if it is changed, it can only be changed to *TEST. That limitation of only two values is indicated to the right of the entry line, where *PROD and *TEST are specified. If there were more possible values that could be used, and there were too many to put into this small help space, as many as possible would be listed followed by an ellipses (…) to indicate there are more.

The last parameter, TEXT 'DESCRIPTION' has *BLANK filled in. The entry line is also quite long. The *BLANK default value will cause the text or description of the library created to be left blank. Text descriptions should be used whenever they are encountered.

One thing about parameters that this screen leaves off is that they each have unique names. All prompted command screens favor the brief help text on the right rather than the command names—because when a command is entered from a prompted screen, the user does not need to know the parameter names. If you are curious, press the F11 key and the prompted screen will change to one similar to the one shown in Figure 3-5.

```
                           Create Library (CRTLIB)

 Type choices, press Enter.

 Library . . . . . . . . . . . . LIB            __________
 Library type . . . . . . . . . . TYPE          *PROD
 Text 'description' . . . . . . . TEXT          *BLANK










                                                                    Bottom
 F3=Exit   F4=Prompt   F5=Refresh   F10=Additional parameters   F12=Cancel
 F13=How to use this display        F24=More keys
```

Figure 3-5: Keywords displayed on Create Library screen.

Notice that the helpful words on the right dropped off, and the parameter names appeared to the immediate left of the entry fields.

The AS/400 has two more options for help other than what appears on the screen. To use either one, place the cursor on the field in question. If you just want a quick list of the possible parameter values (*parameter list*), enter a question mark (?) and press Enter. If you do so on the type of library, you would get the screen shown in Figure 3-6.

```
                         Specify Value for Parameter TYPE

 Type choice, press Enter.


 Library type . . . . . . . . . .   *PROD

   *PROD
   *TEST










 F3=Exit   F5=Refresh   F12=Cancel   F13=How to use this display   F24=More keys
```

Figure 3-6: Permissible values for LIBRARY parameter of Create Library command.

If you really do not know what to do, your other option is to press the F1(Help) key with the cursor on the field. In either case, you will get a very detailed description of what to put in the field and what it means. Figure 3-7 contains a sample of that level of help.

```
                            Create Library (CRTLIB)

 Type choices, press Enter.

 Library . . . . . . . . . . . . LIB            __________
 Library type . . . . . . . . . . TYPE           *PROD
 Text 'descrip ..........................................................
               :                 Library type (TYPE) - Help             :
               :                                                        :
               :  Specifies the type of library being created.          :
               :                                                        :
               :  *PROD                                                 :
               :      This is a production library.  Database files in  :
               :      production libraries cannot be opened for updating if :
               :      a user is in debug mode and he requested that     :
               :      production libraries be protected.  A user can protect :
               :      all database files in production libraries by     :
               :      specifying UPDPROD(*NO) on the Start Debug (STRDBG) :
               :      command to begin testing. However, this protection :
               :                                              More...   :
               :  F2=Extended help   F10=Move to top   F11=InfoSeeker   :
 F3=Exit   F4= :  F12=Cancel         F20=Enlarge       F24=More keys    :
 F13=How to us :                                                        :
               :........................................................:
```

Figure 3-7: Field level help screen.

Some command parameters are *optional parameters*, and some are *required parameters*. To quickly know which is which, press Enter without entering anything. Required fields will be displayed bright, in reverse image. Generally speaking, command parameters are displayed in order required and most often used at the top, down to optional and rarely used.

The example command has some rarely used parameters that are not shown on the display. To view them, press the F10 (Additional Parameters) key. Figure 3-8 contains a sample of the additional parameters for the CRTLIB command.

```
                        Create Library (CRTLIB)

 Type choices, press Enter.

 Library . . . . . . . . . . . . LIB            __________
 Library type . . . . . . . . . TYPE           *PROD
 Text 'description' . . . . . . . TEXT           *BLANK

                         Additional Parameters

 Authority . . . . . . . . . . . AUT            *LIBCRTAUT
 Auxiliary storage pool ID . . . ASP            1
 Create authority . . . . . . . . CRTAUT         *SYSVAL
 Create object auditing . . . . . CRTOBJAUD      *SYSVAL



                                                                 Bottom
 F3=Exit   F4=Prompt   F5=Refresh   F12=Cancel   F13=How to use this display
 F24=More keys
```

Figure 3-8: Additional parameters displayed.

Some complex commands also bring up parameters in response to what values are entered for earlier parameters. If you are impatient and want to preview those parameters, press F9 (Display All Parameters) and they will appear. This is a common function key assignment, although the previous examples did not include it.

Prompted commands can have parameters that extend to many screens. If there are more parameter screens to follow, the lower-right section of the screen will display `More...`. In Figure 3-8, there are no more parameter screens, so the word `Bottom` is displayed.

If you are ever in doubt about a command and how to use it, prompt it first. After doing this a few times, you will be familiar enough with a command to simply enter it on the command line.

Entering a command on the command line is easy: enter the command name and the parameters, then press Enter.

There are three ways to enter command parameters on the command line:

- Keywords.
- Positional.
- Combination of keywords and positional.

The *keywords* are the parameter names you encountered on previous screens. Here is an example of the CRTLIB command using keywords (*keyword notation*).

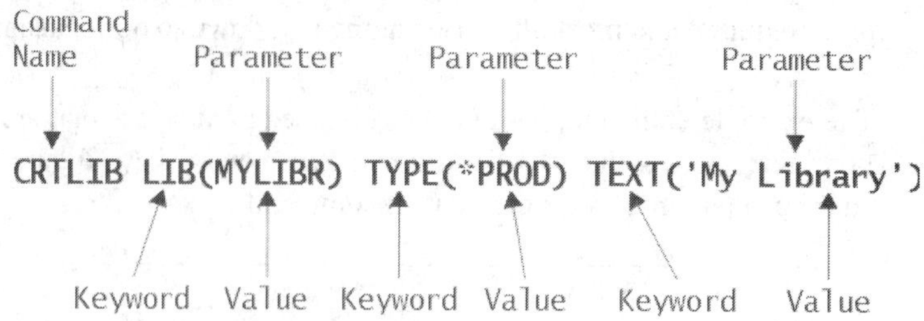

That is easy for the computer; it simply places the values you entered in the parameters you named.

Here is the same command using positional parameters (*positional notation*).

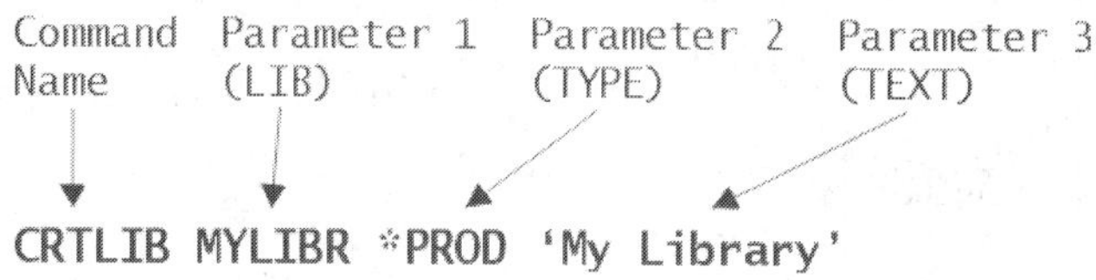

Assuming you put in at least one space between the command name and each of the parameters, the AS/400 assigns each one in order to the first three parameters of the command. The danger with this method is mixing up the parameters.

Also, parameters cannot be skipped using this method. If, in the example, you entered the library and text and did not enter the type parameter (thus, taking the default), you would have to use keyword notation. You can mix keyword with positional parameters in any command.

```
CRTLIB MYLIBR TYPE(*PROD) TEXT('My Library')
```

There is a rule to remember when you mix parameter entry types: once you use your first keyword parameter ("TYPE (*PROD)" in the example), you cannot go back to using positional parameters/notation. This would be incorrect:

```
CRTLIB MYLIBR TYPE(*PROD) 'My Library'
```

The AS/400 would attempt to place the character string MYLIBR in the first parameter, LIB; and *PROD in the second parameter, TYPE. Then it would not know what to do with the character string ('My Library').

You see correctly mixed parameters used when someone really knows the *command structure* and wants to skip one or more parameters. The user will use positional parameters as long as possible, then switch (after the first skipped parameter) to keyword parameters. If you wanted to skip the TYPE parameter in the example, you would enter the command this way:

```
CRTLIB MYLIBR TEXT('My Library')
```

MASTERING THE UNKNOWN IN CL

In the previous section, you started with a command about which you knew little and used prompting to help you use it. Assume you know next to nothing about an AS/400, but you want to take a giant leap—you want to do something with the machine but do not know where to start.

Here is another CL function to try from any command line—there are no menus for this. On a blank command line, press the F4 key. The system will produce a menu like the one shown in Figure 3-9.

```
MAJOR                         Major Command Groups
                                                          System:   BIGBLUE
 Select one of the following:

      1. Select Command by Name                                   SLTCMD
      2. Verb Commands                                            VERB
      3. Subject Commands                                         SUBJECT
      4. Object Management Commands                               CMDOBJMGT
      5. File Commands                                            CMDFILE
      6. Save and Restore Commands                                CMDSAVRST
      7. Work Management Commands                                 CMDWRKMGT
      8. Data Management Commands                                 CMDDTAMGT
      9. Security Commands                                        CMDSEC
     10. Print Commands                                           CMDPRT
     11. Spooling Commands                                        CMDSPL
     12. System Control Commands                                  CMDSYSCTL
     13. Program Commands                                         CMDPGM
                                                                     More...
 Selection or command
 ===> ____________________________________________________________________

 F3=Exit   F4=Prompt   F9=Retrieve   F12=Cancel   F13=Information Assistant
 F16=AS/400 Main menu
 (C) COPYRIGHT IBM CORP. 1980, 1998.
```

Figure 3-9: Major command menu.

Each menu selection will display a group of related commands. Many operators use options 2 and 3 to find commands when they are not sure of the verb, or they know the verb but are not sure of the noun. Or, someone will know enough about the AS/400 to know to work with libraries but does not know where to start. A quick way into an overview of all the commands about libraries is to bring up the major menu. Select option 3 from the major menu and page down (with the Page Down key) until `Libraries` is encountered, and enter that option (which is 214). A screen similar to the one shown in Figure 3-10 will appear.

```
CMDLIB                          Library Commands

 Select one of the following:

   Commands
      1. Change Current Library                                 CHGCURLIB
      2. Change Library                                         CHGLIB

      4. Clear Library                                          CLRLIB
      5. Copy Library                                           CPYLIB
      6. Create Library                                         CRTLIB
      7. Delete library                                         DLTLIB
      8. Display Library                                        DSPLIB
      9. Display Library Description                            DSPLIBD
     10. Query Document Library                                 QRYDOCLIB
     11. Reclaim Library                                        RCLLIB
     12. Restore Library                                        RSTLIB
     13. Restore S/36 Library Members                           RSTS36LIBM
                                                                   More...
 Selection or command
 ===> ____________________________________________________________________

 F3=Exit   F4=Prompt   F9=Retrieve   F12=Cancel   F16=Major menu
 Command prompting ended when user pressed F12.
```

Figure 3-10: Library Commands menu.

Figure 3-10 lists all the commands that do something with libraries. If one looks like the desired one, enter its option number and press Enter; the command will come up in a prompted form. Our favorite, CRTLIB, is option 6. If we type that and press Enter, we will get a screen similar to the one in Figure 3-4.

A SHORTCUT FOR COMMAND ENTRY

System operators spend a large part of the day interacting with the AS/400 through commands. They quickly learn the commands so well that they forego prompting every one. Most operators just key the command and its parameters on a command line.

Even this can get tedious and represent a lot of typing. The AS/400 has a great shortcut built into it. The F9 key is reserved on all screens with a command line. This is the Retrieve key. When pressed, it will bring up the last used command. If you press it from the screen shown in Figure 3-11, you will retrieve the last command you entered. Refer to Figure 3-11 for a sample.

Pressing the Enter key from this screen will make the system try to run the command again. In this case, it would result in an error because library MYLIBR already exists.

By pressing F9 again, you will get the previous command to that one. F9 is useful in several situations:

- To run the same command several times—just changing one or two parameters slightly each time.
- When an inputting error occurs on a complex command—rather than retype it, use F9 and correct the bad parameter.

- When the operator needs to recall exactly what was done previously. For example, if you were asked to create a library called MYLIBR, thought you did so, then could not find it, you could "F9" back through your work to see if you misidentified the name.

```
CMDLIB                          Library Commands

 Select one of the following:

   Commands
      1. Change Current Library                                      CHGCURLIB
      2. Change Library                                              CHGLIB

      4. Clear Library                                               CLRLIB
      5. Copy Library                                                CPYLIB
      6. Create Library                                              CRTLIB
      7. Delete library                                              DLTLIB
      8. Display Library                                             DSPLIB
      9. Display Library Description                                 DSPLIBD
     10. Query Document Library                                      QRYDOCLIB
     11. Reclaim Library                                             RCLLIB
     12. Restore Library                                             RSTLIB
     13. Restore S/36 Library Members                                RSTS36LIBM
                                                                        More...
 Selection or command
 ===> CRTLIB MYLIBR TEXT('My Library')

 F3=Exit   F4=Prompt   F9=Retrieve   F12=Cancel   F16=Major menu
 Command prompting ended when user pressed F12.
```

Figure 3-11: Library Commands menu.

Notice that the command retrieved in Figure 3-11 shows the command and its parameters. Even if the command had been entered through prompting, the F9 key first presents it in its unprompted form. It can again be prompted by pressing the F4 key.

COMMAND LINE VERSUS COMMAND ENTRY DISPLAY

All users except limited users (refer to chapter 11, Security and Security System Values) can enter and prompt commands directly at the command line of any displayed menu, and from many other system-supplied displays.

There is also a specialized display that can be used when a user is entering commands at a workstation. It is called the *Command Entry display*. The Command Entry display is an optional entry panel for commands. To use this panel, simply enter CALL QCMD on the command line. A screen similar to the one shown in Figure 3-12 will appear.

```
                              Command Entry                        BIGBLUE
                                                        Request level:   7
 Previous commands and messages:
All previous commands and messages:
  4 > CPYF FROMFILE(ASDF) TOFILE(*PRINT)
      From-file ASDF in *LIBL not found.
      Copy command ended because of error.
  4 > gomajorOMFILE(ASDF) TOFILE(*PRINT)
      String beginning 'GOMAJOROMF' not valid command name.
      Error found on *N command.
  4 > go major
  5 > /*     */
  7 > go cmdcpy
  7 > call qcmd
  8 > CPYF FROMFILE(OPRLIB/INTRO) TOFILE(*PRINT)
      5 records copied from member TESTPE1.
  4 > CRTLIB MYLIBR TYPE(*PROD) TEXT('My Library')
  4 > CRTLIB MYLIBR TEXT('My Library')
                                                                    Bottom
 Type command, press Enter.
 ===> ____________________________________________________________________
 _________________________________________________________________________
 _________________________________________________________________________
 _________________________________________________________________________
 F3=Exit   F4=Prompt   F9=Retrieve   F10=Include detailed messages
 F11=Display full      F12=Cancel    F13=Information Assistant   F24=More keys
```

Figure 3-12: Command Entry screen.

This is a pure command screen; there is no menu on it. The empty space above the command line is used to display previously issued commands in the order they were issued (latest at the bottom).

The F9 (Retrieve) key can be used on this display, just as on the command line. The difference is that you can position the cursor on any previously entered command and press F9. You won't have to scroll through all commands as you saw earlier.

The F10 (Include Detailed Messages) key includes all messages the user has received in response to this interactive work at the display station. Message help can also be called from this display by placing the cursor on the message and pressing the F1 (Help) key.

The F11 (Display Full) key changes the mode of the Command Entry display, so that the maximum amount of space is available on the screen for command entry.

LAB #3: OS/400 COMMAND STRUCTURE AND CONTROL LANGUAGE

Upon completion of this lab, you should be able to:

- Explore the group command menus.
- Create a library.
- Demonstrate how to create and manage spool files.
- Explain how to move files to a printer.

- Use the command line to execute commands.
- Use the Command Entry display.
- Use user-defined, system-defined, and special values in commands.
- Use command prompting.
- Explore command structure.

THE COMMAND MENUS

MAJOR MENU

The AS/400 provides you with a variety of ways to find commands easily. There are a series of command menus that provide the user with an easy method to find the command needed to perform a specific task. This section explores the various command menus. First, start by exploring the Major menu, which lists commands by category.

To access the Major menu, enter the following command, as shown in Figure L3-1.

- Enter `GO MAJOR` on the Selection or command line ===>.
- Press Enter.

```
MAIN                          AS/400 Main Menu
                                                        System:   BLUE400
Select one of the following:

     1. User tasks
     2. Office tasks
     3. General system tasks
     4. Files, libraries, and folders
     5. Programming
     6. Communications
     7. Define or change the system
     8. Problem handling
     9. Display a menu
    10. Information Assistant options
    11. Client Access tasks

    90. Sign off

Selection or command
===> GO MAJOR

F3=Exit   F4=Prompt   F9=Retrieve   F12=Cancel   F13=Information Assistant
F23=Set initial menu
(C) COPYRIGHT IBM CORP. 1980, 1994.
```

Figure L3-1: Entering the command to access the Major command menu.

The system displays the Major command menu. This menu allows you to access commands that have been organized by groups.

- Review the various groups of commands available on the Major menu.
- List three groups of command menus available on the Major menu.

____

____

To better understand the command groups, spend some time exploring the options on the Major menu. Each of the options leads to another command menu. All menus are objects on the AS/400 and have an associated object name. The standard format for menus is to display the menu's object name in the upper-left corner. Select one of the menu groups and select that menu option.

- Enter the Option number of a menu group on the command line.
- Press Enter.
- What is the name of the menu group that you selected from the Major menu?

____

____

- What is the menu object's name?

____

Remember that a menu can be accessed directly by typing GO followed by the *object name* of the menu. Now that you know the object name of a command group menu, it can be accessed directly from the command line in the future.

Using what you have learned in the previous chapters, determine the answers to the following questions.

- Return to the Main Menu.
- Enter `4` on the Selection or command ===> line.
- Press Enter.The `Files, Libraries and Folders` menu appears.
- What is the object name of this menu?

____

- What is the command you would use to directly access this menu?

____

COMMAND MENUS

To find OS/400 commands, you can use the group command menus or go directly to commands organized by the command type. To go to the WORK command menu, use the command GO followed by CMDXXX (XXX is the command type you want). To access the WORK command menu, the command would be GO CMDWRK. Following this example, to access the SAVE commands, you would enter GO CMDSAV. You can use a generic search character string (a wildcard) to find either all the menus or a group of menus.

- Enter `GO CMD*` on the Selection or command ===> line. A listing of all the command menus is displayed.
- Enter `GO CMDC*` on the Selection or command ===> line.
- List three command menus displayed.

  ____

  ____

Explore the various command menus available on the AS/400. Use the preceding command menu pattern and the group menus to find the commands in Figure L3-2.

- Use the command menus available on the system to complete Figure L3-2.

Work with Active Jobs	
Work with Configuration Status	
Clear an Out Queue	
Send a Message	
Work with Writer	
Save a Library	
Move an Object	
Display a Library List	
Create a Display File	
Create a Duplicate Object	
Change Current Library	
Work with Spool Files	
Change Job Description	
Clear Message Queue	
Copy File	
Add Library List Entry	
Restore Library	
Remove Job Queue Entry	
Create Physical File	
Work with Submitted Jobs	
Work with Systems Status	
Initialize Tape	

Figure L3-2: Identification of commands.

Use the command menus and information in this chapter to list commands.

- Write what each command stands for in Figure L3-3.

DSPMSG	
DLTLIB	
WRKOUTQ	
HLDJOBQ	
RLSOUTQ	
RNMOBJ	
CHGMSGQ	
DSPTAP	
RMVLIBLE	
DLTF	
DSPJOBD	
SBMJOB	
HLDWTR	
STRPRTWTR	
SNDBRKMSG	
DSPOBJD	
DSPDTAARA	
DSPFFD	
WRKDEVD	
WRKDSKSTS	

Figure L3-3: Commands and what they mean.

COMMAND STRUCTURE

Commands consist of the command name as well as the command parameters. Parameters are broken into keywords and values. This section explores command structure. Now that you know how to write command names, they won't always be provided. For questions on the actual command, refer to the previous section.

- Enter the `Copy File` command on the Selection or command ===> line.
- Press F4 to prompt the command.

Use the F11 key to toggle between the keywords and permissible values.

- Press F11 to display the keywords.
- What are the keywords of the first two parameters for this command?
  ______________________ ______________________
- Press F12.
- Enter the command to `Create a Duplicate Object` on the Selection or command ===> line.
- Press F4 (Prompt) key on that command.
- Toggle between keywords and values using the F11 key.
- List the keywords for the five parameters.
  ____
  ______________________ ______________________
  ______________________ ______________________

Commands have required and optional parameters. Generally, the required parameters are displayed first and when prompting on the command, the field is white—in contrast to the optional parameters, which are green. Optional parameters already have been assigned a default value that you have the option to change. Frequently, the permissible values, displayed to the right of the parameter field, are special values. Figure L3-4 lists a few of the command special values you will encounter.

- List the meaning of the special values in Figure L3-4.

*CURLIB	
*LIBL	
*FILE	
*OBJ	
*JOBD	
*PRINT	
*CHAR	
*SYSOPR	
*WRKSTN	
*OUTQ	

Figure L3-4: Special values' meanings.

USING COMMANDS TO PERFORM TASKS

USING THE COPY FILE COMMAND

Copy the INTRO file located in the OPRLIB to print. This will produce a printout in the class out queue. To accomplish this, enter CPYF on the command line then press F4 to prompt. The screen in Figure L3-5 will be displayed.

- Enter CPYF on the Selection or command ===> line.
- Press the F4 (Prompt) key.
- Complete the fields as shown in Figure L3-5.
- Press Enter.

```
                          Copy File (CPYF)

Type choices, press Enter.

From file . . . . . . . . . . .   intro        Name
  Library . . . . . . . . . . .     oprlib     Name, *LIBL, *CURLIB
To file . . . . . . . . . . . .   *print       Name, *PRINT
  Library . . . . . . . . . . .     *LIBL      Name, *LIBL, *CURLIB
From member . . . . . . . . . .   *FIRST       Name, generic*, *FIRST, *ALL
To member or label . . . . . . .  *FIRST       Name, *FIRST, *FROMMBR
Replace or add records . . . . .  *NONE        *NONE, *ADD, *REPLACE...
Create file . . . . . . . . . .   *NO          *NO, *YES
Print format . . . . . . . . . .  *CHAR        *CHAR, *HEX
```

Figure L3-5: Using Copy File command to copy OPRLIB/INTRO to the spool file.

PRINTING THE INTRO FILE

In this class, the printouts do not go directly to a printer, they go to an out queue. You should always view your printout in the out queue before you direct it to a printer. Everything produced may not be worth printing and would be better deleted. Each site can use a variety of printer types. There are AS/400 printers, which are attached to the AS/400; and TCP/IP network printers that are defined to the AS/400 and use out queues defined on the AS/400. More information about TCP/IP printers is found in chapter 19. Check with your instructor to determine the method of printing at your facility.

You need to print the contents of the INTRO file, which was produced in the previous step. To access the files in the out queue(s), the WRKSPLF command is used. The Work with All Spooled Files screen is shown in Figure L3-6.

```
                        Work with All Spooled Files

Type options, press Enter.
  1=Send   2=Change   3=Hold   4=Delete   5=Display   6=Release   7=Messages
  8=Attributes        9=Work with printing status

                                Device or                       Total    Cur
Opt  File         User          Queue        User Data    Sts   Pages    Page  Copy
___  QPJOBLOG     HOHLY#M       QEZJOBLOG    QPADEV0013   RDY       1             1
___  OPRSRC       HOHLY#M       FACOUTQ                   RDY       1             1
___  OPRSRC       HOHLY#M       FACOUTQ                   RDY       2             1
___  OPRSRC       HOHLY#M       FACOUTQ                   RDY       2             1
___  OPRSRC       HOHLY#M       FACOUTQ                   RDY       2             1
___  QPJOBLOG     HOHLY#M       QEZJOBLOG    QPADEV0004   RDY       4             1
5__  QSYSPRT      HOHLY#M       FACOUTQ                   RDY       1             1


                                                                             Bottom
Parameters for options 1, 2, 3 or command
===> ______________________________________________________________________
F3=Exit   F10=View 3   F11=View 2   F12=Cancel   F22=Printers   F24=More keys
```

Figure L3-6: Work with All Spooled Files screen shows a series of spool files.

- Enter `WRKSPLF` on the Selection or command ===> line.
- Press Enter.
- Place a `5` (View) to the left of the last file.
- View and verify that it is the INTRO file. If this is not the correct file, view the other files until you determine which is the contents of the INTRO file.
- Return to the `Work with All Spooled Files` display.

The Work with All Spooled Files screen displays the printouts in your spool files. Once you have determined which file you want to print, you then need to move the file to a printer. To send a file in your spool file to the printer, use one of the following methods.

USING PRT01 PRINTER—A SYSTEM PRINTER

PRT01 is a directly connected AS/400 system printer. Generally, PRT01 is the default system printer. The method shown in Figure L3-7 is used with the system printer.

- Place a `2` to the left of the file you selected to print.
- Press Enter.
- Change the value of the PRINTER parameter to PRT01.
- Press Enter.

```
              Change Spooled File Attributes (CHGSPLFA)

Type choices, press Enter.

Spooled file . . . . . . . . . . > GPCRTOPS     Name, *SELECT
Job name . . . . . . . . . . . . > GPCRTOPS     Name, *
  User . . . . . . . . . . . . . >   HOHLY      Name
  Number . . . . . . . . . . . . >   266972     000000-999999
Spooled file number  . . . . . . > 1            1-9999, *ONLY, *LAST
Printer  . . . . . . . . . . . .   PRT01        Name, *SAME, *OUTQ
Print sequence . . . . . . . . .   *SAME        *SAME, *NEXT
Form type  . . . . . . . . . . .   *STD         Form type, *SAME, *STD
Copies . . . . . . . . . . . . .   1            1-255, *SAME
Restart printing . . . . . . . .   *STRPAGE     Number, *SAME, *STRPAGE...

                         Additional Parameters

Output queue . . . . . . . . . .   FACULTY      Name, *SAME, *DEV
  Library  . . . . . . . . . . .     QGPL       Name, *LIBL, *CURLIB

                                                                  Bottom
F3=Exit   F4=Prompt   F5=Refresh   F10=Additional parameters   F12=Cancel
F13=How to use this display        F24=More keys
```

Figure L3-7: Changing the spooled file to the system printer.

USING A TCP/IP NETWORK PRINTER

TCP/IP network printers are identified by their IP address to the hosts and users on the network. It can be accessed by not only an AS/400, but PCs and other hosts on the network. To print from an AS/400 to a network printer, an out queue is defined. To print a file, it must be moved to the printer out queue. More information on network printing can be found in chapter 6.

- Place a 2 at the left of the file you selected to print.
- Press Enter.
- Press F10 (Additional Parameters) key.
- Change the value of the OUTPUT QUEUE parameter to PRT03.
- Press Enter.

In this example, the network TCP/IP printer is using the PRT03 output queue. *Note*: PRT03 is an out queue rather than a printer. The PRINTER parameter is left unchanged. See Figure L3-8.

```
                    Change Spooled File Attributes (CHGSPLFA)

 Type choices, press Enter.

 Spooled file . . . . . . . . . . > GPCRTOPS    Name, *SELECT
 Job name . . . . . . . . . . . . > GPCRTOPS    Name, *
   User . . . . . . . . . . . . . >   HOHLY     Name
   Number . . . . . . . . . . . . >   266972    000000-999999
 Spooled file number  . . . . . . > 1           1-9999, *ONLY, *LAST
 Printer  . . . . . . . . . . . .   *OUTQ       Name, *SAME, *OUTQ
 Print sequence . . . . . . . . .   *SAME       *SAME, *NEXT
 Form type  . . . . . . . . . . .   *STD        Form type, *SAME, *STD
 Copies . . . . . . . . . . . . .   1           1-255, *SAME
 Restart printing . . . . . . . .   *STRPAGE    Number, *SAME, *STRPAGE...

                          Additional Parameters

 Output queue . . . . . . . . . .   PRT03       Name, *SAME, *DEV
   Library  . . . . . . . . . . .     QGPL      Name, *LIBL, *CURLIB

                                                                   Bottom
 F3=Exit   F4=Prompt   F5=Refresh   F10=Additional parameters   F12=Cancel
 F13=How to use this display        F24=More keys
```

Figure L3-8: Changing a spool file to a network printer.

- Retrieve the printout from the printer.
- Attach the printout to the submission sheet and label it #1.

EXPLORING MORE COMMANDS

Enter the command to display the library list. Information that is displayed on the screen can be printed through a screen print. While the library list is on the screen, do a screen print. A screen print is generated by the use of a Ctrl-Scroll Lock key sequence. Hold down the Ctrl key, tap the Scroll Lock key, and then release both keys.

Now that you are more experienced with commands, you will be asked to determine the command.

- Enter the command to `Display the Library List` on the command line.
- Press Enter.
- Press Ctrl-Scroll Lock keys together.
- Use the printing instruction above to obtain a printout of the library list.
- Attach the printout to the submission sheet and label it #2.

CREATING A LIBRARY

The shortest and simplest method to create a library is to enter the CL command directly onto a command line. The CRTLIB command, as with all other commands, can only be entered on a screen that contains a command line at the bottom of the screen. To create a library with the Create Library (CRTLIB) entry screen:

- Enter CRTLIB on the Selection or command ===> line.
- Press F4 (Prompt).

Next you need to specify the library to be created.

- Enter USERIDZZZ (where "zzz" are your initials).
- Press the Tab key twice to go to the Text description line.
- Enter a brief description of the library on the Text description line (e.g., Lab 3 practice library).

The above command sequence is shown in Figure L3-9.

```
                         Create Library (CRTLIB)
Type choices, press Enter.

Library . . . . . . . . . . . . .   USERIDZZZ      Name
Library type . . . . . . . . . .    *PROD        *PROD, *TEST
Text 'description' . . . . . . . Lab 3 practice library
```

Figure L3-9: Completed Create Library (CRTLIB) entry screen.

The Library type defaults to *PROD for "production." If all options were successful, you will be returned to the screen from which you executed the CRTLIB command, and the message Library USERIDZZZ created is displayed at the bottom of the screen.

Guideline

System libraries start with the letter Q, so it is not good practice for user-defined libraries to start with that letter. Therefore, you should not name your library with anything that starts with a Q.

LIBRARY EXISTENCE

To demonstrate that you have created the above library, do a screen print of the results of the Work with Objects command. This is shown in Figure L3-10.

- Enter the `Work with Objects` command on a command line.
- Press F4 (Prompt) key.
- Fill in the OBJECT parameter with USER*.

A list of libraries that start with the USER character string and that you have authority to is shown. To get a printout of this screen, use the print screen technique outlined above.

```
                    Work with Objects (WRKOBJ)

Type choices, press Enter.

Object . . . . . . . . . . . . .   user*          Name, generic*, *ALL
  Library  . . . . . . . . . . .     *LIBL        Name, *LIBL, *CURLIB...
Object type  . . . . . . . . . .   *ALL           *ALL, *ALRTBL, *AUTL...
```

Figure L3-10: Work with Objects command.

- Attach this printout and label it #3.

Now is the time to demonstrate that you are getting comfortable with the use of commands.

- Use the `Delete Library` command to eliminate the USERIDZZZ library you just created.
- Use the `Work with Objects` command to display the list of libraries.
- Obtain a screen print of the list of libraries starting with the USER character string.
- The library list should not include the USERIDZZZ library.
- Attach the printout and label it #4.

USING THE COMMAND ENTRY DISPLAY

The Command Entry display, shown in Figure L3-11, allows you an easy interface to enter commands, view resulting messages, and repeat previous commands. The top of the screen displays all commands and messages issued since you logged on. After you issue a command, it is displayed followed by the resulting message. To view these commands and messages, you can page through them. Place your cursor on a command and use the F9 (Retrieve) key to retrieve the command to the command line; or press the F4 (Prompt) key to retrieve the command, prompt that command, and modify the parameters of the command. Now it is time to explore using the Command Entry display.

Let's use the Command Entry display to enter commands and view their outcome. To bring up this screen, you need to enter CALL QCMD on a command line.

- Enter `CALL QCMD` on a command line.
- Press Enter.
- Press F10 (Display Messages) key.

This displays the Command Entry screen. Pressing F10 displays all commands entered and their respective messages since you logged on, as shown in Figure L3-11.

```
                                   Command Entry                         BIGBLUE
                                                               Request level:   8
All previous commands and messages:
 4 > CPYF FROMFILE(ASDF) TOFILE(*PRINT)
     From-file ASDF in *LIBL not found.
     Copy command ended because of error.
 4 > gomajorOMFILE(ASDF) TOFILE(*PRINT)
     String beginning 'GOMAJOROMF' not valid command name.
     Error found on *N command.
 4 > go major
 5 > /*      */
 7 > go cmdcpy
 7 > call qcmd
 8 > CPYF FROMFILE(OPRLIB/INTRO) TOFILE(*PRINT)
     5 records copied from member TESTPE1.
                                                                          Bottom
Type command, press Enter.
===> ____________________________________________________________________________
________________________________________________________________________________
________________________________________________________________________________
________________________________________________________________________________

F3=Exit   F4=Prompt    F9=Retrieve   F10=Exclude detailed messages
F11=Display full       F12=Cancel    F13=Information Assistant   F24=More keys
```

Figure L3-11: Command Entry screen with messages displayed.

Note that in Figure L3-11, the Copy File command has been both successfully and unsuccessfully executed. The messages below the command indicate the success and reasons for nonsuccess.

Let us intentionally issue an incorrect command so that we can generate an error message.

- Enter the `Copy File` command on the command line.
- Press F4 (Prompt).
- Complete the parameters as shown in Figure L3-12.
- Press Enter.

```
                         Copy File (CPYF)

Type choices, press Enter.

From file . . . . . . . . . . . > ASDF          Name
  Library . . . . . . . . . . .     *LIBL       Name, *LIBL, *CURLIB
To file . . . . . . . . . . . . > *PRINT        Name, *PRINT
  Library . . . . . . . . . . .                 Name, *LIBL, *CURLIB
From member . . . . . . . . . .   *FIRST        Name, generic*, *FIRST, *ALL
To member or label . . . . . .    *FIRST        Name, *FIRST, *FROMMBR
Replace or add records . . . .    *NONE         *NONE, *ADD, *REPLACE...
Create file . . . . . . . . . .   *NO           *NO, *YES
Print format . . . . . . . . .    *CHAR         *CHAR, *HEX
```

Figure L3-12: Copy File command with a fictitious file name.

You will notice that both the command and error message are displayed in the top portion of the Command Entry display. Page up and down to explore the commands you have entered since you logged in.

- What error message resulted from this command?
  ____
  ____
  ____

Next, let's retrieve the incorrect command, prompt, and correct the command.

- Place your cursor on the command you just issued.
- Press F4 (Prompt) to retrieve and display the last command.
- Change the `File Name` to INTRO and the `Library` to your library (USERID).
- Leave the TO FILE at *PRINT.
- Press Enter.

This above exercise allowed you to view both a successful and unsuccessful execution of a command, and retrieve and modify a command, among other things. The Command Entry screen can be quite useful.

END-OF-CHAPTER AIDS

CHAPTER SUMMARY

This chapter is different because several different topics have been discussed with very few words. CL is the "heart" of the AS/400; it is what we use to make the system go.

CL is huge, complex, and impossible to teach. The subject is discussed in five volumes in the AS/400 documentation. This chapter shows that once you understand the basic command structure and how to work the AS/400, you do not have to know anything about CL.

You can get to any command quickly through many menus. If you know the command but are weak in how it is used, the AS/400 will walk you through it. If you do not even know the command, the AS/400 will show you quickly what you are looking for (and then walk you through it).

Important concept? Consider this: Any computer's prime interface is some kind of control language. How good you are on a computer usually translates into how well you have memorized the computer's control language. Since you do not have to memorize anything about CL, the AS/400 is yours any time you need it.

Do not feel shy about not knowing every little thing about every command on the AS/400. It is not uncommon to find the most seasoned AS/400 professionals pressing F4. Unlike other systems, this practice does not brand one as weak, it shows that the person is smart enough to let the computer do the work—which is why we have computers in the first place.

KEY TERMS

CL commands
CL Program (CLP)
Command Entry display
command line
command name
command structure
commands
Control Language (CL)
default value
keyword notation
keywords
logical file
object name
optional parameter
parameter list
parameters
physical file
positional notation
prompting
required parameter
special values
syntax
values

CHAPTER SELF-TEST

Solutions to these self-test questions are in appendix D.

True-False Questions

___ 1. A command name consists of an action (verb) and an object (noun).

___ 2. A parameter consists of a keyword and a value.

___ 3. A parameter value can be either a user-defined value or a system-defined value. User-defined values begin with an asterisk.

___ 4. All commands have required parameters.

___ 5. The Major menu organizes commands into groups for easy access.

___ 6. When you do not know a command, you can press the F4 (Prompt) key on a blank command line and the Verb menu will appear.

___ 7. A CL command is used to perform a prescribed set of operations.

Fill in the Blanks

1. When entering a command, you can press the __________ key to prompt on a command.

2. To access the Command Entry display, you would enter ________________ at the command line of any screen.

3. CL stands for ________________ ____________________.

4. When you write a command and do not include the keywords and enter the parameters in the proper order, it is referred to as ______________ ____________.

5. Values which begin with an asterisk (*) are called __________ __________.

6. A command parameter consists of a ________________ and a value.

Chapter Review Questions

1. Explain the following terms:
   a. Parameter.
   b. Parameter list.
   c. Keyword notation.
   d. Positional notation.
   e. User-defined value.
   f. Special value.
   g. Optional parameter.
   h. Required parameter.
   i. Syntax.

2. What is the meaning of the term "command syntax?"

3. What is the difference between user-defined values and system-defined values (special values)?

4. What is the difference between a required parameter and optional parameter?

5. Give five examples of special values.

6. What is meant by a "parameter list?"

4

OBJECTS, LIBRARIES, AND LIBRARY LISTS

CHAPTER OBJECTIVES

Upon completion of this chapter, you should be able to:

- Describe the structure and purpose of a typical library, source physical file, source member, and object.
- Describe the structure and use of a library list.
- Explore object retrieval using library lists.
- Explore commands related to manipulating objects.
- Explore library-related commands.
- Describe various types of libraries.
- Describe object naming.

AS/400 OBJECTS AND OBJECT MANAGEMENT

Everything on the AS/400 system that can be stored or retrieved is defined as an object. By definition, an *object* is a named unit that consists of a set of characteristics that describe the object, in many cases, data. An object is anything that exists, occupies storage, and on which operations (commands) can be performed. Different *object types* have different operational characteristics. These differences make each object type unique. For example, a file object contains *records* while a program object contains computer instructions. The implicit uniqueness between the two is set early on—the AS/400 will never allow a program to be read like a file or a file's records to be executed like a program.

Object management provides the functions (commands) necessary to place objects in storage and to locate objects when they are needed for processing. An object consists of two parts: the *object header portion* (or description) and the *functional object portion*. The object header contains a description of the object including the type, owner, creation date, object size, and other attributes that govern the way the object can be used. This allows the system to perform operations collectively on all objects, as well as permitting each object to be tailored for its own purpose. Examples of functional portions of an object would be the file's records, or a program's instructions. See Figure 4-1.

Object name, type, owner, library, etc.	Object header Portion
This could be a file's data, program statements, etc.	Function portion of object

Figure 4-1: Object structure.

Common object header attributes are:

- Name
- Type
- Owner name
- Creation time
- Save time
- Text description
- Library
- Attributes
- Creation date
- Save date
- Offline size
- Change date

Each object has a name. On the AS/400, objects are referred to by their *qualified name* that consists of the *library* and the *object* name. The format is library/object name. For example, a file named INTRO stored in the STUDENT library would have the following qualified name: STUDENT/INTRO.

Usually, an object name has the library/object name pair. Within the AS/400, object names also include the object type. For that reason, the system will allow two objects in the same library with the same name, as long as they are different object types. Like a file and a program both named EMPMST. Objects that are of the same type and stored in the same library must have unique names. That is, every program (object type *PGM) stored in a specific library must have a unique name, as does every file stored in the same library. While two *data files* in the same library can't have the same name, a data file and a program in the same library can have the same name.

Refer to Figure 4-2 where the data file EMPMST (object type *FILE) and RPG program EMPMST (object type *PGM) have the same name. This is allowed because they are two different types of objects. The OS/400 operating system knows which object to use based on the object's type. For example, if the user tries to execute (with the CALL command) the program EMPMST, the AS/400 attempts to run the EMPMST that is the object type program because it's the only object type that can be executed. The AS/400 would ignore the object named EMPMST with object type *FILE.

Before continuing on the subject of object naming, note that the *object attribute* is one aspect of objects that doesn't contribute to the name, but can cause problems. Not all, but some, objects have attributes to further define them. The classic example is in the case of data files. All data files have an object type *FILE, but a *physical file* has an attribute of PF and a *logical file* has an attribute of LF. The naming rules still hold true, but system operators sometimes forget that the type used to determine name uniqueness is *FILE, not the attribute (*LF/*PF). See Figure 4-2.

Contents of Library EMPPAYLIB	
EMPMST(*PGM)	EMPMST(*FILE)
EMPPGM1(*PGM)	QDDSSRC(*FILE)
EMPPGM2(*PGM)	QCBLSRC(*FILE)

Objects in Library EMPPAYLIB		
Object Type	Object Name	
*PGM *FILE	EMPMST EMPMST	The same name can be used for different object types. Since the first object is a program and the second object is a file, they are allowed to have the same name. The AS/400 determines which operations can be performed on the object based on its type.
*PGM *PGM	EMPPGM1 EMPPGM2	All objects of the same type must have different names.
*PGM (RPG IV) *PGM (CL)	UPDPROG UPDPROG	These two objects cannot have the same name because they are the same object types. Although the first program is an RPG IV program and the second program is a CL program, they are considered PGM objects since the AS/400 does not distinguish between subobject types.

Figure 4-2: Contents and objects of EMPPAYLIB.

Keep in mind, this discussion of duplicate names is for illustrative purposes only. Typically, it would be very strange to have different object types with identical names on an AS/400. There would be no problem from the AS/400's point of view, but it would be very confusing to those supporting it. Some objects are supplied with the AS/400 and IBM assigns their names. The user names customer-created objects at creation time.

IBM-supplied objects begin with the letter Q, whether they are libraries, user profiles, programs, etc. Although a user is free to name his/her objects anything, it is not considered wise to name them after an IBM object or even to name them with the first letter Q. This practice will cause problems in the future.

A library is a special type of object (object type *LIB) that serves as a directory for a set of objects. When an object is requested, the specified library is searched for the object. QSYS is the main *system library* and serves as a master directory to all libraries. More about libraries will be provided later in this chapter. Generally, each object is independent of all other objects; however, in some cases, objects are related. When they are related, they can affect each other so that certain commands must be performed in sequence.

An example of *related objects* would be two types of files, physical and logical. A physical file on the AS/400 contains actual data; a logical file contains a set of pointers to that data. Physical and logical files are the same object type (*FILE), so they cannot be named the same. More importantly, a logical file cannot be created without a physical file being present, nor can a physical file be deleted if it has a logical file attached. So the implicit sequence derived from this relationship is to always create the physical file first, then any logical files. To delete them, delete all logical files before deleting the physical file.

OBJECT COMMANDS

There are many, many objects on the AS/400 system. The challenge is to find them quickly. To find objects or information about objects, use the WRKOBJ (Work with Objects) command. Just enter it on the command line and press F4 to prompt it. The screen shown in Figure 4-3 is displayed.

```
                       Work with Objects (WRKOBJ)

 Type choices, press Enter.

 Object . . . . . . . . . . . . . __________   Name, generic*, *ALL
   Library  . . . . . . . . . . .   *LIBL      Name, *LIBL, *CURLIB...
 Object type  . . . . . . . . . . *All         *ALL, *ALRTBL, *AUTL...




                                                                  Bottom
F3=Exit  F4=Prompt   F5=Refresh   F12=Cancel   F13=How to use this display
F24=More keys
```

Figure 4-3: Work with Objects (WRKOBJ) screen.

To see the list of all object types on the AS/400, put the cursor on the object type parameter and press F4. A list of over 50 object types will be displayed. The AS/400 architecture supports a great variety of objects. Each object has a *type identifier*. The type identifier always begins with an asterisk and is followed by an abbreviated name (such as PGM for program). Therefore, the object type for a program is *PGM. These are also referred to as special values. See Figure 4-4.

FUNCTIONS THAT CAN BE PERFORMED ON OBJECTS

We discussed about simply reading or executing functions, but many other functions can be performed on objects. The system performs some functions automatically and others are requested through CL commands. The functions the system performs automatically ensure that an object is processed in a consistent, secure, and proper way.

System Functions Performed on Objects

1. Object Type Verification: The system checks the type of object and the type of function being performed on the object to verify that function can be performed on that type of object.

2. Object Authority Verification: The system checks the object, function, and user to verify that the user can perform that function on that object.

3. Object Lock Enforcement: The system ensures that the integrity of an object is preserved when two or more users try to use an object at the same time. Simultaneous changes to an object are locked out; users cannot use an object while it is being changed.

4. Object Damage Detection and Notification: The system monitors for errors during the processing of objects and communicates any unplanned failures that result from the unrecognized contents of objects.

Object Type	Type Identifier
Authorization List	*AUTL
Class	*CLS
Command	*CMD
Controller Description	*CTLD
Device Description	*DEVD
Document	*DOC
Data Area	*DTAARA
Data Queue	*DTAQ
File	*FILE
Folder	*FLR
Job Description	*JOBD
Job Queue	*JOBQ
Journal and Journal Receiver	*JRN and *JRNRCV
Library	*LIB
Line Description	*LIND
Menu	*MENU
Message File	*MSGF
Message Queue	*MSGQ
Module	*MODULE
Output Queue	*OUTQ
Program	*PGM
Panel Group	*PNLGRP
Subsystem Description	*SBSD
Service Program	*SRVPGM
User Profile	*USRPRF

Figure 4-4: Object types and type identifiers.

User-Requested Functions on Objects

1. Specific Functions: Specific functions are functions that apply to a specific object type; for example, creating, changing, displaying, and deleting an object. The functions and object types are implied in most AS/400 commands. For example, the Create Library (CRTLIB) command will create (that is the function) a library (object type *LIB). The object type *LIB need not be specified.

2. Common Functions Apply to All Objects in General: You must specify the object type in the command. For example: displaying or changing an object's description, creating a duplicate object, renaming an object, moving objects, displaying object authority, changing object authority, saving/restoring objects, and more. Any command that has the word Object (OBJ) in it can be performed on many object types and requires that an object type be specified.

As a final word, objects quickly multiply on AS/400s. It is a good idea to manage the objects on your system by minimizing them. Periodically review queues, libraries, and logs, and delete those that are not being used.

MANAGING SYSTEM OBJECTS

In addition to managing user-created objects, there are several system objects that must be managed.

A feature called Operational Assistant (OA) is a "friendly" way to navigate your way around the AS/400. To access it, type GO SETUP on any command line, press Enter, and Figure 4-5 is displayed.

```
SETUP              Customize Your System, Users, and Devices
                                                     System:   BIGBLUE
 To select an option, type its number below and press Enter:

      1. Change system options
      2. Cleanup tasks
      3. Power on and off tasks
      4. Disk space tasks
      5. Backup tasks

     10. Work with user enrollment
     11. Change passwords for IBM-supplied users

     20. Communications configuration tasks


 Type a menu option below
     ___

 F1=Help   F3=Exit   F9=Command line   F12=Cancel
```

Figure 4-5: Setup menu.

Most of the options on this menu run IBM-supplied CL programs to do tasks for beginning users. In reality, it is probably better to use the system menus and commands to do these same functions—this keeps overhead to a minimum and allows a greater degree of control. However, you should decide for yourself.

LIBRARIES

The basic building block of your work on the AS/400 is the library (object type *LIB). A library, which is itself an object, is a container for objects. It is not really a container, it is more a set of addresses; but it helps to think of it as a container of objects, similar to directories on a PC. The AS/400 can contain any number of libraries, with each library containing any number of objects. Libraries can contain any number of objects, but they cannot contain other libraries. Consider the example library PAYLIB and the objects it contains, shown in Figure 4-6.

PAYLIB		
Object Name	**Object Type**	**Object Address**
PAYROLL	*PGM	Address
PAYMSTR	*FILE	Address
PAYTRANS	*FILE	Address
PAYOUTQ	*OUTQ	Address

Figure 4-6: Library Directory Structure.

IBM ships AS/400s with some libraries already installed. All IBM-supplied libraries have names beginning with the letter Q. The reverse (all libraries that have names beginning with Q are IBM's) is not necessarily true. You can use the Create Library (CRTLIB) command to create a *user library* and give it any name you want (even if it begins with Q). However, the following are good practices:

- Do not give your own libraries names beginning with the letter Q. You can name objects any way you want (even with Q at the beginning) but not libraries.

- Be careful when deleting an IBM-supplied library. Although many are meant to be deleted easily (and should be), others should be de-installed because the deletion will delete a licensed program. For more information on working with licensed programs, refer to chapter 9.

There are a variety of libraries supplied by IBM. Some of the most important system libraries are:

QSYS: As the system library, QSYS is the most important library on the AS/400. QSYS contains OS/400, and it serves as a directory to all other libraries on the system. It cannot be deleted or renamed. An AS/400 cannot operate without QSYS present. There are several types of objects that cannot be placed anywhere but in QSYS:

- User profiles.
- Device descriptions.
- Authorization lists.
- Library object descriptions.

Do not add or delete objects in QSYS. Unless you really know what you are doing, the results are unpredictable.

QUSRSYS: QUSRSYS is a library where the users can place their objects and still consider them, more or less, "system" objects. Typically, QUSRSYS contains message queues for user profiles and some data files used by the system (which can be deleted in most cases).

QHLPSYS: QHLPSYS contains all the help information (which is extensive) that is provided by the system at the touch of the Help key. QHLPSYS contains most of this information in the form of panel group and search index objects.

QHLPSYS is not essential to run the system. If it is not present, there will be no help available. The system-supplied help support is so convenient, however, that it is easy to take for granted.

QGPL: QGPL stands for *General Purpose Library*. As this name implies, QGPL contains a collection of miscellaneous objects that can be used either by the system or by the users at various times. QGPL contains objects such as job queues, subsystem descriptions, source physical files, and output queues.

QGPL should not be cluttered with user objects. Do not use it to store personal objects unless there is a compelling reason to do so. Do not delete or rename this library.

QSPL: SPL (Spooling Library) contains several *database files* used by the system to store reports and other printed *output* waiting to be printed. The database files in QSPL actually make up the system's spooling support.

QDOC: OfficeVision/400 and Client Access/400 are licensed products that use folders and documents. Folders and documents cannot be stored just anywhere; they must be created and maintained in library QDOC.

QTEMP: The QTEMP library is created for every active job on the system; it lasts only for the duration of the job. This library cannot be accessed by any other jobs on the system. It is mainly a "scratch pad," used for temporary objects, like sort work files, etc.

Most AS/400s have hundreds of jobs running at any time, so there are hundreds of QTEMP libraries.

Because QTEMP is created when a job starts and deleted when a job ends, it cannot be named on the standard CRTLIB (Create Library) or DLTLIB (Delete Library). QTEMP is a handy place to keep temporary objects unique to the job running. That is convenient because temporary work files to support processing can be placed and built there, and they will automatically go away when the job ends.

For security reasons, users cannot access the contents of any object in other jobs' QTEMP libraries. A lot of system-related objects get placed in QTEMP during a job. Again, these are temporary and when the job ends, they go away when the library does.

PRODUCT LIBRARIES

IBM-licensed program products are self-contained software packages. Each comes in a separate library called a *product library*.

For example, the *Application Development Tools* program product, also known as PDM (Program Development Manager), lives in library QPDA. The RPG IV (ILE RPG) compiler and RPG IV support come in library QRPGLE.

USER LIBRARIES

Aside from system libraries, the AS/400 can have any number of libraries the users create or which are provided with purchased software (usually non-IBM purchased software). These libraries are referred to as USER libraries.

CREATING LIBRARIES

To create a library, use the CRTLIB command and press the F4 key to prompt it. The system will produce a screen similar to the example shown in Figure 4-7.

```
                          Create Library (CRTLIB)

Type choices, press Enter.

Library . . . . . . . . . . .   __________      Name
Library type . . . . . . . . .  *PROD           *PROD, *TEST
Text 'description' . . . . . .  *BLANK

                          Additional Parameters

Authority . . . . . . . . . .   *LIBCRTAUT  Name, *LIBCRTAUT, *CHANGE...
Auxiliary storage pool ID . . .    1        1-16
Create authority . . . . . . .  *SYSVAL     Name, *SYSVAL, *CHANGE...
Create object auditing . . . .  *SYSVAL     Character value, *SYSVAL...

                                                              Bottom
F3=Exit  F4=Prompt  F5=Refresh  F12=Cancel  F13=How to use this display
F24=More keys
```

Figure 4-7: Create Library (CRTLIB) screen.

This command creates a library called MYLIB and gives it a text description of `My library`.

WORKING WITH LIBRARIES

There are a variety of commands that can be used to manage libraries: CHGLIB, DLTLIB, CLRLIB, DSPLIB, WRKLIB, and RNMLIB are just a few of the commands. To do all these functions from a single screen, use the WRKLIB (Work with Libraries) command and press F4 to prompt for the requested library, as shown in Figure 4-8.

```
                        Work with Libraries (WRKLIB)

 Type choices, press Enter.

 Library . . . . . . . . . . .   *LIBL        Name, generic*, *LIBL...










                                                                     Bottom
 F3=Exit   F4=Prompt   F5=Refresh   F12=Cancel   F13=How to use this display
 F24=More keys
```

Figure 4-8: Work with Libraries (WRKLIB) screen.

Using this command, the operator can manage all aspects of a library or a group of libraries. Simply key in the name, *generic name*, or IBM keyword and press Enter.

The screen, as shown in Figure 4-9, is for the All User Libraries (*ALLUSR) parameter. The WRKLIB command produces a list of libraries. In the LIB parameter of the command, the operator can specify which library or libraries to work with. For example, to work with all user libraries on the system, enter:

```
WRKLIB LIB(*ALLUSR)
```

This command automatically filters out IBM-supplied libraries. Or, to work with all libraries that have names beginning with Q, enter the generic:

```
WRKLIB LIB(Q*)
```

```
                    Work with Libraries

 Type options, press Enter.
   1=Create   2=Change   3=Copy    4=Delete   5=Display   6=Print
   8=Display library description   9=Save     10=Restore
   11=Save changed objects         12=Work with objects    14=Clear

 Opt  Library      Attribute   Text

 __   #LIBRARY     PROD
 __   AAA1234LIB   PROD
 __   ADA3574LIB   PROD
 __   AGTMSTP      PROD
 __   ANJ2529LIB   PROD        Rob Anderson library
 __   AUL1496LIB   PROD        RPG Library
 __   BCDSUPPT     PROD        Electronic Support library
 __   BEA3051LIB   PROD
 __   BILL         PROD        BILLS TEST LIB
                                                               More...
 Parameters for options 1, 2, 3, 5, 8, 9, 10, 11 and 12 or command
 ===> ____________________________________________________________
 F3=Exit   F4=Prompt   F5=Refresh   F9=Retrieve   F11=Display names only
 F12=Cancel   F16=Repeat position to   F17=Position to
```

Figure 4-9: Work with Libraries (WRKLIB) screen with *ALLUSR parameter to show all user libraries.

To work with the objects in a library, type a 12 in the Option column next to the library, and press Enter. The system produces a screen similar to Figure 4-10.

```
                      Work with Objects

 Type options, press Enter.
   2=Edit authority        3=Copy   4=Delete   5=Display authority   7=Rename
   8=Display description   13=Change description

 Opt  Object       Type      Library    Attribute   Text
 _    QSQJRN0001   *JRNRCV   APPDTA                 COLLECTION - created by SQL
 _    QSQJRN0002   *JRNRCV   APPDTA                 COLLECTION - created by SQL
 _    QSQJRN0003   *JRNRCV   APPDTA                 COLLECTION - created by SQL
 _    QSQJRN0004   *JRNRCV   APPDTA                 COLLECTION - created by SQL
 _    QSQJRN0005   *JRNRCV   APPDTA                 COLLECTION - created by SQL
 _    QSQJRN       *JRN      APPDTA                 COLLECTION - created by SQL
 _    CUSTOMER     *FILE     APPDTA     PF
 _    CUSTSLT      *FILE     APPDTA     LF
 _    SYSCHKCST    *FILE     APPDTA     LF          SQL catalog view
 _    SYSCOLUMNS   *FILE     APPDTA     LF          SQL catalog view
 _    SYSCST       *FILE     APPDTA     LF          SQL catalog view
                                                                     More...
 Parameters for options 5, 7 and 13 or command
 ===>_____________________________________________________________________
 F3=Exit   F4=Prompt   F5=Refresh   F9=Retrieve   F11=Display names and types
 F12=Cancel   F16=Repeat position to   F17=Position to
```

Figure 4-10: Work with Objects from WRKLIB screen.

DISPLAYING LIBRARIES

Users and operators often work with objects within a library. But in real life, neither knows exactly what objects are in a library. To find out, use the Display Library (DSPLIB) command.

This command presents a list of objects and their sizes. This command has a parameter, OUTPUT, which is used to direct the information about the library contents either to the screen or a printer. If this list is directed to the screen, that information is all you get. If the list is directed to the printer, however, the listing also contains the total of all the object sizes. This is a good tool to use when determining the disk space each library takes. Here is an example of the DSPLIB command:

```
DSPLIB LIB(ARLIB) OUTPUT(*PRINT)
```

DELETING LIBRARIES

Deleting a library not only deletes the library itself, but all the objects contained in it. For this reason, the process of deleting a library can take a considerable amount of time. To keep from tying up a terminal (or bogging down the system), submit a library deletion to the batch subsystem with the SBMJOB (Submit Job) command. More information on the SBMJOB command is provided in chapter 12.

The DLTLIB (Delete Library) command only requires one parameter: the name of the library to delete.

- Never, under any circumstances, delete an IBM library (name beginning with Q).

If you want to delete a licensed product, use the Delete Licensed Program (DLTLICPGM) instead of DLTLIB. DLTLICPGM will do a more thorough deletion of the products and related objects. To access this command, use the LICPGM menu. Invoke that menu by typing on the command line:

```
GO LICPGM
```

and press the Enter key.

LIBRARY LIST

Remember we said that every object on the AS/400 had to be referenced by a library/name combination? In real life, many commands work with object names, without a library being specified. The way this is possible is with a *library list*—which is another object type (*LIBL).

It is true that the AS/400 must have both names to locate an object, but the AS/400 is user friendly enough to give us an easy way to default the library onto an object name. The library list is, as the name implies, a list of libraries. Every job and user has an attached library list. When someone (or a program) issues a command or names an object without naming a library, the system uses the library list to find an object with a matching name. Library lists are your friends.

A library list is a list of system and user libraries that indicate which libraries are to be searched and the order in which they are to be searched. The library list can have a maximum of forty names and is always scanned from top to bottom. As soon as the system finds the object it is looking for in one of the libraries in the list, it searches no further. Therefore, the scanning process always stops at the first match. Within this list, there is a structure:

1. A System Libraries Portion: This portion must exist and must at least contain system library QSYS. It can have from one to fourteen other libraries. It is set through the system value QSYSLIBL. Keep this portion as short as possible. Place in it only the libraries that all users need to access. Note: System libraries that only some users need access to can be placed in the user library portion (discussed below).

2. A Product Libraries Portion: Optional. This library list can be temporary. It comes into being when a menu or command is invoked that uses a product library. When the menu or command completes, this portion goes away.

3. A Current Library: Optional. The *current library* contains the name of one library that is to be considered current at the time. There is a parameter on the user profile, CURLIB (refer to chapter 11), that sets this. Also, the command CHGCURLIB (Change Current Library) can be used to change it at any time.

4. A User Library Portion: Required. It will always at least have QTEMP in it and can contain from 1 to 25 library names. The *user portion* of the library list should be used for libraries that depend on the nature of the job being performed. Each user can have a different set of libraries in the user portion of the library list.

So if the AS/400 is asked to do something with an object and a library is not specified with the object's name, the AS/400 would start looking for it in the system, product, current, then user library portions of the library list until it is found.

That is nice, but what about creating new objects? When the library qualification is not specified with the name, the library list can cause some confusion if the current library is not set. The current library (object type *CURLIB) in the library list is optional. The library named as the current library is the default library name for new objects that do not have their library specified. If the current library slot is not set (filled), system library QGPL is used.

Be wary of not specifying the library when you create an object. That is one way the system library QGPL gets full. In addition, you just cannot be sure of where the created objects are being placed.

SETTING UP A LIBRARY LIST

When setting up a library list, remember these points:

1. The libraries you name must exist on the system. This has two implications: One, you cannot add a library to a list if it does not exist. Two, you cannot delete a library that is a part of any library list.

2. The libraries in a library list must be authorized to all users who need them (at least *USE authority).

3. System performance is better when the library list is kept as short as possible. Only specify relevant libraries.

CHANGING THE LIBRARY LIST

Any job's system portion of the library list can be changed with the Change System Library List (CHGSYSLIBL) command. This command only affects the current job. All the other jobs remain intact. The CHGSYSLIBL command can add a library at the very top of the system portion of the library list, or remove a library from it. It will not control where in the system portion the library is added. The library always goes to the top of the list.

At any time during the life of a job, the nonsystem portion of the library list can be changed with the Change Library List (CHGLIBL) or Edit Library List (EDTLIBL) command. These commands replace the whole set of the user portion of the library list in a single stroke.

For single changes (such as adding or removing a library), use the Add Library List Entry (ADDLIBLE) or Remove Library List Entry (RMVLIBLE) command. The ADDLIBLE command allows the user to indicate if the new library will be placed at the first or last position of the list. Remember how library lists are searched by the system—libraries at the top get searched first; those at the bottom, last. These two commands modify the User Portion of the library list only.

When manipulating objects, the system needs to be told which library contains the object being manipulated; for example, to delete a file named COMPANY, the system could have a number of files named COMPANY located in different libraries. How would it know which one to delete?

There are two ways to reach the right file: by qualifying its name with the name of the library where it resides, or by qualifying it with *LIBL, as follows:

```
DLTF FILE(MYLIB/COMPANY)
```

or

```
DLTF FILE(*LIBL/COMPANY)
```

The command's default library value is *LIBL so this is an equivalent command:

```
DLTF FILE(COMPANY)
```

In the first case, the system expects to find the file, COMPANY, in library MYLIB. If COMPANY is not there, the command ends in error.

In the second and third instances, the system scans the libraries in the library list for the job, from top to bottom, until it finds a file named COMPANY. When the system finds the file, it deletes it and ends. If the system runs out of libraries without finding COMPANY, the command ends in error.

DISPLAYING A LIBRARY LIST

The Display Library List (DSPLIBL) and Display Job (DSPJOB) commands can be used to display the library list for a job currently running, as shown in Figure 4-11.

```
                                Display Library List
                                                              System:   BLUE400

 Type options, press Enter.
   5=Display objects in library

 Opt  Library     Type       Text
  _    QSYS        SYS        System Library
  _    QSYS2       SYS        System Library for CPI's
  _    QHLPSYS     SYS
  _    QUSRSYS     SYS        SYSTEM LIBRARY FOR USERS
  _    QDDSSRC     CUR        Personal Library for DDS
  _    QGPL        USR        General Purpose Library
  _    QTEMP       USR



                                                                        Bottom
 F3=Exit   F12=Cancel   F17=Top   F18=Bottom
 (C) COPYRIGHT IBM CORP. 1980, 1994.
```

Figure 4-11: Display Library List screen as a result of executing the DSPLIBL command.

USING THE LIBRARY LIST

Library lists are used for powerful results with little work. When applications are worked on, like a payroll application, the developer probably does not want to test the work against the production files but would like as real-life test scenario as possible during testing. One way to do this is to have all the payroll production files in a library called PAYROLL. All users who do PAYROLL work have this library at the top of their library list's User Portion.

The shop would probably have another set of payroll files just for testing. These files would be placed in a library called PAYTEST. When a developer makes a change to the payroll application, he/she would keep PAYTEST at the top of the library list. Any time a program is executed, it would access payroll files located in PAYTEST; it would never see the ones in PAYROLL (in fact, for security, most shops would prohibit developers from any access to the PAYROLL library files).

When the change is moved into production, the users access the new program, but because their library lists are set up with PAYROLL and not PAYTEST in them, they automatically work on the production files. That way, no programming changes have to be made on programs going from test to live.

Another way library lists are commonly used is with packaged software used in companies that have multiple companies or divisions—let us call them business units. Although the same programs are used across the whole business, each business unit is only allowed access to its own data, no others (for the example, this is a business rule, not a technical one). The solution is to group each unit's data into a unique library. The business unit in New York City finds its files in library NYNYDATA while the Phoenix unit finds its in the PXAZDATA library. When the corporate office wants to consolidate data, it can cycle through each library and pull what it needs. Everyone is happy and no special programming has to be done.

Object names, types, libraries, and library lists make a powerful tool on the AS/400. Take your time to use them well as you will see permutations of them over and over in your career.

LAB #4: OBJECTS, LIBRARIES, AND LIBRARY LISTS

Upon completion of this lab, you should be able to:

- Demonstrate how to create and delete libraries.
- Demonstrate how to create and delete objects.
- Demonstrate how to copy, move, and rename objects.
- Demonstrate the relationship of objects to libraries.
- Explain how to use a library list.
- Use the library list to access objects.
- Modify library lists.
- Explore system values' and user profiles' relationships to library list.

WORKING WITH OBJECTS

Objects are the basic unit on the AS/400. To better understand what makes up an object, let us look at the components that define an object. Remember that all objects reside in a library, or another way to say that is they are *associated with* a library. Each object must be one of the defined object types on the AS/400. Object types' values are defined with special values, for example *FILE, *PGM, etc.

OBJECT TYPES

Now to explore some of the object types available on the AS/400. Since you have finished the command chapter, you are often expected to determine the command needed to perform the requested task.

- Sign on to the system.
- Enter the command to call the Command Entry display. (Hint: CALL QCMD.)
- Enter WRKOBJ on the command line.
- Press F4 (Prompt). The Work with Objects (WRKOBJ) screen appears.

```
                         Work with Objects (WRKOBJ)

Type choices, press Enter.

Object . . . . . . . . . . . . .   USERID        Name, generic*, *ALL
  Library  . . . . . . . . . . .     *LIBL        Name, *LIBL, *CURLIB...
Object type  . . . . . . . . . .   *ALL           *ALL, *ALRTBL, *AUTL...
```

Figure L4-1: Work with Objects (WRKOBJ) screen.

- Enter `UserID` (your user ID) for the `Object name`.
- Move the cursor to the `object type` field.
- Press F4 (Prompt).

The screen shows the possible special values of the object types available on the system.

- Find the IBM-defined `Object type` special value for each of the following object types.
- Place your answers in the spaces that follow:

Library	__________	Device description	__________
File	__________	Job queue	__________
Program	__________	Output queue	__________
Message queue	__________	User profile	__________

Now we will explore your user profile. Remember that a user profile is just another object to the AS/400. You need to look through the values for object types until you find the value for the user profile type.

- Enter the special value for a `User profile type` object.
- Press Enter twice.

OBJECT DESCRIPTION INFORMATION

The Work with Objects screen is shown. From this screen, you can work with most aspects of object management.

- Enter the option number that displays the object's description. Place the option to the left of your user profile.
- Press Enter.

The screen shown in Figure L4-2 displays the object header information.

```
                         Display Object Description - Full
                                                              Library 1 of 1
Object . . . . . . . :   OPR0001         Attribute  . . . . . :
  Library  . . . . . :     QSYS          Owner  . . . . . . . :   HOHLY#M
Type . . . . . . . . :   *USRPRF         Primary group  . . . :   *NONE

User-defined information:
  Attribute  . . . . . . . . . . . . :
  Text . . . . . . . . . . . . . . . :   Operation student Marge

Creation information:
  Creation date/time . . . . . . . . :   01/10/99  21:30:46
  Created by user  . . . . . . . . . :   HOHLY#M
  System created on  . . . . . . . . :   BIGBLUE
  Object domain  . . . . . . . . . . :   *SYSTEM

                                                                     More...
Press Enter to continue.

F3=Exit   F12=Cancel
```

Figure L4-2: The Display Object Description screen.

- Page through the information stored for any object.
- Identify the six categories of information in the object description (object header).
- List the categories in the space that follows:

________________________ ________________________

________________________ ________________________

________________________ ________________________

- Press F3 (Exit) until you get to a screen with a command line.
- Enter the command to call the `Command Entry` screen.

From the command line, we want to work with all objects that start with the OPR character string. To do this, you will use a GENERIC* search criteria. For example, if you were looking for all objects that began with the letter "A," the search criteria would be `A*` for the object name.

- Enter WRKOBJ on the Selection or command ===> line.
- Press F4 (Prompt).
- Enter USER* for the Object field.
- Enter *USRPRF for Object Type field.
- Press Enter.
- Enter 8 (Display Description) to the left of your user profile.
- Press Enter.
- Page down through the description.
- What is the value for Days Used Count? ____________________
- Press F3 (Exit).

Now that you have found the value requested, return to the Work with Objects screen. Now switch to working with another object that starts with the OPR string. Page down until you find your message queue. *Hint*: It has the same name as your user profile.

- Enter the Change Description option number to the left of your message queue.
- Press Enter.
- Tab to the Text Desciption field.
- Enter your name's message queue for this field.
- Tab to the Days Used Count field.
- Enter *RESET.
- Press Enter.

Now view the changes made in the above series of commands. You should be viewing the Work with Objects screen that contains the objects starting with OPR string.

- Enter the Display Description option number to the left of your message queue.
- Press Enter.
- Page through the values.
- What is the current value of Days Used Count? ______________
- What is the Date Use Count Reset value? ________________
- Exit from this screen.

MANIPULATING OBJECTS

In this section, you will be working with three different libraries. The libraries are OPRLIB, USERID, and a new library USERIDLIB. The OPRLIB is a master library that has objects you will need to copy to your library. Once the object is in your library, you will use a variety of object commands on that object. You will be copying and moving it between your library and the newly created library.

Before we begin, you will need to verify that you do not have a library called USERIDLIB. If the library is present, you will need to clear its contents. If not there, you will need to create it.

- Enter WRKLIB on the Selection or command ===> line.
- Press F4 (Prompt).
- Enter USERIDLIB at the prompt.
- Press Enter.

If you do not have a USERIDLIB library, skip the next set of instructions. If you do have a USERIDLIB, the next step is to clear out all of the contents.

- Place the option 14 (Clear) to the left of USERIDLIB.
- Press Enter.

The next steps will create the USERIDLIB.

- Enter CRTLIB on the Selection or command ===> line.
- Press F4 (Prompt).
- Enter USERIDLIB for the library name.
- Leave the library type *PROD.
- Enter Your name 2nd library in the Text Description field.
- Press Enter.

The screen for creating the USERIDLIB is shown in Figure L4-3.

```
                          Create Library (CRTLIB)

 Type choices, press Enter.

 Library . . . . . . . . . . . .   UserIDLIB   Name
 Library type . . . . . . . . . .  *PROD          *PROD, *TEST
 Text 'description' . . . . . . .  Your name 2nd library
```

Figure L4-3: Create Library screen to create USER00XXLIB library.

Next you need to check to see if your library (USERID) contains an object named INTRO. If the INTRO file is not present in your library, you will need to copy it from the OPRLIB to your library.

- Enter WRKOBJ on the command line.
- Press F4 (Prompt).
- Enter INTRO in the Object field.
- Tab to the Library field.
- Enter your library (USERID).
- Press Enter.

If you did not find the INTRO file in your library, you will need to copy it from the OPRLIB to your library. Make sure that you copy the data with the file. The command is shown in Figure L4-4.

```
                     Create Duplicate Object (CRTDUPOBJ)

Type choices, press Enter.

From object  . . . . . . . . . . . > INTRO          Name, generic*, *ALL
From library . . . . . . . . . . . > OPRLIB         Name, *CURLIB
Object type  . . . . . . . . . . . > *FILE          *ALL, *ALRTBL, *AUTL...
               + for more values
To library . . . . . . . . . . . . > UserID       Name, *SAME, *FROMLIB...
New object . . . . . . . . . . .     *OBJ           Name, *SAME, *OBJ
Duplicate data . . . . . . . . .     *YES           *NO, *YES
```

Figure L4-4: Copying the intro file from OPRLIB to your library using the Create Duplicate Object command.

- Enter the Create Duplicate Object command on the command line.
- Press F4 (Prompt).
- Complete the screen as shown in Figure L4-4.
- Press Enter.
- The Duplicate Data field will appear.
- Enter *YES in the Duplicate Data field.
- Press Enter.

You now have the following situation:

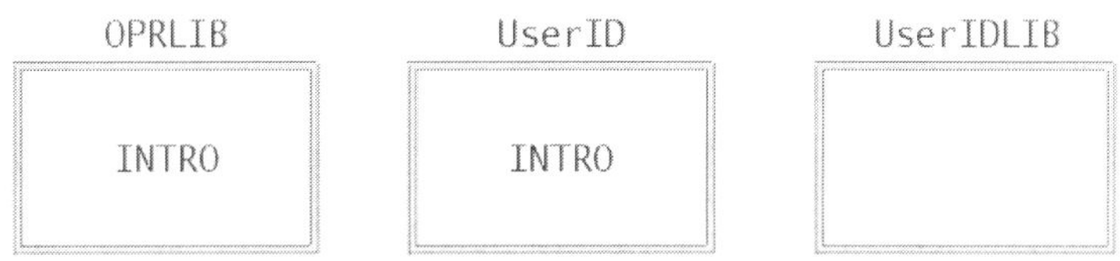

In the next step, you are going to copy the INTRO file from your library to the new library, USERIDLIB, using the Work with Objects command. Also, remember to copy the data.

- Enter the `Work with Objects` command on a command line.
- Press F4 (Prompt).
- Place `*ALL` in the `Object` field.
- Tab to the `Library` field.
- Enter your library (USERID).
- Press Enter.
- Enter option `3` (Copy) on the line to the left of the INTRO file.
- Press Enter.
- Complete the screen as in Figure L4-4, except the `From Library` is your library (USERID) and the `To Library` is USERIDLIB.
- *Hint*: Remember to copy the data.
- Press Enter.
- The following message should appear at the bottom of your screen.
  `Object INTRO in USERIDLIB type *FILE created.`
- What command did you use to make the copy? ________________

You've just copied an object to a new library. The resulting library contents follow:

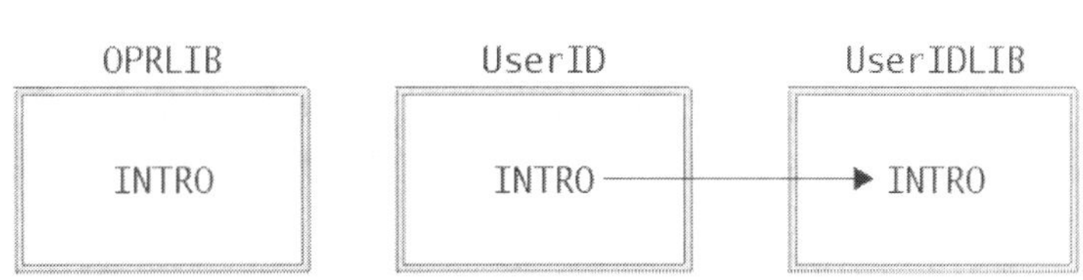

Next you are to copy the INTRO file from your library to the USER00XXLIB and change the name of the object in the same step. A graphical representation of what you need to do is shown below.

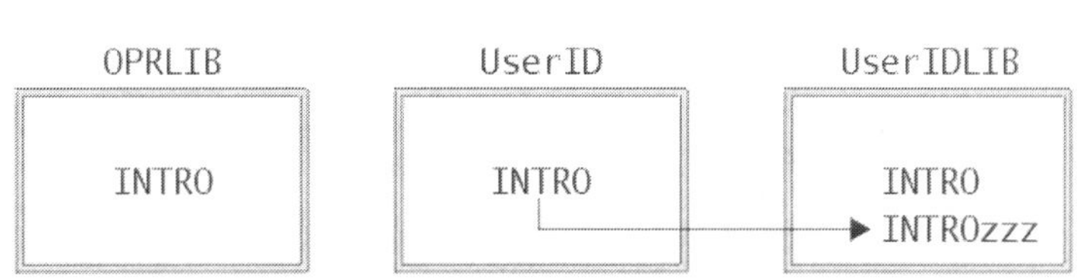

You should still be on the Work with Objects screen showing the INTRO file in your library.

- Enter option 3 (Copy) on the line to the left of the INTRO file.
- Press Enter.
- Complete the screen as shown in Figure L4-5, where zzz stands for your initials.
- Press Enter.

```
                    Create Duplicate Object (CRTDUPOBJ)

Type choices, press Enter.

From object . . . . . . . . . . > INTRO          Name, generic*, *ALL
From library . . . . . . . . . . > USERID         Name, *CURLIB
Object type . . . . . . . . . . > *FILE          *ALL, *ALRTBL, *AUTL...
To library . . . . . . . . . .     USERIDLIB      Name, *SAME, *FROMLIB...
New object . . . . . . . . . .     INTROzzz       Name, *SAME, *OBJ
Duplicate data . . . . . . . .     *YES           *NO, *YES
```

Figure L4-5: Copying an object with name change to a new library using the Create Duplicate Object command.

Next you are to rename the INTRO file in your new library (USER00XXLIB) using the rename command.

- Enter the RNMOBJ command on the command line.
- Press F4 (Prompt).
- Complete the screen to rename the INTRO *FILE to INTROXX in your USERIDLIB (where xx is your number).
- Press Enter twice. You should get the following message:
  `Object INTRO in USERIDLIB type *FILE renamed INTROXX`. This indicates that you have successfully renamed this object.

The results of the above command should have your library contents as follows:

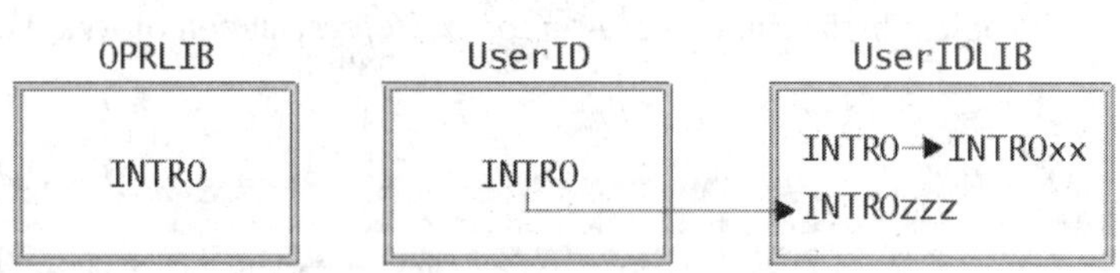

At this point, your USERIDLIB should contain two objects named INTROXX and INTROZZZ. Next, print the contents of your USERIDLIB to show the contents.

- Enter WRKLIB LIB(USERID*) on the command line.
- Press Enter.
- Use the option number to print the contents of the USERIDLIB library.
- Enter the command to `Work with Your Spool Files`.
- Place option 5 (View) to the left of the printout. Verify that this is the correct printout.
- Place option 2 (Change) to the left of the correct printout.
- Complete the screen to direct the printout to your printer. (*Reminder*: Printing was discussed in chapter 3 lab. Review the instructions if you have questions.)
- Attach this as printout #1 to the lab submission sheet.

Next you need to move the INTRO file in your library (USERID) to the new library USERIDLIB. Below is a graphical representation of what you are doing.

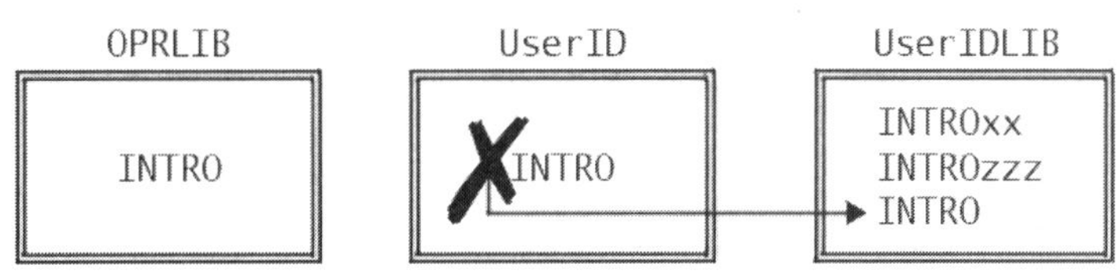

- Enter MOVOBJ on the command line.
- Press F4 (Prompt).
- Enter INTRO in the `Object` field.
- Tab to the `Library` field
- Enter USERID.
- Tab to the `Object Type` field
- Enter *FILE.
- Tab to the `To Library` field.
- Enter USERIDLIB.
- Press Enter. You should get the following message: `Object intro in OPR0001 type *file moved to library OPR0001LIB`. This message indicates you were successful.
- The USERIDLIB should contain three objects.
- Obtain a printout of the USERIDLIB as you did above. Attach this as printout #2 to the lab submission sheet.

Now it is time to test your command knowledge. You need to generate a printed copy of the INTRO file contents in the USERIDLIB.

- Enter CPYF on the command line.
- Press the F4 (Prompt) function key.
- Complete the screen to copy the INTRO file to the printer.
- Obtain a printout of the file contents.
- Attach this as printout #3 to the lab submission sheet.

WORKING WITH LIBRARIES

A library is a special type of object that serves as a directory for a set of objects. To start exploring libraries, we need to explore some of the library commands. Start first with the Work with Library command. To start, this section uses the command to display the Command Entry display.

- Call the `Command Entry` display.
- Press F10 to display messages.
- Enter WRKLIB on the command line.
- Press F4 (Prompt).
- With your cursor in the `Library` field, press F4 (Prompt) function key again.
- What are the six permissible values for the `Library` field?
  ______________________ ______________________
  ______________________ ______________________
  ______________________ ______________________
- Enter your library (USERID) in the `Library` field.
- Press Enter twice.
- The `Work with Libraries` screen is displayed.
- What option would you use to `Create a Library`? ______________________
- What are the options available on this screen?
  Place your answer on the lines below.
  ____
  ____
  ____

Now that you can create a library, you are going to apply this knowledge and create a new library INTROXX, where `xx` is your assigned number.

- Enter the option number to `Create a Library` on the first option line.
- Tab to the `Library` line and key in INTROXX.
- Press Enter.

- The `Create Library` command screen is displayed.
- Enter your name in the TEXT DESCRIPTION parameter.
- Press Enter.

Now that you have created another new library, you will need to copy objects into that library. This is an opportunity to use some of the object commands from the previous section.

- Enter WRKLIB LIB(USERID*) on the command line.
- Press Enter.
- Enter the option number to `Work with Objects` to the left of the USERIDLIB library.
- Enter `3` (Copy) to the left of all objects in the library.
- Press Enter.
- Enter INTROXX in the `To Library` field.
- Tab to the `Duplicate Data` field.
- Enter *YES.
- Press Enter.
- Repeat three previous steps until all objects have been copied to the INTROXX library.
- Enter WRKLIB LIB(INTROXX) on the command line.
- Press Enter.
- Enter the option to `Print` to the left of the INTROXX library.
- Attach this as printout #4 to the submission sheet for this lab.

Now that you have demonstrated that you can create a library and copy objects to that library, you are going to clear the library. This can be done from the Work with Libraries screen. If you are not at that screen, you will need to key in the above commands.

- From the `Work with Libraries` screen, what is the option to clear the objects from a library? ____
- Enter the above option to the left of the INTROXX library.
- Press F4 (Prompt).
- What command is used to clear all objects from a library? _______________
- Press Enter.
- The `Confirm Clear of Libraries` display is shown.
- Press Enter, and the library will be cleared.

Now that you have cleared the contents of the INTROXX library, you need to obtain a printout to demonstrate your success.

- Print the contents of the cleared library (INTROXX).
- Attach printout #5 to the submission sheet for this lab.

WORKING WITH LIBRARY LISTS

Every active job on the system has a library list associated with it. There are many ways to display your current job's library list. From the Command Entry display, use the Display Library List command to view the library list.

- Enter DSPLIBL on the command line.
- Press Enter.

PORTIONS OF THE LIBRARY LIST

The library list consists of three main sections: the system portion (SYS), current library (CUR), and the user portion (USR). An example of a library list is shown in Figure L4-6.

```
                         Display Library List


Type options, press Enter.
  5=Display objects in library

Opt  Library     Type      Text
___  QSYS        SYS       System Library
___  QSYS2       SYS       System Library for CPI's
___  QHLPSYS     SYS
___  QUSRSYS     SYS
___  UserID      CUR       Your name's default library
___  COMMONLIB   USR
___  QGPL        USR
___  QTEMP       USR
```

Figure L4-6: Example of a library list.

Compare your library list with the example list.

- What libraries are in the user portion of your library list? _______________
  ____

The library list generally has the three sections shown above; however, when products are started, they may alter the library list to make the libraries containing these products available for your easy use.

- Enter STRPDM (Start Programming Development Manager) on the command line.
- Press Enter.
- Enter the command to `Display the Library List` on the command line.
- What has changed about the list? ______________________________

LIBRARY LIST COMMANDS

To start exploring the commands you can use with a library list, you should bring up the Library List Command menu.

- Enter GO CMDLIBL command on the command line.
- From the `Library List Command` menu, answer the following questions. How do you:
  a. Add a library to the library list? ______________________________
  b. Change a library list? ______________________________
  c. Change the system portion of the library list?______________________
  d. Edit the library list?______________________________
  e. Remove a library from the library list?_________________________

Now that you know the commands available to use with a library list, it is time to practice using them.

- Enter the command to add OPRLIB to your library list.
- Press Enter.
- Enter the command to `Display your Library List` to verify the list has been modified.
- What is the name of your current library? _________________________
- What portion of the library list is the OPRLIB in? ____________________

Now print the revised library list that was created.

- Enter DSPLIBL on the command line.
- Press F4 (Prompt).
- Change the `Output` field to *PRINT.
- Press Enter.

You now have a spool file containing a copy of the modified library list.

- Attach printout #6 to the submission sheet for this lab.

- Enter WRKLIB on the command line.
- Press F4 (Prompt).
- Enter *USRLIBL in the `Library` prompt.
- Press Enter.
- Which libraries are displayed?

  ____

  ____

  ____

Library list allows you to execute commands without specifying the library and using only the object name. You will be using the library list to execute a program.

- Enter the command to add the LAB4 library to your library list.
- Press Enter.
- Enter CALL PAYMEMO on the command line.
- Press Enter.
- Enter WRKSPLF to display your spool files. Look for the output file as shown in Figure L4-7.
- Attach printout #7 to the submission sheet for this lab.

```
                        Work with All Spooled Files

Type options, press Enter.
  1=Send   2=Change   3=Hold   4=Delete   5=Display   6=Release   7=Messages
  8=Attributes        9=Work with printing status

                                 Device or                     Total     Cur
Opt  File          User          Queue         User Data  Sts   Pages    Page  Copy
___  QSYSPRT       HOHLY#M       FACOUTQ       PAYMEMO    RDY     1               1
```

Figure L4-7: Spool Files showing output of the PAYMEMO program.

A library included in a library list cannot be deleted from the system. Before this lab is finished, you need to delete the libraries you created. The first step is to determine if these libraries are included in the library list. If they are in the list, they first must be removed from the library list and then deleted from the system. Different commands are required for the different sections of the library list. For example, Remove Library List Entry is only valid for the User Portion of the list, and Change Current Library is used for the Current Library Portion.

- Enter the command to `Display the Library List` on the command line.
- Press Enter.
- Note if any of the following libraries are included in the User Portion of the library list: USERIDLIB, INTROXX, or any other library you created in this lab.
- Enter RMVLIBLE on the command line.
- Press F4 (Prompt).
- Enter the library you found in the User Portion of the library list.
- Press Enter.
- Repeat the above command if more than one library was found in the User Portion of the library list.

You now need to display your library list again to determine if there are still libraries you created in the list. If they are still in the list, they are in the Current section of the list. You will have to replace that library with your library.

- Enter the command to `Display the Library List` on the command line.
- Press Enter.
- If the USERIDLIB, INTROXX, or any other library you created in this lab is included in the library list, complete the following steps:
- Enter CHGCURLIB on the command line.
- Press F4 (Prompt).
- Enter USERID in the `Library` field.
- Press Enter.

Using the WRKLIB command, check to see if the following libraries still exist: USERIDLIB, OPRLIBXX, INTROXX, or any other library which you created during this lab. If you find these libraries, use the delete option or DLTLIB command to delete them from the system.

- Enter WRKLIB on the command line.
- Press F4 (Prompt).
- Enter USER* in the `Library` field.
- Press Enter.
- Check to ensure the libraries listed above are not present. If present, continue; otherwise, skip to the next section.
- Enter DLTLIB on the command line.
- Press F4 (Prompt).
- Enter the library to be deleted in the `Library` field.

- Press Enter.
- The `Confirm Delete of Libraries` display is shown.
- Press Enter to confirm the deletion.
- Repeat the above command if more than one library was found.

You are to repeat the above sequence of commands to delete the libraries created in this lab beginning with the INT* character string.

- Enter WRKLIB on the command line.
- Press F4 (Prompt).
- Enter INT* in the `Library` field.
- Press Enter.
- Check that the libraries listed above are not present. If present, continue; otherwise, skip to the next section.
- Enter DLTLIB on the command line.
- Press F4 (Prompt) function key.
- Enter the library to be deleted in the `Library` field.
- Press Enter.
- The `Confirm Delete of Libraries` display is shown.
- Press Enter to confirm the deletion.
- Repeat the above command if more than one library was found.

You should only have your library USERID left.

END-OF-CHAPTER AIDS

CHAPTER SUMMARY

1. Everything stored and used by the AS/400 is an object.
2. Objects have a variety of types. These types determine their operational characteristics.
3. An object consists of two parts:
   a. Object header portion that contains the object description.
   b. Functional portion that contains the contents of the object.
4. No two objects of the same type residing in the same library may have the same name.
5. A library is a special type of object that serves as a directory for a set of objects.

6. Libraries can be used to:
   a. Group certain objects for individual users.
   b. Group all objects used for an individual application.
   c. Ensure security.
   d. Simplify the SAVE/RESTORE process by grouping objects that are saved and restored at the same time.
   e. Use multiple libraries for testing and production.
7. Libraries are the highest-level objects on the AS/400.
8. There are a variety of IBM-supplied system libraries which perform important roles on the AS/400.
9. A library list is a list of system and user libraries that are searched in order for an object when the library is not specified.
10. The library list consists of the following portions in search order:
    a. System libraries.
    b. Product libraries (optional).
    c. Current library (optional).
    d. User libraries.

KEY TERMS

Application Development Tools	library list	physical file
current library	logical file	product library
data files	object	qualified name
database files	object attribute	records
functional object portion	object header portion	related objects
General Purpose Library	object management	special value
generic name	object name	system library
library	object type	type identifier
	output	user library

CHAPTER SELF-TEST

Self-test question solutions are in appendix D.

True-False Questions

___ 1. A library is an object.

___ 2. The qualified name of an object consists of the name of the object and the type of the object.

___ 3. A physical file named EMPMST can be stored in the same library as a logical file by the same name.

___ 4. The library list contains a list of available libraries.

___ 5. The "Move Object" can be used on any object on the system.

___ 6. For better object management, it is good to group objects in libraries. If a subset of objects within a library is closely related, it is best to form a separate library within the first library for these objects.

___ 7. IBM-supplied libraries are named with a Q as the first letter.

___ 8. There is no limit to the number of libraries on the system.

___ 9. When a library is listed in the library list, it cannot be deleted from the system.

Fill in the Blanks

1. The master directory of all libraries is stored in the ________________ library.

2. ___________ ____________ keeps two people from accessing the same object at the same time.

3. The ______________ library often contains user message queues.

4. The __________________ library is created for every active job on the system. This library cannot be created by the CRTLIB command.

5. If you enter DSPLIBL on a command line and press Enter, you will get ____________________________.

6. The __________ and ___________ commands can be used to change the libraries in the user portion of the library list.

Chapter Review Questions

1. Define the following terms:
   a. Special values.
   b. Object.
   c. Library list.
   d. Qualified name.
   e. Library.

2. Why is QSYS the most important library on your system?

3. The WRKLIB command allows you to perform a variety of functions from one screen. List several of these functions.

4. Identify five types of objects that can be stored on an AS/400.

5. Name the sections of a library list in the order it is searched.

6. List commands that can be used to change the User Portion of the library list.

7. List the command used to change the current library within a library list.

8. Consider the following library list:

QSYS QHLPSYS QUSRSYS	System libraries
OPR0060	Current library
QTEMP QGPL	User libraries

For the above library list, answer the following questions.

a. What command would you use if you wanted the current library to be INTRO60?

____

b. What command would you use to have the user library list consist of the following libraries: LAB4, QTEMP, and QGPL? ______________________________________

____

5

Message Handling

Chapter Objectives

Upon completion of this chapter, you should be able to:

- Demonstrate how to display system messages.
- Demonstrate how to send a message to another user on the AS/400.
- Describe the purpose of the message queue.
- Demonstrate how to respond to a user's message.
- Explain the types of messages and their uses.

Messages

Although the AS/400 is easy to use, its internal architecture is very complex. It does not have single (or even dual) processors—the number varies by model—but a single AS/400 can have thousands of separate processors working together. These processors aren't the multiple CPUs higher-end AS/400s come with; they run the support devices like the controllers, the IO processors, and so on. Each device uses an independent processor. Obviously, a method is needed for coordinating all the work they do.

Messages form the backbone of this coordination. Messages are used to command other processors, request information, and deliver information. Not only processors rely on messages—many of the thousands of AS/400 objects are capable of sending/receiving messages.

Every addressable (capable of receiving a message) object in the AS/400 has a unique message queue attached. Messages are always sent to the recipient's message queue for ultimate delivery. After messages are sent or received, they often end up in *logs*. Logs, like *history* and *job logs*, are repositories of thousands of messages. Anyone reading these *job messages* can get a pretty clear idea of what was happening in the system at any time.

The messaging system is to the AS/400 what the central nervous system is to humans. And, like humans, even if everything else is in place, without the appropriate messaging ability, nothing would happen.

Most AS/400 *system messages* are internal (called *system-to-system messaging*), but the AS/400 also communicates with users via messages. Going one step further, users can communicate to other users via messages. When a user receives a message, it can come in one of two modes: break or notify .

Break messages are easy to spot—the AS/400 session gets interrupted and the message appears. The user cannot continue with his work until he or she acknowledges the message or answers it. The user can resume work after examining the message and replying to it (if necessary).

Notify messages are a little subtler. The left side of the bottom line of the AS/400 workstation screen contains some special icons or letters. There may be an "SA" or something indicating the System Available—more explicitly that the workstation is connected to the system. When Enter is pressed, an "X" or the letters "II" (Input Inhibited) will appear. These only appear briefly and indicate that your workstation is temporarily under control of the AS/400, and until that control is released, further work is not allowed. Finally, getting to the message information, a message delivered in notify mode will cause either an "MW" (Message Waiting) or an icon that is supposed to look like a message to appear. (These options—letters versus icons—are due to differences in terminal emulation software.) When either appears, there is a notify message in the background. The user has to do something special to display it.

The typical way to display messages is with the Display Message (DSPMSG) command. Enter DSPMSG on the command line and press Enter. The message will appear along with a reply line if it needs a reply.

When reading a message, its meaning may not be completely understood. Messages typically have two text versions called *levels*. Level one (the simplest) is always displayed first. If level one is not clear enough, place the cursor on the message text and press the Help (F1) key. The second level (or level two) message will appear, and it is generally longer and more descriptive.

Whether a message is delivered in break or notify mode, what has to be done with it depends on its type. There are two major types of messages on the AS/400: inquiry and informational.

An *inquiry message* requires an answer. An *informational message* only contains information and does not require a reply.

Here is an example of a situation for each:

Inquiry—The system is doing a backup to tape cartridge. It has filled a cartridge and would like the operator to insert a second cartridge so it can continue. The operator has to physically remove the filled cartridge, insert a new one, and respond to the message so that the system can continue.

Info—The same backup is complete and the operator gets a message saying so. While the operator doesn't have to respond to the message, the operator probably will want to gather up the cartridges, label them, and file them. Messages can be further separated into two types of messages:

- Predefined messages.
- Impromptu messages.

Predefined Messages

Predefined messages are just those—messages that are used commonly enough that they are predefined in the system. A large set of predefined messages is supplied with every AS/400, and software developers can create their own. Generally, as you add packaged software to your system, the vendor has included his own message file(s).

Predefined messages live in objects called *message files*. Messages are organized into different message files based on the category of messages. For example, messages used by the ILE C compiler are grouped into the QC2MSGF file. To browse all the message files on any system, use the Work with Message Files (WRKMSGF) or Display Object (DSPOBJ) command. Predefined messages have a definite structure:

- Message identifier.
- Message text—level one.
- Message text—level two.
- Cause text.
- Recovery text.
- Message variables.
- Message reply variables.
- Severity.

The *message identifier* is a unique message key, usually composed of three letters followed by four numbers. The three letters indicate the message category. For example, messages CPA through CPZ represent messages sent from the operating system. The remaining four digits indicate the sequence number of the message within the message file.

The *message text—level one* is the first, shortest message text displayed. The thinking is that most users quickly get accustomed to what the AS/400 is telling them so shorter is better.

Message text—level two is a longer version of the message.

The message *cause text* is optional. If it is present, it is contained in the level two *message description* text. It is a brief description of what may have happened to cause the message to appear.

The message *recovery text* is also optional. If it is present, it is contained in the level two message description text. It is a brief description of what the operator can do in response to the message.

Messages may have *variables* to increase their usefulness. For example, a very common problem that the system encounters is a file or library is missing. Instead of having a unique message for every possible file and library that may be missing, a single message uses variables. The raw message description contains these variables that are represented by a sequential number preceded by an "&" symbol. For example, consider the message:

```
From-file &1 in &2 not found.
```

The message variables are the &1 and &2. By substituting file and library names, this single message can be used for many situations. For example, the same message, using variables, can look like any of these:

```
From-file EMPMST in PRDLIB not found.

From-file DLYCSH in ARLIB not found.
```

The *message reply variables* of a message provide two options for message replies:

- A variable to hold the reply.
- Valid values for the reply.

Optionally, the message description for a message that takes a reply will have meanings of the various reply values, especially when they are codified.

Finally, messages have *severity codes*. Severity codes below 30 are usually informational or warning messages—the programs or jobs continue. Messages with severity codes 30 and above will generally end a program or job.

Figure 5-1 lists severity code values and what they mean. Also, particular messages with a severity code 60 or greater are always sent to the system operator's *message queue* so that they can be dealt with immediately.

Message Severity Code		**Message Sent To QSYSOPR Only**	
Informational message	00	System status	60
Warning	10	Device integrity	70
Error	20	System alert	80
Severe error	30	System integrity and user messages	90
Severe error—abnormal end of program function	40	Action	99
Abnormal end of job or program	50		

Figure 5-1: Message severity codes.

Figure 5-2 shows an example of an informational message that does not require a response from the user. Once the user has read the message and decides what to do, the user can press Enter, F12 (Cancel), or F3 (Exit) to return to the screen that was displayed before the message was displayed.

```
                     Additional Message Information

Message ID . . . . . . :   CPF2802       Severity . . . . . . . :   30
Message type . . . . . :   Diagnostic
Date sent  . . . . . . :   06/30/99      Time sent  . . . . . . :   00:53:05

Message . . . . :   From-file ASDF in OPRLIB not found.
Cause . . . . . :   Either the file or the library does not exist.
Recovery  . . . :   Change the file name or the library name.  Then try the
  request again.

                                                                      Bottom
Press Enter to continue.

F3=Exit   F6=Print   F9=Display message details
F10=Display messages in job log   F12=Cancel   F21=Select assistance level
```

Figure 5-2: Example of a predefined message.

Impromptu Messages

The user can also communicate with other users through messages that are created at the same time they are sent. These are called *impromptu messages.*

The commands used for impromptu messages, SNDMSG (Send Message) and SNDBRKMSG (Send Break Message), are explored later in this chapter.

MESSAGE QUEUES

Messages are not delivered directly to their destinations. Each destination has a *message queue* attached and messages go directly there. A message queue is like a mailbox for messages. They are objects on the system; their object type is *MSGQ. Some of the message queues we deal with every day are:

- Each workstation has a message queue with the same name as the workstation ID.
- Each user has a message queue named the same as the user profile.
- The system operator has a special message queue name QSYSOPR.
- Each program (object *PGM) has its own message queue.
- Each job (object *JOB) has two message queues:
    - An internal one to communicate with the system.
    - An external one to communicate with users.

Whenever a user signs onto the system, he or she has a personal message queue as part of his/her user profile to hold messages sent. In addition, every workstation has a message queue to hold *workstation messages* that have been sent to the workstation. The workstation must have a person signed onto it to have a message queue. The delivery of a message (whether break [*BREAK] or notify [*NOTIFY]) depends upon the *delivery mode* of the receiver's message queue.

DISPLAYING MESSAGES

Here is an example of how to work with messages. Sometimes a simple drilldown technique will clarify even the most cryptic-appearing messages. Let's assume you've started a program from the command line (using the CALL command), and that the program fails because a file is missing. You would get a *break inquiry message* from the system. See Figure 5-3.

```
                         Display Program Messages

Job 137811/DAWSON#M/QPADEV0004 started on 03/16/99 at 20:06:18 in subsystem
 CPF2817 received by FIG0501 at 200. (C D I R)








Type reply, press Enter.
  Reply . . .
_______________________________________________________________________

F3=Exit   F12=Cancel
```

Figure 5-3: A predefined message from the system.

We admit, this is a pretty cryptic message. The system is also waiting for a response to the message with either a C, D, I, or R. Let's assume we don't know anything about this message. Place the cursor on the message text and press the F1 key. Figure 5-4 shows the level-two version of the same message.

Now we have something to work with. The section labeled CAUSE tells us program, library, and program line number that caused the error. Near the bottom of the screen, we see what the effects of the possible responses are. Now we can make a more educated guess about how to respond.

By the way, in most AS/400 shops, the people who execute programs are not the same as those who develop or maintain them. The custom in this case would be to call the developer responsible (even in the middle of the night) and inform him of the problem. Whatever he tells you to do, he will probably want a screen-shot of the level two message. Produce one by pressing the Print Screen key—take it off the printer and leave it for the software developer.

```
                    Additional Message Information

 Message ID . . . . . . :   CPA0701      Severity . . . . . . . :   99
 Message type . . . . . :   Inquiry
 Date sent  . . . . . . :   03/16/99     Time sent  . . . . . . :   20:22:57

 Message . . . . :   CPF2817 received by FIG0501 at 200. (C D I R)
 Cause . . . . . :   Control language (CL) program FIG0501 in library DAWSON#M
   detected an error at statement number 200. Message text for CPF2817 is: Copy
   command ended because of error.
 Recovery  . . . :   This inquiry message can be avoided by changing the
   program. Monitor for the error (MONMSG command) and perform error recovery
   within the program. To continue, choose a reply value.
 Possible choices for replying to message . . . . . . . . . . . . . . . :
   C - Cancel the CL program.
   D - Dump the CL program variables and cancel the CL program.
   I - Ignore the failing command.
   R - Try the failing command again.
                                                                   Bottom
 Press Enter to continue.

 F3=Exit   F6=Print   F9=Display message details
 F10=Display messages in job log   F12=Cancel   F21=Select assistance level
```

Figure 5-4: Level two of our predefined message.

Back to the level-two text shown in Figure 5-4. Something has happened. The top of the screen is actually for CPA0701 and its severity is 99. Remember the severity rule, anything 30 and over will probably kill the program? There is no hope for this program continuing. When that happens, the system often sends messages in pairs—one with the original problem and one that says in effect, "Due to a previously encountered problem, this program is dead." That is what we see here.

At this point, the operator's most likely reaction to the message shown in Figure 5-4 would be to cancel the program, by entering the letter C, or to cancel the program and obtain a program dump by entering the letter D. Either response would be appropriate. Requesting the dump would yield more information about the problem (AS/400 program dumps are easy to read). Either response will cause the message display to go away and the original screen (presumably with a command line) to return. The other two responses, Ignore (I) and Retry (R) should be taken only if you have a deep understanding of the failing program. Not many programs will really "ignore" a level 99 message. Nor will any program continue successfully after a "retry" unless either the operator or the programmer has taken some action.

If we want to really look at the original message, we would use the WRKMSGD (Work with Message Descriptions) command and specify the desired message. For example, enter this on the command line:

```
WRKMSGD CPF2817
```

- Press Enter and the `Work with Message Descriptions` screen in Figure 5-5 appears.

```
                         Work with Message Descriptions
                                                          System:   BIGBLUE
 Message file:   QCPFMSG        Library:   QSYS

 Position to . . . . . . .              Message ID

 Type options, press Enter.
   2=Change   4=Delete   5=Display details   6=Print

 Opt  Message ID  Severity  Message Text
  5     CPF2817       40      Copy command ended because of error.
  _     CPF2818       40      *FROMMBR value is not allowed on TOMBR parameter.
  _     CPF2819       30      &3 not allowed on TOMBR for &1 in &2.
  _     CPF2820       30      &3 not allowed on FROMMBR for inline file.
  _     CPF2821       30      &3 not allowed on RCDFMT for &1 in &2.
  _     CPF2822       30      COMPRESS(*NO) not valid for specified files.
  _     CPF2823       30      Multiple from-members not allowed.
  _     CPF2825       30      SRCOPT value not allowed for &1 in &2.

More...
 Parameters or command
 ===> ____________________________________________________________
 F3=Exit   F5=Refresh   F6=Add   F12=Cancel   F24=More keys
```

Figure 5-5: Work with Message Descriptions screen of the WRKMSGD command.

Notice that we can look at one of several messages; the command positions us at an alphabetical break. By entering a 5 (see the options list in Figure 5-5), we can request the details on message CPF2817. Press Enter from this screen to get another menu similar to the one shown in Figure 5-6.

```
                        Select Message Details to Display
                                                          System:   BIGBLUE
 Message ID . . . . . . . . . :   CPF2817
 Message file . . . . . . . . :   QCPFMSG
   Library  . . . . . . . . . :     QSYS
 Message text . . . . . . . . :   Copy command ended because of error.


 Select one of the following:

      1. Display message text
      2. Display field data

      5. Display message attributes

     30. All of the above



 Selection  ________________________________________________________


 F3=Exit   F12=Cancel
```

Figure 5-6: Menu to display sections of a message.

Type 1 on the Selection line and press Enter. The message text will appear on a screen similar to Figure 5-7.

```
                    Display Formatted Message Text
                                                        System:   BIGBLUE
Message ID . . . . . . . . . :   CPF2817
Message file . . . . . . . . :   QCPFMSG
  Library  . . . . . . . . . :     QSYS


Message . . . . :   Copy command ended because of error.
Cause . . . . . :   An error occurred while the file was being copied.
Recovery  . . . :   See the messages previously listed.  Correct the errors,
  and then try the request again.
```

Figure 5-7: Details of message text for CPF2817.

Refer to the menu shown in Figure 5-6; taking other options will show other views of the message. For now, let us move on.

Messages are collected into logs. One of the primary logs is the job log. While a user is signed onto a workstation, he has a job log that is building with messages and the commands he runs. He can check out the job log built during these simple exercises by typing DSPJOBLOG on the command line and pressing Enter. The system will produce a display similar to the one shown in Figure 5-8.

```
                          Display All Messages
                                                   System:   BIGBLUE
Job . . :   QPADEV0004  User . . :   DAWSON#M   Number . . . :   137811

    CPF2817 received by FIG0501 at 200. (C D I R)
  ? C
4 > wrkjoblog
    Command WRKJOBLOG in library *LIBL not found.
    Error found on WRKJOBLOG command.
4 > dspjoblog
4 > wrkmsgd cpf2817
4 > call fig0501
    From-file FILEA in DAWSON#M not found.
    Copy command ended because of error.
    CPF2817 received by FIG0501 at 200. (C D I R)
  ? C
4 > wrkmsgd cpg2817
4 > wrkmsgd cpf2817

                                                          More . . .
Press Enter to continue.

F3=Exit   F5=Refresh   F12=Cancel   F17=Top   F18=Bottom
```

Figure 5-8: Details of a job log.

Notice the job log is all commands and messages. Together, an operator can pretty much reconstruct anything that happened on an AS/400 at any time.

In the example shown in Figure 5-8, note that the program FIG0501 was called (the command is `CALL FIG0501`).

Immediately after that, we see the first message, `From-file FILEA in DAWSON#M not found.`

That was a fatal error, so the next message is a high-level one from the system, `Copy command ended because of error.`

Then the predefined message that the user received is displayed, `CPF2817 received by FIG0501 at 200. (C D I R).`

Finally, the next line starts with a question mark (?) followed by the letter C. That tells us a reply was requested (indicated by the question mark) and that the user responded with a C, which cancelled the job. Everything goes into the job log.

Here are several commands that will help you work with messages, message files, and message queues:

- Create and Change Messages Queues (CRTMSGQ, CHGMSGQ, WRKMSGQ).
- Change Message Descriptions (CHGMSGD).
- Remove Message Descriptions (RMVMSGD).
- Create Message Files (CRTMSGF).
- Delete Message Files (DLTMSGF).
- Add Message Descriptions (ADDMSGD).
- Send Impromptu Messages (SNDMSG, SNDBRKMSG).
- Display Messages and Print Messages Descriptions (DSPMSG, DSPMSGD, WRKMSGF).
- Add Default Replies for Predefined Messages Using the System Reply List (WRKRPYLE).

There is no need to memorize these commands (no need other than to pass the chapter quiz, that is). If you are unsure about them, just use the Message menu. To invoke it, enter

```
GO MESSAGE
```

on the command line and press Enter.

The system will produce a menu similar to the one shown in Figure 5-9 from which you can do almost anything with messages.

SENDING IMPROMPTU OR USER MESSAGES

There are two commands you can use to send impromptu messages to users, Send Message (SNDMSG) and Send Break Message (SNDBRKMSG).

```
MESSAGE                              Messages
                                                              System:   BIGBLUE
 Select one of the following:

      1. Send a message
      2. Send a break message
      3. Display messages
      4. Display system operator messages
      5- Send a network message
      6. Work with message queues
      7. Create a message queue
      8. Work with message descriptions

     70. Related commands




 Selection or command
 ===>  ____________________________________________________________________
 ____________________________________________________________________________

 F3=Exit   F4=Prompt   F9=Retrieve   F12=Cancel   F13=Information Assistant
```

Figure 5-9: Message menu.

SNDMSG COMMAND

The SNDMSG command is used to send a message from your display station to one or more message queues, including both display station and *user message queues*. The SNDMSG command has five parameters, but for most practical purposes there are only four of them to note:

- The Message Text (MSG) parameter used to specify the actual message.
- The To User Profile (TOUSR) parameter identifies who should receive the message.
- The Message Type (MSGTYPE) parameter indicates the type of message: informational (*INFO) or inquiry (*INQ). The default value is *INFO, so the only time this parameter needs to be specified is when an inquiry message is being sent.
- The Reply Message Queue (RPYMSGQ) parameter indicates which message queue will receive the reply message. This is used for inquiry messages only. The default value is *WRKSTN. If workstations are dynamically allocated, it is a good practice to change the reply message queue to a specific user message queue.

Let us consider how the SNDMSG command is used to send informational and inquiry messages to other users on the system. The system operator may want to send a message to a user for many reasons. For example, he may need to inform the user that his report has finished printing and is ready to be picked up, or he may need to tell all users that the system will be shut down at 5:30 P.M. for a release upgrade.

Suppose one user wants to send an informational message to user JWILSON to tell JWILSON that the AS/400 lab assignment is finished. The CL command in Figure 5-10 could be used.

```
                         Send Message (SNDMSG)

Type choices, press Enter.

Message text . . . . . . . . . .  I have finished my lab assignment






To user profile  . . . . . . . .  JWILSON       Name, *SYSOPR, *ALLACT...

                         Additional Parameters

To message queue . . . . . . . .  ________               Name, *SYSOPR
  Library  . . . . . . . . . . .    *LIBL       Name, *LIBL, *CURLIB
             + for more values    ________
                                    *LIBL
Message type . . . . . . . . . .    *INFO            *INFO, *INQ
                                                                     More...
F3=Exit   F4=Prompt   F5=Refresh   F12=Cancel   F13=How to use this display
F24=More keys
```

Figure 5-10: The SNDMSG command using MSG and TOUSR parameters.

The two parameters that have been used are Message Text (to describe the text of the message), and To User Profile (to indicate which user receives the message). Notice that the default value for the message type is *INFO (informational)—that means the recipient does not have to respond.

Sending to Multiple Users

The To User Profile parameter has a limitation of only one user profile (one addressee by profile). Although this parameter looks like it only allows a single user profile, system-generic names that imply more than one profile can be used. These are not names but keywords that invoke many profile names. They are sometimes referred to as *special users*, not to be confused with the users themselves being special. Valid special users supplied by IBM for the AS/400 are:

- *SYSOPR to send a message to the system operator.
- *ALLUSR to send a message to all users whether they are currently signed on or not.
- *ALLACT to send a message to all users currently signed on. (*Note*: This special user designation may not be used on the SNDBRKMSG command.)
- *ALLWS to send a message to all workstations whether they are currently active or not.

The most common use of special users is to communicate with the system operator. All you need to do is specify TOUSR(*SYSOPR) or TOMSGQ(*SYSOPR). The system operator actually has two profile names: his own and the generic QSYSOPR. His message queue also has the same two names. The nice thing about this feature is that the users don't have to know who the system operator is at any time, they just address the special name, *SYSOPR.

Messages sent to *ALLUSR really go to all users, even those who are not signed on. How does that happen? The messages wait in their queues in "Hold" status until they eventually sign on, then they get the messages. Usually, you want to use *ALLACT, rarely use *ALLUSR.

Another parameter, To Message Queue, can accept many addresses. If the message queues are known, the system operator could use the To Message Queue parameter to send the same message to several users. Or, more accurately, to their message queues (either their personal message queue based on their user profile or their workstation's message queue):

```
SNDMSG MSG('Time to start our meeting in the Computer +
Room.') TOMSGQ(JUNG JUAN JENNIFER JUSTIN)
```

Note that this message example was typed straight in on the command line. Do not be thrown by the use of the parameter names like MSG and TOMSGQ. Remember the material in chapter 3 about using CL commands. Each parameter has its own name. Press the F11 key to show names.

In this example, the same message would be sent to message queues JUNG, JUAN, JENNIFER, and JUSTIN: "Time to start our meeting in the computer room."

The distinction between the user profile and message queue is important. When the security administrator creates a user profile, a message queue has to be assigned for the new user. The name of the message queue defaults to the user profile name. A user named JUSTIN would have a message queue of the same name. In this case, it makes no difference whether you use the TOUSR or the TOMSGQ parameter, because the names are identical. Keep in mind, however, that this similarity is not automatic and not followed in every shop.

Sending Inquiry Messages

When the sender of an impromptu message wants an answer, the message inquiry is made on the SNDMSG command. For example, the following inquiry message to user LUIS requires an answer:

```
SNDMSG MSG('I need to shut down the system. How much +
        longer are you going to use it?') +
        TOUSR(LUIS) +
        MSGTYPE(*INQ)
```

When LUIS sees this message, the system provides an input field that goes all the way across the screen, right below the message text as shown in Figure 5-11.

```
                              Display Messages
                                                         System:   BIGBLUE
 Queue . . . . . :   QPADEV0018              Program . . . . :   *DSPMSG
   Library . . . :     QSYS                    Library . . . :
 Severity  . . . :   00                      Delivery  . . . :   *NOTIFY

 Type reply (if required), press Enter.
   From  . . . :   DAWSON#M       03/17/99   20:49:08
   I need to shut down the system. How much longer are you going to use it?
     Reply . . :   _____________________________________________________________

                                                                        Bottom
 F3=Exit              F11=Remove a message                   F12=Cancel
 F13=Remove all       F16=Remove all except unanswered       F24=More keys
```

Figure 5-11: Receiving an inquiry type message.

LUIS can then type the answer and press Enter; when he does that, the user gets the answer at his terminal.

If the sender wants the reply to come to a different workstation than the one the message was sent from, it can be specified with the RPYMSGQ parameter. This parameter always defaults to *WRKSTN, which means that the sending display station's message queue receives the reply.

Sending inquiry messages has two restrictions. Special user *ALLACT cannot be used on parameter TOUSR. Also, more than one name cannot be used in the TOMSGQ parameter because of the implied flood of answers that could generate.

Inquiry messages can only be sent to single users or workstations. Only informational messages may be sent to multiple users.

Break Messages

The Send Break Message (SNDBRKMSG) command is used to send a break message to a workstation message queue. Because break messages interrupt work, they are only used for important messages. Also, break messages are only sent to workstation message queues; they cannot be used to send to users' personal message queues. This means that if a break message is to be sent to user MGARCIA, the sender must first find out where MGARCIA is signed on. The command to do this is Work with User Job (WRKUSRJOB). Here is an example of using it from the command line to find out where MGARCIA's current workstation message queue is:

```
WRKUSRJOB USER(MGARCIA) STATUS(*ACTIVE)
```

The STATUS parameter could be omitted, but in that case, the system would return all of MGARCIA's jobs (she may have dozens of jobs that are either completed or waiting in a job queue). When the system displays the list of jobs, it can be visually scanned for interactive jobs (type INTER). The job name is always the same as the workstation message queue name so make note of it.

The system operator uses the SNDBRKMSG command quite often when a systemwide message needs to be sent to all active users. For example, if the system operator needed to inform all users to sign off for a particular reason, he or she would send a break message to all active workstation message queues. If a workstation is active (someone is signed onto the workstation) at the time of delivery, the break message interrupts the current job and displays the message.

With this knowledge, run the SNDBRKMSG command to send Maria Garcia a break message. For an example, refer to Figure 5-12.

Like SNDMSG, the same break message can be sent to more than one place. The TOMSGQ parameter accepts a list of display station names (to send the same break message to several specific display stations).

SNDBRKMSG also can send an inquiry message. Specify MSGTYPE(*INQ) to only one display station at a time.

```
                      Send Break Message (SNDBRKMSG)

 Type choices, press Enter.

 Message text . . . . . . . . . .   Maria, let's do lunch!






 To work station message queue  .   QPADEV0017     Name, *ALLWS
   Library  . . . . . . . . . . .     *LIBL        Name, *LIBL
              + for more values
                                          *LIBL
 Message type . . . . . . . . . .   *INFO         *INFO, *INQ
 Message queue to get reply . . .   QSYSOPR       Name
   Library  . . . . . . . . . . .     *LIBL       Name, *LIBL


                                                                 Bottom
 F3=Exit   F4=Prompt   F5=Refresh   F10=Additional parameters   F12=Cancel
 F13=How to use this display        F24=More keys
```

Figure 5-12: Send Break Message screen.

System Reply List

Some system-generated inquiry messages start to get in the way because they come up constantly, hanging up programs until the user or system operator responds to them. The response to these messages is almost always the same, so all they do is delay processing.

The AS/400 has a *system reply list* that allows us to provide automatic responses to many messages. An example would be a message to change forms on a laser printer that only contains blank white stock paper. However, a message to change forms on a line printer in the computer room will not be so predictable. A line printer usually prints on many paper types; it is up to the system to inform the operator when it wants to print to a special paper type, and up to the operator to actually change the paper, ensure correct line up, and tell the system this information.

With the System Reply list, the system can be forced to give the same response every time the question comes up. In the case of the two printers' messages, the operator can also have the system parse out information to determine which ones to have the system respond to and which ones to pass on to the user or system operator.

Not all jobs use the System Reply list. A job has to have the parameter INQMSGRPY(*SYSRPYL) specified or it will ignore this list. Most jobs do not have this set; use the Change Job (CHGJOB) command to set it. The AS/400 comes with a basic System Reply list that looks like Figure 5-13.

Sequence Number	Message Identifier	Compare Value	Reply	Dump
10	CPA0700	*NONE	D	*YES
20	RPG0000	*NONE	D	*YES
30	CBE0000	*NONE	D	*YES
40	PLI0000	*NONE	D	*YES

Figure 5-13: System Reply list.

Figure 5-13 is not too intuitive. It means that any error starting with the error number's trailing zeros and going to the 9s in those spaces will receive a response. In other words, the first line says that all messages CPA07<u>00</u> through CPA07<u>99</u> from any job with INQMSGRPY(*SYSRPYL) will be answered automatically with a "D" (for a program dump). Reply list entries are added with the ADDRPYLE command.

To illustrate, assume we want the AS/400 to automatically respond to an align-forms message (CPA4002) received for any printer except the line printer in the computer room (which in our example, we will assume is named QSYSPRT).

If the align-forms message is not for QSYSPRT, it must be for a laser printer and the system will just reply with an "I" for ignore.

If the align-forms message is for QSYSPRT, it is for the line printer and the message will be passed on through to the intended destination, probably the system operator.

No problem. Just look inside the message identification, CPA4002, at its MSGDTA area. The command is WRKMSGD CPA4002. Figure 5-14 shows its first menu screen.

```
                        Work with Message Descriptions
                                                               System:   BIGBLUE
 Message file:   QCPFMSG         Library:   QSYS

 Position to . . . . . . .              Message ID

 Type options, press Enter.
   2=Change   4=Delete   5=Display details   6=Print

 Opt  Message ID  Severity   Message Text
  5_    CPA4002       99     Verify alignment on printer &3. (I G N R E C)
  _     CPA4003       99     Form feed attachment &4 required on printer &3. (C
  _     CPA4004       99     End of ribbon on printer &3. (C H I PAGE 1-9999999)
  _     CPA4005       99     End of ribbon on printer &3. (C I)
  _     CPA4006       99     Volume &5 density is not correct. (C R)
  _     CPA4007       99     Paper jam on printer &3. (C R)
  _     CPA4008       99     Open cover on printer &3. (C H PAGE 1-9999999)
  _     CPA4009       99     Open cover on printer &3. (C R)
                                                                        More...
 Parameters or command
 ===> ____________________________________________________________________________
 F3=Exit   F5=Refresh   F6=Add   F12=Cancel   F24=More keys
```

Figure 5-14: WRKMSGD menu.

Take option 5, then option 1 from the next displayed screen to see the full message text. See Figure 5-15.

```
                         Display Formatted Message Text
                                                            System:   BIGBLUE
Message ID . . . . . . . . . :   CPA4002
Message file . . . . . . . . :   QCPFMSG
  Library  . . . . . . . . . :     QSYS

Message . . . . :   Verify alignment on printer &3. (I G N R E C)
Cause . . . . . :   The forms may not be aligned correctly.  The first line
  for the file is &4.
Possible choices for replying to message . . . . . . . . . . . . . . . :
  I - To continue printing aligned forms starting with the next line of the
    file, type an I.
  G - To continue printing aligned forms skipping to the next form and
    printing the first line again, type a G.
  N - To print the first line again on the next form and to verify the
    alignment,
    1. Press Stop only if Start and Stop are two keys, or press Reset.
    2. Advance the paper to the next form by pressing Form Feed/New Page.
    3. Adjust the alignment with the forms adjust control.
                                                                      More...
Press Enter to continue.

F3=Exit   F11=Display unformatted message text   F12=Cancel
```

Figure 5-15: Message text for message ID CPA4002.

Press the F12 key to go back to the menu (Figure 5-14) and take option 2 to see the MSGDTA layout. This is where the compare value will come from. Refer to Figure 5-16 for a sample of the MSGDTA layout.

```
                          Display Field Data

Message ID . . . . . . . . . :   CPA4002
Message file . . . . . . . . :   QCPFMSG
  Library  . . . . . . . . . :     QSYS


                                    Decimal       Vary
Field     Data Type      Length     Positions     Length      Dump
 &1       *CHAR            10                                  *NO
 &2       *CHAR            10                                  *NO
 &3       *CHAR            10                                  *NO
 &4       *BIN              2                                  *NO
 &5       *CHAR            10                                  *NO
 &6       *CHAR            10                                  *NO
 &7       *CHAR             0                                  *NO
 &8       *CHAR             0                                  *NO
 &9       *CHAR             0                                  *NO
 &10      *CHAR             0                                  *NO
                                                                    More ...
Press Enter to continue.

F3=Exit   F12=Cancel
```

Figure 5-16: Layout of MSGDTA for message ID CPA4002.

Now add two reply message entries to the System Reply list shown in Table 5-13. One for the laser printer that always gets an answer of "G" and one for the line printer that we want the user or system operator to see and respond to. Add message CPA4002 immediately after CPA0700. When the operating system goes through the list, the first time it gets a hit, it stops searching. In our example, we want to qualify one instance of the message (when the printer's name is QSYSPRT) and leave the other instance (for all other printers) unqualified. To do this, we must put the qualified instance first—if the unqualified instance is first, the system will always be satisfied on that one and never look past it. So the first instance for this printer example will be the qualified one or the QSYSPRT message. Here is the command:

```
ADDRPYLE SEQNBR(12) MSGID(CPA4002) RPY(*RQD) CMPDTA('QSYSPRT' 21)
```

Refer to Figures 5-15 and 5-16. The message text on Figure 5-15 has an &3 as the variable that contained the printer name. In Figure 5-16, that variable is third in the list, and it starts on column 21 (the first two fields are ten characters each, 10 + 10 is 20, so the third field must start on 21). When this message is intended for the system printer, it will have the word QSYSPRT in column 21, so that is where we specify the comparison.

The RPY(*RQD) parameter of this Reply List entry effectively tells the system there is no automatic reply for this message. Seeing that, the system forwards it to the recipient, usually the system operator.

Here is the Reply List entry without the compare message to catch CPA4002's for the other printers:

```
ADDRPYLE SEQNBR(14) MSGID(CPA4002) RPY(G)
```

This Reply List entry makes no comparison for the printer device name. Figure 5-17 shows the System Reply list after those changes.

Sequence Number	Message Identifier	Compare Value	Reply	Dump
10	CPA0700	*NONE	D	*YES
12	CPA4002	'QSYSPRT' 21	&RQD	*NO
14	CPA4002	*NONE	G	*NO
20	RPG0000	*NONE	D	*YES
30	CBE0000	*NONE	D	*YES
40	PLI0000	*NONE	D	*YES

Table 5-17: System Reply list after changes.

That was easy. For other messages, be very careful about their placement. Remember that RPG0000, on sequence 20, implicitly includes all RPG messages (RPG0000 through RPG9999). The trailing zeros automatically create that range. Therefore, a message RPG0120 would include RPG0120 through RPG0129. In this case, any new RPG would have to be placed prior to the RPG0000 ahead of sequence 20. Once a message traps, the system quits looking any further.

LAB #5: MESSAGE HANDLING

Upon completion of this lab, you should be able to:

- Demonstrate how to display system messages.
- Demonstrate how to send a message to another user on the AS/400.
- Explain the types of messages and their uses.
- Describe the purpose of the message queue.
- Demonstrate how to respond to a message.
- Use the Command Entry display.
- Use user-defined, system-defined, and special values in commands.
- Use command prompting.
- Explore message command structure.

MESSAGE HANDLING

Messages are the backbone of system coordination and are used to command other processors, request information, and deliver information. Remember that messages are delivered to message queues. To start to investigate messages, we will explore the command that is used to display messages and the queues that they can be delivered to.

- Enter the command to call the `Command Entry` screen.
- Enter DSPMSG on the command line.
- Press F4 (Prompt).

The Display Messages command prompt screen as shown in Figure L5-1.

```
                          Display Messages (DSPMSG)

 Type choices, press Enter.

 Message queue . . . . . . . . .   *WRKUSR       Name, *WRKUSR, *SYSOPR...
   Library . . . . . . . . . . .   __________    Name, *LIBL, *CURLIB
 Output . . . . . . . . . . . .    *             *, *PRINT, *PRTWRAP







                                                                      Bottom
 F3=Exit   F4=Prompt   F5=Refresh   F10=Additional parameters   F12=Cancel
 F13=How to use this display        F24=More keys
```

Figure L5-1: Display Messages prompt screen.

- Place the cursor in the Message Queue field.
- Press Help.
- Read through the help text and complete the chart shown in Figure L5-2.

Message Queue Values	Define and Identify Restrictions (Where Appropriate)

Figure L5-2: List and define the five types of message queues.

- Exit help.
- Press F10 (Additional Parameters).

Now, all the parameter values for the Display Messages command are displayed. From here, you can control what messages are displayed and how they are displayed. For example, you can control the sequence in which messages are displayed or filter the messages and only look at messages with a severity greater than the value you enter.

- Press Enter until the Display Messages screen is displayed.

When you use the DSPMSG command from a workstation, by default, the command displays the messages available in both the workstation and user message queues. To determine which message queue you are viewing, look at the Queue field in the upper-left corner of the screen. See Figure L5-3.

Figure L5-3 shows the messages in the workstation queue called QPADEV0004. If you are viewing the workstation message queue, you will need to press Enter to view the messages in your message queue. Your message queue has the same name as your user profile.

- Return to the Command Entry screen.

```
                          Display Messages
                                                 System:   BIGBLUE
Queue . . . . . :   QPADEV0004             Program . . . . :   *DSPMSG
  Library . . . :     QSYS                   Library . . . :
Severity  . . . :   00                     Delivery  . . . :   *NOTIFY

Type reply (if required), press Enter.
  From  . . . :   OPR0001        07/22/99   02:23:21
   Do you want a cup of coffee?

    Reply . . :   Yes, hope your are buying.

  From  . . . :   HOHLY#M        07/22/99   20:50:21
  hi, how are you?
    Reply . . . ________________________________________________________



                                                                 Bottom
F3=Exit                F11=Remove a message                 F12=Cancel
F13=Remove all         F16=Remove all except unanswered     F24=More keys
```

Figure L5-3: Display Messages screen showing the workstation queue QPADEV0004'S messages.

SENDING A MESSAGE

Now let's send an impromptu message using the Send Message command. This command can send messages to either the message queue specified in a user profile, *system operator message queue*, all active users, or the sender of the message. If this parameter is not selected, the alternative choice is to send the message to a message queue that is specified. Messages can be sent in either an informational or inquiry mode. When sending an inquiry message, you need to specify that it is an inquiry message. Placing a question mark at the end of the text does not make it a question.

- Enter SNDMSG on the command line.
- Press F4 (Prompt) (shown in Figure L5-4).
- Enter a question in the message text field, for example, `Would you like a cup of coffee?`
- Enter *REQUESTER in the `User Profile` field.
- Press F10 (Additional Parameters).
- Enter *INQ for the message type.
- Press Enter.

```
                    Send Message (SNDMSG)

Type choices, press Enter.

Message text . . . . . . . . . . ______________________________
_____________________________________________________________
_____________________________________________________________
_____________________________________________________________
_____________________________________________________________
_____________________________________________________________
_____________________________________________________________
To user profile  . . . . . . . . __________  Name, *SYSOPR, *ALLACT...




                                                          Bottom
F3=Exit   F4=Prompt   F5=Refresh   F10=Additional parameters   F12=Cancel
F13=How to use this display        F24=More keys
```

Figure L5-4: Sending a message with SNDMSG command.

This will send the question to your message queue, allow you to view the message you sent, and also reply to the message. The message will not automatically display, rather it will turn on the MW (Message Waiting) symbol on the bottom line of your screen and beep, which signals the arrival of a message.

- On the command line, enter DSPMSG.
- Press Enter.
- Press F16 to remove all but unanswered messages (as shown in Figure L5-5).
- Press Enter again.

This will bring up the Reply screen.

```
                         Display Messages
                                               System:   BIGBLUE
Queue . . . . . :   OPR0001               Program . . . . :   *DSPMSG
  Library . . . :     QUSRSYS               Library . . . :
Severity  . . . :   00                    Delivery  . . . :   *NOTIFY

Type reply (if required), press Enter.
  From  . . . :   OPR0001        07/22/99   02:23:21
   Would you like a cup of coffee?
    Reply . . . _____________________________________________




                                                            Bottom
F3=Exit            F11=Remove a message                 F12=Cancel
F13=Remove all     F16=Remove all except unanswered     F24=More keys
```

Figure L5-5: F16 removes all except unanswered messages on the Display Messages screen.

- Enter your answer on the line provided.
- Press Enter twice.

Waiting in your message queue is your new message that requires a reply. The MW symbol is displayed on the bottom line accompanied by a beep. These are your clues that you have received another message. The message you received was delivered to you in the notify mode.

- Enter DSPMSG on the command line.
- Press Enter until your message and its reply are displayed.
- Enter your message answer.
- Press Enter.

Note that you should be seeing messages in your message queue as well as those in the workstation queue. The message queue name appears in the upper-left corner of the screen.

- Remove all messages from your message queue. (*Note*: Check upper-left corner to determine which queue you are viewing.)

You should also periodically check your workstation message queue. Next, you will be asked to clean out your workstation message queue.

- Enter the DSPMSG command.
- Press F4 (Prompt).
- Enter the `keyword identifier` for the workstation message queue.
- Press Enter.
- Delete all messages in the workstation message queue. (*Hint*: Use function keys.)
- Return to the `Command Entry` screen.

Again, messages are sent to message queues. The way you receive your messages is influenced by the delivery mode of your message queue. You can determine the delivery mode of messages on your message queue. Next, you will be experiencing these modes. Remember that your message queue is named the same as your user profile and usually stored in QUSRSYS library.

- Enter the command to `Change your Message Queue` on the command line.
- Press F4 (Prompt).
- Enter `USERID` for the message queue name.
- Change the delivery mode parameter to *BREAK.
- Press Enter.

- Using the SNDMSG command, send yourself an informational message.
- What happened? ______________________________

Now that you know how the break mode works, you will be changing your message queue to experience other modes. You will be using the procedure you used above.

- Use the command to `Change your Message Queue` again.
- Change the delivery mode parameter to *HOLD.
- Using the SNDMSG command, send yourself an informational message.
- What happened? ______________________________
- Display your message queue.
- Did you receive the message? ______________________________

Now that you have experienced several of the modes of message delivery, it is time to do some cleanup and put your message queue back to its original condition.

- Delete all messages in your message queue.
- Change your message queue delivery mode back to *NOTIFY. (*Note*: Use above procedure.)

You have to send a message using the USER PROFILE parameter to determine who will receive your message. You can also send a message using the TO MESSAGE QUEUE parameter. In this next section, you will be determining the message queue of the workstation of another student in the class. Then you will send an inquiry message to that workstation. Remember, you can always test this by sending a trial message to your workstation message queue. In determining the recipient of the message, you can use either the TO USER PROFILE or TO MESSAGE QUEUE parameters, never both. Before starting, let's look at the command you use to send the message. To see the TO MESSAGE QUEUE parameter, you need to view the additional parameters. See Figure L5-6.

Also, before you begin, you will need to ask the person to whom you are sending a message `What is their User ID`? Then you will need to find their workstation job name. There are many ways to determine this information. Let's use one of the methods in this section. Because your fellow student is actively working on the system, one of the methods to find the information you need is to use the Work with Active Jobs command as shown in Figure L5-7.

```
                         Send Message (SNDMSG)

 Type choices, press Enter.

 Message text . . . . . . . . . _______________________________________
 ______________________________________________________________________
 ______________________________________________________________________
 ______________________________________________________________________
 ______________________________________________________________________
 ______________________________________________________________________
 ______________________________________________________________________
 To user profile  . . . . . . . __________    Name, *SYSOPR, *ALLACT...

                        Additional Parameters

 To message queue . . . . . . .  __________    Name, *SYSOPR
   Library  . . . . . . . . . .   *LIBL        Name, *LIBL, *CURLIB
              + for more values  __________
                                  *LIBL
 Message type . . . . . . . . .  *INFO         *INFO, *INQ
                                                                More...
 F3=Exit   F4=Prompt   F5=Refresh   F12=Cancel   F13=How to use this display
 F24=More keys
```

Figure L5-6: Send Message command including the additional parameters.

```
                        Work with Active Jobs                    BIGBLUE
                                                       07/23/99  03:00:00
 CPU %:      .0      Elapsed time:   00:00:00     Active jobs:   115

 Type options, press Enter.
   2=Change    3=Hold    4=End    5=Work with    6=Release    7=Display message
   8=Work with spooled files    13=Disconnect ...

 Opt  Subsystem/Job  User        Type  CPU %  Function        Status
 __   QBASE          QSYS        SBS      .0                   DEQW
 __   QBATCH         QSYS        SBS      .0                   DEQW
 __   QCMN           QSYS        SBS      .0                   DEQW
 __   QCTL           QSYS        SBS      .0                   DEQW
 __     QSYSSCD      QPGMR       BCH      .0  PGM-QEZSCNEP     EVTW
 __   QINTER         QSYS        SBS      .0                   DEQW
 __     QPADEV0004   HOHLY#M     INT      .0  CMD-WRKACTJOB    RUN
 __   QPGMR          QSYS        SBS      .0                   DEQW
 __   QSERVER        QSYS        SBS      .0                   DEQW
                                                               More...
 Parameters or command
 ===> _________________________________________________________________
 F3=Exit   F5=Refresh       F7=Find      F10=Restart statistics
 F11=Display elapsed data   F12=Cancel   F23=More options   F24=More keys
```

Figure L5-7: Determine workstation name for HOHLY#M by using WRKACTJOB.

You will notice that one of the authors is active on the system and the name of the workstation job for HOHLY#M is QPADEV0004. Now it is your turn to determine the workstation of the other student.

- Enter the WRKACTJOB command on the command line.
- Press Enter.
- Page down until you find the other student user ID.
- What is the workstation job name for the other student? ____________________

Now compose and send the inquiry message to the other student.

- Enter SNDMSG on the command line.
- Press F4 (Prompt) (shown in Figure L5-4).
- For the message text, enter a question.
- Press F10 (Additional Parameters).
- Enter the workstation job name for the other student in the `To message queue` field.
- Remember to leave the `User Profile` field blank.
- Enter *INQ for the message type.
- Press Enter.

Chances are, messages have been sent to you. You will need to check your messages to answer any inquiry messages you have received.

- Enter the command that displays your message queue.
- Press the function key to `Remove all except unanswered` messages.
- If you have received any inquiry messages, respond to them.
- Press Enter.
- Clear your message queue.

SENDING A BREAK MESSAGE

Operators are often required to send messages to users. Often the message is important and the user must receive the message immediately. Also, everyone should know how to send a break message in case they ever need to get someone's attention immediately. When this is the case, the operator will use a break message. A break message "pops" up on the screen. Break messages cannot be sent to a user, they can only be sent to an interactive job (workstation message queue, not the user message queue). Before you send a message to a person, you need to know the name of their interactive job name. In a previous section, you found the user interactive (workstation) job through the use of the Work with Active Jobs command (refer to Figure L5-7). This is not the only method available. The Work with User Jobs command also allows us to determine what interactive jobs are on the system. This command is shown in Figure L5-8.

```
                     Work with User Jobs (WRKUSRJOB)

 Type choices, press Enter.

 User whose jobs to display . . . > *ALL          Name, *, *ALL
 Status of user jobs  . . . . . . > *ACTIVE       *ALL, *ACTIVE, *JOBQ, *OUTQ
 Output . . . . . . . . . . . . .   *             *, *PRINT
 Job type . . . . . . . . . . . . > *INTERACT     *ALL, *INTERACT, *BATCH









                                                                        Bottom
 F3=Exit   F4=Prompt   F5=Refresh   F10=Additional parameters   F12=Cancel
 F13=How to use this display        F24=More keys
```

Figure L5-8: Work with User Jobs to display the interactive jobs on the system.

- Enter WRKUSRJOB USER(*ALL) STATUS(*ACTIVE) JOBTYPE(*INTERACT) command on the command line (as shown in L5-8).
- Press Enter.
- Page down until you find the other student user ID.
- What is the job name for the other student? ____________________________

Now that you have determined where to send your break message, let's get on with the creation of the message. Before we enter the command, let's look at the parameters of this command. See Figure L5-9.

```
                     Send Break Message (SNDBRKMSG)

 Type choices, press Enter.

 Message text . . . . . . . . . .   When is the coffee break in this class?
 ______________________________________________________________________________
 ______________________________________________________________________________
 ______________________________________________________________________________
 ______________________________________________________________________________
 ______________________________________________________________________________
 ______________________________________________________________________________
 To work station message queue  .   QPADEV0004    Name, *ALLWS
   Library  . . . . . . . . . . .     *LIBL       Name, *LIBL
              + for more values     __________
                                      *LIBL
 Message type . . . . . . . . . .   *INFO         *INFO, *INQ
 Message queue to get reply . . .   QSYSOPR       Name
   Library  . . . . . . . . . . .     *LIBL       Name, *LIBL


                                                                        Bottom
 F3=Exit   F4=Prompt   F5=Refresh   F10=Additional parameters   F12=Cancel
 F13=How to use this display        F24=More keys
```

Figure L5-9: Send Break Message screen.

Note that to send an inquiry break message, there are several parameters with which you must be concerned. Of course, the message is important as well as who receives the message. Two other parameters need to be considered: first the message type that must be changed to *INQ, and an often forgotten second parameter, the MESSAGE QUEUE TO GET REPLY. Remember that when you ask a question, you expect to get a reply. You will note that the default reply goes to the system operator. As the operator, you may not want to receive everyone's messages. You must change this parameter to your message queue in order to receive the reply to your message.

- Enter SNDBRKMSG on the command line.
- Press F4 (Prompt).
- Enter your message. Remember to make it a question.
- Enter the `To Work Station Message Queue` with the interactive job name of the person receiving your message. (*Note*: You found this information above.)
- Change the message type parameter to *INQ.
- Enter your message queue in the MESSAGE QUEUE TO GET REPLY parameter. (*Note*: Your message queue is your user ID.)
- Press Enter.

Remember that you may receive messages from others in your class. If you get a break message, follow the instructions below.

- Read your message.
- Reply to any inquiry messages.
- Press Enter.

Now let's see what you have learned. Below is a message you need to send.

- Send an inquiry type message to `Your Instructor` or workstation `DSP01`.
- Your instructor will reply to your message.
- Use the print screen process to print a copy of your replied to message.
- Attach the replied-to message to your lab submission sheet labeled printout #1.

MESSAGE MENU

The Message menu provides easy access to a variety of message handler functions. You will notice that this menu provides access to many of the commands you have been previously using in the lab. Take a moment to explore this menu.

- Enter the command to display the `Message` menu.
- Press Enter.
- Identify four functions available from this menu. ________________ ____
- Select the `Related Command Menu` option.
- Press Enter.
- What menu accesses message files? ________________________________

MESSAGE FILES

When one of the system error-handling programs encounters an error, it sends a message to the appropriate queue. Messages sent this way, and from some application programs, use prewritten text. The message program substitutes values provided by the error-handling program into the message at predefined locations. The most frequently used message file is QCPFMSG. This message file contains messages for the operating system and machine errors. Other message files contain RPG, COBOL, or other messages. The key to any message file is the message ID, a value beginning with a three-character field identifying the error-handling program, followed by a four-digit number identifying the specific error. To find message files, you can use the command WRKMSGF.

- Enter WRKMSGF on the command line.
- Press F4.
- On the `Message File` prompt, key in the generic name Q*.
- Press Enter.
- Find the message file QCPFMSG.
- Enter the option to `Display the Message Descriptions` next to the above message file.
- Press Enter.
- Enter CPF2802 in the `Position to` field.
- Press Enter.
- What is the predefined message that corresponds to this message ID? ____
- Place a `5` to the left of CPF2802.
- Press Enter.
- Select option `1` (`Display Message Text`).
- Press Enter.
- Screen print the message text and attach it to your lab submission sheet.
- Label screen print as printout #2.
- Exit and go to the `Command Entry` screen.

ADDITIONAL LAB ASSIGNMENTS

Now try your skills at working with messages:

1. Issue the command WRKMSG and prompt it with F4.
   a. Which message queues can you work with?
   b. Select the option *WKRKUSR.
      i. Which queues will this work with?
   c. Use the function key to select *BASIC assistance.
      i. Which function key did you use?
      ii. What sequence are entry displays?
   d. Use the function key to select *INTERMEDIATE assistance.
      i. Which function key did you use?
      ii. What sequence are entry displays?
   e. Use the function key to display list details.
      i. What queues are reported on?
      ii. How are messages delivered on each queue?
      iii. What severity of message is delivered on each queue?
2. Repeat question 1 for the message queue QSYSOPR.
3. Experimenting with message files:
   a. Issue the command DLTF BANANA.
   b. Write down the message at the bottom of your screen.
   c. Move your cursor to the message and press F1 (to get more details).
   d. What is the message severity?
   e. What is the message type?
   f. Write down the message ID and print the message.
   g. Use the command WRKMSGF to display all message files. List at least five of them and what types of messages they contain.
   h. Work with the message file QCPFMSG.
   i. Use the search capability to find the message ID that you wrote down in 3f.
   j. Display and print all the information about that message.
4. Sending Messages:
   a. Send a break message to the person sitting next to you. To do that, you will have to get their interactive job name. (This will be displayed if that individual types DSPJOB.) You might have to send a message to an individual to check the status of their job. Make your break message type INQUIRY so the recipient can

respond to you. (*Note*: This demonstrates another method of finding the user's interactive job [workstation] name.)

b. Send a break message to all active displays; tell them `HI from (Your Name) in the Operations Class`. This should be an INFO message. Operators have to send messages to all active users at times to tell them things like "The system will not be available from 10 P.M. till 5 A.M. today."

c. Send a message to the user ID of the person sitting next to you.

d. How did the break message and nonbreak message vary?

END-OF-CHAPTER AIDS

CHAPTER SUMMARY

Messages are the life of any AS/400. They will become second nature to you as you work with the machine and solve day-to-day problems. They are not as intuitive as AS/400 commands are, but you also do not have to create them as much. For the most part, your role will be passive, responding to messages from the system. That saves you having to memorize message IDs or variables. For the most part, the same messages come up all the time—you will be taking action and responding to them without thinking too much about it.

Message Summary

1. Informational messages do not need a reply.
2. Inquiry messages need a reply.
3. Both informational and inquiry messages are found in your message queue, which can be viewed from the Work with Messages display.
4. Messages can come from three sources.
5. Messages can be displayed in three ways:
   a. Message line.
   b. Break Message display.
   c. Work with Messages display.
6. You send messages from the Send a Message display.
7. You can view your messages using the DSPMSG command.
8. Break messages (interrupt user messages) should be sent only when necessary.
9. The way you receive messages depends on the delivery mode:
   a. Notify.
   b. Break.

c. Hold.

d. Default.

10. You cannot send Inquiry messages to multiple users/workstations.

11. From the Work with Messages or Display Messages display, you can delete messages.

12. You press F16 to remove all messages not needing a reply.

KEY TERMS

*BREAK
break inquiry message
break messages
cause text
delivery mode
DSPMSG
history
impromptu messages
informational message
inquiry message
job logs
job messages
levels
logs
message description
message files
message identifier
message queue
message reply variable
message text—level one
message text—level two
message type (MSGTYPE) parameter
messages
*NOTIFY
notify messages
predefined messages
recovery text
severity code
SNDBRKMSG
SNDMSG
special users
system messages
system operator message queue
system reply list
system-to-system messaging
user message queues
variables
workstation message
WRKMSGF

CHAPTER SELF-TEST

Solutions to these self-test questions are in appendix D.

True-False Questions

___ 1. The SNDBRKMSG sends messages to user profiles and message queues.

___ 2. An inquiry message can be sent to all the students in your class.

___ 3. When a user signs onto the system, they have a job log that is collecting all messages received and commands issued.

___ 4. A message sent to a user goes directly to the user's message queue.

___ 5. You receive the following message on your screen message line: `From-file empmst in *LIBL not found`. This is an example of a level one message.

___ 6. The System Reply list is a convenient way to respond to messages that have the same reply all the time.

___ 7. Messages with a severity code forty and below are informational or warnings.

Fill in the Blanks

1. You are in the process of saving some libraries to tape; your display suddenly changes and displays a message. This is an example of a _____________ message.

2. The SNDMSG command is used to send a(n) (impromptu/predefined) message.

3. The Message ID CPF2802 identifies the following message. The message text is `From-file FUN in *libl not found`. This is an example of a message from the/a(n) (user/system operator/system/application program).

4. The System Reply list contains a list of only _________________ messages.

5. To display the system operator's messages, enter ____________________ on the command line.

6. A(n) ______________ message does not require an answer.

7. Predefined messages are stored in a ______________ ______________.

8. Messages with a severity code of _________________________ are sent to the system operator.

Chapter Review Questions

1. Explain the following terms:
   a. Informational message.
   b. Inquiry message.
   c. User message.
   d. System message.
   e. Workstation message.
   f. Break message.

2. What is the purpose of a message in the OS/400 operating system?

3. Why is the order of messages important when using the System Reply list?

4. How do you change your message queue to interrupt you whenever you receive a message?

5. When would you send a break message?

6

Handling Spooled Files and Printing Functions

Chapter Objectives

Upon completion of this chapter, you should be able to:

- Identify the role and functions of output queues.
- Describe controlling printer writers.
- Explain how to manage printed output.
- Use directly connected printers and network printers.

Overview

Chapter 1 briefly mentions that there are two major types of jobs on the AS/400: interactive and batch. Jobs are sets of one or more programs. We also said that interactive jobs are jobs that tie up a workstation—the user can do nothing until the job is finished (these are also said to be running in the *foreground*). Batch jobs are simply jobs that do not tie up a workstation because they run deep in the AS/400 (they run in the *background*).

This chapter describes what happens to those jobs' printed output—where it goes, how it gets printed, and ways to control it. Not every job produces output that needs to be printed, but when it does, even if it is only a single summary page, that output is handled in the same basic way. Let us call any output that needs to be printed a *report*. Anyone signed on to the AS/400 is an *AS/400 job*. If a user presses the Print Screen key to print out what is on the screen at that moment, that is a report, too.

Also, before we get too far into the subject, let us point out something about the AS/400. Every other computer in the world has a dedicated printer called a *system printer*. This is a printer that is plugged directly into the computer, and if a report is not sent to any other printer, the system printer automatically prints it.

Although the AS/400 can designate any printer a system printer, it does not have a facility for any printer to be connected or printed to in any way that is special from other printers. No printer has a special connection point, and any printer is capable of being the system printer.

On an AS/400, programs never send output directly to a printer. Printed output always goes to the hard disk, in an area known as an *output queue*. Another system program later delivers the content of that report to a printer.

This method of printing is a way of helping programs run faster. Writing to a fast device, like disk, is better than writing to a slow device, such as a printer.

This method is referred to as *spooling*. The output files sitting in the output queues waiting to get printed are known as *spooled files*.

THE PRINTING PROCESS

When an AS/400 job produces a report, that output goes into an output queue where it lives as a spooled file. A program later sends the queued report to a printer for printing. *Later* may be instantaneous, if the queue is empty and the printer attached to it is ready. The point is that there are two separate functions: program to queue, and queue to printer.

An AS/400 typically has many output queues, but it only has a small number of physical printers. Several output queues come configured on the AS/400 from IBM. They are easy to spot; they all start with the letter Q. The most commonly used IBM output queue is QPRINT followed closely by QSYSPRT, the output queue for the system printer.

The operator can name output queues anything as long as it doesn't start with the letter Q. For example, INVOICES could be a name for an output queue that only holds invoices ready to be printed. Or queues can be named for their department, i.e., ARQ for the accounts receivable output queue. If the system is very distributed, queues can be named after the city from which the reports come.

The printer that prints is, of course, a physical printer. We will refer to the *logical device* that the AS/400 sees; that is the *printer writer*.

Because there are a set number of physical printers, there are usually fewer printer writers than there are output queues. Printer writers must be attached to an output queue in order for them to print anything. If there is nothing in the queue they are attached to, they are not going to print—they will just wait until a report enters the queue.

Figure 6-1 represents a typical job/queue/printer writer configuration.

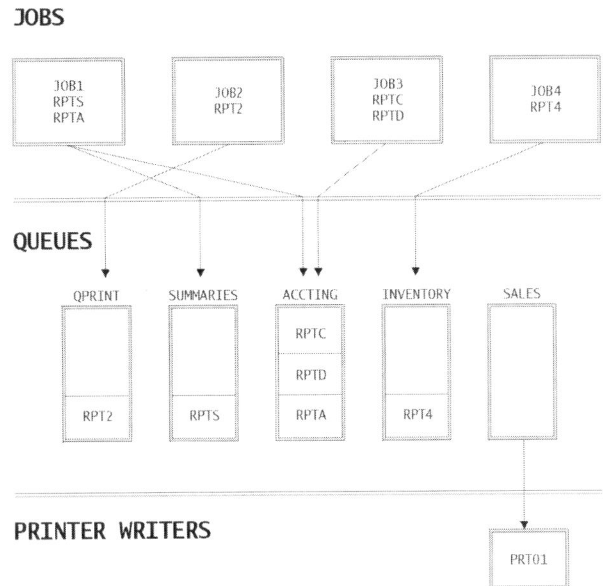

Figure 6-1: Jobs, queues, and printer writers.

In this configuration, there are four jobs: JOB1, JOB2, JOB3, and JOB4. There are five output queues: QPRINT, SUMMARIES, ACCTING, INVENTORY, and SALES. There is one printer writer, PRT01.

JOB1 produces two reports: RPTS and RPTA. RPTS is directed to output queue SUMMARIES, and RPTA to ACCTING. JOB2 produces one report: RPT2 and it is sent off to output queue QPRINT. JOB3 produces two reports: RPTC and RPTD, both of which go to output queue ACCTING (the same output queue JOB1 directed one of its reports to). Finally, JOB4 produces one report: RPT4, and directs it to output queue INVENTORY.

As a result of the jobs running in the time frame represented in Figure 6-1, three of the output queues, QPRINT, SUMMARIES, and INVENTORIES, have one report each waiting to print. Output queue ACCTING has three reports, and queue SALES has none.

The only printer writer on this system, PRT01 is attached to the empty output queue, SALES, so it is just waiting at the moment.

We will cover several queue and printer commands, then return to this configuration for examples of how an operator would use combinations of commands to get these reports printed.

COMMANDS FOR PRINTING

One thing no one can do when working with spooled files, output queues, and printers on the AS/400 is change the contents of the reports. So we will start/stop printing, look at the contents of reports, and maintain the infrastructure (queues and writers), but we will not change anything inside a report.

OUTPUT QUEUE COMMANDS

Output queues need to be created; occasionally, they also need to be deleted. Use the Create Output Queue (CRTOUTQ) command to create one and the Delete Output Queue (DLTOUTQ) command to delete one.

There is not much to these—when creating an output queue, just name it. There are some parameters about the maximum number of printed pages the queue can hold. Use these parameters sparingly. They are meant to help keep disk utilization under control—users tend to generate large reports and keep them in their personal queues forever. The problem with using parameters to control disk usage comes when a user legitimately needs an exceptionally large amount of printed pages in their queue. It is a better idea to manually monitor and control the size of output queues than to put an arbitrary cap on them.

The DLTOUTQ command is equally easy—just name the output queue to delete. The output queue's spooled files should be deleted or printed first, though.

More than likely, the system operator will want to drill down from a high-level view of all queues to locate an individual queue to inquire or make changes. The AS/400 has individual commands for these functions: Change Output Queue (CHGOUTQ) and Display Output Queue (DSPOUTQ). But it is easier and more logical to "drill down" through all output queues.

The Work with Output Queue (WRKOUTQ) is the do-everything command, and it comes in two forms. If the operator knows nothing else about the system, the parameter *ALL should be used on this command. If the desired queue name is known, use that name when using this command.

Here is an example of each. To look at all output queues, type this on the command line:

```
WRKOUTQ *ALL
```

To start looking at the spool files held in output queue QPRINT, enter this on the command line:

```
WRKOUTQ QPRINT
```

This command will produce a screen similar to the one shown in Figure 6-2.

There are several interesting things about this screen other than ID; it displays the *queues* on this system. Remember, the queues that do not start with the letter Q were created and named by the user. The user created only COBOLOUTQ, CPAOUTA, OPROUTQ, and FACOUTQ.

The `Files` column refers to how many spooled files (or individual reports) are in each queue. Most of the queues are empty, but three of them—CPAOUTQ, FACOUTQ, and QPRINT—have quite a few spooled reports.

This system has one printer writer active, PRT01, in the `Writer` column. Notice that it is attached to output queue COBOLOUTQ and that queue is empty at the time. So we assume PRT01 is just sitting there.

```
                          Work with All Output Queues

 Type options, press Enter.
   2=Change   3=Hold    4=Delete   5=Work with   6=Release   8=Description
   9=Work with Writers   14=Clear

 Opt     Queue          Library         Files      Writer        Status
  _      QDMT           QDMT                0                      RLS
  _      COBOLOUTQ      QGPL                0      PRT01           RLS
  _      CPAOUTQ        QGPL              741                      RLS
  _      FACOUTQ        QGPL               61                      RLS
  _      OPROUTQ        QGPL                0                      RLS
  _      QDKT           QGPL                0                      RLS
  _      QPFROUTQ       QGPL                0                      RLS
  2      QPRINT         QGPL               62                      RLS
  _      QPRINTS        QGPL                0                      RLS
  _      QPRINT2        QGPL                0                      RLS
  _      CPAOUTQ        QUSRSYS             0                      RLS
  _      CPQOUTQ        QUSRSYS             0                      RLS

                                                                 More ...
 Command
 ===> ________________________________________________________________
 F3=Exit   F4=Prompt   F5=Refresh   F12=Cancel   F24=More keys
```

*Figure 6-2: Sample of the WRKOUTQ *ALL command. This shows all output queues on an AS/400.*

Finally, the `Status` column shows that all queues are in a Released (RLS) state. They could be in a Hold (HLD) state, but in the example, they are released. In other words, they are active, accepting new reports, and if they contain reports, are ready to deliver them to any printer writer that gets attached to them.

The left-most column, the `Opt` column, allows the operator to enter options to do something with each queue. Valid options for this screen are documented above the main screen area.

We have mentioned deleting an output queue. The options shown in Figure 6-2 can save time. For example, option 4 from this screen will delete an output queue without the need to type in the command.

Options 3 (Hold) and 6 (Release) are related. Option 3 holds the output queue—nothing gets printed from it. Option 6 releases it again. These change the status of the queue as shown under the `Status` column in Figure 6-2.

Option 9 (Work with Writers) kind of segues out of the output queues into the printer writers. The equivalent command is Work with Writers (WRKWTR) with *PTR parameter.

Option 14 (Clear) is a dangerous one. It will call the Clear Output Queue (CLROUTQ) command and clear all the spool files from the queue. Use this one judiciously for two reasons: One, make sure everything in the queue is to be deleted, because the command makes no distinction. Two, if this is issued for an output queue that has a lot of spool files (QPJOBLOG can have more than 10,000 files), it is going to run for a long time and may cause system degradation.

The two most common options are 2 (Change) and 5 (Work with). Option 2 (Change) is a quick way to invoke the Change Output Queue (CHGOUTQ) command to change many attributes of the output queue. Option 5 (Work with), on the other hand, invokes the Work with Output Queue (WRKOUTQ) command and allows work to be done with the spooled files within the output queue.

Those are the two major differences between the two: Option 2 changes attributes of the output queue itself; option 5 works with the spool files inside the queue. Option 8 (Description) is similar to option 2 (Change) except that nothing can be changed—the data is display only.

Let us look at the screens from options 2 (Change) and 5 (Work with). First, Figure 6-3 contains the change screen we get after typing a 2 next to the QPRINT queue and pressing Enter from Figure 6-2.

```
                     Change Output Queue (CHGOUTQ)

 Type choices, press Enter.

 Output queue . . . . . . . . . . > QPRINT        Name
   Library  . . . . . . . . . . . >   QGPL        Name, *LIBL, *CURLIB
 Maximum spooled file size:
   Number of pages  . . . . . . .   *SAME         Number, *SAME, *NONE
   Starting time  . . . . . . . .   ______        Time
   Ending time  . . . . . . . . .   ______        Time
              + for more values   _
 Order of files on queue  . . . .   *SAME         *SAME, *JOBNBR, *FIFO
 Remote system  . . . . . . . . .   *SAME



                                                                Bottom
 F3=Exit   F4=Prompt   F5=Refresh   F10=Additional parameters   F12=Cancel
 F13=How to use this display        F24=More keys
```

Figure 6-3: Change screen for QPRINT queue.

Remember, on these screens, the only values that can be changed are underlined.

Override the queue's initial `Maximum spooled file size` parameter with a new value representing the maximum number of pages the user can have. The value *NONE means there is not a maximum. A nice feature of this parameter is that the maximum number of pages specified can go into effect for a specific duration. These start and end times are specified with the two parameters, `Starting time` and `Ending time`. If a maximum number of pages and a start/end time are specified, that page limit starts and ends on the times specified. Multiple limits and time blocks can be issued by putting a plus sign (+) on the `+ for more values` line.

The `Order of files on queue` parameter specifies the order that the spooled files will be processed from the queue. The default is *FIFO. Like inventories, this means First In, First Out. This parameter allows the order to be overridden to *JOBNBR order. Every job that runs on the AS/400 has a unique job number that is assigned sequentially. Jobs may start in sequential order but can finish in any order since some run for a short time and some for a long time. This option ensures that the spooled files are placed on the output queue in the order of their job number.

Note: This is not a cure-all for job sequence ordering. For example: if jobs 1, 2, and 3 all feed the same output queue and they are started in that order, but jobs 2 and 3 finish quickly while job 1 runs for several hours, jobs 2 and 3 will print long before job 1.

Finally, the `Remote system` parameter specifies the address of the remote system to send spool files to when the remote printer writer is started. Network printing is an advanced subject and will be covered in a later chapter.

Now, go back and take option 5 (Work with) from the screen shown in Figure 6-2. You will get a screen similar to the one shown in Figure 6-4.

```
                           Work with Output Queue

Queue:   QPRINT          Library:   QGPL           Status:   RLS

Type options, press Enter.
  1=Send  2=Change  3=Hold  4=Delete   5=Display  6=Release   7=Messages
  8=Attributes     9=Work with printing status

Opt  File        User      User Data  Sts    Pages     Copies  Form Type  Pty
 5   QPDZDTALOG  A97001080            RDY        1          1  *STD         5
 _   R1404DSP    A97001080            RDY        8          1  *STD         5
 _   R1505       A97001080            RDY       12          1  *STD         5
 _   R1404DSP    A97001080            RDY        8          1  *STD         5
 _   R1505       A97001080            RDY       12          1  *STD         5
 _   R1505       A97001080            RDY       12          1  *STD         5
 _   R1404PF     A82322260            RDY        3          1  *STD         5
 _   R1505DIS    A82322260            RDY        6          1  *STD         5
 _   R1505       A82322260            RDY        9          1  *STD         5
                                                                   More . . .
Parameters for options 1, 2, 3 or command
===> ____________________________________________________________________
F3=Exit    F11=View 2   F12=Cancel   F20=Writers    F22=Printers
F24=More keys
```

Figure 6-4: Option 5 (Work with) shows the contents of an output queue.

The difference between Figure 6-2 and Figure 6-4 is that Figure 6-2 allows the operator to work with all output queues; Figure 6-4 only allows the operator to work with the queue selected (QPRINT in this case).

Before we get too much into this screen, there is more information available. Press the F11 (View 2) function key (note the F-key documentation under the command line) to get the screen shown in Figure 6-5.

```
                           Work with Output Queue

Queue:   QPRINT          Library:   QGPL           Status:   RLS

Type options, press Enter.
  1=Send  2=Change 3=Hold   4=Delete   5=Display   6=Release   7=Messages
  8=Attributes     9=Work with printing status

Opt  File        File Nbr  Job         User       Number  Date      Time
 5   QPDZDTALOG         5  QPADEV001J  A97001080  150998  03/30/99  19:06:14
 _   R1404DSP           1  R1404DSP    A97001080  151164  03/30/99  19:09:17
 _   R1505              1  R1505       A97001080  151204  03/30/99  19:16:01
 _   R1404DSP           1  R1404DSP    A97001080  151243  03/30/99  19:22:52
 _   R1505              1  R1505       A97001080  151251  03/30/99  19:24:50
 _   R1505              1  R1505       A97001080  151260  03/30/99  19:26:21
 _   R1404PF            1  R1404PF     A82322260  151266  03/30/99  19:26:53
 _   R1505DIS           1  R1505DIS    A82322260  151270  03/30/99  19:28:39
 _   R1505              1  R1505       A82322260  151272  03/30/99  19:28:47
                                                                   More. . .
Parameters for options 1, 2, 3 or command
===> ____________________________________________________________________
F3=Exit    F11=View 1   F12=Cancel   F20=Writers    F22=Printers
F24=More keys
```

Figure 6-5: Second view of spooled files in queue QPRINT.

There is only one reason to get View 2 of the spool files—that is when using an older command that identifies a spool file through a combination of parameters. The columns for those parameters are marked in bold in Figure 6-5. Figure 6-6 shows a sample of one of these commands, the DSPSPLF command.

```
                        Display Spooled File (DSPSPLF)

 Type choices, press Enter.

 Spooled file . . . . . . . . . .   ___________   Name
 Job name . . . . . . . . . . . .   *__________   Name, *
   User . . . . . . . . . . . . .   __________    Name
   Number . . . . . . . . . . . .   __________    000000-999999
 Spooled file number  . . . . . .   *ONLY         1-9999, *ONLY, *LAST




                                                                   Bottom
F3=Exit   F4=Prompt   F5=Refresh   F10=Additional parameters   F12=Cancel
 F13=How to use this display        F24=More keys
```

Figure 6-6: Five fields had to be used to qualify this command.

In order to make this command work, the operator has to supply up to these five fields of information. This is fairly inconvenient.

Alternatively, when drilling down through the Work with menu to this command, the command still needs the five fields, but the AS/400 supplies them, making the job easier.

If a command like this must be used from the command line, get the View 2 of the Work with Output Queue (WRKOUTQ) shown in Figure 6-5, write down the information, then use the command. By the way, the parameters in Figure 6-6 do not exactly match up with the column headings in Figure 6-5. Figure 6-7 lists the translation.

Column Headings from Fig. 6-5	Matching Parameters from Fig. 6-6
File	Spooled file
Job name	Job
User	User
Number	Number
File number	Spooled file number

Figure 6-7: Work with Output Queue column names match to parameter names.

These commands will want a combination of data to identify which spool file to work with. Figure 6-8 lists the commands that require this information.

Command	Description
CHGSPLFA	Change Spool File Attributes
CPYSPLF	Copy Spool File
DLTSPLF	Delete Spool File
DSPSPLF	Display Spool File
HLDSPLF	Hold Spool File
RLSSPLF	Release Spool File
SNDNETSPLF	Send Network Spool File
SNDTCPSPLF	Send TCP Spool File
WRKPRTSTS	Work with Printer Status

Figure 6-8: Commands that, if not used through the Work with command, require a lot of detail to identify spool files.

That was a long side trip, but it was a point that needed to be made. Let us return to Figure 6-4. We typed a 5 for a spooled file that we want to display—note the option descriptions above, 5 (Display). This shows the report data. Figure 6-9 shows the result from Figure 6-4.

```
                              Display Spooled File
File  . . . . . :   QPDZDTALOG                        Page/Line   1/1
Control . . . . .   ____________________________      Columns     1 - 78
Find  . . . . . .   ______________________________________________________
*...+....1....+....2....+....3....+....4....+....5....+....6....+....7....
 5769SS1     V4R2M0  980228                                AUDIT LOG
  Library/File . . . . .   WAT1080LIB/R1404PF
  Member . . . . . . . .   R1404PF
  Job Title  . . . . . .   WORK WITH DATA IN A FILE
                SSNO      COURSE NUMBER TERM DATE COURSE NAME          IN
 Changed      ********       101          52297    COMPUTER SCIENCE I
                          CSC101
 Changed      ********       110         121597    MICROCOMPUTERS I
                          DPS110
 Changed      ********       310         121597    ADVANCED C
                          CSC310
 Changed      ********       210          52297    INTRO TO C
                          CSC210
 Changed      ********       201          52297    CALCULUS I
                          MTH201
 Changed      ********       202         121597    COMPUTER SCIENCE II
                                                               More. . .
F3=Exit   F12=Cancel   F19=Left   F20=Right   F24=More keys
```

Figure 6-9: Contents of spooled file.

Notice that Figure 6-9 is almost what the printer is going to print. The only exception is that blank lines are removed for viewing.

The nice thing about browsing a spooled file is it reduces printing. Quite often, users only want to look at the bottom (or top) of a report, they do not need the entire report printed unless there is a problem. Also, a user skilled in working with spool files can find his or her way around much faster than through a stack of paper.

There are two dedicated navigation fields on the screen: CONTROL and FIND. Let us explore the *Control field* first. Just enter a simple number—10, for example—on the CONTROL line and press Enter. The tenth line of the spooled file will be at the top of the screen, under the rule line. The 10 will stay in place—press Enter again and nothing will change—the same tenth line stays at the top. This is an *absolute command.*

Put a plus (+) or minus (-) in front of the 10 and it becomes a *relative command*. Now, every time Enter is pressed, the spool file will reposition itself with the next tenth line at the top (or previous tenth line when a minus is entered). A document can be scrolled through in ten-line increments by entering +10 and repeatedly pressing Enter.

Now, put a P to the left of the number and the scroll file will advance (or backup) a number of pages at a time. The same rule applies for the absolute versus relative movement. For example, P10 will present the tenth page (not line) of the report. P+10 will advance to the tenth page past the current page.

Instead of a P, put a W on the front of the number to control the horizontal movement of the screen. W35 will position the scroll file so the thirty-fifth column is the left-most column of the screen. This is a common way of looking at the right side of a 132-column report. A W1 will return the spool file to the image in Figure 6-9. A W+2 will move the spooled file to the right in two-column increments every time Enter is pressed. A W-2 will scroll it to the left two columns at a time.

Finally, to really move around a report, put a T on the control line, and you will see the top (or first page) of the report will be shown. A B will produce the bottom (or last page). Figure 6-10 lists a summary of the spool file control line commands.

Command	Action
T	Takes you to the top of the report (first page).
B	Takes you to the bottom of the report (last page).
xx	Puts line xx at the top of the screen.
+xx	Advances xx lines from the current line.
-xx	Goes back xx lines from the current line.
Pxx	Goes to the xx page of the report.
P+xx	Advances xx pages from the current page.
P-xx	Goes back xx pages from the current page.
Wxx	Puts the xx column on the left side of the screen.
W+xx	Shifts the report to the right xx columns.
W-xx	Shifts the report to the left xx columns.

Table 6-10: Commands for spool files.

There is another line on the screen shown in Figure 6-9, the *Find field*. Put any word or phrase here and press the F16 function key to locate it in the document. It is not necessary to put phrases in quotes. The AS/400 trims off the right-most blanks until it hits the first nonblank character, then it takes what is left as a search string.

Through the use of very few commands, anyone can quickly find their way around an AS/400 spool file.

Let us go back to Figure 6-4 and see the changes that can be made to the spool files. Remember, the report contents cannot be changed—only *attributes* of the spool file can be changed. Get to this by entering an option 2 (Change) on any spool file and pressing Enter. Figure 6-11 contains a sample of the resulting Change Spooled File Attributes screen. This is the same screen that would appear if the command version of it were typed on the command line, CHGSPLFA (Change Spool File Attributes).

```
                Change Spooled File Attributes (CHGSPLFA)

Type choices, press Enter.

Spooled file . . . . . . . . . . > QPDZDTALOG     Name, *SELECT
Job name . . . . . . . . . . . . > QPADEV0004     Name, *
  User . . . . . . . . . . . . . >   A91001170    Name
  Number . . . . . . . . . . . . >   150687       000000-999999
Spooled file number  . . . . . . > 1              1-9999, *ONLY, *LAST
Printer  . . . . . . . . . . . .   *OUTQ          Name, *SAME, *OUTQ
Print sequence . . . . . . . . .   *SAME          *SAME, *NEXT
Form type  . . . . . . . . . . .   *STD           Form type, *SAME, *STD
Copies . . . . . . . . . . . . .   1              1-255, *SAME
Restart printing . . . . . . . .   *STRPAGE       Number,*SAME,*STRPAGE...

                         Additional Parameters

Output queue . . . . . . . . . .   QPRINT         Name, *SAME, *DEV
  Library  . . . . . . . . . . .     QGPL         Name, *LIBL, *CURLIB
File separators  . . . . . . . .   0              0-9, *SAME

                                                              More. . .
F3=Exit   F4=Prompt   F5=Refresh   F12=Cancel
  F13=How to use this display F24=More keys
```

Figure 6-11: Change Spooled File Attributes command—screen 1.

The nice thing about invoking this command via the menu (instead of keying it on the command line) is that the five parameters that identify the spool file whose attributes you are changing are automatically filled in. In Figure 6-11, they are the five parameters that are not underlined and are marked with the ">" symbol.

On these screens, any of the underlined fields can be changed. We will just talk about the most commonly changed spool file parameters. Also, we will give the parameter names that would appear if the F11 key were pressed on any of these screens. The first parameter from this screen that is used often is the Form Type (FORMTYPE). This allows the operator to change the form on which a report is to print. Programmers can specify in their programs which form a report is to print on—for example, they can specify that a "report" be printed on letterhead stationery. They may have specified the form type of LTRHEAD.

When that report starts to print, the system will issue a message requesting that the form be loaded on the printer. It may also request that an alignment check be made. If the report is being produced for a test or for any reason that letterhead is not to be actually used, this value can be changed to

*STD prior to printing and the system will not request a form type change. The COPIES parameter, logically enough, specifies how many copies of a report will be printed.

Restart printing (RESTART) is interesting. Printers are mechanical devices and often the most trouble-prone equipment in the computer room. When a jam is fixed, or any problem that caused the system to hold the print job is cleared, the operator may not want to start from the beginning of the report when printing resumes. With this parameter, he can specify the page number printing should start on.

Probably the most used parameter is the Output Queue (OUTQ). This moves a spool file from one output queue to another. Typically, from an output queue that does not have a printer writer attached to one that does—and thereby, gets it printed.

When we press the F10 (Additional Parameters) key, we bring up all the extra things about the spool file that can be changed. Figures 6-12 and 6-13 contain the second and third screens of this command.

```
                     Change Spooled File Attributes (CHGSPLFA)

Type choices, press Enter.

Page range to print:
  Starting page . . . . . . . .   1           Number, *SAME, *ENDPAGE
  Ending page . . . . . . . . .   *END        Number, *SAME, *END
File becomes available . . . .   *FILEEND    *SAME, *JOBEND, *FILEEND...
Save file . . . . . . . . . . .   *NO         *SAME, *NO, *YES
Output priority . . . . . . . .   5           1-9, *SAME, *JOB
User data . . . . . . . . . . .   '          'User data, *SAME
Align page . . . . . . . . . . .   *NO         *SAME, *NO, *YES
Print quality . . . . . . . . .   *STD        *SAME,*STD,*DEVD,*DRAFT...
Form feed . . . . . . . . . . .   *DEVD       *SAME,*DEVD,*CONT,*CUT...
Source drawer . . . . . . . . .   1           1-255, *SAME, *E1, *FORMDF
Print fidelity . . . . . . . . .   *CONTENT    *SAME, *ABSOLUTE, *CONTENT
Print on both sides . . . . . .   *NO         *SAME,*NO,*YES,*TUMBLE...
Pages per side . . . . . . . . .   1           1-4, *SAME
Form definition . . . . . . . .   *NONE       Name,*SAME,*NONE,*DEVD...
  Library . . . . . . . . . . .     ____      Name, *LIBL, *CURLIB
                                                               More. . .
F3=Exit F4=Prompt   F5=Refresh   F12=Cancel   F13=How to use this display
F24=More keys
```

Figure 6-12: Change Spooled File Attributes command—screen 2.

The Page Range to Print (PAGERANGE) parameter is nice to print a portion of the report. Programmers use this a lot while debugging—users can use it to capture pieces of a report. This is a two-part parameter; both the starting page and ending page are parts of the single parameter, PAGERANGE. Usually when a spool file prints, it disappears from the output queue. With the Save File (SAVE) parameter, the system will save the file after it is printed. The file is saved in a HOLD status.

Each spool file has an attribute known as the *output queue priority* (OUTPTY). This partly determines where it will sit on the output queue. Earlier, we said that spool files arrive and pass through output queues in a FIFO method. That is partly true. They are also arranged first by their output priority. This is a number between 1 and 9, with the lower numbers being the higher priority. Often, software developers use these numbers to control what gets printed when. All spool files with priority 1 will get printed before any priority 2 spool files get printed and so on.

When specific spool file output queue priorities are not assigned, they have a default priority of 5. Spool files of the same priority pass through output queues in FIFO order. To print one spool file ahead of the others, simply use the Output Priority (OUTPTY) parameter to override the priority to a lower number—one low enough to force the file to the bottom (closest to the printer) of the queue.

Access to this command and this parameter is generally not something users should have. When it is allowed, all spool files end up with an output priority of 1! Also, users tend to manipulate other users' spool file priorities.

We talked about forms. When printers used continuous forms, it was often a hit-or-miss process to get the page break exactly lined up with the printing. The AS/400 would print a test line of print, then, via message, ask the operator if the printer was lined up. The operator would look at it, if it was not lined up physically, adjust it, and reply "NO." The system would eject a page and print another test line. This would keep up until the operator responded with a "YES." With laser printers, we do not have to worry about aligning forms because they use individual sheets. If the Align Page (ALIGN) parameter is overridden to *NO, the system will not stop and ask to verify the printer alignment.

```
                  Change Spooled File Attributes (CHGSPLFA)

 Type choices, press Enter.

 Front side overlay:
   Overlay . . . . . . . . . . .   *NONE      Name, *NONE, *SAME
     Library . . . . . . . . . .    ______    Name, *LIBL, *CURLIB
   Offset down . . . . . . . . .   ________   0.00-57.79, *SAME
   Offset across . . . . . . . .   ________   0.00-57.79, *SAME
 Back side overlay:
   Overlay . . . . . . . . . . .   *FRONTOVL  Name,*FRONTOVL,*NONE,*SAME
     Library . . . . . . . . . .    ______    Name, *LIBL, *CURLIB
   Offset down . . . . . . . . .   ________   0.00-57.79, *SAME
   Offset across . . . . . . . .   ________   0.00-57.79, *SAME
 User defined option . . . . . .   *NONE      Option, *SAME, *NONE
               + for more values   _
 User defined object:
   Object . . . . . . . . . . . .   *NONE      Name, *NONE, *SAME
     Library . . . . . . . . . .    ________  Name, *LIBL, *CURLIB
   Object type . . . . . . . . .   _________  *DTAARA, *DTAQ, *FILE...
                                                              Bottom
F3=Exit  F4=Prompt   F5=Refresh   F12=Cancel   F13=How to use this display
 F24=More keys
```

Figure 6-13: Change Spooled File Attributes command—screen 3.

This screen is dedicated to controlling overlays—graphical pages that are combined with printed text. This is a very advanced (and obscure) topic and will not be covered in this book. Before leaving the subject, here is a trick that can be done from Work with Output Queue (see Figure 6-4).

If the appropriate parameter of the Change Spooled File Attributes command is known, changes to many files can be made at once. To move many spooled files to another output queue, the parameter name is OUTQ. Place a 2 (Change) in the option field of the files to change, then type in the new output queue on the command line. Figure 6-14 shows an example.

```
                          Work with Output Queue

Queue:   QPRINT          Library:   QGPL                Status:   RLS

Type options, press Enter.
  1=Send  2=Change  3=Hold  4=Delete   5=Display   6=Release   7=Messages
  8=Attributes      9=Work with printing status

Opt  File        User       User Data  Sts    Pages    Copies   Form Type   Pty
 2   QPDZDTALOG  A97001080             RDY        1        1    *STD          5
 _   R1404DSP    A97001080             RDY        8        1    *STD          5
 2   R1505       A97001080             RDY       12        1    *STD          5
 _   R1404DSP    A97001080             RDY        8        1    *STD          5
 2   R1505       A97001080             RDY       12        1    *STD          5
 2   R1505       A97001080             RDY       12        1    *STD          5
 _   R1404PF     A82322260             RDY        3        1    *STD          5
 2   R1505DIS    A82322260             RDY        6        1    *STD          5
 _   R1505       A82322260             RDY        9        1    *STD          5
                                                                     More . . .
Parameters for options 1, 2, 3 or command
===> OUTQ(SYSPRT)
F3=Exit    F11=View 2   F12=Cancel   F20=Writers   F22=Printers
F24=More keys
```

Figure 6-14: Multiple changes in one operation from a Work with... menu.

In the example, five spooled files will be moved from output queue QPRINT to output queue SYSPRT.

PRINTER WRITER COMMANDS

Before the AS/400 can communicate with a printer, that printer must be created. That sounds funny because the printer is, of course, already created—you can see it and touch it. But creating it on the AS/400 means making it known to the AS/400.

Any hardware device the AS/400 is asked to communicate with must be created or made known to the AS/400. We will see this later with workstations, lines, and controllers. All of these devices are generically known to the AS/400 as *devices*.

There are two ways to create a printer device on the AS/400. One is the masochist's way—using the Create Device Print (CRTDEVPRT). Forget for now we ever mentioned it. The only reason to use this command is to have absolute control over printer naming schemes.

Most AS/400 customers let the AS/400 do its own configuration. That is right—the AS/400, when it IPLs, will go out and meet any new devices and configure them. The naming scheme for printers is PRT01, PRT02, etc. The sequential numbers are assigned in the order the AS/400 encounters them.

This capability is unique to the AS/400 and is known as *automatic configuration*. It can be turned on (automatic configuration happens) or off (automatic configuration does not happen). Automatic configuration is set with the system value QAUTOCFG. Look at this system value with the Display System Value (DSPSYSVAL) command, and change it with the Change System Value

(CHGSYSVAL) command. If it is set to a 1, automatic configuration is on; if it is set to a 0, automatic configuration is off.

A physical printer is a device to the AS/400; the software that communicates with this device is a *writer*. From an operations point of view, the term "printer writer" is often used for a printer. It sounds funny, but that is how operations addresses a physical printer.

To look at all the printer devices known to your AS/400, use the Work with Writers (WRKWTR) command, specifying the *PRT parameter. Here is how it is entered on the command line:

```
WRKWTR *PRT
```

The system will instantly display the printer writers and their current statuses. Once a printer writer is created (made known to the system) and before it will do anything, it must meet three conditions:

1. It must be started.
2. It must be in a Released status (*RLS).
3. It must be connected to an output queue that:
   a. Has something to be printed and that spooled file is in a Released status (*RLS).
   b. Is in a Released status (*RLS).

Use the Start Printer Writer (STRPRTWTR) to start a printer writer. Figure 6-15 shows a sample of that command.

```
                        Start Printer Writer (STRPRTWTR)

 Type choices, press Enter.

 Printer . . . . . . . . . . . .   PRT01         Name, *ALL, *SYSVAL
 Output queue . . . . . . . . . .  QPRINT        Name, *DEV
   Library . . . . . . . . . . .     ______      Name, *LIBL, *CURLIB
 Queue for writer messages . . .   *DEVD         Name, *DEVD, *REQUESTER
   Library . . . . . . . . . . .     ______      Name, *LIBL, *CURLIB
 Form type options:
   Form type . . . . . . . . . .   *ALL          Form type, *ALL, *STD, *FORMS
   Message option . . . . . . . .  *INQMSG       *INQMSG, *MSG, *NOMSG...
 File separators . . . . . . . .   *FILE         0-9, *FILE
 Drawer for separators . . . . .   *DEVD         1-255, *DEVD, *FILE




                                                                  Bottom
 F3=Exit   F4=Prompt   F5=Refresh   F10=Additional parameters   F12=Cancel
F13=How to use this display        F24=More keys
```

Figure 6-15: Prompted version of the Start Printer Writer command.

The two most important parameters are the printer to start (PRT01, for example) and the output queue (QPRINT in this example). When the printer device is created, it has a specific output queue associated with it. With automatic configured devices, an output queue is created with the same name as the device.

When new to the AS/400, it is sometimes hard to remember that printer writers are associated with output queues, not to individual spool files. What and in what order spool files come out of the queues depend on their order, status, and priority within the queue. If their print order is important, set that up within the queue through the use of the output queue priority settings before attaching a printer writer to it.

If their print order is important and it is a bother to rearrange the contents of the output queue, an alternative is to have a printer writer attached to an empty queue and manually send each spool file to it in the order they should be printed.

The example command in Figure 6-15 starts printer writer PRT01 and associates it with output queue QPRINT. As soon as the command is issued (the Enter key is pressed), the printer device PRT01 will start printing any unheld spool file requests in output queue QPRINT. By the way, refer back to Figure 6-2 and note that output queue QPRINT has 62 spooled files ready to print. The customer probably does not want all 62 actually printed. For this reason, printer writers are often (but do not have to be) associated with output queues that are normally empty. We want to physically review spooled output requests and move them before printing.

End or stop a printer writer with the End Printer Writer (ENDPRTWTR) command. It is not uncommon for a printer writer to end itself during the processing day. When some laser printers jam or overheat, they will cause the printer writer to end. Do not be alarmed when checking out a printer problem to find that the printer writer that was running in the morning is no longer active. The remedy is to issue another Start Printer Writer (STRPRTWTR) command.

Like output queues, printer writers can be held and released. To hold a printer writer, use the Hold Printer Writer (HLDPRTWTR) command; to release one, use the Release Printer Writer (RLSPRTWTR) command. Better yet, you can hold or release them from the Work with Writers (WRKWTR) menu.

If a printer writer is started and something about it needs to be changed, use either the Change Writer (CHGWTR) command or option 2 (Change) from the Work with Writers (WRKWTR) command. Most of the time, the operator will only want to change the output queue it is attached to or the form it is printing.

Printer Messages

When a printer needs a forms change, jams, runs out of paper, or generally flakes out, the system operator should know right away so he can fix the condition and keep going. Printer messages are sent to specific printer message queues. They can all be sent to QSYSOPR, thinking that keeping printers going is an operations assignment; or they can go to other queues, thinking that the department where the printer is located should keep them going.

In real life, we see all combinations. If the printer's message queue is not known, it can be determined with the Work with Writers (WRKWTR) command—select option 5 (Display).

Unfortunately, unless the printer's message queue happens to be the system operator's own (the printer writer can be changed so this is the case), there will not be any indication of messages pending for printers. Most people never know there is a problem until someone complains.

There are two ways of looking at printer messages: go look for them or have the system alert the system operator when there is one. The choice between the two is not so easy. If the system passes every printer message, real work will be interrupted too often. If the operator is in the same room as the printer (or perhaps has the printer on a desktop), the operator can see when something is not right with the printer and may not want the interruptions. If the operator cannot physically see the printer, then it is better to have the system interrupt you with all messages.

Printer messages can be checked through either the Work with Output Queue (WRKOUTQ) or Work with Writers (WRKWTR) command. Look at a message with the Display Message (DSPMSG) command—but be sure to specify the printer's output queue.

For example, our printer PRT01 sends its messages to a message queue named PRT01. To read and respond to messages on that queue, type the command:

```
DSPMSG PRT01
```

and press Enter.

Keep in mind that most printer messages require a reply. For example, the printer may run out of paper. The system operator not only has to refill the paper supply, a message has to be sent telling the writer it is OK to continue printing.

The other way to handle printer messages is to force them to come to a workstation in break mode (remember from the previous chapter, these messages will display automatically, interrupting work). This ensures a printer message is never missed. If the printer device PRT01 used a message queue named the same, force the system to send all its messages to a specific message queue with the Change Message Queue (CHGMSGQ) command. Here is an example of how to key it on the command line:

```
CHGMSGQ MSGQ(PRT01) DLVRY(*BREAK) PGM(*DSPMSG)
```

An Example of Restarting a Printer

Sometimes things really get out of whack with printers. A really good jam is an example. Two or three pages are mangled in the printer, and the printer writer has ended. Suppose the jam occurred on page 500 of a 2,000-page report. If we clear the jam and have the printer restart, we do not want it to reprint the first 500 pages. You can use a combination of the commands we have discussed to have the printer start printing on page 501. Here are those steps:

1. On the physical printer, clear the jam. Make sure it is powered on and on-line, or ready.

2. On the AS/400, hold the report either by selecting option 3 (Hold) from the Work with Output Queue (WRKOUTQ) command (naming the output queue).

3. Change the spool file attribute with either option 2 (Change) from the Work with Output Queue (WRKOUTQ) command which has a parameter called RESTART PRINTING. Set it to

the page the printer is to start printing (501 in our example). Figure 6-16 contains an example of this screen.

4. If the printer writer has ended, restart it with the Start Printer Writer (STRPRTWTR) command. If you do this, make sure you associate it with the output queue containing the spool file you want the restart on.

5. Release the spool file with either option 6 (Release) or from the Work with Output Queue (WRKOUTQ) command (naming the output queue).

```
                    Change Spooled File Attributes (CHGSPLFA)

 Type choices, press Enter.

 Spooled file . . . . . . . . . . > STDCRSPF      Name, *SELECT
 Job name . . . . . . . . . . . . > STDCRSPF      Name, *
   User . . . . . . . . . . . . . >   A91001170   Name
   Number . . . . . . . . . . . . >   149683      000000-999999
 Spooled file number  . . . . . . > 1             1-9999, *ONLY, *LAST
 Printer  . . . . . . . . . . . .   *OUTQ         Name, *SAME, *OUTQ
 Print sequence . . . . . . . . .   *SAME         *SAME, *NEXT
 Form type  . . . . . . . . . . .   *STD          Form type, *SAME, *STD
 Copies . . . . . . . . . . . . .   1             1-255, *SAME
 Restart printing . . . . . . . .   501           Number, *SAME, *STRPAGE...

                              Additional Parameters

 Output queue . . . . . . . . . .   QPRINT        Name, *SAME, *DEV
   Library  . . . . . . . . . . .     QGPL        Name, *LIBL, *CURLIB

                                                                       Bottom
 F3=Exit   F4=Prompt   F5=Refresh   F10=Additional parameters   F12=Cancel
 F13=How to use this display        F24=More keys
```

Figure 6-16: Example to change a spool file to cause it to start printing on page 501.

LAB #6: HANDLING SPOOLED FILES AND PRINTING FUNCTIONS

Upon completion of this lab, you should be able to:

- Use a program to create reports/spool files.
- Change output queue priorities.
- Change spool file status.
- Demonstrate the ability to move spool files between output queues.
- Create, clear, and delete output queues.
- Demonstrate the ability to print multiple documents in one operation.

BASIC PRINTING

Printing was a critical skill needed to print the previous lab reports, so basic printing was discussed. For completeness, we will briefly review printing on the AS/400 and then go on to new topics.

CREATING A SPOOL FILE

To review printing, you must have a spool file in your output queue ready to print. Create this spool file using the Copy File command to make an image of the data in the EMPMST file.

- Enter CPYF on the command line.
- Press F4 (Prompt).
- Enter EMPMST in the `From File` field.
- Enter OPRLIB for the `Library` field.
- Enter *PRINT for the `To File` field.
- Press Enter.

You now have a spool file in the output queue that you can print.

PRINTING A SPOOL FILE

Each site can use a variety of printer types. There are AS/400 printers, which are attached to the AS/400 and TCP/IP network printers that are defined to the AS/400 and use output queues defined on the AS/400. For more information about TCP/IP printers, see chapter 19.

Check with your instructor to determine the method of printing at your facility. You need to print the contents of the EMPMST file, which was produced in the previous step. To access the files in output queue(s), the WRKSPLF command is used. The Work with All Spooled Files screen is shown in Figure L6-1.

```
                        Work with All Spooled Files

 Type options, press Enter.
   1=Send   2=Change   3=Hold   4=Delete   5=Display   6=Release   7=Messages
   8=Attributes        9=Work with printing status

                                 Device or                          Total     Cur
 Opt  File        User           Queue       User Data   Sts      Pages     Page  Copy
 ___  QSYSPRT     OPR0001        OPROUTQ                 RDY          1              1
 ___  QSYSPRT     OPR0001        OPROUTQ                 RDY          1              1
 ___  QSYSPRT     OPR0001        OPROUTQ                 RDY          1              1
 ___  QSYSPRT     OPR0001        OPROUTQ                 RDY          1              1
 ___  QSYSPRT     OPR0001        OPROUTQ     CPYF        RDY          3              1
 ___  QSYSPRT     OPR0001        OPROUTQ     CPYF        RDY          4              1
 ___  QSYSPRT     OPR0001        OPROUTQ     CPYF        RDY          1              1
                                                                              More...
 Parameters for options 1, 2, 3 or command
 ===> ____________________________________________________________________________
 F3=Exit   F10=View 4   F11=View 2   F12=Cancel   F22=Printers   F24=More keys
```

Figure L6-1: Work with All Spooled Files screen shows printout produced by the Copy File command.

The Work with All Spooled Files command will bring up a screen displaying the printouts (spool files) located in output queues. It is recommended that you view the file before printing. This will allow you to verify that you are printing the correct file. Always view the spool file before you move the file to the printer. To view the file, place a 5 on the option line before the file you want to view.

- Enter WRKSPLF on the command line.
- Press Enter.
- Place a 5 (View) to the left of the last file. (*Note*: It has CPYF in the `User Data` field.)
- View and verify that it is the correct file.
- If this is not the correct file, view the other files until you determine which is the copy of the contents of the EMPMST file.

To send a spool file to the printer, use one of the following methods.

USING PRT01 PRINTER—A SYSTEM PRINTER

PRT01 is a directly connected AS/400 system default printer. The method shown in Figure L6-2 is used with a system printer.

- Place a 2 to the left of the file you selected to print.
- Change the value of the PRINTER parameter to PRT01.
- Press Enter.

```
                 Change Spooled File Attributes (CHGSPLFA)

Type choices, press Enter.

Spooled file . . . . . . . . . . > QSYSPRT      Name, *SELECT
Job name . . . . . . . . . . . . > QPADEV0012   Name, *
  User . . . . . . . . . . . . . >   HOHLY      Name
  Number . . . . . . . . . . . . >   266972     000000-999999
Spooled file number  . . . . . . > 1            1-9999, *ONLY, *LAST
Printer  . . . . . . . . . . . .   PRT01        Name, *SAME, *OUTQ
Print sequence . . . . . . . . .   *SAME        *SAME, *NEXT
Form type  . . . . . . . . . . .   *STD         Form type, *SAME, *STD
Copies . . . . . . . . . . . . .   1            1-255, *SAME
Restart printing . . . . . . . .   *STRPAGE     Number, *SAME, *STRPAGE...

                        Additional Parameters

Output queue . . . . . . . . . .   OPROUTQ      Name, *SAME, *DEV
  Library  . . . . . . . . . . .     QGPL       Name, *LIBL, *CURLIB

                                                                  Bottom
F3=Exit   F4=Prompt   F5=Refresh   F10=Additional parameters   F12=Cancel
F13=How to use this display        F24=More keys
```

Figure L6-2: Changing the spooled file to the system printer.

USING A TCP/IP NETWORK PRINTER

A TCP/IP network printer is identified to the hosts and user on the network by its IP address. It can be accessed by an AS/400, PCs on the network, and other hosts on the network. For users of an AS/400 to print to a network printer, an output queue must be defined for the printer. In order to have a file print, it must be moved to the printer queue. More information on network printing will be found in chapter 19.

- Enter 2 at the left of the file you selected to print.
- Press F10 (Additional Parameters).
- Change the value of the QUTPUT QUEUE parameter to PRT03.
- Press Enter.

In this example, the network TCP/IP printer is using the PRT03 output queue. *Note*: PRT03 is an output queue rather than a printer. The PRINTER parameter is left unchanged, as shown in Figure L6-3.

```
                Change Spooled File Attributes (CHGSPLFA)

Type choices, press Enter.

Spooled file . . . . . . . . . . > QSYSPRT       Name, *SELECT
Job name . . . . . . . . . . . . > QPADEV0012    Name, *
  User . . . . . . . . . . . . . >   HOHLY       Name
  Number . . . . . . . . . . . . >   266972      000000-999999
Spooled file number  . . . . . . > 1             1-9999, *ONLY, *LAST
Printer  . . . . . . . . . . . .   *OUTQ         Name, *SAME, *OUTQ
Print sequence . . . . . . . . .   *SAME         *SAME, *NEXT
Form type  . . . . . . . . . . .   *STD          Form type, *SAME, *STD
Copies . . . . . . . . . . . . .   1             1-255, *SAME
Restart printing . . . . . . . .   *STRPAGE      Number, *SAME, *STRPAGE...

                         Additional Parameters

Output queue . . . . . . . . . .   PRT03         Name, *SAME, *DEV
  Library  . . . . . . . . . . .     QGPL        Name, *LIBL, *CURLIB

                                                                  Bottom
F3=Exit   F4=Prompt   F5=Refresh   F10=Additional parameters   F12=Cancel
F13=How to use this display        F24=More keys
```

Figure L6-3: Changing a spool file to a network printer output queue.

- Retrieve the printout from the printer.
- Label it as printout #1.
- Attach this printout to the submission form for this lab.

PRINTING REPORTS

Let's do a review of some of the major printing concepts. When you execute a job that produces printed output or a report, that output is referred to as a spool file. A spool file is a print image. Spool files are owned by the person who created them and can be controlled by that person or any user with *SPLCTL authority. More about authorities will be discussed in chapter 11. Spool files are stored in output queues. These reports/spool files go directly to the printer if the output queue has an active printer writer and the report is in the Ready (RDY) status.

Let's do some printing before we complete the review. The first step is to generate several reports to print in this section. The OPRLIB library contains a program called ADDRESS1 that will produce a report showing the new students that added the AS/400 Operations Online Class. Since this program is not in your library, you need to run the program from the OPRLIB library. Run this program several times to load your output queue with copies of this report. Multiple spool files to work with are needed in this lab.

- Enter the command to add the OPRLIB library to your library list.
- Call the ADDRESS1 program.
- Repeat the above step at least four more times.

Now you should have at least five copies of the AS/400 Operations Online Class New Students Report in your output queue. Prior to printing a report, let's explore the output queues where the reports went.

OUTPUT QUEUES

The printouts you just created were sent directly to the output queue specified in your user profile. More about your user profile is found in chapter 11. If the output queue that received the reports is ready and has an active printer writer, the reports will go directly from the output queue to the printer.

An output queue can be associated with a printer writer. If the writer is *varied on* (or started), then the spool software will print the spool files from that output queue. The printer writer will only select spool files that have the status of ready and the correct form type.

In this class, and frequently in companies, the printouts don't go directly to a printer but to an output queue without a printer writer assigned. This queue could be referred to as a holding queue. Before you direct reports or spool files to a printer, you should always view your printouts in the output queue. Everything produced may not be worth printing and would be better deleted. As shown in Figure 6-1 in this chapter, the output of several jobs goes to output queues without assigned printer writers. All of these reports are waiting to be sequenced on the SALES output queue. Remember that the SALES output queue has an active printer writer and directs the report to printer PRT01.

OUTPUT QUEUE PRIORITY

Spool files wait on the output queue in the order of output queue priority and the time they were created. The priorities range from 1 to 9, where 1 would be first.

Let us explore the priorities of the reports you created above. You will be changing the priority of these files and see the effect on their sequence in the queue and the effect it has on the order they print.

- Enter WRKSPLF on the command line.
- Press Enter.
- Locate the five reports produced by the ADDRESS1 program.

Figure L6-4 shows the five reports produced by the ADDRESS1 program. Using the F-11 function key, change to View 2 to display the priority of each report. You will next be changing the priority of these files to 5, 6, 7, 8, and 9. Also, change the USER DATA field to reflect the priority of the reports respectively. For example, a report at priority 5 would have USER DATA of ADDRESS5, etc. Now let's experiment with priority.

```
                        Work with All Spooled Files

 Type options, press Enter.
   1=Send    2=Change    3=Hold    4=Delete    5=Display    6=Release    7=Messages
   8=Attributes          9=Work with printing status

                                     Device or                          Total      Cur
 Opt  File          User         Queue         User Data    Sts    Pages      Page  Copy
 ___  QSYSPRT       OPR0001      OPROUTQ                    RDY        1               1
 ___  QSYSPRT       OPR0001      OPROUTQ                    RDY        1               1
 ___  QPBKIPRTF     OPR0001      OPROUTQ                    RDY        3               1
 ___  QSYSPRT       OPR0001      OPROUTQ       PGMGARDEN    RDY        1               1
 ___  QSYSPRT       OPR0001      OPROUTQ       ADDRESS1     RDY        1               1
 ___  QSYSPRT       OPR0001      OPROUTQ       ADDRESS1     RDY        1               1
 ___  QSYSPRT       OPR0001      OPROUTQ       ADDRESS1     RDY        1               1
 ___  QSYSPRT       OPR0001      OPROUTQ       ADDRESS1     RDY        1               1
 ___  QSYSPRT       OPR0001      OPROUTQ       ADDRESS1     RDY        1               1
                                                                                  Bottom
 Parameters for options 1, 2, 3 or command
 ===> ____________________________________________________________________________
 F3=Exit    F10=View 4    F11=View 2    F12=Cancel    F22=Printers    F24=More keys
```

Figure L6-4: Five reports created by the ADDRESS1 program in the OPROUTQ output queue.

- Enter 2 (Change) to the left of the first of the five reports.
- Press F11 (View 2).
- What are the priorities of the five reports? ______________________________
- Press Enter.
- Press F10 (Additional Parameters).
- Page down to the next screen.

Notice that when you changed to View 2, the priority of each spool file was shown. Initially, all the reports are at the priority established by your user profile. You will be changing each report to a different priority. The first report is at priority 5, so leave the priority alone but change the USER DATA field to reflect the priority of 5. Next, you will change the priority of the remaining reports to priorities 6 through 9 and their USER DATA to ADDRESS6 through ADDRESS9 respectively. This will easily identify the priority of each file.

Also, change the status to Hold (HLD) for all five reports/spool files. Spool files can be in several statuses in an output queue—they can be RDY (Ready to print), HLD (Held, cannot print until released), and SAV (Saved, has been printed and saved, can be reprinted by releasing it).

Once you have completed the steps above, Figure L6-5 screen is displayed. You will be asked to edit this screen for each of the five reports.

```
                  Change Spooled File Attributes (CHGSPLFA)

 Type choices, press Enter.

 Page range to print:
   Starting page  . . . . . . . .   1              Number, *SAME, *ENDPAGE
   Ending page  . . . . . . . . .   *END           Number, *SAME, *END
 File becomes available . . . . .   *FILEEND       *SAME, *JOBEND, *FILEEND...
 Save file  . . . . . . . . . . .   *NO            *SAME, *NO, *YES
 Output priority  . . . . . . . .   5              1-9, *SAME, *JOB
 User data  . . . . . . . . . . .   'ADDRESS5   '  User data, *SAME
 Align page . . . . . . . . . . .   *NO            *SAME, *NO, *YES
 Print quality  . . . . . . . . .   *STD           *SAME, *STD, *DEVD, *DRAFT...
 Form feed  . . . . . . . . . . .   *DEVD          *SAME, *DEVD, *CONT, *CUT...
 Source drawer  . . . . . . . . .   1              1-255, *SAME, *E1, *FORMDF
 Print fidelity . . . . . . . . .   *CONTENT       *SAME, *ABSOLUTE, *CONTENT
 Print on both sides  . . . . . .   *NO            *SAME, *NO, *YES, *TUMBLE...
 Pages per side . . . . . . . . .   1              1-4, *SAME
 Form definition  . . . . . . . .   *NONE          Name, *SAME, *NONE, *DEVD...
   Library  . . . . . . . . . . .                  Name, *LIBL, *CURLIB
                                                                        More...
 F3=Exit   F4=Prompt   F5=Refresh   F12=Cancel   F13=How to use this display
 F24=More keys
```

Figure L6-5: Second screen of option 2 (Change) from the Work with All Spooled Files screen.

- Change the USER DATA field to ADDRESS5.
- Press Enter.
- Enter 2 (Change) to the left of the next report.
- Press Enter.
- Page down to the next screen.
- Enter 6 in the PRIORITY field.
- Enter ADDRESS6 in the USER DATA field.
- Press Enter.
- Repeat the above steps until you have changed the next three reports to priorities 7, 8, and 9. (Remember to change USER DATA respectively, also.)

To verify that you have completed the above steps, print the screen showing the revised report priorities.

- Enter WRKSPLF on the command line.
- Press Enter.
- Press F11 (View 2).
- Press Ctrl-Scroll Lock to create a screen print.
- Press F5 (Refresh).

- Where is this screen print in relationship to the five reports?
- Label it as printout #2.
- Attach this printout to the submission form for this lab.
- Press the Error Reset key.

____

____

Remember that you can view the spool files in the output queue to determine their contents.

Next, let's change the priorities of the reports from 8 and 9 back to 5, but leave the USER DATA unchanged. This allows you to see the effect changing priorities has on the sequence of the files in the queue.

- Make sure that you are at the `Work with All Spooled Files` screen.
- Enter 2 (Change) to the left of the ADDRESS8 report.
- Press Enter.
- Page down to the next screen.
- Enter 5 in the `PRIORITY` field.
- Leave the `USER DATA` field unchanged.
- Press Enter.
- Repeat the above steps for the ADDRESS9 report.
- Press F5 (Refresh).
- Press Ctrl-Scroll Lock to create a screen print.
- Press the Error Reset key.
- Press F5 (Refresh).
- Label it as printout #3.
- Attach this printout to the submission form for this lab.

At this point, you should have three reports at priority 5, and two reports at higher priorities.

- What happened to the five reports' sequence?

____

____

OUTPUT QUEUE COMMANDS

An output queue is an object in a library. It is of the type *OUTQ. Output queues can be held or released. If released, and they have a printer writer assigned, the files in the output queue are available to print. First, let's create an output queue in your library. Next, you will move some spool files to that queue.

- Enter CRTOUTQ on the command line.
- Press F4 (Prompt).
- Enter USERID for the output queue. (*Note*: This is your user profile plus a Q.)
- Press F10 (Additional Parameters).
- Page down to the next screen.
- Change the TEXT 'DESCRIPTION' field to Lab 6-output queue.
- Press Enter.

Now that you have an output queue in your library, the next step is to move some spool files to that queue. The output queue that you just created does not have a printer writer associated with it, so it functions as a holding queue. All spool files in that queue, regardless of their status, will not be printed directly. Also, there is no effect on printing to hold this queue. These commands only have an effect when the output queue is capable of printing.

- Enter WRKSPLF on the command line.
- Press Enter.
- Enter 2 to the left of both reports with USER DATA ADDRESS8 and ADDRESS9.
- Tab to the command line.
- Enter OUTQ(*CURLIB/USERIDQ).
- Press Enter.
- Press F5 (Refresh).
- What change is shown in the ADDRESS8 and ADDRESS9 spool files? ____
- Enter WRKOUTQ *ALL on the command line.
- Press Enter.

- Page down until your new output queue is seen on the screen.
- Press Ctrl-Scroll Lock to create a screen print.
- Press the Error Reset key.
- Press F5 (Refresh).
- Label it as printout #4.
- Attach this printout to the submission form for this lab.

Let me draw attention to that fact that you moved two spool files to your new output queue in a single step. When you know the files you want to modify for multiple entries on a list screen, place the option number to the left of the multiple entries to change. Next, put the parameter being changed on the command line.

This latest printout will show that you have created an output queue in your library. It also shows two files are currently in this output queue. Now you will have a chance to use the command that clears an output queue. This will delete all the spool files in that queue.

- Enter the command to `Clear an Output Queue` on the command line.
- Press F4.
- Enter `USERIDQ` for the output queue.
- Press Enter.
- Enter the command to `Work with All Output Queues`.
- Press Enter.
- Press F5 (Refresh).
- Repeat the procedure above to obtain a screen print of the Work with Output Queue screen showing that there are no files in your new output queue `USERID`.
- Press the Error Reset key.
- Press F5 (Refresh).
- Label it as printout #5.
- Attach this printout to the submission form for this lab.

You can explore the HLDOUTQ, RLSOUTQ, and CHGOUTQ commands if you like. This will provide some practice using these commands. To help keep your system clean, you should delete unneeded objects. Now, it is time to delete the output queue that you created in this section.

- Enter DLTOUTQ on the command line.
- Press F4 (Prompt).
- Enter the name of the output queue you created in your library. (*Note*: The library should be your current library.)
- Press Enter.

To demonstrate that the output queue is no longer on the system, print the Work with Output Queue screen.

- Enter the command to `Display all Output Queues on the System.`
- Do a print screen of this screen.
- Press the Error Reset key.
- Press F5 (Refresh).
- Label it as printout #6.
- Attach this printout to the submission form for this lab.

PRIORITIES WHILE PRINTING

To see the sequence of objects being printed based on priority, move the three remaining reports to a printer in one step. This will sequence them together.

- Enter the command to `Display your spool files.`
- Place a `2` to the left of the three remaining reports from the address1 program.
- On the command line, enter the parameter to `Direct the reports to the printer.`
- Are there other printouts in the printer queue? ______________________
- Retrieve at least one copy of the AS/400 Operations Online Class New Students Report from the printer.
- Label it as printout #7.
- Attach this printout to the submission form for this lab.
- What order were your reports printed? ______________________

  ____
- Did they print together? ______________________

WORKING WITH SPOOL FILES

The Work with Spooled Files command allows a user to view the spool files/printouts in a variety of output queues and the printers they were sent to, among other criteria. You could use this same command to view printouts by who directed them to the output queue. See Figure L6-6 for more on the choices.

```
                      Work with Spooled Files (WRKSPLF)

 Type choices, press Enter.

 Select files for:
   User . . . . . . . . . . . . . .   *CURRENT      Name, *CURRENT, *ALL
   Print device . . . . . . . . . .   *ALL          Name, *ALL, *OUTQ
   Form type  . . . . . . . . . . .   *ALL          Form type, *ALL, *STD
   User data  . . . . . . . . . . .   *ALL          User data, *ALL
   ASP  . . . . . . . . . . . . . .   *ALL          1-16, *ALL
 Output . . . . . . . . . . . . . .   *             *, *PRINT







                                                                       Bottom
 F3=Exit   F4=Prompt   F5=Refresh   F10=Additional parameters   F12=Cancel
 F13=How to use this display        F24=More keys
```

Figure L6-6: Prompted version of the Work with Spooled Files screen.

- Enter the `Work with Spooled Files` command on the command line.
- Press F4 (Prompt).

To view the printouts waiting in output queue for any user, you can enter the user's ID on the above screen. From here, you can choose to work with your spooled files, or anyone's, given the correct authority.

- Enter QSECOFR for the USER parameter.
- Press Enter.
- Could you view the contents of the spool files? ____________________
- Exit the current screen.

All spool files, on any and all output queues, are displayed for that user. Using this command, you can find anyone's output. Now let's explore other portions of this screen.

- Enter the `Work with Spooled Files` command on the command line.
- Press Enter.
- Enter a `2` (Change) next to one of the spool files to printer. *Note*: If there are no spool files, create two as done previously in this lab.
- Press Enter.
- Direct the spool file to a printer.
- Press F5 (Refresh).

The resulting screen shows only those files left in the output queue. Before proceeding to the next section make sure there is at least one printout in your spool files. If the queue is empty, create another printout as before in this lab.

- Move the cursor to the `Status` column.
- Press F1 (Help).
- Read through the different statuses.
- What is the difference between WTR and PRT status?____________________
- ____
- When MSGW is displayed, what option should you take to display the file's message? ____
- Enter `8` (Attributes) next to one of the files.
- Read the information that is presented.
- What is the device type? ____
  ____
- Return to the `Work with All Spooled Files` screen.
- Enter `9` (Work with Printing Status) next to a file in the output queue.
- The `Work with Printing Status` display is shown.
- Enter `5` (Display). The `Display Detailed Description` screen is shown.
- Read through the information.
- Exit `Display Detailed Description` screen.
- Why is the file not printing? ____

WORK WRITER COMMAND

The Work with Writer command leads you to the Work with All Printers screen. This will list the printers attached to your AS/400.

- Enter the `Work with Writer` command.
- Press Enter.
- What printers are shown? ______________________________
- What is the status of each printer? ______________________________

____

ADDITIONAL LAB ASSIGNMENTS

Now try your skills at working with printing concepts.

1. Issue the command WRKWTR.
   a. What printers are defined to the system?
   b. What is the status of PRT01?
   c. If the status of PRT01 is as shown below, what options would you use to correct/change the situation?
      i. END.
      ii. HLD.
      iii. MSGW.
   d. You want to work with the spool files in the queue for printer PRT01. Which option would you use?
2. You are using TCP/IP network printing, and your network printer is PRT03. What output queue would this printer be using?
3. Create two spool files in your output queue. You can either run a program or copy a file to the printer. Change the priority and user data of at least one of the files to priority 6. Which spool file would print first?

END-OF-CHAPTER AIDS

CHAPTER SUMMARY

Let us return to the configuration example shown at the start of this chapter. Here it is again as Figure L6-7.

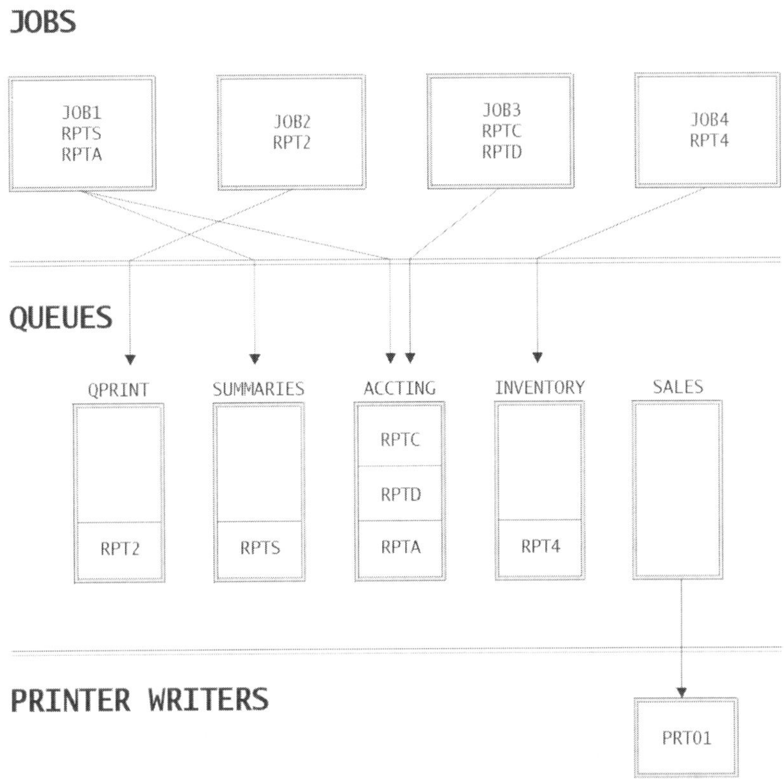

Figure L6-7: Jobs, queues, and printer writers.

Here are some real-life situations you may encounter and how to work with them.

Example 1: JOB2 has completed. Print report RPT2.

There are two ways to do this:

1. Change the printer writer (PRT01) assignment from empty queue SALES to queue QPRINT. From the Work with Writer (WRKWTR) command, select option 2 (Change). See Figure L6-8.

```
                        Change Printer Writer (CHGPRTWTR)

Type choices, press Enter.

Printer . . . . . . . . . . . . .   PRT01         Name, *ALL, *SYSVAL
Output queue . . . . . . . . . .   QPRINT        Name, *DEV
  Library . . . . . . . . . . .     ______      Name, *LIBL, *CURLIB
Queue for writer messages . . .   *DEVD         Name, *DEVD, *REQUESTER
  Library . . . . . . . . . . .     ______      Name, *LIBL, *CURLIB
Form type options:
  Form type . . . . . . . . . .   *ALL          Form type, *ALL, *STD, *FORMS
  Message option . . . . . . . .   *INQMSG       *INQMSG, *MSG, *NOMSG...
File separators . . . . . . . .   *FILE         0-9, *FILE
Drawer for separators . . . . .   *DEVD         1-255, *DEVD, *FILE

                                                                  Bottom
F3=Exit   F4=Prompt   F5=Refresh   F10=Additional parameters   F12=Cancel
F13=How to use this display        F24=More keys
```

Figure L6-8: Move Printer Writer PRT01 to output queue QPRINT.

2. Move the report from output queue QPRINT to output queue SALES, where printer writer PRT01 can print it. Drill down from the Work with Output Queue (WRKOUTQ) command or enter the command WRKOUTQ QPRINT on the command line. From the screen, enter option 2 (Change) on spool file RPT2. From the change screen, enter the new output queue. See Figure L6-9.

```
                  Change Spooled File Attributes (CHGSPLFA)

Type choices, press Enter.

Spooled file . . . . . . . . . . > RPT2          Name, *SELECT
Job name . . . . . . . . . . . . > JOB2          Name, *
  User . . . . . . . . . . . . . >   A91001181   Name
  Number . . . . . . . . . . . . >   149607      000000-999999
Spooled file number . . . . . . > 1             1-9999, *ONLY, *LAST
Printer . . . . . . . . . . . .   *SAME         Name, *SAME, *OUTQ
Print sequence . . . . . . . . .   *SAME         *SAME, *NEXT
Form type . . . . . . . . . . .   *SAME         Form type, *SAME, *STD
Copies . . . . . . . . . . . . .   *SAME         1-255, *SAME
Restart printing . . . . . . . .   *SAME         Number, *SAME, *STRPAGE...

                           Additional Parameters

Output queue . . . . . . . . . .   SALES       Name, *SAME, *DEV
  Library . . . . . . . . . . .     QGPL        Name, *LIBL, *CURLIB

                                                                  Bottom
F3=Exit   F4=Prompt   F5=Refresh   F10=Additional parameters   F12=Cancel
F13=How to use this display        F24=More keys
```

Figure L6-9: Send report RPT2 from output queue QPRINT to output queue SALES.

Example 2: Jobs JOB1 and JOB3 have completed. Print their reports as a set.

In a similar way to option 1 of Example 1, change the printer writer (PRT01) assignment from empty queue SALES to queue ACCTING.

Move all three reports from output queue ACCTING to output queue SALES. Do so in one move. Use the Work with Output Queue (WRKOUTQ) command and drill down to the output queue, or use the command and specify the queue you want to work with. Once you are at the Work with Output Queue screen with a display of the spool files in the queue, change their output queue assignments as shown in Figure L6-10.

```
                          Work with Output Queue

Queue:   ACCTING            Library:   QGPL             Status:   RLS

Type options, press Enter.
  1=Send  2=Change  3=Hold  4=Delete   5=Display   6=Release   7=Messages
  8=Attributes     9=Work with printing status

Opt  File        User      User Data  Sts   Pages   Copies  Form Type  Pty
 2   RPTC        MDAWSON              RDY       1        1  *STD         5
 2   RPTD        MDAWSON              RDY       8        1  *STD         5
 2   RPTA        MDAWSON              RDY      12        1  *STD         5
                                                                More . . .
Parameters for options 1, 2, 3 or command
===> OUTQ(SALES)
F3=Exit   F11=View 2   F12=Cancel   F20=Writers   F22=Printers
F24=More keys
```

Figure L6-10: Move three reports to output queue SALES.

Example 3, same as Example 2. Print the reports in this order: RPTA, RPTC, RPTD.

1. Move all three reports from output queue ACCTING to output queue SALES, but do so in three separate moves. Use the Work with Output Queue (WRKOUTQ) command and drill down to the output queue, or use the command and specify the queue you want to work with. Once you are at the Work with Output Queue screen with a display of the spool files in the queue, change output queue assignments one at a time as shown in Figure L6-11.

```
                          Work with Output Queue

Queue:   ACCTING            Library:   QGPL             Status:   RLS

Type options, press Enter.
  1=Send  2=Change  3=Hold  4=Delete   5=Display   6=Release   7=Messages
  8=Attributes     9=Work with printing status

Opt  File        User      User Data  Sts   Pages   Copies  Form Type  Pty
 _   RPTC        MDAWSON              RDY       1        1  *STD         5
 _   RPTD        MDAWSON              RDY       8        1  *STD         5
 2   RPTA        MDAWSON              RDY      12        1  *STD         5



                                                                More . . .
Parameters for options 1, 2, 3 or command
===> OUTQ(SALES)
F3=Exit   F11=View 2   F12=Cancel   F20=Writers   F22=Printers
F24=More keys
```

Figure L6-11: Move reports one at a time to output queue SALES. (Note: This step will be repeated for RPTC and RPTD, in that order.)

1. Notice in the right-most column in Figure L6-11, all reports have the same output queue priority of 5. Change their print order by changing their priorities, again, by drilling down through the Work with Output Queue command to the screen that shows the spooled files. Then, individually select option 2 (Change) on each. Make priority assignments like this:

   RPTA priority 1

   RPTC priority 2

   RPTD priority 3

Figure L6-12 shows an example of changing report RPTA.

```
                 Change Spooled File Attributes (CHGSPLFA)

 Type choices, press Enter.

 Page range to print:
   Starting page . . . . . . . .   1______    Number, *SAME, *ENDPAGE
   Ending page . . . . . . . . .   *END       Number, *SAME, *END
 File becomes available . . . . .  *FILEEND   *SAME, *JOBEND, *FILEEND...
 Save file . . . . . . . . . . .   *NO        *SAME, *NO, *YES
 Output priority . . . . . . . .   1_         1-9, *SAME, *JOB
 User data . . . . . . . . . . .   '_________'User data, *SAME
 Align page . . . . . . . . . . .  *NO        *SAME, *NO, *YES
 Print quality . . . . . . . . .   *STD       *SAME,*STD,*DEVD,*DRAFT...
 Form feed . . . . . . . . . . .   *DEVD      *SAME,*DEVD,*CONT,*CUT...
 Source drawer . . . . . . . . .   1_         1-255, *SAME, *E1, *FORMDF
 Print fidelity . . . . . . . . .  *CONTENT   *SAME, *ABSOLUTE, *CONTENT
 Print on both sides . . . . . .   *NO        *SAME,*NO,*YES,*TUMBLE...
 Pages per side . . . . . . . . .  1_         1-4, *SAME
 Form definition . . . . . . . .   *NONE      Name,*SAME,*NONE,*DEVD...
   Library . . . . . . . . . . .     ____     Name, *LIBL, *CURLIB

                                                                More. . .
 F3=Exit F4=Prompt   F5=Refresh   F12=Cancel   F13=How to use this display
 F24=More keys
```

Figure L6-12: Change output priority of report RPTA to 1, forcing it to the highest priority (and an earlier print position).

Repeat the operation shown in Figure L6-12 for the other two reports, giving them output priorities of 2 and 3. Then, you can either change the printer writer from SALES to ACCTING (Example 1, option 1), or move all three reports to output queue SALES (Example 2, option 2).

If, after you have arranged reports in order by resetting their priorities, you choose to print them by moving them to another queue, it is critical that you move them all as a block.

KEY TERMS

absolute command	Find field	queues
attributes	foreground	relative command
automatic configuration	logical device	spooled files
background	output queue	spooling
Control field	output queue priority	system printer
devices	printer writer	writer

CHAPTER SELF-TEST

Solutions to these self-test questions are in appendix D.

True-False Questions

___ 1. All jobs on the system produce output.

___ 2. The AS/400 can designate a printer to be the system printer.

___ 3. A report produced by a program or a job on the system can be sent directly to a printer.

___ 4. A report in an output queue is referred to as a spool file.

___ 5. The number of output queues and printers are the same for most systems.

___ 6. Reports on an output queue with different priorities will print in FIFO order.

___ 7. To view the messages for the system operator, a user would type DSPMSG *SYSOPR.

Fill in the Blanks

1. A report that is generated by either a program or a job is sent to a(n) ______________.

2. A report waiting on an output queue with no attached printer writer (will/will not) print.

3. A report in a held queue with an attached writer will print the report if the queue is ______________________.

4. While viewing a spool file, you would place ______________ on the Control line to move the file forward fifteen lines.

5. On the Control line of a spool file, a __________ is placed to move you to the end of the document.

6. To search a spool file for a character string, you would place the string on the Field line and press the ________________ function key.

7. The ________________ command allows you to change the number of copies, the starting page, and/or the output queue of a spool file to be printed.

8. If a printer writer has ended, the ____________________ command would make it begin.

Chapter Review Questions

1. Define the following terms:

   a. Logical device.

   b. Background versus foreground.

   c. FIFO.

   d. System printer.

   e. Output queue priority.

2. List the steps in the printing process on the AS/400.

3. What effect does priority have on the sequence for printing?

4. If you want to move five reports from the Invoice output queue to the Sales output queue in one move, how would you do it?

5. What things should you consider before you clear an output queue?

6. How is a report different when viewed on-line versus its appearance when printed?

7. Why would you hold or release a spooled output file?

8. Why is a print writer important?

7

MANAGING DEVICES

CHAPTER OBJECTIVES

Upon completion of this chapter, you should be able to:

- Explain the function of controllers.
- Explain what a device is.
- Describe device configuration.
- Explain the relationship between lines, controllers, and devices.
- Demonstrate how to display device descriptions.
- Demonstrate how to copy a device description.
- Demonstrate how to create descriptions for new hardware.
- Demonstrate how to display the hardware configuration.
- Define the hardware configuration.
- Demonstrate how to configure DASD and ASPs.
- Describe user and system ASPs.
- Demonstrate how to work with user and system ASPs.

INTRODUCTION

The AS/400, like any computer, is made up of hardware *devices* (things you can touch) and software products. Within the definition of hardware, the AS/400 makes another distinction. Imagine the basic AS/400, a black monolith. It contains the basic CPU and RAM, plus other hardware pieces such as *Direct Access Storage Device* (*DASD*), memory, cabling, a power supply, fans, and so on. All these things inside the black box are considered *internal hardware.*

External hardware pieces attached to the AS/400 are considered devices. Examples of devices are printers, workstations, diskette readers, and tape devices. Things that support communications, like lines and controllers, are also considered devices on an AS/400.

Everything an AS/400 is supposed to support is considered a device and must be made known to the AS/400 before it can be used.

A device becomes known to the AS/400 through an object type called a *device description* (type *DEVD). A device description contains basic things like device name, address, attached controller, and many other values that may be unique to the type of device. Writing a device description is also referred to as *configuring* the device.

Locally connected devices (that is, devices not attaching through a dial-up modem or a router or gateway) have two ways of getting configured—automatic and manual. All remote devices must be configured manually.

AUTOMATIC CONFIGURATION

Automatic configuration (referred to as *autoconfig*) is turned on and off through an AS/400 system value, QAUTOCFG. If this system value contains a “0,” auto configuration is disabled; if “1,” it is enabled.

When automatic configuration is turned on (and only when it is turned on), another system value, QDEVNAMING, determines the name format that the AS/400 will assign to those devices it automatically configures. Valid values for this system value and the names they dictate are:

1. *NORMAL—Native AS/400 device names are used. For example: DSPnn, PRTnn, TAPnn, DKTnn.

2. *DEVADR—The actual device address is used. DSPccppdd, PRTccppdd, where cc is controller number, pp is the port number, and dd is the device address.

3. *S36—Type device naming is used. Wn, Pn, Tn, etc.

There are a couple definite advantages to using automatic configuration over *manual configuration*: One, when setting up a new system, there can be hundreds of devices. Autoconfig can save the operator many hours of work configuring those devices. Two, for a quick connection of an additional workstation or printer, it is easier to plug the device in and turn it on. Within a minute, it will be usable through the AS/400.

On the other hand, there are one or two disadvantages to using autoconfig. The major disadvantage is that as devices are swapped, if their model types are not the same, autoconfig will delete the old device descriptions and create new ones when it senses that the models have moved. The result of such a swap/rename could be that two display stations named DSP12 and DSP15 may become DSP88 and DSP89. If the original names meant something to the shop, this arbitrary renaming could get very confusing. Shops that really have a problem with autoconfig's naming are those where devices are getting moved around a lot. Such a shop will suddenly see device names ballooning with little apparent regard for logic.

The second disadvantage to autoconfig is when a shop really wants to name its devices in a meaningful way. Autoconfig takes away the capability of having custom device names.

Many, if not most, shops prefer autoconfig but do not like the gapped names it can produce. A compromise solves that problem—turn on autoconfig when the system first comes up, then turn it off. Only turn it on again for special, controlled circumstances.

MANUALLY CREATING DEVICE DESCRIPTIONS

Manually create device descriptions with one version of the Create Device command. The root of this command is CRTDEVXXX (xxx is replaced by a value listed in Figure 7-1). In this way, the same root command uses the suffix values to become four separate commands. Figure 7-1 lists the valid command abbreviations for devices.

Device	Description
DKT	Diskette
DSP	Display
PRT	Printer
TAP	Tape

Figure 7-1: Device types.

Through the suffixes plus the root, the four commands that are created are:

```
CRTDEVDKT
CRTDEVDSP
CRTDEVPRT
CRTDEVTAP
```

Communications, remote and local, on an AS/400 always happen through two devices: the *communication controller* and the *line*. Logically enough, there must be a physical line to connect devices and the line must be described to the AS/400 so it knows things like the type of line, its maximum speed, etc. A workstation controller is less obvious, especially for students with no prior exposure to an AS/400. A controller is a computer itself. It off-loads a lot of the communication work from the AS/400.

Lines and controllers are configured with their own create commands: Create Line xxx (CRTLINXXX) and Create Controller (CRTCTLXXX). The xxx suffix denotes what kind of line and controller we are configuring. This is fairly advanced and will be covered later in the communication chapter.

The first attempt to create device descriptions can be intimidating because the AS/400 wants to know a lot about a device. Refer to the physical documentation that comes with new devices for the details.

In general, there are several items that are common to many devices. These items are the *item description* and its *address*.

Item description usually consists of three parameters: CLASS, TYPE, and MODEL. These come together to describe a device to the AS/400 (for example, a 3477 Model FC).

Addresses are the connection location on the AS/400. Devices on AS/400s are always attached to a *controller*. More specifically, to a port on a controller. Generally speaking, controllers have eight ports. Twinax devices (the AS/400's original local network protocol was 5250, or twinax, a dying protocol) also want a switch setting. When a twinax switch setting is specified, that tells the AS/400 to what the dip switches internal to the device will be set.

Non-twinax devices also need the LOCADR parameter set. This is a two-character value—valid values are dependent on the type of controller to which the device is attached.

When configuring printer devices, pay attention to their MSGQ parameter. This is the name of the message queue that is to receive the messages the system issues when something goes wrong with the printer (such as running out of paper or having a ribbon jam). There are three possible strategies for naming a printer message queue:

- Use QSYSOPR, which tells the system to use the same centralized message queue for all the messages related to printers. This is nice if the system operator is responsible for maintaining all printers. But if that is not the case, this practice could result in printer messages that just get lost because QSYSOPR tends to be overly busy all the time.
- Use one message queue (other than QSYSOPR) for all printers. Doing this relieves QSYSOPR from that burden. Because any user with enough authority can display messages from the message queue, anyone can take corrective action (especially someone near the printer). A disadvantage of this scheme is that it provides little security. By replying to inquiry messages in this message queue, anyone authorized to do so would indirectly control all printers.
- Create a separate message queue for each printer. Separate message queues give the best possible control and is not as bad as it sounds, especially if the message queue is named after the printer it controls. If the Receiving Department's printer is called RCVPRT01, create a message queue called RCVPRT01 and make it the message queue for the printer. When the system operator needs to display messages for RCVPRT01, he or she will know which message queue to display.

Logically enough, most large shops create a separate message queue for each printer; small shops (with only one or two printers) use QSYSOPR for the printer message queue.

MAINTAINING DEVICE DESCRIPTIONS

Create, change, delete, and display device descriptions at any time. Whatever changes made become effective immediately. The system does not require any major chore for the changes to take effect. If at any time of the day a department needs an additional display station, configure it (either by the operator or autoconfig), plug it in, connect it to the system, turn it on, and begin using it.

Even though a device may be connected and turned on, sometimes the AS/400 will not communicate to it. The reason may be that the device is not varied on.

The term *vary*, used as a verb on the AS/400, means to logically turn on a device or to make it ready. Devices are always varied on from a workstation, often the system console. Printers, when they jam or overheat, are prone to becoming varied off automatically by the system. If a device is connected and turned on but not working, always check its status in terms of if it is varied on or not. A device can be *reset* by varying it off, then on again.

The command for varying a device on and off is the Vary Configuration (VRYCFG) command.

Many (but not all) device description settings can be changed after a device is created by using the corresponding Change Device Description xxx (CHGDEVXXX) command. Again, xxx can be replaced by one of the device types previously listed.

A device description can be displayed with the Display Device Description (DSPDEVD) command or deleted with the Delete Device Description (DLTDEVD) command. Neither has the XXX variations mentioned in other commands.

Occasionally, especially if autoconfig has caused a problem, a device needs to be renamed. This is done with the Rename Object (RNMOBJ) command. Be sure to vary off the device before renaming it and vary it back on afterward.

For example, if automatic configuration created DSP42 and it should be named ADMDSP03, run the following command:

```
RNMOBJ OBJ(DSP42) OBJTYPE(*DEVD) NEWNAME(ADMDSP03)
```

LISTING DEVICE DESCRIPTIONS

The number of device descriptions can be in the hundreds, even thousands. As soon as a new (or changed) AS/400 stabilizes, it is nice to have a list of them for reference. Such a list can be produced in three ways:

- Run the Display Object Description (DSPOBJD) command, and specify OBJ(QSYS/*ALL) OBJTYPE(*DEVD). Direct the output to the display (the default) or to the printer by specifying OUTPUT(*PRINT).
- Run the Print Device Address (PRTDEVADR) command. This command produces a printed grid that lists all device descriptions attached to a particular local workstation controller. The command only has one parameter, CTL, where the desired workstation controller is named. Supply a value like CTL01. The disadvantage to this command is it only lists the devices on one controller at a time—it must be rerun for each controller to get the big picture.
- Run the Work with Configuration Status (WRKCFGSTS) command, specifying CFGTYPE(*DEVD) CFGD(*ALL). Like the DSPOBJD command, direct the output to the display or to the printer by entering * or *PRINT in the output parameter.

None of these commands give much information about the actual configuration of the devices. DSPOBJD generates a list that shows only the device description names and text descriptions. It does not show any of their configuration settings. However, when maintenance problems occur, such a list can be key to getting started.

WORK WITH DEVICE DESCRIPTIONS

Taking charge of this maintenance is made easier with the Work with Device Descriptions (WRKDEVD) command. It displays all available device descriptions on the screen and allows functional operations to all. Figure 7-2 shows a sample of this command screen.

```
                         Work with Device Descriptions
                                                        System:   BIGBLUE
Position to  . . . . . ____________  Starting characters

Type options, press Enter.
  2=Change   3=Copy    4=Delete   5=Display   6=Print   7=Rename
  8=Work with status   9=Retrieve source

Opt  Device       Type        Text
 _   A98003873    3179        Device created for BIGBLUE.
 _   BIGBLUE      3477        Device created for BIGBLUE.
 _   CPAOUTQ      3812        Device created for BIGBLUE.
 _   CPQOUTQ      3812        Device created for BIGBLUE.
 _   DSP01        3179        CREATED BY AUTO-CONFIGURATION
 _   ETHLITCP     *NET        CREATED BY AUTO-CONFIGURATION
 _   EXODUS       *INTRA      Exodus TCP/IP Server Intrasystems Com Dev
 _   GIL1         3179        Device created for BIGBLUE.
 _   OPT01        6321        CREATED BY AUTO-CONFIGURATION
                                                              More . . .
Parameters or command
===> _________________________________________________________________
F3=Exit   F4=Prompt   F5=Refresh   F6=Create   F9=Retrieve   F12=Cancel
F14=Work with status
```

Figure 7-2: Basic screen for WRKDEVD command.

There can be thousands of devices connected to an AS/400, so this command can have hundreds of pages. To help navigate quickly to the desired device(s) to work with, this command comes with a positioning facility (it is not a search facility). At the top of the screen is a blank line with the caption `Position to`. Generic searches or fuzzy logic cannot be used; enter the name of the device, press Enter, and it will be displayed at the top of a new screen. *TOP and *BOT are keywords that will quickly display the top or bottom pages of this list.

The lesson here is: know the device names. It's another reason to keep and maintain a list.

One of the device description commands that can be easily performed from this menu that will save a lot of work is the Copy (option 3). Use this function when either creating a large number of similar devices or configuring a new, unfamiliar device. As long as one similar device already exists on the system, this is a handy function. For example, most people do not add diskette drives every day. If a shop had to and one was already on the system, the first thing the operator could do to start configuring the new drive is make a copy of the existing one, but name it with the new device's name. From there, he can make whatever changes are necessary to correctly create the new drive's device description.

WORKING WITH DEVICES

Devices are created once and not changed very often after that. During daily operations, the system operator works quite a bit with *device statuses*. Each device type has its own menus and commands to work with its devices and statuses. Until one gets familiar with the AS/400, just type:

```
GO DEVICE
```

on any command line and press Enter. Use this method to learn the device type menus, then the device type commands. We will give a high-level view of GO DEVICE but point out how to go direct to devices later. Figure 7-3 contains a sample menu (named DEVICE) that the command GO DEVICE produces.

```
DEVICE                    Device Operations
                                                        System:   BIGBLUE
 Select one of the following:

      1. Work with device status
      2. Work with displays
      3. Printer
      4. Tape
      5. Diskette
      6. Configure PC connections
      7. Optical

     70. Related commands



 Selection or command
 ===> ____________________________________________________________

 F3=Exit  F4=Prompt  F9=Retrieve  F12=Cancel  F13=Information Assistant
 F16=AS/400 Main menu
(C) COPYRIGHT IBM CORP. 1980, 1990.
```

Figure 7-3: Device menu.

The menu shown in Figure 7-3 provides seven ways to work with different device type statuses. Option one calls a command directly, Work with Device Status. Even this command is an overall one, providing access to all devices. Figure 7-4 contains a sample of WRKCFGSTS's screen. This screen will appear either if option one is taken from the GO DEVICE menu or the command WRKCFGSTS is typed directly on any command line.

```
                    Work with Configuration Status (WRKCFGSTS)

 Type choices, press Enter.

 Type . . . . . . . . . . . . . . . > *DEV       *NWS, *NWI, *LIN, *CTL, *DEV
 Configuration description  . . . > *ALL       Name, generic*, *ALL, ...
 Output . . . . . . . . . . . . .   *          *, *PRINT
 Range  . . . . . . . . . . . . .   *NET       *NET, *OBJ
 Status . . . . . . . . . . . . .   *ALL       *ALL, *ACTIVE, *FAILED...
```

Figure 7-4: Work with Configuration Status screen.

The parameters in WRKCFGSTS enable you, the operator, to send the requested status information to a printer through the OUTPUT parameter. Or, with the RANGE parameter, the RANGE to work with can be limited to local objects (*OBJ) or expanded to networked objects (*NET). Finally, the operator can specify that he or she only wants to work with objects with a specific status. Although the figure shows the default, *ALL, he or she may want to work only with objects that are active (*ACTIVE), that means turned on and capable of being used. Or he or she can work with objects with a failed status (*FAILED). In real life, both *ACTIVE and *FAILED are used as filters much more often than the broader *ALL.

If the type of the device is known, just name it on the first TYPE parameter. More typically, the name of the device(s) to work with is not known. Then the second parameter, CONFIGURATION DESCRIPTION, will help. Most customers at least know the general kind of device they want to work with and put it on this parameter.

Let's assume you want to work with display stations. Change the value *ALL to *DSP so we can look at all display devices currently known to the system. When you press Enter, you get a screen similar to the one shown in Figure 7-5.

```
                Work with Configuration Status                    BIGBLUE
                                                       05/06/99  23:02:39
Position to  . . . . .  ___________  Starting characters

Type options, press Enter.
  1=Vary on    2=Vary off    5=Work with job    8=Work with description
  9=Display mode status      13=Work with APPN status...

Opt  Description       Status            -------Job-------
 _   A98003873         VARIED OFF
 _   BIGBLUE           VARIED OFF
 _   DSP01             SIGNON DISPLAY
 _   GIL1              VARIED OFF
 _   QCONSOLE          VARIED OFF
 _   QPADEV000A        VARIED OFF
 _   QPADEV000B        SIGNON DISPLAY
 _   QPADEV000C        VARIED OFF
 _   QPADEV000D        SIGNON DISPLAY
                                                               More . . .

Parameters or command
===> ____________________________________________________________________
F3=Exit   F4=Prompt   F12=Cancel   F23=More options   F24=More keys
```

Figure 7-5: All display devices and their status currently on AS/400 named BIGBLUE.

Similar to the Work with Device Descriptions previously shown in Figure 7-2, this screen allows the operator to position to a device quickly (if its name is known) by using the `Position to` field.

Compare the options at the top between Figure 7-2 and Figure 7-5. The screen in Figure 7-4 deals primarily with statuses and, in the case of workstations, their statuses are mostly varied on or off. A status of `Signon Display` means the workstation is not in use but is displaying a sign-on screen.

The sign-on display status is unique to workstations. A printer could never have a sign-on display status, but it may have a status of `ready`. Although most AS/400 devices will have `Varied On` and `Varied Off` as statuses, some will have statuses unique to what they do, like this one.

But the purpose of the screen shown in Figure 7-2 was to work with device descriptions; the purpose of the screen shown in Figure 7-5 is to work with their statuses. Note option 8 on Figure 7-5. If the operator was on this screen checking statuses and decided to look at the device description for one of the displays, the operator would put 8 on the option line to the left of the device he or she was interested in and press Enter. From there, the operator would work with the device description as if it had been entered through the Work with Device Descriptions shown in Figure 7-2.

Before we leave Figure 7-5, if a workstation is turned off, it may have a status of `Varied Off` as many do in the figure. There are three ways a device may be in a varied off status:

- It is on and ready but varied off.
- It is turned off.
- It is plugged in, turned on, but the network connection has failed.

If the operator takes option 2 to try to vary on a varied-off device and the status changes to `Varied On`, he is in business. If the status changes to `Vary On Pending`, the workstation is not turned on. If the device is turned on and plugged in and this message appears, there is a network or controller problem.

As shown in Figure 7-3, most of these options ultimately present the single command, WRKCFGSTS. They have simply supplied the Configuration Description parameter with an appropriate value.

Rather than slog through a litany of the same resulting screens, Figure 7-6 lists the menus and by which each option finds its way to that command and the value for the parameter that makes it work. Within the WRKCFGSTS command, the CONFIGURATION DESCRIPTION parameter is known as CFGD (see Figure 7-6). This might help demystify the navigation from this screen; it helps invoke commands directly.

Figure 7-3 Option	Invokes Menu	Menu Option	Invokes Command	CFGD Value
1			WRKCFGSTS	<BLANK>
2			WRKCFGSTS	*DSP
3	PRINTER	4	WRKCFGSTS	*PRT
4	TAPE	6	WRKCFGSTS	*TAP
5	DISKETTE	6	WRKCFGSTS	*DKT
6	CFGPCS			
7	OPTICAL	5	WRKCFGSTS	*OPT

Figure 7-6: Device menu options and commands.

The one ringer in the menu is option 6. Option 6 does nothing with statuses; it configures communication devices.

As is apparent from Figure 7-6, although GO DEVICE is handy when new to the AS/400, most people quickly graduate to putting the WRKCFGSTS command directly on the command line.

LEARNING ABOUT AS/400 HARDWARE

Any AS/400 can have literally thousands of separate hardware pieces. The system operators do not concern themselves with this trivia day to day, but they should generally know what is on an AS/400 and be able to quickly find out what pieces are installed if they do not know.

Like all other areas of system operation, the AS/400's hardware configuration is easily displayed through several menu interfaces and commands:

1. Work with Hardware Products (WRKHDWPRD).
2. Work with Hardware Resources (WRKHDWRSC).
3. Display Hardware Resources (DSPHDWRSC).
4. GO CMDHDW.
5. GO CMDHDWRSC.
6. GO HARDWARE.

To work with the features installed on a system, use the WRKHDWPRD command. For the larger AS/400 model, 9406 system unit, the rack configuration is displayed in a screen similar to that shown in Figure 7-7.

```
                         Work with Hardware Products
                                                        System:   BIGBLUE
Select one of the following:

     1. Work with rack configuration
     2. Copy rack configuration
     3. Replace rack configuration



Selection ________


F3=Exit   F12=Cancel
(C) COPYRIGHT IBM CORP. 1980, 1998.
```

Figure 7-7: WRKHDWPRD command for an AS/400 9406 model.

Smaller AS/400 models, like the 9404 or 9402, have a system unit configuration that will be displayed in a screen similar to that shown in Figure 7-8.

```
                    Work with Hardware Products
                                                        System:
Select one of the following:

     1. Work with system configuration
     2. Copy system configuration
     3. Replace system configuration
     4. Display description label locations
     5. Change description label locations



Selection ________


F3=Exit   F12=Cancel
(C) COPYRIGHT IBM CORP. 1980, 1998.
```

Figure 7-8: WRKHDWPRD for small AS/400s, models 9402 and 9404.

To work with the installed configuration from either type of system screen, take option 1.

Option 4 (`Display description label locations`) for a server model from Figure 7-8 results in a screen similar to that shown in Figure 7-9.

```
                  Display Description Label Locations
                                                     System:   BIGBLUE
System type-model/serial . . . . . . . :   9406-S20 / 10-2HZ5M

--------Location---------
Frame    EIA      Device     Card
 ID    Location  Position  Position  Port  Label
1                            C01       1   ETHLINE
1                            C05       1   *NONE
1                            C05       2   *NONE
1                            C09           CTL01
1                            C09       1   QESLINE, QTILINE,
                                             VISA
1                  D01                     TAP01
1                  D02                     OPT01



                                                                  Bottom
F3=Exit   F11=Display types/serial numbers   F12=Cancel   F17=Print
```

Figure 7-9: Description label locations, option 4 from WRKHDWPRD.

Use this command to get a listing of the AS/400's current configuration on any unfamiliar machine. This includes brand-new systems as this is also a good way to verify that the AS/400 received was the AS/400 ordered. As we said earlier, this research is not done that often; when it is, the resultant information is usually archived. Use the F17 key (shown at the bottom right of the figure) to print the configuration. File the resultant report for future reference.

As the AS/400 is modified, either through upgrades, regular maintenance, or necessary repairs, this command will be used to update the configuration and to document those changes. (Generally, service personnel make these changes.)

Many areas of hardware configuration can be displayed or changed. From the command line of any menu, key in:

```
GO HARDWARE
```

The Hardware menu is shown in Figure 7-10.

```
HARDWARE                        Hardware Resources
                                                          System:   BIGBLUE
 Select one of the following:

      1. Work with communication resources
      2. Work with local workstation resources
      3. Work with storage resources
      4. Work with processor resources
      5. Work with token ring LAN adapter resources
      6. Work with DDI LAN adapter resources
      7. Work with all LAN adapter resources
      8. Work with coupled system adapter

     70. Related commands




 Selection or command
 ===> ________________________________________________________________________

 F3=Exit   F4=Prompt   F9=Retrieve   F12=Cancel   F13=Information Assistant
 F16=AS/400 Main menu
 (C) COPYRIGHT IBM CORP. 1980, 1998.
```

Figure 7-10: Hardware menu.

This menu itemizes all of the resources that can be displayed. The system operator can select an option corresponding to the resource he or she would like to work with. Most operators prefer to use the command directly, however. That command is the Work with Hardware Resource (WRKHDWRSC). On any command line, enter WRKHDWRSC and press F4. The screen shown in Figure 7-11 will be displayed.

```
                    Work with Hardware Resources (WRKHDWRSC)

 Type choices, press Enter.

 Type . . . . . . . . . . . . . .   ______          *CMN, *CSA, *LAN, *LWS...



                                                                        Bottom
 F3=Exit   F4=Prompt   F5=Refresh   F12=Cancel   F13=How to use this display
 F24=More keys
```

Figure 7-11: The prompted version of the WRKHDWRSC command.

From this screen, simply key in the desired resource and press Enter. The resource types are kind of coded. If what is available is not known, place the cursor on the TYPE parameter input line and press the F4 key for a quick list. If more information is needed, place the cursor on the TYPE parameter input line and press the F1 (Help) key.

For our example, assume we want to work with communication resources whose object type is *CMN. We key that in on the TYPE parameter and press Enter. A display similar to the one shown in Figure 7-12 appears.

```
                       Work with Communication Resources
                                                        System:   BIGBLUE
Type options, press Enter.
  5=Work with configuration descriptions   7=Display resource detail

Opt  Resource        Type  Status              Text
__   CMB01           9164  Operational         Combined function IOP
__     LIN01         2721  Operational         Comm Adapter
__       CMN01       2721  Operational         V.24 Port
__   CMB02           2809  Operational         MFIO Processor
__     LIN02         2721  Operational         Comm Adapter
__       CMN02       2721  Operational         Comm Port
__       CMN03       2721  Operational         Comm Port
__     LIN03         2838  Operational         LAN Adapter
__       CMN04       2838  Operational         Ethernet Port




                                                                   Bottom
F3=Exit   F5=Refresh   F6=Print   F12=Cancel
```

Figure 7-12: Work with all communications hardware resources.

This command also displays the current status of each feature type specified on the command. Along with documenting what's on the system, this command can be used in an emergency to scan the status of all devices of a certain type. For example, if the network is down, this command will quickly display the statuses of all communication devices, from the workstations themselves, to the network devices (like gateways and routers), to the communication controller within the AS/400.

From these commands, WRKHDRPRD and WRKHDWRSC, the operator can change the hardware configuration—a very powerful activity. As a result, in practice, most AS/400 shops restrict the use of the WRKHDWPRD and WRKHDWRSC commands to the system operator. The general user, even the programmers, don't get to use them. The general command, Display Hardware Resources (DSPHDWRSC), is often not restricted, and it's the one non-operations people can use. But with it, hardware resources can only be displayed; their configuration cannot be altered. To use this command, type DSPHDWRSC on any command line and press F4. See Figure 7-13.

```
                 Display Hardware Resources (DSPHDWRSC)

Type choices, press Enter.

Type . . . . . . . . . . . . . . > *AHW     *AHW, *CMN, *CSA, *LAN...
Output . . . . . . . . . . . . .   *______  *, *PRINT, *OUTFILE




                                                                  Bottom
F3=Exit F4=Prompt F5=Refresh F12=Cancel F13=How to use this display
F24=More keys
```

Figure 7-13: DSPHDWRSC command.

Like the other commands, this one asks what hardware resource type to display. Unlike the others, this one has one for all hardware or *AHW. If we took that option from the screen shown in Figure 7-13, we would get a screen similar to the one shown in Figure 7-14.

```
                      Display All Hardware Resources
                                                       System:   BIGBLUE
Type options, press Enter.
  7=Display resource detail

Opt  Resource        Type-Model  Status             Text
___  CEC01            9406-S20   Operational        Main Card Enclosure
___  PN01             2468-001   Operational        System Control Panel
___  MP01             2161-000   Operational        System Processor Card
___  SP01             9164-001   Operational        Service Processor Card
___  BCC01                       Operational        Bus Extender
___  MS01              3002-000  Operational        Next Level Main Storage
___  MS02              3002-000  Operational        Next Level Main Storage
___  MS03              3002-000  Operational        Next Level Main Storage
___  MS04              3002-000  Operational        Next Level Main Storage
___  MS05              3002-000  Operational        Next Level Main Storage
___  MS06              3002-000  Operational        Next Level Main Storage
___  CMB01             9164-001  Operational        Combined function IOP
___  LIN01             2721-001  Operational        Comm Adapter
___  CMN01             2721-001  Operational        V.24 Port
___  CMB02             2809-001  Operational        MFIO Processor
                                                                 More...
F3=Exit    F5=Refresh    F6=Print    F12=Cancel
```

*Figure 7-14: DSPHDWRSC *AHW screen.*

With these tools, the system operator can easily document the hardware on an AS/400 and make changes to the hardware configuration. It is a good idea to keep a hard copy of the hardware configuration of every AS/400 in the shop. Also, if the shop should ever order hardware from a vendor unfamiliar with the current installation, the vendor will often ask for such a list.

DASD AND USER AUXILIARY STORAGE POOLS

When new AS/400 DASD is purchased, someone from the supplying company usually comes out to install it. A problem comes in with the definition of "install." Some installers work with the customer and do not leave until the DASD is in and the AS/400 is up and ready to use. More and more frequently, installers are cutting corners and only installing DASD physically, leaving a lot of work up to the customer. Left in this state, the new DASD is said to be *unconfigured*. Another more precise way to describe the situation is the DASD is configured but not assigned.

If the DASD is to be left in any condition other than up and running, the system operator has to finish the job. Refer to the IBM manual *OS/400 Backup and Recovery V4R3, Procedures for Configuring Disks and Disk Protection* for detailed information.

Having to do the configuration can be seen as an opportunity when it allows the operator to configure the DASD into a particular or *Auxiliary Storage Pool* (*ASP*). To understand ASPs, let us review how the AS/400 stores data on DASD.

The AS/400 stores data and programs on disk with a process called *data striping*. This is one of the benefits of the AS/400's single-level store architecture. With data striping, the customer does not allocate files to specific disk volumes. Actually, the customer is not even aware of disk volumes. When the system writes to a file, it finds the least-used disk volume and writes it there. Therefore, pieces of any file are located all over the system. The benefits of striping are:

- All volumes are always balanced, with no effort from the customer.
- Read/write activities automatically make use of multiple arms, resulting in faster throughput.

The disadvantages of data striping are:

- If a disk drive is lost, the whole system is lost. The customer must have adequate backup.
- The objects from some tasks, such as keeping a journal or saving, would perform better if they could be dedicated to specific disk volumes.

User auxiliary storage pools (ASPs) rectify these disadvantages. An ASP is a way to assign physical drives for specific applications or functions. Typically, specific objects are stored in specific ASPs. ASPs are not for those new to the AS/400 who are fond of dedicating every volume to a specific set of files.

ASPs reduce the impact to the system due to a single drive failure. If one drive that is part of an ASP fails, the system operator only has to worry about restoring the libraries and objects stored in that ASP. The rest of the system would be untouched. Like we said, customers new to the AS/400 can misuse ASPs. Try to limit ASPs to these situations:

- An ASP dedicated to save files (type *SAVF).
  - Backups can be done faster to a save file than to tape, and an ASP dedicated to this minimizes the time a library is held up during backups.

- An ASP could be designated to hold only journals and receivers. There are two advantages to this:
    - Performance improves on a machine using journaling heavily because the journaling DASD operations are always assured of dedicated read/write arms and heads.
    - Backups are more efficient. Typically, journal receivers and library data are saved to tape in separate times and operations. By keeping journaling physically out of the data library, this function is easier to manage.
- A *user ASP* to ensure user objects are separate from system objects (that are held in a *system ASP*).

ASPs are created only after a manual IPL using the *Dedicated Service Tools* (*DST*). Also, ASPs are usually created with a lot of thought given to the physical hardware.

There are three types of ASPs:

1. ASP 1 is always referred to as the system ASP. The system creates this automatically whenever it IPLs. All configured disk drives that are not otherwise assigned to an ASP are placed in ASP 1.

2. ASPs 2 through 16. These are called user ASPs and they come in two types:
    a. Library-user ASPs.
    b. Non-library-user ASPs.

Create ASPs through the DST at IPL time. If the first thing moved into a new ASP is a library, then the system designates that as a library user ASP. If the first thing moved into the ASP is a journal, journal receiver, or save file, then the ASP is designated a non-library-user ASP.

CONTROLLING ASPS

Never let an ASP fill up. If it does, the recovery is rough and can't be accomplished without some serious downtime. When an ASP fills up, it is marked as "damaged" by the system. It also overflows. When a nonsystem ASP fills up, it overflows into the system ASP. If the system ASP overflows, the system goes down.

To recover after either ASP overflow, the AS/400 must be IPLed (refer to chapter 8, Starting and Stopping the AS/400) then the excess objects that caused the ASP to overflow must be removed. It must then be re-IPLed again to get it right. These activities constitute hours of the AS/400 being "down" to users—a situation unacceptable in most organizations. Three are two areas to protect an ASP from overflowing:

- Set a threshold, a percentage, that when the ASP level exceeds that percentage, the system will send a system operator message every hour until the condition is fixed (objects removed from the ASP).
- Two system values, QSTGLOWLMT and QSTGLOWACN, tell the system how to actively monitor the system ASP. QSTGLOWLMT sets the limit above which an ASP cannot fill. QSTGLOWACN describes the action the system should take when this limit is reached. These are explained below.

SETTING ASP THRESHOLDS

Set ASP thresholds through either the *System Service Tools (SST)* or DST. While both are similar, only DST can be started by performing a manual IPL (refer to chapter 8). When the system menu comes up, select option 3 (Use Dedicated Service Tools) and take the menu options from there.

To start SST, simply type the command STRSST on any command line. Figure 7-15 contains a sample of the SST screen.

```
                         System Service Tools (SST)

 Select one of the following:

      1. Start a service tool
      2. Work with active service tools
      3. Work with disk units
      4. Work with diskette data recovery







 Selection
      _

 F3=Exit          F10=Command entry          F12=Cancel
```

Figure 7-15: Main screen of the STRSST command.

From this screen, select option 3 (Work with Disk Units). Figure 7-16 contains a sample of the resulting screen.

```
                              Work with Disk Units

 Select one of the following:

      1. Display disk configuration
      2. Work with disk configuration
      3. Work with disk unit recovery







 Selection
      _

 F3=Exit          F12=Cancel
```

Figure 7-16: Work with Disk Units screen from SST.

From that screen, select option 2 (Work with Disk Configuration). Figure 7-17 contains a sample of the resulting screen.

```
                         Work with Disk Configuration

Select one of the following:

     1. Display disk configuration
     2. Add units to ASPs
     3. Work with ASP threshold
     4. Include unit in device parity protection
     5. Enable remote load source mirroring
     6. Disable remote load source mirroring
     7. Start compression on non-configured units






Selection
    _

F3=Exit          F12=Cancel
```

Figure 7-17: Work with Disk Configuration screen from SST.

Finally, select option 3 (Work with ASP Threshold). The resulting screen will be similar to the one shown in Figure 7-18.

```
                       Select ASP to Change Threshold

Type option, press Enter.
  1=Select

                                       --Protected--  --Unprotected-
Option  ASP  Threshold  Overflow          Size  %Used         Size  %Used
   1     1        90%   No               29360 15.31%            0  0.00%









F3=Exit          F12=Cancel
```

Figure 7-18: Display of the ASPs and their thresholds (all ASPs will display).

To change the threshold percentage, enter 1 on the selection line to the left of the desired ASP. Press Enter and the system will display a screen similar to the one shown in Figure 7-19.

```
                         Change Storage Threshold

                        --Protected--  --Unprotected-
ASP  Threshold  Overflow      Size  %Used       Size  %Used
  1       90%   No           29360 15.31%          0  0.00%

This is a mirrored ASP.  The threshold represents the amount
of protected storage used before an attention message is sent
to the system operator.

Type choice, press Enter.

  New threshold . . . . . . . .   ______  1-100





F3=Exit   F11=Display disk configuration status   F12=Cancel
```

Figure 7-19: Screen to change the ASP threshold.

Just enter the desired new threshold percentage and press Enter.

Making System ASP Proactive

Thresholds only issue warnings. To really protect a system, use the two system values we mentioned previously.

QSTGLOWLMT—Sets the system ASP limit. This has nothing to do with the threshold. The threshold is normally set at 90 percent and this value to 95. If the operator does not respond quickly enough to the first message, the system will kick in at 95 percent.

QSTGLOWACN—Tells the AS/400 what action to take when the percentage specified in QSTGLOWLMT is reached. Possible values are:

- *MSG—The system sends message CPI099C to the QSYSMSG and QSYSOPR message queues. (It sends this anyway when any of the other options are chosen.)
- *CRITMSG—Sends the message CPI099B to the user specified to receive critical messages.
- *REGFAC—The system calls the program registered for the QIBM_QWC_QSTGLOWACN exit point.
- *ENDSYS—The system comes to a restricted state.
- *PWRDWNSYS—The system is powered down immediately and restarts.

  *PWRDWNSYS may seem like the same action that is taken when the system has no protection, but there is a big difference. It is better to power down the system before the system ASP gets labeled as damaged. Recovery is easier. Many times ASPs fill up due to runaway programs. In these cases, either *ENDSYS or *PWRDWNSYS will stop the offending program and the operator will have a chance to identify the program and alert the developers before allowing it to start again.

Creating User ASPs

There are many ways to create or change ASPs, and we will not go into them here. For more information, refer to the *OS/400 Backup and Recovery V4R3*, *Procedures for Configuring Disks and Disk Protection*, and *Working with Auxiliary Storage Pools* for more information.

The problem is, there are different steps to go through for setting up ASPs on a new AS/400, adding new disk units to existing ASPs, moving disk units from one ASP to another, or removing disk units.

To create a new ASP, refer to the section in the manual mentioned above regarding adding disk units to an ASP. Do not create ASPs directly. When disk units are added to an ASP that doesn't exist, the system creates the ASP for you. In general, do this:

- Have a plan.
- Know the disk units currently on the system. Use the WRKHDWRSC *STG command to get this.
- Have a current system backup.
- When adding new disks, know if they are configured or not. If not, there will be some extra steps to go through. Nonconfigured disk units are not recognized by the system.

Use SST or DST to do the ASP work. Although SST is easier to start, both require an IPL anyway. For this reason, we prefer just to IPL the system and use DST.

Other ASP Considerations

Not every type of object can exist in a user ASP. The *OS/400Backup and Recovery V4R2*, section 4, has a list of object types that are not allowed in a user ASP.

Be especially careful of ASPs used for journals/journal receivers. They are most apt to overflow unexpectedly. User ASPs cause developers headaches in two areas.

- Dependent database files cannot exist across ASPs. Therefore, all logical files that belong to a physical file must reside in the same ASP as the physical file.
- Objects cannot be moved (MOVOBJ) or duplicated (CRTDUPOBJ) across ASPs.

A disk drive on the AS/400 can actually have several storage devices within one physical unit. When creating an ASP to enhance recovery, include all the devices within each unit as part of the ASP.

LAB #7: MANAGING DEVICES

Upon completion of this lab, you should be able to:

- Demonstrate the ability to display the AS/400 hardware configuration.
- Use commands to manage and display device configuration.
- Navigate communication resources.

- Navigate local workstation resources.
- Navigate memory and storage devices.
- Explore system values related to hardware.

EXPLORE YOUR AS/400 HARDWARE

This exercise is designed to familiarize you with the commands necessary to work with AS/400 hardware, software, and devices.

SYSTEM CONFIGURATION

Now is the time to explore the AS/400 at your facility. You may find that you have some restrictions on what access you have. Often, you can find a lot about your system using display commands.

- Enter CALL QCMD on the command line.
- Press Enter.
- Press F10 (Include Detailed Messages).
- Enter GO CMDHDW to go to the Hardware Command menu.
- Press Enter.
- Enter 1 (Hardware Resource Commands) on the command line.
- Press Enter.
- Enter 1 (Display Hardware Resources) on the command line.
- Press Enter.
- Enter *AHW for the TYPE parameter.
- Write the complete command just entered. ______________________________

  ____
- Press Enter.
- Enter WRKHDWRSC on the command line.
- Press F4.
- Enter *PRC for the TYPE parameter.
- Press Enter.
- What is the total amount of memory?

  ____

This screen shows you the component parts of the AS/400 at your site. Page through the screens and review the available options. Use the information you found to answer the following questions. As systems vary from site to site and if you cannot find some of the information below, check with your instructor.

- What is the total amount of memory? ______________________________
- What is the model and type of the tape drive? ______________________________

____

- What is the description of CTL01? ______________________________
- Does your system have a CD drive? (*Hint*: This will appear under another name.)

____

- What is the resource name for the CD drive? ______________________________
- Press F12 (Cancel).

You should be back at the `Hardware Resource Commands menu`. Option 3 (Work with Hardware Resources) on the menu allows you to explore the internal components and how devices connect to the AS/400.

- What is the object name of the `Hardware Resource Commands` menu?

____

- Enter 3 (`Work with Hardware Resources`) on the command line.
- Press Enter.
- What is the command to get to this screen directly? ______________________________

____

- What resources are available from the parameter values? Complete the chart below:

Complete the chart shown in Figure L7-1 with the type of resources available on your AS/400.

Type	Description
*CMN	
*CSA	
*LAN	
*LWS	
*PRC	
*STG	

Figure L7-1: Fill in the type of resources available on your AS/400.

COMMUNICATION RESOURCES

- What is the command to go directly to the above screen? ________________

  ____

- Place *CMN in the TYPE parameter.
- Press F11 (Keywords).
- What changes about the display? ______________________________

  ____

- Press Enter.
- How many communication controllers (Processors or IOP) are there? ______
- ____
- Do you have a Token-Ring or Ethernet Port?____________________
- Which controller and line handles the Ethernet or Token-Ring communications?

  ____

- Press F12.

LOCAL WORKSTATION RESOURCES

Now that you have explored the communication lines and controllers, we will move on to look at the Local Workstation resources.

- Enter DSPHDWRSC on the command line.
- Press F4 (Prompt).
- Enter the Local Workstation value for the TYPE parameter.
- What are the resource names of the Workstation Controllers?

  ____

- There may be more than one controller.
- Place 5 (Display Controller Descriptions) to the left of CTL01.
- Press Enter.
- Place 8 (Work with Configuration Status) to the left of CTL01.
- Press Enter.
- What is the name (description) and status of the device(s)? _______________

  ____

- Press F12.

- Place 9 (Display Associated Descriptions) to the left of CTL01.
- Press Enter.
- What is the name (description) and text of the device(s) attached to CTL01?

  ____
- Press F12.
- Using the above procedure, what is the name (description), text, and status of the devices attached to QCTL? ______________________________

  ____

MEMORY AND STORAGE DEVICES

Let us continue looking at your AS/400's hardware. Next, you will explore the memory and DASD on the system. In this section, the printout that you create will not contain your user ID. In light of this, you should view the spool file prior to printing. This will assist you in identifying your output.

- Enter DSPHDWRSC on the command line.
- Press F4 (Prompt).
- Enter *PRC for the TYPE parameter.
- Enter *PRINT for the OUTPUT parameter.
- Press Enter.
- What type of information is displayed? ______________________

  ____
- If the information is available, how much memory is there on this AS/400? ____

  ____
- Retrieve a copy of the Processor Resources List produced above.
- Attach the printout to your submission form for this lab.
- Label it as printout #1.
- Using the procedures above, what type of information is displayed if the TYPE field is *STG? ______________________________________

  ____
- How many disk drives does your AS/400 have? ________________
- What is the resource name of your tape drive? ________________
- What is the resource name of your CD drive? ________________

DEVICE CONNECTIONS

When configuring a device, you need to create a device description. You will need to have an address for the device that you will be connecting to the AS/400. Devices on AS/400s are always attached to a controller. More to the point, it is connected to a port on a controller. Now let us look at the controller CTL01 and see what devices are attached and what ports are available.

- Enter the command to go to the `Command Hardware Resources` (CMDHDWRSC) menu.
- Press Enter.
- Select the option to `Print Device Addresses`.
- Press Enter.
- Enter CTL01 for the Controller Description parameter.
- Press Enter.
- Print and retrieve the printout you just produced from your spool files. (*Note*: Your user ID will not appear on this printout. You should view it prior to printing.)
- Attach the printout to your submission form for this lab.
- Label it as printout #2.

Now that you have retrieved the CTL01 controller address grid, use it to answer the following questions.

- How many ports exist on the controller? ______________________________
- How many switch settings are available? ______________________________

Device addresses consist of the name of the controller, port, and switch setting. For example, a device on controller CTL01, port 3, and switch 5 would have the following address: CTL010305.

- Review the devices on the grid.
- What is the address of either the Console (DSP01) or Printer (PRT01)?

  ____

HARDWARE AND DEVICE SYSTEM VALUES

System values are used to define the basic environment on your AS/400. Let's see how the AS/400 at your site has been defined by looking at several system values.

- Enter the DSPSYSVAL command on the command line.
- Press F4 (Prompt).
- Complete the chart of system values (shown in Figure L7-2).

System Value	Values on your AS/400
QAUTOCFG	
QTSEPOOL	
QDEVNAMING	
QTOTJOB	
QUSRLIBL	
QIPLTYPE	

Figure L7-2: Fill in the system values on your AS/400.

MANAGING DEVICES

We have been describing a lot of the internal hardware on your AS/400. It's now time to switch to explore the external hardware. You could consider external hardware pieces that are attached to your AS/400. They are often referred to as devices. This might be a bit confusing, as we have been viewing some devices in the previous sections. Before a device becomes known to the AS/400, a device description must be defined. While the device menu organizes device tasks, it can be cumbersome when you want to work with a specific device. So you can use the WRKCFGSTS command directly.

- Enter WRKCFGSTS on the command line.
- Press F4 (Prompt).
- Complete the screen as shown in Figure L7-3.

```
                  Work with Configuration Status (WRKCFGSTS)

Type choices, press Enter.
 Type . . . . . . . . . . . . . . > *DEV          *NWS, *NWI, *LIN, *CTL, *DEV
 Configuration description  . . . > *ALL          Name, generic*, *ALL, *CMN...
 Output . . . . . . . . . . . . .   *             *, *PRINT
```

Figure L7-3: Work with Configuration Status screen to display all the devices on this AS/400.

- Press Enter.

From here you can manage virtually all aspects of a device. Take a look at this command's available information. Start exploring:

- Move the cursor to the Status column.
- Press the F1 (Help).
- Read through the status help.

- What does "Vary on Pending" mean? ______________________________

  ____

- Examine the following devices and determine their status.

Device Description	Status
DSP01	
ETHLITCP	
OPT01	
QCONSOLE	
QPADEV0001	
QPADEV0015	
QPADEV0045	
PRT01	
TAP01	
QQAHOST	
QTIDA	

Figure L7-4: Fill in the status for the device descriptions.

- If you want to make a device unavailable for use, what option would you use?

  ____

- Print the device description of one of the devices in the chart above.
- Attach the printout to your submission form for this lab.
- Label it as printout #3.

ADDITIONAL LAB ASSIGNMENTS

Now try your skills at working with internal and external hardware.

1. Issue the command WRKCFGSTS.
   a. What is the device name and type of your current workstation?
   b. How many workstations are active at this time?
   c. How many workstations of the type you are using are defined to the system?
   d. Use the help function to explore the possible status for devices.
      i. What does RCYPND mean?
      ii. List six of the most common statuses.
   e. What is the complete command to vary off the tape drive?

2. You need to add a new system printer to your AS/400 and have its device description created automatically. What system value would you change and what value would you set it to?

3. If you were using AS/400 standard (native) naming conventions, what are the prefixes for the following types of devices: printer, tape drives, and CD drives?

4. What types of functions are available on the Device menu? What would be some reasons to use this menu?

5. If you wanted to check the status of various devices easily from a menu, what menu would you use? (*Hint*: Menu name begins with a "D.")

6. Vary off your display.

   a. What is the message you receive?

   b. Point at the message and press F1. Why did you get the message?

   c. How could you vary off a display with an active job?

END-OF-CHAPTER AIDS

CHAPTER SUMMARY

Although the material in this chapter might seem rather basic, two things are important: One is that you know what a device is and how broad the definition spreads. Two, depending on your position as an AS/400 operator, most of your work might well be centered around working with devices, getting them up, and keeping them up. Other than a limited amount of physical activity (turning on devices, changing paper and tapes, for example), most of the work is done from a workstation using the techniques outlined in this chapter.

KEY TERMS

address
autoconfig
automatic configuration
Auxiliary Storage Pool (ASP)
communication controller
configuring
controller
data striping
Dedicated Service Tools (DST)
device
device description
device statuses
Direct Access Storage Device (DASD)
external hardware
internal hardware
item description
line
manual configuration
reset
system ASP
System Service Tools (SST)
unconfigured
user ASP
vary

CHAPTER SELF-TEST

Solutions to these self-test questions are in appendix D.

True-False Questions

___ 1. After you change a device description, you must IPL the system for the changes to take effect.

___ 2. To produce a printed copy of information available on a screen, you change the output field from * to *PRINT.

___ 3. A device whose status is varied on pending is powered on and ready for use.

___ 4. An ASP that is overfilled is marked by the system as damaged.

___ 5. There are no steps that can be taken to keep an ASP from overflowing or overfilling except just being careful and doing cleanup.

___ 6. QDEVNAMING is only referenced when automatic configuration is enabled.

___ 7. To determine if a workstation is available for use, you would enter WRKCFGSTS *DEV on the command line.

Fill in the Blanks

1. A device is defined to the system through its ______________________ ___________________.
2. To display devices that are active, the command would be WRKCFGSTS CFGTYPE(*DEV) CFGD(*ALL) STATUS(_________________).
3. To assign a physical drive for a specific use is known as a(n) ______________.
4. To determine if automatic configuration is enabled, you would check the __________________ system value.
5. The following ____________ and _________ commands cannot be used across ASPs.
6. To manually create a device configuration for a new printer, you would use the ___________________ command.

Chapter Review Questions

1. Define the following terms:
   a. ASP.
   b. Data striping.
   c. Device description.
   d. Internal hardware.
   e. External hardware.
2. What are the advantages and disadvantages of using automatic configuration?
3. What are the advantages and disadvantages of data striping?
4. Give an example of when it would be a good idea to have an ASP.
5. What are the three most common statuses for a device, and what do they mean?

8

STARTING AND STOPPING THE AS/400

CHAPTER OBJECTIVES

Upon completion of this chapter, you should be able to:

- Explain what IPL means and what happens during an IPL.
- Describe the different approaches used to IPL the system.
- Describe the system values important to IPLs.
- Demonstrate how to change the startup program and explain how it can be used.
- Explain how to stop and start subsystems.
- Explain how to power down the system.
- Explain how to set up the automatic power schedule.

OVERVIEW

Starting an AS/400 is referred to as *IPLing*. The abbreviation comes from the term *initial program load* (*IPL*). This is similar to booting a PC except that an IPL does many more tasks, so it takes a lot more time and is done less frequently.

Many of these tasks concern system housekeeping. Without a periodic IPL to clean things up, any AS/400 will start to experience degraded performance after a few weeks (sooner if it is heavily loaded). So AS/400s need to be IPLed periodically for their general health. When the IPL is finished, the sign-on display is shown on the console.

WHAT AN IPL DOES

An AS/400 IPL does more than start the operating system. Additionally, it:

- Resets disk storage. This results in increasing available disk storage.
- Recognizes new licensed program products.
- Optionally applies delayed *Program Temporary Fixes* (*PTF*s).
- Recognizes some changes in system values.
- Returns unused addresses to the system.

WHEN TO IPL

In general, the AS/400 runs 24 hours per day, seven days per week. IPLs should be scheduled at least monthly but weekly is best. This schedule will keep performance healthy. Other than these planned IPLs, also do so:

- After a *power failure* or any *abnormal end* (abnormal shut down).
- After installing delayed PTFs at the direction of the PTF installation instructions.
- After installing a new *licensed program product* (*LPP*) from IBM.
- When there is a problem with the system—at IBM support's direction.
- The ADDRESSES USED reaches 90 percent.
- The SYSTEM AUXILIARY STORAGE reaches 95 percent.

Think of the IPL as one half of a pair of operations—power down, power up/IPL. The IPL cannot be separated from powering up. Ideally, the system is powered down in an orderly manner and later (or instantly) powered back up again. This is normal and the IPL does not take that much time.

Anytime an AS/400 IPLs after it has gone down from a power failure or any abnormal end, the IPL will take a long time. That may sound logical enough; after all, most computers take longer to come up after they have ended improperly. The trick with the AS/400 is in the definition of abnormal end—it may not be something as obvious as pulling the plug.

Occasionally, a program will have a bug (or the data will be bad), and the only way the operator can end it is with the command End Job Abnormally (ENDJOBABN). That command ends a stubborn job but also sends a flag that indicates the AS/400 to be in an abnormal state. The next IPL, even if it is days or weeks later and even if it follows a normal shutdown, will take a long time. For this reason, many AS/400 shops have two absolute rules:

- End jobs with the ENDJOBABN only when nothing else works.
- After ENDJOBABN is used, schedule an extra IPL as soon as possible to clear the abnormal indication.

ADDRESSES USED is also mentioned above. Addresses are not a concept unique to the AS/400, but how they are treated is unique.

As an overview on the subject, any object a computer creates has a unique address. A program sitting out on disk has an address, but programs are not run directly from disk, they are loaded into memory and executed there. When a program moves from its disk address into a memory location, a copy of it is made and that copy has its own address. When the program ends, the operating system deletes the memory copy of it. What happens to the address? In all non-AS/400 computers, the address is made available for reuse by the system. In AS/400s, it is marked as "used" and cannot be reused by the system.

Reusing old addresses has caused internal problems in computers for years, not the least of which are security issues. As a result, complex algorithms have been developed to help deal with a problem that really does not go away. AS/400s deal with the problem by not reusing old addresses. The downside to this is that there are only a finite set of possible addresses (determined by the word-length of the computer) available, and any operating system can generate millions of addresses in a day. So the AS/400 can end up without any available addresses. IBM deals with the problem by having the IPL regenerate addresses across the system. During an IPL, every object on the AS/400 is re-addressed and the system comes up with no used addresses. Other than the inconvenience of mandatory periodic IPLs, this system has resulted in fewer overall problems than any other address-handling method.

When the ADDRESSES USED approaches 90 percent, plan an IPL within 24 hours. When this value reaches 90 percent and above, the operator will receive periodic warning messages from the system.

A similar situation is encountered when the amount of *system auxiliary storage* (read that as disk space) used becomes excessive. The system uses some of your disk space normally to do its work. An IPL recovers these system temporary libraries and *work control blocks*. The effect of IPLing on available disk space is not nearly as dramatic as the result of IPLing to reclaim addresses. Usually the system only returns 5–10 percent. Too full disks are almost always due to something the customer is doing, not the system. So combine the IPL with a serious effort to clean up customer data.

Both the ADDRESSES USED and the SYSTEM AUXILIARY STORAGE can be quickly checked with the Work with System Status (WRKSYSSTS) command. Figure 8-1 contains a sample of that command.

```
                          Work with System Status                       BIGBLUE
                                                    05/01/99  23:28:51
 % CPU used . . . . . . :          1.3  Auxiliary storage:
 Elapsed time . . . . . :     00:00:01    System ASP . . . . . . :       29.36 G
 Jobs in system . . . . :          807    % system ASP used  . . :       15.8592
 % addresses used:                        Total  . . . . . . . . :       29.36 G
   Permanent  . . . . . :         .007  Current unprotect used  :         354 M
   Temporary  . . . . . :         .013  Maximum unprotect  . .  :         624 M

 Type changes (if allowed), press Enter.

 System     Pool   Reserved    Max   ---DB---   --Non-DB--
  Pool   Size (K)  Size (K)  Active  Fault  Pages  Fault  Pages
    1      80108     46904    +++++     .0     .0     .0     .0
    2     666748         0       68     .0     .0     .0     .0
    3        256         0        2     .0     .0     .0     .0
    4      39320         0       26     .0     .0    4.4    4.4

                                                                    Bottom
 Command
 ===>___________________________________________________________________________
 F3=Exit   F4=Prompt             F5=Refresh   F9=Retrieve    F10=Restart
 F11=Display transition data   F12=Cancel   F24=More keys
```

Figure 8-1: Sample of WRKSYSSTS command.

Note that the permanent and temporary address percentages are shown as the fourth and fifth items in the upper-left column. When we said that should not exceed 90 percent, we meant these two percentages totaled should not exceed 90 percent.

The SYSTEM AUXILIARY STORAGE is shown as an absolute number and as a percentage on the top two fields of the right column. This is the percentage that should not be allowed to get above 95 percent.

The solution to both of these situations is to re-IPL as soon as possible. However, like we mentioned above, SYSTEM AUXILIARY STORAGE may not come down that much. If it does not, the problem is with your shop, not the system. When an operator encounters this, he or she should alert someone that additional DASD needs to be purchased. In the meantime, the system needs some adjustments. Here are some things an operator can do:

- Check system libraries (the ones that start with the letter Q, like QSYS) for user libraries or files. Move or archive/delete those libraries/files.
- Check for unnecessary user libraries/files that can be archived/deleted. Some examples would be:
  - Obsolete libraries used for vendor demos, training, or testing.
  - Programmers' personal libraries.
  - Various system logs.
  - Large audit files.
- There should be a minimum of two ASPs on any AS/400, named ASP 1 and ASP 2. ASP 1 should contain only system objects; make sure that it does not contain user objects.

The real life of most AS/400 shops is that their computers are often on the cusp of being overloaded. Do not be surprised that addresses are over 90 percent too often—a model upgrade will take care of that. Also, SYSTEM AUXILIARY STORAGE chronically hovering around 93 percent may be "normal"—additional DASD will take care of that. But budget money to upgrade the computer does not grow on trees. At-capacity AS/400s often keep the system operator fairly busy cleaning old objects and IPLing quite often, even daily.

CONTROL PANEL

In every discussion of AS/400 IPLing, there are two items that many people confuse: *control panel* and *control console*. The control panel is the area on the front of every AS/400, old and new. This panel differs slightly from model to model but, in general, has some common components:

- An LCD screen to display information. This screen can be used to:
  - View statuses of the system.
  - Assist in problem analysis.
  - Make IPL function/mode selections.
  - Display stages of an IPL.
- A slot for a physical key or key stick (a plastic device with an embedded chip, used as a key).
- Selection dial or buttons.
- Power on/off button (rarely used).

A control console is a workstation direct-connected to the first port of the first controller. Optionally, another workstation can be designated as the secondary console.

An IPL is technically "complete" when a sign-on screen is presented on the control console. The AS/400 has a system value, QSTRUPPGM, where an initial program can be named to run. That is, a nonsystem program that does some other initial tasks. This program is automatically invoked by the system when the IPL is "complete." The typical use of this program is to start all subsystems, which indirectly starts all workstations, communications lines, and printers.

The AS/400 is a platform that encompasses a wide range of hardware options. There are multiple models available for each system type. In fact, IBM has been announcing new models in the AS/400 product line at a rigorous pace. We will show two "typical" control panels in Figures 8-2 and 8-3, but keep in mind that your AS/400 may differ. More information about the current control panels can be found on the Internet at:

```
http://publib.boulder.ibm.com/pubs/html/as400/online/v4r4eng.htm
```

and in the manual: *AS/400 Basic System Operation, Administration, and Problem Handling V4R4,* SC41-5206-03. This can be found by the following book path:

```
/home/publib/epubs/book/QB3AG003.BOO
```

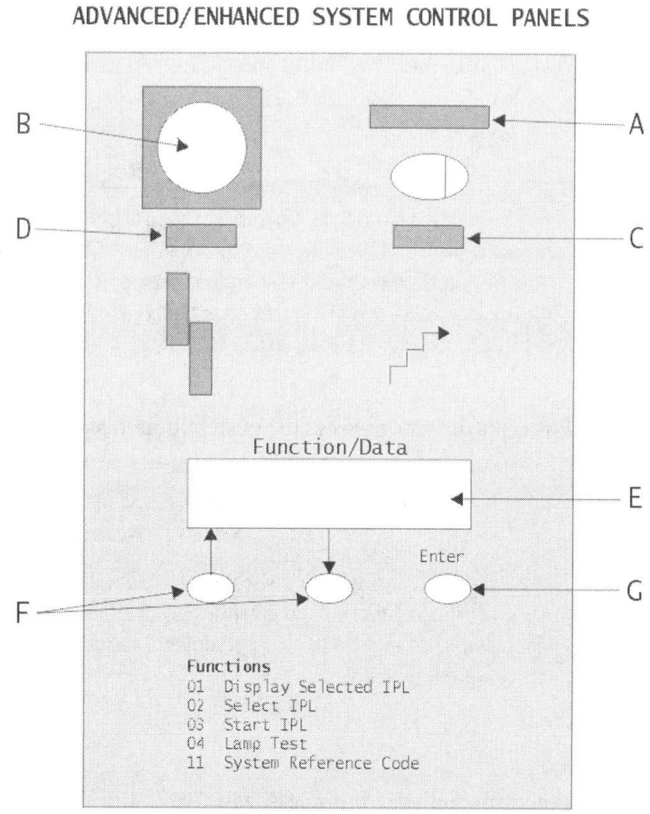

Figure 8-2: 9402 Model 2xx control panel.

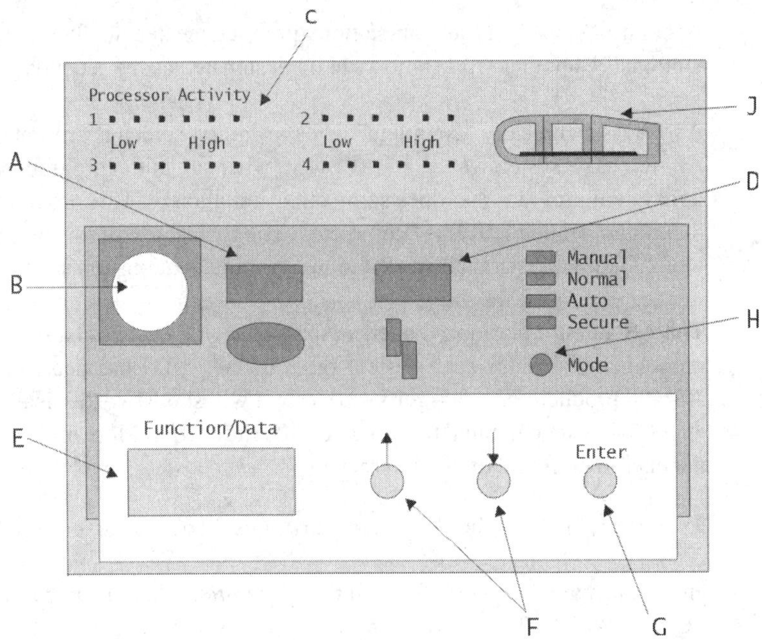

Figure 8-3: 9404 Model 4xx control panel.

CONTROL PANEL AREAS

A. Power On Light: This light comes on when there is power to the system unit.

> **Note:**
>
> The Power On Light blinks when the system is being started up and when the system is manually turned off. Another way to power down the system is to use the Power Down System (PWRDWNSYS) command or the options on the Power On and Off Tasks (POWER) menu. In these cases, the Power On Light does not blink.

B. Power Push Button: Press the push button to start the system.

> **Note:**
>
> Most of the time, forget this switch exists. You will be cycling (turning it off then on) the AS/400 primarily through commands. Never use this button to power off an AS/400 unless instructed to do so by a service person, and only use it to power on when the AS/400 is sitting in a powered-off state.

C. Processor Activity or Processor Active Light: The 9402/9404 Models 2xx and 4xx System Units have one Processor Active Light. This light comes on and blinks when programs are running. Some 9404/9406 Models 3xx and 5xx System Units have the Processor Activity Lights that provide a graphical display of the processor activity, and some have only one Processor Active Light.

D. System Attention Light: This light comes on when the system requires operator attention, such as correcting a severe system failure.

E. Function/Data Display: When one of the increment/decrement push buttons (F) is pressed, a function number appears in the Function/Data display. When the Enter push button (G) is pressed, the current function number is sent to the processing unit and it disappears. Only the function numbers that can be used in the present mode (H) are displayed, so function numbers may appear to be skipped. System Reference Codes (SRCs) and other information from the processing unit are also displayed in the Function/Data display.

F. Increment/Decrement: This is used to increase or decrease the number shown in the Function/Data display. The push button (Increment or Decrement) can also be used to change the data shown in the Function/Data display when selecting an IPL type.

G. Enter Push Button: This sends the function information shown in the Function display to the processing unit.

H. Mode: On most of the AS/400 system units, there are four modes available— Manual, Normal, Auto, and Secure. Continually press this button and the Mode light will move. To use this switch, the key or key stick must be inserted.

J. Electronic Key Stick: On the 9494/9406 Models 3xx and 5xx, the key stick contains a small circuit card that activates a control panel for use. *Note*: Many shops just leave this key stick in the panel—this should be considered physical security and its use thoroughly thought out.

Mode Positions (H)

There are four possible modes of IPLing the AS/400: Manual, Normal, Auto, and Secure. These are chosen from the control panel with the Mode switch. The modes and what they mean are:

1. Normal: The Normal mode is for day-to-day operations. This should be the default mode of the AS/400. In other words, whenever another mode IPL is performed, when it is finished, return the mode switch to Normal. The Normal mode allows the power to be manually turned on and the *automatic operations* enabled. Examples of automatic operations are starting the system from another system (called a *remote* IPL), an IPL scheduled by date and time, or an IPL after a power failure.

   To stop the system when the mode is set to Normal, use the Power Down System (PWRDWNSYS) command at any display station. The authority to do this is often limited to the system operations staff and security officer.

2. Manual: When the mode is set to Manual, the system allows manual IPLs (such as an operator-attended IPL from disk or tape), and manual control functions (such as select an IPL or display the kind of IPL that the system is set to run). However, automatic operations cannot be done.

3. Auto: The Auto (Automatic) mode allows an automatic operation, but it will not allow:

   - Starting the system by doing an IPL manually.

- Stopping the system by using the Power push button.
- Selecting a different IPL type by using the Increment/Decrement buttons.

4. Secure: The Secure mode locks the control panel on the system unit. The system can only be stopped from a display station by using the Power Down System (PWRDWNSYS) command.

A *normal IPL* is also referred to as an *automatic IPL* or *unattended IPL*. If the mode switch is in this position, the system will automatically IPL from DASD when the power is turned on.

A *manual IPL* is also referred to as a "manual" or *attended IPL*. After the power is turned on, the system will start the IPL from DASD or tape. During the IPL, the system shows menus and displays on the control console. Manual IPLs are normally done when you want to change IPL options, install the operating system, or use dedicated service tools.

For this to occur, QIPLTYPE is set to "1," and the mode is in the Manual position when the power is turned on. The attended IPL will bring a sign-on display up on the control console before it brings up the rest of the system. This is the system operator's opportunity to get in and make changes to the system before it gets all the way up.

Set the AS/400 to the desired IPL by changing the IPL mode on the AS/400 control panel.

To set the mode on a black (newer) AS/400, the key stick must be in the slot when the MODE switch (H) is pressed. Press it until a light illuminates next to the word MANUAL. On the gray (older) models, turn the key to the MANUAL position.

In addition to selecting the mode through the switch, a system value must be set to agree with the mode selection. System Value IPL Type (QIPLTYPE) must be set to "1" to do a manual IPL, "0" for a normal IPL. Use the Work with System Values (WRKSYSVAL) command to display and change this value.

Remember:

MANUAL = ATTENDED

NORMAL = UNATTENDED

TIP:

Make it standard practice to leave the mode in NORMAL and the System Value QIPLTYPE = 0.

IPL STORAGE AREAS

An IPL can be made from one of two system storage areas: the A side or the B side. This is an area that causes many AS/400 operations professionals' headaches, but it is really very simple.

A copy of the operating system is kept in each area. System storage area A is referred to as the *permanent storage area* or the "permanent side," while B is the *temporary storage area*. This whole issue is most relevant to PTFs (refer to chapter 9). PTFs can be installed temporarily or permanently to either side. When they are in side B, even "permanent" PTFs can be removed if a problem develops with one. The same PTFs installed in side A cannot be removed. Typically, instructions for installing PTFs are very specific about side A/side B.

There are two reasons for having storage areas A and B: One, the copy of OS/400 that is to receive a PTF cannot be running when the PTF is applied. Therefore, the storage areas give the capability of running on one version of the operating system, freeing the other for updates. The second reason is that the ability to apply PTFs temporarily gives a buffer where the PTFs can be tested and "proven" before they are permanently applied. With two storage areas, if a PTF proves to be a bad one, it can be easily removed without having to restore the system from a pre-PTF backup tape.

There is another "storage area" option when IPLing an AS/400, and that is storage area D. It is not really a storage area as much as it is a way to bring up an AS/400 from a copy of OS/400 located on a tape drive. Figure 8-4 summarizes the storage areas.

Storage Area	Description
*PANEL	Uses the storage area (A, B, or D) currently shown on the control panel.
A	Temporarily applies unapplied PTFs or removes specific previously temporarily applied PTFs.
B	Permanently applies previously temporarily applied PTFs.
D	System is started from a tape device.

Figure 8-4: Storage areas.

Normal operation is from the B side unless advised otherwise; even then, side A will be used only one time. To change the IPL storage area on the AS/400 control panel:

- Put the machine in Manual mode (with the key in the slot, press the `Mode` button).
- Select function `02` (with the Increment/Decrement button).
- Press the Enter button.
- Select storage area `A`, `B`, or `D` (with the Increment/Decrement button).
- Press the Enter button.
- Return the machine to the Normal mode (with the key in the slot, press the `Mode` button).

STOPPING THE AS/400

There are four ways of stopping, or powering off, the AS/400:

- Power failure.
- Unplugging the machine.
- Pressing the power switch on the control panel.
- Using the Power Down System (PWRDWNSYS) command.

While power failures do happen from time to time, hopefully, the AS/400 is protected with some sort of *uninterruptible power supply* (*UPS*). For obvious reasons, we do not like to see the first two methods happen. The third, using the power switch, is also not desirable. This method is used rarely when, for some reason, the machine has some sort of serious problem and will not come down otherwise.

That leaves us with the fourth method, the PWRDWNSYS command. This is the preferred method of stopping an AS/400.

This and other power commands are accessible through the Power menu. To access this, type:

```
GO POWER
```

on the command line and press Enter. For this discussion, we will focus on the commands.

Figure 8-5 shows a prompted version of the PWRDWNSYS command.

```
                         Power Down System (PWRDWNSYS)

Type choices, press Enter.

How to end . . . . . . . . . . .   *CNTRLD       *CNTRLD, *IMMED
Delay time, if *CNTRLD . . . . .   3600          Seconds, *NOLIMIT
Restart options:
  Restart after power down . . .   *NO           *NO, *YES
  Restart type . . . . . . . . .   ______        *IPLA, *SYS, *FULL
IPL source . . . . . . . . . . .   *PANEL        *PANEL, A, B, D




                                                                  Bottom
F3=Exit F4=Prompt F5=Refresh F10=Additional parameters F12=Cancel
F13=How to use this display        F24=More keys
```

Figure 8-5: Power Down System command screen.

Before this command takes effect, the system must be placed in what is known as a *restricted state*. That is, all subsystems except QSYS are ended. In order to end any subsystem, all programs running within it must be ended. So the bottom line is all programs must be ended and all users signed off before the AS/400 can be powered down. The PWRDWNSYS command ensures this happens.

The first parameter, HOW TO END, allows the choice of a controlled (*CNTRLD) or immediate (*IMMED) power down. Although the choice may seem obvious (controlled seems the more conservative approach), in practice, immediate is preferred.

When *CNTRLD is selected, the AS/400 waits for programs to finish normally before ending the subsystems they are in. The parameter delay time governs how long the system will wait. 3600 is one hour. At that time, the system will forcibly end programs still running. So *CNTRLD takes a long time and may end programs abnormally anyway. PWRDWNSYS with an immediate end is preferred because it happens right away. The responsibility this adds to the operator is that he or she, personally, must ensure that all programs are ended normally and all subsystems are ended.

Most shops end all batch programs and get the users to sign off manually. They do this with the Work with Active Jobs (WRKACTJOB) command to view active programs and users. The operator should have a sense of what jobs are important, which are not, as well as how long each will run before completing normally. Users are sent messages or phoned to ask them to sign off. In the case where a user has walked away from his workstation for the evening without signing off, the operator has to end the job. End jobs with option 4 on the WRKACTJOB screen, but press F4 before you press Enter. Override the *CNTRLD value with *IMMED on the screen, then press Enter.

When all programs within a subsystem are ended, the subsystem can be ended with the End Subsystem (ENDSBS) command. Figure 8-6 contains a sample of that command.

```
                        End Subsystem (ENDSBS)

Type choices, press Enter.

Subsystem . . . . . . . . . .   __________    Name, *ALL
How to end . . . . . . . . . .   *CNTRLD       *CNTRLD, *IMMED
Delay time, if *CNTRLD . . . . .   *NOLIMIT      Seconds, *NOLIMIT






                                                     Bottom
F3=Exit F4=Prompt F5=Refresh F10=Additional parameters F12=Cancel
F13=How to use this display       F24=More keys
```

Figure 8-6: Sample of the prompted version of the ENDSBS command.

With this command, name the subsystem to end (using the parameter *ALL causes all subsystems to end), then specify whether the subsystem should end controlled or immediate. This is similar to the choices for PWRDWNSYS and, for the same reasons, immediate (*IMMED) is preferred. This again puts the responsibility on the operator to properly end all programs running in each subsystem before invoking it.

When all subsystems except QSYS are ended, use the PWRDWNSYS command with the *IMMED option to turn the AS/400 off.

If the AS/400 absolutely must be turned off with the power switch, make sure tapes and diskettes are out of their drives and the Control Panel mode is set to Manual. Then press the power button. The control panel will give you a cryptic warning by displaying 0? To continue with the power down sequence, press the power button again. If you want to stop the power down, press any other button on the control console.

After pressing the power button the second time or after issuing the PWRDWNSYS command, the power light on the console will flash as the AS/400 powers down. When the power is off, the light will be off. If the light continues to flash for 30 minutes, the System Attention Light on the control panel will light. If that happens, you have a problem beyond the scope of this book. Call for service.

STARTING THE AS/400

How an AS/400 is started depends on a combination of how it went down and the condition of certain settings. If the AS/400 is to start automatically after it has been powered down, the following will have to be in place:

- System value QIPLTYPE must be set to "0" to allow an unattended IPL.
- If the system went down due to a power failure, system value QPWRRSTIPL must be set to "1." *Note*: A power failure is a true power failure or circuit failure; it is not that the system went down from pressing the power switch or issuing the PWRDWNSYS command
- The mode switch on the control panel must be set to NORMAL.

If an automatic IPL is expected and doesn't happen, one or more of these values is not set correctly. In that case, here is what the operator should do:

1. Turn on all power to displays, printers, tape, disks, and controllers.
2. Make sure the mode on the control panel is set to NORMAL.
3. Press the power button to turn the system ON.
4. Depending on the value in the system value QIPLTYPE, which cannot be seen before starting, the system will either:
    a. IPL. When done, the sign-on display will be shown (QIPLTYPE = 0).
    b. Display a menu for service called Dedicated Service Tools (DST) (QIPLTYPE = 1 or 2). Either work with DST functions or just exit out of the menu to continue the IPL, but someone must physically be present to do either.

Usually, we intentionally IPL the system. AS/400s do not have soft-boot commands—the only way to re-IPL one is to power it down then let it come back up. Here are the steps to perform a fully automatic IPL for an AS/400 that is running:

- Ensure that the mode switch is set to NORMAL.
- Ensure that system value QIPLTYPE is set to 0.
- Ensure you have either Security Officer (SECOFR) or Security Administrator (SECADM) authority in your user profile.
- End all jobs in all subsystems except QSYS.
- End all subsystems except QSYS.
- Enter the following command on the command line and press Enter:

```
PWRDWNSYS OPTION(*IMMED) RESTART(*YES  *IPLA)
```

Refer back to Figure 8-5 for a sample of the prompted version of this command. Previously, we were only interested in powering the machine off. Now we want it to come back up. There is a double parameter on this command (called RESTART) that provides you with some control in the restart. First, you can say *YES or *NO to the choice to restart the machine after it has powered down. Assuming you do want to restart, specify how a restart will occur. The choices are:

- *SYS. The AS/400 is restarted. Any attached hardware devices that can be restarted are done so only if there is a pending PTF that requires it.
- *FULL. The AS/400 and all restartable hardware devices are restarted.
- *IPLA. The Restart Type (*SYS or *FULL) is taken from the IPL Attributes table stored in the AS/400. The IPL Attributes provides the ability to change many of the IPL options without doing a manual IPL. This is accomplished through the use of the Change IPL Attributes (CHGIPLA) command as shown in Figure 8-7. The values set by this command are implemented when the *IPLA parameter is selected within the RESTART parameter.

```
                     Change IPL Attributes (CHGIPLA)

 Type choices, press Enter.

 Restart type . . . . . . . *SYS          *SAME, *SYS, *FULL
 Keylock position . . . . . *NORMAL       *SAME, *NORMAL, *AUTO...
 Hardware diagnostics . . . *MIN          *SAME, *MIN, *ALL
 Compress job tables  . . . *NONE         *SAME, *NONE, *NORMAL...
 Check job tables . . . . . *ABNORMAL *SAME, *ABNORMAL, *ALL, *SYNC
 Rebuild product directory .*NONE         *SAME, *NONE, *NORMAL...
 Mail Server Framework recovery   *NONE  *SAME, *NONE, *ABNORMAL
 Clear job queues . . . . . *NO           *SAME, *YES, *NO
 Clear output queues  . . . *NO           *SAME, *YES, *NO
 Clear incomplete joblogs . *NO           *SAME, *YES, *NO
 Start print writers  . . . *YES          *SAME, *YES, *NO
 Start to restricted state. *NO           *SAME, *YES, *NO


                                                            Bottom
F3=Exit F4=Prompt F5=Refresh F12=Cancel F13=How to use this display
F24=More keys
```

Figure 8-7: Change IPL Attributes command screen.

Many of the devices attached to an AS/400 are computers in their own right. Communication controllers, for example, are powerful, standalone processors that only do one thing: control communication. Like the AS/400, these devices can be brought down then up to IPL. That is why there are the options of *SYS and *ALL—the operator may or may not want an IPL to extend to all attached, rebootable devices.

Sometimes the operator will want to (or be instructed to) IPL the AS/400 in a Manual mode. The procedure is the same for an automatic IPL except the mode switch on the control panel must be set to MANUAL. As the IPL is progressing, he/she will be presented with the IPL/Install menu. A sample of that menu is shown in Figure 8-8.

```
                      IPL or Install the System

 Select one of the following:

 1.  Perform an IPL
 2.  Install the operating system
 3.  Use Dedicated Service Tools
 4.  Perform automatic installation of the operating system


 Selection  ____________
```

Figure 8-8: Manual IPL screen.

To continue with the attended IPL, select option 1 and press Enter. The IPL sign-on display is shown next—sign onto the system. When you sign on, the IPL Options menu will be displayed on your workstation. A sample is shown in Figure 8-9.

```
                              IPL Options

 Type choices, press Enter

   System date . . . . . . . . . . . . . . . . 05/02/99  MM/DD/YY
   System time . . . . . . . . . . . . . . . . 12:00:00  HH/MM.SS
   Clear job queues. . . . . . . . . . . . . . N                   Y= Yes, N= No
   Clean output queues . . . . . . . . . . . . N                   Y= Yes, N= No
   Clear incomplete job logs . . . . . . . . . N                   Y= Yes, N= No
   Start print writers . . . . . . . . . . . . Y                   Y= Yes, N= No
   Start this device only. . . . . . . . . . . N                   Y= Yes, N= No
   Start the system to a restricted state. . . N                   Y= Yes, N= No
   Run #STRTUP1 procedure. . . . . . . . . . . Y                   Y= Yes, N= No
   Run #STRTUP2 procedure. . . . . . . . . . . Y                   Y= Yes, N= No
   Set Major System Options. . . . . . . . . . N                   Y= Yes, N= No
   Define or Change System at IPL. . . . . . . N                   Y= Yes, N= No
```

Figure 8-9: IPL options that can be changed.

To change an option, simply position the cursor over it and type the new value. What appears next depends on what was entered for the SET MAJOR SYSTEM OPTIONS parameter on the screen shown in Figure 8-9. If it was set to No (N), the normal main menu will appear just like any normal sign on.

If SET MAJOR SYSTEM OPTIONS was set to Yes (Y), the menu shown in Figure 8-10 will appear before the IPL is complete.

```
                          Set Major System Options

 Type choices, press Enter
     Enable automatic configuration . . . . . . Y          Y= Yes, N= No
     Device configuration naming. . . . . . . . *NORMAL    *NORMAL, *S36, *DEVADR
     Default special environment. . . . . . . . *NONE      *NONE, *S36
```

Figure 8-10: Set Major System Options screen.

Enable automatic configuration tells the AS/400 to automatically configure any devices that start communicating with it that it does not know already. If automatic configuration is selected, the AS/400 will want to know how you would like it to name the devices it creates.

Do this with the next two parameters. On the DEVICE CONFIGURATION NAMING parameter, valid values are:

- *NORMAL (most common in AS/400 shops) names devices with a three-character prefix and a rotating numeric suffix. For example, displays are named DSP01, DSP02, etc., while printers are named PRT01, PRT02, etc.
- *S36 names devices with System/36 naming conventions. For example, displays are W1, W2, etc., while printers are P1, P2, etc.

- *DEVADR names devices using the device resource name. Examples would be DSP010203, PRT010204, etc. For additional information on resource names, see chapter 18, Communications: SNA, APPC, and APPN.

The last parameter, DEFAULT SPECIAL ENVIRONMENT, sets up a System/36 environment for customers migrating from a System/36 who need to run the SSP operating system on the AS/400.

When changing options on this screen, the operator is overriding default values specified in the system values QAUTOCFG, QDEVNAMING, and QSPCENV. After making desired changes, press Enter.

If DEFINE OR CHANGE SYSTEM AT IPL was set to Y from the screen shown in Figure 8-9, the menu shown in Figure 8-11 will appear.

```
                         Define or Change the System at IPL

 Select one of the following:

         1. Configuration commands
         2. Change user profile
         3. System value commands
         4. Network attributes commands
         5. General objects commands
         6. Work with shared pool

 Selection:

               ______

 F3 = Exit and continue IPL
```

Figure 8-11: Define or Change the System at IPL screen.

Of these six options, option 3 allows system values to be changed; it is the most useful of these options.

As a choice is typed and Enter is pressed, the AS/400 presents menus and entry displays. Simply read the screens and make desired changes. When done with each menu option task, the system will return to this menu.

When finished making all selections, press F3 to continue the IPL—the system will not respond to Enter.

AUTOMATICALLY POWERING YOUR SYSTEM OFF AND ON

We have been talking about powering your system off to restart it. Even "automatic" IPLs require someone to be at the AS/400 to start the power-down sequence. This can be taken one step further and truly automatic power down/up cycles can be chosen through AS/400 power scheduling.

This method is very nice because it really is automatic, but it has a potential flaw. A problem can occur if the automatic power off happens in the middle of a nightly process that, for some reason, goes beyond its scheduled end time and is still running when the system decides it is time to power-down. Automatic power on and off is better suited for weekend and holiday shutdowns and for eight-hour shops. This method is not used very much in 24-hour AS/400 shops or even 16-hour shops. To set up a power on and off schedule, enter:

```
GO POWER
```

on any command line and select option 2 (`Change Power On and Off Schedule`). From that screen, immediately press the F10 (`Change Power On/Off Defaults`). A screen similar to the one shown in Figure 8-12 will appear.

Changing Power On and Off Schedule Defaults: To set up a power on and off schedule, select option 2 (`Change Power On and Off Schedule`) on the Power On and Off Tasks (POWER) menu. On the Change Power On/Off Schedule display, press F10 (`Change Power On/Off Defaults`). Figure 8-12 shows the Change Power On/Off Defaults display.

```
                         Change Power On/Off Defaults
                                                          System:   BIGBLUE
 Type choices below, then press Enter.

 First day of week . . . . . . . .   1  1=Sunday, 2=Monday, 3=Tuesday,
                                        4=Wednesday, 5=Thursday, 6=Friday,
                                        7=Saturday

 Minutes before power off to send
   message . . . . . . . . . . . .   30    0-60

                        Default       Default
 Week                   Power         Power
 Day                    On            Off
 Sunday                 ________      ________
 Monday                 05:30:00      ________
 Tuesday                ________      ________
 Wednesday              ________      ________
 Thursday               ________      ________
 Friday                 ________      23:00:00
 Saturday               ________      ________

 F1=Help   F3=Exit   F12=Cancel
```

Figure 8-12: Change Power On/Off Defaults screen.

In this example, we put in the times 05:30:00 and 23:00:00. Normally, the command would display these lines blank or a previously entered schedule.

The "schedule" is predicated on the same thing happening each day of the week. In the example, the system is set to power off at 11:00 P.M. Friday and to power itself back on at 5:30 A.M. Monday. Prior to going down on Friday evening, the system will send a message to all users 30 minutes prior to shutting down. Note the MINUTES BEFORE POWER OFF TO SEND MESSAGE parameter in the upper part of the figure. The value can be changed from no message (zero minutes) to 60 minutes.

When the message appears, a Security Administrator (SECADMIN) or Security Officer (SECOFR) can delay shutdown for up to three hours. But that is the last opportunity to delay a shutdown before the system comes down.

In this example, assuming the mode switch is set to NORMAL and system value QIPLTYPE is set to 0, the system will take itself down properly at 11:00 P.M. Friday and bring itself back up at 5:30 A.M. Monday.

SYSTEM VALUES IMPORTANT TO IPLS

There are several system values that pertain specifically to IPLs on the AS/400. Display the current values of these and change them by using the Work with System Values (WRKSYSVAL) command. Appendices B and C provide an overview of all system values. Figure 8-13 lists those that affect IPLs.

QIPLDATTIM	IPL date and time. This is the date and time when the system will IPL itself automatically. Default value: *NONE.
QIPLSTS	IPL status displays the way the system did the last IPL. This cannot be changed; it can only be displayed. Here are the codes and what they mean: 0—an IPL from the control panel of the AS/400. 1—an unattended IPL after a power failure (refer to system value QPWRRSTIPL). 2—an unattended IPL after the PWRDWNSYS command with the RESTART(*YES) parameter. 3—an unattended scheduled IPL as a result of system value QIPLDATTIM being used. 4—an unattended remote IPL, with system value QRMTIPL being set to 1.
QIPLTYPE	Defines the type of IPL the system will do from the control panel: 0—an unattended IPL. No one needs to be there. However, if the control panel is set to manual mode, the IPL will be attended, manual. 1—an attended IPL with dedicated service tools (DST). However, if the IPL is done via a remote AS/400 due to a value in QIPLDATTIM being reached or after a power failure, an unattended, normal mode IPL will be done regardless of this system value. 2—an attended IPL in debug mode. Set this only if you are experiencing problems with your AS/400 and only at the direction of the IBM CE or Rochester support.
QPWRRSTIPL	Will the system automatically restart itself after a power failure? 0—No automatic IPL after a power failure (most common setting). 1—Automatic IPL after a power failure.
QRMTIPL	Can a remote system start the AS/400? 0—A remote system cannot start the AS/400. 1—A remote system can start the AS/400.
QSTRUPPGM	Name of program to start when IPL is complete and before the system is turned over to the users. *NONE—No program starts. library/name—The name and library location of the program to start automatically.
QUPSDLYTIM	If the AS/400 is connected to a smart, uninterruptible power supply (UPS), there is a set amount of time it will wait before it starts saving main storage and entering a controlled shutdown. *BASIC or *CALC—*CALC is the default. Neither of these are very popular options. A numeric value is preferred. *NOMAX—Used when a user-written program controls the shutdown or when a generator will take over for the UPS after a few seconds. 0—Automatic system shutdown starts as soon as the UPS kicks in. 1-99999—The delay time in seconds before the system starts to shut itself down. This is the preferable method in most shops that rely only on a UPS. Work with your UPS engineer about the power consumption of your AS/400 and the rating of the UPS for a good time-delay figure.
QUPSMSGQ	The message queue that receives messages about a power interruption. Specify this as library/message queue

Figure 8-13: System values that are important to IPLs.

LICENSE KEY

New with Version 4 is the requirement for a license authorization code, or *license key,* to be entered into AS/400s upgrading from V3 and prior to V4. (New AS/400 customers do not have to worry about this as IBM preloads the password and provides a 70-day grace period).

That means the AS/400 without a license key will power up and IPL for 70 days. After 70 days, the AS/400 will not IPL again, although it will keep running until it is taken down for a re-IPL.

There is an ongoing penalty for running the AS/400 without a license key. Within the 70-day grace period, the AS/400 will issue a message every four hours to the system operator (and possibly the users as well) stating that a valid key has not been supplied. After day 70, the AS/400 will issue the message every hour.

To add the license key, just enter in ADDLICKEY on any command line on the AS/400 and press the F4 key. Fill in the blanks on the screen and press Enter. If the code is forgotten or for any reason you do not have one, contact the company that sold the AS/400 as soon as possible.

LAB #8: STARTING AND STOPPING THE AS/400

Upon completion of this lab, you should be able to:

- Demonstrate the use of the power schedule.
- Describe the system values related to performing an IPL.
- Describe the commands to power down the system.
- Demonstrate the power-down procedure.

INTRODUCTION

While many of the topics in this chapter are very important to an operator, they do not lend themselves to hands-on lab work in an academic environment. For example, it would be a poor practice to give access to the PWRDWNSYS command to a student and risk the system being unexpectedly powered down. This is the same situation in most companies. This command is restricted to a few people. The nature of this chapter does not lend itself easily to hands-on lab exercises. We have provided some exercises that require greater authority than may be possible at some site. By their nature, it may be that one person actually touches the keys, and the remaining students watch and learn by viewing the activities rather than actually doing the activities.

POWER SCHEDULE

Many facilities IPL their systems on a regular basis. In fact, they schedule these IPLs to occur on specific days at specific times. This allows the user to schedule the IPLs. Let's look at the Power Schedule capabilities, shown in Figure L8-1.

```
POWER                         Power On and Off Tasks
                                                          System:   BIGBLUE
 To select one of the following, type its number below and press Enter:

      1. Display power on and off schedule
      2. Change power on and off schedule
      3. Power off the system immediately
      4. Power off the system immediately and then power on








 Type a menu option below
      ____________________________________________________________

 F1=Help   F3=Exit   F9=Command line   F12=Cancel
```

Figure L8-1: Power menu easily allows the operator to control the schedule.

With the proper authority, you will be able to use option 2 to change the power on and off schedule. Just in case your authority is limited, let's look at the screen, shown in Figure L8-2, which is displayed when option 2 is selected.

```
                          Change Power On/Off Schedule                BIGBLUE
                                                             08/04/99  03:09:14
 Start list at  . . . . . . . .                 Date

 Change times and descriptions below, then press Enter.  To change defaults,
   press F10.

                     Power     Power
 Date       Day      On        Off        Description
 08/04/99   Wed      _______   _______    ______________________________
 08/05/99   Thu      _______   _______    ______________________________
 08/06/99   Fri      _______   _______    ______________________________
 08/07/99   Sat      _______   23:00:00   ______________________________

 08/08/99   Sun      02:00:00  _______    ______________________________
 08/09/99   Mon      _______   _______    ______________________________
 08/10/99   Tue      _______   _______    ______________________________
 08/11/99   Wed      _______   _______    ______________________________
 08/12/99   Thu      _______   _______    ______________________________
 08/13/99   Fri      _______   _______    ______________________________
 08/14/99   Sat      _______   23:00:00   ______________________________
                                                                     More...
 F1=Help   F3=Exit   F10=Change power on/off defaults   F12=Cancel
```

Figure L8-2: Change Power On/Off Schedule screen.

You will notice that the schedule shown in Figure L8-2 performs a weekly IPL at a time when users are not generally on the system. Now let's explore what you can do with the power on/off schedule.

- Enter GO POWER on the command line.
- Press Enter.
- Select the Display Power On and Off Schedule option.
- What time is your system set to power off? ____________________
- What time is your system set to power on? ____________________

POWERING DOWN YOUR SYSTEM

Power Down System is not a command you would generally be allowed access to, so Figures L8-3 and L8-4 provide you with the prompted PWRDWNSYS command.

```
                         Power Down System (PWRDWNSYS)

 Type choices, press Enter.

 How to end . . . . . . . . . . .   *CNTRLD       *CNTRLD, *IMMED
 Delay time, if *CNTRLD . . . . .   3600          Seconds, *NOLIMIT
 Restart options:
   Restart after power down . . .   *NO           *NO, *YES
   Restart type . . . . . . . . .   ________      *IPLA, *SYS, *FULL
 IPL source . . . . . . . . . . .   *PANEL        *PANEL, A, B, D



                                                                        Bottom
 F3=Exit   F4=Prompt   F5=Refresh   F10=Additional parameters   F12=Cancel
 F13=How to use this display        F24=More keys
```

Figure L8-3: Power Down System command screen with permissible values displayed.

```
                         Power Down System (PWRDWNSYS)

 Type choices, press Enter.

 How to end . . . . . . . . . . . OPTION          *CNTRLD
 Delay time, if *CNTRLD . . . . . DELAY           3600
 Restart options:                 RESTART
   Restart after power down . . .                 *NO
   Restart type . . . . . . . . .                 ________
 IPL source . . . . . . . . . . . IPLSRC          *PANEL



                                                                        Bottom
 F3=Exit   F4=Prompt   F5=Refresh   F10=Additional parameters   F12=Cancel
 F13=How to use this display        F24=More keys
```

Figure L8-4: Keyword format of the Power Down System command.

- Using Figures L8-3 and L8-4, answer the following.
- Write the command that will power down your system immediately and restart the system using the option previously defined on the `Change IPL Attributes` command. ____

  ____
- Revise the command above to restart the system from the A storage area.

EXPLORING IPL-RELATED SYSTEM VALUES

In this, we have looked at which system values are important to an IPL. To learn more about your system, let's explore the values for it.

- Enter `DSPSYSVAL` on the command line.
- Press F4 (Prompt).
- Enter each of the system values and determine their assigned values on your system. Include what the assigned value(s) means also. Place these values in the chart shown in Figure L8-5.

System Value	Your AS/400's Assigned Value and Meaning
QIPLDATTIM	
QIPLSTS	
QIPLTYPE	
QPWRRSTIPL	
QRMTIPL	
QSTRUPPGM	
QUPSDLYTIM	
QUPSMSGQ	

Figure L8-5: Enter system values and assigned values and meanings.

ADDITIONAL LAB ASSIGNMENTS

This section focuses on exercises that require special authority or should be demonstrated by your instructor. Check with your instructor to determine if you can perform these assignments.

The method of doing this section may vary from site to site. Your instructor will let you know which system and terminal to use. Your instructor will have to log on to the system for you to provide adequate authority to perform this section of the lab.

This section takes you through the steps for a normal IPL with a restart. Remember that when you power down the system, you cannot have any users on the system.

1. Use the console that has been signed onto as either QSECOFR or a user with Security Officer authority.

2. Use the Work with Active Jobs command to determine if there are any active users on the system. If you find active users, send a BREAK message to direct the active users to log off the system within five minutes. Check the system again in five minutes. If the users are still on the system, check with your instructor prior to ending the user jobs.

3. Before you issue the command to power down the system, you should explore the parameters. Using the help function, determine what happens when you select the Restart Type *SYS.

4. Issue the command to power down the system immediately and change the RESTART parameter to *YES and *SYS.

5. After a period of time, the sign-on screen will be displayed.

6. Have the Security Officer log on to the console. Verify that everything started correctly. Include the following in your check:

   a. Using Work with Active Jobs, verify that TCP/IP is up and active. *Hint*: Check that there are several jobs running in the QSYSWRK under user QTCP.

      i. If not active and if your site is normally running TCP/IP, issue the command to start TCP/IP.

   b. Verify that the subsystems are active. In particular, check to see that QINTER is among these subsystems.

      i. If the subsystems are not active, issue the command to start all subsystems.

7. Go to another terminal or workstation attached to the AS/400 you just IPLed and sign on. If you are successful, then you have successfully completed this assignment. If not, check with your instructor.

END-OF-CHAPTER AIDS

CHAPTER SUMMARY

Powering an AS/400 down and back up is a healthy routine AS/400 shops regularly perform. With the tools IBM makes available, it is a painless process. For example, from the discussion, you can see how most shops would develop standards, such as always leave the mode switch in the Normal position, that favor automatic IPLs.

KEY TERMS

abnormal end
attended IPL
automatic IPL
automatic operations
control console
control panel
initial program load (IPL)
IPLing
license key
licensed program product (LPP)
manual IPL
normal IPL
permanent storage area
power failure
Program Temporary Fixes (PTFs)
remote IPL
restricted state
system auxiliary storage
system reference codes (SRCs)
temporary storage area
unattended IPL
uninterruptible power supply (UPS)
work control blocks

CHAPTER SELF-TEST

Solutions to these self-test questions are in appendix D.

True-False Questions

___ 1. To stop the AS/400 when it is in Normal mode, you should use the PWRDWNSYS command.

___ 2. IPLs should be scheduled and performed on a regular basis.

___ 3. You can only change IPL options by performing a manual IPL.

___ 4. When an object is deleted from memory, its address space is returned to the unused address pool.

___ 5. When a job ends abnormally, it sends a flag that causes the next IPL to be longer.

___ 6. An IPL can regenerate memory addresses and free up loads of space on the DASD. These are two of the reasons a regular IPL is important.

Fill in the Blanks

1. An AS/400 is currently powered off. The operator goes to the control panel and presses the power push button, then goes back to work. This is referred to as an (attended/unattended) __________________ IPL.

2. You cannot do an automatic IPL when your system is in the _____________ mode.

3. The system value _________________ is used to determine the type of IPL.

4. When upgrading from V3 to V4, a customer will need to enter _____________ ________________.

5. The __________________ command is used to check both the addresses used and the system auxiliary storage.

6. The complete command to have the system power down immediately is ____.

Chapter Review Questions

1. Define the following terms:
   a. IPL.
   b. Storage area.
   c. License key.
   d. Attended IPL.
   e. Unattended IPL.
2. What is QSTRUPPGM and what does it usually do?
3. What normally occurs during an IPL?
4. Why are there two copies of the operating system on an AS/400?
5. What does "0?" mean when displayed in the LCD on the control panel?

9

Operating System, Licensed Program Products, and PTFs

Chapter Objectives

Upon completion of this chapter, you should be able to:

- Describe the typical procedure for installing OS/400.
- Describe how to quickly determine what system products are installed on any AS/400.
- Describe software upgrades and PTFs.
- Describe types of system software available on your AS/400.
- Describe what PTFs are and how to maintain them at current levels on your system.

Overview

The software on an AS/400 consists of IBM-supplied software and software from other vendors. This book focuses on only the IBM-supplied software and its support software. These components consist of four main parts:

- The operating system, OS/400.
- Optional *Licensed Program Products* (*LPP*).

- Optional *Programming Request for Price Quotations* (*PRPQ*).
- Program Temporary Fixes (PTFs).

An operating system is simply a collection of manufacturer-supplied programs installed on a system. Its purpose is to control overall operation of the computer and all its resources.

LPPs are other software items that the customer purchases in addition to OS/400. LPPs include things like compilers, OfficeVision, Backup/Recovery Management System (BRMS), and many others.

PRPQs are basically utilities that either IBM developed on its own or, more likely, a customer was willing to pay IBM to develop. In either case, IBM then decided the product would be profitable to sell to other customers, but not profitable enough to support. So PRPQs are offered to everyone for a low price and are unsupported. These three basic pieces of software are continually improved through periodic releases of the software and through ongoing PTFs.

OS/400

OVERVIEW

The basic operating system, OS/400, has quite a lot in it. To say it is an operating system like other operating systems is to understate what OS/400 is. While all operating systems do the same thing—they make their computers work—they still have a wide range of strength and functionality. They range from the simplest, like the older DOS that could only run one program at a time, to those that allow many users to run different programs at the same time. This upper end of functionality includes the OS/400 and is referred to as *multiuser, multitasking*.

But OS/400 is unique in that it also comes with additional functionality not found in any other operating system available today. For example, a complete relational database management system called DB2/400 comes built into it. Customers on other computers have to purchase the database management system in addition to the operating system. OS/400 also includes the industry's highest-level security. Remember one thing about AS/400 security—no AS/400 has ever been hacked into.

Some other, not minor, built-in OS/400 functions are network and communication support, the ability to serve PC and UNIX files outside of its database, and program scheduling. Unlike other computers, any business application can run on the AS/400 with nothing more than the basic OS/400. The major functions of an operating system are:

- Running more than one program at a time concurrently.
- Handling printed output (spooling).
- Scheduling work on the system.
- Communicating with the user.

The operating system runs more than one program at a time by allowing programs to share the CPU and main memory. It is OS/400 that allocates the computer's processor, main storage, I/O devices, and data resources to various users in the most efficient manner possible.

One way that OS/400 does this is through *virtual memory management*. In other words, OS/400 recognizes that "running" programs spend most of their time waiting for something and not running at all. They wait for records to be read from or written to disk. They wait computer-eternities for users to respond to something on a screen and press Enter. When OS/400 finds a program waiting for something, it will save that program to disk and make its memory and CPU power available to other programs that really need to run. When the waiting program needs to run again, other waiting programs are moved out to make room for it.

Handling printer output, or spooling, is not as simple as it sounds. Most AS/400s have several printers available to produce reports. While some are attached directly to the AS/400, most are LAN-based printers. There are usually hundreds of users producing thousands of reports. These reports range from large (thousands of pages) to small (one page), some are very important, others are routine, some require that special paper forms (like checks) be loaded into the printers before they are printed. Then there are printer problems like their tendency to periodically run out of paper. OS/400 provides the mechanism to handle all this. When it cannot make decisions on its own, it communicates to the most logical person—the user or the system operator—to find out what it needs to know.

The AS/400 provides the ability for the user to schedule work in many ways. A program or series of programs can be scheduled to start at 6:00 P.M., for example. Or a series of programs can be structured to run concurrently and/or sequentially. Internally, as we said, the AS/400 knows which programs are waiting and, therefore, are in a low priority; and which are running and, therefore, are in a high priority. When the system gets very busy, it also knows which programs have been inactive due to the fact that they have been waiting for resources, and it will raise those programs' priorities to ensure they get an equal chance to run.

All communication to the users and operational staff is handled through OS/400. This is true whether that communication is to workstations directly attached or attached via a LAN. This communication can be in the form of supporting application input/output screens or messages that OS/400 sends when it needs to know something.

MONITORING OS/400

OS/400 is continually updated with new versions. These versions have three internal levels to their name: Version, Release, and Modification. Used together, these levels indicate the *release level* of OS/400. When people speak of a release level, they use at least two of these—often dropping the third, modification. To further shorten the naming, they refer to version as the letter V and release as the letter R. Modification would be referred to with the letter M but, unless it is very important, it is usually dropped. For example, Version 4, Release 4, Modification 0 of the operating system is referred to as "V4R4."

Another popular acronym concerning OS/400 is *Licensed Internal Code* (*LIC*). This is kind of a slippery term, sometimes it refers to the code below the machine interface layer (which is way down in the machine, or close to the hardware); other times, it refers to generally all the IBM-supplied software on the AS/400. For our purposes, the letter will be the meaning we assign to LIC.

To find out what release of the operating system that is running on an AS/400, type:

```
GO LICPGM
```

on the command line and press Enter. The system will produce a screen similar to that shown in Figure 9-1.

```
LICPGM                    Work with Licensed Programs
                                                          System:   BIGBLUE
 Select one of the following:

   Manual Install
      1. Install all

   Preparation
      5. Prepare for install

   Licensed Programs
     10. Display installed licensed programs
     11. Install licensed programs
     12. Delete licensed programs
     13. Save licensed programs


                                                                   More...
 Selection or command
 ===> _________________________________________________________________

 F3=Exit   F4=Prompt   F9=Retrieve   F12=Cancel   F13=Information Assistant
 F16=AS/400 Main menu
```

Figure 9-1: Sample of the LICPGM menu.

Option 10 (`Display Installed Licensed Programs`) from this screen will result in a screen similar to the one shown in Figure 9-2.

```
                 Display Installed Licensed Programs
                                                     System:   BIGBLUE
 Licensed  Installed
 Program   Status       Description
 5769SS1   *COMPATIBLE  OS/400 - Library QGPL
 5769SS1   *COMPATIBLE  OS/400 - Library QUSRSYS
 5769SS1   *COMPATIBLE  Operating System/400
 5769SS1   *COMPATIBLE  OS/400 - Extended Base Support
 5769SS1   *COMPATIBLE  OS/400 - Online Information
 5769SS1   *COMPATIBLE  OS/400 - Extended Base Directory Support
 5769SS1   *COMPATIBLE  OS/400 - Example Tools Library
 5769SS1   *COMPATIBLE  OS/400 - AFP Compatibility Fonts
 5769SS1   *COMPATIBLE  OS/400 - *PRV CL Compiler Support
 5769SS1   *COMPATIBLE  OS/400 - Host Servers
 5769SS1   *COMPATIBLE  OS/400 - System Openness Includes
 5769SS1   *COMPATIBLE  OS/400 - GDDM
 5769SS1   *COMPATIBLE  OS/400 - Ultimedia System Facilities
 5769SS1   *COMPATIBLE  OS/400 - Extended NLS Support

 More...
 Press Enter to continue.

 F3=Exit   F11=Display release   F12=Cancel   F19=Display trademarks

 (C) COPYRIGHT IBM CORP. 1980, 1998.
```

Figure 9-2: Sample of the Display Installed Licensed Programs screen.

This screen is mostly informational but lists several function keys near the bottom. To get the current release of the operating system, press the F11 key. The screen will change to one similar to Figure 9-3.

```
                  Display Installed Licensed Programs
                                                    System:   BIGBLUE
 Licensed  Installed
 Program   Release     Description
 5769SS1   V4R2M0      OS/400 - Library QGPL
 5769SS1   V4R2M0      OS/400 - Library QUSRSYS
 5769SS1   V4R2M0      Operating System/400
 5769SS1   V4R2M0      OS/400 - Extended Base Support
 5769SS1   V4R2M0      OS/400 - Online Information
 5769SS1   V4R2M0      OS/400 - Extended Base Directory Support
 5769SS1   V4R2M0      OS/400 - Example Tools Library
 5769SS1   V4R2M0      OS/400 - AFP Compatibility Fonts
 5769SS1   V4R2M0      OS/400 - *PRV CL Compiler Support
 5769SS1   V4R2M0      OS/400 - Host Servers
 5769SS1   V4R2M0      OS/400 - System Openness Includes
 5769SS1   V4R2M0      OS/400 - GDDM
 5769SS1   V4R2M0      OS/400 - Ultimedia System Facilities
 5769SS1   V4R2M0      OS/400 - Extended NLS Support

More...
 Press Enter to continue.

 F3=Exit   F11=Display option   F12=Cancel   F19=Display trademarks
```

Figure 9-3: Sample of the current release inquiry screen.

This particular AS/400 is running V4R2 of OS/400. Note the number/letter code in the left column. Although we casually refer to our current OS/400 as "VxRx," this code is the actual product number that is used when ordering a new release.

To make it easier to keep up with new versions of the operating system, IBM offers a service known as *Preventive Service Planning (PSP).* It offers help for keeping up with general information about licensed program products, new releases of the operating system, and so on. Also, the service provides tips and techniques about the operating system and, from time to time, reviews what Rochester is doing about developing the software on the system.

ORDERING OS/400

New OS/400 releases are offered in roughly 18-month intervals. When they are available, they come with a lot of fanfare from local IBM branches and every AS/400 news medium. It is almost impossible to miss a new release of OS/400.

Because they are available for years, the customer can decide when he or she would like to install a new operating system release. A good rule of thumb when dealing with new releases is never be the first to get it and never be the last. Give all releases a while to settle in. Let other customers find out how stable the release is before installing it. An order of a new release of the operating system comes with:

- OS/400.
- All current PTFs for the new OS/400.
- LPP(s).
- All current PTFs for LPP(s).
- PRPQs and all current PTFs for them.

Orders are placed directly through the independent reseller (IR), value-added reseller (VAR), or IBM. They are placed over the phone and followed up with a letter specifying the order in writing.

As a follow-up, print a hardcopy of the order and send it to the IR, VAR, or IBM. This should be verified for completeness and accuracy.

An order for a new release of OS/400 is no simple thing. For one thing, all the other IBM program products the customer owns usually need to be upgraded as well. Then there is the issue that not all customers have the same set of products on their AS/400s.

When the customer orders a new release of OS/400, it is done with a phone call. The company actually making the order runs it through a computer program that automatically orders all the other materials that particular customer should receive. The tool that makes this happen is the *customer profile*.

The problem comes in when the company making the OS/400 order does not have the customer's complete profile. Some items will not be ordered.

Any customer ordering a new release of OS/400 should ask for a hardcopy of the order details and double check that the order is complete. The customer should review this hardcopy of the order for completeness. The ultimate responsibility for a correct order is the customer's.

INSTALLATION OF OS/400

Installing a new version of OS/400 is typically done over a weekend. The OS/400 media (tape or CD) comes with a document called the *Installation Guide*. This is the reference for installing that particular release. It provides:

- Step-by-step installation instructions.
- Estimates of how long each step should take.
- Instructions on how to use the planning utilities.

From the Installation Guide, the operator should be able to determine:

- How long the installation will take.
- How to schedule the workload (try to have very long sections run overnight unattended).
- How much additional disk space the new release will use.
- How much faster the AS/400 should run after the new release is installed.

New releases come with software utilities that provide installation sizing, timing, and performance information. Their purpose is to provide very accurate sizing and timing information—as those can be dependent on the model and current capacity of the AS/400. Use the timing figures from the utility intelligently to work out a project plan and schedule of the install. Also, use the sizing information, combined with the current amount of disk space available on the AS/400, to determine if the new release will even fit. It is not uncommon for an AS/400 shop to have to either do some serious disk cleanup or purchase additional disk drives prior to putting on a new release.

Although the guide and utilities cover a lot of the machine-specific detail for an installation, there are some general things that apply to every OS/400 installation.

Probably the first thing the operations' staff should determine is whether it is even possible to install the new release based on the release level already on the system compared with the desired new release.

Depending on the OS/400 version currently on an AS/400, the new version may or may not be able to be loaded. For example, when V3R1 came out, it could be installed only on AS/400s that already had V2R1M0, V2R2M1, V2R2M0, or V2R3M0. At that time, any Version 1 machines had to go to one of those V2Rx releases before it could go to V3R1. That makes two separate orders and two weekends (or one very full one) of OS/400 loads.

Part of the preinstallation process should include cleaning up junk on the system. Examples are: test files that software developers have built, used, then forgotten; and libraries that were set up for vendor demos, then forgotten. Also, old system logs seem to never get cleaned up and should be deleted prior to the new release install.

Part of the package of OS/400 material includes a current PTF cumulative package if one is available. Check that this is there and read the Installation Guide for:

- PTFs that need to be applied before the new relase can be installed. Do not continue if the minimum-required PTFs are not installed.
- If the AS/400 connects to one or more other AS/400s on a network of any kind and they are not being upgraded together, check for the interoperability between the two machines after installation. *Interoperability* refers to the ability of the two machines to send/receive or save/restore each other's data.

PTFs can be quite complex. The person or persons who will install the release must either be the security officer or security administrator.

Also, users QSECOFR and QLPINSTL must be named in the system directory entries. Verify that they are with the Display Directory Entries (DSPDIRE) command. It will display a screen similar to the one shown in Figure 9-4.

```
                        Display Directory Entries

Type options, press Enter.
  5=Display details   6=Print details

Opt  User ID   Address   Description
___  HOHLY#M   CERRITOS  Marge Hohly Cerritos College
___  KEMPE#H   BIGBLUE   Herman Kempe
___  LAVERGNE  BIGBLUE   Lavergne, Marc
___  QDFTOWN   QDFTOWN   Default Owner
___  QDOC      QDOC      Internal Document Owner
___  QLPAUTO   QLPAUTO   Licensed Program Automatic User
___  QLPINSTL  QLPINSTL  Licensed Program Install       <----
___  QSECOFR   QSECOFR   Security Officer               <----
___  QSYS      QSYS      Internal System User Profile
___  QUMB      QUMB      ULTIMEDIA SYSTEM FACILITIES
___  QUSER     QUSER     Default user for PC Support

                                                            Bottom
F3=Exit   F5=Refresh   F9=Display nicknames   F10=Search directory
F12=Cancel  F13=Display departments  F17=Position to  F24=More keys
```

Figure 9-4: Output from DSPDIRE command.

If either is not present, add them with the following appropriate commands:

```
ADDDIRE USRID(QSECOFR QSECOFR) USRD('Security +
   USER(QSECOFR)
ADDDIRE USRID(QLPINSTL QLPINSTL) USRD('Licensed +
   Program Install')  USER(QLPINSTL)
```

Even with all the planning, mistakes are sometimes made and things are lost installing a new version of OS/400. The reason this happens is usually lack of planning and/or a lack of properly administering the AS/400 on a day-to-day basis.

When OS/400 installs, it replaces all Q-libraries (remember, these are IBM's libraries) except for two: QGPL and QUSRSYS. Customer-made changes and customer-made objects that are stored in the replaced Q-libraries will be lost. Make it a practice of not using the libraries for storing non-IBM objects. When it becomes necessary to make changes to IBM objects (like subsystems' descriptions), record those changes. Here are some examples of "normal" things that the new OS/400 will replace:

- Changes to subsystem descriptions.
- Changes to IBM-supplied printers (like QPRINT) for things like rotation, lines per inch, and characters per inch.
- Some customers make duplicates of IBM commands and store them in Q-libraries other than the two mentioned above. Those commands will be lost.
- Logical files the customer has built over IBM-supplied physical files by using commands that have OUTPUT(*OUTFILE) capability.

The preceding are just some examples, there may be more. If these type changes are present, either save the objects for separate restoration later or document the changes so they can be redone after the installation.

After the installation is planned, and immediately before it is started, the system should be saved with the SAVSYS command. If there is any problem with the installation, use this tape to restore the system. Of course, this step is not for customers installing OS/400 on new machines. See chapter 10 for details.

One thing that the Installation Guide will reference is whether the actual installation is to be done in AUTOMATIC or MANUAL Mode.

AUTOMATIC (sometimes called NORMAL) is used most of the time; it is the faster method. Like the name implies, AUTOMATIC will do all of the work.

MANUAL Mode installation interrupts the installation process to give the operator a chance to do something special to the AS/400. A MANUAL Mode installation must be performed any time the operator wants to:

- Add DASD using mirroring, device parity, or user ASP.
- Change the primary language (national, not programming) of the machine.
- Change the environment of the AS/400 (to S/36, for example) or change system default values or system configuration.

- Use tapes that were created with the SAVSYS (Save System) command.
- Determine if the IBM libraries (the ones that start with a Q) have been duplicated on the system.
- Install one or more LPPs for the first time.

LICENSED PROGRAM PRODUCT (LPP)

OVERVIEW

Although OS/400 can be thought of as a Licensed Program Product (LPP) because it is, it is usually referred to as the operating system. Other software products that provide AS/400 functionality not under the OS/400 umbrella are commonly referred to as LPPs.

Another way to put the distinction is that, although OS/400 has a fixed price, all functionality is included whether it is used or not; but each LPP has a single (or limited) functionality and is purchased individually. Some examples of LPPs are:

- Client Access/400.
- All program compilers.
- Query products.
- OfficeVision/400.
- Advanced backup/recovery tools.

Client Access/400 provides many powerful workstation support features on the AS/400.

Computer programs are written in a human-readable format (a programming language) and kept in files of *source code*. A *compiler* takes this human-readable format and changes it into a machine-readable format. The human-readable formats are as structured as another language, like German or French. To make this conversion of formats, the computer uses a compiler dedicated to the human-readable language.

Query products are tools that help users, operators, and software developers quickly, with a minimum of knowledge, produce reports or analysis of one or more database files.

MONITOR

To see what LPPs are currently on any AS/400, type:

```
GO LICPGM
```

on the command line and press Enter. Figure 9-5 contains a sample of the resulting menu.

```
LICPGM                       Work with Licensed Programs
                                                            System:   BIGBLUE
 Select one of the following:

   Manual Install
      1. Install all

   Preparation
      5. Prepare for install

   Licensed Programs
     10. Display installed licensed programs
     11. Install licensed programs
     12. Delete licensed programs
     13. Save licensed programs

                                                                   More . . .
 Selection or command
 ===>___________________________________________________________________________
F3=Exit   F4=Prompt   F9=Retrieve   F12=Cancel   F13=Information Assistant
 F16=AS/400 Main menu
 (C) COPYRIGHT IBM CORP. 1980, 1998.
```

Figure 9-5: Sample of the LICPGM menu.

Choose option 10 (`Display Installed Licensed Programs`). The system will present a screen that shows every LPP installed on it and OS/400 objects together. The objects that are part of OS/400 will have a description that starts with "OS/400."

The rest, the purchased LPPs, will have no such preface. Figure 9-6 contains a sample of some OS/400 and some LPP products.

The figure is actually page 2 or 3 from an AS/400. The first three objects, ObjectConnect, Integration of FlowMark, and Domain Name System, are products bundled within OS/400. This customer has also purchased the following LPPs:

- COBOL program compiler.
- VisualAge C++ program compiler.
- Performance Tools.
- Application Development Toolset.

No doubt if we paged down, we would find more LPPs installed. This menu is a good way to get acquainted with an unfamiliar AS/400.

```
                    Display Installed Licensed Programs
                                                               System:   BIGBLUE
Licensed  Installed
Program   Status        Description
5769SS1   *COMPATIBLE   OS/400 - ObjectConnect
5769SS1   *COMPATIBLE   OS/400 - Integration of FlowMark
5769SS1   *COMPATIBLE   OS/400 - Domain Name System
5769CB1   *COMPATIBLE   ILE COBOL for AS/400
5769CB1   *COMPATIBLE   OPM COBOL for AS/400
5716CX5   *COMPATIBLE   VisualAge C++ for AS/400
5716CX5   *COMPATIBLE   VisualAge C++ Windows 95/NT Client
5769PM1   *COMPATIBLE   Performance Management/400
5769PT1   *COMPATIBLE   Performance Tools for AS/400
5769PT1   *COMPATIBLE   Performance Tools - Manager Feature
5769PW1   *COMPATIBLE   App Dev ToolSet for AS/400 - SEU
5769PW1   *COMPATIBLE   App Dev ToolSet for AS/400 - Others
5769PW1   *COMPATIBLE   App Dev ToolSet for AS/400 - App Dev Manager
5769PW1   *COMPATIBLE   App Dev ToolSet for AS/400 - AppDict Services
                                                                       More...
Press Enter to continue.

F3=Exit   F11=Display release   F12=Cancel   F19=Display trademarks
```

Figure 9-6: Sample of installed LPPs.

ORDERING LPPS

LPPs are purchased new through the normal business partner, whether it is IBM or one of the many VARs and IRs around the country.

Updates to those LPPs are included within a new release of the OS/400. Generally, that is the only time LPPs need updating. For that reason, when a new OS/400 release is ordered, orders for the new version of all your LPPs are automatically generated.

As we mentioned before, what makes this "automatic" is the customer profile that the company accepting the order has on the AS/400 customer. This may not be up to date, especially for customers who shop around for hardware and software. The only items on the business partner's profile are those that were transferred when the account was taken over, items the business partner sold to the customer, and the items the customer asked the business partner to add.

A smart AS/400 operations person will ask for a hardcopy confirmation of the OS/400 order and verify that the LPPs that will ship are complete. If any are missing, have the business partner add it to the order and update the customer profile.

Another rule of thumb about this automatic LPP ordering is that the first time a shop orders a new release of OS/400 after purchasing the LPP, the LPP will probably not be part of the upgrade package.

This is important to AS/400 operations because—although good faith in the business partner is a part of every transaction—ultimately, the completeness of the order is the customer's responsibility.

INSTALLATION OF LPPS

When LPPs are new, they are installed stand-alone, not part of an OS upgrade. Each will come with its own installation instructions. Use these to do adequate planning prior to attempting to load the LPP.

The person doing the actual installation must have security officer (QSECOFR) authority. Most LPP installations are done with the system in a restricted state (refer to chapter 8, Stopping the AS/400 section).

The load process will issue messages that should not be missed. To ensure they appear on the operator's screen, change the operator's message queue in this way:

- Type on the command line:
  ```
  CHGMSGQ QSYSOPR *BREAK SEV(60)
  ```
  press Enter.
- Then type on the command line:
  ```
  CHGMSGQ  QSYSOPR  *BREAK  SEV(95)
  ```
  press Enter.

From this point, follow the installation instructions that came with the LPP.

After the LPP is installed, most come with a set of PTFs that must be applied as well. Again, follow the installation instructions.

Most new LPPs will not run until the AS/400 is re-IPLed. An IPL is required to run the Initialize System (INZSYS) process. Expect to spend some time doing this.

Also, the AS/400 system should be saved (see chapter 10) before the LPP load is started and after the last IPL is made. These are stored in case there is a problem with the AS/400 after the LPP is installed.

PROGRAMMING REQUEST FOR PRICE QUOTATIONS (PRPQS)

OVERVIEW

As we said earlier, PRPQs are smaller, single-function programs that are available for purchase (usually inexpensively). They are not "supported" by IBM, although, if one has a serious problem or just will not run, IBM will usually provide assistance.

Sometimes, lowly PRPQs grow in complexity until IBM eventually makes them a real product, offered either in OS/400 or sold as an LPP. Performance Explorer is one example of this—it started life as a PRPQ called Timing and Paging Statistics Tool.

MONITOR

There is no definite way to monitor the current status of PRPQs other than to ask your business partner or IBM about their availability. PRPQs are stable—once they are loaded and run the first time, they rarely present a problem. If they do, however, call for support. There may be a PTF out for them that no one knew about. Again, this is relatively rare.

ORDERING

PRPQs are ordered and installed individually. When the operating system is upgraded, their new versions should be automatically shipped. However, double-check the order. PRPQs are not automatically included on OS/400 orders.

INSTALLATION

New or upgraded PRPQs come with their own PTFs and an installation guide for both the PRPQ and its PTFs. Make this installation guide your reference source.

PROGRAM TEMPORARY FIX: PTF

OVERVIEW

PTF stands for Program Temporary Fix. The reason they are called "temporary" is because IBM takes note of a problem and makes sure that the next release or modification of the software does not have the same bug. In other words, a "permanent" fix will be made in the future. Until then, PTFs themselves can be installed permanently or temporarily.

PTFs are a complex topic because they are not just installed like other software; there are *loaded PTFs*, and then there are *applied PTFs*. When applied, they can be *permanently applied PTFs* or *temporarily applied PTFs*. In case of a problem with one (one that causes more problems than it fixes—it happens, though rarely), a PTF can be a *removed PTF* (the opposite of applied). When PTFs are removed, they can be removed permanently or temporarily. PTFs also can be *delayed PTFs* or *immediate PTFs*. Immediate means they take effect as soon as they are applied. Delayed means the AS/400 has to re-IPL for them to take effect. Handling different permutations of these scenarios make up the bulk of this section.

PTFs start when IBM becomes aware of a bug in its software (either a bug discovered by IBM or reported to IBM by a customer). IBM first creates an *authorized program analysis report* (*APAR*) to study the problem and, if warranted, creates a PTF that eradicates it.

PTFs are designed as replacements for specific objects within OS/400 or LPPs. PTFs come out at any time in any frequency. They become available with little fanfare and most customers can go a long time without even being aware of them. They have weird codified names, and it takes effort to know what problem each one fixes.

PTFs are important to keep up with but difficult to track. For this reason, IBM offers a periodic cumulative tape of all current PTFs. It is sensitive to the customer. That means when the customer orders a current cumulative tape, he receives all PTFs new to him, not new in general.

Along with all the ways PTFs can be loaded, there are also two types of them: *normal PTFs* and *high-impact pervasive PTFs* (better known as *HIPER*). HIPERs are PTFs that are quite serious. Whenever a new HIPER PTF becomes known, install it on the system as soon as possible.

Always follow the instructions that come with PTFs. Learn how they are applied and how previous temporary PTFs are to be treated. Temporary PTFs might have to be permanently applied, or they might have to be removed before applying any new PTFs.

This section refers to several specific commands. An optional path to the same commands is to type:

```
GO PTF
```

on the command line. This command produces a menu from which the operator can easily get to the PTF functions (ordering, loading, applying, etc.)

MONITOR

If it is hard to know when PTFs are available or what they do, how does one keep on top of PTFs? The same IBM service offered for operating systems and LPPs—PSP—helps keep up with PTFs. PSP has general information about *cumulative PTF tapes*. The service reports new HIPERs discovered on the operating system or LPPs and will report any previous PTFs that were found to be in error. Also, the service gives tips and techniques to install PTFs. The tips and techniques should be reviewed prior to installing a cumulative PTF tape.

Sometimes IBM issues PTFs that do more damage than good. These PTFs are reported in the HIPER PTF packages as "PTFs in error."

The operator will probably want to know two things about PTFs:

- What PTFs are currently on the AS/400 and their status.
- What PTFs are currently available and their relative importance—normal or HIPERs.

To display the current PTFs on the system, use the Display PTF (DSPPTF) command. To see all the PTFs on the system, type:

```
DSPPTF *ALL
```

on the command line and press Enter. Figure 9-7 has a sample of the resulting screen.

This screen gives a quick glance of the PTFs by their codified names and their current status on the system. Near the top of this screen is IPL source, showing the storage area side in use by this current set of PTFs. In the figure, ##MACH#B indicates storage side B.

Refer to the discussion in chapter 8, IPL Storage Areas. A problem that may come up routinely is that the system is running different than normal. The problem may be that the AS/400 was IPLed from the wrong storage side the last time it came up. This command is one way to display the storage side that was last used to IPL the machine. Remember, there are two copies of OS/400 on an AS/400. IPLing the machine from the wrong side of storage could make things confusing. The AS/400 that produced the screen shown in Figure 9-7 is running a copy of OS/400 that is in storage area B and has these (and more) PTFs installed.

```
                        Display PTF Status
                                                System:   BIGBLUE
Product ID . . . . . . . . . . . . . :    5769999
IPL source . . . . . . . . . . . . . :    ##MACH#B
Release of base option . . . . . . . :    V4R2M0 L00


Type options, press Enter.
  5=Display PTF details  6=Print cover letter   8=Display cover letter

     PTF                                                  IPL
Opt  ID       Status                                      Action
 _   TL98140  Permanently applied                         None
 _   TL98132  Superseded                                  None
 _   TL98083  Superseded                                  None
 _   TL98045  Superseded                                  None
 _   TL98041  Superseded                                  None
 _   TL98028  Superseded                                  None
 _   RE98079  Permanently applied                         None
 _   RE98033  Permanently applied                         None
 _   RE97357  Permanently applied                         None
                                                             More...
F3=Exit   F11=Display alternate view   F17=Position to   F12=Cancel
```

Figure 9-7: Screen showing all PTFs on an AS/400.

Note that from this and other PTF screens, putting a 5, 6, or 8 in the Option column will display that PTF's details, print its cover letter, or display its cover letter to read on the screen. Figure 9-8 shows a sample of option 5 (`Display PTF Details`).

```
                        Display PTF Details

Product ID/PTF ID . . . . . . . . . :   5769999   TL98140
Release . . . . . . . . . . . . . . :   V4R2M0

Select one of the following:

     1. General information

     4. Superseded PTFs

     6. PTF Objects
     7. Symptom strings

     9. APARs fixed

    20. All of the above

                                                           Bottom
Selection
   __

F3=Exit   F12=Cancel
```

Figure 9-8: Menu to display PTF details.

From this screen, we can get up to five sets of PTF detail information for PTF TL98140. For everyday use, options 1 (`General Information`) and 4 (`Superseded PTFs`) are commonly used. Figure 9-9 contains a sample of the General Information screen.

```
                          General information


Product ID/PTF ID . . . . . . . . . . :   5769999  TL98140
Release . . . . . . . . . . . . . . . :   V4R2MO

On order . . . . . . . . . . . . . . . :   No
PTF save file . . . . . . . . . . . . :   No
PTF status . . . . . . . . . . . . . . :   Permanently applied
Status date/time . . . . . . . . . . . :   03/15/99  20:27:14
Type . . . . . . . . . . . . . . . . . :   Delayed
Unattended IPL action . . . . . . . . :   None
Optional part . . . . . . . . . . . . :   *BASE
PTF library . . . . . . . . . . . . . :   QGPL
Cover letter . . . . . . . . . . . . . :   No
Mandatory instructions . . . . . . . . :   No
Test Fix . . . . . . . . . . . . . . . :   No
Action pending . . . . . . . . . . . . :   No
Action required . . . . . . . . . . . :   No
                                                              More...

Press Enter to continue

F3=Exit   F12=Cancel
```

Figure 9-9: Primary screen of PTF general information.

From this screen, we know if the PTF is on order or not. This one is not on order, so we assume it is in-house. In fact, it must be because its status is "Permanently applied." It was applied on 03/15/99 at 20:27:14. It was a delayed PTF, meaning when it was installed, the AS/400 had to be re-IPLed for it to take effect. There is no cover letter with it, and there are no mandatory instructions. The cover letter was probably deleted after installation.

Did this PTF supersede other PTFs—replacing them? Take option 4 (`Superseded PTFs`) and take a look. Figure 9-10 contains a sample of that screen.

```
                     Display Superseded PTFs

Product ID/PTF ID . . . . . . . . . . :   5769999  TL98140
Release . . . . . . . . . . . . . . . :   V4R2MO

PTF ID                                    PTF ID
TL98132
TL98083
TL98045
TL98041
TL98028
```

Figure 9-10: PTFs superseded by PTF TL98140.

PTF TL98140 must be a pretty strong one, because it replaced five older PTFs. We do not know what they are for at this point; if we wanted to know, we could go back to the screen shown in Figure 9-7 and get information about them.

Returning to Figure 9-7, cover letters are valuable documentation about what each PTF does. Option 6 (`Print Cover Letter`) from that screen will produce a hardcopy of one. More commonly used is option 8 (`Display Cover Letter`) from that Figure.

We got into this by displaying all the PTFs on the system. Maybe we only want to look at certain types of PTFs. The informational content will remain about the same so we will just show the difference in the main screens.

To display LIC PTFs, key in DSPPTF 5769999. This command will display only those PTFs directly related to the LIC. If we did this on this AS/400, the information would be exactly the same as shown on Figure 9-7. When all PTFs are displayed, OS/400 PTFs are displayed first.

To see OS/400 PTFs, key in DSPPTF 5769SS1 and press Enter. Figure 9-11 contains a sample of the resulting screen.

```
                         Display PTF Status
                                                 System:   BIGBLUE
Product ID . . . . . . . . . . . . . . :   5769SS1
IPL source . . . . . . . . . . . . . . :   ##MACH#B
Release of base option . . . . . . . . :   V4R2M0 L00


Type options, press Enter.
  5=Display PTF details   6=Print cover letter   8=Display cover letter

     PTF                                               IPL
Opt  ID        Status                                  Action
 _   TC98140   Permanently applied                     None
 _   TC98132   Superseded                              None
 _   TC98083   Superseded                              None
 _   TC98045   Superseded                              None
 _   TC98041   Superseded                              None
 _   TC98028   Superseded                              None
 _   TA98140   Permanently applied                     None
 _   TA98132   Superseded                              None
 _   TA98083   Superseded                              None
                                                         More...
F3=Exit   F11=Display alternate view   F17=Position to   F12=Cancel
```

Figure 9-11: The first screen of the PTFs dedicated to OS/400.

This screen starts to show some filtering of the PTFs. If you want to look at the PTFs applied for an LPP, first determine the LPP's correct name. We displayed LPPs in Figure 9-6; this AS/400 had the COBOL compiler installed. Refer to that figure now—the ID for that LPP is 5769CB1. Key on the command line:

```
DSPPTF 5769CB1
```

and press Enter. Figure 9-12 contains a sample of the resulting screen.

```
                          Display PTF Status
                                                  System:   BIGBLUE
Product ID . . . . . . . . . . . . . . :    5769CB1
IPL source . . . . . . . . . . . . . . :    ##MACH#B
Release of base option . . . . . . . . :    V4R2M0


Type options, press Enter.
  5=Display PTF details   6=Print cover letter   8=Display cover letter

     PTF                                                    IPL
Opt  ID       Status                                        Action
 _   SF47614  Permanently applied                           None
 _   SF47486  Permanently applied                           None
 _   SF47284  Permanently applied                           None
 _   SF46742  Permanently applied                           None
 _   SF46577  Permanently applied                           None
 _   SF46307  Permanently applied                           None
 _   SF46047  Permanently applied                           None
 _   SF45995  Superseded                                    None
 _   SF45502  Superseded                                    None
                                                               More...
F3=Exit   F11=Display alternate view   F17=Position to   F12=Cancel
```

Figure 9-12: PTFs currently on the AS/400 to support the COBOL compiler.

When PTFs are ordered by Electronic Customer Service (ECS) modem, the cover letter is placed in file QAPZCOVER (library QGPL), in a member named with a P followed by the PTF number. The cover letter can be displayed with the Display Physical File Member (DSPPFM) command. It can also be printed with the Copy File (CPYF) command, which specifies TOFILE(QSYSPRT). Many shops order one or several PTFs, then print or display their cover letters before installing them.

Other than the PSP service and networking with business partners, another way to keep current with HIPERs is through the Internet at:

```
http://www.as400service.ibm.com
```

ORDERING PTFs

All that PTF jargon sounds intimidating, but in reality keeping up with PTFs can be an important but low-impact job.

There are two ways to keep up with PTFs. One is to periodically order a cumulative tape of all PTFs not currently on the system and install it. This is the most common method because most OS/400 bugs, while they should be fixed, have little effect on the AS/400 or its applications.

How often is "periodically?" Three months is adequate in most cases. However, sometimes, a new release of OS/400 or an LPP is a little "rough." In those cases, order and install the cumulative tape more frequently. The customer who does wait three months may find the installation task unwieldy.

The other way to keep up with PTFs is when reporting a problem to IBM or the business partner. They will research the problem and, if a PTF solution exists, provide its number. In that case, order that PTF and install it as quickly as possible. Order PTFs through:

- The ECS modem on the AS/400 (this may be the most convenient way).
- A marketing representative.
- A telephone call to AS/400 Service.
- The Internet at: `http://www.as400service.ibm.com`.

The easiest and most convenient way to order PTFs is through ECS using the Send PTF Order (SNDPTFORD) command. Figure 9-13 contains a sample of that screen.

```
                    Send PTF Order (SNDPTFORD)

Type choices, press Enter.

PTF description:
  PTF identifier . . . . . . . . > TL98576       Character value
  Product  . . . . . . . . . . .   *ONLYPRD      F4 for list
  Release  . . . . . . . . . . .   *ONLYRLS      *ONLYRLS, VxRxMx
               + for more values   _

PTF parts  . . . . . . . . . . . > *ALL          *ALL, *CVRLTR
Remote control point . . . . . .   *IBMSRV       Name, *IBMSRV,*SELECT
Remote network identifier  . . .   *NETATR       Name, *NETATR

                      Additional Parameters

Delivery method  . . . . . . . .   *ANY          *ANY, *LINKONLY
Order  . . . . . . . . . . . . .   *REQUIRED     *REQUIRED, *PTFID
Reorder  . . . . . . . . . . . .   *NO           *NO, *YES
Check PTF  . . . . . . . . . . .   *NO           *NO, *YES

                                                               Bottom
F3=Exit   F4=Prompt F5=Refresh F12=Cancel F13=How to use this display
F24=More keys
```

Figure 9-13: Sample screen to send a PTF order.

No matter how specific PTFs are requested (not the cumulative tape), there must be a PTF number to place the order.

With this command example shown in Figure 9-13, the customer is ordering one PTF: TL98576. Parameter PTF PARTS (*ALL) means that the customer wants to receive both the cover letter and the actual PTF code. The customer could also request PTF PARTS (*CVRLTR). In this case, only the cover letter would be received.

DELIVERY METHOD (*ANY) indicates that if the PTF is small enough, it should be transmitted to you through the ECS line. This transmission avoids the need for the operator to load the PTF into the system. If the PTF is too large (for example, a cumulative PTF package), IBM may (at its option) send it on a tape or CD-ROM, which normally arrives within 48 hours, and will frequently arrive in only 24 hours. If DELIVERY (*LINKONLY) is specified, the PTF is sent through the ECS line. If the PTF is too big, IBM service will call for further instructions.

If *LINKONLY for DELIVERY METHOD is specified and the order is too large to ship via the link, the customer will get a message right away at the bottom of the order screen. The operator can then break the order into several smaller orders. Specifying *REQUIRED on the ORDER parameter tells IBM that if the PTF being ordered has another PTF as a prerequisite, both PTFs should be sent. For example, if PTF B is being ordered but IBM has decided that in order to install B, PTF A is required, use ORDER (*REQUIRED) to get both.

On the other hand, if a PTF that has been superseded is being ordered, its replacement will not be shipped. For example, if PTF B is ordered and it requires that PTF A be installed before it, the customer will get PTFs B and A. However, if PTF B has been superseded by PTF C, he will not get PTF C.

Two things to keep in mind: One, know the whole set of available PTFs by reviewing cover letters or investigating on the Internet. Two, always work off a current cumulative package.

The opposite value is ORDER (*PTFID), which only gets the PTF ordered, even if it has a prerequisite. Use *PTFID when the prerequisites are known and the PTFs installed are known.

With REORDER(*NO), the customer indicates that this is the original order for this PTF. The system will check that the PTF is already loaded and/or applied. If it is, the SNDPTFORD command ends in error because the system is trying to avoid a duplicate order. REORDE(*YES) comes in handy when the PTF is loaded. Lost cover letters can be reordered; specify PTFPART (*CVRLTR) and indicate REORDER (*YES).

SPECIAL PTF NUMBERS

IBM has created some "reserved" PTF numbers that expand what can be ordered through SNDPTFORD. As listed in Figure 9-14, "v" is the OS/400 version number, "r" is the release number, and "m" is the modification level. The modification cannot be dropped from the convention. Therefore, for V4R4M0, "vrm" would be replaced by "440."

Reserved PTF Number	Description
MF98vrm	Cumulative HIPER PTF package for reported hardware problems.
SF97vrm	Software PTF summary listing. It tells you the number of the latest cumulative PTF package, when it became available, and when you can expect the next cumulative package.
SF98vrm	Cumulative HIPER PTF package for reported software problems.
SF99vrm	Cumulative PTF package for other software problems (not HIPER).

Figure 9-14: Reserved PTF numbers.

Common PTF Order Screens

Whether the order is for cover letters, cumulative packages, or specific PTFs, use the SNDPTFORD command. Handle the first screen as described above. When Enter is pressed, the system will produce two verification screens common to all order types. The first common screen, shown in Figure 9-15, allows the customer to change the shipping address and contact person.

```
                         Verify Contact Information
                                                    System:   BIGBLUE
 Type changes, press Enter.

   Company . . . . . . . . . .   World Wide Widgets,Inc.
   Contact . . . . . . . . . .   Mike Dawson
   Mailing address:
     Street address  . . . . .   999 N. Any Drive
                                 
                                 
     City/State  . . . . . . .   Scottsdale,AZ
     Country . . . . . . . . .   USA
     Zip code  . . . . . . . .   85999
   Telephone numbers:
     Primary . . . . . . . . .   602-555-1234
     Alternative . . . . . . .   602-555-1234
   Fax telephone numbers:
     Primary . . . . . . . . .   602-555-1234
     Alternative . . . . . . .   
   National language version     2924   F4 for list
                                                               Bottom
 F3=Exit   F4=Prompt   F5=Refresh   F12=Cancel

 (C) COPYRIGHT IBM CORP. 1980, 1998.
```

Figure 9-15: Shipping and contact information change after sndptford.

After pressing Enter from the screen shown in Figure 9-15, the system provides one last chance to send or not send the order. Refer to the screen shown in Figure 9-16.

```
                          Select Reporting Option
                                                    System: BIGBLUE
 Problem ID . . . . . . . . . :   9915850345
 Current status . . . . . . . :   READY
 Problem  . . . . . . . . . . :   PTF summary information requested.




 Select one of the following:

      1. Send service request now
      2. Do not send service request
      3. Report service request by voice




 Selection ______


 F3=Exit   F12=Cancel
```

Figure 9-16: Verification screen before the order is sent.

To continue with the order, just type 1 and press Enter.

INSTALLATION OF PTFs

PTFs must be loaded then applied to make them active. ECS-delivered PTFs are already "loaded." It is crucial that you read the cover letter that comes with the PTFs and that any instructions contained in it are followed. PTF installation is complex and tends to vary widely from PTF to PTF, and installing one PTF usually involves doing something with one or more other PTFs. But there are general guidelines to follow. Before loading or applying any PTFs, do the following:

- Make a backup of your system with the SAVSYS command.
- Have all users sign off the AS/400. It is less critical but a good idea to also make sure no batch jobs are running.
- Make sure the person who is going to install the PTFs signs onto the AS/400 with SECOFR authority.

There are two operations needed to install a PTF:

- Load PTF (LODPTF).
- Apply PTF (APYPTF).

Even if a large number of PTFs are sitting around the AS/400 unapplied, all or some can be selected for installation.

Figure 9-17 shows a sample of the prompted LODPTF command. The operator should know which PTFs are for what products. If there is any doubt, check the documentation that comes with the PTF or press F4.

```
                 Load Program Temporary Fix (LODPTF)

Type choices, press Enter.

Product . . . . . . . . . . . . . ________     F4 for list
Device  . . . . . . . . . . . . . *SERVICE     Name, *SERVICE, *SAVF
PTF numbers to select . . . . . . *ALL____     Character value, *ALL
              + for more values   ________
PTF numbers to omit . . . . . . . ________     Character value
              + for more values   ________
Superseded PTFs . . . . . . . . . *APYPERM     *APYPERM, *NOAPY
Release . . . . . . . . . . . . . *ONLY___     *ONLY, VxRyMz
```

Figure 9-17: The prompted version of command LODPTF.

DEVICE tells the system where it can find the PTF to load. It can be in *SERVICE (delivered from the ECS), *SAVF (a save file from another AS/400), or a device such as a CD-ROM drive. They can be in a *SAVF in a multiple-CPU system. In that case, they were loaded from a device, then saved, and physically moved to the system (or moved via SNDNETF).

For the most part, customers take the defaults on the rest of the keywords when installing individual PTFs. When installing PTFs from a cumulative tape, make more use of these fields. Here is a summary of what they do. With PTF NUMBERS TO SELECT, select only specific PTFs from a cumulative package.

Some PTFs are sent with their own mandatory special instructions. If IBM really wants those instructions read, those PTFs will not be installed from the command when the parameter USE PTF NUMBERS TO SELECT is set to *ALL in the figure. These must be installed individually.

The PTF NUMBERS TO OMIT parameter allows specific PTFs to be omitted from a cumulative tape. This is used for superseded PTFs. If it has been a long time since any PTFs were installed and the cumulative tape contains earlier PTFs, there will be PTFs that have been superseded by newer PTFs. This is why the individual cumulative tape installation instructions are crucial.

Finally, the SUPERSEDED PTFs field refers to PTFs that have been applied to your system prior to this load. This field instructs the system to apply them permanently or to not apply them. Remember, PTFs that have been permanently applied cannot be removed. Follow any installation instructions to the letter.

Applying PTFs

After PTFs are loaded, they must be applied. PTFs are applied in two conditions:

- Temporary:
  - Takes a little longer when they run.
  - Can be removed in the future.
- Permanent:
  - Becomes a permanent part of the program product.
  - Runs fast.
  - Cannot be removed.

Most customers apply PTFs temporarily at least for a few weeks to see how they affect the system. Before any PTFs are applied permanently, make a system backup. In the unlikely event a permanently applied PTF must be backed out, the only way it can be is to restore the system from a SAVSYS taken prior to making the PTF permanent. Only apply PTFs permanently when the installation instructions say to, and then only after letting them settle in for a week or more. Do not apply PTFs permanently under any circumstances if the installation instructions do not say to. PTFs are further defined as two types:

- Immediate—Once applied, they take effect immediately.
- Delayed—Once applied, they do not take effect until after the next IPL. PTFs become delayed when the program they are fixing is active—PTFs cannot be applied to active programs. At IPL time, the program will not be active.

The command to apply PTFs is APYPTF. Figure 9-18 shows an example of its prompted screen.

```
                 Apply Program Temporary Fix (APYPTF)

 Type choices, press Enter.

 Product  . . . . . . . . . . . . > 5769SS1       F4 for list
 Release  . . . . . . . . . . . .   *ONLY         *ONLY, VxRxMx
 PTF numbers to select  . . . . .   *ALL          Character value, *ALL
                + for more values
 PTF numbers to omit  . . . . . .                 Character value
                + for more values
 Extent of change . . . . . . . .   *TEMP         *TEMP, *PERM
 Delayed PTFs . . . . . . . . . .   *NO           *NO, *YES, *IMMDLY
 IPL apply options:
   Apply at unattended IPL  . . .   *YES          *NO, *YES
   Prerequisite lic int code  . .   *APYPERM      *APYPERM, *NOAPY
 Apply requisite PTFs . . . . . .   *NO           *NO, *YES



                                                                  Bottom
 F9=All parameters   F11=Keywords   F14=Command string   F24=More keys
```

Figure 9-18: Command APYPTF after supplying the product code.

In the example shown in this Figure 9-18, the product is OS/400 itself. To apply an individual PTF, put that number in PTF NUMBERS TO SELECT. To load a cumulative tape, follow the instructions shipped with the tape. Generally, there will only be one release of the operating system installed. Therefore, *ONLY is sufficient for the RELEASE keyword. Select *ALL PTFS and do not OMIT any (next two keywords). However, specific cumulative tape instructions could, and probably will, change this.

The EXTENT OF CHANGE keyword determines whether the PTF(s) applied will be temporary or permanent.

This command will immediately apply any PTFs it can. If a PTF cannot be immediately applied because the operating system or LPP is active, it will be marked as not applied and designated as a delayed PTF.

The DELAYED PTFs keyword concerns applying PTFs that have been previously designated as delayed. These can be applied at the next IPL. In the case of LPPs, delayed PTFs can be applied anytime that the particular product is inactive.

Most PTFs are delayed and require a re-IPL in order to make them take effect. *Note*: There is a power menu on the AS/400 that will power the system down. Do not use this to start an IPL that will apply PTFs; it does not invoke the APYPTF command. When you IPL to apply delayed PTFs, use the following command after you have ended all subsystems:

```
PWRDWNSYS *IMMED RESTART(*YES) IPLSRC(x)
```

Refer to chapter 8, IPL Storage Areas section, for details on the IPLSRC(x) parameter. Although the installation guide will have the instruction concerning which storage area to use, always defer to the guide.

After IPLing the system for the last time (as directed by the installation instructions you received), verify that the PTF installation was successful. Use the Display PTF (DSPPTF) command to check statuses as we did in Figure 9-7.

Applying PTFs Permanently

PTFs are applied temporarily by default. The system keeps two versions of the system objects affected by PTFs. The old one is in IPL storage area A, and the new one is in area B. Because the system has the two versions, it is easy to go back to a status prior to the application of a particular PTF.

When applying a PTF permanently, however, the system replaces the original object with the new one and there is no going back. To apply a PTF temporarily and then decide to apply it permanently, the objects that were in IPL area B are copied to area A, and the space in area B is freed. Applying PTFs permanently gives additional disk space.

When ready to apply PTFs permanently, use the DSPPTF to find out what PTFs have an "applied temporarily" status.

If delayed PTFs are to be permanently applied, first IPL from storage area A—that will apply them temporarily. Then re-IPL from storage area B to get them applied permanently.

If you have any outstanding PTFs that have not been applied (they were delayed) or have been temporarily applied, the system will show a Work With PTFs display. From this screen, apply PTFs permanently or remove them temporarily or permanently.

PTF activation might not work every time. PTFs only get applied when the IPL is a result of a PWRDWNSYS command. Even then, they will not apply if:

- The system came down from a power failure.
- The power down part of the PWRDWNSYS command did not complete normally (power to the machine failed before it sucessfully powered down).
- Any abnormal condition existed in the AS/400 prior to issuing the PWRDWNSYS command. This can be due to:
    - A job ended at any time before the power down (even weeks) using the End Job Abnormal (ENDJOBABN) command.
    - The system ending previously with any function check in the controlling subsystem.
    - The system going down while rebuilding database files during another abnormal IPL.

Removing PTFs

Occasionally, there will be a problem with a PTF and it should be removed. Or sometimes the installation guide will instruct the operator to remove a previous PTF before loading a new one.

Only PTFs that have not been applied permanently can be removed. Like applications, PTF removal can be done temporarily or permanently. When a PTF is removed, the original object the PTF replaced is restored. When the PTF is removed temporarily, it reverts back to being loaded but nonapplied. When the PTF is removed permanently, it disappears—nonloaded and nonapplied.

There are a couple of rules about removing PTFs. A PTF that has another PTF dependent on it cannot be removed. Or, a PTF that has its related operating system or LPP active cannot be removed. Finally, operating system PTFs can only be removed permanently. Figure 9-19 summarizes these and other rules. The command to remove PTFs is Remove PTF (RMVPTF). It is almost identical to the APYPTF command shown in Figure 9-18.

When removing a PTF that was delayed when it was originally applied (that is, it could not be fully applied until an IPL was performed), an IPL will have to be performed (with the IPL storage area set to B) to complete the removal. If in doubt, check the status of the PTF after RMVPTF completes.

Condition/Type of PTF	Remove Description
Permanently applied	Cannot remove
Operating system PTF	Remove permanently only
Delayed PTF, applied temporarily	Remove temporarily only
Delayed PTF, applied temporarily, then removed temporarily	Remove permanently
Immediate PTF, applied temporarily	Remove temporarily or permanently
Immediate PTF, loaded but not applied	Remove permanently

Figure 9-19: PTF remove—temporary/permanent rules grid.

LAB #9: OS/400 OPERATING SYSTEM, LICENSED PROGRAM PRODUCTS, AND PTFS

Upon completion of this lab, you should be able to:

- Demonstrate the use of the Licensed Program menu to manage LPPs.
- List software on your AS/400.
- Demonstrate the method to download a PTF and cover letter.
- Use the informational PTF to plan a PTF order.
- Demonstrate the method of installing and removing a PTF.

NAMING CONVENTIONS FOR THIS LAB

During the lab, every time you encounter one of the lab names that begin with USER, substitute it with your assigned name. You should note that the convention adopted in this text is to have your user ID match your user library. As you complete the lab assignment, you will explore using commands on the system. See Figure L9-1.

	Lab Name: Identified in Commands as:	Your Assigned Name:
Profile (User ID)	USERID	
Library Name	USERID	
Output Queue	USEROUTQ	
Printer	PRT01	

Figure L9-1: Naming conventions.

LICENSED PROGRAMS

The software on the AS/400 consists of several types, including the operating system, Licensed Program Products (LPPs), and other vendor software. Let's start exploring what software is on your AS/400. Primarily, we will focus on the LPP software. Let's use the Licensed Program menu that controls access and management of the LPP software. You can display the installed software on the system by using the Licensed Program menu or the Display Software Resources command. If you are not allowed access to the Licensed Program menu to display LPPs, use the Display Software Resources command that provides most of the same information.

DISPLAYING INSTALLED LPP

The installed software on your system can be managed from the Licensed Program menu. This provides a consistent method of installing, deleting, and displaying LPPs on your system. You will notice that when you plan to install software, this menu automates the preinstallation process. We will be using this menu to display the LLPs on your system.

- Enter GO LICPGM on the command line.
- Press Enter.
- Enter 10 (`Display Installed Licensed Programs`).
- Press Enter.

ALTERNATE METHOD TO DISPLAY LPP

If you don't have access to the Licensed Program (LICPGM) menu, you can still display the LPPs on your system. This method does not provide the ability to manage your software as the above method provides.

- Enter DSPSFWRSC on the command line.
- Press Enter.

EXPLORING LPP ON YOUR SYSTEM

Each LPP has a product identifier that consists of four digits followed by three characters/numbers. The three characters/numbers portion is related to the product; for example, SS1 for OS/400, CB1 for COBOL, etc. The first four digits are related to the version of the operating system. You will be using the Display Licensed Program screen to complete this section.

- For the installed software on your system, what is the four-digit portion of the licensed products' IDs? ______________________________
- Press F11 (`Display Release`).

- What is the release of the software on your AS/400? ____________________
- Complete the chart shown in Figure L9-2 with information about the LPPs installed on your AS/400. Find software products to match the categories requested.

Software Type	Software Name/Description	Software Release
Program Compiler (List 2)		
Query Product		
Development Tools		
Performance Tool/Software		
Client Access/400		

Figure L9-2: LPP information.

PTF SUMMARY LISTING

Working with the PTF summary listing, there are two basic steps. First, you must send a request to IBM for a copy of the informational PTF to be downloaded to your system. Second, you will work with the downloaded document to review the information provided.

SENDING A PTF ORDER

This section requires that your AS/400 has an ECS modem connected to a phone line. If this is not the setup at your site, skip to the next portion of this lab. The capability to send a PTF order is often reserved for those who have adequate authority. You would not want just anyone in the company to be downloading PTFs or upgrading the software on your system. To do this section, you will either need adequate access, have your instructor demonstrate this portion of the assignment, or have your instructor make arrangements to allow you to perform this section.

You can request informational PTFs as well as request a specific PTF or a cover letter by using the SNDPTFORD command. You will be requesting an informational PTF. To be more specific, you will be requesting the `Software PTF Summary Listing`. Let's get started.

- Enter SNDPTFORD on the command line.
- Press F4 (Prompt).
- Enter `SF97vrm`, where v = version, r = release, and m = modification for the operating system on your system. (*Hint*: This was determined in 9-14.)
- Press F10 (`Additional Parameters`).
- Enter *LINKONLY for the DELIVERY METHOD parameter.

- Press Enter.
- Complete the information on the Verify Contact Information screen.
- Press Enter.
- Enter `1` (`Send Service Request Now`) on the command line.
- Press Enter.

Watch the messages as they are displayed on your screen. You will be told when the download of the `Software PTF Summary Listing` is complete.

EXPLORING AN INFORMATIONAL PTF

An informational PTF was downloaded to your AS/400 in the previous section. PTFs are downloaded as members of the QAPZCOVER file in QGPL library. Actual software PTFs can be downloaded in the same manner if they are small enough. You will be reviewing the contents of this informational PTF.

- Enter WRKOBJPDM on the command line.
- Press F4 (Prompt).
- Enter QGPL for the LIBRARY parameter.
- Enter QAPZCOVER for the OBJECT parameter.
- Enter *FILE for the OBJECT TYPE parameter.
- Press Enter.
- Place `12` (`Work With`) to the left of QAPZCOVER.
- Press Enter.
- Locate the member SF97vrm, where v = version, r = release, and m = modification for your AS/400.
- Place `5` (`Display`) to the left of the PTF you located above.
- Press Enter.
- When was this document last updated? ______________________________
- What is the number of the latest cumulative package available? ______________________________
- If you were placing an order for the latest cumulative package, which one would you order? ______________________________
- When did the latest cumulative package ship? ______________________________
- Are there any other cumulative PTFs planned for this version of the operating system? ______________________________

- The PTFs can be viewed through the Internet. What was the URL provided?
  ____
- What is the PTF number for the `Read First - Memo to Users`?
  ____
- Press F3 (Exit).

You should spend some time reviewing the type of information available in this PTF. Now that you have done your first download, you are ready to move on to actually requesting a fix through the ECS modem when a future need arises.

ADDITIONAL LAB ASSIGNMENTS

This section focuses on exercises that require special authority. Your instructor should demonstrate them or other special arrangements should be made. Check with your instructor to determine if you can perform these assignments. The method of doing this section may vary from site to site. Your instructor will let you know which system to use and which terminal. Your instructor will have to log onto the system for you to provide you adequate authority to perform this section of the lab.

This section takes you through the steps of downloading a PTF and applying it temporarily. After installing the PTF, this lab will ask you to remove the downloaded PTF, thus returning the system to its original condition.

As a safety factor, your system should have a good backup prior to doing this exercise. You instructor will prepare the system for this exercise.

To do this exercise, you will need to have all users off the system, so you will need either a second AS/400 or a time to perform this lab when other classes do not need to access the system. In most companies, when the system is being upgraded, it is scheduled for times when the system can be down for a reasonable period of time. Frequently, these upgrades are scheduled for weekends or over company vacations. You may find this lab needs to be scheduled for a weekend also and performed by the class as a group.

1. Obtain from your instructor the product ID and PTF ID of the PTF you will be downloading. The instructor can assign different PTFs to each student. (*Note*: Do not use dependent PTFs.)
2. Use the DSPPTF command to verify that this PTF does not currently exist on your system. If you find the PTF on your system, check with your instructor for further instructions.
3. Print the screen showing that the PTF does not exist on your system. Label the printout #1.

4. Use SNDPTFORD to download the assigned PTF.
   - Use the procedures in 9-17 to complete the download of the PTF.
   - Make sure that the PTF PARTS parameter is set to *ALL.
   - Verify that the PTF arrived and is located in QGPL/QAPZCOVER.
   - Verify that you did receive the cover letter with the PTF.
5. Using the WRKOBJPDM command, locate the cover letter for the PTF.
6. Print out the cover letter. (This will be submitted with your assignment. Label it printout #2, after you have completed the lab.)
7. Because ECS-delivered PTFs are already loaded, you already have a portion of the install completed.
8. You should verify that there is a good backup available.
   - If this is not the case, check with your instructor for further instructions.
9. Have all users sign off the AS/400.
10. Make sure that the person doing the install is signed on as QSECOFR. Your instructor will usually sign on for you to do this assignment.
11. Follow the instructions contained in the cover letter to install the PTF. It is very important that you do not use other procedures.
12. When asked to apply the PTF, make sure that you apply it only temporarily.
13. Verify that the installation completed successfully.
14. Issue the command to start the controlling subsystem. The command should be STRSBS QCTL.
   - If your controlling subsystem is not QCTL, modify the command to reflect the controlling subsystem on your AS/400.
15. Use the DSPPTF command to show that the PTF is on your system. Attach a printout of the screen print showing the PTF existence and label it printout #3.
16. Use the RMVPTF command to remove the PTF you just applied.
17. Use the DSPPTF command to obtain a screen print showing that the PTF is no longer on your system. Attach the printout and label it #4.
18. You have successfully completed your additional assignment.

END-OF-CHAPTER AIDS

CHAPTER SUMMARY

OS/400 is the most functionally rich operating system in the industry. It grows in stages marked by releases. Interim (between releases) fixes are made through PTFs. Likewise, AS/400 utilities, compilers, and other support programs from IBM grow and are repaired in the same manner. These Licensed Program Products (LPPs) do not have to grow in step with the operating system but generally do.

An important part of any system operator's job is to keep this software comfortably current. That involves some knowledge of what is current as well as strategy. For OS/400, know the current release and the release your shop is on. Know what is important to you in the new release and how successful other customers have been installing the new release.

OS/400 is easy to keep up with. Keeping up with PTFs for it and LPPs are another story. There are a lot of them out there and while, theoretically, each one is important, the smart system operator will know which PTFs are important to his shop and which can be delayed.

As involved as the material in this chapter may seem, and as important as the activity is, the actual process for this takes up a small portion of a system operator's day. Just make the effort to keep up as best you can. Whatever you do, don't let OS/400 releases or PTFs go unattended for a long time.

KEY TERMS

applied PTFs
authorized program analysis report (APAR)
compiler
cumulative PTF tapes
customer profile
delayed PTFs
high-impact pervasive PTFs (HIPER)
immediate PTFs
Installation Guide
interoperability
Licensed Internal Code (LIC)
Licensed Program Products (LPPs)
loaded PTFs
multitasking
multiuser
normal PTFs
permanently applied PTFs
Preventive Service Planning (PSP)
Programming Request for Price Quotations (PRPQ)
release level
removed PTF
source code
temporarily applied PTFs
virtual memory management

CHAPTER SELF-TEST

Solutions to the self-test questions are in appendix D.

True-False Questions

___ 1. Query/400 is an example of an LPP.

___ 2. Prior to upgrading your operating system or LPPs, you should make sure that all required PTFs have been installed.

___ 3. OS/400 has built into it a complete relational database management system called Sequel.

___ 4. LIC is another name for the operating system.

___ 5. Before and after installing PTFs, do a complete system backup.

___ 6. All PTFs can be loaded immediately.

___ 7. When ordering an upgrade to your operating system, you must specifically order the latest PTF or they will not be included in your order.

Fill in the Blanks

1. The AS/400 is capable of concurrently running more than one job at a time. This is referred to as ____________________________.

2. Before upgrading your operating system, be sure that ____________________ and ____________________ are named in the system directory entries.

3. Enter _________________________ on the command line to determine the Licensed Program Products loaded on your system.

4. Installing PTFs is a two-step process; they are ________________, then they are ________________________.

5. The most serious PTFs are called ________________________.

6. Using the SNDPTFORD command to order both the cumulative PTF packages for a system at V4R1M0, you would order the ________________ and _______________ PTF numbers.

7. Enter ________on the command line to determine what PTFs are on your system.

Chapter Review Questions

1. Define the following terms:
    a. Interoperability.
    b. Temporary PTF.
    c. Permanent PTF.
    d. Multiuser.
    e. Multitasking.
    f. APAR.

2. What is Licensed Internal Code?

3. What is the purpose of a Program Temporary Fix? Why are they important?

4. Why are there two storage areas? What relationship do these areas have to the upgrading of software?

5. Why should you not name your libraries staring with the letter Q?

6. What is the difference between a temporarily and permanently applied PTF?

7. How can you determine the latest PTFs available?

10

BACKUP AND RECOVERY

CHAPTER OBJECTIVES

Upon completion of this chapter, you should be able to:

- Explain the purpose of backup and recovery procedures.
- Describe how to establish a backup strategy.
- Explain tape concepts and tape initialization.
- Explain how to set up a backup procedure.
- Demonstrate save commands.
- Explain the purpose of Save-While-Active procedure.
- Demonstrate restore commands.
- Demonstrate how to restore different object types.

INTRODUCTION

To *backup* is to copy some or all of a computer's software to a storage location independent of the computer. To *restore* is to copy that remotely stored data back onto the computer and be able to use it. The reasons why some or all of the saved software would have to be restored are:

- Object Failure: This is the most common reason. An object or isolated group of objects became erroneously deleted, damaged, or corrupted to the point that they cannot be used.

- Object Movement: Saving an object or group of objects to *magnetic media* then shipping that media to another site or company is a popular way of moving objects from one AS/400 to another.
- Site Movement: This happens when a company moves its operations from one computer to another. This is common for *disaster recovery* and for off-loading very high-impact data processing. Although no objects are damaged or lost, the new computer has none of the objects on it. The way to initially populate it is to do a full restore.
- Efficiently Save Infrequently Used Information: Sometimes large objects take up disk space and they are infrequently used. They can be backed up, stored, and deleted from disk. That frees up valuable disk space until those objects can be restored as the need arises.
- System Failure: Much less common, but it does happen. Power can be lost or disk units fail and, as a result of either, one or many objects become damaged and must be replaced.
- Site Loss: This is extremely rare, but it does happen. Flood, fire, riots, and so on can destroy a computer or its peripherals. The result would also be a partial or complete loss of software objects.

One point about the backup/recovery process is that it could be accomplished by simply copying files, but it rarely is. Backup/recovery is accomplished through its own mechanism, different from copying. This mechanism provides for some system-management functions of the data backed up and restored. It also provides very efficient data compression techniques, minimizing the amount of space the backed up objects require as well as the time it takes to do a backup or restore.

Those items make backup files unreadable without using the appropriate *restore command*. That is probably the most significant difference between copied and saved files. If a file were "backed up" using a *copy command*, the computer would have two copies of the file; either could be accessed at any time. Data in files created by a backup command cannot be accessed by any means other than one of the restore commands.

Backups on the AS/400 are done with the Save command (prefix SAV). Recoveries are made with the Restore command (prefix RST). There are six object categories on the system that should be considered when planning any backup and recovery strategy:

- ***Operating objects*** include the model-unique licensed internal code (MULIC) and the licensed internal code (MICROCODE).
- ***System objects*** include OS/400 licensed program, user profiles, private authorities, device configurations, system values, and network values. These are things the customer developed mostly through configuration.
- ***Support objects*** include all system libraries required for normal operation of the system, the compiler, and utilities. The set of backup/restore commands and programs are examples of support object utilities.
- ***Production objects*** include production data files, data areas, job descriptions, programs, and other objects necessary for running the production applications.
- ***Development objects*** include source file objects. Source files belong to programmers and are compiled into executable (by the computer) objects known as programs. If source files are lost, future maintenance and development of programs is impossible.
- ***User objects*** include data associated with applications such as office functions, queries, and graphic applications.

BACKUP

There is a wide range of options for backing up (or saving, the terms are used interchangeably) individual AS/400 objects, files, libraries, or the entire system. Objects can be saved onto one or more *diskettes*, optical disks, tape reels, and cartridges. However, it is not practical for all objects to be equally savable to all *storage media*. Sometimes the media just does not make sense and is, therefore, not allowed. For example, it would be foolish to try to save the entire system to diskettes. It would probably take about a thousand of them before it finished, so the AS/400 just will not allow system saves to diskettes. In the sections that follow, we will indicate what media each type of save can be performed to. In general, objects can be saved to:

- Magnetic tape.
- DASD (through a save file).
- Diskette.
- Another AS/400.
- Optical media.

The term *Save File* (object type *SAVF) deserves some special mention. It is a special file created on the DASD to hold the saved objects. The idea is that writing to DASD is faster than writing to other magnetic media. This results in the save completing faster. When the save to Save File is complete, the Save File itself is saved to magnetic media (like tape), and the Save File is deleted from the system. Saving the Save File to *tape* is a simple operation; it does not involve another save.

Save Files' contents are like other data saved to other media; it is not data anyone can access. The only purpose of Save Files is to speed up the save/restore process.

Saves to be done to other AS/400s over network connections utilize optical connections for fast data transfer rates.

Magnetic media that is to be used as a recipient of saved data must be initialized in a special way. That format is the Save/Restore (*SAVRST) format. The exception to this is the media that receives a save file—it must not be initialized to *SAVRST.

To format a tape, use the Initialize Tape (INZTAP) command. Figure 10-1 contains a sample of that prompted command.

```
                         Initialize Tape (INZTAP)

 Type choices, press Enter.

 Device . . . . . . . . . . . . . . _______        Name
 New volume identifier  . . . . .  *NONE           Character value, *NONE...
 New owner . . . . . .  *BLANK
 Volume identifier identifier . . . . . . .  *MOUNTED     Character value,
*MOUNTED
 Check for active files . . . . .  *YES            *YES, *NO, *FIRST
 Tape density . . . . . . . . . .  *DEVTYPE        *DEVTYPE, *CTGTYPE, *QIC120...
 Code . . . . . . . . . . . . . .  *EBCDIC         *EBCDIC, *ASCII
 End of tape option . . . . . . .  *REWIND         *REWIND, *UNLOAD
 Clear  . . . . . . . . . . . . .  *NO             *NO, *YES




                                                                        Bottom
 F3=Exit   F4=Prompt   F5=Refresh   F12=Cancel   F13=How to use this display
 F24=More keys
```

Figure 10-1: Initialize Tape screen.

To format a diskette, use the Initialize Diskette (INZDKT) command. Figure 10-2 contains a sample screen from that command.

```
                       Initialize Diskette (INZDKT)

 Type choices, press Enter.

 Diskette device  . . . . . . . .  _______         Name
 New volume identifier  . . . . .  *NONE           Character value, *NONE
 New owner identifier . . . . . .  *BLANK
 Diskette format  . . . . . . . .  *DATA           *DATA, 1, 2, 2D, *DATA2...
 Sector size  . . . . . . . . . .  *STD            *STD, 128, 256, 512, 1024
 Check for active files . . . . .  *YES            *YES, *NO
 Code . . . . . . . . . . . . . .  *EBCDIC         *EBCDIC, *ASCII




                                                                        Bottom
 F3=Exit   F4=Prompt   F5=Refresh   F12=Cancel   F13=How to use this display
 F24=More keys
```

Figure 10-2: Initialize Diskette screen.

In the screens shown in Figures 10-1 and 10-2, there are only two parameters to worry about:

- The TAPE DEVICE/DISKETTE DEVICE is the hardware device where the media will be mounted. Typically, they have names like TAP01 or DKT01.
- CHECK FOR ACTIVE FILES: Note the default is *YES. It will not *initialize media* that contains active files. The system does this check, and it is a very good idea to always accept the default. Otherwise, live data may be lost.

Tapes and diskettes can be stored separately from the system and are useful for transporting data from one system to another when the machines are close together.

SAVE COMMAND MENU

Almost all save functions can be accessed through system menus. To work with the Save menu, type on the command line:

```
GO SAVE
```

Figure 10-3 contains a sample of the Save command menu.

```
SAVE                                  Save
                                                       System:   BIGBLUE
 Select one of the following:

   Save Data
      1. Files
      2. Libraries
      3. Documents and folders
      4. Programs
      5. Other objects
      6. Changed objects only
      7. Licensed programs
      8. Security data
      9. Storage
     10. Configuration
     11. Objects in directories
```

```
Save System and User Data
     20. Define save system and user data defaults
     21. Entire system
     22. System data only
     23. All user data

   Save Document Library Objects
     30. All documents, folders, and mail
     31. New and changed documents, new folders, all mail
     32. Documents and folders
     33. Mail only
     34. Calendars
```

```
Save Libraries
  40. All libraries other than system library
  41. All IBM libraries other than system library
  42. All user libraries
  43. All changed objects in user libraries

Save for Different Systems
  50. Save in System/36 format

Related Commands
  70. Related commands

Bottom
Selection or command
===> ____________________________________________________________

F3=Exit   F4=Prompt   F9=Retrieve   F12=Cancel   F13=Information Assistant
F16=AS/400 Main menu
```

Figure 10-3: SAVE menu screens 1, 2, and 3.

We will focus on the individual Save commands that underlie the menu selections in this chapter. Before we begin with the individual commands, let us draw attention to the option 21 that saves the entire system. This is a combination of several of the commands that follow. The command this option actually calls is as follows:

```
SAVSYS, SAVLIB *NONSYS and SAVDLO DLO(ALL) FLR(*ANY)
```

SAVE COMMANDS

In the set of Save commands, there is quite a bit of overlap and gaps. Figure 10-4 contains a summary of the Save commands and these overlaps and gaps. Use it as a reference as we discuss the actual commands.

Although listed in Figure 10-4, the Save Storage (SAVSTG) command is rarely used. It saves the entire system but does so by saving an exact image of all the permanent objects on disks. This save is actually a sector-by-sector mirror image of all the DASD.

There are two problems with this that make it an undesirable normal operation. One, there is almost never a reason to save the entire system with all system and user data together. Even large saves focus on all user or all system objects, but not both. The second problem is that the system saved with this command can only be restored to the system that made the save. Quite often, saves are done with the intent to restore on a different AS/400.

The perfect application for SAVSTG is when a company expects to waste its entire system and then rebuild it. In that case, SAVSTG offers the fastest time to totally rebuild the system. But planning such an event ahead of time would be extremely rare. SAVSTG, when it is done at all, is done at the direction of hardware service people.

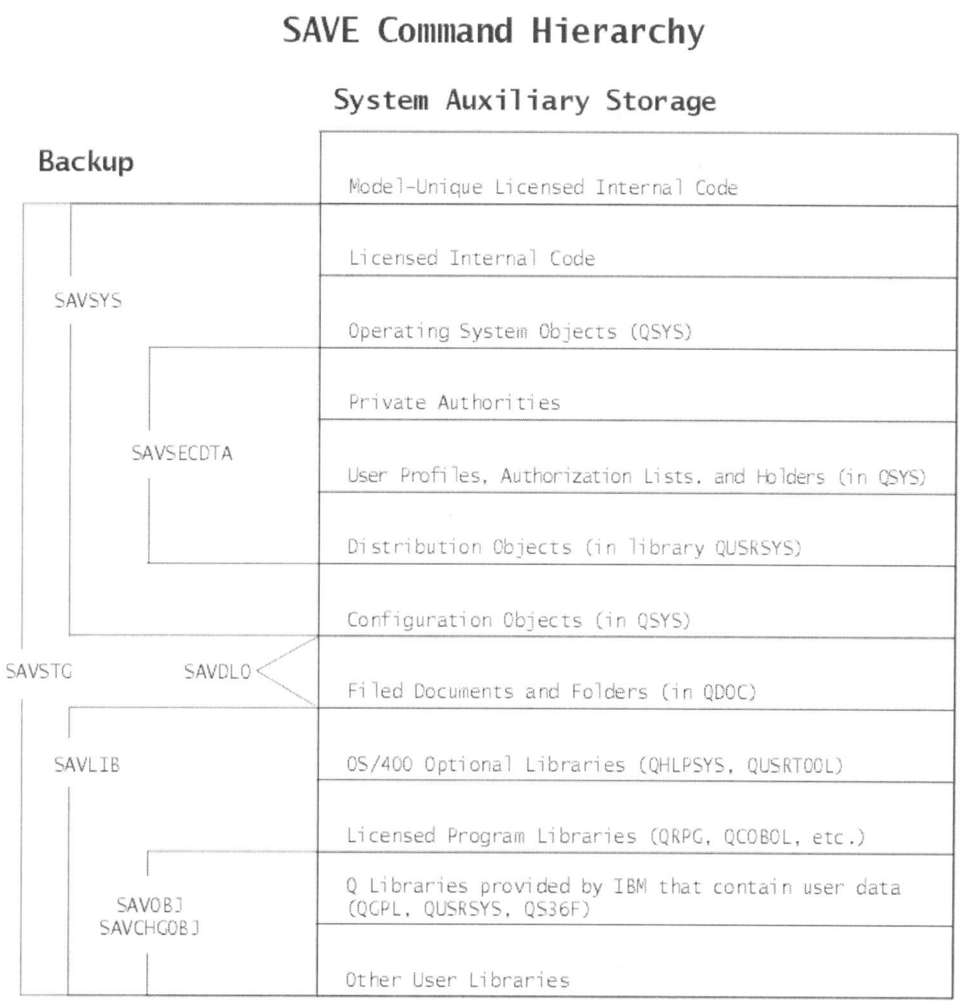

Figure 10-4: Save commands and their relationship to objects saved.

SAVE SYSTEM (SAVSYS)

After a new load of the operating system or after PTFs are applied, the system usually needs to be saved. In general terms, the "system" is the IBM parts of the system, not the user parts. The command, Save System (SAVSYS), must be run with the system in a *restricted state*. Save System (SAVSYS) saves the system libraries. It will save:

- OS/400 system objects.
- Licensed internal code.
- Optionally, the system configuration. For additional information, see SAVCFG section.
- System resource management objects.
- Optionally, security objects. For additional information, see SAVSECDTA section.
- All PTFs. For additional information, see chapter 9, Operating System, Licensed Program Products, and PTFs.

But it will not save:

- IBM-licensed programs (such as compilers).
- Any optional parts of OS/400.
- Folders.
- Libraries QGPL and QUSRSYS. *Note*: Although they start with a Q, they are not really system libraries.
- Any user libraries.

Figure 10-5 shows the prompted version of SAVSYS.

```
                           Save System (SAVSYS)

Type choices, press Enter.

Tape device . . . . . . . . . .   TAP01         Name
              + for more values   _______
Volume identifier . . . . . . .   *MOUNTED      Character value, *MOUNTED
              + for more values   _______
File expiration date . . . . . .  *PERM         Date, *PERM
End of tape option . . . . . . .  *REWIND       *REWIND, *LEAVE, *UNLOAD
Use optimum block . . . . . . .   *YES          *YES, *NO
Omit . . . . . . . . . . . . . .  *NONE         *NONE, *CFG, *SECDTA

Output . . . . . . . . . . . . .  *NONE         *NONE, *PRINT, *OUTFILE

                         Additional Parameters

Clear . . . . . . . . . . . . .   *NONE         *NONE, *ALL, *AFTER
Data compression . . . . . . . .  *DEV          *DEV, *NO, *YES
Data compaction . . . . . . . .   *DEV          *DEV, *NO
                                                                  Bottom
F3=Exit   F4=Prompt   F5=Refresh   F12=Cancel   F13=How to use this display
F24=More keys
```

Figure 10-5: Prompted version of SAVSYS command.

Note the first parameter says TAPE DEVICE. System saves can only be performed to a reel or cartridge tape. If the tape device names were not known, the Work with Hardware Products (WRKHDWPRD) command would help find it. Usually, TAP01 is used as the device name in most organizations. The parameter names are pretty self-explanatory, but here is a little more explanation for some of them:

- END OF TAPE OPTION—This tells the AS/400 what it should do with the tape after it completes the save command. The options are:
  - *REWIND—The tape is rewound but left on the drive in a ready state.
  - *LEAVE—The tape is left where it is when the save completes.
  - *UNLOAD—The tape is rewound completely and the drive is set offline. The drive door may be opened for you or the cartridge may be extended into an output tray.
- USE OPTIMUM BLOCK—This makes for more efficient save operations. The system takes over and blocks the records to the drive in a way that is optimum for that drive. Note: This method relies on the hardware type and capabilities so the result can be tapes that are unreadable by other drives.
- OMIT—Allows you to optionally omit saving system configurations and security data (refer to SAVCFG and SAVSEC below). These two are usually omitted from a system save.

SAVCFG

A SAVSYS takes a long time and, for the most part, it is not necessary to do very often. The operating system is quite stable. However, system operators routinely change parts of the operating system—such as device configurations, user profiles, and authorities—and should keep a current backup of them. Because a simple configuration backup takes about two minutes, it would be foolish to spend hours doing a whole SAVSYS.

In order to save time, the AS/400 offers the Save Configuration (SAVCFG) command. This is similar to the SAVSYS command discussed previously, but it only saves device configurations such as:

- Line descriptions.
- Controller descriptions.
- Device descriptions.
- Mode descriptions.
- Class-of-service descriptions.
- Network interface descriptions.
- Connection lists.
- Configuration lists.
- System configuration.
- Hardware resources.
- Token-Ring adapter data.

Figure 10-6 shows a prompted version of SAVCFG.

```
                       Save Configuration (SAVCFG)

Type choices, press Enter.

Device . . . . . . . . . . . . .   ________     Name, *SAVF
             + for more values     ________
Volume identifier  . . . . . . .   *MOUNTED     Character value, *MOUNTED
             + for more values     ________
Sequence number  . . . . . . . .   *END         1-16777215, *END
File expiration date . . . . . .   *PERM        Date, *PERM
End of tape option . . . . . . .   *REWIND      *REWIND, *LEAVE, *UNLOAD
Use optimum block  . . . . . . .   *YES         *YES, *NO
Save file  . . . . . . . . . . .   ________     Name
  Library  . . . . . . . . . . .     *LIBL      Name, *LIBL, *CURLIB

                         Additional Parameters

Clear  . . . . . . . . . . . . .   *NONE        *NONE, *ALL, *AFTER
Object pre-check . . . . . . . .   *NO          *NO, *YES
Data compression . . . . . . . .   *DEV         *DEV, *NO, *YES
                                                                  More...
F3=Exit   F4=Prompt   F5=Refresh   F12=Cancel   F13=How to use this display
F24=More keys
```

```
Data compaction  . . . . . . . .   *DEV         *DEV, *NO
 Output . . . . . . . . . . . . .   *NONE        *NONE, *PRINT, *OUTFILE
 File to receive output . . . . .   ________     Name
   Library  . . . . . . . . . . .     *LIBL      Name, *LIBL, *CURLIB
 Output member options:
   Member to receive output . . .   *FIRST       Name, *FIRST
   Replace or add records . . . .   *REPLACE     *REPLACE, *ADD
```

Figure 10-6: Prompted version of SAVCFG command (parts 1 and 2).

Configuration data can be saved to:

- Tape.
- Save File.

The parameter names are basically self-explanatory, but following is further explanation for some of them:

- SEQUENCE NUMBER—This is the sequential number of the file on the tape or cassette media to place this saved data. Individual saves result in files on the tape numbered sequentially from one to 1,677,215. This parameter allows the output from the command to be exactly at one of these files. More likely, the operator specifies *END and allows the system to place the saved data at the end of the media (or in the event the media [tape reel] is newly initialized, the file will be the one and only file on the media).
- END OF TAPE OPTION—Refer to this parameter under command SAVSYS.

- SAVE FILE—Saves done to a Save File must have *SAVF specified on the DEVICE parameter and name the Save File here. Optionally, the Save File library can also be named. Save Files have to exist before they are named as a parameter on these commands. If the desired one does not exist, create it with the Create Save File (CRTSAVF) command.
- USE OPTIMUM BLOCK—Refer to this parameter under command SAVSYS.

SAVSECDTA

Similar to the SAVCFG command, Save Security Data (SAVSECDTA) presumes that security data is a system component that is subject to change and, rather than require a complete SAVSYS each time a user profile is added or dropped, SAVSECDTA will only save system security information. The items saved are:

- User profiles.
- Private authorities to objects.
- Authorization lists.

These are the things that the system operator typically creates but they end up in the system portion of the AS/400. Figure 10-7 shows a prompted version of the SAVSECDTA command.

```
                     Save Security Data (SAVSECDTA)

Type choices, press Enter.

Device . . . . . . . . . . . . .   __________    Name, *SAVF
               + for more values   ________
Volume identifier  . . . . . . .   *MOUNTED      Character value, *MOUNTED
               + for more values   ________

Sequence number  . . . . . . . .   *END          1-16777215, *END
File expiration date . . . . . .   *PERM         Date, *PERM
End of tape option . . . . . . .   *REWIND       *REWIND, *LEAVE, *UNLOAD
Use optimum block  . . . . . . .   *YES          *YES, *NO
Save file  . . . . . . . . . . .   __________    Name
  Library  . . . . . . . . . . .     *LIBL       Name, *LIBL, *CURLIB

                        Additional Parameters

Clear  . . . . . . . . . . . . .   *NONE         *NONE, *ALL, *AFTER
Object pre-check . . . . . . . .   *NO           *NO, *YES
Data compression . . . . . . . .   *DEV          *DEV, *NO, *YES
                                                                  More...
F3=Exit   F4=Prompt   F5=Refresh   F12=Cancel   F13=How to use this display
F24=More keys
```

```
Data compaction  . . . . . . . .   *DEV          *DEV, *NO
Output . . . . . . . . . . . . .   *NONE         *NONE, *PRINT, *OUTFILE
File to receive output . . . . .   __________    Name
  Library  . . . . . . . . . . .     *LIBL       Name, *LIBL, *CURLIB
Output member options:
  Member to receive output . . .   *FIRST        Name, *FIRST
  Replace or add records . . . .   *REPLACE      *REPLACE, *ADD
```

Figure 10-7: Prompted version of SAVSECDTA command (parts 1 and 2).

Security data can be saved to:

- Tape.
- Save File.

The parameter names are basically self-explanatory, but following is further explanation for the more common ones:

- NUMBER—Refer to this parameter under command SAVCFG.
- END OF TAPE OPTION—Refer to this parameter under command SAVSYS.
- SAVE FILE—Refer to this parameter under command SAVCFG.
- USE OPTIMUM BLOCK—Refer to this parameter under command SAVSYS.

SAVLIB

This command is used to save specific named libraries. These can be the libraries that SAVSYS did not save and any user-created libraries. Figure 10-8 contains samples of the three screens that make up this command.

```
                        Save Library (SAVLIB)

Type choices, press Enter.

Library . . . . . . . . . . .   __________    Name, generic*, *NONSYS...
               + for more values  _________
Device . . . . . . . . . . . .  __________    Name, *SAVF
               + for more values  _________
Volume identifier . . . . . . . *MOUNTED
               + for more values  _________
Sequence number . . . . . . . . *END          1-16777215, *END
Label . . . . . . . . . . . . . *LIB
File expiration date . . . . . .*PERM         Date, *PERM
End of tape option . . . . . . .*REWIND       *REWIND, *LEAVE, *UNLOAD
Starting library . . . . . . . .*FIRST        Name, *FIRST
Save file . . . . . . . . . . . __________    Name
  Library . . . . . . . . . . .   *LIBL       Name, *LIBL, *CURLIB
Optical file . . . . . . . . . .__________

Use optimum block . . . . . . . *YES          *YES, *NO
                                                                 More...
F9=All parameters   F11=Keywords   F14=Command string   F24=More keys
```

```
                         Save Library (SAVLIB)

 Type choices, press Enter.

                        Additional Parameters

 Target release . . . . . . . . .   *CURRENT     *CURRENT, *PRV, V3R2M0...
 Update history . . . . . . . . .   *YES         *YES, *NO
 Clear  . . . . . . . . . . . . .   *NONE        *NONE, *ALL, *AFTER
 Object pre-check . . . . . . . .   *NO          *NO, *YES
 Save active  . . . . . . . . . .   *NO          *NO, *LIB, *SYNCLIB, *SYSDFN
 Save active wait time  . . . . .   120          0-99999, *NOMAX
 Save active message queue  . . .   *NONE        Name, *NONE, *WRKSTN
   Library  . . . . . . . . . . .     *LIBL      Name, *LIBL, *CURLIB
 Save access paths  . . . . . . .   *NO          *NO, *YES
 Save file data . . . . . . . . .   *YES         *YES, *NO
 Storage  . . . . . . . . . . . .   *KEEP        *KEEP, *FREE
 Data compression . . . . . . . .   *DEV         *DEV, *NO, *YES
 Data compaction  . . . . . . . .   *DEV         *DEV, *NO
                                                                     More...
 F9=All parameters   F11=Keywords   F14=Command string   F24=More keys
```

```
                         Save Library (SAVLIB)

 Type choices, press Enter.

 Libraries to omit  . . . . . . .   *NONE        Name, generic*, *NONE
               + for more values
 Objects to omit:
   Object . . . . . . . . . . . .   *NONE        Name, generic*, *NONE, *ALL
     Library  . . . . . . . . . .     *ALL       Name, generic*, *ALL
   Object type  . . . . . . . . .   *ALL         *ALL, *ALRTBL, *BNDDIR...
               + for more values
 Output . . . . . . . . . . . . .   *NONE        *NONE, *PRINT, *OUTFILE
 File to receive output . . . . .                Name
   Library  . . . . . . . . . . .     *LIBL      Name, *LIBL, *CURLIB
 Output member options:
   Member to receive output . . .   *FIRST       Name, *FIRST
   Replace or add records . . . .   *REPLACE     *REPLACE, *ADD
 Type of output information . . .   *OBJ         *OBJ, *LIB, *MBR, *ERR


                                                                      Bottom
 F9=All parameters   F11=Keywords   F14=Command string   F24=More keys
```

Figure 10-8: The prompted version of the SAVLIB command (screens 1, 2, and 3).

Libraries can be saved to:

- Tape.
- Diskette.
- Save File.
- Optical media—but only if the command parameter LIB is not set to the generic values:
  - SAVE-WHILE-ACTIVE FEATURE *ALLUSR.
  - *IBM.
  - *NONSYS.

For information on the Save-While-Active feature, refer to a later section on the topic. SAVLIB cannot be used to save these libraries:

- QSYS.
- QDOC.
- QSPL.
- QRPLOBJ.
- QTEMP.
- QSRV.
- QRECOVERY.

The parameter names are basically self-explanatory, but following is further explanation for the more common ones:

- LIB names the library or libraries to be saved. The possible values are:
  - The names of up to 300 libraries to save.
  - *NONSYS.
    - Saves all nonsystem libraries in alphabetical order.
    - Must be run with the system in a restricted state.
  - *ALLUSR.
    - Saves all libraries including: QDSNX, QGPL, QGPL38, QPFRDATA, QRCL, QS36F, QUSER38, QUSERSYS, QUSRVXRXMX, and any other library that doesn't begin with a Q or #.
  - *IBM.
    - Saves libraries starting with a # symbol.
    - Saves all Q-libraries except the ones saved by *ALLUSR.
    - Should be run when libraries it saves are not being used.
- DEVICE names the device that will do the save. Possible values are:
  - Device name.

- *SAVF indicating a Save File is to receive the saved data. When this is used, the operator will be asked for the Save File name and library.
- SEQUENCE number—Refer to this parameter under command SAVCFG.
- END OF TAPE OPTION—Refer to this parameter under command SAVSYS.
- TARGET RELEASE—Allows saving objects for movement to another system that is not at the same version as the system making the save.
- OMIT LIBRARIES—Optional parameter that appears whenever one of the three generic values (*NONSYS, *ALLUSR, *IBM) is specified for the parameter LIB. With this parameter, up to 300 specific libraries can be excluded from the save.

Although it is necessary to have the system in a restricted state only when saving with the LIB(*NONSYS) parameter, in practice, the other parameters are almost as limited. Technically, a library can be saved while some of its objects are in use. The ones that are active will not be saved. But in those cases, the successful completion message would be false.

The system may think it finished successfully, but none of the objects that were in use at the time were saved. For that reason, when backing up any library, make sure no one is using any of its objects. *Note*: The way around this problem is called *Save-While-Active*. For additional information, see section on Save-While-Active.

All these library options can get confusing. Figure 10-9 lists a summary of the libraries that are saved with the SAVLIB parameter values.

Library Name	SAVLIB LIB(xx) SAVLIB LIB(*NONSYS)		SAVLIB LIB(*IBM)		SAVLIB LIB(*ALLUSR)	
	Saved	Not Saved	Saved	Not Saved	Saved	Not Saved
QDOC		x		x		x
QGPL	x			x	x	
QGPLTEMP	x		x			x
QGPL38	x			x	x	
QPFRDATA	x			x	x	
QRCL	x			x	x	
QRECOVERY		x		x		x
QRPLOBJ		x		x		x
QSPL		x		x		x
QSRV		x		x		x
QSYS		x		x		x

Figure 10-9: What objects are saved and not saved when various IBM values are used for the library parameter.

Library Name	SAVLIB LIB(xx) SAVLIB LIB(*NONSYS)		SAVLIB LIB(*IBM)		SAVLIB LIB(*ALLUSR)	
	Saved	Not Saved	Saved	Not Saved	Saved	Not Saved
QSYS2	x		x			x
QS36F	x			x	x	
QTEMP		x		x		x
QUSR38	x			x	x	
QUSRSYS	x			x	x	
QUSRTEMP	x		x			x
QDSNX	x			x	x	
#LIBRARY	x			x	x	
#CGULIB	x		x			x
#COBLIB	x		x			x
#DFULIB	x		x			x
#RPGLIB	x		x			x
#SDALIB	x		x			x
#SEULIB	x		x			x
#DSULIB	x		x			x
QXXXXXXXXX	x		x			x

Figure 10-9: What objects are saved and not saved when various IBM values are used for the library parameter (continued).

SAVCHGOBJ

The Save Changed Objects (SAVCHGOBJ) command is used to save any object changed—such as a file with records added, changed, or deleted since the previous save. Most companies specify *ALLUSR but specific libraries can be identified. When using *ALLUSR, the optional OMITLIB parameter allows specific libraries to be excluded. Figure 10-10 shows the prompted version.

```
                    Save Changed Objects (SAVCHGOBJ)

Type choices, press Enter.

Objects . . . . . . . . . . .   __________    Name, generic*, *ALL
               + for more values  __________
Library . . . . . . . . . . .                 Name, generic*, *ALLUSR
               + for more values  _________
Device . . . . . . . . . . . .  __________    Name, *SAVF
               + for more values  _________
Object types . . . . . . . . .  *ALL          *ALL, *ALRTBL, *BNDDIR...
               + for more values  _________
Journaled objects  . . . . . .  *NO           *NO, *YES
Reference date . . . . . . . .  *SAVLIB       Date, *SAVLIB
Reference time . . . . . . . .  *NONE         Time, *NONE
Volume identifier  . . . . . .  *MOUNTED
               + for more values  _________
Sequence number  . . . . . . .  *END          1-16777215, *END
Label  . . . . . . . . . . . .  *LIB
File expiration date . . . . .  *PERM         Date, *PERM
                                                                 More...
F3=Exit   F4=Prompt   F5=Refresh   F12=Cancel   F13=How to use this display
F24=More keys
```

```
                    Save Changed Objects (SAVCHGOBJ)

Type choices, press Enter.

End of tape option . . . . . .  *REWIND       *REWIND, *LEAVE, *UNLOAD
Starting library . . . . . . .  *FIRST        Name, *FIRST
Save file  . . . . . . . . . .  _________     Name
  Library  . . . . . . . . . .    *LIBL       Name, *LIBL, *CURLIB
Optical file . . . . . . . . .  _______

Use optimum block  . . . . . .  *YES          *YES, *NO

                          Additional Parameters

Target release . . . . . . . .  *CURRENT      *CURRENT, *PRV, V3R2M0...
Update history . . . . . . . .  *YES          *YES, *NO
Clear  . . . . . . . . . . . .  *NONE         *NONE, *ALL, *AFTER
Object pre-check . . . . . . .  *NO           *NO, *YES
Save active  . . . . . . . . .  *NO           *NO, *LIB, *SYNCLIB, *SYSDFN
Save active wait time  . . . .  120           0-99999, *NOMAX
                                                                 More...
F3=Exit   F4=Prompt   F5=Refresh   F12=Cancel   F13=How to use this display
F24=More keys
```

```
                    Save Changed Objects (SAVCHGOBJ)

Type choices, press Enter.

Save active message queue . . .   *NONE        Name, *NONE, *WRKSTN
  Library . . . . . . . . . . .     *LIBL      Name, *LIBL, *CURLIB
Save access paths . . . . . . .   *NO          *NO, *YES
Save file data . . . . . . . . .  *YES         *YES, *NO
Data compression . . . . . . . .  *DEV         *DEV, *NO, *YES
Data compaction . . . . . . . .   *DEV         *DEV, *NO
Libraries to omit . . . . . . .   *NONE        Name, generic*, *NONE
               + for more values  __________

Objects to omit:
  Object . . . . . . . . . . . .  *NONE        Name, generic*, *NONE, *ALL
    Library . . . . . . . . . .     *ALL       Name, generic*, *ALL
  Object type . . . . . . . . .   *ALL         *ALL, *ALRTBL, *BNDDIR...
               + for more values  __________

Output . . . . . . . . . . . . .  *NONE        *NONE, *PRINT, *OUTFILE
File to receive output . . . . .  __________   Name
  Library . . . . . . . . . . .     *LIBL      Name, *LIBL, *CURLIB
                                                                  More...
F3=Exit   F4=Prompt   F5=Refresh   F12=Cancel   F13=How to use this display
F24=More keys
```

```
                    Save Changed Objects (SAVCHGOBJ)

Type choices, press Enter.

Output member options:
  Member to receive output . . .  *FIRST       Name, *FIRST
  Replace or add records . . . .  *REPLACE     *REPLACE, *ADD
Type of output information . . .  *OBJ         *OBJ, *LIB, *MBR, *ERR






                                                                   Bottom
F3=Exit   F4=Prompt   F5=Refresh   F12=Cancel   F13=How to use this display
F24=More keys
```

Figure 10-10: Prompted version of the SAVCHGOBJ command (screens 1-4).

Changed objects can be saved to:

- Tape.
- Diskette.
- Save File.
- Optical media.

Save-While-Active feature is possible, refer to the Save-While-Active section for more information. The parameter names are basically self-explanatory, but following is further explanation for the more common ones:

- JOURNALED OBJECTS—Files currently being journaled can be saved or not. If this parameter is set to *NO, they will not be saved.
- SEQUENCE NUMBER—Refer to this parameter under command SAVCFG.
- END OF TAPE OPTION—Refer to this parameter under command SAVSYS.
- SAVE FILE—Refer to this parameter under command SAVCFG.
- OPTICAL FILE—If an optical device was named in the DEVICE parameter, this must contain the path to that device.
- USE OPTIMUM BLOCK—Refer to this parameter under command SAVSYS.
- OBJECT TO OMIT—A list of objects to be omitted from the save.
- TARGET RELEASE—To save objects for movement to another system that is not at the same version, this parameter allows an earlier release level to be specified. This parameter is only required when saving for restoration on an earlier release of OS. Ignore it when saving/restoring across equal releases or when the target system has a higher release OS installed.

SAVOBJ

While not always considered part of backup or recovery, the Save Object (SAVOBJ) command, nevertheless, has an ancillary role. SAVOBJ saves individual objects within libraries. A good *backup strategy* will use the other commands, but this one fills a niche as a backup tool.

Saving something on the AS/400 is not always done for disaster-recovery reasons. SAVOBJ is often done just because it is a convenient way of saving or transporting a set of objects.

When two AS/400s are linked or networked, the operator should find it easy to save several objects in a Save File, send the Save File to the other machine, and restore the objects there. Do not attempt something like the SAVLIB (which will save a whole library as a minimum). SAVOBJ allows the operator to save exactly the desired objects. Figure 10-11 shows a prompted view of the SAVOBJ command.

```
                          Save Object (SAVOBJ)

Type choices, press Enter.

Objects . . . . . . . . . . . . . ________    Name, generic*, *ALL
               + for more values  ________
Library . . . . . . . . . . . . . ________    Name, generic*
               + for more values  ________
Device . . . . . . . . . . . . .  ________    Name, *SAVF
               + for more values  ________
Object types . . . . . . . . . .  *ALL        *ALL, *ALRTBL, *BNDDIR...
               + for more values  ________
Volume identifier  . . . . . . .  *MOUNTED
               + for more values  ________
Sequence number  . . . . . . . .  *END        1-16777215, *END
Label  . . . . . . . . . . . . .  *LIB
File expiration date . . . . . .  *PERM       Date, *PERM
End of tape option . . . . . . .  *REWIND     *REWIND, *LEAVE, *UNLOAD
Save file  . . . . . . . . . . .  ________    Name
  Library  . . . . . . . . . . .    *LIBL     Name, *LIBL, *CURLIB
                                                                More...
F3=Exit   F4=Prompt   F5=Refresh   F12=Cancel   F13=How to use this display
F24=More keys
```

```
                          Save Object (SAVOBJ)

Type choices, press Enter.

Optical file . . . . . . . . . .

Use optimum block  . . . . . . .  *YES        *YES, *NO

                        Additional Parameters

Target release . . . . . . . . .  *CURRENT    *CURRENT, *PRV, V3R2M0...
Update history . . . . . . . . .  *YES        *YES, *NO
Clear  . . . . . . . . . . . . .  *NONE       *NONE, *ALL, *AFTER
Object pre-check . . . . . . . .  *NO         *NO, *YES
Save active  . . . . . . . . . .  *NO         *NO, *LIB, *SYNCLIB, *SYSDFN
Save active wait time  . . . . .  120         0-99999, *NOMAX
Save active message queue  . . .  *NONE       Name, *NONE, *WRKSTN
  Library  . . . . . . . . . . .    *LIBL     Name, *LIBL, *CURLIB


                                                                More...
F3=Exit   F4=Prompt   F5=Refresh   F12=Cancel   F13=How to use this display
F24=More keys
```

```
                         Save Object (SAVOBJ)

 Type choices, press Enter.

 File member:
   File . . . . . . . . . . . . . .   *ALL          Name, *ALL
   Member . . . . . . . . . . . . .   *ALL          Name, generic*, *ALL, *NONE
                 + for more values

 Save access paths  . . . . . . . .   *NO           *NO, *YES
 Save file data . . . . . . . . . .   *YES          *YES, *NO
 Storage  . . . . . . . . . . . . .   *KEEP         *KEEP, *FREE
 Data compression . . . . . . . . .   *DEV          *DEV, *NO, *YES
 Data compaction  . . . . . . . . .   *DEV          *DEV, *NO
 Libraries to omit  . . . . . . . .   *NONE         Name, generic*, *NONE
                 + for more values

                                                                       More...
 F3=Exit   F4=Prompt   F5=Refresh   F12=Cancel   F13=How to use this display
 F24=More keys
```

```
                         Save Object (SAVOBJ)

 Type choices, press Enter.

 Objects to omit:
   Object . . . . . . . . . . . . .   *NONE         Name, generic*, *NONE, *ALL
     Library  . . . . . . . . . . .     *ALL        Name, generic*, *ALL
   Object type  . . . . . . . . . .   *ALL          *ALL, *ALRTBL, *BNDDIR...
                 + for more values
 Output . . . . . . . . . . . . . .   *NONE         *NONE, *PRINT, *OUTFILE
 File to receive output . . . . . .                 Name
   Library  . . . . . . . . . . . .     *LIBL       Name, *LIBL, *CURLIB
 Output member options:
   Member to receive output . . . .   *FIRST        Name, *FIRST
   Replace or add records . . . . .   *REPLACE      *REPLACE, *ADD
 Type of output information . . . .   *OBJ          *OBJ, *LIB, *MBR, *ERR

                                                                        Bottom
 F3=Exit   F4=Prompt   F5=Refresh   F12=Cancel   F13=How to use this display
 F24=More keys
```

Figure 10-11: Prompted version of SAVOBJ command (parts 1-4).

Objects can be saved to:

- Tape.
- Diskette.
- Save File.
- Optical media.

Save-While-Active feature is possible, refer to Save-While-Active section for more information. The parameter names are basically self-explanatory, but following is further explanation for the more common ones:

- SEQUENCE NUMBER— Refer to this parameter under command SAVCFG.
- END OF TAPE OPTION— Refer to this parameter under command SAVSYS.
- SAVE FILE— Refer to this parameter under command SAVCFG.
- OPTICAL FILE—If an optical device was named in the DEVICE parameter, this must contain the path to that device.
- USE OPTIMUM BLOCK— Refer to this parameter under command SAVSYS.
- OBJECT TO OMIT—Objects can be omitted from the save.
- TARGET RELEASE—Refer to this parameter under command SAVCHGOBJ.

Although it might look completely functional, there are a couple of restrictions on the command's parameters that limit its use.

- If more than one library is specified, all objects OBJ(*ALL) must also be specified regarding the objects to be saved within those libraries.
- To save to a Save File (*SAVF), only a single library can be specified.

SAVSAVFDTA

When saves are done to a Save File, the Save File should be moved to tape. Do this with the Save Save File Data (SAVSAVFDTA) command. Basically, it adds some system information to the file and copies it to tape or diskette. Save a Save File with the Save Save File Data (SAVSAVFDTA) command. Figure 10-12 contains sample of a prompted version of it.

```
                     Save Save File Data (SAVSAVFDTA)

Type choices, press Enter.

Save file . . . . . . . . . . .   __________     Name
  Library . . . . . . . . . . .     *LIBL        Name, *LIBL, *CURLIB
Device . . . . . . . . . . . . .  __________     Name
               + for more values  __________
Volume identifier . . . . . . .   *MOUNTED       Character value, *MOUNTED
               + for more values  __________
Sequence number . . . . . . . .   *END           1-16777215, *END
End of tape option . . . . . . .  *REWIND        *REWIND, *LEAVE, *UNLOAD
Use optimum block . . . . . . .   *YES           *YES, *NO
Clear . . . . . . . . . . . . .   *NONE          *NONE, *ALL, *AFTER

                         Additional Parameters

File expiration date . . . . . .  *PERM          Date, *PERM
Data compaction . . . . . . . .   *DEV           *DEV, *NO
Output . . . . . . . . . . . . .  *NONE          *NONE, *PRINT, *OUTFILE
                                                                More...
F3=Exit   F4=Prompt   F5=Refresh   F12=Cancel   F13=How to use this display
F24=More keys
```

```
                     Save Save File Data (SAVSAVFDTA)

Type choices, press Enter.

File to receive output . . . . .  __________     Name
  Library . . . . . . . . . . .     *LIBL        Name, *LIBL, *CURLIB
Output member options:
  Member to receive output . . .  *FIRST         Name, *FIRST
  Replace or add records . . . .  *REPLACE       *REPLACE, *ADD







                                                                 Bottom
F3=Exit   F4=Prompt   F5=Refresh   F12=Cancel   F13=How to use this display
F24=More keys
```

Figure 10-12: Prompted version of SAVSAVFDTA command (parts 1 and 2).

Save Files can be saved to:

- Tape.
- Diskette—except for Save Files containing SAVCFG and SAVSEC data.

SAVLICPGM

This command Saves Licensed Program Products (LPPs). The unique thing about it is it saves them in a format that makes them restorable with the Restore Licensed Program (RSTLICPGM) command. Figure 10-13 shows a prompted view of the SAVLICPGM command.

```
                       Save Licensed Program (SAVLICPGM)

Type choices, press Enter.

Product . . . . . . . . . . .   _________     Character value
Device . . . . . . . . . . . .  _________     Name, *SAVF
               + for more values ________

Optional part to be saved  . . . *BASE        *BASE, 1, 2, 3, 4, 5, 6, 7...
Release  . . . . . . . . . . .  *ONLY        Character value, *ONLY
Language for licensed program  . *PRIMARY    Character value, *PRIMARY...
Object type  . . . . . . . . .  *ALL         *ALL, *PGM, *LNG

                                                                     Bottom
F3=Exit   F4=Prompt   F5=Refresh   F12=Cancel   F13=How to use this display
F24=More keys
```

Figure 10-13: Prompted version of the SAVLICPGM command.

Objects can be saved to:

- Tape.
- Save File.

SAV

This Save (SAV) command saves the contents of the *Integrated File System (IFS)*. To use this command, the operator must use the IFS file naming conventions for files and devices. This command is to the IFS what all the other Save commands are to the traditional AS/400—it can save the IFS system, libraries (or directories), and objects.

We will not go into great detail here, but for example, instead of naming the tape device DEVICE(TAP01), the operator would say, DEV('/QSYS.LIB/TAP01.DEVD'). Figure 10-14 shows a prompted view of the SAV command.

```
                        Save Object (SAV)

 Type choices, press Enter.

 Device . . . . . . . . . . . . . ______________________________
 ___________
               + for more values ______________________________
 ___________
 Objects:
   Name . . . . . . . . . . . . .   '*'________________________
 ___________
   Include or omit . . . . . . .   *INCLUDE      *INCLUDE, *OMIT
               + for more values
 Directory subtree . . . . . . .   *ALL          *ALL, *DIR, *NONE, *OBJ
 Save active . . . . . . . . . .   *NO           *NO, *YES, *SYNC
 Output . . . . . . . . . . . . .  *NONE__________________________
 ___________
 Volume identifier . . . . . . .   *MOUNTED
               + for more values
 Label . . . . . . . . . . . . .   *GEN
                                                             More...
 F3=Exit   F4=Prompt   F5=Refresh   F12=Cancel   F13=How to use this display
 F24=More keys
```

```
                        Save Object (SAV)

 Type choices, press Enter.

 Optical file . . . . . . . . . . ______________________________
 ___________
 Sequence number . . . . . . . .   *END          1-16777215, *END
 File expiration date . . . . . .  *PERM         Date, *PERM
 End of tape option . . . . . . .  *REWIND       *REWIND, *LEAVE, *UNLOAD
 Use optimum block . . . . . . .   *YES          *YES, *NO

                        Additional Parameters

 System . . . . . . . . . . . . .  *LCL          *ALL, *LCL, *RMT
 Time period for last change:
   Start date . . . . . . . . . .  *ALL          Date, *ALL, *LASTSAVE
   Start time . . . . . . . . . .  *ALL          Time, *ALL
   End date . . . . . . . . . . .  *ALL          Date, *ALL
   End time . . . . . . . . . . .  *ALL          Time, *ALL
 Object pre-check . . . . . . . .  *NO           *NO, *YES
                                                             More...
 F3=Exit   F4=Prompt   F5=Refresh   F12=Cancel   F13=How to use this display
 F24=More keys
```

```
                         Save Object (SAV)

 Type choices, press Enter.

 Target release . . . . . . . . .   *CURRENT      *CURRENT, *PRV, V3R2M0...
 Update history . . . . . . . . .   *NO           *NO, *YES, *SYS, *PC

 Clear  . . . . . . . . . . . . .   *NONE         *NONE, *ALL, *AFTER
 Data compression . . . . . . . .   *DEV          *DEV, *NO, *YES
 Data compaction  . . . . . . . .   *DEV          *DEV, *NO

                                                                    Bottom
 F3=Exit   F4=Prompt   F5=Refresh   F12=Cancel   F13=How to use this display
 F24=More keys
```

Figure 10-14: Prompted version of the SAV command (screens 1-3).

Objects can be saved to:

- Tape.
- Diskette.
- Save File.
- Optical media.

Save-While-Active feature is possible, refer to Save-While-Active section for more information.

SAVDLO

The Save Document Library Object (SAVDLO) command saves specific folders and documents, or all documents in *ANY folders found. This command by itself is not used often, but it is a part of the entire system backup, so it warrants some mention.

SAVE-WHILE-ACTIVE

The AS/400 has a nice feature that allows an object to be saved while it is being accessed (even updated) by users. The feature is called Save-While-Active. The Save-While-Active command saves the same type of objects as the other save commands. Backups typically take a long time, and many companies running twenty-four hours a day simply cannot afford the downtime it causes. With Save-While-Active, users can have minimal or no downtime while the system backs itself up.

When Save commands run, they try to grab an exclusive lock on whatever object they are saving. If they cannot obtain a lock, they will not save that object. If a command can obtain a lock, it will not release it until the object is saved. By implication, then, the operator should wait until an entire object or library set is free before saving anything. This is the procedure for most companies and saves are done during off-hours. However, there are plenty of twenty-four-hour companies where this would not work.

Save-While-Active cannot be performed if parameters STG(*FREE) or STG(*DELETE) are also specified on the Save command.

SAVE-WHILE-ACTIVE SAVE

Save-While-Active is only available on these Save commands:

- SAVLIB.
- SAVOBJ.
- SAVCHGOBJ.
- SAV.

Three parameters on each command refer to Save-While-Active:

- SAVACT—Starts/stops Save-While-Active and sets the synchronization level of the database files being saved. Possible values are:
  - *NO—Save-While-Active is not in effect. Other parameters have no effect on the command
  - *LIB—Save-While-Active is in effect and the synchronization level of the files being saved are at the library level. This assumes that the files being saved all reside in the same library.
  - *SYNCLIB—Save-While-Active is in effect and the synchronization level of the files being saved are at the multiple library level. This assumes that the files being saved reside in different libraries.
  - *SYSDFN—Save-While-Active is in effect and the synchronization level of the files being saved are set by the system.
- SAVACTWAIT—Determines how many seconds the system will wait for a lock issue to be resolved. The default is 120, the range is zero–99,999.
- SAVACTMSGQ—Names the message queue to receive Save-While-Active messages.

Let us consider the completeness of the Save-While-Active because saving multiple database files while they are being updated carries a unique set of considerations.

The first consideration is how Save-While-Active works (from a 50-thousand-foot level). It relies on an internal set of *checkpoints*. Internal, that is, to the applications updating the files being saved. The checkpoints are similar to commitment control that we will cover later in chapter 17, Journaling. These checkpoints, set by the system if commitment control is not on, seek to define the boundaries of a *transaction*. That is, they establish all the files that are updated for every transaction that a user enters (a single order entry would be a transaction).

The first rule of an AS/400 is that it will never save a partially updated record. That is, one where some of the fields have been changed, and others are supposed to but have not at the time of the save.

The second consideration is that an application may, in processing a single transaction, update multiple database files. This is where the system checkpoints come into play. They define the intervals where application file updates are complete, none are waiting in buffers.

These checkpoints ensure what is known as *database synchronization*. For this reason, the operator has control with the SAVACT parameter to specify what kind of synchronization level the system should do.

A third consideration is the customer's. That is, with the application boundary. Although the system can make a pretty good guess about the synchronization level, there is no way it can absolutely determine the application boundary. Only the customer, through knowledge of the application, can know for sure.

Just by turning on Save-While-Active, some sort of synchronization level comes into play and that may be enough. But the customer who needs something further for a complex application would be wise to journal the transaction and use commitment control.

If the saved files are journaled, make saving the journal receiver an automatic feature as soon as the Save-While-Active completes. *Note*: Do not try to save a journal receiver with Save-While-Active on.

TIP:

Use SAVACT(*LIB) if all files are in one library.

Use SAVACT(*SYNCLIB) if all files are in multiple libraries and no journaling is in effect.

Use SAVACT(*SYSDFN) if all files are journaled.

Although there is a parameter that tells the system how long to wait for a lock conflict, it is possible that a lock will not be released in the allotted time. If that is the case, the Save command does not save that file and moves on to the next, just like if Save-While-Active were not in place.

TIP:

Do not trust the system; double-check the results of the save even if doing Save-While-Active.

A user or a program can monitor a message queue, create a special one with the Create Message Queue (CRTMSGQ), and name that on the SAVACTMSGQ parameter. Three messages that will appear in that queue are of special interest to the operator:

- If SAVACT(*SYNCLIB), CPI3712 when the checkpoint image is completed.
- If SAVACT(*LIB) or SAVACT(*SYSDFN), CPI3710 when the checkpoint image is completed.
- If the checkpoint image does not complete normally, CPI3711 is issued for all Save commands except SAV, which gets CPI3712 for an abnormal completion.

That brings up another consideration about Save-While-Active. Originally, it was a full Save-While-Active feature intended for companies where twenty-four-hour uptime was critical. However, Save-While-Active took a long time to run. Many companies were willing to allow a minimum downtime for the save for a trade-off of a faster save.

For that reason, plan carefully how a Save command will run using Save-While-Active. If the users can be talked into getting off an application for a couple minutes, do so; the save will be cleaner and run faster. But if the company absolutely cannot endure any downtime, go for Save-While-Active while they are up. It will do the job. Here is an example of how to do each:

- Some downtime:
  - Have all users sign off, stop the application.
  - Set parameter SAVACTWAIT(0) and name the message queue on the SAVACTMSGQ.
  - Start the save and monitor the message queue.
  - When a successful message hits the message queue, restart the application, and let the users back on.
- No downtime:
  - Start the save, monitor the message queue.
  - If the database files were journaled, save the journal receiver.
  - Double-check the job log or message queue for unsaved files.

Save-While-Active Save Performance Considerations

Here are some things that will improve the performance of the Save-While-Active feature:

- Only start the save when the system is at its lowest utilization.
- Only start the save if the system has plenty of available disk space (20 percent or better of the total DASD installed on the system).
- Move at least 1500KB of memory into the machine pool.
- To save multiple libraries, try to start individual SAVLIB jobs and have them all going to their own tape drive (if there are enough drives). *Note*: If related database files are spread across libraries, the Save commands should not be broken up.
- It is better to save a small number of large files than a large number of small files.

THINGS NOT SAVED

Not everything gets saved by the Save commands. While all AS/400 objects will be technically saved, their contents are not always saved. Sometimes you can get around these, sometimes you cannot. The items that will give trouble when saving their contents are:

- The contents of queues.
  - Queues can be saved, but not their contents. The queues on the AS/400 are:
    - Data
    - Job.
    - Message.
    - Output.
    - User.

- Two lists held within journals.
- Logical files.
- Sometimes Save Files (*SAVF).

To save the contents of spooled output files before deleting them, use the Copy Spool File (CPYSPLF) first. This command copies the spool file records to a database file. The operator then can save the database file. Although the contents of journal receivers (*JRNRCV) save completely, some things are lost when saving journals (*JRN). These are:

- The list of journaled objects.
- The list of associated journal receivers.

Logical files are themselves never saved, they are saved when their associated physical files are saved—as long as the operator specifies that the save should include the physical files' access paths. Save Files (*SAVF) are only saved when parameter SAVFDTA is made *YES on the Save command.

RESTORE COMMANDS

To work with the Restore menu, type on the command line:

```
GO RESTORE
```

Figure 10-15 contains a sample of that menu.

```
RESTORE                                 Restore
                                                         System:   BIGBLUE
 Select one of the following:

   Restore Data
      1. Files
      2. Libraries
      3. Documents and folders
      4. Programs
      5. Other objects
      6. Licensed programs
      7. Configuration
      8. User profiles
      9. Objects in directories

   Restore System and User Data
     21. System and user data
                                                                  More...
 Selection or command
 ===> ____________________________________________________________________

 F3=Exit   F4=Prompt   F9=Retrieve   F12=Cancel   F13=Information Assistant
 F16=AS/400 Main menu
 (C) COPYRIGHT IBM CORP. 1980, 1998.
```

```
RESTORE                            Restore
                                                          System:   BIGBLUE
 Select one of the following:

     22. System data only
     23. All user data

   Restore Office Data
     30. All documents, folders, and mail
     31. Documents and folders
     32. Mail only
     33. Calendars

   Restore Libraries
     40. All libraries other than system library
     41. All IBM libraries other than system library
     42. All user libraries
                                                                   More...
 Selection or command
 ===> ________________________________________________________________________

 F3=Exit   F4=Prompt   F9=Retrieve   F12=Cancel   F13=Information Assistant
 F16=AS/400 Main menu
```

```
RESTORE                            Restore
                                                          System:   BIGBLUE
 Select one of the following:

   Restore from Different Systems
     50. Restore from System/36 format

   Related Commands
     70. Related commands


                                                                    Bottom
 Selection or command
 ===> ________________________________________________________________________

 F3=Exit   F4=Prompt   F9=Retrieve   F12=Cancel   F13=Information Assistant
 F16=AS/400 Main menu
```

Figure 10-15: Restore menu (screens 1, 2, and 3).

Like the Save commands, there are some overlaps and gaps. Also, specific Restore commands must be used for data saved with specific Save commands. Figure 10-16 shows these overlaps, gaps, and command dependencies.

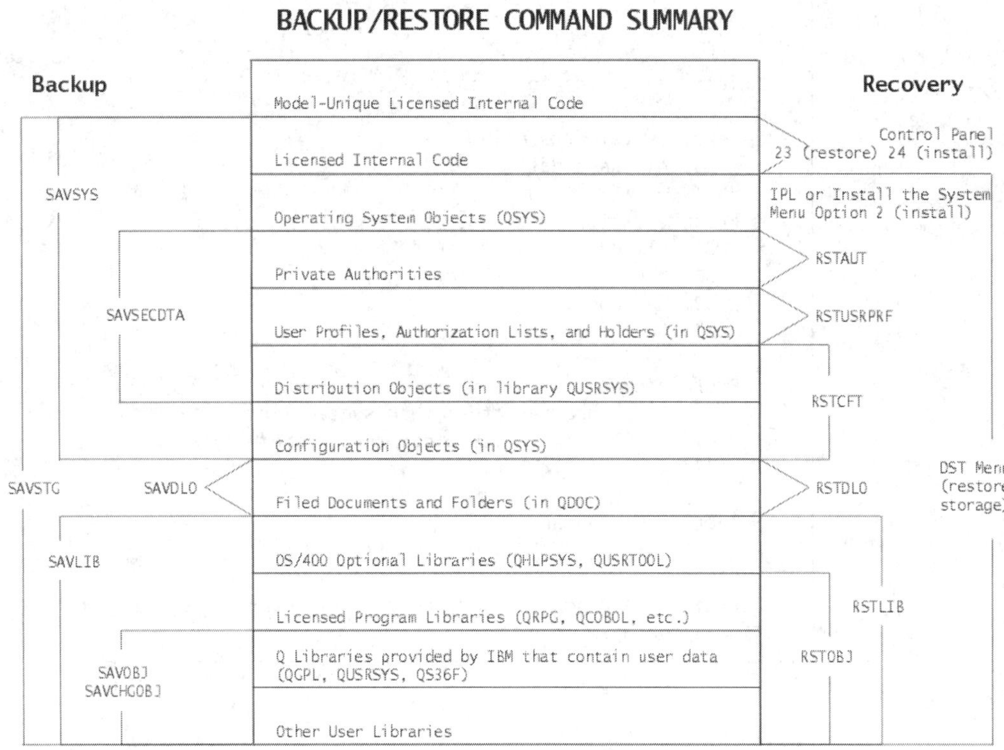

Figure 10-16: Summary of Save and Restore commands and the objects they affect.

Restore functions allow the saved copy to be restored to the system. Objects that were saved by separate commands must be restored by separate commands. The system that will be restoring objects must be at the same or higher release level than the system from which the objects were originally saved.

RESTORES

The opposite of save (or backup) is restore. Most of the Save commands covered so far have a counterpart with a prefix RST (for restore). For example, SAVLIB can be restored with a RSTLIB. Here is a list of the common Restore commands:

- RST—Restores objects from the IFS.
- RSTLIB—Restores one or more libraries.
- RSTOBJ—Restores one or more objects from one or more libraries.
- RSTLICPGM—Restores saved licensed programs.
- Security restores:
    - RSTAUT—Restores authorizations.
    - RSTCFG—Restores configurations.
    - RSTUSRPRF—Restores user profiles.

SAVSYS does not have a direct Restore counterpart, although the system can be restored (refer to Figure 10-3). These commands are fairly simple, but RSTOBJ has two important parameters to understand:

- OPTION—Used to control what objects are restored. It refers to the objects on the system the restore is being done to. Its allowed values are:
  - *ALL—The default. All objects on the save media requested to be restored will be restored. Most of the time, just accept this default and all items the operator wants restored will be.
  - *NEW—Only objects that do not exist on the system will be restored.
  - *OLD—Only objects that do exist on the system will be restored.
  - *FREE—Only objects that exist on the system with their storage freed will be restored.
- DATABASE MEMBER OPTION—Refers to the objects on the media the restore is being done from. This parameter is only in effect when restoring database files, and it will cause some grief to the operator who is careless. Here are its possible values and what they mean:
  - *MATCH—The default. Database files to be restored will only be restored if the member lists exactly match the member lists on the system. For example, if file TRNFILE is to be restored and its saved version has four members, it will only be restored if TRNFILE on the system also has four members with the same names.
  - *ALL—All members of a saved file are restored.
  - *NEW—Only members of a saved file that are not members of the file on the system are restored.
  - *OLD—Only members of a saved file that are also members of the file on the system are restored.

System operators who forget to override the default from *MATCH to something else spend a lot of time wondering why their restores were not successful. Just pay attention to this parameter— if a matched restore is desired, leave it; if not, replace it with *ALL.

When restoring user profiles, there are two commands. The Restore User Profile (RSTUSRPRF) restores the actual user profiles. The Restore Authorities (RSTAUT) re-grants profile authorities.

Restore-While-Active

We talked in the SAVE section about the Save-While-Active option. Objects can be restored while they are being used. The three Restore commands that allow Restore-While-Active are:

- RSTOBJ.
- RSTLIB.
- RST.

These will restore the objects. If the restoration is being done after a disaster, journal entries may have to be applied to bring the restored database up to currency. To do this, apply or remove journal changes. We cover this in depth in chapter 17, Journaling. For now, here is the thumbnail version.

If the journal receiver in effect at the time of the save is no longer on the system, restore it first. Do whatever your procedure is for bringing the restored files up to the application boundary—this may involve Applying Journal Changes (APYJRNCHG) or Removing Journal Changes (RMVJRNCHG). Most commonly, companies that do this are applying changes. In most companies, a simple, synchronized save and restore is enough to bring the system back to its original condition. It is up to the customer to think through a save/restore plan that will work.

BACKUP STRATEGIES

The goal of any *recovery strategy* is that, following any type of failure, the information exists that will allow system recovery based on the company's availability requirements. All user and system objects must be considered in the save/restore procedures. Any backup strategy consists of:

- Goals/deliverables:
  - How much time will be spent each day/week/month doing backups?
  - In the event of a disaster requiring recovering some or all of the system, how long can the users wait?
- Plans:
  - How long will backups be kept?
  - How many *generations of backups* will be kept?
  - Where will the backup media be kept and how accessible is it?
  - If the computer is destroyed, where and how quickly will another be available?
- Activities:
  - Save the entire system on a regular basis.
  - Save libraries.
  - Save objects.
  - Save changed objects.
  - Save documents' library objects.
  - Save distribution objects associated with mail.
  - Contract for a standby AS/400.
- Verification:
  - Is everything really available on the backup media?
  - Is the media in good condition or is it getting worn from too much use?
  - If the media is stored off-site (it usually is), is it obtainable during off-hours?

Of all these, the most common mistake is the verifying. Every company that has its first serious problem realizes something important was not backed up and, therefore, is not available. Double- and triple-checking what is backed up cannot be stressed enough.

In the event of a disaster, basically, the backup is the system. When a system is lost, whatever is not on the backup is not part of the new system.

That is very extreme, though. We have not heard of an AS/400 going down that hard—the machine is just too reliable. On a more realistic level, most recoveries are made possible from applications' errors or even developers' errors. And frankly, most save/restore activities are primarily directed at moving objects from one machine to another.

Disasters are one thing—about half of the backup strategy. While the risk of damage from a disaster is huge, most of the time, the company will want to backup routinely for other, nondisaster reasons—prior to testing, for example.

Some companies use save/restore commands and media to move data from one machine to another. Others plan to save large files used only in month-end processing and restore them prior to the next month-end. This keeps their machine DASD utilization lower.

Part of the routine backup strategy should be to rotate through several tapes and keep at least three generations. In the event a restore of objects, files, or libraries goes bad—the tape is bad or becomes bad during the process—at least there will be another tape. While that data will be somewhat obsolete, it'll be better than nothing.

Use media rotation and store one or more of the rotated sets off-site. Three generations of backup media are typical. This will ensure backups survive an on-site disaster. A simple, typical backup strategy is:

- Whenever a new release of the operating system, a new licensed program, or some new PTFs are installed, the system should be backed up with SAVSYS.
- Monthly—Save the production libraries before and after month-end processing.
- Weekly—Save all production libraries. These include libraries for users and programmers, as well as libraries for all applications.
- Daily—Save all objects that were changed that day. Save journal receivers.

Backups take away resources from normal processing, and heavy, normal processing and backups do not get along well; each one makes the other run slowly. Therefore, time backups to the night or other hours when work on the system is at its lightest. Even when a company runs the computer system 24 hours a day, the demand on the system is lightest during evening hours. Normal system activity and the processing required to do backups conflict with each other.

VERIFY THE BACKUP STRATEGY

It is rare for a company to actually lose their AS/400 to the extent that they really need to reload their systems from the backup media. However, when it does happen, a high percentage of users find that one or more important things were not backed up. This is not a good time to discover backup problems. Check and double-check the backup strategy periodically to determine four points:

- Are the planned saves completing? Surprisingly, too many companies go for months with incomplete saves.
- Are the objects that are intended to be saved, in fact, getting saved? For example, are all user libraries really getting saved? How about all libraries containing source code? All developers' libraries?
- Are the save tapes readable?
- Is the tape drive in good condition?

These checks can be partially automated. Regardless, make them happen soon after every backup to ensure that the strategy works. At least be as sure as anyone can be without going through an actual disaster. There are products available from third parties that do nothing but analyze and report on the save status of all objects on a system.

Do not forget to include people in the strategy. Who does what when? How long will the restore take? Bosses like to know this information.

Try to schedule a surprise disaster drill on a weekend and see how everything works. DO NOT cause a real disaster. Just call some people in, get some tapes, check their contents manually against what the system would lose if it had gone down.

While a disaster drill is a simple concept and almost seems like a waste of time, dumb things will surface that no one ever considered. Like the company that stored their tapes off-site. The off-site storage company was very security conscious. So much so that, during the Saturday drill, no one was in place (including the VP of MIS who was present) with enough security clearance to actually receive the tapes.

Are the Tapes and Drives OK?

The last weak link in any backup and recovery strategy is with the media or drives themselves. No one relies on tapes for everyday data processing like they used to. Tapes and drives have been relegated strictly to backup and recovery. If the recovery side of that equation is rare, no one can be really sure it will work.

Tapes and Diskettes

Verify that the save tapes and diskettes are good. Companies reuse the same tapes and diskettes for repeated saves without taking into account that magnetic media wears thin over time. Unfortunately, drive units will write onto unreadable tapes—they just will not read from them.

The AS/400 has a built-in error-reporting feature that helps track the diminishing quality of oft-used tapes and diskettes.

Start with new, not used and not reconditioned, magnetic media. Every time they are used in a save, the system will record any errors it encounters when writing to them. Individual errors are not the problem, but a lot of errors are a signal. Look for a trend. New, fresh tapes will not have many errors; older ones will have many. As errors increase, replace the entire set. Tapes are cheap. Do not mix old tapes with new tapes.

Verify tapes after the save by checking the error log. The tapes do not have to be on the drives to be verified. Any errors are already in the system. Start the System Service Tools (STRSST) and select option 1, Start a Service Tool. From there, select option 1, Error Log Utility; and then option 5, Display or Print Tape or Diskette Session Statistics.

The default time period to look at errors is the previous 24 hours. Override this to the backup period. The utility will print a report of each drive's read/write errors, errors corrected, as well as number of bytes written to tapes. This report can be printed and stored with the backup tape set.

Tape Drives and Diskette Drives

Again, there is a potential problem with tape drives that are only used to create save tapes. If the company has more than one tape drive and uses tapes frequently, or if tapes are processed periodically from other sites, the drives are constantly being validated. Therefore, they are probably all right. However, if the company only has one drive and it is only used to create save tapes, it may be in bad shape and no one knows. The company would have a huge, unrecognized exposure.

Think about the kind of disasters from which a recovery may be necessary. Is it possible the company will not have access to the same drive that created the backup tapes? If a drive gets out of adjustment, it often can read the tapes it creates, but no other drive can read them. Periodically verify drives by taking the tapes they create and have them read on other drives. These small steps protect the company not only from out-of-adjustment drives, but also from having a drive that suddenly decides to eat tapes while restoring from a disaster.

BACKUP AND RECOVER TIME-SAVERS

Just assume that there is never enough time for backups. Here are some ways to speed things up. For more items specific to Save-While-Active, refer to Save-While-Active Save Performance Considerations.

Some Save commands require that the system first be in a restricted state, others are not so picky. But any backup or recovery command can run faster if the system is in a restricted state. For maximum system uptime for the users, objects can be backed up with the Save-While-Active function. While granting maximum uptime to those users, this produces the slowest backups. A compromise solution is to end the application updating the files to be saved, start the save with Save-While-Active on, monitor its message queue, and restart the application when it is finished making the checkpoint image. This produces some (although minimal) downtime to the users but a much faster save.

Saving many libraries at once will go faster by using a single SAVLIB command for all of them (rather than one SAVLIB for each library). Saving only changed objects daily with the SAVCHGOBJ command is faster than saving entire libraries.

Do not forget the restore requirements when planning the backup strategy. Saving access paths will definitely lengthen the backup process, but it will also shorten the restore time. Actually, in most cases, saving access paths will enhance the restore function many times more than it degrades the backup function.

Note: To successfully save/restore logical files, the physical file save must have ACCPTH(*YES) specified on both the Save and Restore commands. The logical file must be built with MAINT(*IMMED) or MAINT(*DELAY). To check logical files' MAINT value, use the Display File Description (DSPFD) command. To change logical files' MAINT value, use the Change Logical File (CHGLF) command.

If the person doing the backups has special authority, *SAVSYS in his or her user profile, security checking on each object will be bypassed and the save operation will be faster. For more information on special authorities, see chapter 11.

Data compression can reduce the amount of media required to save objects, files, or libraries but it will slow down the backup. The three data compression choices are:

- Software data compression done by the CPU. Slows the backups down the most.
- Hardware data compression performed by the AS/400 adapter (with the attachment feature). Faster save times.
- Hardware data compacting performed by the 3480/3490 and 3590 tape units. The faster and more elaborate the data compression algorithm, the shorter the save times.

LAB #10: BACKUP AND RECOVERY

Upon completion of this lab, you should be able to:

- Demonstrate the use of some Save commands.
- Demonstrate the use of some Restore commands.
- Demonstrate the ability to restore selectively.
- Demonstrate the ability to display tape.
- Create and use a Save File to perform backup and recovery operations.

NAMING CONVENTIONS FOR THIS LAB

During the lab, every time you encounter one of the lab names that contains xx, replace the xx with the number that has been assigned (Figure L10-1). As you complete the lab assignment, you will create and modify your environment to reflect your specific assigned names.

	Lab Name: Identified in Commands as:	Your Assigned Name:
Profile (User ID)	user00xx	
Library Name	user00xx	
Output Queue	userOUTQ	
Tape Drive	TAP01	

Figure L10-1: Naming conventions.

INTRODUCTION

For an operator, learning backup procedures is one of the most important labs. Clearly, backup is an activity to which many operators dedicate a large percentage of their time. Ideally, you'll spend less of your time doing restores. In this lab, you are asked to perform two series of save and restore activities. You will use a different set of commands in each of the sets. This lab introduces you to a series of commands as listed in Figure L10-2.

Command	Description
CRTDUPOBJ	Create Duplicate Object
INZTAP	Initialize Tape — Students will not use this command during this lab.
DSPTAP	Display Tape
SAVLIB	Save Library
SAVOBJ	Save Object
STRPDM	Start Programming Development Manager
RSTLIB	Restore Library
RSTOBJ	Restore Object

Figure L10-2: Save and Restore commands.

LAB PROCEDURES

There will be quite a few printouts generated in this lab. Make sure that you retrieve the printouts and label them when they are created to simplify assembling this assignment for submission.

The printouts generated in this assignment should be separated, numbered, stapled, and neatly folded at the back of the submission sheet. The order of the listings will be indicated during the course of this assignment; please submit the attachments in the correct order.

Several of these activities need to be completed on the same day, so watch your time. If you do not have adequate time to complete a sequence of steps, wait until the next lab session. The sequences that need to be completed on the same day will be identified in the lab prior to starting that section. Also, remember the sequence of operations is critical for this lab. Your instructor will be checking to see that the printouts reflect times in keeping with the designated sequence of operations.

This lab is a bit unusual in that save and restore operations are usually performed by a single person in a company at any given time. You would normally never have 20 or 30 people doing save or restore operations concurrently. To accommodate multiple people doing this lab at the same time, the lab is performed in the batch mode using one job queue. This avoids conflicts and locks on devices.

Students wishing to complete this assignment on their employers' systems need to see their instructor to make arrangements. Students need to have specific objects loaded in designated libraries for this lab.

GETTING READY

Before we start this lab, it is important to have a set of known objects in your library. You will need objects of a variety of types, some of which will need to have required names.

- Enter the command to display the `Command Entry` screen.
- Press F10 (Additional Parameters).

There are five objects in the OPRLIB library that you need to duplicate in your library. (Hint: You may want to check your library to see if any of these objects are already there.)

- Enter CRTDUPOBJ on the command line.
- Press F4 (Prompt).
- Press F11 (Keywords). See Figure L10-3.

```
Create Duplicate Object (CRTDUPOBJ)

 Type choices, press Enter.

 From object . . . . . . . . . . OBJ            __________
 From library . . . . . . . . . . FROMLIB        __________
 Object type . . . . . . . . . . OBJTYPE        __________
                       + for more values        __________
 To library . . . . . . . . . . . TOLIB          *FROMLIB__
 New object . . . . . . . . . . . NEWOBJ         *OBJ______

                                                              Bottom
 F3=Exit   F4=Prompt   F5=Refresh   F12=Cancel   F13=How to use this display
 F24=More keys
```

Figure L10-3: Create Duplicate Object screen showing keywords.

Before copying the following object into your library, you should display the contents of your library and determine if they are already present.

- Check to see if DINVEN is already in your library. If it is, skip this block of instructions.
- Complete the screen shown in Figure L10-3 as follows:
- Enter DINVEN in the `Obj` parameter.

- Enter OPRLIB in the Fromlib parameter.
- Enter *FILE in the Objtype parameter.
- Enter USER00XX in the Tolib parameter.
- Enter *SAME in the Newobj parameter.
- Press Enter.
- The Duplicate Data (DATA) prompt will then be displayed.
- Change the Data parameter to *YES.
- Press Enter.

The command will execute on-line. When done, the Command Entry screen will be displayed again. You should see a message on your screen indicating that the duplication of the DINVEN file was successful. If the message indicated an error condition, review that error message. Resolve the error and repeat. Use the Create Duplicate Object command to duplicate the following four objects from the OPRLIB to your library.

Remember to duplicate data for objects that contain data and accept the default (not to duplicate data) for those that do not. (*Hint*: *FILE type objects have data.) Duplicate the four objects in the chart shown in Figure L10-4 from OPRLIB library to your library.

Object Name	Object Name	Duplicate Data
DRPG2	*FILE	*YES
DRPG7	*FILE	*YES
DRPGPGM1	*PGM	*NO
AS400JQ	*JOBQ	*NO

Figure L10-4: Duplicate data for objects.

Now, to verify that the objects were successfully duplicated, print a copy of the contents of your library. You should review the printout to verify that all five of the above objects exist in your library.

- Return to the Command Entry screen.
- Enter STRPDM on the command line.
- Press Enter.

PDM (Programming Development Manager) is one of the Application Development Toolsets (ADTS). ADTS is an optional software product that not all companies have installed. If your company is doing any programming, these tools will generally be installed. AS/400 PDM provides you three starting points: libraries, objects, and members. To review the hierarchy, libraries contain objects, and some objects contain members. As your interest is in printing the contents of your library, we will start at the library level (option 1).

- Enter `1` on the command line.
- Enter `USER00XX` (your library).
- Press Enter.
- Enter `12` (`Work With`) to the left of your library (`USER00XX`).
- Press Enter.

This will bring up the Work with Objects Using PDM screen. Verify that all the objects specified above are in your library. Use F24 (More Keys) to view the various function keys available on this screen. You will notice that F21 (Print List) allows you to generate a printout showing the objects in your library.

- Press F21 (Print List).
- Use the `Work with Spool Files` command to print the listing.
- Retrieve the printout showing the contents of your library.
- Attach the printout to your submission form for this lab.
- Label it as printout #1.

INITIALIZE TAPE

Since this lab is being done by a group of students, your instructor will initialize the tape at the start of the lab session. Check with your instructor to see that the tape has been initialized and loaded in the drive prior to continuing with the lab.

Note:

Do not reinitialize the tape during the lab period. This will erase your fellow students' work.

Remember that the tape will be reinitialized for every class period. This means items saved will not be retained on the tape from class to class. Make sure that you check the time prior to starting a save operation that will require a restore operation. If adequate time is not available for BOTH the save and restore operations, wait until the next class period to start the save. The SAVE and RESTORE *must* be completed within the same class period.

Note:

All save, restore, and display operations to tape are to be submitted to batch. Don't run these interactively.

Note:

The Tape Drive is assumed to be TAP01 and the Job Queue is QBATCH. Verify the Tape Drive and Job Queue with your instructor.

SAVE LIBRARY

When you start this section, you must complete it or wait until the next lab session.

- Enter SBMJOB on the command line.
- Press F4 (Prompt).
- Enter SAVLIB in the `Command to Run` parameter.
- Press F4 (Prompt).
- Press F11 (Keywords).
- Press F10 (Additional Parameters).

The Save Library screen is shown. Notice `Level: 2` in the upper-right corner.

- What does Level: 2 stand for? ________________________________

Next, you need to enter the parameters to define the save operation. Enter the following values for the Keyword parameters:

- Enter `user00xx` (your library) for LIB parameter.
- Enter TAP01 for Dev.
- Enter *MOUNTED for `Vol`.
- Enter *LIB for `Label`.
- Enter a date or use the default *PERM for `Expdate`.
- Leave the remaining parameters at their default value.
- Press Enter twice.

When using the SAVLIB command, there are several IBM-supplied libraries that cannot be specified on the Library Name prompt.

- Name three of the IBM-supplied libraries that cannot be saved with the SAVLIB command. ______________________________
____

DISPLAY TAPE

Now to find out if you were successful in your save operation. You will need to display the tape to verify that your library is truly on the tape. There are two options to display a tape. The Data parameter's two choices are *LABELS, that identifies the library the saved objects were in; or *SAVRST, that lists the objects in the library that were saved. You will be doing two displays utilizing both options of the Data parameter. Remember that saving to a tape is a sequential operation and that many students are sharing the tape with you, so there will be many libraries displayed.

Generally, the *LABELS printout will be a single page, while the *SAVRST will produce a separate page for each library on the tape. If the printout from the tape display consists of multiple pages, only print the page(s) that shows your library. Note that if you perform multiple saves, there will be multiple saves/pages of yours in the spool file. Depending on the requirement of the save, select and print only the requested save/page.

Note:

Do not submit copies of other students' libraries, unless they are on the same page as your save.

Now it is time to get started using the Display Tape command.

- Enter SBMJOB on the command line.
- Press F4 (Prompt).
- Enter DSPTAP for the `Command to Run` parameter.
- Press F4 (Prompt).
- Press F11 (Keywords).

Enter the following values for the Keyword parameters:

- Enter TAP01 for `Dev`.
- Enter *ALL for `Label`.

- Enter *LABELS for Data.
- Enter *PRINT for Output.
- Press Enter twice.
- Retrieve a copy of the contents of the tape.
- Attach the printout to your submission form for this lab.
- Label it as printout #2.

The printout will contain a listing of the libraries saved to the tape. Note the Sequence number if you have multiple saves on the tape. Now that you have done one Display Tape operation, you will repeat the procedure—only this time, change the Data parameter to *SAVRST.

If you have performed multiple saves to the tape, you will need to select the one you want to print. Note the Sequence number if you have multiple saves on the tape. Since there are only a few objects in your library, each library fits on a single page; thus, in a multiple-page printout, the Sequence number will also be the page number. Use the WRKSPLF command to view your printouts. Use option 5 (Display) to view the contents. Page through your spool file to verify the specific page to be printed by placing P*x*, where *x* stands for the page number, on the Control line at the top.

When you have determined the page you are going to print, exit the Display screen. Select option 2 (Change) to select the page to print then direct it to the printer. On the Change Spooled File Attributes (CHGSPLFA) screen, press F10 (Additional Parameters), and then page down. See Figure L10-5. Place the page number of the selected page in the Starting Page and Ending Page parameters and press Enter. On a system printer, you will get only the selected page. If using Operations Navigator, use the Current Page option while viewing the printout.

```
                  Change Spooled File Attributes (CHGSPLFA)

Type choices, press Enter.

Page range to print:
  Starting page . . . . . . . .   1            Number, *SAME, *ENDPAGE
  Ending page . . . . . . . . .   *END         Number, *SAME, *END
File becomes available . . . . .  *FILEEND     *SAME, *JOBEND, *FILEEND...
Save file . . . . . . . . . . .   *NO          *SAME, *NO, *YES
Output priority . . . . . . . .   5            1-9, *SAME, *JOB
User data . . . . . . . . . . .   '          ' User data, *SAME
Align page . . . . . . . . . . .  *NO          *SAME, *NO, *YES
Print quality . . . . . . . . .   *STD         *SAME, *STD, *DEVD, *DRAFT...
Form feed . . . . . . . . . . .   *DEVD        *SAME, *DEVD, *CONT, *CUT...
Source drawer . . . . . . . . .   1            1-255, *SAME, *E1, *FORMDF
Print fidelity . . . . . . . . .  *CONTENT     *SAME, *ABSOLUTE, *CONTENT
Print on both sides . . . . . .   *NO          *SAME, *NO, *YES, *TUMBLE...
Pages per side . . . . . . . . .  1            1-4, *SAME
Form definition . . . . . . . .   *NONE        Name, *SAME, *NONE, *DEVD...
  Library . . . . . . . . . . .                Name, *LIBL, *CURLIB
                                                                     More...
F3=Exit   F4=Prompt   F5=Refresh   F12=Cancel   F13=How to use this display
F24=More keys
```

Figure L10-5: Second page of the Work with Spooled File command shows parameter that controls the range of pages printed.

- Repeat the steps above.
- Use *SAVRST for the Data parameter.
- Retrieve a copy of the contents of the tape.
- Attach the printout to your submission form for this lab.
- Label it as printout #3.

Printout #3 will contain the library contents.

DELETING OBJECTS IN YOUR LIBRARY

Do not start this step until you have printed or viewed the above two printouts. If your library does not appear on the above printouts, then repeat and/or look into the reason. Now you are going to delete objects from your library. Later, you will restore them from the tape.

- Return to the Command Entry screen.
- Press F10 (Additional Parameters).
- Enter STRPDM on the command line.
- Press Enter.
- Select option 1.
- Press Enter.
- Enter your Library Name.
- Press Enter.

This brings you to the Work with Libraries Using PDM screen showing your library. Next, you need to display the contents of the library.

- Enter 12 (Work with) in the Opt column next to your library name.
- Press Enter.

The Work with Objects Using PDM screen is shown, listing the current contents of your library. You now want to delete all files from your library.

- Enter option 4 (Delete) next to ALL the *FILE type objects.
- Press Enter.
- Press Enter again to confirm the delete.

The updated Work with Objects display is shown. Now you need to obtain a printout of the updated contents of the library showing that the files have been deleted. This can be accomplished using the function keys.

- Press F21 (Print List) to print a listing of your library to the spool file.
- Retrieve a copy of the updated contents of your library showing the deletion.
- Attach the printout to your submission form for this lab.
- Label it as printout #4.
- Return to the `Command Entry` screen.

RESTORE LIBRARY

To complete the save and restore sequence, you still need to restore the deleted objects from the tape. To restore your library to its pre-deleted-objects condition, use the procedure that follows.

- Enter SBMJOB on the command line.
- Press F4 (Prompt).
- Enter RSTLIB in the `Command to Run` parameter.
- Press F4 (Prompt).
- Press F11 (Keywords).
- Then press F10 (Additional Parameters).

Now you are ready to complete the parameters of the Restore Library command. Since you have come this far in this lab, it is time to test your understanding. You will be completing the following parameters with values previously used in this lab and appropriate to restore you library to its original condition. Complete the parameter values below:

- Supply the value for the `Savlib` parameter.
- Supply the value for the `Dev` parameter.
- Leave `Vol` as *MOUNTED.
- Leave `Label` at its default value.
- Press Enter until the command executes.

The library will be restored as a batch operation. When the restoration is complete, you will receive a message to that effect. Use the DSPMSG to view the message. The message should be similar to this: `Job 189770/OPR0001/OPRJOBD completed normally on 08/09/99 at 12:16:52.`

Use the Restore commands to answer the following questions:

- On the RSTOBJ command, when the Allow Object Differences (ALWOBJDIF) parameter is specified as *ALL, what are the allowable object differences?
____
____
____

- What is the purpose of the Restore Licensed Program (RSTLICPGM) command?
____
____

DEMONSTRATE LIBRARY WAS RESTORED

Use PDM to show that the objects have been restored to your library. Use the procedure you previously used.

- Use the STRPDM command.
- Select the option to `Work with Your Library.`
- Select the option to `Work with Objects.`
- Use the function key to get a listing of your library, showing the current (restored) objects.
- Retrieve and attach the printout labeled as #5 to your submission sheet.
- Return to the `Command Entry` screen.

SAVE OBJECT

The sequence of the following operations is very similar to the sequence in the operations you've just completed. The Save and Restore commands have changed; however, most of the information provided above applies in the save and restore of objects. Once you start this section, you will need to complete it. If you won't have time to complete it, wait until the next lab session to start.

- Enter SBMJOB on the command line.
- Press F4 (Prompt).
- Enter SAVOBJ on the `Command to Run` parameter.
- Press F4 (Prompt).
- Then press F11 (Keywords).
- Also press F10 (Additional Parameters).

You are going to save all the files beginning with the characters DRPG. So, enter a generic name (DRPG*) for the OBJ parameter. Complete the remaining parameters with the appropriate values. Remember that all the objects are being saved from the same library. Below are the parameters you need to complete.

- Enter appropriate values for the `Lib` and `Dev` parameters.
- Enter the appropriate `Objtype` parameter. (*Hint*: You want to save files.)
- The `Vol` parameter should be *MOUNTED.
- Press F10 (Additional Parameters).
- Leave the `Label` prompt at its default value.
- Enter a date or use the default for the `Expdate` parameter.
- Press Enter until the command executes.

When done, a message will be received notifying you that the job completed normally. Make sure that your message indicator is clear so that you will know when this message has been received. View the message to see that it completed normally.

DISPLAY TAPE AGAIN

You should be good at this procedure by now. This is just a rerun of a previous section.

- Enter SBMJOB on the command line.
- Press F4 (Prompt).
- Enter DSPTAP on the `Command to Run` parameter.
- Press F4 (Prompt).
- Then press F11 (Keywords).

You need to change the following keyword parameters:

- Enter the tape device name for `Dev` parameter.
- Change `Label` parameter to *ALL.
- Leave `Data` parameter the default value.
- Select the value for the `Output` parameter to get a printout.
- Press Enter twice.
- This listing should be labeled #6.
- Attach to your lab submission sheet for this lab.

Next, you will repeat the above command, only change the Data parameter to `DISPLAY` and print the objects saved in the library.

- Repeat the above command.
- Change the `Data` parameter to *SAVRST.
- Label it printout #7.
- Attach to your submission sheet for this lab.

DELETE OBJECTS

Delete all the objects from your library.

- Use the STRPDM command.
- Select `Work with Objects`.
- Use an option to delete all objects.

You should get a message indicating that the objects were deleted.

VERIFY OBJECTS DELETION

Now, from PDM, get a current listing of your library contents showing the absence of the deleted objects.

- Use the STRPDM command.
- Select `Work with Objects`.
- Use function key to Print List.
- Retrieve printout and label it #8.
- Attach printout to your submission form.

RESTORE SELECTED OBJECTS

You are going to restore selected objects to your library. In other words, all objects that you saved will not be restored. Again, submit your command to batch.

- Enter SBMJOB on the command line.
- Press F4 (Prompt).
- Enter RSTOBJ in the `Command to Run` parameter.
- Press F4 (Prompt).
- Press F11 (Keyword).

You saved all objects beginning with DRPG and you only want to restore the files that start with DRPG. This will not restore all the objects you saved.

- Enter SBMJOB on the command line.
- Press Enter.
- Enter `Restore Object in the Command to Run` parameter.
- Press F4 (Prompt).
- Press F10 (Additional Parameters) and F11 (Keywords).

You want to restore all the files beginning with the characters DRPG. So, enter a generic name for the Object parameter.

- Enter `generic name` for files beginning with the characters DRPG.
- Enter the appropriate values for the `Savlib, Dev`, and `Objtype` parameters.
- Press F10 (Additional Parameters) and F11 (Keywords).
- Leave the `volume identifier` at its default value.
- Leave the `Label` prompt at its default value.
- Press Enter twice to submit the command to execute.
- Return to the `Command Entry` screen.

VALIDATE RESTORE

Once again, you need a printout to demonstrate that you successfully restored the files beginning with DRPG only.

- Use the STRPDM command
- Print out a current listing of the objects in your library.
- Retrieve the printout, label it #9, and attach to your submission form.

You now have successfully performed backup and recovery activities. You are ready to apply your knowledge in the workplace or in the additional assignments.

You are ready to submit your assignment. Remember that each sheet of paper generated by the assignment steps must be labeled with the number of the printout. Submit these printouts in the correct sequence, stapled in the upper-left corner.

ADDITIONAL LAB ASSIGNMENTS

Check with your instructor to determine if there are restrictions or special information needed to do these additional assignments.

1. Do your backup and recovery operations interactively to a Save File located in your library rather than to tape.
   a. Create a Save File called LAB10 in your library.
   b. Save File commands you should use are:
      i. CLRSAVF to clear the contents of a Save File. One of the major differences between a Save File and tape is that a Save File can contain the results of ONLY ONE save operation. It must be cleared before the next operation is performed.
      ii. DSPSAVF is used to view the contents of the Save File. There is an OUTPUT parameter that directs the results either to the screen or the spool file. DSPSAVF is used in place of the DSPTAP command.
   c. Make sure that the following objects are in your library:
      i. DINVEN *FILE.
      ii. DRPG2 *FILE.
      iii. DRPG7 *FILE.
      iv. DRPGRGM1 *PGM.
      v. AS400JQ *JOBQ.
   d. Backup/recovery operation choices:
      i. SAVLIB/RSTLIB choice.
         (1) Save the contents of your library without saving the Save File LAB10.
         (2) Display and print the Save File.
         (3) Delete all objects in your library starting with a D.
         (4) Print the contents of your library.
         (5) Restore the library.
         (6) Print the contents of your library.
         (7) Clear the Save File.
         (8) Print the contents of the Save File.

ii. SAVOBJ/RSTOBJ choices:

(1) Save all objects in your library beginning with a D.

(2) Display and print the Save File.

(3) Delete all objects except LAB10 (the Save File).

(4) Print the contents of your library.

(5) Restore only the programs to your library.

(6) Print the contents of your library.

(7) Restore the files beginning with a D.

(8) Print the contents of your library.

(9) Clear the Save File.

(10) Print the contents of the Save File.

2. Use the Save File LAB10 in your library. Do the following backup/recovery activity. The save should be done in one step, so combine steps b, c, and d.

   a. Make sure your library has the objects listed in Additional Lab Assignments 1c.

   b. Use the *LIB value for the Save-While-Active parameter. Leave the remaining Save-While-Active parameters at their default value.

   c. Save the objects to a previous release of the operating system.

   d. Save all objects starting with a D.

   e. If any object did not get saved, print the error message showing the reason.

   f. Display and print the contents of the Save File.

   g. Delete all files (except the Save File).

   h. Print the contents of your library.

   i. Restore the DINVEN file.

   j. Print the contents of your library.

3. When designated by your instructor, you can initialize the tape. You instructor will provide you with the needed format information.

END-OF-CHAPTER AIDS

CHAPTER SUMMARY

New AS/400 customers sometimes feel that things are not progressing well when they first do a backup or a restore. Feelings of uncertainty are especially evident in customers who backup or recover to reel tapes where they can watch the tape drive's progress. The AS/400 backup and restore programs do some preliminary processing and post-processing that makes the drive seem a little erratic.

When saving objects, files, and libraries, the backup process builds directories about the objects being saved. When each directory is complete, it is written to the save media and the objects follow. Many small objects take a long time (usually longer than a few large objects). When a new AS/400 customer views the tape progress, it advances a few inches when the process starts and then sits for several minutes before rapidly continuing. The tape might stop again for a few minutes and then continue. These "minutes" can be an hour or more—no wonder people get nervous.

Restores are similar. The tape drive will read a few inches of information and then digest it for several minutes before continuing. The same behavior happens on diskettes and tape cartridges (even Save Files), but these cannot be observed like tape reels can.

AS/400 backups and recoveries are rich in function but, when you boil them down to what is required, they become a routine nightly function. You will hardly think about them.

But do spend the time to develop a strategy, spend the time to implement its actions, and especially spend the time to verify that backups are happening according to the strategy. Remember, backups are boring—no one cares, everyone resents the time they take. But restores, on the other hand, will make or break several people's careers.

KEY TERMS

backup
backup strategy
checkpoints
copy command
database synchronization
development objects
disaster recovery
diskettes
end of tape option
generations of backups
initialize media
Integrated File System (IFS)
magnetic media
omit libraries
operating objects
production objects
recovery
recovery strategy
restore
restore command
restricted state
save command
Save File (*SAVF)
Save-While-Active
sequence number
storage media
support objects
system objects
tape
target release
transaction
user objects

CHAPTER SELF-TEST

Solutions to these self-test questions are in appendix D.

True-False Questions

___ 1. You would use the RSTSYS command to restore objects saved with the SAVSYS command.

___ 2. Saturday evening, you saved the system using the SAVSTG command. A user contacts you Monday afternoon requesting that you restore an object he/she just deleted in error. You can restore the user's object from the Saturday tape with no problem.

___ 3. The most common reason for a backup is to restore an object or group of objects that have erroneously been deleted or damaged.

___ 4. One of the constraints of the SAVSYS command is that it must run in a restricted state.

___ 5. A more efficient save is done when setting the Use Optimum Block parameter to *YES. Tapes prepared using this parameter are good for moving information between multiple AS/400s regardless of the tape drives.

___ 6. Before you do a save to a Save File, the Save File must exist on the system.

___ 7. A tape or diskette needs to be initialized prior to its initial use.

___ 8. A user printed a spooled report Monday morning that was generated on Friday. The system was completely backed up over the weekend. The user calls the operator Monday afternoon in a panic as the report he/she printed in the morning was misplaced, and he/she had deleted the spool file from the output queue after printing. You are able to help this user by restoring the spool file to the output queue.

Fill in the Blanks

1. You are making a copy of a library on a V4R3 system to be restored on a V4R1 system. The operator can use the __________________ command and would need to indicate the require release on the __________________ parameter.

2. The system performs the Save-While-Active function by maintaining an image of the object being saved as it existed at a single point in time. This point in time is called the ____________ for an object, and the image of the object is called the ____________ ____________.

3. The SAVSYS command can be done in parts. When using this command, you can choose to not include the save of ________________ ________________ and ____________ ____________, thus, having them saved with separate commands later.

4. An object saved using the SAVCHGOBJ command would be restored using the __________________ command.

5. Objects saved with either the SAVOBJ or SAVCHGOBJ can be restored with the __________________ command.

6. ____________ ____________ are never saved themselves. Instead, they are saved when you save the physical file they are built over and specify on the Save command that you want to save access paths.

Chapter Review Questions

1. Define the following terms:

   a. Save-While-Active.

   b. Checkpoint.

   c. Backup.

   d. Backup/recovery strategy.

   e. Backup media.

f. Restricted state.

g. Device configurations (with respect to the SAVCFG command).

h. Save File.

2. When would you use the SAVSTG command, and what are the limitations of this command?

3. Before you start to upgrade your operating system, you should do a current backup of your system. How would you do this? Include the commands you would use and why.

4. What are the advantages and disadvantages of using the Save-While-Active option in many commands?

5. The SAVLIB command can be used to save all libraries except?

6. An entire system backup consists of what commands? *Note*: This is the same as option 21 on the Save menu.

7. How is the SAVLICPGM command different from the other save commands?

8. How could an operator believe that he/she performed a restoration of an object to the system and was not successful? (*Hint*: Database member option.)

9. Propose a backup strategy for your college AS/400.

10. When do you use the Omit parameter on the Save commands? What are the constraints?

11. What is the difference between the use of SAVOBJ and SAVCHGOBJ commands, and when would you use which command?

12. Briefly describe the difference between the SAVSTG command and the SAVSYS command.

13. Which command can be used to restore user profiles from SAVSYS media?

14. What are Save Files (*SAVF) and how are they created?

15. What does the term "freeing storage" mean?

16. When saving to tape using IBM Save commands, there is a parameter called Clear. What is its purpose?

17. List the five types of configuration objects that are saved when the SAVSYS command is used.

11

SECURITY AND SECURITY SYSTEM VALUES

CHAPTER OBJECTIVES

Upon completion of this chapter, you should be able to:

- Explain the importance of security on a computer system.
- Describe the various AS/400 security levels.
- Explain what system values are and how they are used.
- Explain the system values related to system management and security.
- Describe specific and special authorities.
- Explain the purpose of the predefined profiles including QSYSOPR and QSECOFR.
- Explain how the following can be used to control security:
  - User and group profiles.
  - User classes.
  - Object authority.
  - Job descriptions.
  - Library lists.
  - Authorization lists.
  - Adopted authority.

INTRODUCTION

System security consists of the safeguards to control who can access devices, data, and programs. This control is necessary to prevent accidental—or intentional—changes to, or loss or destruction of, system resources. Security prevents access to objects by users who don't have *authority* and keeps the integrity of the system's data. Security has two broad areas: physical security and data security.

Physical security involves protecting the computer, its devices, and media from damage. The system should be located in a secure area, physically locked, and free from risk of fire, flood, etc. The control panel on the system unit should be kept locked during normal operation, and the key(s) and/or key stick should be stored in a secure location.

Data security is the protection of the logical (nonhardware) pieces that make up a computer system. Some examples of these are: programs, operating systems, data, passwords, and utilities. Data security extends to concepts like database integrity (the data is there, and it should be good, too) and access to the computer.

Data security can focus on the objects on a system. When it does, it is referred to as *object-based security*. Object-based security is very strong because even if someone was to hack into the system, every object on the system knows who can access it, so security occurs at a very low level. The alternative is security attached to each user ID, or *user-based security*. User-based security identifies the user when an attempt to sign in is made. When a successful entry to the computer is achieved, the rules that govern what that user can or cannot do are established and follow the user while signed on. This method is more flexible but weaker than object-based security, because once such a security system is hacked into, the whole computer is at the disposal of the hacker. The AS/400 uses a combination of both security approaches.

Physical and data security elements often work together. The tape backup of important software will be more secure when it is also kept physically away from harm, like in a locked vault. Just having a recent version of the system available in case of a catastrophic data loss is data security. Physical security, how much is done, is a project involving the company's physical space, budgets, and needs. Data security, on the other hand, is taken care of within the AS/400. This is the area discussed in this chapter. To start with, data security is comprised of three broad areas:

- System Level: The *system level* is a very high-level security decision made through OS/400 *system values*. These decisions affect everyone accessing the AS/400 and have a great effect on how the AS/400 looks and feels.
- User Profiles: Each user has a *user profile* that should be unique. Among other things, it can give the user the authority to use very powerful system functions (or not use them). It also determines ownership of objects created by the user. A user signs onto the system and is known to the system by this user profile.
- Object: Every object on the AS/400 contains a list of users (actually their user profiles) who can access it. On this list is also what each can do to the object. It can also specify what access (if any) a user can have who is not on the list. The object's owners' and previous owners' current authorities are also carried with each object.

Working together, these three security forces and set of system values provide the most flexible security matrix in the industry. The customer can set up very lax security or extremely (defense department "C2") tight security.

SYSTEM SECURITY LEVEL

The level of system security determines, in general terms, what the security of the AS/400 will be. This level is often referred to as the system's *level of security*. It is controlled by the system value QSECURITY. The two-digit value in this system value sets the security level of the whole machine. Here are the valid values for it and a brief description of each level:

- Security Level 20 (SL20): The user must sign on with a valid user ID and password. Once in, the user has access—except for functions reserved just for the all-powerful security officer—to everything on the system.

- Security Level 30 (SL30): This is the first level that provides real system security. The user must sign on with a valid user ID and password. Users have access to objects only when the objects have been designated as usable by the individual user or by *PUBLIC (anyone). When objects are restored, there is a parameter on the Restore command running under SL30 that is not on SL20. This is the Allow Object Differences parameter, and it is defaulted to a *YES. For an example of how this parameter works, consider restoring a file that has been changed since the backup was made. If the option is still *YES (the default), the system will complete the restore. If the parameter was changed to *NO, the system will not restore the object. This is the security level that is most common with AS/400 customers.

- Security Level 40 (SL40): The user must sign on with a valid user ID and password. Users have access to objects only when the objects have been designated as usable by the individual user or by *PUBLIC (anyone). When files are restored, the same Allow Object Differences option is defaulted to a *NO and must be changed if the object has been changed since it was last saved. This is a small thing, but it can make simple restores cumbersome. The biggest thing SL40 does over the others is it prevents applications from using "unauthorized" low-level programming techniques that are sometimes employed by software vendors for improved performance.

- Security Level 50 (SL50): Also called "C2," this level was developed for the Department of Defense, and it is finding acceptance where AS/400 systems allow open access to remote users. SL50 is the same as SL40 except:

  - Users can only access objects to which they have been given explicit access. This eliminates many of the shortcuts and defaults with SL30 and SL40.

  - Programs will abend if they access unauthorized low-level functions.

  - Programs will abend if they access AS/400 Application Programming Interfaces (APIs) or functions and they do not pass exactly the right number of parameters. APIs are the doors to those low-level functions. They require very advanced programming skills to use. Holding software to a number of parameters when using APIs can be a problem when IBM adds new parameters to existing APIs in a new OS/400 release. This happens from time to time, usually with no effect because the number of API parameters is optional on all but SL50 AS/400s. When it does happen on an SL50 AS/400, existing programs may start to fail.

Once the system's basic security level is set, the operator is ready to begin to work with other components of security.

USER PROFILES

The second piece of the AS/400 security matrix is the user profile. These are individual objects, object type *USRPRF. All user profiles reside in system library, QSYS. The name of this object is the name the user needs to sign onto the AS/400. The user profile defines the user's rights on the system and sets several values for a user's work environment:

- Basic security information about the person.
- Special authorities granted to the person.
- Job processing information specific to the person, such as:
  - Job queue.
  - Output queue.
  - Initial program or menu to call.
  - Current library.

We have seen job queues, output queues, and current library in discussions about jobs. These can be specified on job descriptions or on the Submit Job (SBMJOB) command; when they are, those specified items are used. But job descriptions and the SBMJOB command can also specify *USERDEF instead of naming specific objects. When that happens, the user profile is where the system will go to determine the jobs' queues and current library.

The AS/400 can support as simple or as complex a set of users as the company needs. An organization with few IT personnel will have one or two people who have access to everything. Large organizations will have many subsets of users, each with a very definite set of rights and accesses.

IBM supplies several user profiles known as *default profiles* on every AS/400. They all start with the letter Q and reside in the library QSYS. Here is the typical mix of user roles on an AS/400. The user profiles that start with the letter Q are supplied by IBM with every AS/400:

- *Security Officer*: The IBM-supplied user profile is QSECOFR. Referred to as "Sec-Offer," this user can do anything on the system except service functions. Service functions are better left to the IBM or reseller CE (customer engineer). The security officer has unlimited power to access objects on the system. Most AS/400 IT departments only have one or two security officers.

- *System Operator*: The *IBM system-supplied profile* is QSYSOPR. The system operator has authority to control jobs, print files, and do backup and restore functions.

- *Programmers*: The IBM system-supplied profile is QPGMR. This user is a developer who can create programs and database files and generally has broad access in the development libraries. This user usually does not have access to production libraries. This dichotomy makes a complex issue and many organizations purchase CMS (Change Management Systems) to give them real sophistication in the area.

- *Users*: The system-supplied profile is QUSER. A user can be defined as anyone not in the computer department.

These user profiles, except for QSECOFR, do not have passwords from IBM when the system is received. QSECOFR's password is QSECOFR and must be changed the first time someone signs onto a new AS/400.

These user profiles from IBM are basic examples of the user profiles that are really needed to set up an AS/400. They are not intended to be used as actual user profiles; they are meant to be merely referenced, copied, possibly renamed, and activated with passwords before use. Used either way, the default profiles are an excellent basis from which to start creating user profiles.

In addition to the user profiles mentioned above, the AS/400 comes with these special service user profiles:

- QSRV— Services (all functions). This is the profile that the person who services the AS/400 will use.

- QSRVBAS—Services (limited functions). This is the profile that the person who services the AS/400 will use.

There are several additional IBM-supplied user profiles that are not to be turned into user profiles that someone can sign onto the system with. They are to be used internally by the AS/400 to do special functions. Often when the system starts a system job, the "owner" of the job will be one of these AS/400 user profiles. The system operator does not have to do anything with these user profiles. Just recognize them when they appear from time to time.

- QAUTPROF—IBM General Authority Profile.
- QBRMS—Backup Recovery Media (BRM) Profile.
- QDBSHR—Database Share Profile.
- QDFTOWN—All objects on the AS/400 must be owned by a legitimate user. If a user profile is no longer valid, its objects' ownership is changed to QDFTOWN.
- QDOC—Document Profile.
- QDSNX—Distributed System Node Executive.
- QFNC—Finance Profile.
- QGATE—User profile to bridge into PROFS (VM/MVS on mainframes).
- QLPAUTO—Licensed Program Auto-installation User (see chapter 9).
- QLPINSTALL—Licensed Program Installation User (see chapter 9).
- QMSF—Mail Server Framework Profile.
- QNETSPLF—Network Spooling Profile.
- QNFSANON—NFS User Profile.
- QSNADS—SNADS User.
- QSPL—Spooling User.
- QSPLJOB—Spooling Readers/Writers Job User Profile.
- QSYS—Internal System User.
- QTCP—TCP/IP User.

Do not change or delete these profiles. If they are changed or deleted, internal functions will probably stop working.

SPECIAL AUTHORITIES AND USER CLASSES

Inflexible security—like this person can do this but cannot do that—is nice for most things, but it ignores the need for something special in order to have both adequate security and still allow people to do their jobs. Consider that object level security only creates a dilemma.

Many of the real distinctions between user types are achieved through the granting of special authorities. An example of this is the system operator who needs to save and restore files. System operators typically are excluded from access to production files (the thinking is it would not be wise to give one full access to the payroll file). But if the system operator really was excluded, that would also mean that he/she would not be able to save the payroll file (because he/she has no access rights to it). He/she especially would not be able to restore the payroll file (because the restore can imply deleting an existing copy).

In this case, the special authority, *SAVSYS, allows the operator to do system-level tasks like save/restore but not read any records and certainly not change, add, or delete them. That something special is called the *special authorities*, and a user profile can have up to ten of them. While most AS/400 security is object-based, special authorities are user-based. Here is what they do:

- *ALLOBJ: The user can do anything to any object. This is reserved for SECOFR. This special authority overrides all private/public authorities on the system, so be careful who is granted this authority level. (*Note*: When the system security level is set to 20, all users have *ALLOBJ special authority.)
- *AUDIT: The user can change system values that control auditing. This gives the user the necessary authority to perform auditing functions such as changing QAUDXXX system value and changing user profile or object auditing. The user can execute the commands CHGOBJAUD and CHGUSRAUD.
- *IOSYSCFG: The user can change system configuration issues including network and communications devices, controllers, and lines. Note that if the AS/400 supports Internet access, anyone with this special authority can configure the communication devices and the TCP/IP server.
- *JOBCTL: Allows a user to manage jobs running on the system. Gives the user authorization to maintain other users' jobs. It allows a user to change jobs to other job queues and change output to different queues. The user can cancel or alter running jobs or change their priorities with this authority. On the system, the user can start/stop the entire subsystem, load the operating system, and so on. This authority is usually given to system operators.
- *SAVSYS: Allows the user to perform backup/restore operations on all objects even if the user has no authority to an object. This authority is usually given to system operators.
- *SECADM: Allows user to create and alter user profiles. Some AS/400 IT departments have a person dedicated to this function. Only a user with both *SECADM and *ALLOBJ authorities can grant *SECADM authority to another user. *SECADM allows a user to:
  - Create, change, and delete user profiles.
  - Add users to the system distribution directory.
  - Change or display authority for documents or folders.
  - Add and remove access codes on the system.
  - Delete documents and folders.

  - Delete document lists.
  - Change distribution lists created by other users.
  - Change security-related system values and network attributes.
- *SERVICE: This allows service and dump functions. It gives a user the authority to run the service functions such as the System Service Tools (SST). These are never given to someone who is not extremely knowledgeable about the system. This authorization is more often extended to the IBM service representatives than to anyone in-house.
- *SPLCTL: This allows a user to manage output queues. These users can display, move, print, release, and cancel spooled output. This is commonly granted to all users who need to be able to browse their reports directly in output queues. The problem that can come up is one user browsing other users' output, even confidential files. The solution to that is to build "restricted" output queues. Then users with *SPLCTL can browse only nonrestricted output queues.

User class is a user profile parameter that is used to quickly specify the default special authorities for a user and control what menu options are shown to the user. This does not necessarily limit the use of other authorities. Each user class has certain special authorities that are automatically invoked when one of these user classes is named. The user classes that determine which system control operations and menu options a user can access are:

- *SECOFR.
- *SECADM.
- *PGMR.
- *SYSOPR.
- *USER.

The special authorities granted to each class change with the security level of the AS/400. Figures 11-1 and 11-2 list the special authorities granted based on the AS/400 security level.

Special Authorities at Level 20							
User Class	*ALLOBJ	*AUDIT	*SECADM	*SAVSYS	*JOBCTL	*SPLCTL	*SERVICE
*SECOFR	x	x	x	x	x	x	x
*SECADM	x			x	x		
*PGMR	x			x	x		
*SYSOPR	x			x	x		
*USER	x			x			

Figure 11-1: Special authorities granted to user classes in SL20 AS/400s.

Special Authorities at Level 30, 40, or 50							
User Class	*ALLOBJ	*AUDIT	*SECADM	*SAVSYS	*JOBCTL	*SPLCTL	*SERVICE
*SECOFR	x	x	x	x	x	x	x
*SECADM			x	x	x		
*PGMR				x	x		
*SYSOPR				x	x		
*USER	*** No Special Authorities for "User" ***						

Figure 11-2: Special authorities granted to user classes in all other AS/400 security levels.

GROUP PROFILES

The use of *group profiles* can speed up user profile creation and enhance security. Profiles contain a lot of information about each user. A small amount of it is unique to the user, most of it is similar for many users and can be shared. The group profile allows these attributes common to a group of similar users to be shared. For example, if all the users in the accounts receivable department were to have common characteristics, a group profile for that department would be set up. Then, when the user profiles are created, they would reference the same group profile. Individual user profiles could still be maintained but most of the detail would be in the group profile.

Group members are not necessarily all equal in security. For example, the manager of the department could belong to the same group and have more authority given in his/her user profile. A nice feature about having many users referencing a common group profile is that changes to the group can be made once by changing the group profile, rather than many times by individually changing the user profiles.

One big impact of group profiles is that they change *object ownership*. This is an important issue and is best understood considering setting up a group of developers. Object ownership is important because the creator of the object is usually the owner, and the object's owner can do anything to the object: read it, change it, or delete it. Anyone else, the nonowners, must be granted access to the object. One developer may start on a project, but others may work with him or may actually finish the work. It would be very cumbersome if all object access had to be manually granted to others.

When all developers are in the same group and object ownership is set to the group profile, not the user profile, then the group owns objects—not the individual who creates them. This allows for a much more dynamic programming environment. Group profiles begin life as regular user profiles except that they do not have passwords. This is done through the parameter PASSWORD with the Create command set to *NONE. They become group profiles when they are specified on the GRPPRF parameter on a regular user profile.

If we wanted to create a group profile for developers called PGM, we would create a user profile called PGM that does not have a password. Then, for every individual user profile we create, we would specify PGM as the GRPPRF parameter.

TIP:

User profiles that are members of a group profile inherit the group profile's authorities. Do not create a group profile with a lot of authority, like *ALLOBJ, or you'll inadvertently give it to all members of that group.

OBJECT SECURITY

Every AS/400 object carries its own list of who can do what to it. This is referred to as its *authorities*. These are different from user profile authorities. Where user profile authorities name broad-based powers for each user (or group of users), objects carry a list of users (or groups of users) and what functions those users can do to the object. The user names can be in several contexts on the object:

- Ownership:
    - Every object is owned by one user profile.
    - An object may contain a previous owner's name.
- Named users and specific authorities—A list of users and what they can do to the object.
- Authorization lists—A way of externally listing users and their specific authorities to the object.
- Public authority—A user profile not found on the object's ownership or list of users, or the authorization list is considered public (*PUBLIC). The *PUBLIC (the un-named users) has its own *specific authority*.

OWNERSHIP—SINGLE AND GROUP

The first item in an object's authority is who owns it. *Ownership* consists of one of four categories:

- The person who created it.
- Previous owners' authorities (optional).
- The group user profile of the creator.
- If the owning user profile gets deleted, the system changes the object's owner to the system default owner, QDFTOWN.

The owner automatically has all rights to the objects he/she creates. He/she can read, write, or change records as well as delete or change the object itself.

Object ownership can be changed with the Change Object Owner (CHGOBJOWN) command and often times will be when an object moves from development into production. When ownership is changed, the system gives the operator the opportunity to revoke or keep the previous owner's authorities. If the operator wants to retain the previous owner's authorities (or a modified version of them), the object will carry a single owner (the new one) and the previous owner's name and current authorities.

Here is a twist to object ownership. We do not want unauthorized people changing production jobs or data. Therefore, when programs or files are moved from a development (or quality assurance) library into production, object ownership should be changed to some nonperson owner. This "owner" would be a user profile without a password (so a real person could never sign onto the system with it). Those who can access the object can only do so by being named on the object (or having special authorities on their user profile).

But consider how program fixes and enhancements are made. First, they are not made in production. They must be moved or *checked out* from production to development. The programmer works on them there, tests the results, then moves (or *promotes*) the program to either a quality control area or production. When the program object is checked out, the programmer is granted total authority over it. When it is promoted, any authority to it is stripped. This is often done by changing object ownership during the process. Object ownership can be a little complex and the smart IT department will seriously consider a good change-management system (CMS) to do all the housekeeping for it.

The ownership of an object has a lot to do with what is considered a *user's storage*. This is the maximum amount of storage a user can have. It is optional and, if it is set, is done so with the Maximum Storage (MAXSTSG) parameter of either the Create User Profile (CRTUSRPRF) or Change User Profile (CHGUSRPRF) commands. If the user's objects are owned by the user alone, their size contributes to the amount of storage being carried—it is this figure the system will attempt to limit. If an object is owned by the group profile, its storage is assigned to the group (and usually MAXSTG is set to *NOMAX for group profiles). Group ownership adds a twist to this, however, if MAXSTG is set for the development staff. Do not think this will allow individuals unlimited storage because all new objects are owned by the group. When an individual creates a file object by copying an existing file, that individual owns it during the creation process. If ultimate object ownership will belong to the group, ownership is transferred as soon as the object is created. This can mean that a developer creating a large object may exceed the individual MAXSTG limit, even though the object is meant to be owned by the group. The way around this is to have the developer create a shell (an empty file) then fill it after creation. Another solution is to temporarily set the developer's MAXSTG to *NOMAX until the large object is created and ownership is made under the group profile.

Named Users and Specific Authorities

There are plenty of users on a system and only one of them (or several through a group profile) can have ownership at one time. Access to others (nonowners) is granted through specific authorities attached to each object.

Specific authorities are a list (attached to the object) of user profiles or group user profiles with specific access authorities for each. Although an object can only have one owner, it can have many individual specific users, and each user has his/her own access level.

Objects really have two sets of authorities that we are concerned with. One, management authority, determines who can do what with the object's existence. This authority has nothing to do with the contents of the object—it governs who can change its attributes (like how big a file can be), delete it, or even use it. Possible management authorities that can be assigned to a named user are:

- *Operational Authority*—The user can look at a description of the object and can use it as determined by other specific authorities.

- *Management Authority*—The user can specify security for the object, can move it, or rename it. If the object is a database file, the user can add members to it.

- *Existence Authority*—The user can delete the object, change the object's owner, free its storage, and perform save/restore functions on the object.

- *Authority List Management*—The user can attach an *authority list* to the object and add/change/delete users and their authorities within the list.

- *Alter Authority*—The user can change the attributes of database files or add/remove stored triggers (a programming function).

- *Reference Authority*—The user can name a database table as the parent in a referential integrity situation (a programming or database administration function).

The other authority set we have to be concerned with is the *data authorities*. These govern what the named user can do with the contents of the object. Some common sense must be used here as these authorities can change as the object type changes. For example, a user cannot be granted the right to read the contents of a program object but can be given the right to execute the program. On the other hand, it makes perfect sense that a user can be granted the right to read the records in a database table, but it makes no sense to allow that user the right to execute the table. The possible data authorities that can be assigned to a named user are:

*READ—The user can read the contents of the object.

*ADD—The user can add to the contents of the object.

*UPD—The user can make changes to the contents of the object.

*DLT—The user can delete all or pieces of the contents of the object.

*EXECUTE—The user can execute the object.

That is eleven separate object authorities to think through on every object. To make the process easier, IBM gives us four *predefined specific authorities* that, once one is specified, the system fills in what it feels are appropriate management and data authorities. These predefined specific authorities are:

- *ALL—The user has all management and all data authorities.

- *CHANGE—The user has operational authority and all data authorities.

- *USE—The user has operational, read, and execute authorities but cannot add/change/delete pieces of the object's contents.

- *EXCLUDE—The user has no access to the object.

We will visit these authorities in greater detail in the second half of this chapter, which deals with security commands.

TIP:

User profiles have special authorities.

Objects have specific authorities.

Special authorities define what the user can do.

Specific authorities define what can be done to the object.

Authorization Lists

The list of individual users authorized to each object can be quite lengthy, so AS/400 objects can be secured through *authorization* lists. An authorization list is a type of object itself (*AUTL) that always resides in QSYS. It contains a list of user IDs and authorizations. By attaching the authorization list to an object, the system operator is automatically attaching the users and their authorities to the object.

Applications that have hundreds of objects and hundreds of users can be set up with one authorization list of all valid users and their authorizations. By attaching the list to each of the hundreds of objects, the operator can avoid rekeying the same set of users for each object. When new objects are created in that application, the same authorization list can just be attached to it, and most security needs will be met. When a user leaves a group, his/her access can be cancelled for all objects just by deleting his/her user profile or removing his/her name one time from the authorization list. When either occurs, that user will be denied any authorization to objects the list was attached to (except where that user was also named on the object or those objects that allow authorization to *PUBLIC).

The contents of authorization lists are integrated with the user profiles. When a user profile is deleted, it automatically deletes from any authorization list on which it appears. Special authorities can be mixed with authorization lists. The same users can even be named in both places. Such practice is common in real life but redundant. The system searches for a user's authorities in the authorization list first. If it finds the user in the list, it will not look further into its list of named users. This can be confusing when a customer attempts to grant a user some kind of special access to an object. If that user is already named in an authorization list that the object uses, the new authority will be ignored.

Public Authority

Besides ownership, specific authorities, and authorization lists, objects have public authority. This is the amount of authority the object will allow someone who is not recognized in any other category. The system default is *NONE, the public has no access to the object. Public access *EXCLUDE also leaves the public with no access.

The object owner, the SECOFR, or applications such as a CMS can change the public authority on any object even if not otherwise named.

TIP:

Review your authorization lists against each object's special authorities, especially in regard to the authority *PUBLIC has. *PUBLIC is often repeated in authorization lists and object lists, with the authorization list determining the authority the *PUBLIC actually has. *PUBLIC should be mentioned once; we prefer at the object level.

Specific Data Authorities Summary

Figure 11-3 lists a summary of the specific authorities that can be granted users, groups, and the public.

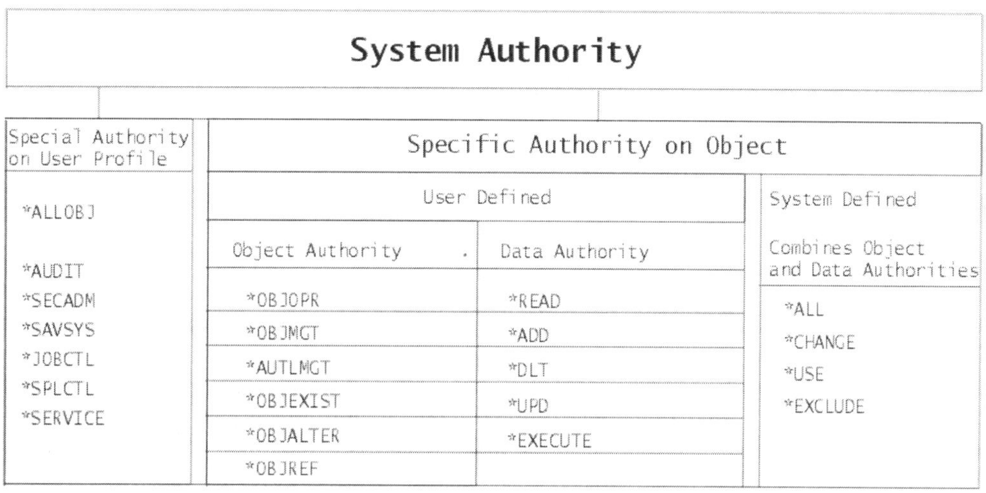

Figure 11-3: System authority structure.

ADOPTED AUTHORITIES

Besides naming users and authorities to objects, another way to allow access to file objects is through *adopted authorities*. In concept, adopted authority is a little different than the others in that it affects (and resides in) executing programs only. When a program runs, it has authority and a user ID. Typically, the user who starts the program becomes the "user" of the program, and that user's authority is used to determine the "authority" the program has to files.

Let us consider two users, Bob and Sue, who work in different departments in a large insurance company. Bob works in the claims department, and Sue works in policies. Normally, Bob has access to claim records but not policies, and Sue has access to policy records but not claim records. That could present a huge problem because in this application, very few programs do not at least look at policy and claim records.

One solution would be to give access to these records to each other's departments, but this particular insurance company sees that as a dilution of its security strategy. Another solution is to have the executing programs take their user ID not from the user executing them, but rather from the user profile of their owner. A developer can make a program adopt authority in one of two ways:

- On program creation, by specifying it on the USRPRF parameter.
- After the program has been created with the Change Program (CHGPGM) command:

```
CHGPGM <library/program name> USEADPAUT(*YES)
```

When an adopt authority program executes, no matter who started it, it will use the user ID of the program owner, usually the developer. There are, however, some risks and potential problems with adopting authority:

- The adopted owner's authority will be in effect for all programs the program using adopted authority calls and all programs those programs call. This can be a problem in complex applications that allow hot keys for fast screen navigation. Such hot keys can inadvertently provide a user with a back door into security he should not have. Be particularly careful in applications where a user can bring up a command line while in the program. That user will have the program owner's authority while on the command line and will be able to run any commands the owner can.
- When a program that adopts authority calls another program, that call must have the library specified. The system will not search a library list.
- Many IT departments grant their developers QSECOFR authority (by giving their user profiles special authority [*ALLOBJ]). Just be aware that programs in those environments that adopt authority are adopting full security officer authority.
- The authority that programs adopt is not only the developer's authority to objects but all of his special authorities as well.
- When a program using adopted authorities passes control to another program through the Transfer Control (TRFCTL) command (instead of the CALL command), an authority adoption does not follow.
- Programs get re-created as a result of production emergencies. When these happen, do not forget to reset the program's adopted authority or the fixed programs will not work in production.
- Change management systems assign an owner to the production version of all programs. In IT departments without a CMS, the developers do the final production compile themselves. In those cases, be careful of developers that have unequal authorities. The program may work or not work depending on the "strength" of the last developer to create it.

SYSTEM VALUES AND SYSTEM SECURITY

System values are global items containing information the system needs to know. They are objects; their type is *SYSVAL. There are many system values directly affecting security but not all do. We discuss security system values and the commands to work with them. These same commands work for all system values. Appendixes A and B contain a comprehensive list of all system values.

Fortunately, all system values are shipped with basic default settings, which will enable the system to run. The system operator will want to change some system values right away, others will be changed on a regular basis, and some may never be changed at all. When a system value needs to be changed, there are several commands in addition to the menu interface available.

To view various system values from any command line, type DSPSYSVAL, press F4, fill in the system value, then press the Enter key. There are hundreds of system values. When not sure which one is appropriate, place the cursor in the field and press F4. Work with system values with these commands:

- DSPSYSVAL (Display System Value).
- CHGSYSVAL (Change System Value).
- WRKSYSVAL (Work with System Value). This command combines all the system value functions—add, change, delete, and so on. Its menu provides a one-stop kind of shopping for working with system values.
- RTVSYSVAL (Retrieve System Value). This command is used within a CL program to collect a specific system value and put it into a CL variable. The CL program can then use the contents of the variable directly in its processing or pass it along to another program to use.

System values can provide default values for command keywords. For example, the Create User Profile (CRTUSRPRF) command has the Assistance Level (ASTLVL) parameter where the assistance level available to the user can be specified. Possible values are:

- *BASIC.
- *INTERMEDIATE.
- *ADVANCED.
- *SYSVAL.

The last option causes the system to look in system value QASTLVL for the assistance level. This system value will contain one of the first three choices. In this way, system values can speed up adding new users. To give all or most users *INTERMEDIATE assistance levels, set the system value, and do not do anything on the field when creating a new user profile; *SYSVAL is the default.

QAUDLVL—Keeping a Security Audit

System value QAUDLVL sets up a security audit. The audit can contain many parameters that tell the system what events it should record. Also, the security audit can monitor object activity, user activity, or any combination of the two. The audit records the event, who did it, when, and from what terminal. The audit journal is named QAUDJRN and it lives in library QSYS.

QAUTOVRT—Auto configuration of Virtual Devices

Determines if virtual device descriptions are created automatically.

QDSPSGNINF—Sign-on Display Information Control

Determines if a user can sign on information that is displayed.

QINACTITV—Inactive Job Time-out Interval

This system value sets the amount of time in minutes a job can be inactive before the system takes action and signs it off.

This may seem a great security tool when supporting TCP/IP connection to the Internet. However, FTP jobs are not covered under this system value. FTP jobs' inactivity intervals are set through the INACTTIMO parameter of the Change FTP Attributes (CHGFTPA) command.

QINACTMSGQ—Inactive Job Message Queue

If a message queue is specified, a message will be sent indicating when a terminal is inactive longer than the number of minutes specified in the QINACTITV system value.

QLMTDEVSSN—Limits Device Sessions

QLMTDEVSSN determines if a user can have more than one device session (workstation) occurring at one time.

QLMTSECOFR—Limits Security Officer Device Access

QLMTSECOFR determines if user with *ALLOBJ or *SERVICE special authority can sign onto any device.

QMAXSIGN—Maximum Sign-On Attempts

QMAXSIGN declares the number of times a user can unsuccessfully attempt to sign onto the AS/400 before that user profile is deactivated. Once the user ID has been deactivated, only the SECOFR or *system administrator* can reactivate it.

QMAXSGNACN—Maximum Sign-On Failed Action

QMAXSGNACN determines the action taken by the system when the maximum sign-on attempts are reached. The device, the user profile, or both can be disabled.

QPWDEXPITV—Password Expiration Interval

QPWDEXPITV specifies how many days the system will allow a user to go without changing his or her password. After this interval, the user can still sign on, but the only option available is to access the Change Password function. Once the password has been changed, the user can continue as usual.

QPWDLMAJC—Limit Adjacent Characters in Password

If system value QPWDLMAJC is set to a one, users cannot create passwords (such as 12345) that are not very secure.

QPWDLMREP—Limit Repeated Characters in Password

If system value QPWDLMREP is set to a one, users cannot create passwords (such as 11111) that are not very secure.

QPWDLMTCHR—Invalid Password Characters

System value QPWDLMTCHR allows up to ten characters to be listed that the users may never use as part of a password. These can be any ten characters (such as @, #, S, %, ^, or &) but the idea is to block special characters.

QPWDMAXLEN—Maximum Password Length

QPWDMAXLEN specifies the maximum length of a password. It can range from one to ten characters. While this requirement might seem a little weak, the AS/400 will need this setting to match the smaller password lengths of the other machines if it is networked with other non-AS/400 machines.

QPWDMINLEN—Minimum Password Length

QPWDMINLEN specifies the minimum length of a password. It can range from one to ten characters. The longer a password is, the harder it is to guess.

QPWDPOSDIP—Force all New Password Characters to Be Different

If system value QPWDPOSDIF is set to one, users cannot create new passwords with any character the same as the old password. This prevents sequential passwords like FRANK01, FRANK02, etc.

QPWDRQDDGT— Force the Use of at Least One Number in a Password

System value QPWDRQDDGT, set to one, requires the user to build passwords that include at least one number. The number can be in any position and more than one number can be included, but there must be at least one number.

QPWDRQDDIF—Expired Password Must Be Changed

When the maximum time for a password has expired and the user is asked to change his or her password, if system value QPWDRQDDIF is set to one (instead of zero), the new password must be different from any of the previous thirty-two passwords. If QPWDRQDDIF is set to a zero, the new password can be the same.

QPWDVLDPGM—User Program to Validate Passwords

If the system does not give enough control on the construction of passwords, the IT department may elect to use a program it developed to validate new passwords to some other criteria. If such a program is used, its name is specified on this system value. A validation program can be used to give the user additional instructions for creating a new password. This is not often used.

QRETSVRSEC—Retain Server Security Data

QRETSVRSEC specifies whether encrypted authentication information associated with user profiles or validation list (*VLDL) entries can be retained on the host system. (The AS/400 user profile password is not affected.)

QSECURITY—Security Level

This sets the security level for the whole machine.

QUSEADPAUT—Use Adopted Authority

This system value contains the name of an authorization list that names the users that can create a program that adopts authority. Optionally, this system value can contain the value *NONE, meaning that any user who can create or change a program can designate a program as one that adopts authority.

Notice that there are several system values that directly control passwords. These are bypassed when a user profile's password is changed through the Change User Profile (CHGUSRPRF) command.

SECURITY COMMANDS

There are many commands available to work with security objects, including user profiles; however, operators new to the AS/400 have the Security menu for a high-level entry to all functions. From the command line of any menu, simply enter:

```
GO SECURITY
```

and press the Enter key. Figure 11-4 contains a sample of the Security menu.

```
SECURITY                                Security
                                                           System:   BIGBLUE
 Select one of the following:

      1. Work with object authority
      2. Work with authorization lists
      3. Office security
      4. Change your password
      5. Change your user profile
      6. Work with user profiles
      7. Work with system values
      8. Security tools

     70. Related commands


 Selection or command
 ===>______________________________________________________________


 F3=Exit   F4=Prompt   F9=Retrieve   F12=Cancel   F13=Information Assistant
 F16=AS/400 Main menu
 (C) COPYRIGHT IBM CORP. 1980, 1998.
```

Figure 11-4: Security menu.

Rather than discuss the options (topics) found in Figure 11-4, we will defer to the more detailed coverage later in the chapter.

Changing the Passwords of IBM-Supplied Profiles

The security officer user profile, QSECOFR, comes with the password QSECOFR, but that password is set to *EXPIRED on the user profile. The first time that password is used, it must be changed. Use a bit of planning so that one person does not keep the new password a secret, leaving the others without access.

Many of the IBM-supplied profiles can be changed from something called the *setup menu*. To get to the menu, enter:

```
GO SETUP
```

on the command line. Press the Enter key. Select option 11 (`Change Passwords for IBM-Supplied Users`) and change all the passwords from the same screen. Figure 11-5 shows a sample of the screen to change IBM-supplied user profile passwords.

```
                    Change Passwords for IBM-Supplied Users
                                                         System:   BIGBLUE
Type new password below for IBM-supplied user, type password again to verify
  Change, then press Enter.

New security officer (QSECOFR) password  . . . . . . . . . .
  New password (to verify) . . . . . . . . . . . . . . . . .

New system operator (QSYSOPR) password . . . . . . . . . . .
  New password (to verify) . . . . . . . . . . . . . . . . .

New programmer (QPGMR) password  . . . . . . . . . . . . . .
  New password (to verify) . . . . . . . . . . . . . . . . .

New user (QUSER) password  . . . . . . . . . . . . . . . . .
  New password (to verify) . . . . . . . . . . . . . . . . .

New service (QSRV) password  . . . . . . . . . . . . . . . .
  New password (to verify) . . . . . . . . . . . . . . . . .


                                                                  More...
F1=Help   F3=Exit   F5=Refresh   F12=Cancel
```

Figure 11-5: Screen from Setup menu to change IBM-supplied passwords.

To change any or all of these passwords, type the new password twice (the second time for verification). If the new password and the verification are not exactly the same, the system will not change the password and will ask that the operator rekey the password. Change those values again whenever a key AS/400 person (who may know the passwords) terminates his or her association with the organization.

MANAGING USER PROFILES

There are six user profile commands:

- CRTUSRPRF (Create User Profile).
- CHGUSRPRF (Change User Profile).
- DLTUSRPRF (Delete User Profile).
- DSPUSRPRF (Display User Profile).
- RSTUSRPRF (Restore User Profile).
- RTVUSRPRF (Retrieve User Profile). CL programs only.

A seventh user profile command, Work with User Profile (WRKUSRPRF), presents the user profiles and provides a method to perform any of these commands with it (as well as to create a new profile).

DETAILED LOOK AT THE CREATE USER PROFILE COMMAND

Before starting to create user profiles, study the predefined user profiles that already exist on the system. They can act as a model for the creation of user profiles.

The user profile information is fairly standard across all the commands. The CRTUSRPRF gives an idea of what these are. Here are the four screens it takes to collect all profile information, with a brief discussion of what each parameter does. Refer to Figures 11-6 through 11-9.

```
                     Create User Profile (CRTUSRPRF)

Type choices, press Enter.

User profile . . . . . . . . . .   __________     Name
User password  . . . . . . . . .   *USRPRF        Name, *USRPRF, *NONE
Set password to expired  . . . .   *NO            *NO, *YES
Status . . . . . . . . . . . . .   *ENABLED       *ENABLED, *DISABLED
User class . . . . . . . . . . .   *USER          *USER, *SYSOPR, *PGMR...
Assistance level . . . . . . . .   *SYSVAL        *SYSVAL, *BASIC, *INTERMED...
Current library  . . . . . . . .   *CRTDFT        Name, *CRTDFT
Initial program to call  . . . .   *NONE          Name, *NONE
  Library  . . . . . . . . . . .     __________   Name, *LIBL, *CURLIB
Initial menu . . . . . . . . . .   MAIN           Name, *SIGNOFF
  Library  . . . . . . . . . . .     *LIBL        Name, *LIBL, *CURLIB
Limit capabilities . . . . . . .   *NO            *NO, *PARTIAL, *YES
Text 'description' . . . . . . .   *BLANK

                                                                     Bottom
F3=Exit   F4=Prompt   F5=Refresh   F10=Additional parameters   F12=Cancel
F13=How to use this display        F24=More keys
```

Figure 11-6: Prompted version of command CRTUSRPRF (part 1 of 4).

- User Profile (USRPRF). Up to ten characters in length, the user profile name can contain any letter, number, or symbol. Although a user profile cannot start with a number, the operator can create one that contains all numbers but starts with the letter Q. The user then can sign on with just the numbers. Example: user profile Q12345 can be used as 12345. In real life, try not to exceed eight characters in length. Do not use special characters, and the user profile name does not have to be cryptic. Use a standard that means something (a user's initials and department code are popular choices).

- User Password (PASSWORD). Passwords can have up to ten characters. There are many system values that affect password constructions, as discussed earlier.

- Set Password to Expired (PWDEXP). The security officer or security administrator can use (PWDEXP[*YES]) to force the user to change the user's password the next time the user signs on. This is the typical way to set up a new user.

- Status (STATUS). The profile may be allowed to sign on (STATUS[*ENABLED]) or not be allowed to sign on (STATUS[*DISABLED]). The system may disable a profile if the user exceeds the maximum number of unsuccessful sign-on attempts. Or the security officer or system administrator may make a profile disabled. Changing the Status from *DISABLED to *ENABLED can be done only by a security officer or system administrator and allows the user to sign on again.

- User Class (USRCLS). Controls the menu options the user sees on AS/400 menus. Possible values for this parameter are: *SECOFR, *SECADM, *PGMR, *SYSOPR, and *USER. *USER is the default value. Note the following:
  - This value alone doesn't determine what commands the user can access.
  - This parameter can implicitly assign special authorities to a user.

- Assistance Level (ASTLVL). Three possible values:
  - Job *BASIC is best for new or occasional users. AS/400 Operational Assistant is used to provide step-by-step help.
  - *INTERMED is the default value. It provides complete information and capabilities to users. All options are available and displayed.
  - *ADVANCED is only for very experienced users. All options are available, but possible options might not be displayed in order to make room for more information.

- Initial Program to Call (INLPGM). This is a two-variable library/file parameter. It is used to automatically invoke a program when the user signs on. When it is used, it is almost always for users rather than for developers, operators, security officers, or system administrators.

- Initial Menu (INLMNU). This is a two-variable library/file parameter. If an INLPGM is not specified, the default MAIN (the AS/400 Main Menu) is displayed when the user signs on. This parameter is used to present the user a personalized Initial menu.

- Limit Capabilities (LMTCPB). Limit Capabilities restricts the user's capacity to execute commands from a command line. Possible values are *NO (the default), *PARTIAL, and *YES.

- Text (TEXT). The Text parameter contains up to fifty characters. Use this wisely. Spell out the user's name and perhaps his or her phone extension or LAN connection address. Decide early on whether to use "last name first" to facilitate alphabetic searching of user profiles.

```
                    Create User Profile (CRTUSRPRF)

 Type choices, press Enter.

                         Additional Parameters

 Special authority . . . . . . .   *USRCLS      *USRCLS, *NONE, *ALLOBJ...
              + for more values   
 Special environment  . . . . . .   *SYSVAL      *SYSVAL, *NONE, *S36
 Display sign-on information  . .   *SYSVAL      *SYSVAL, *NO, *YES
 Password expiration interval . .   *SYSVAL      1-366, *SYSVAL, *NOMAX
 Limit device sessions  . . . . .   *SYSVAL      *SYSVAL, *YES, *NO
 Keyboard buffering . . . . . . .   *SYSVAL      *SYSVAL, *NO, *TYPEAHEAD...
 Maximum allowed storage  . . . .   *NOMAX       Kilobytes, *NOMAX
 Highest schedule priority  . . .   3            0-9
 Job description  . . . . . . . .   QDFTJOBD     Name
   Library  . . . . . . . . . . .     *LIBL      Name, *LIBL, *CURLIB
 Group profile  . . . . . . . . .   *NONE        Name, *NONE
 Owner  . . . . . . . . . . . . .   *USRPRF      *USRPRF, *GRPPRF
                                                                     More...
 F3=Exit   F4=Prompt   F5=Refresh   F12=Cancel   F13=How to use this display
 F24=More keys
```

Figure 11-7: Prompted version of command CRTUSRPRF—Additional Parameters (part 2 of 4).

- Special Authority (SPCAUT). This parameter has up to ten character values. See section on Special Authorities. Note the "+ for More Values" line. By putting a plus sign (+) in that field and pressing Enter, authorities 2–10 can be assigned.

- Special Environment (SPCENT). This parameter specifies whether the user can run in a System/36 environment.

- Display Sign-On Information (DSPSGNINF). Determines whether sign-on information is displayed when the user signs on. Sign-on information is a brief display of when the last date/time was that the user signed on to the system. *Note*: When a password is within days of expiring, it will display regardless of this value.

- Password Expiration Interval (PWDEXPITV). This parameter establishes how many days the password can be used before the system makes the user change it. Many IT departments leave this at the default, *SYSVAL, which relies on the number of days specified in the QPWDEXPITV system value. Do not use the *NOMAX value—the user will never have to change his or her password. Valid values are from one through 366 days.

> **TIP:**
>
> Set this to a shorter interval for all user profiles that have *SERVICE, *SAVSYS, and *ALLOBJ Special Authorities. Refer to section on Special Authorities for more information.

- Limit Device Sessions (LMTDEVSSN). This prevents a user from signing onto the system from more than one device at one time. This does not prevent the user from starting multiple sessions from the same workstation or from using the System Request Attention key to start another session.

- Keyboard Buffering (KBDBUF). This allows or disallows a user who types ahead of the system (like when the Input Inhibited Light is on) to have his keystrokes stored. This parameter separately allows or disallows buffering of the System Request Attention key. If it is buffered, all keys are buffered and the System Request Attention key is handled just like any other key. If that key is not buffered, when it is pressed it flows into the AS/400 immediately, regardless of the status of other buffering or the input capabilities of the keyboard.

- Maximum Storage (MAXSTG). This parameter is numeric, up to eleven digits, and it specifies the amount of storage in KB a user's owned objects can take in DASD. This parameter is used in large IT departments and is placed on the profile of any user who can create and own objects. Typically, that is the development staff, but it can be power users as well. Maximum storage is nice for enabling a small staff to manage DASD utilization.
- Priority Limit (PTYLMT). This limits the highest priority that users' jobs can have. A job has three priorities and this limits them all. The three priorities are:
  - Job—The priority of the job while on the job queue.
  - Run—The priority of the job while running.
  - Output—The priority of the printed output of the job while on the output queue.
- Job Description (JOBD). This parameter allows up to ten characters for a job description. Many IT departments use the system default QDFTJOBD. When the user signs onto the system, the subsystem's workstation entry contains the job description the system will use. If that value is *USRPRF, the system will get the job description specified on this parameter. For more information, see chapter 12, Working with Jobs.
- User Group (GRPPRF). This parameter has up to ten characters, and it makes the user a member of a group. *Note*: A group user profile must already exist.
- Owner (OWNER). This parameter has up to ten characters. If the user is a member of a group, specify whether any object created by the user is owned by the user profile or the group user profile. Possible values are *USRPRF (the default) and *GRPPRF.

```
                     Create User Profile (CRTUSRPRF)

Type choices, press Enter.

Group authority  . . . . . . . .   *NONE        *NONE, *ALL, *CHANGE, *USE...
Group authority type . . . . . .   *PRIVATE     *PRIVATE, *PGP
Supplemental groups  . . . . . .   *NONE        Name, *NONE
               + for more values   ________
Accounting code  . . . . . . . .   *BLANK
Document password  . . . . . . .   *NONE        Name, *NONE
Message queue  . . . . . . . . .   *USRPRF      Name, *USRPRF
  Library  . . . . . . . . . . .     ________   Name, *LIBL, *CURLIB
Delivery . . . . . . . . . . . .   *NOTIFY      *NOTIFY, *BREAK, *HOLD, *DFT
Severity code filter . . . . . .   0            0-99
Print device . . . . . . . . . .   *WRKSTN      Name, *WRKSTN, *SYSVAL
Output queue . . . . . . . . . .   *WRKSTN      Name, *WRKSTN, *DEV
  Library  . . . . . . . . . . .     _______    Name, *LIBL, *CURLIB
Attention program  . . . . . . .   *SYSVAL      Name, *NONE, *SYSVAL, *ASSIST
  Library  . . . . . . . . . . .     _______    Name, *LIBL, *CURLIB

                                                                      More...
F3=Exit   F4=Prompt   F5=Refresh   F12=Cancel   F13=How to use this display
F24=More keys
```

Figure 11-8: Prompted version of command CRTUSRPRF (part 3 of 4).

- Group Authority (GRPAUT). If the user profile is a member of a group user profile and the ownership is set to *USRPRF, this parameter dictates what authority is granted to other members of the same group as the creator of an object. Possible values are:
  - *ALL—Group members have all rights to objects created by the user.
  - *CHANGE—Group members can change the objects.
  - *USE—Group members can use objects created by the user.
  - *NONE—The default. No specific authority is given to the group profile. (This is the same as queue *EXCLUDE.)
  - *EXCLUDE—Group members are denied access to objects created by the user.
- Group Authority Type (GRPAUTTYP). When a user creates an object, he/she is the owner of that object and, if he/she is a member of a group, the group shares object ownership. This parameter optionally limits granting that ownership to other group members. Possible values are:
  - *PRIVATE—The Group Profile (GRPPRF) of the creating user is given private authority over the object, although the group does not become the owner of the object. The amount of authority the group has over the object is determined by the GRPAUT parameter of the creating user's profile.
  - *PGP—The Group Profile of the creating user becomes the primary group of the object.
- Supplemental Groups (SUPGRPPRF). User profiles can be a member of a group and, as such, receive authorities to objects created by other group members. This parameter allows up to fifteen supplemental groups to be specified from which this user profile will derive authorities.
- Accounting Code (ACGCDE). Up to fifteen characters can be used to specify an accounting code for the user. This supports Job Accounting, which should be active (or plan to be active) for this to make sense.
- Document Password (DOCPWD). This allows the users to specify the password he/she is using to password-protect document objects.
- Message Queue (MSGQ). Up to ten characters can be qualified with a library name. Specify the message queue for a user profile. This is where any messages from other users or programs will be placed. Most of the time, just use the default, *USRPRF, which means the message queue should be the same name as the user profile. Otherwise, specify the message queue and library to which messages should go. If the message queue is specified, also specify a unique message queue for each user.
- Delivery (DLVRY). This specifies in what way messages on the queue are delivered to the user. Possible values are:
  - *NOTIFY—The default. An alarm is sounded at the workstation and a message icon is displayed on the lower-left corner of the screen. The user must use the DSPMSG (Display Message) command to see the message.
  - *BREAK—The user's workstation is interrupted by the incoming message. It goes blank and displays the message.
  - *HOLD—Messages are held in the message queue until the user requests them with the DSPMSG command.

  - *DFT—Messages requiring replies are automatically responded to with their default reply value. Informational messages are ignored.

- Severity (SEV). When DLVRY is set to *NOTIFY or *BREAK only, this determines the lowest level message that is delivered to the user. The default is 00 (or all messages). Set this to only receive more serious messages (like 30 for level 30 and above).

- Print Device (PRTDEV). Use up to ten characters to specify the name of the printer used to print this user's output. Possible values are:

  - *WRKSTN—The default. All printed output is sent to a printer device with the same name as the workstation.

  - *SYSVAL—All printed output is sent to the system printer (as defined in the system value QPRTDEV).

  - Print Device name.

- Output Queue (OUTQ). Up to ten characters can be qualified with a library name to define the output queue to which the printed output for the user will go. The possible values are the same as those for the PRTDEV parameter.

- Attention Program (ATNPGM). This is the program that is activated when the user presses the Attention key. The parameter is large enough to contain a library/program name combination (twenty characters).

```
                          Create User Profile (CRTUSRPRF)

Type choices, press Enter.

Sort sequence . . . . . . . . .   *SYSVAL      Name, *SYSVAL, *HEX...
  Library . . . . . . . . . . .   ______       Name, *LIBL, *CURLIB
Language ID . . . . . . . . . .   *SYSVAL      *SYSVAL...
Country ID . . . . . . . . . . .  *SYSVAL      *SYSVAL...
Coded character set ID . . . . .  *SYSVAL      *SYSVAL, *HEX...
Character identifier control . .  *SYSVAL      *SYSVAL, *DEVD, *JOBCCSID
Locale job attributes . . . . .   *SYSVAL      *SYSVAL, *NONE, *CCSID...
              + for more values   ______
Locale . . . . . . . . . . . . .  *SYSVAL

User options . . . . . . . . . .  *NONE        *NONE, *CLKWD, *EXPERT...
              + for more values   ______
User ID number . . . . . . . . .  *GEN         1-4294967294, *GEN
Group ID number . . . . . . . .   *NONE        1-4294967294, *NONE, *GEN
Home directory . . . . . . . . .  *USRPRF

                                                                     More...
F3=Exit   F4=Prompt   F5=Refresh   F12=Cancel   F13=How to use this display
F24=More keys
```

Figure 11-9: Partial prompted version of command CRTUSRPRF (part 4 of 4).

- Sort Sequence (SRTSEQ). This allows the user's data ordering to be done optionally by the sort associated with his/her native language or by hexadecimal.

- Language ID (LANGID). This allows the user to specify a language unique to him/her to be used whenever he/she signs on. For a list of valid language codes, press the F4 key when the cursor is positioned on this parameter.

- Country ID (CNTRID). This allows the user to specify a unique country that the system will support while that user is signed on. For a list of valid country codes, press the F4 key when the cursor is positioned on this parameter.
- Coded Character Set ID (CCSID). This specifies a CCSID different from the systemwide CCSID and unique to this user. For a list of valid CCSID codes, press the F4 key when the cursor is positioned on this parameter.
- Locale Job Attributes (SETJOBATR). This parameter accepts up to 16 ten-character job attributes. This parameter specifies what job attributes are to be taken from the locale parameter.
- Locale (LOCALE). This specifies the path name of the locale that is assigned to the LANG environment variable for the user.
- User Options (USROPT). Accepts 250 ten-character values. This parameter allows the user's display and some functions to be customized.
- User ID Number (UID). For users to be on a system that uses the integrated file system (IFS), that user must have a UID number. That number is used by the IFS to determine authorities. If the AS/400 is not part of an AS/400 network, use *GEN for this parameter. For networked AS/400s, the operator must calculate a unique UID for each user and enter it here.
- Group ID Number (GID). User profiles that are used as part of group profiles need to have this unique number assigned. (See description of UID above.)
- Home Directory (HOMEDIR). This is the user's initial home directory when he/she signs on for accessing data in the IFS.
- Authority (AUT). Specifies the authority the public will have when accessing this profile.

USER PROFILE PARAMETER CONSIDERATIONS

Any user who adds, changes, or deletes user profiles must have *SECADM as one of the special authorities in his own user profile.

There is no way to learn a profile's password. Even security officers, who have all rights to everything on the system, cannot learn it.

For new users and for users who have forgotten their passwords, the procedure is as follows:

- For new users, create the user profile with any generic password.
- For forgetful users, change the user profile to any generic password.
- For both, set the parameter PWDEXP(*YES), then tell the user the generic password. The next time he/she signs on, the system will force him/her to change it.

To really restrict users to one application, INLPGM and INLMNU can be used together. Name the application the user will access as the INLPGM and name *SIGNOFF as the INLMNU. When that user signs on, he or she will only see the application's menu (or main screen). When the user exits the application, he or she is automatically signed off.

TIP:

INLPGM = <name of application main program>

INLMNU = *SIGNOFF

For PRTDEV and OUTQ parameters, most IT departments do not worry much about the PRTDEV, opting instead to send all printed output to one of two types of output queues. Developers and others who do not expect to print everything they generate can have a queue named the same as their user profile. When they want to print something, they move it—with the CHGSPLFA (Change Spool File Attributes) command—to a queue with an attached printer. Users who expect immediate output from their reports can get a designated output queue that normally has a printer attached.

User profiles have another, hidden, parameter not set with the CRTUSRPRF or CHGUSRPRF commands. This parameter concerns security auditing and it is AUDLVL. It is only set with the CHGUSRAUD (Change User Audit) command.

SHORTCUTS TO ENTERING USER PROFILES

Simply using the CRTUSRPRF command means a lot of data entry for every new user profile. In reality, many user profiles share many parameter values. If someone really keyed them all in, most of that keying would be repetitious.

One reason IBM loads the AS/400 with default user profiles is to give the customer (even the experienced ones) a basis on which to start. On a new AS/400, operators often use Work with User Profiles (WRKUSRPRF) to copy QUSER into the first user profiles. However, QUSER (and the other supplied profiles) are in library QSYS. Copy them out to library QGPL and create user profiles there. That will save a major headache the next time a new version of the operating system is loaded (which replaces library QSYS).

Save time creating user profiles by copying existing profiles with option 3 (Copy) on the Work with User Profiles (WRKUSRPRF) command. Let us say a new user, Jennie A. Jung, works in Accounts Receivable. Let us also assume the IT department has a naming standard that says use the user's initials followed by a department code. So the operator would create a user profile for her named JAJAR by copying profile QUSER to JAJAR and making any changes.

For all subsequent users, the work gets easier. Use the Work with User Profiles (WRKUSRPRF) OPTION 3 TO COPY JAJAR and create another user profile for the next user. Then just use option 2 (Change) to make the minor changes that make the new user unique from JAJAR (probably the name and password).

DELETING USER PROFILES

Use the DLTUSRPRF (Delete User Profile) command or option 4 from the WRKUSRPRF command to delete a user profile. This is easy, but know that behind the scenes, the system removes the user profile as owner of any objects and from any authorization lists. Objects must be owned by someone. Therefore, the system changes the ownership to QDFTUSER (one of the IBM-supplied profiles).

USER PROFILE PARAMETERS AND OBJECT SECURITY

All this ownership can be confusing, so here are three examples of profiles and security. First, refer to Figure 11-10, where user profile MDAWSON is set so that ownership of the objects it creates goes to *GRPPRF. MDAWSON is in group NEWGRP, and creates a physical file, MSTFLE. When we do a Display Object Authority (DSPOBJAUT) on object MSTFLE, we get the screen shown in Figure 11-10.

```
                         Edit Object Authority

Object . . . . . . . :   MSTFLE          Owner  . . . . . . . :   NEWGRP
  Library  . . . . . :     MDAWSON       Primary group  . . . :   *NONE
Object type  . . . . :   *FILE

Type changes to current authorities, press Enter.

  Object secured by authorization list  . . . . . . . . . . . .   *NONE

                         Object
User        Group        Authority
NEWGRP                   *ALL
*PUBLIC                  *CHANGE
```

Figure 11-10: Displaying object authority on MSTFLE.

From the figure, we see that object MSTFLE is owned by NEWGRP. There are no authorization lists attached to it. Owner NEWGRP has all authority to the object. Members of the group have all access to the object. If NEWGRP is a user, only that user has all access to it. Anyone else is considered the Public (*PUBLIC) and can change the object.

In Figure 11-11, user profile MDAWSON is set so ownership of the objects it creates goes to *USRPRF. Any group authority will be *CHANGE—parameter GRPAUT stores that information. Parameter GRPAUTTYP is set to *PRIVATE to give the group profile private authority. When user MDAWSON recreates the same file, MSTFLE, and you again display its authority, the result is as shown in Figure 11-11.

```
Edit Object Authority

Object . . . . . . . :   MSTFLE          Owner  . . . . . . . :   MDAWSON

  Library  . . . . . :     MDAWSON       Primary group  . . . :   *NONE
Object type  . . . . :   *FILE

Type changes to current authorities, press Enter.

  Object secured by authorization list  . . . . . . . . . . . .   *NONE

                         Object
User        Group        Authority
MDAWSON                  *ALL
NEWGRP                   *CHANGE

*PUBLIC                  *CHANGE
```

Figure 11-11: Displaying object MSTFLE's authorities.

Figure 11-11 shows that object MSTFLE is owned by MDAWSON. The creator's group, NEWGRP, has *CHANGE authority. Anyone who is not MDAWSON or a member of NEWGRP will also have *CHANGE authority.

If user profile MDAWSON is again changed— this time the parameter GRPAUTTYP is set to *PGP—we see a primary group. Displaying its authority (Figure 11-12) shows that owner is user MDAWSON. The group NEWGRP is shown as having *CHANGE authority and also as the primary group for the object.

```
                          Edit Object Authority

Object . . . . . . . :   MSTFLE          Owner  . . . . . . . :   MDAWSON
  Library  . . . . . :     MDAWSON       Primary group  . . . :   NEWGRP
Object type  . . . . :   *FILE

Type changes to current authorities, press Enter.

  Object secured by authorization list  . . . . . . . . . . . .   *NONE

                         Object
User         Group       Authority
NEWGRP                   *ALL
MDAWSON                  *CHANGE
*PUBLIC                  *CHANGE
```

Figure 11-12: Displaying object MSTFLE's authorities.

Finally, object MSTFLE is owned by user MDAWSON, and NEWGRP is named as the primary group for the object. That group has *CHANGE authority. Object authority is granted, revoked, or changed in a real-time mode through the following commands:

- GRTOBJAUT (Grant Object Authority).
- RVKOBJAUT (Revoke Object Authority).
- EDTOBJAUT (Edit Object Authority).
- WRKOBJ (Work with Objects, then take options for authorities).

Granting, revoking, and changing object authority is done to individual objects.

Note that when a user's specific authority is removed from an object—if the user is not the SECOFR or owner—the user's authority reverts to whatever *PUBLIC authority is set. Here are three scenarios illustrating the implications of that fact:

- An object has these specific authorities: User TOM has *USE authority, user *PUBLIC has *USE authority. Remove TOM from the object's authority list. Result: user TOM still has *USE authority as a member of the *PUBLIC.
- An object has these specific authorities: User TOM has *USE authority, user *PUBLIC has *ALL authority. Remove TOM from the object's authority list. Result: user TOM's authority has been increased from *USE to *ALL.
- An object has these specific authorities: User TOM has *USE authority, user *PUBLIC has *EXCLUDE authority. Remove TOM from the object's authority list. Result: user TOM still has no authority to the object.

For that reason, many AS/400 customers set public (*PUBLIC) authority to *EXCLUDE on all objects.

After looking at the possible specific authorities available for an object, let's look at how the authorities for any given object can be displayed. To edit the specific authority for an object, use the Edit Object Authority (EDTOBJAUT) command and press F4. Figure 11-13 is displayed.

```
                     Edit Object Authority (EDTOBJAUT)

 Type choices, press Enter.

 Object . . . . . . . . . . . . .   OPRLIB        Name
   Library  . . . . . . . . . . .     *LIBL       Name, *LIBL, *CURLIB
 Object type  . . . . . . . . . .   *LIB          *ALRTBL, *AUTL, *BNDDIR...









                                                                      Bottom
 F3=Exit   F4=Prompt   F5=Refresh   F12=Cancel   F13=How to use this display
 F24=More keys
```

Figure 11-13: The Edit Object Authority screen.

To view and edit the authorities for a given object, key in the object to work with and press Enter. The following screen in Figure 11-14 is displayed.

```
                            Edit Object Authority

 Object . . . . . . . :   OPRLIB          Owner  . . . . . . . :   HOHLY#M
   Library  . . . . . :     QSYS          Primary group  . . . :   *NONE
 Object type  . . . . :   *LIB

 Type changes to current authorities, press Enter.

   Object secured by authorization list  . . . . . . . . . . . .   *NONE

                         Object
 User        Group       Authority
 HOHLY#M                 *ALL
 QSYSOPR                 USER DEF
 OPR0060                 *CHANGE
 OPR0059                 *USE
 *PUBLIC                 *EXCLUDE



                                                                      Bottom
 F3=Exit   F5=Refresh   F6=Add new users     F10=Grant with reference object
 F11=Display detail object authorities   F12=Cancel   F17=Top   F18=Bottom
```

Figure 11-14: Object authorities of the OPRLIB.

The Figure describes an object named OPRLIB that is owned by user HOHLY#M. It does not have an authorization list attached. As owner, HOHLY#M has all authority to the object. The system operator (QSYSOPR) has been granted authority only from the special authorities in his profile (USERDEF). User OPR0060 has been granted *CHANGE authority and user OPR0059 has been granted *USE authority. The public is EXCLUDED from the object.

This object, a library named OPRLIB, has five named users. They have object authorities assigned through the use of IBM's predefined specific authorities. To see the details of these authorities, press the F11 key. The system will produce a screen similar to the one shown in Figure 11-15.

```
                          Edit Object Authority

Object . . . . . . . :   OPRLIB          Owner . . . . . . . :   HOHLY#M
  Library  . . . . . :     QSYS          Primary group . . . :   *NONE
Object type  . . . . :   *LIB

Type changes to current authorities, press Enter.

  Object secured by authorization list . . . . . . . . . . . .   *NONE

                         Object      -----Object------
User        Group        Authority  Opr  Mgt  Exist  Alter  Ref
HOHLY#M                  *ALL        X    X     X      X     X
QSYSOPR                  USER DEF    X    _     _      _     _
OPR0060                  *CHANGE     X    _     _      _     _
OPR0059                  *USE        X    _     _      _     _
*PUBLIC                  *EXCLUDE    _    _     _      _     _

                                                                     Bottom
F3=Exit   F5=Refresh   F6=Add new users     F10=Grant with reference object
F11=Display data authorities   F12=Cancel   F17=Top   F18=Bottom
```

Figure 11-15: Object authorities of the OPRLIB.

Figure 11-15 shows the details of the management authorities. There are blank lines on the screen. The system operator can change these defaulted authorities by taking out an X, or add new authorities by putting in an X. To do either, place the cursor on the line and either delete the X or enter an X. Notice that the F11 text has changed. To see the data authorities, press the F11 key again. The result will be a screen similar to the one shown in Figure 11-16.

```
                        Edit Object Authority

Object . . . . . . . :   OPRLIB         Owner  . . . . . . . :   HOHLY#M
  Library  . . . . . :     QSYS         Primary group  . . . :   *NONE
Object type  . . . . :   *LIB

Type changes to current authorities, press Enter.

  Object secured by authorization list  . . . . . . . . . . . .  *NONE

                          Object     ---------Data---------
User        Group         Authority  Read  Add  Update  Delete  Execute
HOHLY#M                   *ALL        X     X     X       X        X
QSYSOPR                   USER DEF    X     _     _       _        _
OPR0060                   *CHANGE     X     X     X       X        X
OPR0059                   *USE        X     _     _       _        X
*PUBLIC                   *EXCLUDE    _     _     _       _        _

                                                                  Bottom
F3=Exit   F5=Refresh      F6=Add new users   F10=Grant with reference object
F11=Nondisplay detail     F12=Cancel         F17=Top    F18=Bottom
```

Figure 11-16: Data authorities of the OPRLIB.

Again, the data authorities can be changed from this screen. The predefined specific authorities saved us some keying but if there are many users to authorize to a group of objects, use authorization lists or group profiles. In any event, some planning needs to go into implementing the security on the system. Authorization lists are used quite extensively on AS/400 security. Figure 11-17 shows a sample authorization list named MCAUTLST.

```
                        Edit Authorization List

Object . . . . . . . :   MCAUTLST       Owner  . . . . . . . :   PGM
  Library  . . . . . :     QSYS         Primary group  . . . :   *NONE

Type changes to current authorities, press Enter.

              Object    List
User          Authority Mgt
PGM           *ALL       X
BWEBER        *USE       _
HOHLY#M       *ALL       _
*PUBLIC       *EXCLUDE   _
```

Figure 11-17: Sample authorization list, MCAUTLST, displayed using the EDTAUTL command.

The owner of the authorization list is PGM. PGM is not a user profile, but a group user profile for all the users in a department. Therefore, any user in that group has all access to any object that has this authorization list on it. Notice the X (to the right of PGM) under the `List Mgt` column. This symbol indicates this user (or, in this case, a group of users) can change the authorization list. Anyone not so marked may not change the list. On an authorization list, this is referred to as list *management rights*.

User BWEBER, a programmer, can read any records on any files that use this list, but cannot delete those records or files or change their descriptions. In addition, the public (anyone not named on the list) is excluded (*EXCLUDE) from access to this file. Investigate further and see what objects use the authorization list by pressing the F15 key. See Figure 11-18.

```
Display Authorization List Objects

 Authorization list . . . . . . . . :   MCAUTLST
   Library  . . . . . . . . . . . . :     QSYS
 Owner  . . . . . . . . . . . . . . :   PGM
 Primary group  . . . . . . . . . . :   *NONE

                                                    Primary
 Object       Library      Type        Owner        group        Text
 ONERPGPGM    MDAWSON      *PGM        PGM          *NONE        One RPG program
 STARTUP      MDAWSON      *PGM        PGM          *NONE        PROGRAM to start sub
```

Figure 11-18: Result of pressing F15 from Figure 11-17—EDTAUTL. Objects that use the authorization list MCAUTLST.

In this case, two objects use it and they are both programs. No one else has access because the public was excluded in the authorization list shown in Figure 11-17. To see what security is attached to an object, use either the EDTOBJAUT (Edit Object Authority) or WRKOBJ (Work with Object) command. Either command will produce the screen shown in Figure 11-19.

```
                              Edit Object Authority

 Object . . . . . . . :   STARTUP          Owner  . . . . . . . :   PGM
   Library  . . . . . :     MDAWSON        Primary group  . . . :   *NONE
 Object type  . . . . :   *PGM

 Type changes to current authorities, press Enter.

   Object secured by authorization list  . . . . . . . . . . . .   MCAUTLST

                          Object
 User         Group       Authority
 TCLARK                   *ALL
 *GROUP       PGM         *ALL
 *PUBLIC                  *EXCLUDE
```

Figure 11-19: Object authority from object viewpoint.

At the top right, the owner is specified as PGM. The object is secured with authorization list MCAUTLST, shown on Figure 11-17. TCLARK is a user ID with access to the program object. The public is excluded from the object, but because *PUBLIC was specified on the authorization list (Figure 11-17), this is redundant.

> **TIP:**
>
> This is a common source of security confusion (if not problems) on AS/400s. If an object is secured with an authorization list, that list is checked first for authorities, nothing is checked later. The *PUBLIC authority the user specifies on the object has no meaning because the *PUBLIC authority specified on the authorization list has priority.

LAB #11: SECURITY AND SYSTEM VALUES

Upon completion of this lab, you should be able to:

- Explore the definition of a user profile.
- Explore the use of system values and their role in security.
- Explore object security.
- Explore the role of authority lists in securing objects.
- Create an authorization list.
- Secure an object with an authorization list.
- Change object authority.

NAMING CONVENTIONS FOR THIS LAB

During the lab, every time you encounter one of the lab names that contains xx, replace the xx with the number that has been assigned. As you complete the lab assignment, you will create and modify your environment to reflect your specific assigned names. See Figure L11-1.

	Lab Name: Identified in Commands as:	Your Assigned Name:
Profile (User ID)	USERID	
Library Name	USERID	
Output Queue	USEROUTQ	

Figure L11-1: Naming conventions.

DISPLAY YOUR USER PROFILE

User profiles are an important component of any AS/400's security system. Let's start by investigating your user profile to determine what steps were taken to provide and/or limit your access to the system.

- Enter the command to display the `Command Entry` screen.
- Press F10 (Additional Parameters).
- Enter the `WRKUSRPRF` command.
- Press F4 (Prompt).
- Enter `USERID` (your user ID).
- Press Enter.

This will bring you to the Work with User Profiles screen. With the appropriate authority, from this screen, you can change, copy, create, delete, change the profile description, or work with objects by owner. Now let us explore how your user profile was defined.

- Place a `5` in the `Option` column next to your user profile.
- Press F4 (Prompt).
- The `Display User Profile` screen is shown.
- Change the `Type of Output` parameter from *BASIC to *ALL.
- Press Enter.
- Your user profile is shown. Read through the information and answer the following questions:

  a. What is your user class? ____________
  b. What are your special authorities? _____________
  c. What is your current library? _____________
  d. What is your group profile? ____________
  e. Are you a limited user? __________________
  f. What is your job description name? ______________
  g. What library is used to store your message queue? _____________
  h. What is your maximum allowed storage? ______________
  i. When did you last sign on? Give date and time. ____________
  j. When was your password last changed? __________________
  k. What is your scheduling priority? _____________________

Now that you have found what many of the values that define your environment are, let's find out more about the Output Queue parameter.

- Move the cursor to the `Output Queue` parameter.
- Press the Help key.
- Read the information presented.
- If *WRKSTN is specified for the `Output Queue` prompt, where does the system look for the default output queue? ______________________________ ______________________________
- Exit Help.
- Place your cursor on the `User Options` parameter.
- Press the Help key.
- List three user options that you would like to have available in your user profile. ______________________________ ______________________________ ______________________________
- Exit Help.
- Place your cursor on the `Home Directory` parameter.
- Press the Help key.
- What is the name of the `Home Directory`? ______________________________
- What is your `Home Directory`? ______________________________
- Exit Help.
- Press Enter.

Your user profile also has a variety of information about what you can and cannot do associated with it. Let's look at what other authorities or access you have been granted. For example, if you are provided specific authority to any commands, they will be listed.

- Press Enter.
- Any commands for which you have been given specific authority are shown.
- Press Enter.
- Any devices for which you have been given specific authority are shown.
- Press Enter.
- All objects you are authorized to are displayed. (These objects are not owned by you.)
- What are the objects that you are authorized to? List a maximum of five. ______________________________ ______________________________ ______________________________

- Press Enter.
- List the Object Name, Library, and Type for five of the object(s) that you own. If you own more than five objects, make sure you include at least one of each type.

  ____

  ____

  ____

- Press Enter.
- Display Primary Group Objects screen is shown.
- Press Enter.
- The Work with User Profiles screen is shown again.

OBJECT AUTHORITY

The user profile establishes the access and authority a user will have on your AS/400, but it is not the whole story. Another component is object security. Access to and use of an object is based on the user authority to that object. Let us explore object authority in this section.

Before we start working with object authority, you will need to have an object you create and, thus, own in your library. The object you will be using in this lab is a data file called EMPLOYEE. You will be copying a source file, named LAB11SRC, containing the EMPLOYEE file source member to your library. You will compile the source code and create the EMPLOYEE file.

- Enter the Create Duplicate Object command.
- Press F4 (Prompt).
- Enter the following values for the parameter: From Object is LAB11SRC, From Library is OPRLIB, Object Type is *FILE, To Library is USERID (your library), and Duplicate Data is *YES.
- Press Enter.
- Enter Work Object PDM command.
- Press F4 (Prompt).
- Enter USERID for the Library parameter.
- Press Enter.
- Place 12 (Work with) to the left of LAB11SRC.
- Press Enter.
- Place 14 (Compile) to the left of EMPLOYEE.
- Press Enter.

You now have an object, EMPLOYEE, in your library that you own. As the owner of an object, you have the authority to change access to the object as well as grant others access to that object. When you created this object, you had authority; however, the public is excluded. Before we go on, let's look at what other objects you have authority to. Let's start exploring the other objects that you own.

- Enter the `Work with User Profiles` command.
- Press F4 (Prompt).
- Enter your profile (`USERID`).
- Press Enter.
- Place a `12` (Work with Objects by Owner) next to your profile.
- Press Enter.
- The `Work with Objects by Owner` screen is shown.
- If multiple objects are listed, find the *MSGQ object.
- Place a `5` (Display Authority) to the left of the *MSGQ object.
- Press Enter.
- Press F11 (Display Detail Object Authorities) to determine the object component authority.
- Enter the `Object Authority` in the chart below.
- Press F11 (Display Data Authorities) to determine the data component authority.
- Enter them in the chart shown in Figure L11-2.
- To complete the chart, you will need to look at the object authority of some other objects.
- Enter the `Work with Object` command on the command line.
- Press F4 (Prompt).
- Enter your user ID (`USERID`).
- Press Enter.
- Place a `5` (Display Authority) to the left of your user ID (`USERID`).
- Press Enter.
- Complete the chart below with the Object and Data authorities.
- Repeat the above steps for the OBJ object in the OPRLIB library.
- Complete object authority shown in Figure L11-2.

When possible, select a different combination type. For example, try selecting *USE, *ALL, *CHANGE, and *EXCLUDE.

		Object					Data				
Object Name	Type	Obj	Mgt	Exist	Alter	Ref	Read	Add	Update	Delete	Execute
user00xx *MSGQ											
user00xx *USRPRF											
user00xx *USRPRF											
OBJ											

Figure L11-2: Object authority.

AUTHORIZATION LIST

Authorization lists are an important method of controlling object authority for a group of users. It determines what user and level of authority they will have to an object. You are going to create an authorization list and secure the EMPLOYEE file you created with the list.

- Enter CRTAUTL on the command line.
- Press F4 (Prompt).
- Enter `USERID` for the authorization list name.
- Enter descriptive text that includes your name.
- Enter `Work with Objects` command on the command line.
- Press F4 (Prompt).
- Enter the `Generic*` USER* (the first three to four characters of your user ID).
- Press Enter.
- Find your authorization list. In what library is your authorization list located?
  ____

You will pair with another student for this section of the lab. You will add the other student and some other user profiles to your newly created authorization list.

- Write down the user ID of the student with whom you are working.
  ____
- From the `Work with Objects` screen, place a 2 (Edit Authority) to the left of your authorization list.
- Press Enter.

- This takes you to the Edit Authorization List screen.
- Press F6 (Add New User).
- Enter the student's user ID with authority *USE, and QSYSOPR authority *CHANGE.
- Change Public authority to *EXCLUDE.
- Press Enter until you are back at the Edit Authorization List screen.
- Print the screen of the Edit Authorization List.
- Attach to the submission sheet.
- Label it printout #1.
- What user has List Management authority? ______________________________

You're ready to secure the EMPLOYEE file with this newly created authorization list.

- Enter Work with Objects command on the command line.
- Press F4 (Prompt).
- Enter *ALL for the Object and USERID for the Library parameters.
- Press Enter.
- Rename the EMPLOYEE *FILE to EMPLOYEEXX (where xx is your user ID number).
- Press Enter.
- Place a 2 (Edit Authority) to the left of EMPLOYEEXX *FILE.
- Press Enter.
- Enter your authorization list name (USERID) for the Object Secured by Authorization List parameter.
- Copy EMPLOYEEXX *FILE to the LAB11 library.
- Using the Work with Objects command, place a 5 (Display Authority) to the left of EMPLOYEEXX IN LAB11 library.
- Press F4 (Prompt).
- Change the Output parameter to *PRINT.
- Press Enter.
- Retrieve and print the spool file you just created.
- Attach to submission sheet and label as printout #2.
- Have the other class member attempt to move the EMPLOYEEXX from LAB11 to his/her library. What happened? ______________________________

DISPLAY SECURITY-RELATED SYSTEM VALUES

System values determine the AS/400's overall security level. To determine how your AS/400's security was set up, let us explore the system values.

- Go to the `Command Entry` screen.
- Enter DSPSYSVAL on the command line.
- Press F4 (Prompt).
- `Display System Value` command prompt is displayed.
- Complete the screen for the system values in the chart below.
- Use the DSPSYSVAL command to complete the chart shown in Figure L11-3.

System Value	Description	Current Value	Optional Values	What Does This Value Do?
QSECURITY				
QINACTITV				
QINACTMSGQ				
QLMTDEVSSN				
QMAXSIGN				

Figure L11-3: System values.

ADDITIONAL LAB ASSIGNMENTS

1. Fill out the form shown in Figure L11-4 using the WRKSYSVAL command viewing each value and using help on the values.

System Value	Description	Current Value	OptionalValues	What Does This Value Do?
QCRTAUT				
QDSPSGNINF				
QLMTSECOFR				
QMAXSGNACN				
QPWDEXPITV				
QPWDLMTAJC				
QPWDLMTCHR				
QPWDLMTREP				
QPWDMAXLEN				

System Value	Description	Current Value	OptionalValues	What Does This Value Do?
QPWDMINLEN				
QPWDPOSDIF				
QPWDRQDDGT				
QPWDRQDDIF				
QPWDVLDPGM				
QRETSVRSEC				
QRMTSIGN				
QUSEADPAUT				

Figure L11-4: Use the WRKSYSVAL command.

2. Experiments in Object Authority:
   - Work with another student.
   - Have him/her attempt to work with your library. What happened?
   - Check to see if you have a library called USER00XXLIB. Create this library if it does not exit. Clear the library if it exists.
   - Copy your library and its contents to a new library, USER00XXLIB.
   - Use EDTOBJAUT command to allow the student *USE authority to USER00XXLIB.
   - Have the student attempt to work with your library. What happened?
   - Use EDTOBJAUT to exclude the student from the OBJECT LAB11SRC in your library.
   - Have the student attempt to use the WRKMBRPDM on USER00XX/LAB11SRC. What happened?
   - Use EDTOBJAUT command to exclude that student *USE authority on USER00XXLIB library.
   - When you complete this lab, you should delete the USER00XXLIB.
3. Program Authority:
   - Select a program in your library.
   - Display the program with the command DSPPGM or by typing a 5 next to the program in WRKOBJPDM.
   - Who is the owner of this program?
   - Change the User Profile parameter from *USER to *OWNER. What command did you use to change this parameter?
   - What does the User Profile parameter do?
   - What is the value of USE adopted authority for this program?
   - What does USE adopted authority do?
4. Profiles and Security:
   - Display your user profile.

- What is either QSECOFR or QSYSOPR user class?
- What are the valid values for user class?
- What is the group profile?
- What special authorities does the security officer or system operator have?
- List the special authority values.

END-OF-CHAPTER AIDS

CHAPTER SUMMARY

The AS/400 comes with the most sophisticated, multitiered approach to security in the industry. The customer must implement it in a way that balances protection with ability to work. Each aspect of AS/400 security is easy to understand. What cannot be expressed enough in writing is that when skilled operators manipulate these aspects, the range of security solutions is as diverse as there are AS/400s.

KEY TERMS

adopted authorities
alter authority
authorities
authority
authority list
authority list management
authorization lists
checked out
data authorities
data security
default profiles
existence authority
group profiles
IBM system-supplied profile
level of security
list management rights
management authority
object-based security
object ownership
operational authority
ownership
physical security
predefined specific authorities
private authority
programmer
promotes
public authority
QPGMR
QSECOFR
QSECURITY
QSYSOPR
QUSER
reference authority
security officer
setup menu
special authorities
specific authority
system administrator
system level
system operator
system values
user-based security
user class
user profile
users
user's storage

CHAPTER SELF-TEST

Solutions to these self-test questions are in appendix D.

True-False Questions

___ 1. *SECADM special authority is reserved for only the QSECOFR.

___ 2. *SPLCTL authority provides the user with the ability to manage job queues.

___ 3. A user with user class USER noticed that the menu options on their menus were fewer than menus shown in this textbook. For example, the Security menu would display only the option to `Change your Password`.

___ 4. You always own any object you create.

___ 5. The security officer has been asked to give you access to the Employee Master file. You are allowed to update the data in the file, but you will not be allowed to delete the file from the system. Using the Grant Object Authority command, the security officer provided you with *CHANGE authority to meet these requirements.

___ 6. Authorization lists, object type *AUTL, are stored in QSYS library.

___ 7. If a user unsuccessfully attempts to sign onto the AS/400 repeatedly, his/her user profile is deactivated. The number of attempts is set by the QMAXSIGN system value.

Fill in the Blanks

1. Special authorities are (user-based/object-based) ____________ authorities.

2. The system operator needs to have _______________ and ______________ special authorities to do their job.

3. When configuring a device on the system, you first need ____________ special authority before you get started.

4. When using group profiles, the individual has an individual user profile and becomes a member of a group. When authority or access issues arise, the (group/user) _____________ profile over rides the (group/user) ___________ profile's authority.

5. You need to run a program that we created. The program accesses objects you currently have authority to use. You would generally need _____________ authority to access or run this program.

6. You created a program to look up the job title and phone extension of any employee in the company. All company employees use this program. You want to simplify your work and maintain security. You want to limit the ability to modify the program, while still allowing wide use. To meet these requirements, you would set the (special/specific/public/private*)* _______________ authority of the program (OBJECT) to ____________________.

7. A user in the MIS department has been granted *CHANGE authority to the payroll database file. The payroll file is also secured by the PAYROLL authorization list. The user changes jobs from the MIS department to the payroll department. With this move, the only change is the user's profile is added to the PAYROLL authorization list with *USE authority. To review, the user has *CHANGE authority to the file and *USE authority through the authorization list. The __________ authority would apply when the user accesses this object.

8. The college staff and students are allowed to sign onto more than one workstation at one time. For this to occur, the security officer would need to set the ____________________ system value to ____________.

9. If a student gets up and leaves his/her workstation for more than thirty minutes, the college wants the student to be automatically logged off. To accomplish this, the security officer would set the ____________________ system value to ________________.

10. If the maximum attempts to sign onto the AS/400 are exceeded, the ____________________ system value determines what consequence occurs.

Chapter Review Questions

1. Define the following terms:

   a. Special authority.

   b. Specific authority.

   c. Group profile.

   d. Authorization list.

   e. Adopted authority.

   f. System values.

   g. Object-based authority.

   h. User-based authority.

2. What is the difference between PRIVATE and PUBLIC authority?

3. What is the concern with a user having *ALLOBJ authority?

4. Why is level 20 not considered secure? Include the relationship to special authorities in your answer.

5. List several reasons why a company or college would use group profiles.

6. AXYZ company has a group of contract employees that work for them periodically. The same contract employees work for XYZ. The term of employment varies for these contract workers; they rarely work independently on individual projects, but most often, they work together on group projects. How would you handle/design their user profiles? You want to allow them to work together, and maintain security on the system. You also want to assure the company boss when the projects are complete and the contract employees are deleted from the system that all the objects they worked on and/or created continue to remain on the system and function as expected.

7. You outsourced the Y2K conversion of your company's custom software. A user profile was created for each individual programmer from the consulting company. What would the Object Ownership parameter be set to for the user? If the user were going to be gone for a month then return to the project, would you delete or change the programmer's user profile? If you would change the profile, what would be the changes?

8. What are the advantages and disadvantages of adopted authority?

9. List the system values that affect the user value for their password. What effect does each system have on the password?

10. What happens on your AS/400 when you delete a user profile?

11. If you were given the task to design a user profile for a student at your college, what values would you use in the parameters shown in Figure L11-5? Your instructor may ask you to explain your choices for designated parameters.

Parameter	Value
a. Set password to expire	
b. Status	
c. User class	
d. Assistance level	
e. Limit capabilities	
f. Special authority	
g. Password expiration interval	
h. Limit device sessions	
I. Maximum allowed storage	
j. Group profile	
k. Owner	
l. Group authority (if using group profiles)	
m. Delivery	
n. Severity	
o. Print device	
p. Output queue	
q. Attention program	
r. Home directory	
s. Authority	

Figure L11-5: Parameters and values for a user profile.

12

WORKING WITH JOBS

CHAPTER OBJECTIVES

Upon completion of this chapter, you should be able to:

- Explain what a job is, including batch, interactive, and communication jobs.
- Describe what a job description is and what it provides the system.
- Describe what job classes are and how they are used.
- Demonstrate how to work with jobs by status.
- Demonstrate how to change job sequence.
- Describe what job queues are and how they are used.
- Explain how jobs are submitted and scheduled.
- Demonstrate how to work with signed-on users.
- Explain the commands that are used in managing jobs.

OVERVIEW

Jobs are the basic work unit of the AS/400. By grouping one or more programs into related sets called jobs, the AS/400 gives the system operator a unique method of controlling how and when work gets through. The operator can easily schedule jobs and assign system resources to them (or take away system resources). Most of what an operator does in a normal day can be categorized as working with jobs.

JOB TYPES

There are four major job types system operators concern themselves with:

- Interactive.
- Batch.
- Communication.
- System.

An *interactive job* runs in the foreground. That is, it utilizes a terminal session while it runs. It usually does so because input from the user is critical to what the job does. A data entry program is an example of an interactive job. An interactive job is started when the user signs onto the terminal. While running under this job, the user can execute programs via the CALL *command*. When this happens, the CALLED programs also run interactively because, as subjobs of the main job, they assume its job type. All interactive jobs tie up the workstation screen until they finish.

A *batch job* runs in the *background*. Background processing means the job does not tie up a terminal. It may have been submitted (as opposed to CALLed) from a terminal, but it runs independently of that terminal. A month-end check-printing program would be an example of a batch program.

An interactive user can start a batch job to the AS/400 via the Submit Job (SBMJOB) command. We will discuss these commands later in the chapter. A *communication job* is a batch job that has been started by a remote AS/400. It is similar to a batch job in most other respects.

A *system job* is always a batch job and it is one the AS/400 starts. Its name usually starts with the letter Q, like other AS/400 objects. Generally, these come and go within the Q-named *subsystems*. For the most part, even system operators do not work with them. An example of a system job that it might be nice to know is around is when a spool file is sent to a printer for printing. A system job does the actual printing. When the printing is done, the system job ends. As another example, when a backup is started, a system job actually does the backup.

System jobs are not critical to master because we can do nothing with them for performance. But it is nice to be aware of them when monitoring the system for performance. An example may be when a system backup is started during the day. Interactive users may start to complain about response time. The system operator looks at what is going on in the system and notes that none of the non-IBM jobs are taking any computer resources at all. But the operator may notice that a Q-job is using about 70 percent of the system.

If the system operator knows about jobs and system jobs, he/she would realize the backup command that was started in turn started its own Q-job, and that is what is taking up system resources. The only choice to improve performance is to cancel the backup and try it later (if possible). Whatever the situation, it's better to realize that jobs can have a system job doing all the work in the background.

JOB DESCRIPTIONS

Job descriptions contain the attributes a job will have. These are called *job attributes* and are not to be confused with a job's other set of attributes—*runtime attributes*. Before a job can be recognized by the AS/400, it will have both sets of attributes. Both sets stay with the job throughout its life, although the run attributes are mostly meaningless when the job is not running, and the job attributes are mostly meaningless when it is running. Exceptions to this rule are the few job attributes, like the job name and start date, that are in effect throughout the job's life.

Along with job attributes, the job description contains *routing data* that helps the AS/400 locate runtime attributes for it. All jobs have a job description even if it is only the IBM-supplied default, QDFTJOBD. The primary elements of a job description are:

- Job description name.
- Job date.
- Job date format.
- User ID.
- Starting information:
  - Job queue in which the job will be placed (for batch jobs).
  - Priority of the job while it is on the job queue (but not its run priority).
  - Status on job queue. (It can be on HOLD, in which case it will not run until it is released.)
- Output information:
  - Output queue.
  - Print device.
  - Output queue priority.
  - Routing data.
  - Accounting code.
- Message logging level. Whether to log a lot of information to the job log or a little (see chapter 15).

Figures 12-1 through 12-3 show the screens used to create a job description with the Create Job Description (CRTJOBD) command.

```
                    Create Job Description (CRTJOBD)

 Type choices, press Enter.

 Job description . . . . . . . .   NEWJOB       Name
   Library . . . . . . . . . . .     *CURLIB    Name, *CURLIB
 Job queue . . . . . . . . . . .   QBATCH       Name
   Library . . . . . . . . . . .     *LIBL      Name, *LIBL, *CURLIB
 Job priority (on JOBQ) . . . . .   5            1-9
 Output priority (on OUTQ)  . . .   5            1-9
 Print device . . . . . . . . . .   *USRPRF      Name, *USRPRF, *SYSVAL...
 Output queue . . . . . . . . . .   *USRPRF      Name, *USRPRF, *DEV, *WRKSTN
   Library . . . . . . . . . . .                Name, *LIBL, *CURLIB
 Text 'description' . . . . . . .   *BLANK

                          Additional Parameters

 User . . . . . . . . . . . . . .   *RQD         Name, *RQD
 Print text . . . . . . . . . . .   *SYSVAL
                                                                More...
 F3=Exit   F4=Prompt   F5=Refresh   F12=Cancel   F13=How to use this display
 F24=More keys
```

Figure 12-1: Prompted version of the CRTJOBD command (part 1 of 3).

All this command really has to have is the Job Description name, but if that is all that you know about the job, use the IBM Default Job Description (QDFTJOBD) previously mentioned. Chances are, at least a few of the parameters on a new job description will be set for a particular need. Here is a rundown of the more commonly used parameters of this command:

- *Job Queue* (JOBQ). Name of the job queue into which the job will go before it goes into a subsystem for execution.
- *Job Priority* (JOBPTY). Number from 1 to 9 indicating the priority of the job while it is in the job queue. Priority 1 is the highest priority, 9 is the lowest.
- *Output Priority* (OUTPTY). Number from 1 to 9 indicating the priority of the output while it is in the output queue. Priority 1 is the highest priority, 9 is the lowest.
- *Output Queue* (OUTQ). Name of the output queue into which the job's printed output will go.
- *Print Device* (PRTDEV). An optional way of naming the output destination. Name a print device and any spooled output will automatically go to the output queue associated with that device (the queue will have the same name as the device).
- *Text* (TEXT). Short, plain language description of the job.

```
                    Create Job Description (CRTJOBD)

                         Type choices, press Enter.

Accounting code  . . . . . . . .   *USRPRF
Routing data . . . . . . . . . .   QCMDI

Request data or command  . . . .   *NONE



CL syntax check  . . . . . . . .   *NOCHK         0-99, *NOCHK
Initial library list . . . . . .   *SYSVAL        Name, *SYSVAL, *NONE
               + for more values
End severity . . . . . . . . . .   30             0-99
Message logging:
  Level  . . . . . . . . . . . .   4              0-4
  Severity . . . . . . . . . . .   0              0-99
  Text . . . . . . . . . . . . .   *NOLIST        *NOLIST, *MSG, *SECLVL
Log CL program commands  . . . .   *NO            *NO, *YES
                                                                More...
F3=Exit   F4=Prompt   F5=Refresh   F12=Cancel   F13=How to use this display
F24=More keys
```

Figure 12-2: Prompted version of the CRTJOBD command (part 2 of 3).

- *Routing Data* (RTGDTA). Contains the information to be used later by the *job class* to locate its runtime attributes. Refer to chapter 13 and chapter 14 for more information on routing data and its relationship to routing entries.
- *Initial Library List* (INLLIBL). This allows the operator to set the library list that the job's programs will use. This is both a security and a testing feature. For security purposes, this disallows the programs from access files. For testing, test libraries can be inserted here and, therefore, keep the programs from accessing production data. Later, when the programs are tested, the test libraries can be replaced with production libraries.
- *Message Logging* (LOG). This determines what messages (if any) are logged about the job's execution. Refer to chapter 15 for more information about these values.

```
                    Create Job Description (CRTJOBD)

                         Type choices, press Enter.

 Inquiry message reply . . . . .   *RQD          *RQD, *DFT, *SYSRPYL
 Hold on job queue . . . . . . .   *NO           *NO, *YES
 Job date . . . . . . . . . . .    *SYSVAL       Date, *SYSVAL
 Job switches . . . . . . . . .    00000000      Character value
 Device recovery action . . . . .  *SYSVAL
 Time slice end pool . . . . . .   *SYSVAL       *SYSVAL, *NONE, *BASE
 Authority . . . . . . . . . . .   *LIBCRTAUT    Name, *LIBCRTAUT, *CHANGE...
 Job message queue maximum size    *SYSVAL       2-64, *SYSVAL
 Job message queue full action .   *SYSVAL       *SYSVAL, *NOWRAP, *WRAP...
 Allow multiple threads . . . . .  *NO           *NO, *YES


                                                                    Bottom
 F3=Exit   F4=Prompt   F5=Refresh   F12=Cancel   F13=How to use this display
 F24=More keys
```

Figure 12-3: Prompted version of the CRTJOBD command (part 3 of 3).

- *Hold on Job Queue* (HOLD). The job enters the job queue in a *HOLD status. Jobs with this status will not start in a subsystem until they are released. Sometimes several jobs are submitted into a queue that are in a hold status, then their order is manipulated before they are made available for execution by being released.

Any job description parameters can be changed with either the CHGJOBD or the WRKJOBD command. CHGJOBD looks a lot like the CRTJOBD. Some customers prefer the WRKJOBD because it gives a quick overview of many job descriptions. This is especially helpful when the exact spelling of a job name has been forgotten or when just browsing for a job description. Figure 12-4 shows a sample of WRKJOBD.

```
                         Work with Job Descriptions

 Type options, press Enter.
   1=Create   2=Change   3=Copy   4=Delete   5=Display

        Job
 Opt  Description  Library     Text

  _   QAMTJOBD     QSYS        Job description to allow multiple threads.
  _   QCTL         QSYS        Controlling Subsystem Job Description
  _   QDIRJOBD     QSYS        Job description for Directory Services
  _   QESAUTON     QSYS        Job Description for Automatic Problem Notificati
  _   QFSIOPWK     QSYS        File Sever I/O Processor job description
  _   QIMGJOBD     QSYS        PostScript interpreter job description
  _   QIZAJOBD     QSYS        UPGRADE ASSISTANT FOR OS/400 JOBD
  _   QIZAJOBR     QSYS        UPGRADE ASSISTANT FOR OS/400 JOBD
  _   QJSCCPY      QSYS        COPY SCREEN
  _   QLPINSTALL   QSYS        Job description for LP Install
                                                                     More...
 Parameters for options 1, 2, 3 and 5 or command
 ===>____________________________________________________________________

 F3=Exit      F4=Prompt    F5=Refresh    F9=Retrieve    F11=Display names only
 F12=Cancel   F16=Repeat position to    F17=Position to    F24=More keys
```

Figure 12-4: The WRKJOBD command.

Make a change to a job description by putting a 2 to the left of it, then pressing F4. The AS/400 comes with several job descriptions already created and ready for use. They are listed in appendix C of *OS/400 Work Management V4R4.*

JOB NAMES AND NUMBERS

Jobs get their names from several sources:

- Interactive jobs are named after the workstation from which they are started.
- Batch jobs can be:
  - Named by the person submitting them.
  - Obtained from the job description.

Each job also has a unique job number assigned by the system. There can be multiple jobs with the same name, but each job will have a unique job number. The system operator has no control over the job number but may be asked for it on some AS/400 commands. We will demonstrate how to find this number.

JOB CLASSES

A job class is an object that provides runtime attributes. Runtime attributes consist of three primary elements:

- *Runtime Priority*. This is the priority the job will have when it is active in the subsystem.
- *Time Slice* in milliseconds. This shows how long the CPU will work on this job before going onto another one. The CPU will come back to this job when it can; the time slice measurement is just how much continuous time it can spend executing the job.
- *Eligible for Purge*. Always leave this at the default *YES. If the system needs to purge a job, it will, regardless of this value.

Job Classes are created with the Create Class (CRTCLS) command. Figure 12-5 contains a sample of that prompted command.

As with other creation commands, not every parameter is crucial. Here are the common class parameters:

- *Class* (CLASS). The name of the class.
- *Run Priority* (RUNPTY). A number ranging from one through ninety-nine indicating the runtime priority of the job. (The highest priority is 1, 99 is the lowest.) *Caution*: Do not use a runtime priority of less than 10 unless you are very sure of what you are doing. This priority area, from 1 to 10, is the area of system job priorities. Although a system operator can assign one of those priorities to a user job, he/she should be very sure before doing so.
- *Time Slice* (TIMESLICE). The amount of time in milliseconds that the system will work on the job continuously before going onto another job. Interactive jobs usually default to 2,000; batch and communication jobs to 5,000.

```
                          Create Class (CRTCLS)

Type choices, press Enter.

Class . . . . . . . . . . . . . ________    Name
  Library . . . . . . . . . . .   *CURLIB   Name, *CURLIB
Run priority . . . . . . . . .  50          1-99
Time slice . . . . . . . . . .  2000        Milliseconds
Eligible for purge . . . . . .  *YES        *YES, *NO
Default wait time  . . . . . .  30          Seconds, *NOMAX
Maximum CPU time . . . . . . .  *NOMAX      Milliseconds, *NOMAX
Maximum temporary storage  . .  *NOMAX      Kilobytes, *NOMAX
Maximum threads  . . . . . . .  *NOMAX      1-32767, *NOMAX
Text 'description' . . . . . .  *BLANK


                                                                Bottom
F3=Exit   F4=Prompt   F5=Refresh   F10=Additional parameters   F12=Cancel
F13=How to use this display        F24=More keys
```

Figure 12-5: Prompted version of CRTCLS.

- *Eligible for Purge* (PURGE). Always leave this *YES. This refers to how the system will purge the job if it needs to make room for other jobs.

- *Default Wait Time* (DFTWAIT). This is the amount of time the system will wait for a command to execute. In computer-time, the default, thirty seconds, is an eternity. Leave this default for most jobs. Think of it this way: If a file that this job needs to open is locked by another job, how long is this job to sit and wait for it? Thirty seconds is long enough.

- *Text* (TEXT). Short, plain language description of the job class.

  IBM has filled in some fairly decent default values for the default class—
  enough to make them work. Before creating custom classes, however, try the IBM-supplied ones (listed in appendix C of the *OS/400 Work Management V4R2).*

JOB QUEUES (BATCH JOBS ONLY)

Before a batch job becomes active in a batch subsystem, it must pass through a job queue. A job queue is simply a holding place for jobs entering the system. Think of a job queue as a funnel above a subsystem. Each job queue can only funnel jobs into one subsystem, but one subsystem may be fed by several job queues.

Sometimes the queue and subsystem are empty and a job falls right through the queue into the subsystem where it starts running. Other times, a queue will be full of pending jobs and a new job entering will take its place in the queue. And yet at other times, a subsystem will be too busy to accept new jobs, so even though a job enters an empty job queue, it will not start until the subsystem is ready to receive it.

Each job has a *job queue priority* assignment that comes from its job description. Jobs in the queue will be released to the subsystem in ascending order of these priorities. Jobs with equal priority will be released in *first in, first out* (*FIFO*) order.

The system operator can manipulate jobs on a queue. If there were five jobs on a queue with equal priority and a sixth one entered with the same priority, the sixth one will not start until after the other five have started (and the subsystem is ready to accept another job). If the sixth job is very important and must be started ahead of the others, the system operator can change its priority to a number lower than the priorities of the other five jobs. Another thing the operator can do is hold all five jobs and allow the sixth to start ahead of them.

Anyone who is going to manipulate jobs on a queue, however, must have special authority, *Job Control* (JOBCTL), on his user ID. System operators do have this authority. For more on authorities, see chapter 11.

Job queues are created with the Create Job Queue (CRTJOBQ) command. Figure 12-6 shows its format.

Job queues are really simple things—to create one, all that is needed is the name, its library, and a short text; that is all most AS/400 customers actually do.

Creating a job queue is only half the work, though. They have to be assigned to a batch subsystem after they are created. To do this, the batch subsystem description must already be created—refer to chapter 13, Subsystems. Add a job queue to an existing subsystem description with the Add Job Queue Entry (ADDJOBQE) command. Its basic format is simple:

```
ADDJOBQE <library>/<batch subsystem><library>/<job queue name>
```

Prompt it by pressing the F4 key to more easily view the command parameters. As an aid to getting started, the AS/400 comes with several job queues to use directly or modify as needed. They are listed in *OS/400 Work Management V4R4.*

WORKING WITH JOBS

SUBMITTING JOBS

Interactive jobs are not submitted, they are started automatically when the user signs on. Within an interactive job, a user can start a program via the CALL command. Ultimately, the only way to start a program is through the CALL command or by executing a command (like the commands we have discussed throughout this book), which implicitly "calls" a program to do its work.

When an interactive user is signed on, that user is running an interactive job. When the user CALLS a program or issues a command from the command line, the resulting program runs interactively. If the interactive user wants to start a program and have it run in batch, the user has to submit that same CALL or command into the system with the Submit Job (SBMJOB) command.

Similarly, within a job, the program that is running can start another program with the CALL command or by issuing a command. When it does, the program that runs is part of the job and carries its characteristics. Think about that as it relates to the original job type. A job running in batch that invokes another job or program, whether it submits a job or calls a program, will result in the new job or program running in batch. An interactive job submitting a job will result in the submitted job running in batch. An interactive job calling a program will result in the called program running interactively, as a subjob of the parent interactive job.

A running job can start another batch job only through the Submit Job (SBMJOB) command, just like humans. We will not go into the construction of the command language or programming language within a job that does this; we will just discuss the command.

Batch jobs begin their lives when they are submitted. The command to submit a job is the Submit Job (SBMJOB) command. Figures12-7 through 12-10 contain a sample of it in the prompted version.

```
                         Create Job Queue (CRTJOBQ)

 Type choices, press Enter.

 Job queue . . . . . . . . . . .  __________    Name
   Library . . . . . . . . . . .    *CURLIB     Name, *CURLIB
 Text 'description' . . . . . . . *BLANK______________________________
```

Figure 12-6: Prompted version of the CRTJOBQ command.

```
                            Submit Job (SBMJOB)

 Type choices, press Enter.

 Command to run . . . . . . ____________________________________________
 ______________________________________________________________________
 ______________________________________________________________________
 ______________________________________________________________________
 ______________________________________________________________________
                                                                   ...
 Job name . . . . . . . . . . . . *JOBD        Name, *JOBD
 Job description  . . . . . . . . *USRPRF      Name, *USRPRF
   Library  . . . . . . . . . . .   ________    Name, *LIBL, *CURLIB
 Job queue  . . . . . . . . . . . *JOBD        Name, *JOBD
   Library  . . . . . . . . . . .   ________    Name, *LIBL, *CURLIB
 Job priority (on JOBQ) . . . . . *JOBD        1-9, *JOBD
 Output priority (on OUTQ)  . . . *JOBD        1-9, *JOBD
 Print device . . . . . . . . . . *CURRENT     Name, *CURRENT, *USRPRF...

                                                                  More...
 F3=Exit   F4=Prompt   F5=Refresh   F10=Additional parameters   F12=Cancel
 F13=How to use this display        F24=More keys
```

Figure 12-7: Prompted version of the SBMJOB command (screen 1 of 4).

Here are the common Submit Job parameters:

- *Command to Run* (CMD). This is the CALL <program name> or other command. It is important to note that a submitted job, which becomes a batch job, does not have to be an application or a programmer-written job; it can be an AS/400 command. Because of the length of time they take to complete, many long-running AS/400 commands are submitted to batch to run.

- *Job Name* (JOB). This is the name of the job. It is optional and if it is not given, the system will attempt to go to the Job Description (next parameter) for the name.
- *Job Description* (JOBD). This is the job description the system is to access to obtain the nonrunning attributes of the job. Again, this is optional, if it is not given, the default, *USRPRF, will be used by the system. That is, the system will go to the user's profile and use that job description for this job.
- *Job Queue* (JOBQ). Name of the job queue into which the job will go before it goes into a subsystem for execution. This is optional and if the default is not changed, the system goes to the job description for the job queue name.
- *Job Priority* (JOBPTY). Number from 1 to 9 indicating the priority of the job while it is in the job queue.
- *Output Queue* (OUTQ). Name of the output queue into which the job's printed output will go. Note: We skipped the Print Device parameter because most IT departments just send output to an output queue and let the printer attached to that queue print it. In other words, they prefer to control the printer device through the output queue, not the job itself.

```
                           Submit Job (SBMJOB)
Type choices, press Enter.

Output queue . . . . . . . . . .   *CURRENT      Name, *CURRENT, *USRPRF...
  Library  . . . . . . . . . . .   __________    Name, *LIBL, *CURLIB

                        Additional Parameters

User . . . . . . . . . . . . . .   *CURRENT      Name, *CURRENT, *JOBD
Print text . . . . . . . . . . .   *CURRENT
Routing data . . . . . . . . . .   QCMDB

Request data or command  . . . .   *CMD
_______________________________________________________________________
_______________________________________________________________________
_______________________________________________________________________
_______________________________________________________________________
_______________________________________________________________________

                                                                    ...
                                                               More...
F3=Exit   F4=Prompt   F5=Refresh   F12=Cancel   F13=How to use this display
F24=More keys
```

Figure 12-8: Prompted version of the SBMJOB command (screen 2 of 4).

```
                          Submit Job (SBMJOB)

Type choices, press Enter.

System library list . . . . . .   *CURRENT      *CURRENT, *SYSVAL
Current library . . . . . . . .   *CURRENT      Name, *CURRENT, *USRPRF...
Initial library list . . . . . .  *CURRENT      Name, *CURRENT, *JOBD...
               + for more values  __________
Message logging:
  Level . . . . . . . . . . . .   *JOBD         0-4, *JOBD
  Severity . . . . . . . . . . .  *JOBD         0-99, *JOBD
  Text . . . . . . . . . . . . .  *JOBD         *JOBD, *MSG, *SECLVL, *NOLIST
Log CL program commands . . . .   *JOBD         *JOBD, *NO, *YES
Inquiry message reply . . . . .   *JOBD         *JOBD, *RQD, *DFT, *SYSRPYL
Hold on job queue . . . . . . .   *JOBD         *JOBD, *NO, *YES
Schedule date . . . . . . . . .   *CURRENT      Date, *CURRENT, *MONTHSTR...
Schedule time . . . . . . . . .   *CURRENT      Time, *CURRENT
Job date . . . . . . . . . . . .  *JOBD         Date, *JOBD, *SYSVAL
Job switches . . . . . . . . . .  *JOBD         Character value, *JOBD
Allow display by WRKSBMJOB . . .  *YES          *YES, *NO
                                                                    More...
F3=Exit   F4=Prompt   F5=Refresh   F12=Cancel   F13=How to use this display
F24=More keys
```

Figure 12-9: Prompted version of the SBMJOB command (screen 3 of 4).

- *Current Library* (CURLIB). Allows the current library (the preferred one from the job's library list) to be specified. If one is not specified, the library list in effect for the submitter of the job is used.
- *Initial Library List* (INLLIBL). Specifies the library list the job is to use. If one is not specified, the library list in effect for the submitter of the job is used.
- *Message Logging* (LOG). This determines what messages (if any) are logged about the job's execution. Refer to Chapter 15, Messages, Logs, and Cleanup, for more information about these values.
- *Hold on Job Queue* (HOLD). The job enters the job queue in a *HOLD status. Jobs with this status will not start in a subsystem until they are released. Sometimes several jobs are submitted into a queue in a hold status, and then their order is manipulated before they are made available for execution by being released.
- *Schedule Date* (SCDDATE). The date the job is to start. This is used in conjunction with the Schedule Time (next). If no time is specified, the job will start at 12:01 A.M. on the date indicated here.
- *Schedule Time* (SCDTIME). The time the job is to start. This is used in conjunction with the Schedule Date (previous). If no schedule date is specified, the job will start when the specified time is reached.
- *Allow Display by* WRKSBMJOB (DSPSBMJOB). When the DSPSBMJOB command is used to display active jobs and the value is set to *NO, this job will not display. Unless you have a very good reason, do not mark jobs *NO on this parameter.

```
                           Submit Job (SBMJOB)

 Type choices, press Enter.

 Message queue . . . . . . . . .   *USRPRF       Name, *USRPRF, *WRKSTN, *NONE
   Library . . . . . . . . . . .   __________    Name, *LIBL, *CURLIB
 Sort sequence . . . . . . . . .   *CURRENT      Name, *CURRENT, *USRPRF...
   Library . . . . . . . . . . .   __________    Name, *LIBL, *CURLIB
 Language ID . . . . . . . . . .   *CURRENT      *CURRENT, *SYSVAL...
 Country ID . . . . . . . . . . .  *CURRENT      *CURRENT, *SYSVAL...
 Coded character set ID . . . . .  *CURRENT      *CURRENT, *USRPRF, *SYSVAL...
 Submitted for . . . . . . . . .   *CURRENT      Name, *CURRENT
   User . . . . . . . . . . . . .  ________      Name
   Number . . . . . . . . . . . .  ________      000000-999999
 Job message queue maximum size    *JOBD         2-64, *JOBD, *SYSVAL
 Job message queue full action  .  *JOBD         *JOBD, *SYSVAL, *NOWRAP...
 Copy environment variables . . .  *NO           *NO, *YES
 Allow multiple threads . . . . .  *JOBD         *JOBD, *NO, *YES

                                                                        Bottom
 F3=Exit   F4=Prompt   F5=Refresh   F12=Cancel   F13=How to use this display
 F24=More keys
```

Figure 12-10: Prompted version of the SBMJOB command (screen 4 of 4).

Notice that many parameters are exactly the same as corresponding parameters on the Job Description command. The reason for the redundant data in multiple locations is so that SBMJOB information can be specified or implied to come from a variety of places. In that way, AS/400 jobs can be tailored to fit a wide range of operating conditions.

Two parameters, SCDDATE and SCDTIME, are used together to indicate that the job will start at some future date and time. These are optional and if not used, the job starts as soon as it can.

SCDDATE has some system values that can be used instead of specifying an actual date. They are:

- *CURRENT—Today's date.
- *MONTHSTR—First day of the month.
- *MONTHEND—Last day of the month.
- *MON through *SUN—The next occurrence of the day specified.

SCHTIME only has one value other than specifying an actual start time:

- *CURRENT—Current time.

In Figure 12-9, the default values for SCDDATE and SCDTIME are system values *CURRENT, which imply they will start immediately if those values are not changed.

Scheduling Jobs

The SBMJOB command submits the job right away or has rudimentary job scheduling features in the SCDDATE and SCDTIME parameters.

That makes it pretty powerful, but sometimes AS/400 IT departments want more sophistication in their job scheduling. The job scheduler does that. *Job scheduling* is the process of scheduling jobs to submit themselves on a predetermined schedule. Jobs set up in the job scheduler submit and run themselves in schedules with varying degrees of complexity. The thing to remember about the job scheduler is that, sophisticated as it is, it ultimately starts jobs with the same SBMJOB command we just discussed.

The heart of the job scheduler is an IBM object located in library QUSRSYS, named QDFTJOBSCD. Because it is an IBM object, we cannot create, change, duplicate, delete, or rename it. To use it, we have to add, change, and remove entries to it. The following set of commands help us do that:

- ADDJOBSCDE. Adds a job and its schedule to the job schedule.
- CHGJOBSCDE. Changes a job and its schedule already on the job schedule.
- HLDJOBSCDE. Holds a job already on the job schedule, preventing it from starting at its appointed time.
- RLSJOBSCDE. Releases a job and its schedule already on the job schedule and previously held.
- RMVJOBSCDE. Removes a job and its schedule from the job schedule.
- WRKJOBSCDE. Work with many jobs and their schedules already on the job schedule.

The WRKJOBSCDE provides a quick overview of all scheduled jobs on the system. Figure 12-11 contains a sample of its screen on a typical AS/400.

```
                         Work with Job Schedule Entries                  BIGBLUE
                                                             07/03/99  16:39:05


 Type options, press Enter.
   2=Change   3=Hold   4=Remove    5=Display details    6=Release
   8=Work with last submission     10=Submit immediately

                                                                        Next
                           ---Schedule---             Recovery  Submit
 Opt  Job          Status  Date        Time       Frequency   Action    Date
 __   QCLRSPLF      SCD    *ALL        06:00:00   *WEEKLY     *SBMRLS   07/04/99
 __   SAVRPG        SCD    *FRI        21:00:00   *WEEKLY     *SBMRLS   07/09/99
```

Figure 12-11: Jobs and their schedules on an AS/400.

Notice that through the options, we can go directly to the other job schedule commands. From this figure, we see two jobs that are scheduled. Their statuses are SCD, or scheduled, indicating they are not currently in a held status. One job, QCLRSPLF (an IBM system job that clears spool files), starts every day (Date *ALL) at 6 A.M. (Time 06:00:00). The date this command was run was 07/03/99 (from upper-right corner, second line), and the next time this job will run will be 07/04/99, which is shown in the right-most column, Next Submit Date.

The other job, SAVRPG, is also scheduled and will run on Fridays (*FRI) at 21:00, or 9 P.M. Running weekly (*WEEKLY), it happens every Friday. The next time it's scheduled to run is 07/09/99, the date of the next Friday. Both jobs have the same Recovery Action as specified in the seventh column, *SBMRLS. Recovery Action tells the system what to do with the job if the system is unavailable as scheduled. Obviously, nothing happens until the system is available, but then the *SBMRLS value will have the system submit the job even though it missed its appointed time, and it will submit it in a normal, or released, state—meaning it will be ready to run.

Let's add a new job to the scheduler. Remember, the scheduler ultimately submits the job so we will see a lot of the SBMJOB parameters on the add command we use. That command is Add Job Scheduler Entry (ADDJOBSCDE) and Figures 12-12 and 12-13 contain a sample of its screens.

Earlier, we discussed the Submit Job (SBMJOB) command and its parameters. This command uses many of those same parameters; it only introduces a couple new ones to accomplish job scheduling. We will not go over the common parameters to both commands, just the important new ones. They are:

- *Frequency* (FREQ). The frequency that the scheduling will recur. The options are *ONCE, *WEEKLY, and *MONTHLY.
- *Schedule Date* (SCDDATE). The date the job is scheduled to run. Possible values are the same as those for SCDDATE in the SBMJOB command. This parameter is mutually exclusive of the next. Use one or the other, but not both.
- *Schedule Day* (SCDDAY). The day the job is scheduled to run. Possible values are the day of the week (indicated with *MON through *SUN or *ALL for every day).

```
                       Add Job Schedule Entry (ADDJOBSCDE)

Type choices, press Enter.

Job name . . . . . . . . . . . . __________      Name, *JOBD
Command to run . . . . . . . . . ____________________________________________
_____________________________________________________________________________
_____________________________________________________________________________
_____________________________________________________________________________
_____________________________________________________________________________
_____________________________________________________________________________

Frequency . . . . . . . . . . .  _________       *ONCE, *WEEKLY, *MONTHLY
Schedule date, or . . . . . . .  *CURRENT        Date, *CURRENT, *MONTHSTR...
Schedule day . . . . . . . . . . *NONE           *NONE, *ALL, *MON, *TUE...
               + for more values _________
Schedule time . . . . . . . . .  *CURRENT        Time, *CURRENT
Save . . . . . . . . . . . . . . *NO             *NO, *YES

                                                                     More...
F3=Exit   F4=Prompt   F5=Refresh   F12=Cancel   F13=How to use this display
F24=More keys
```

Figure 12-12: Jobs and their schedules on an AS/400 (screen 1 of 2).

```
                    Add Job Schedule Entry (ADDJOBSCDE)

Type choices, press Enter.

                        Additional Parameters

Omit date . . . . . . . . . . .  *NONE        Date, *NONE
             + for more values
Recovery action . . . . . . . .  *SBMRLS      *SBMRLS, *SBMHLD, *NOSBM
Job description . . . . . . . .  *USRPRF      Name, *USRPRF
  Library . . . . . . . . . . .               Name, *LIBL, *CURLIB
Job queue . . . . . . . . . . .  *JOBD        Name, *JOBD
  Library . . . . . . . . . . .               Name, *LIBL, *CURLIB
User . . . . . . . . . . . . . .  *CURRENT     Name, *JOBD, *CURRENT
Message queue . . . . . . . . .  *USRPRF      Name, *USRPRF, *NONE
  Library . . . . . . . . . . .               Name, *LIBL, *CURLIB
Text 'description' . . . . . . .  *BLANK
```

Figure 12-13: Jobs and their schedules on an AS/400 (screen 2 of 2).

WORK WITH JOBS

There are several ways to work with jobs on the AS/400. Probably a good place to start is with the general Work with Active Jobs (WRKACTJOB) command. Figure 12-14 contains a sample of that command.

```
                         Work with Active Jobs                    BIGBLUE
                                                        07/03/99  17:47:11
CPU %:     .0     Elapsed time:   00:00:00     Active jobs:   112

Type options, press Enter.
  2=Change   3=Hold   4=End   5=Work with   6=Release   7=Display message
  8=Work with spooled files   13=Disconnect ...

Opt  Subsystem/Job  User       Type  CPU %  Function        Status
 _   QBASE          QSYS       SBS      .0                   DEQW
 _   QBATCH         QSYS       SBS      .0                   DEQW
 _   QCMN           QSYS       SBS      .0                   DEQW
 _   QCTL           QSYS       SBS      .0                   DEQW
 _     QSYSSCD      QPGMR      BCH      .0  PGM-QEZSCNEP     EVTW
 _   QINTER         QSYS       SBS      .0                   DEQW
 _     QPADEV0004   DAWSON#M   INT      .0  CMD-WRKACTJOB    RUN
 _   QPGMR          QSYS       SBS      .0                   DEQW
 _   QSERVER        QSYS       SBS      .0                   DEQW
                                                                   More...
Parameters or command
===>
F3=Exit   F5=Refresh        F7=Find       F10=Restart statistics
F11=Display elapsed data    F12=Cancel    F23=More options   F24=More keys
```

Figure 12-14: Jobs and subsystems active (from the WRKACTJOB command).

This screen shows all active jobs and their subsystems. The jobs are indented below their respective subsystems so the viewer can easily see which are subsystems and which are jobs. In case the visual clue is missed, subsystems are marked with a type of SBS, interactive jobs with INT, and batch jobs as BCH.

In this figure, we see some jobs named with the letter Q. These are system jobs or subsystems. We also see one of the authors is running a job named QADEV0004, under subsystem QINTER, the interactive subsystem. The job name comes from the workstation device technically, but in this case, he/she is signed on remotely, so the name adopts the name of the remote communication controller he/she came in through. Notice under the Function column, we can see what the author is doing—running command WRKACTJOB—what a coincidence! At the top are options for several functions. Let us take option 5 (`Work with`) to see what we can see. Figure 12-15 contains a sample of that screen.

At the top of the screen are the three elements that make up a job name to the AS/400: the name, the user, and the system-assigned job number. This is a menu of further options, depending on what we want to see about the job. We will look at the commonly used options. If we use option 1 (`Display Job Status Attributes`), we get a screen similar to that shown in Figure 12-16.

```
                              Work with Job
                                                             System:   BIGBLUE
 Job:   QPADEV0004      User:    DAWSON#M        Number:   187515

 Select one of the following:

      1. Display job status attributes
      2. Display job definition attributes
      3. Display job run attributes, if active
      4. Work with spooled files

     10. Display job log, if active or on job queue
     11. Display call stack, if active
     12. Work with locks, if active
     13. Display library list, if active
     14. Display open files, if active
     15. Display file overrides, if active
     16. Display commitment control status, if active
                                                                      More...
 Selection or command
 ===> ____________________________________________________________________

 F3=Exit   F4=Prompt   F9=Retrieve   F12=Cancel
```

Figure 12-15: Menu for displaying job QPADEV0004.

```
Display Job Status Attributes
                                                      System:   BIGBLUE
 Job:   QPADEV0004    User:   DAWSON#M      Number:   187515

 Status of job . . . . . . . . . . . . . . . :   ACTIVE
 Current user profile  . . . . . . . . . . . :   DAWSON#M
 Job user identity . . . . . . . . . . . . . :   DAWSON#M
   Set by  . . . . . . . . . . . . . . . . . :     *DEFAULT
 Entered system:
   Date  . . . . . . . . . . . . . . . . . . :   07/03/99
   Time  . . . . . . . . . . . . . . . . . . :   12:01:54
 Started:
   Date  . . . . . . . . . . . . . . . . . . :   07/03/99
   Time  . . . . . . . . . . . . . . . . . . :   12:01:54
 Subsystem . . . . . . . . . . . . . . . . . :   QINTER
   Subsystem pool ID . . . . . . . . . . . . :     2
 Type of job . . . . . . . . . . . . . . . . :   INTER
 Special environment . . . . . . . . . . . . :   *NONE
 Program return code . . . . . . . . . . . . :   0
                                                                  More...
 Press Enter to continue.

 F3=Exit   F5=Refresh   F12=Cancel   F16=Job menu
```

Figure 12-16: Job status attributes for job QPADEV0004.

Here we see that the job is active, who the user is, the date/time the job entered the system, the date/time it started, and subsystem memory pool ID it is running in (refer to chapter 13 for more information about memory pools). We also see that it is an interactive (INTER) type job. So we have an active job from the Work with Job screen (Figure 12-15). We may want to take option 3 (`Display Job Run Attributes`) to see how the job is configured to run. If we did, we would get a screen similar to the one shown in Figure 12-17.

```
                           Display Job Run Attributes
                                                      System:   BIGBLUE
 Job:   QPADEV0004    User:   DAWSON#M      Number:   187515

 Run priority  . . . . . . . . . . . . . . . . . :   20
 Time slice in milliseconds  . . . . . . . . . . :   2000
 Eligible for purge  . . . . . . . . . . . . . . :   *YES
 Default wait time in seconds  . . . . . . . . . :   30
 Maximum CPU time in milliseconds  . . . . . . . :   *NOMAX
   CPU time used . . . . . . . . . . . . . . . . :     2299
 Maximum temporary storage in K bytes  . . . . . :   *NOMAX
   Temporary storage used  . . . . . . . . . . . :     660
 Maximum threads . . . . . . . . . . . . . . . . :   *NOMAX
   Threads . . . . . . . . . . . . . . . . . . . :     1








 Press Enter to continue.

 F3=Exit   F5=Refresh   F9=Change job   F12=Cancel   F16=Job menu
```

Figure 12-17: Job run attributes for job QPADEV0004.

The job's run priority is a 20, which is normal for interactive jobs. The time slice is set to 2,000 milliseconds, it is eligible for purge, and will wait thirty seconds for any command that is unable to finish. There is no maximum CPU usage or temporary storage (by the *NOMAX parameter values), although the job has currently used 2,299 milliseconds of CPU and 660Kbs of memory. All this is fairly normal for interactive jobs. Batch jobs run at a priority of around 50, and have their time slices set to around 5,000 milliseconds.

Let us look at more about this job from Figure 12-15. Selection 2 (`Display Job Definition Attributes`) will bring up some familiar pieces of information. Refer to Figure 12-18.

We have been saying that the system operator does not have to create every little thing, like job descriptions, that the AS/400 comes preloaded with default job descriptions that work just fine. This job is an example. Apparently, no job description was created for it; the system was told to use the default, which is named QDFTJOBD.

The job queue is not specified because this is an interactive job, and they do not use job queues. The job's priority on the job queue, 5, is ignored for interactive jobs.

Any output the job produces will go to the output queue with a priority 5. Any message of severity 30 or above will end the job. The message logging is typical—it is not logging CL commands, and it will use printer device PRT01 and output queue FACOUTQ.

```
                    Display Job Definition Attributes
                                                          System:   BIGBLUE
 Job:   QPADEV0004     User:   DAWSON#M       Number:   187515

 Job description . . . . . . . . . . . . . . . . . :    QDFTJOBD
   Library . . . . . . . . . . . . . . . . . . . . :      QGPL
 Job queue . . . . . . . . . . . . . . . . . . . . :
   Library . . . . . . . . . . . . . . . . . . . . :
 Job priority (on job queue) . . . . . . . . . . . :    5
 Output priority (on output queue) . . . . . . . . :    5
 End severity  . . . . . . . . . . . . . . . . . . :    30
 Message logging:
   Level . . . . . . . . . . . . . . . . . . . . . :    4
   Severity  . . . . . . . . . . . . . . . . . . . :    0
   Text  . . . . . . . . . . . . . . . . . . . . . :    *NOLIST
 Log CL program commands . . . . . . . . . . . . . :    *NO
 Printer device  . . . . . . . . . . . . . . . . . :    PRT01
 Default output queue  . . . . . . . . . . . . . . :    FACOUTQ
   Library . . . . . . . . . . . . . . . . . . . . :      QGPL
                                                                  More...
 Press Enter to continue.

 F3=Exit   F5=Refresh   F9=Change job   F12=Cancel   F16=Job menu
```

Figure 12-18: Job definition attributes for job QPADEV0004.

Back to Figure 12-15—this job is not doing that much, so there are no messages on the job log to look at. There is also nothing on the output queue to look at. Likewise, no files open or locked. Let us look at the job's library list. We mentioned that every job can have its own library list and that list can come from a variety of sources. We may have a job running and we do not know which library list it ended up with, but we want to make sure that it is processing files from the right libraries. We would take option 13 (`Display Library List`) from that screen. Figure 12-19 contains a sample of the library list for this job.

```
                          Display Library List
                                                   System:   BIGBLUE
Job:   QPADEV0004     User:   DAWSON#M       Number:   187515

Type options, press Enter.
  5=Display objects in library

Opt  Library     Type      Text
__   QSYS        SYS       System Library
__   QSYS2       SYS       System Library for CPI's
__   QHLPSYS     SYS
__   QUSRSYS     SYS
__   COMMONLIB   USR
__   QGPL        USR
__   QTEMP       USR

                                                              Bottom
F3=Exit   F12=Cancel   F16=Job menu   F17=Top   F18=Bottom
(C) COPYRIGHT IBM CORP. 1980, 1998.
```

Figure 12-19: Library list for job QPADEV0004.

From here, we would check that the job is using the right libraries. At the top of all these screens are the same three items: Job Name, User, and Job Number. As mentioned previously, you can pretty much name a job anything you want. The user name is picked up from the user either signing on (for interactive jobs) or submitting a job (for batch jobs). The system assigns the unique job number. All three items together make up the identifier of a job. To illustrate how this is used and why WRKACTJOB is an easier command to use, consider a command that you've been implicitly using all the time: the Work with Job (WRKJOB) command. When we were looking at the WRKACTJOB command just now, that command was actually calling the WRKJOB command. Try to skip the Work with Active Job (WRKACTJOB) command and go directly to the Work with Job (WRKJOB) command. It's a legal command, we're legal users with the appropriate authorities, and we'll just key the command on a command line and press the F4 key. See Figure 12-20 for the result.

```
                         Work with Job (WRKJOB)

Type choices, press Enter.

Job name . . . . . . . . . . . .   *__________    Name, *
  User . . . . . . . . . . . . .     __________   Name
  Number . . . . . . . . . . . .     __________   000000-999999
Output . . . . . . . . . . . . .   *________      *, *PRINT
Option . . . . . . . . . . . . .   *SELECT        *SELECT, *STSA, *DFNA...

                                                              Bottom
F3=Exit   F4=Prompt   F5=Refresh   F10=Additional parameters   F12=Cancel
F13=How to use this display        F24=More keys
```

Figure 12-20: Prompted version of the WRKJOB command.

This command is not going anywhere unless the system operator happens to know the three items that uniquely identify the job. Actually, the operator can get by with just the job name only if it happens to be the only job currently in the system with that name. That is kind of a random thing; most of the time, the operator will have to supply all three items and that will take some research with the WRKACTJOB command anyway. We will fill in the three items and check the result in Figure 12-21. Look familiar?

Normally, we would have to at least go to WRKACTJOB to determine the user and job number anyway, even if we knew the job name. It is much easier just to use WRKACTJOB. The exception to this common preference is a small but distinct one. Unlike WRKACTJOB, WRKJOB allows the system operator to send all job information to a printer. The operator only has to enter *PRINT for the OUTPUT parameter on the command.

```
                               Work with Job
                                                         System:   BIGBLUE
 Job:   QPADEV0004      User:    DAWSON#M       Number:   187515

 Select one of the following:

      1. Display job status attributes
      2. Display job definition attributes
      3. Display job run attributes, if active
      4. Work with spooled files

     10. Display job log, if active or on job queue
     11. Display call stack, if active
     12. Work with locks, if active
     13. Display library list, if active
     14. Display open files, if active
     15. Display file overrides, if active
     16. Display commitment control status, if active
                                                                  More...
 Selection or command
 ===> ________________________________________________________________________

 F3=Exit   F4=Prompt   F9=Retrieve   F12=Cancel
```

Figure 12-21: The Display Job menu screen is identical to the one shown in Figure 12-15.

Revisit Figure 12-14 (Work with Active Jobs) for a bit. We've been playing with the option 5, but there are other options at the top of this screen. Rather than go through all of them, because they're similar to option 5, here are the highlights of each:

- Option 2 (Change). This allows the system operator to make changes to the job. To use this option, enter a 2 on the option line and press the F4 key.
- Option 3 (Hold). This holds a job on the queue. It will not run as long as it is held.
- Option 4 (End). This invokes the ENDJOB command and ends the job.
- Option 6 (Release). This releases a previously held job on the job queue. When it is released, the job is eligible to run.
- Option 7 (Display Messages). If there are messages for this job, option 7 displays them. This is a nice way to cut through the thousands of messages on the system operator's message queue and focus just on messages for a single job.
- Option 8 (Work with Spooled Files). If the job has produced any output, this option will get the operator to those spool files quickly.

Let's move on. Maybe we don't want to look at active jobs. Let's assume a user calls to complain that he or she submitted a job and doesn't know what happened to it. First, find out the user's name as known to the system—it will be the user profile he or she uses when he or she signs on—the user ought to know it. Then use the Work with User Jobs (WRKUSRJOB) command. Figure 12-22 contains a prompted version of that command.

```
                        Work with User Jobs (WRKUSRJOB)

 Type choices, press Enter.

 User whose jobs to display . . .   *            Name, *, *ALL
 Status of user jobs  . . . . . .   *ALL         *ALL, *ACTIVE, *JOBQ, *OUTQ
 Output . . . . . . . . . . . . .   *            *, *PRINT
 Job type . . . . . . . . . . . .   *ALL         *ALL, *INTERACT, *BATCH









                                                                        Bottom
 F3=Exit   F4=Prompt   F5=Refresh   F10=Additional parameters   F12=Cancel
 F13=How to use this display        F24=More keys
```

Figure 12-22: Prompted version of the WRKUSRJOB command.

Assume the user is author HOHLY#M. We will put that in for the first parameter and press the Enter key. We get a screen similar to the one shown in Figure 12-23.

```
                             Work with User Jobs                    BIGBLUE
                                                          07/03/99  18:48:56
 Type options, press Enter.
   2=Change   3=Hold   4=End   5=Work with   6=Release   7=Display message
   8=Work with spooled files   13=Disconnect


 Opt  Job          User        Type     ---Status---   Function
 __   PAYFILE      HOHLY#M     BATCH    OUTQ
 __   PAYJOBD      HOHLY#M     BATCH    JOBQ      HELD
 __   PAYMEMOA     HOHLY#M     BATCH    OUTQ
 __   PAYMEMOA     HOHLY#M     BATCH    OUTQ
 __   PAYMEMOA     HOHLY#M     BATCH    OUTQ
 __   PAYMEMOA     HOHLY#M     BATCH    OUTQ
 __   QDFTJOBD     HOHLY#M     BATCH    JOBQ      HELD
 __   QPADEV0004   HOHLY#M     INTER    OUTQ
 __   QPADEV0004   HOHLY#M     INTER    OUTQ
 __   QPADEV0004   HOHLY#M     INTER    OUTQ
                                                                     More...
 Parameters or command
 ===>_____________________________________________________________________

 F3=Exit     F4=Prompt   F5=Refresh   F9=Retrieve   F11=Display schedule data
 F12=Cancel  F21=Select assistance level
```

Figure 12-23: All jobs known to the system that user HOHLY#M started.

There are two jobs on job queues and they are held; the rest are on an output queue. A job on the output queue usually means it is finished. Refer back to the screen in Figure 12-22—we could further refine our selection by specifying that we only want to look at jobs on the job queue owned by the same user. The result would be a screen similar to the one shown in Figure 12-24.

```
                          Work with User Jobs                          BIGBLUE
                                                             07/03/99  18:51:29
 Type options, press Enter.
   2=Change   3=Hold   4=End   5=Work with   6=Release   7=Display message
   8=Work with spooled files   13=Disconnect


 Opt  Job        User       Type    ---Status---   Function
  _   PAYJOBD    HOHLY#M    BATCH   JOBQ     HELD
  _   QDFTJOBD   HOHLY#M    BATCH   JOBQ     HELD
  _   RPGJOBD    HOHLY#M    BATCH   JOBQ     HELD


                                                                          Bottom
 Parameters or command
 ===> ____________________________________________________________________

 F3=Exit      F4=Prompt   F5=Refresh   F9=Retrieve   F11=Display schedule data
 F12=Cancel   F21=Select assistance level
```

Figure 12-24: All jobs on job queues known to the system that user HOHLY#M started.

User HOHLY#M has three jobs (not two) on job queues. Using option 5 (`Work with`), we could see what queue they are on and investigate further. Refer back to Figure 12-22; we could also filter the search to just interactive or batch jobs.

Don't think the command is limited to one user, either. We could leave the user off and just look for all interactive or batch jobs, jobs on output queues, or jobs about to start and on job queues. Or, we could use the command without changing anything and see all jobs for all users—the result would be so voluminous it would be meaningless, but we could do it.

Let's explore one more way of working with jobs before we leave this section. Suppose we want to zero in on just the jobs running in a particular subsystem, QINTER, for example. Keep in mind, jobs on subsystems are active jobs. We could use the Work with Subsystem Jobs (WRKSBSJOB) command. Figure 12-25 has a prompted version of it.

```
                    Work with Subsystem Jobs (WRKSBSJOB)

 Type choices, press Enter.

 Subsystem  . . . . . . . . . .   QINTER     Name, *ALL, *JOBQ, *OUTQ
 User whose jobs to display . .   *ALL       Name, *ALL
 Output . . . . . . . . . . . .   *          *, *PRINT



                                                                          Bottom
 F3=Exit   F4=Prompt   F5=Refresh   F12=Cancel   F13=How to use this display
 F24=More keys
```

Figure 12-25: Prompted version of the WRKSBSJOB command.

If we key in the name QINTER for the first parameter and press the Enter key, we will get a screen similar to the one shown in Figure 12-26.

```
                        Work with Subsystem Jobs                    BIGBLUE
                                                          07/03/99  19:00:44
Subsystem  . . . . . . . . . . :   QINTER

Type options, press Enter.
  2=Change   3=Hold   4=End    5=Work with    6=Release    7=Display message
  8=Work with spooled files    13=Disconnect


Opt  Job         User        Type      ---Status---   Function
 _   QPADEV0004  DAWSON#M    INTER     ACTIVE             CMD-WRKSBSJOB





                                                                       Bottom
Parameters or command
===>
F3=Exit    F4=Prompt    F5=Refresh    F9=Retrieve    F11=Display schedule data
F12=Cancel
```

Figure 12-26: Jobs currently running in subsystem QINTER.

From this screen, we could look into any job and see what the user is doing and change the runtime parameters.

Work with Jobs on Job Queues

One of a system operator's duties is to manipulate jobs on the various job queues. Let us illustrate the nature of this manipulation and review the subsystem-job queue connection. Figure 12-27 contains a sample of a typical AS/400 system.

Subsystem QBATCH is fed by three job queues: JOBQA, JOBQB, and JOBQC. The three jobs already running in the subsystem have previously made their way through one of the queues. JOBQA has two jobs waiting, JOB5 and JOB7. JOBQB has one, JOB6. With subsystem QBATCH's maximum active jobs set to 3, no other jobs from the three queues will start until one of the current three (JOB1, JOB2, and JOB3) completes. Then the subsystem will take the next job from the next queue's turn for service. Assume JOBQC does not have anything all day, so it would be next if another job were submitted into it. If that does not happen, let us assume the next job the subsystem works on will be JOBQB. In this case, the subsystem would start JOB6.

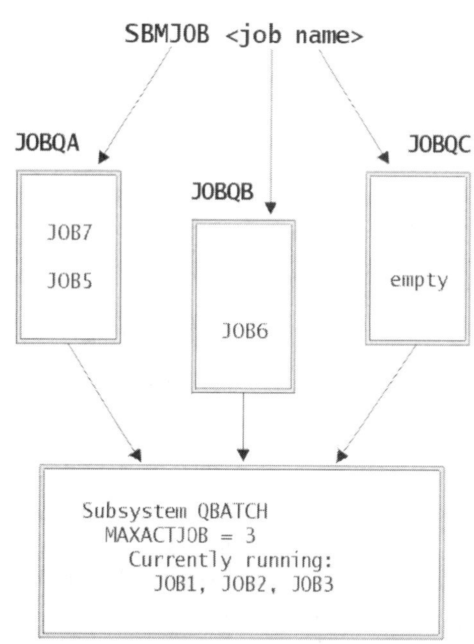

Figure 12-27: Jobs, queues, and subsystem.

Assume that the three jobs in the queues are equal priority and that they arrived in order of their number. In other words, they arrived in this order: JOB5, JOB6, then JOB7. Let's also assume that, in this IT department, the three jobs must run in order so the system operator must ensure that JOB5 starts before JOB6 does, and that nothing that enters JOBQC can start until after JOB7 is complete. The system operator can use the HLDJOBQ command to hold JOBQC:

```
HLDJOBQ JOBQC
```

When a job queue is held, new jobs can enter the queue, but none can start. If JOBQC were held, no jobs from it would start in the subsystem until either they were moved to an active queue or that queue was released. To ensure that the remaining three jobs enter the subsystem in sequence, the operator could do one of two things:

- Hold JOBQB until after JOB5 starts, then release it.
- Move JOB6 to JOBQA and ensure the three jobs' order on the queue by manipulating their priorities.

Holding JOBQB would be similar to holding JOBQC. Let's look at the second option, the Change Job (CHGJOB) command:

```
CHGJOB JOB6
```

then press the F4 key. That would produce a screen similar to the one shown in Figure 12-28.

```
                          Change Job (CHGJOB)

Type choices, press Enter.

Job name . . . . . . . . . . . . > JOB6          Name, *
  User . . . . . . . . . . . . . >   DAWSON#M      Name
  Number . . . . . . . . . . . . >   187412        000000-999999
Job priority (on JOBQ) . . . . .   5             0-9, *SAME
Output priority (on OUTQ)  . . .   5             1-9, *SAME
Print device . . . . . . . . . .   PRT01         Name, *SAME, *USRPRF...
Output queue . . . . . . . . . .   FACOUTQ       Name, *SAME, *USRPRF, *DEV...
  Library  . . . . . . . . . . .     QGPL        Name, *LIBL, *CURLIB
Run priority . . . . . . . . . .   *SAME         1-99, *SAME

                        Additional Parameters

Job queue  . . . . . . . . . . .   JOBQA         Name, *SAME
  Library  . . . . . . . . . . .     QGPL        Name, *LIBL, *CURLIB
Print text . . . . . . . . . . .   *BLANK

                                                                  More...
F3=Exit   F4=Prompt   F5=Refresh   F12=Cancel   F13=How to use this display
F24=More keys
```

Figure 12-28: Screen to change JOB6 to JOBQA.

The actual job queue change is bolded in the figure. To get the job queue parameter to come up, you must press the F10 key (Additional Parameters). If you press the Enter key from the screen shown in the figure, JOB6 leaves JOBQB and appears in JOBQA. Next, use the WRKJOBQ command, specifying JOBQA like this:

```
WRKJOBQ JOBQA
```

You get a screen similar to Figure 12-29 showing the three jobs in job queue JOBQA.

```
                         Work with Job Queue

Queue:   QBATCH        Library:   QGPL          Status:   RLS/SBS

Type options, press Enter.
  2=Change   3=Hold   4=End   5=Work with   6=Release

Opt     Job            User           Number     Priority     Status
 _      JOB6           DAWSON#M       187412        5          HLD
 _      JOB5           DAWSON#M       187413        5          HLD
 _      JOB7           DAWSON#M       187414        5          HLD

                                                                    Bottom
Parameters for options 2, 3 or command
===> ____________________________________________________________________

F3=Exit   F4=Prompt   F6=Submit job   F12=Cancel   F21=Subsystem
F22=Work with job schedule entries    F24=More keys
```

Figure 12-29: New list of jobs in JOBQA.

Now with control of all three jobs in a single job queue, all we have to do is order them. Do so by manipulating their job priority, all of which are now equal at 5. The command, again, is Change Job (CHGJOB), and it will produce a screen similar to the one we saw in Figure 12-28. Either run this command for each of the three jobs or, better, use the Work with User Jobs (WRKUSRJOB) or WRKJOBQ (see Figure 12-29).

Taking option 2 for each job (three times) from either screen still invokes the CHGJOB command, it is just less keying and easier to do changes this way. If we did and changed the three jobs' priorities to priorities that lined up the way we wanted to see them and issued another WRKJOBQ command, we would get a screen similar to the one shown in Figure 12-30.

```
                         Work with Job Queue

Queue:   QBATCH        Library:   QGPL          Status:   RLS/SBS

Type options, press Enter.
  2=Change   3=Hold   4=End   5=Work with   6=Release

Opt     Job            User           Number     Priority     Status
 _      JOB5           DAWSON#M       187412        5          RLS
 _      JOB6           DAWSON#M       187413        6          RLS
 _      JOB7           DAWSON#M       187414        7          RLS

                                                                    Bottom
Parameters for options 2, 3 or command
===>____________________________________________________________________

F3=Exit   F4=Prompt   F6=Submit job   F12=Cancel   F21=Subsystem
F22=Work with job schedule entries    F24=More keys
```

Figure 12-30: Jobs on JOBQA after priorities are changed.

The three jobs in this job queue will start in the desired order. Assume a user calls the system operator at this point. The user is the chief finance officer and says he has just submitted a program (he wouldn't actually submit it, he'd probably have taken a menu option, but bear with us), and he wants it to run right away. Assume you look again at the same JOBQA and see the new job, called NEWJOB, there. The system operator can quickly hold the other three jobs to ensure NEWJOB starts first. The hold option, 3, can be put in for multiple jobs. Refer to Figure 12-31.

```
                           Work with Job Queue

Queue:   QBATCH          Library:   QGPL            Status:   RLS/SBS

Type options, press Enter.
  2=Change   3=Hold   4=End   5=Work with   6=Release

Opt     Job         User          Number      Priority      Status
 _      NEWJOB      CFOUSER       187418          5           RLS
 3      JOB5        DAWSON#M      187412          5           RLS
 3      JOB6        DAWSON#M      187413          6           RLS
 3      JOB7        DAWSON#M      187414          7           RLS

                                                                    Bottom
Parameters for options 2, 3 or command
===>_____________________________________________________________________

F3=Exit   F4=Prompt   F6=Submit job   F12=Cancel   F21=Subsystem
F22=Work with job schedule entries    F24=More keys
```

Figure 12-31: Quickly holding jobs on JOBQA.

Pressing Enter from this screen would hold all three jobs and NEWJOB would be the next job to start in the subsystem, when it is ready. After it starts, all three could again be released with option 6 to resume their normal run schedule. Alternatively, the system operator could have changed NEWJOB's priority to a 4, ensuring it would start before the others.

These are just some ways that system operators manipulate jobs on the job queues for various reasons. One thing to keep in mind about manipulating jobs on a job queue is that, if the subsystem is active and the jobs and queues are not held, they are ready to run. They can start at any time. Most operators making changes to multiple job sequencing will automatically hold the queues first, then work on the jobs. That way, they will not start prematurely.

Ending Jobs

Sometimes jobs must be deleted from a job queue (if they have not started yet) or ended from a subsystem (if they have). A job can be ended from the job queue before it starts just by using option 4 (End) from the WRKJOBQ command. If a job is already started in a subsystem, it is also ended with an option 4 (End), but from the WRKACTJOB command. Never use option 4 (End) without prompting it. Here is why: Suppose we want to end JOB2 from subsystem QBATCH. If we issued the command:

```
WRKSBSJOB QBATCH
```

on the command line, you get a screen similar to the one shown in Figure 12-32.

```
                          Work with Subsystem Jobs                         BIGBLUE
                                                                07/03/99  19:00:44
Subsystem . . . . . . . . . . :   QINTER

Type options, press Enter.
  2=Change   3=Hold   4=End   5=Work with   6=Release   7=Display message
  8=Work with spooled files   13=Disconnect


Opt  Job         User        Type      ---Status---  Function
 _   JOB1        DAWSON#M    INTER     ACTIVE            PGM-RPGJOB1
 4   JOB2        DAWSON#M    INTER     ACTIVE            PGM-RPGJOB2
 _   JOB3        DAWSON#M    INTER     ACTIVE            PGM-RPGJOB3



                                                                        Bottom
Parameters or command
===> 

F3=Exit   F4=Prompt   F5=Refresh   F9=Retrieve   F11=Display schedule data
F12=Cancel
```

Figure 12-32: Jobs running in subsystem QBATCH.

In the figure, we put in the option 4 to end the job. Instead of pressing the Enter key, we press the F4 key. Remember that with these work commands, even though functions are selected with numbers, a command is what is really invoked. When the system operator presses the F4 key after selecting an option, the command is prompted, exactly as if it had been entered on the command line. In this example, we would get a screen similar to the one shown in Figure 12-33.

```
                            End Job (ENDJOB)

Type choices, press Enter.

Job name . . . . . . . . . . . . > JOB2         Name
  User . . . . . . . . . . . . . >   DAWSON#M   Name
  Number . . . . . . . . . . . . >   187534     000000-999999
How to end . . . . . . . . . . .   *IMMED       *CNTRLD, *IMMED
Delay time, if *CNTRLD . . . . .   30           Seconds
Delete spooled files . . . . . .   *NO          *NO, *YES
Maximum log entries  . . . . . .   *SAME        Number, *SAME, *NOMAX
Additional interactive jobs  . .   *NONE        *NONE, *GRPJOB, *ALL




                                                                       Bottom
F3=Exit   F4=Prompt   F5=Refresh   F10=Additional parameters   F12=Cancel
F13=How to use this display        F24=More keys
```

Figure 12-33: Prompted end of job JOB2.

We select *IMMED to end the job, overriding the default, *CNTRLD. This is a judgment call on the part of the system operator. Ending a job *CNTRLD properly closes all files and journals, and ends the program properly. However, it can take a long time. In real life, when we want to end a job, we usually want to end it for one of three reasons:

- It was started in error and just should not be running.
- It has a serious problem.
- For whatever reason, the user wants it ended.

In each case, we want the job ended now and the best way to do that is with *IMMED. *IMMED may not end the job "properly," but we have never experienced any adverse aftereffects from it. Most IT departments use *IMMED to end jobs. The system operator might also consider changing the Maximum Log Entries parameter to zero. If the job is to be ended now, the operator does not want to wait for the system to write a long job log.

As we said, the use of option 4 invokes the command End Job (ENDJOB). The system operator could enter the command on the command line and prompt it to end the job as well. Sometimes a job with a serious problem will not end even with ENDJOB. The only way to end that kind of job may be with the End Job Abnormally (ENDJOBABN) command. We will not go into details of this command, it is too similar to ENDJOB.

Remember this about ENDJOBABN: It sets a flag on the system that says the system is running in an abnormal state. That will affect the next IPL, as IPLs from an abnormal system take longer and often must be performed twice (once to clear the abnormality and once to get a normal IPL). Use ENDJOBABN only if all else failed.

LAB #12: WORKING WITH JOBS

Upon completion of this lab, you should be able to:

- Demonstrate how jobs are submitted and scheduled.
- Demonstrate how to use the Submit Job (SMBJOB) command.
- Demonstrate how to work with jobs including batch, interactive, and communication jobs.
- Demonstrate how to work with job queues.
- Demonstrate how to work with signed-on users.

NAMING CONVENTIONS FOR THIS LAB

During the lab, every time you encounter one of the lab names that contains xx, replace the xx with the number that has been assigned. As you complete the lab assignment, you will create and modify your environment to reflect your specific assigned names (Figure L12-1).

	Lab Name: Identified in Commands as:	Your Assigned Name:
Profile (User ID)	USERID	
Library Name	USERID	
Output Queue	USEROUTQ	
Job Description	USERJOBD	

Figure L12-1: Naming conventions.

INTRODUCTION

Active jobs are allocated a portion of available time based on job run priority 1 through 99, with 1 being most important, and 99 least important—interactive jobs are typically 20, and batch jobs are typically 50. The amount of time a job gets when it is serviced is determined by the time slice; 2,000 is the default time slice for interactive jobs; and 5,000 for batch jobs (the bigger the time slice, the longer the job is likely to run each time it becomes active).

Lowering the run priority and increasing the time slice will typically speed up a batch job. You can find the jobs for a specific user with the command WRKUSRJOB, submitted jobs with the command WRKSMBJOB, by job name with the command WRKJOB, by job queue with the command WRKJOBQ, by subsystem with the command WRKSBJOB.

DISPLAY YOUR JOB DESCRIPTION

Job management is an integral portion of an operator's job. To learn how jobs are controlled, start with exploring the job descriptions that define the job environment—job queues and output queues—and help manage the flow of jobs through the system. Let's get started. For this assignment, begin by exploring your job description.

- Enter the command to call the `Command Entry` screen.
- Press F10 (Include Detailed Messages).
- Enter WRKJOBD on the command line.
- Press F4 (Prompt).
- Enter `userJOBD` for the Job Description parameter.
- Press Enter.
- The `Work with Job Descriptions` display is shown.

With authorization, you can change, copy, delete, or display the job description.

- Place a `5` (Display) in the `Option` column next to the job description.
- Press Enter.
- Your default job description is displayed.

The default job description is used to execute all your interactive and batch jobs.

- Use the information available in your job description to answer the following questions:
  a. What is your default job queue? ______________________
  b. What is your default output queue? ______________________
  c. What is your job's routing data? ______________________
  d. Place your cursor on the `Routing Data` parameter and press `Help`.
     What is it used for? ______________________
  e. What are your job queue and output queue priorities? ______________________
  f. Press `Help` on the `Message Logging Level` prompt.
  g. What are the values that can be specified for `Message Level`? ______________________
     ____
     What do they mean? ______________________
  h. What are the values that can be specified for `Message Text`? ______________________
     ____
     What do they mean ______________________
- Press F3 (Exit).
- Return to the `Command Entry` screen.

MANAGING JOBS

You need jobs to better understand how jobs are managed. Several jobs will be submitted to a batch job queue. A different job description designed for this assignment will be used. This provides you with the opportunity to see how a job description affects the execution of jobs. The job description used in this lab is JOBSLABJD. This job description directs the job to the QBATCH1 job queue that is attached to the QBATCH subsystem. This job queue is held so that you will have time to work with the submitted jobs.

- Enter the command to call the `Command Entry` screen (Call QCMD).
- Press F10 (Include Detailed Messages).
- Enter SBMJOB on the command line.
- Press F4 (Prompt).
- Enter CPYF for the `Command to Run` parameter.
- Press F4 (Prompt).

- Enter the following parameters: DRPG2 for From File; OPRLIB for From Library; and *PRINT for To File.
- Press Enter. The resulting command should appear on the Command to Run parameter: CPYF FROMFILE(OPRLIB/DRPG2) TOFILE(*PRINT).

Look at the different parameters of the Submit Job (SBMJOB) command. With this command, you can give the job a specific name, override the current job description, specify a different job queue, specify an output queue, change a job's priority, plus make many other changes. You will be changing the job description to one designed specifically for this lab assignment.

As you proceed with the next section of commands, you are submitting several jobs to the QBATCH1 job queue. These are the jobs you will manage later in this lab. Let's finish creating the job.

- Enter JOBSLABJD for the Job Description parameter.
- Leave the other parameters at the default values.
- Press Enter.
- Press F9 (Retrieve).
- This will retrieve the previous command.
- Press Enter.
- This will submit the job a second time.
- Repeat above process five more times.

Submitting the command several times will load the job queue with approximately five to seven batch jobs to manage. Next it's time to use some of the job commands.

- Enter the command to call the Command Entry screen.
- Press F10 (Include Detailed Messages).
- Enter WRKUSRJOB (Work User Job) on the command line.
- Press F4 (Prompt).

You can work with the current (*), a specific user's job (name), or all user jobs (*ALL). You can specify a specific job's status, or all jobs. The output from the command can be either displayed or printed. Let us finish the command.

- Leave the defaults and press Enter.

The Work with User Jobs display is next. Any active job (*ACTIVE status), jobs with *JOBQ status, or completed jobs with output to print (*OUTQ status) are displayed.

- Place the cursor to the left of one of the batch jobs (*JOBQ) on the screen.
- Enter 2 (Change) to the left of a job in *JOBQ status.
- Press Enter.
- Press F10 (Additional Parameters).

The Change Job screen has many parameters, and attributes of a job can be changed. Use the page keys to scroll through the parameter.

- Enter QBATCH2 for the `Output Queue` parameter.
- Page down to the `Date Format` parameter.
- Press the `Help` key.
- Change date format to the `Julian` date.
- Press Enter.

The job should process now that you moved it to the QBATCH2 job queue. This is a job queue that is not held and attached to the active subsystem, QBATCH. Next, you will continue working with the submitted jobs and explore other commands.

- Make sure you are on the WRKUSRJOB screen.
- Enter a 5 (Work with Job) to the left of another job in *JOBQ status.
- Press Enter.
- The `Work with Job` menu is displayed.
- List five of the options available from this menu:

  ____

  ____

  ____

- Page down to the second screen of the `Work with Jobs` menu.
- Execute option 30 (To Execute All Menu Options).
- Press Enter repeatedly to display the output from each menu option.

You have just looked at a batch job. For contrast, return to the Work with User Jobs screen, and work with your interactive job. Look at the differences in the screen between the previous batch job and your interactive job.

- Enter the Work with User Jobs command.
- Press Enter.
- Place a 5 (Work with User Jobs) to the left of your Interactive job.
- Press Enter.
- Execute option 30 (To Execute All Menu Options).
- Press Enter repeatedly to display the output from each menu option.
- Do you notice any differences between the interactive job and the batch job on a job queue? ______________________________
- Return to the Command Entry screen.

HOLDING AND RELEASING A JOB (HLDJOB, RLSJOB COMMANDS)

A job with *JOBQ status can be held to make it unavailable for processing. A job with *ACTIVE status can be held to temporarily stop its processing. A job with *OUTQ status cannot be held, but you can hold or delete its spooled output files that are not yet printed. Releasing a job makes it available again for processing. Let us look at working with jobs in these above statuses.

- Enter the WRKUSRJOB (Work with User Jobs) command.
- Press Enter.
- Enter a 3 (Hold) to the left of a batch job in *JOBQ status.
- Press Enter.

The status of the job has changed to *HLD. If you know the job name, simply use the HLDJOB command. This will accomplish the same result.

- Enter a 2 (Change) to the left of the HELD batch job.
- Press Enter.
- Press F10 (Additional Parameters).
- Change the Job Queue to QBATCH2 in library QGPL.
- Press Enter.

Earlier in this lab, you found that moving a job to the QBATCH2 job queue caused the job to execute. Because the job is held when it is moved to the active queue, it still does not execute. When you know the qualified job name, you can use the RLSJOB command.

- Enter 6 (Release) to the left of the HELD job.
- Press F5 (Refresh).
- Did the job status change? ____________________________

The job will execute—watch for its status to change. Once the job executes, the status will change to *OUTQ.

END A USER'S JOB (ENDJOB COMMAND)

You can end a user's job that has a status of *JOBQ or *ACTIVE. Ending a job removes the job from the system. A job with *OUTQ status has already ended, but you can hold, change, or delete the job's spool files. Using the Work with User Jobs display, you can also end a job. You cannot end your current interactive job.

- If not at the WRKURSJOB screen, enter the WRKUSRJOB command and press Enter.
- Enter 4 (End) to the left of a batch job in *JOBQ status.
- Press F4 (Prompt).
- The End Job screen is shown.

Here, you can control how a job will end.

- Change the `How to End` parameter from *CNTRLD to *IMMED.
- Change the `Maximum Log Entries` parameter from *SAME to `1` or `0`.
- Press Enter.

You can also use the ENDJOB command if you know the name of the job. Occasionally, there are times when a job will not end. If, after doing an ENDJOB *IMMED, the job does not end after ten or fifteen minutes, you can use the ENDJOBABN command. This command is not available from any menu or display; it must be keyed in directly. Write down the qualified job name that needs to be ended, then type the command on any command line and press F4 (Prompt); enter the job name and the job will end. Be aware that if the job was updating database files, those databases will probably need to be rolled back.

SCHEDULING A JOB

Now all jobs are run when the command is entered. Often, you want to run a job at a designated time and on a specific date. The scheduling feature is quite handy when the night operator is to run a job that he is not authorized to. This allows the authorized person to schedule the job to run when they are not present, and the night operator is there to monitor its execution. Now it is time for you to schedule one of your remaining jobs in *JOBQ status to execute at a given time.

- Return to the WRKUSRJOB screen.
- Place a 2 (Change) to the left of a job in the *JOBQ status.
- Press Enter.
- Press F10 (Additional Parameters).
- Change the `Job Queue` parameter to an active job queue. For example, active queues are QBATCH2 through QBATCH6.
- Page down to the second screen.
- Change the `Schedule Date` parameter to *CURRENT.
- Change the `Schedule Time` parameter to a time approximately three minutes later than the current time. Remember, you must enter the time in military time. For example: 6 P.M. would be 18:00.
- Press Enter.
- Press F11 (Display Schedule Data).
- Press F5 (Refresh).
- What is the current status for this job? ____________________
- What occurred when you pressed F11? ____________________
- Press F5 (Refresh) repeatedly as you get close to the scheduled time. Keep doing the Refresh until the job executes.
- Did you see the status change and the job execute? ____________________

WORKING WITH JOB QUEUES

Before processing, a batch job waits with other jobs in line on a job queue attached to the subsystem that will process it. The subsystem and its job queue usually have the same name. The waiting job has a status (ready or held) and a priority (its place on the job queue).

It is possible to have more than one job queue attached to a subsystem; however, we will not be discussing that particular work management configuration. You can work with all job queues or work with a specific job queue.

- On the Command Entry screen, enter the command WRKJOBQ *ALL on the command line.
- Press Enter.
- Wait a few minutes.
- A list of all the job queues on the system is shown.

From this display, you can hold, release, or work with the job queue of your choice. When you know the name of the job queue that you want to work with, you can enter the HLDJOBQ, RLSJOBQ, or WRKJOBQ commands and simply specify the job queue name.

- Place the option to Work with the QBATCH1 job queue in the QGPL library.
- Press Enter.

From the Work with Job Queue display, you can work with the individual jobs of your choice. You can change, hold, end, work with, and release individual jobs.

As the lab comes to an end, it is time for some cleanup. The jobs you have been managing have produced printouts that you do not need. You may also have jobs that have not run in the queue. So the next few steps are cleaning up your system.

- If you see any of your own jobs listed in the job queue, End them now.
- Check your spool file for unneeded printouts.
- Delete the printouts generated in this lab.
- These are labeled QSYSPRT and are copies of the DRPG2 file.

Now you should have a good idea about how to work with jobs on the system.

ADDITIONAL LAB ASSIGNMENTS

Batch programs wait in queues until the subsystem assigned to that queue starts the batch program. Typically, the subsystem and queue both are named QBATCH; however, for these assignments, we will use the subsystem QBATCH and the JobQ's QBATCH1 and QBATCH2. See Figure L12-2.

1. Queue QBATCH1 is on Hold.

    a. Submit a batch job to the queue QBATCH1:

    ```
    SBMJOB CMD(CALL XXYYZZ)JOB
    (yourlastname) JOBQ(QBATCH1)
    ```

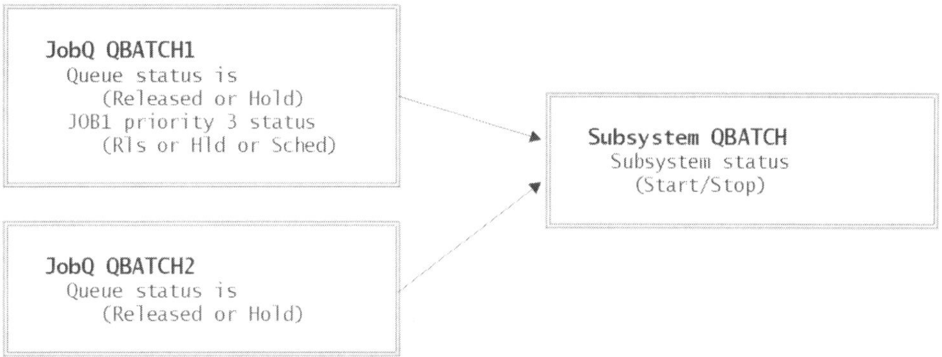

Figure L12-2: Queued batch programs.

2. Working with the jobs waiting on this queue, find your job. What is preventing it from processing?

3. Submit a batch job to the queue QBATCH2:

   ```
   SBMJOB CMD(CALL XXYYZZ) JOB
   (yourlastname)JOBQ(QBATCH2)
   ```

   (This will cause an error message to be sent to you because there is no program named XXYYZZ.)

4. Submit a batch job to the queue QBATCH1 with the job status of Hold:

   ```
   SBMJOB CMD(CALL XXYYZZ) JOB (yourlastname) JOBQ(QBATCH1) HOLD(*YES)
   ```

5. Working with the jobs waiting on this queue, find your job. What is preventing this job from processing?

6. Submit a batch job to be scheduled to be processed at 9:30 P.M. tonight:

7. `SBMJOB CMD(CALLXXYYZZ) JOB(yourlastname) JOBQ(QBATCH2) SCHTIME('21:30:00')`
   When will this job actually run?

8. How would you schedule a job for 7 A.M. tomorrow using QBATCH2 job queue?

9. How would you schedule a job for midnight tonight using QBATCH2 job queue?

10. Enter a job with a job priority of 4, but hold it:

    ```
    SBMJOB CMD(CALLXXYYZZ) JOB(yourlastname)
    JOBQ(QBATCH2) JOBPTY(4) HOLD(*YES)
    ```

11. Look at the JOBQ. How was this job positioned in relationship to jobs with a priority of 5? Where would it be positioned in relationship to jobs with a priority of 6? Which jobs will become active first? Change the priority to 6—what happens?

12. Submit the following to JOBQ(QBATCH2):

    ```
    SBMJOB CMD(CALL TSTFOREVER) JOB(yourlastname) JOBQ(QBATCH2)
    ```

13. End the job (option 4 from Work with Jobs). Does it stop quickly?

14. Press F9 to find the submit command for TSTFOREVER. Submit it again.

15. End the job immediately:

    a. Type a 4; do not press Enter.

    b. Press F4 (Prompt).

    c. Change `How to End` parameter to *IMMED.

16. End all of your jobs in JOBQ's QBATCH1 and QBATCH2 and in subsystem QBATCH.

END-OF-CHAPTER AIDS

CHAPTER SUMMARY

The information about jobs discussed in this chapter represents a large percentage of what a system operator does during a day. Jobs are always being shifted around, held, released, submitted, and ended. When they are running, their priorities and time slices are adjusted fairly routinely to meet some need of the system. One job may be adjusted to take less system resources; another may be adjusted up to finish quickly. Anyone who works with jobs is on the frontline of making the AS/400 responsive to its users.

This chapter serves two purposes. One, from a real-life standpoint, job manipulation is the daily bread and butter of an operator's day. The skills presented are basic ones every operator should master. Two, jobs are the foundation of understanding many AS/400 concepts. As we progress in the next chapters, jobs are one ingredient of other objects and concepts. We will be referring to them and their components with more frequency and familiarity, assuming you, the student, have grasped the definitions and concepts.

KEY TERMS

background
batch job
CALL command
communication job
End Job (ENDJOB)
first in, first out (FIFO)
interactive job
job attributes
job class
Job Control (JOBCTL)
job descriptions
job name
job priority
job queue
job queue priority
job scheduling jobs
routing data
runtime attribute
Submit Job (SBMJOB)
subsystems
system job
time slice
Work with Active Job (WRKACTJOB)
Work with User Jobs (WRKUSRJOB)

CHAPTER SELF-TEST

Solutions to these self-test questions are in appendix D.

True-False Questions

___ 1. Once a job has been placed on the job queue, you can safely remove the job from execution any time prior to the actual startup of the job.

___ 2. Running jobs in a batch mode helps the overall performance of the AS/400 and improves the performance of interactive jobs.

___ 3. All AS/400 systems have a job queue called JOBLOG.

___ 4. When you sign onto the AS/400, you start an interactive job.

___ 5. Batch jobs waiting to execute are held in an output queue.

___ 6. Jobs submitted to a job queue with the same priority process in LIFO (last in, first out) order.

___ 7. The operator can schedule a job to process at a specific date and time by using the SBMJOB command.

Fill in the Blanks

1. The name of a job consists of three parts: job name, user profile, and the job number. The job name for an interactive job comes from the ________________________.

2. The qualified name for a batch job with the following three parts—Job name: Payroll; Job number: 123456; and User ID: ALincoln would be ______________________________.

3. The time slice given to a job is determined by the ___________________________.

4. The ________________________ provides the routing data that helps the AS/400 find the runtime attributes.

5. When several jobs are submitted to a job queue at one time, it is the job ________________________ that determines their order.

6. The security officer wants the paycheck program that generates the employee's paychecks to run after midnight. The system operator will handle the running and printing of the checks during the evening shift. The system operator does not have the authority to the program. To allow the system operator access to this program, the security officer could _____________ the job on the job queue when submitting it to batch.

7. You need to save a particular library every evening at 7 P.M. This is an example of a job that would be well-suited for the ___________________________.

Chapter Review Questions

1. Explain the following terms:

   a. Job class.

   b. Job description.

   c. Job queue.
   d. Job scheduler.
   e. Routing data.
   f. Subsystem.

2. What is the sequence of steps in the execution of a batch job?

3. What types of jobs are best run interactively?

4. What types of jobs are best run in batch?

5. List the primary components of a job description.

6. What is the purpose of the Job Scheduling Entry?

7. A job is scheduled to execute every Friday and the job has been placed on hold on Thursday. The error is discovered on the following Tuesday and the job is released. What happens when it is released?

8. A series of jobs were placed on a job queue. The operator discovered that these jobs needed to process in a sequence different than the current sequence. How could the operator change the sequence to the desired order?

9. When would you use the following commands? They allow you to manage what?
   - WRKACTJOB.
   - WRKUSRJOB.
   - WRKJOBQ.
   - WRKJOB.

13

SUBSYSTEMS

CHAPTER OBJECTIVES

Upon completion of this chapter, you should be able to:

- Explain subsystems and subsystems' descriptions.
- Explain how the CPU uses time slices, run priorities, and job statuses to manage jobs.
- Through the subsystem description (SBSD) commands, explain how the following fit together:
  - Devices.
  - Jobs.
  - Storage.
  - Activity levels.
  - Routing entries/data.
  - Workstation entries.
- Identify and explain the system values related to jobs and work management.
- Explain how jobs run, including batch and interactive jobs.
- Describe what storage pools are and how they are used.
- Demonstrate memory pools and activity levels.

- Describe routing entries and routing data.
- Describe workstation entries.
- Identify and explain the system values related to jobs and work management.

OVERVIEW

To say that the AS/400 is simply a multiuser, multitasking computer is to understate it. That simple definition leaves no allowance for the fact that the machine must also support a wide mix of job types. Large jobs should not become bullies and take system resources away from small jobs. Also, jobs have relevant importance to each other. Important jobs should finish faster than routine jobs and should do so without consuming all the system resources.

Then there are shifting priorities that the AS/400 must recognize and support. For example, consider interactive and *batch jobs*. Interactive jobs have a lot of importance when users are signed on. After all, if their screens do not come back quickly, they complain. Batch jobs should continue to run but can do so at a more leisurely pace. But in the evening, when users go home, batch jobs can become considerably more important. Most of the daily batch processing goes on at night, and it is vital that this work gets done before the users return in the morning. The AS/400 comes with a rich set of tools to support all these shifting demands.

MEMORY: STORAGE POOLS AND ACTIVITY LEVELS

AS/400 memory can be assigned (and dynamically reassigned) to support changing needs for workflow support. It can be set aside for specific programs to finish more quickly. *Activity levels* enhance raw memory allocation by restricting how many programs will vie for the same memory at the same time. The system operator frequently shifts these two values—memory and activity levels—during the day as the job mix changes.

STORAGE POOLS

A *storage pool* is a pool of memory where one type of program or application (a set of programs) runs. AS/400s, like other computers, have a certain amount of memory. But with the AS/400, the system operator can dedicate sections of memory to different jobs. When the machine is delivered from the factory, that memory is divided into two special shared storage pools: *MACHINE and *BASE.

**MACHINE* is the storage pool where the system tasks (tasks the customer has no control over) run. **BASE* can be where everything else runs. Most customers configure their AS/400s by building other pools to support individual job types.

The AS/400 comes with the optimum memory assigned to *MACHINE. This is based on the configuration of the machine. The system operator can reset this, but does not have to and probably should not initially. Later, if he suspects problems with *MACHINE pool, he can adjust its memory within limits.

*MACHINE's memory can never be below a base of 256Kb, plus what the machine thinks it needs (based on the size and model); the system will not allow it. Memory adjustments to *MACHINE are made by changing the system value QMCHPOOL.

The amount of memory in *BASE cannot be adjusted directly because it is the total memory available on the system less the memory used by *MACHINE and any other *private pools* or *shared pools*. The system operator can, however, set system value QBASPOOL to a value below which the system will not allow *BASE to fall. QBASPOOL comes with an IBM set value and should not be changed except under expert advice. In addition to the minimum that can be reset, the system has a built-in minimum limit for *BASE memory below to which no one can set their machine.

TIP:

*MACHINE	= QMCHPOOL	: Set memory
*BASE	= QBASPOOL	: Set memory lower limit

The two original pools, *MACHINE and *BASE, are sufficient to run any AS/400. Beyond them, however, the operator might want to consider using private or shared pools for better performance.

Dividing memory into pools is like fencing the range. Although at first it might look like something is being lost, it is not. Actually, the control will make an AS/400 with a broad job mix run better. Fencing the range allows dissimilar animals to graze "together" within fences better than they would on the open range. Cattle could graze in their space, sheep in theirs, and goats in other places—all without unfair competition. Similarly, dividing memory into pools allows interactive jobs to coexist with batch jobs without either eating the other's grass. The term *pool* is the amount of fenced-in memory.

To illustrate what this means, let us assume an AS/400 company has only the two default pools, *MACHINE and *BASE. In such a system, all the system tasks would run in *MACHINE, and the nonsystem jobs would run in *BASE. The AS/400 will have interactive and batch jobs running together in the same pool, *BASE.

Let us digress for a moment to explain that there are two concepts in memory management that every student ought to know: paging and faulting. *Paging* is when memory pages for a relatively inactive program are written out to DASD so the system can load memory pages for a currently active program. *Faulting* is when the AS/400 is working on a program (or its data) and attempts to go to a new memory page and does not find it. The system has to go look for the page out on DASD and reload it into memory. Some amount of paging and faulting is common but an excess of either degrades the system, so the savvy system operator seeks a balance.

Now that we have a grasp of paging and faulting, let us return to performance and storage pools. Our example was interactive and batch jobs running in their own subsystems, but sharing all memory out of pool *BASE. Interactive jobs typically run at a higher priority than batch jobs and, therefore, get system attention much more often. The AS/400 does not work on one program until it is finished. It will work on one program (actually one for each processor but let us not get too fancy here) until it has to wait for something or until it has spent an amount of time referred to as a *time slice*, then goes on to another program. In this way, all programs get some system attention. The system in the example would run through all interactive jobs—working on them two or three times—before it goes to any batch job.

With all jobs using the same storage pool, when the system needs memory for interactive jobs, it will probably take it from batch jobs. Because batch jobs run at a lower priority, their memory pages would appear "inactive" in relation to the highly active interactive pages, so their memory would get stolen. After several iterations of this, the system would eventually get around to working on a batch job. None of its previously loaded pages are around anymore. The system faults heavily. By the time the system finds them and returns them to memory, the time slice for working on the batch job has expired, and the system returns to the interactive jobs. This excessive faulting is called *thrashing.* It means a lot of work goes on and nothing gets done—at least for the batch programs in this example. The primary symptom of this machine would be very fast online screens, very slow batch programs, and every once in a while, when the system really starts thrashing some batch programs, the whole system bogs down for a minute or two.

Fortunately this is only an example—there are not any AS/400 IT departments in this bad a shape. The typical approach is to have interactive and batch jobs running in their own subsystems, each with its own private memory pool. A *subsystem* is an environment unique to a type of program. It allows some high-level runtime attributes to be applied to all jobs within it, while other jobs in other subsystems keep their own attributes. In this scenario, memory paging for interactive jobs occurs only between interactive jobs. Meanwhile, paging for batch jobs occurs only between batch jobs.

That is the basic description and use of memory pools. Going further, the AS/400 makes some further distinctions concerning pools. Any AS/400 can have these types of pools:

- Shared Pools.
  - *Special shared pools.* The two pools that come with the AS/400, *MACHINE and *BASE, are special shared pools. These are the only special shared pools.
  - *General shared pools.* These have predetermined names like *INTERACT.
- Private Pools.

An AS/400 can only have a total of 64 pools on it. Because the system insists on using *MACHINE and *BASE, it can really only have 62 pools. As far as creating and naming pools:

- Private pools are created and named on the subsystem description—we will discuss subsystems and their descriptions later in this chapter. Their names are simple: 1 through 62. A private pool can only support one subsystem. A shared pool can support multiple subsystems and still maintain thrashing protection from other subsystems' jobs not using the pool. For example, if subsystem HOTRPTS has a private pool and its name is pool 1, no other subsystem can use or refer to pool 1. If an AS/400 has two interactive subsystems, QINTER01 and QINTER02, shared pool *INTERACT can be assigned to both and they will share the memory within it.
- The AS/400 comes with predetermined names and, in two cases, predetermined uses, for shared pools. Here is the list:
  - *INTERACT. Supports interactive subsystems' jobs.
  - *SPOOL. Supports spool writers (printing).
  - *SHRPOOL1 through *SHRPOOL60. Names available for customer-defined shared pools.

Both private or shared pools' memory can be adjusted at any time. The more memory assigned to a pool generally means the more work it can do. It is common to put more memory in the interactive subsystem's pool and take some away from the batch subsystem's pool during the day. By reversing the procedure in the evening, memory is taken away from the interactive pool and given to the batch pool.

Because it contains all the system's memory that is not taken by the other pools, *BASE plays a major part in moving memory around the AS/400. There are specific steps to take memory from one pool and give it to another:

- Adjust one pool down; the adjustment returns memory to *BASE, making it bigger.
- Increase the other pool; the increased memory comes out of *BASE, making it smaller.

ACTIVITY LEVEL

When AS/400 jobs are running, they have three states:

- Active. The job is running.
- Wait. The job is waiting for something to happen. This can be:
  - The user to press the Enter key at the workstation.
  - A file to open or close.
  - A record to be retrieved from or written to disk.
  - A device allocation.
  - A locked record to become unlocked.
  - A message.
- Ineligible.
  - The job is ready to run, but the system is too busy for it.
  - The system has spent its allocated time (its time slice) on the job and will begin working on other jobs.

Every storage pool has an activity level associated with it. An activity level limits the number of job threads the computer will work on at one time within the pool. This is a confusing subject even to experienced AS/400 people, because there is a similar setting on the job queue that limits the maximum number of jobs that can be active at one time. These are not the same values.

TIP:

Job queue's MAXACT (Maximum Active Jobs) = Number of jobs from that queue that can be active in the subsystem at one time.

Storage pool's MAXACTLVL (Maximum Activity Level) = Number of jobs active in the subsystem that the system will work on at the same time.

The batch subsystem, QBATCH, could easily have a maximum of six active jobs, but an activity level of 3. In that case, it would have six jobs running; three would be active and three would be present but either waiting or ineligible. When an active job goes into a wait or ineligible state, the system makes one of the already ineligible jobs active if it can. If the job that entered the wait state returned from that state and the system is working on three other jobs, it goes ineligible until one of the others goes to wait or ineligible.

This is not as choppy as it sounds because jobs go into and out of states all the time and do so very quickly. If someone were monitoring the system we just described, he or she would mostly see six active jobs. He or she would see many waits and only occasionally catch some ineligible statuses.

Overall throughput of any subsystem can be increased greatly by carefully setting the activity level. This is a powerful feature of the AS/400 because it provides another alternative to just throwing memory at jobs that are running slow. Sometimes more memory is simply not available without spending a lot of money. The exception to manipulating activity levels is the *MACHINE pool. It is the pool for system tasks and its activity level cannot be changed.

USING MEMORY AND ACTIVITY LEVELS

Although you would think a private memory pool would have some kind of memory management command, it does not. On the AS/400, it is associated closely with the subsystem and is created or changed through the subsystem's description.

CREATING PRIVATE POOLS/ASSIGNING SHARED POOLS

Subsystem descriptions are created with the CRTSBSD command that we will discuss next. For now, Figure 13-1 shows the section of the command where pools are created and assigned.

```
                     Create Subsystem Description (CRTSBSD)

Type choices, press Enter.

Subsystem description . . . . .   __________   Name
  Library . . . . . . . . . . .   *CURLIB      Name, *CURLIB
Storage pools:                    ___
  Pool identifier . . . . . . .   _________    1-10
  Storage size . . . . . . . . .  _________    Number, *BASE, *NOSTG...
  Activity level . . . . . . . .  _______      Number
             + for more values     _________
Maximum jobs . . . . . . . . . .  *NOMAX       0-1000, *NOMAX
Text 'description' . . . . . . .  *BLANK




                                                                 Bottom
F3=Exit   F4=Prompt   F5=Refresh   F10=Additional parameters   F12=Cancel
F13=How to use this display        F24=More keys
```

Figure 13-1: CRTSBSD command screen for memory pool assignments.

The areas where pools are specified are shown in bold. The operator can define up to 10 pools for each subsystem description. There are three fields on this screen relevant to each storage pool:

- *Pool identifier.* This field is the subsystem pool number (1 through 10) within the subsystem; it is not the system name-number of the pool. Subsystems can have up to 10 pools assigned to them. In reality, not many subsystems have more than three pools assigned to them, and most have two.

- *Storage size.* This field has two forms:
  - To define a private pool (no other subsystems can use it), specify the amount of memory to be in the pool. When the subsystem is started (STRSBS), it will start a private pool for that subsystem with that amount of memory. Do not specify a pool name on this parameter. The name of that private pool will be assigned by the system, and it will be the next available number between 1 and 62.
  - To define a shared storage pool, specify the name of the shared pool (e.g., *INTERACT or *SHRPOOL5) in this parameter. Do not specify the storage size; that is defined on the shared pool itself. Adjust shared pools' memory with the WRKSYSSTS or CHGSHRPOOL commands.
- Activity level is the activity level for that pool.

For more pools, put a plus sign (+) in the `+ For More Values` parameter and the system will prompt for up to 10 subsystem pools.

How do you know starting values if you have never configured a subsystem before? See the IBM manual, *OS/400 Work Management V4R4,* Using Dynamic Tuning Support to Determine the Minimum Storage Pool Size section for a table of these values.

CHANGING POOL MEMORY/ACTIVITY LEVELS

There are three commands that will change memory and activity level settings on pools. Each has its place. They are:

- Work with System Status (WRKSYSSTS).
- Change Subsystem Description (CHGSBSD).
- Change Shared Pool (CHGSHRPOOL).

The two system values that affect the Machine Pool Memory and the Base Pool Activity Levels are:

- Machine Pool (QMCHPOOL).
- Base Activity Level (QBASACTLVL).

Figure 13-2 shows these commands and system values, and where they are used.

Pool Name	Adjustments to Memory	Adjustments to Activity Level
*MACHINE	QMCHPOOL (sv) WRKSYSSTS	—— n/a ——
*BASE	—— n/a ——	QBASACTLVL (sv) WRKSYSSTS
ALL PRIVATE POOLS	WRKSYSSTS CHGSBSD	WRKSYSSTS CHGSBSD
ALL SHARED POOLS	WRKSYSSTS CHGSHRPOOL	WRKSYSSTS CHGSHRPOOL
(sv) = System Value. Use CHGSYSVAL command to change these.		

Figure 13-2: Memory activity level commands.

Figure 13-3 shows an example of using the CHGSHRPOOL command to change attributes of a shared pool. Enter the command:

```
CHGSHRPOOL
```

on a command line and press the F4 key. Just enter in the new values for memory and/or activity levels and the change will take effect immediately.

```
                    Change Shared Storage Pool (CHGSHRPOOL)

 Type choices, press Enter.

 Pool identifier . . . . . . . .   __________  *MACHINE, *BASE, *INTERACT...
 Storage size . . . . . . . . . .  *SAME       Number, *SAME, *NOSTG
 Activity level . . . . . . . . .  *SAME       Number, *SAME
 Paging option . . . . . . . . .   *SAME       *SAME, *FIXED, *CALC
 Text 'description' . . . . . . .  *SAME



                                                                     Bottom
 F3=Exit   F4=Prompt   F5=Refresh   F10=Additional parameters   F12=Cancel
 F13=How to use this display        F24=More keys
```

Figure 13-3: CHGSHRPOOL command.

Private pools are changed within their subsystems. Figure 13-4 shows the relevant screen from the prompted version of the CHGSBSD command.

```
                    Change Subsystem Description (CHGSBSD)

 Type choices, press Enter.

 Subsystem description . . . . . > QINTER         Name
   Library . . . . . . . . . . .     *LIBL        Name, *LIBL, *CURLIB
 Storage pools:                    _

   Pool identifier . . . . . . .   *SAME          1-10, *SAME
   Storage size . . . . . . . . .  _________      Number, *BASE, *NOSTG...
   Activity level . . . . . . . .  _________      Number
              + for more values     _________

 Maximum jobs . . . . . . . . . .  *SAME          0-1000, *SAME, *NOMAX
 Text 'description' . . . . . . .  *SAME



                                                                       Bottom
 F3=Exit   F4=Prompt   F5=Refresh   F10=Additional parameters   F12=Cancel
 F13=How to use this display        F24=More keys
```

Figure 13-4: CHGSBSD command to change private pool sizes.

Only private pools can be changed with this command. Specify the subsystem pool identifier and its new memory or activity level.

DELETING POOLS

- Pools *MACHINE and *BASE cannot be deleted or removed.
- Delete private pools by ending the subsystem in which they run.
- Make shared pools inactive by ending the subsystems in which they run. They still will appear on the WRKSYSSTS command, but they will have zeros for memory and activity level, and there will not be a pool identification associated with them.

POOL NAMES

Nothing confuses AS/400 customers as much as storage pool names. First, the system names pools and it is not very creative. Second, pools are sometimes referred to by their relative pool number within a subsystem and sometimes by their system-generated pool number-name. And, in the case of shared pools, by their shared pool names. Is that confusing? Let us walk through an example. Figure 13-5 shows the command Work with Subsystems (WRKSBS).

```
                          Work with Subsystems
                                                      System:   BIGBLUE
Type options, press Enter.
  4=End subsystem   5=Display subsystem description
  8=Work with subsystem jobs    Subsystem Pool 1
                                   Subsystem Pool 2

                     Total      ------Subsystem Pools------
Opt  Subsystem    Storage (K)   1   2   3   4   5   6   7   8   9  10
 _   QBASE                 0    2   3
 _   QBATCH                0    2
 _   QCMN                  0    2
 _   QCTL                  0    2
 _   QINTER                0    2   3  <-- System Pool 3
 _   QCOMPILE              0    2  11  <-- System Pool 11
 _   QSERVER               0    2
 _   QSPL                  0    2   4
 _   QSYSSBSD              0    2
 _   QSYSWRK               0    2  <-- System Pool 2
                                                                Bottom
Parameters or command
===>
F3=Exit   F5=Refresh   F11=Display system data   F12=Cancel
F14=Work with system status
```

Figure 13-5: Subsystems command.

Here is a list of subsystems and their pools. Columns 1 through 10 refer to the subsystem pools. The numbers under those columns are the system pool names that occupy those subsystem pool slots. Let us look further at subsystem QCOMPILE. It has two subsystem pools: 1 and 2. Its number 1 pool contains system pool identification 2 (which is always *BASE), and its number 2 pool is system pool identification 11.

If we select option 5 (`Display Subsystem Description`), we will see the subsystem's pool definitions. See Figure 13-6 for a sample of the Work with Subsystems (WRKSBS) command, showing a display of QCOMPILE's pool definitions.

```
                          Display Pool Definitions
                                                          System:   BIGBLUE
 Subsystem description:   QCOMPILE          Status:   ACTIVE


 Pool       Storage     Activity
  ID        Size (K)     Level
   1          *BASE
   2       *SHRPOOL2  <--- Shared Pool Names

   ^
   |
  Subsystem Pool Number





                                                                 Bottom
 Press Enter to continue.

 F3=Exit   F12=Cancel
```

Figure 13-6: Command WRKSBS, displaying pool definitions.

Each row shows information about each of QCOMPILE's pools. Each row is a subsystem's pool number. Here you can verify that *BASE is the shared pool for QCOMPILE's subsystem pool 1. The shared pool name for QCOMPILE's subsystem pool 2 is *SHRPOOL2. Remember Figure 13-5 shows the subsystem's pool 1 contains system pool number 2? Figure 13-6 shows that subsystem pool 1 is the shared pool, *BASE. By applying a little logic, you can infer that system pool 2 is shared pool *BASE.

Let's go on. Figure 13-5 shows subsystem pool 2 containing system pool 11. Figure 13-6 shows subsystem pool 2 is really *SHRPOOL2. Apply the same logic and subsystem pool 2 is system pool 11, which is a shared pool called *SHRPOOL2.

Anyone can focus on memory pools—as long as they know the system pool number—with the Work with System Status (WRKSYSSTS) command. Figure 13-7 shows a sample of the WRKSYSSTS command.

Here the memory and activity level is allocated to system pool name 11. It has 50,000Kb of memory and an activity level of four. These lines are underscored to indicate changes to them can be made from this screen.

```
                        Work with System Status                  BIGBLUE
                                                                 07/05/99
12:06:24
 % CPU used . . . . . . . :       63.0   Auxiliary storage:
 Elapsed time . . . . . . :   00:30:01    System ASP . . . . . . :     22357 M
 Jobs in system . . . . . :       9789    % system ASP used  . . :   71.4165
 % addresses used:                        Total  . . . . . . . . :   187375 M
   Permanent  . . . . . . :     22.313    Current unprotect used :     2854 M
   Temporary  . . . . . . :      4.707    Maximum unprotect  . . :     3222 M

 Type changes (if allowed), press Enter.

 System     Pool    Reserved    Max    ---DB---  --Non-DB--
  Pool   Size (K)  Size (K)  Active  Fault  Pages  Fault  Pages
   11     50000          0       4      .0     .3    2.7     .0
   ↑
  System Pool Number
                                                                   Bottom
 Command
 ===>

 F3=Exit   F4=Prompt            F5=Refresh   F9=Retrieve   F10=Restart
 F11=Display transition data    F12=Cancel   F24=More keys
```

Figure 13-7: Command WRKSYSSTS, information about system pools.

Another, more direct, approach to learning about shared pools is through the Work with Shared Pools (WRKSHRPOOL) command. Figure 13-8 contains a sample of it.

```
                            Work Shared Pools
                                                      System:   BIGBLUE
 Main storage size (K)  . :        655360

 Type changes (if allowed), press Enter.

               Defined    Max   Allocated   Pool  -Paging Option-
 Pool         Size (K)  Active  Size (K)     ID   Defined  Current
 *MACHINE       90000    +++++      90000     1   *FIXED   *FIXED
 *BASE          88360       32      88360     2   *FIXED   *FIXED
 *INTERACT      10000        7      10000     8   *FIXED   *FIXED
 *SPOOL         12000        7      12000     3   *FIXED   *FIXED
 *SHRPOOL1     200000       10     200000     4   *CALC    *CALC
 *SHRPOOL2      50000        4      50000    11   *FIXED   *FIXED
 *SHRPOOL3      50000        4      50000    10   *CALC    *CALC
 *SHRPOOL4      40000       10      40000     5   *FIXED   *FIXED
 *SHRPOOL5      70000        7      70000     6   *FIXED   *FIXED
 *SHRPOOL6          0        0          0         *FIXED
                                                                More...
 Command
 ===>
 F3=Exit   F4=Prompt   F5=Refresh   F9=Retrieve   F11=Display tuning data
 F12=Cancel
```

Figure 13-8: Command WRKSHRPOOL.

Here are the shared pool names and the system pool names (pool ID) to which they correspond. Notice three things about the screen in Figure 13-8.

- Like WRKSYSSTS in Figure 13-7, the memory and activity levels are underscored (meaning changes can be made to them).
- *SHRPOOL6, at the bottom of the screen, has no memory or activity level assigned to it. Apparently, its subsystem was stopped at the time this was taken. Also, it has no system pool assigned to it. Therefore, it is dormant and uses no memory.
- The system pool numbers 7 and 9 are missing. These must have been used as private pools for some subsystem(s). The command WRKSHRPOOL only shows shared pools (not private).

SUBSYSTEMS

We will discuss all the objects that subsystems contain, and discuss subsystems themselves. Subsystems are environments where jobs run. The best part about them is that they are environments the customer defines. The system operator can create the optimum environment in which to run batch jobs, and the optimum environment in which to run interactive jobs. There can even be separate environments for different departments' users. This makes it easy to shift computer resources around as needs arise.

Although subsystems are objects themselves, we know them better as subsystem descriptions. The command to create one is Create Subsystem Description (CRTSBSD). See Figure 13-9 for a sample.

```
                   Create Subsystem Description (CRTSBSD)

 Type choices, press Enter.

 Subsystem description . . . . .   NEWSBS        Name
   Library . . . . . . . . . . .     *CURLIB     Name, *CURLIB
 Storage pools:                    _
   Pool identifier . . . . . . .   1             1-10
   Storage size . . . . . . . . .  *BASE         Number, *BASE, *NOSTG...
   Activity level . . . . . . . .                Number
              + for more values
 Maximum jobs . . . . . . . . . .       4        0-1000, *NOMAX
 Text 'description' . . . . . . .  'New Subsystem for test
configuration'

                          Additional Parameters

 Sign-on display file . . . . . .  *QDSIGNON     Name, *QDSIGNON
   Library . . . . . . . . . . .                 Name, *LIBL, *CURLIB
 Subsystem library . . . . . . .   *NONE         Name, *NONE
                                                                 More...
 F3=Exit   F4=Prompt   F5=Refresh   F12=Cancel   F13=How to use this display
 F24=More keys
```

Figure 13-9: Prompted CRTSBSD command.

The operator does not have to do much more than put in the subsystem name and library. In the example, we named the new subsystem NEWSBS. That is the beauty of the AS/400—it has enough built-in defaults that it kind of knows what the customer wants.

However, one should at least specify some memory storage pools. The first pool, whatever it is, always supports the subsystem driver. For a lot of performance reasons, we do not want that activity in a private or general shared pool; it is best if it runs in *BASE. So that gives us a rule about subsystems: any subsystem's number 1 pool should be *BASE. Note the pool definition in Figure 13-9.

Reading down in Figure 13-9, the next parameter, `Maximum Jobs`, is the maximum number of jobs that the subsystem will allow active at any one time. Remember that jobs come into the subsystem from one or more job queues. It would not be very efficient if the users could just flood a subsystem. Therefore, this value sets a limit on the number of jobs that can be in the subsystem at any one time. This value is crucial. How many jobs are allowed in helps determine how much memory the subsystem should have assigned to it.

Don't forget our earlier discussion and confuse maximum jobs with the subsystem's activity level. Maximum Jobs specify how many jobs are in the subsystem, while Activity Level specifies how many of those jobs the subsystem will actually be working on at one time. For performance, the big difference between the two is this:

- Maximum Jobs:
  - Set too low and job queues back up.
  - Set too high and throughput goes down.
- Activity Level:
  - Very little impact on the casual observer because jobs frequently change states.
  - High impact on overall throughput of the subsystem. Even if Maximum Jobs is set too high, if activity levels are set correctly, throughput will be good.

1. From the storage pool screen shown in Figure 13-9, the system operator should put a "+" on the `+ For More Values` parameter and create at least one additional, private storage pool. In Figure 13-10, we have set up this new subsystem with a second storage pool, private system pool 11.

```
                  Specify More Values for Parameter POOLS

 Type choices, press Enter.

 Storage pools:
   Pool identifier . . . . . . . > 1__        1-10
   Storage size . . . . . . . . .  *BASE      Number, *BASE, *NOSTG...
   Activity level . . . . . . . .  ________   Number

   Pool identifier . . . . . . .   2___       1-10
   Storage size . . . . . . . . .  50000__    Number, *BASE, *NOSTG...
   Activity level . . . . . . . .  4_____     Number

   Pool identifier . . . . . . .   ____       1-10
   Storage size . . . . . . . . .  _______    Number, *BASE, *NOSTG...
   Activity level . . . . . . . .  ______     Number

   Pool identifier . . . . . . .   ____       1-10
   Storage size . . . . . . . . .  _______    Number, *BASE, *NOSTG...
   Activity level . . . . . . . .  ______     Number
                                                                More...
 F3=Exit   F4=Prompt   F5=Refresh   F12=Cancel   F13=How to use this display
 F24=More keys
```

Figure 13-10: Adding storage pools to a new subsystem description.

ROUTING ENTRIES

That really is all there is to creating a subsystem description. But other pieces should be attached to it after it is built.

One of these is the *routing entry* to the subsystem description. Routing entries give the subsystem a means to find any job's runtime attributes.

Unlike other pieces we have been discussing, a routing entry is not an object, so it does not have a Create command for it. There are also no default routing entries from IBM that one can use as a starting place.

Add routing entries to an already created subsystem description with the Add Routing Entry (ADDRTGE) command. Do further maintenance on them with the Change Routing Entry (CHGRTGE) and Remove Routing Entry (RMVRTGE) commands.

When a job enters a subsystem, it attempts to make a match between literals held in the *routing data* to those in the routing entries. The routing data may be specified in the job description. If it is, the subsystem compares that data to its list of routing entries. When there is a match, the subsystem associates the job to a job class (specified on the routing entry) to determine what supporting program to invoke and what the job's runtime attributes will be.

In most cases, the initial program the subsystem will call will be QSYS/QCMD. This is the AS/400 Command Processor Program (CPP) that executes commands (running a program is a result of executing a CALL command). Generally, it is named as a routing entry's initial program.

Control a job's *routing* indirectly through these routing entries and the Routing Data parameter on the Job Description (see chapter 12). Figure 13-11 contains a sample of the routing data on a job description.

```
                         Display Job Description
                                                       System:   BIGBLUE
 Job description:   QINTER        Library:   QGPL

 Message logging:
   Level . . . . . . . . . . . . . . . . . . . . :   4
   Severity . . . . . . . . . . . . . . . . . . :   0
   Text . . . . . . . . . . . . . . . . . . . . :   *NOLIST
 Log CL program commands . . . . . . . . . . . :   *NO
 Accounting code . . . . . . . . . . . . . . . :   *USRPRF
 Print text . . . . . . . . . . . . . . . . . . :   *SYSVAL

 Routing data . . . . . . . . . . . . . . . . . :   QCMDI
```

Figure 13-11: A sample of the routing data for a job description.

Figure 13-12 shows a sample of some routing entries from a subsystem. To obtain this, use the Display Subsystem Description (DSPSBSD) command and take the option for Routing Entries.

```
                        Display Routing Entries
                                                      System:   BIGBLUE
Subsystem description:   QINTER        Status:   ACTIVE

Type options, press Enter.
  5=Display details

                                                                 Start
Opt    Seq Nbr    Program      Library      Compare Value          Pos
 _        10      QCMD         QSYS         'QCMDI'                  1
 _        20      QCMD         QSYS         'QS36MRT'                1
 _        40      QARDRIVE     QSYS         '525XTEST'               1
 _       700      QCL          QSYS         'QCMD38'                 1
 _      9999      QCMD         QSYS         *ANY

                                                                Bottom
F3=Exit   F9=Display all detailed descriptions   F12=Cancel
```

Figure 13-12: Routing entries in the subsystem description.

Notice that the value to match is specified on the column under Compare Value (CMPVAL). To the right of that is the compare position of 1. Although the value one is usually what is used, this allows the operator to specify a comparison of different starting positions of the routing data. For more information about a routing entry, put a 5 on the option line and press the Enter key. See Figure 13-13.

```
                      Display Routing Entry Detail
                                                      System:   BIGBLUE
Subsystem description:   QINTER        Status:   ACTIVE

Routing entry sequence number . . . . . . . :   10
Program . . . . . . . . . . . . . . . . . . :   QCMD
  Library . . . . . . . . . . . . . . . . . :     QSYS
Class . . . . . . . . . . . . . . . . . . . :   QPTY35
  Library . . . . . . . . . . . . . . . . . :     QGPL
Maximum active routing steps  . . . . . . . :   *NOMAX
Pool identifier . . . . . . . . . . . . . . :   2
Compare value . . . . . . . . . . . . . . . :   'QCMDI'

Compare start position  . . . . . . . . . . :   1

Press Enter to continue.

F3=Exit   F12=Cancel   F14=Display previous entry
```

Figure 13-13: Expanded routing entries in the subsystem description.

Note the use of this routing entry (a clue to which is provided by the system operator who set this up), QPTY35. Any job with this routing data would get runtime attributes from class QPTY35, which is a modified version of job class QINTER. The only difference is that the runtime priority is 35 (not 20). Apparently it is for low-priority interactive jobs. We discussed job classes in chapter 12, Working with Jobs.

Using multiple routing entries and job classes like this is a fairly advanced procedure. For those new to the AS/400, do not specify routing data information on any job description. Instead, specify a single routing entry on subsystem descriptions with a compare value of *ANY. No check is made because the specification considers any job to be a match.

WORKSTATION ENTRIES (INTERACTIVE JOBS ONLY)

Interactive subsystems are a little different from batch subsystems:

- Jobs do not enter them through job queues; they enter through the signed-on user's workstations.
- Jobs are not born with job descriptions; the AS/400 must be retrieved from somewhere in the system and associate them with the job.

AS/400 workstations are devices. Workstation Entries (WSE) are listed with the subsystem description using a method similar to routing entries. They contain the name of specific displays or generic displays that the subsystem will support. These entries also specify a job description to use when a user attempts to sign on from a supported display.

Most AS/400 IT departments use the system's auto configuration, and it names display station devices something like DSP01, DSP02, DSP03, and so on. The system operator can identify every display station in the organization to the interactive subsystem with one WSE by leaving those names and specifying one workstation entry with the generic name: D*. The asterisk acts like a wildcard indicating any WSE with a name starting with the letter "D" is supported by the subsystem. Alternatively, workstation names can be less generic (DSP0*), or named individually (DSP01).

Most AS/400 IT departments just use the generic name and have one WSE that serves for every display on the system. The WSE's main jobs are:

- Associate valid workstations that the interactive subsystem will support.
- Associate a job description with a user signing on. This is either done by specifying on the WSE:
  - A named job description.
  - *USRPRF, which tells the subsystem to go to the user profile of the signing-on user and get the job description.
  - *SBSD, which tells the subsystem to look at the job description specified on its own description.

STARTING/ENDING SUBSYSTEMS

Subsystems do not become active until they are started. The command for that is STRSBS. See Figure 13-14.

```
                    Start Subsystem (STRSBS)

Type choices, press Enter.

Subsystem description . . . . .   QBATCH        Name
  Library . . . . . . . . . . .     *LIBL       Name, *LIBL, *CURLIB

                                                                  Bottom
F3=Exit   F4=Prompt   F5=Refresh   F12=Cancel   F13=How to use this display
F24=More keys
```

Figure 13-14: Prompted STRSBS command.

The only parameter that must be specified is the subsystem to start. Conversely, end a subsystem with the ENDSBS command. See Figure 13-15.

```
                    End Subsystem (ENDSBS)

Type choices, press Enter.

Subsystem . . . . . . . . . . . > QBATCH        Name, *ALL
How to end . . . . . . . . . . .  *CNTRLD       *CNTRLD, *IMMED
Delay time, if *CNTRLD . . . . .  *NOLIMIT      Seconds, *NOLIMIT

                                                                  Bottom
F3=Exit   F4=Prompt   F5=Refresh   F10=Additional parameters   F12=Cancel
F13=How to use this display        F24=More keys
```

Figure 13-15: Prompted ENDSBS command.

On this command, either specify a subsystem by name (we specified subsystem QBATCH) or the general *ALL. The second parameter, `How to End`, accepts either *CNTRLD or *IMMED. *CNTRLD is for a controlled shutdown. It will have the system properly close any active jobs before it ends. The

*IMMED is for an immediate end to the subsystem. While it may look like *CNTRLD is the way to close a job, in real life, that parameter can take a long time. Most customers end a subsystem by using the WRKACTJOB command to check it first for active jobs. If they find any active jobs, they do whatever will end them normally. Once all jobs in a subsystem are ended, do an ENDSBS with the *IMMED option.

LAB #13: SUBSYSTEMS

Upon completion of this chapter, you should be able to:

- Explore the system's subsystem definitions.
- Explore the definition of runtime attributes of a job.
- Explore routing data.
- Explore shared storage pools.
- Demonstrate the ability to create a subsystem.
- Demonstrate the ability to create a class.
- Determine the controlling subsystem.
- Demonstrate the ability to develop a private pool.
- Demonstrate the ability to add a routing entry to a subsystem.
- Demonstrate the ability to start and end a subsystem.

NAMING CONVENTIONS FOR THIS LAB

During the lab, every time you encounter one of the lab names containing xx, replace the xx with the assigned number (Figure L13-1). As you complete the lab assignment, create and modify your environment to reflect the specific assigned names.

	Lab Name: Identified in Commands as:	Your Assigned Name:
Profile (User ID)	USERID	
Library Name	USERID	
Output Queue	USEROUTQ	
Job Description	USERJOBD	

Figure L13-1: Naming conventions.

INTRODUCTION

The manager of activities (Jobs) on the 400 is a program called QCTL. This type of a program is referred to on the AS/400 as a Subsystem (only specific types of jobs can run in a subsystem). The task of QCTL is to manage the other subsystems. As such, we have little interaction with this subsystem. Once it is started, which would be automatically during an IPL (Initial Program Load),

QCTL will start other subsystems specified to start at IPL. Thus, it is referred to as the *controlling subsystem*.

QBATCH. This subsystem manages batch programs. Actually, any number of batch subsystems can be created and started on the AS/400, QBATCH is the name of the default batch subsystem. Batch subsystems are associated with one or more Job queues. Batch jobs wait on the queue to which they are assigned until activated by the subsystem that is processing that queue. If the JOB queue is not associated with an active subsystem, the jobs in that queue will wait until the queue is associated with an active batch subsystem. Batch subsystems have a maximum number of jobs that can be active at one time.

If a subsystem serves more than one queue, there can also be a limit on the number of active jobs submitted from any specific queue. Thus, if a job queue has a maximum of one job that can be active, no other job can be started in that job queue until the first jobs ends. Jobs wait on the job queue in order of Job Queue priority (1–9 with 1 being first) and order of time of submittal. Jobs that are scheduled to run at a later time become available to the job queue at the time that they are scheduled for; that is, they do not necessarily start at that time but are available and will wait on the queue for an opportunity to start. While a job queue is held, no jobs from that queue will become active. If a subsystem is ended, no jobs will become active from that subsystem.

QINTER. This subsystem manages interactive jobs—except the system console, which is managed by QCTL. When that subsystem is ended, no jobs will become active from that subsystem.

QCMN. Controls communication jobs.

QSPL. Controls spool functions.

SUBSYSTEMS

To start exploring how subsystems work, we will stick to the standard subsystems shipped with all AS/400s. The first subsystem we will look at is QBATCH.

- Enter the command to call the `Command Entry` screen.
- Press F10 (Include Detailed Messages).
- Enter WRKSBSD QSYS/QBATCH on the command line.
- Press Enter
- This brings you to the `Work with Subsystems Descriptions` screen.
- Enter a `5` (Display) in the `Options` column next to qbatch.
- Press Enter.
- The `Display Subsystem Description` screen is shown.
- Press the Help key.
- Read through the Help text and each menu option.

- Briefly describe the information available for the following options on the `Display Subsystem Description` menu.
  Option 1 ____
  ____
  Option 2 ____
  ____
  Option 6 ____
  ____
  Option 7 ____
  ____
- Exit from Help.
- From the `Display Subsystem Description` screen, select option `1` (Operational Attributes).
- Press Enter.
- What is the qualified name of the default sign-on display file? ____________
  ____
- What is the maximum number of jobs allowed in the subsystem? __________
- Return to the `Display Subsystem Description` screen.
- Enter option `2` (Pool Definitions).
- Press Enter.
  What pool is defined as `Subsystem pool 1`? ____________________
- Read and evaluate the following statement: Both the operational attributes of a subsystem and its pool definitions are created using the CRTSBSD command and are changed using the CHGSBSD command. True or False?
- Return to the `Display Subsystem Description` screen.
- Select option `6` (Job Queue Entries).
- Press Enter.

The Display Job Queue Entries screen is shown. This screen lists, in sequence number order, the job queues that can be used as sources of work for the subsystem they are assigned. It is not uncommon to have several job queues attached to a BATCH subsystem, as batch jobs often enter the subsystem via their job queues. Continue exploring the QBATCH subsystem description.

- List at least two of the job queues: ____________________________
  ____
- For the QBATCH *JOBQ, what are the maximum active jobs? ___________
  ____
- Return to the `Display Subsystem Description` screen.
- Read and evaluate the following statement: For a subsystem, AUTOSTART job, workstation name, type, job queue, communications, and PRESTART job entries are Work Entries that must be added to the subsystem description using the appropriate `Change subsystem description` command. True or False?

Let's continue looking at the description of the QBATCH subsystem.

- Return to the `Display Subsystem Description` screen.
- Select option 7 (Display Routing Entries).
- Press Enter.
- Display the details for routing entry sequence number 9999 and answer the following questions:

  What class is used for jobs being started with this entry? ______________
  ____

  What subsystem storage pool is used for jobs being started from this entry?
  ____
  ____

  What does the compare value of *ANY mean? ______________________
  ____
  ____
- Read and evaluate the following statement: Routing entries must be added to a subsystem description using the ADDENTRY CL command. True or False?

Now that you have looked at a BATCH subsystem, let's take a look at another subsystem. It should be of interest to observe the differences between these different subsystem definitions.

- Return to the `Command Entry` screen.
- Press F9 (Retrieve) to retrieve the previous command.
- Press F4 (Prompt).
- Change QSYS/QBATCH to QSYS/QCTL.

- Press Enter.
- On the `Work with Subsystem Description` screen, select option 5 (Display).
- Press Enter.
- Display the pool definitions for QCTL.
- What storage pool is defined? ______________________
- Press Enter.
- Next, display the AUTOSTART job entries for QCTL.
- What AUTOSTART job(s) are listed? ______________________
  ____
- Press Enter.
- Read and evaluate the following statement: Any job specified as an AUTOSTART job will automatically run when the subsystem is started. True or False?
  Next, display the routing entries for QCTL.
- List all information supplied on routing entry sequence number 9999.
  ____
  ____
- Return to the `Command Entry` screen.

In our investigation of the standard subsystems on your AS/400, we will next turn our attention to the QSPL subsystem. You will see how different this subsystem is defined. Now, work with the Spooling Subsystem (QSPL).

- Enter WRKSBSD QSYS/QSPL on the command line.
- Press Enter.
- The `Display the Subsystem Description` screen is shown.
- Display the pool definitions.
- What storage pools are defined? ______________________
- Return to the `Display Subsystem Description` screen.
- Select the option to `Display Job Queue Entries`.
- Press Enter.
- Name a few of the job queues used by QSPL.
  ____
  ____
- Return to the `Command Entry` screen.

QINTER is the interactive subsystem. As you look through the definition of QINTER, you should compare it to QBATCH.

- Enter WRKSBSD QINTER on the command line.
- Enter the option to `Display the Subsystem Description`.
- Press Enter.
- Display the pool definitions.
- What pools are defined for QINTER? ______________________________
  ____
  Are these private pools or shared pools? ______________________
- Return to the `Display the Subsystem Description` screen.

Next, let's look at the routing information for qinter.

- Enter option `7` (Routing Entries).
- Press Enter.
- Enter option `5` (Display Details) next to the routing entry #10.
- Press Enter.
- From the `Display Routing Entry Detail` screen, answer the following questions:
  The Class name is: ________________________
  What are the maximum routing steps? ______________
  What pool IDs are jobs assigned to? ______________
- Press F3 (Exit).
- Return to the `Command Entry` screen.
- Read and evaluate the following statement: Routing entries should be ordered from the most general to the most specific, a sequenced number order. True or False?
- Read and evaluate the following statement: The Class (specified on the routing entry for a job) contains parameters that control the runtime environment for a job. True or False?

RUNTIME ATTRIBUTES—JOB CLASS

A job class is a way of providing runtime attributes. The principle runtime attributes are runtime priority, time slice in milliseconds, and eligible for purge.

- Enter the command to go to the `Command Entry` screen.
- Enter DSPCLS QINTER on the command line.

- Press Enter.
- Use the `Display Class Information` screen to answer the following questions:
  What is the qualified name of the class? ____________________
  What is the time slice specified? ____________________
  What other attributes are specified in the class? ____________________
- Return to the `Command Entry` screen.
- Enter the command to `Display the Class` on the command line.
- Press F4 (`Prompt`).
- Enter QBATCH for the Class parameter.
- Use the QBATCH class to answer the following questions:
  What is the qualified name of the class? ____________________
  What is the run priority? ____________________
  What is the time slice specified? ____________________
- Return to the `Command Entry` screen.

STORAGE POOLS

AS/400 memory is assigned to support the workflow on the system. A pool of memory is called a storage pool and is where programs and applications execute. Memory can be allocated to either shared or private pools. Now, let's explore the pool allocations on your system by using the Work with Shared Pools command.

- From the `Command Entry` screen, enter the WRKSHRPOOL command.
- Press Enter.

If you have authorization, from here you can dynamically change the size and activity level of these pools. You cannot change the activity level of *MACHINE pool or the size of the *BASE pool.

- Complete the chart in Figure L13-2 for the shared pools that have a storage size greater than zero.

Shared Pool	Briefly Define	Size	Activity Level

Figure L13-2: Shared pools.

- Read and evaluate the following statement: All shared storage pools can be used for user jobs. True or False?

SYSTEM VALUES

There are a series of system values that are related to subsystems and work management on the AS/400. We will explore these values now.

- Enter the command to `Display System Values` on the command line.
- Press Enter.
- As shown in Figure L13-3, complete the chart for the system values that affect work management on your system.

System Value	Description of Value	Current Value	Available Values
QMCHPOOL			
QBASPOOL			
QBASACTLVL			

Figure L13-3: System values.

ADDITIONAL LAB ASSIGNMENTS

1. Work with jobs in the subsystem QINTER. What are these jobs? What would happen if you ended one of these jobs?

2. Work with jobs in the subsystem QCMN. What are these jobs? What would happen if you ended one of these jobs?

3. This can only be done with adequate authority. Create a new subsystem description called NEWSUBXX. Define NEWSUBXX as a private pool. To set this subsystem up as a private pool, you need to set up a specific amount of memory for the pool. You also need to have all routing entries point only to the private pool.
   a. Complete the screen as shown Figure L13-4.

```
                    Create Subsystem Description (CRTSBSD)

Type choices, press Enter.

Subsystem description . . . . . > NEWSUBxx      Name
  Library . . . . . . . . . . .      *CURLIB    Name, *CURLIB
Storage pools:
  Pool identifier . . . . . . . > 1             1-10
  Storage size . . . . . . . . . > *BASE        Number, *BASE, *NOSTG...
  Activity level . . . . . . . . > _________    Number

  Pool identifier . . . . . . . > 2             1-10
  Storage size . . . . . . . . . > 1024         Number, *BASE, *NOSTG...
  Activity level . . . . . . . . > 1            Number
              + for more values
Maximum jobs . . . . . . . . . .   *NOMAX       0-1000, *NOMAX
Text 'description' . . . . . . . > 'Chapter 13 subsystem'
```

Figure L13-4: Create subsystem description.

b. Create a class as shown in Figure L13-5.

```
Create Class (CRTCLS)

 Type choices, press Enter.

 Class . . . . . . . . . . . . .   userid       Name
   Library . . . . . . . . . . .     *CURLIB    Name, *CURLIB
 Run priority . . . . . . . . . .  50           1-99
 Time slice . . . . . . . . . . .  2000         Milliseconds
 Eligible for purge . . . . . . .  *YES         *YES, *NO
 Default wait time . . . . . . .   30           Seconds, *NOMAX
 Maximum CPU time . . . . . . . .  *NOMAX       Milliseconds, *NOMAX
 Maximum temporary storage . . .   *NOMAX       Kilobytes, *NOMAX
 Maximum threads . . . . . . . .   *NOMAX       1-32767, *NOMAX
 Text 'description' . . . . . . .  Class for NewSubxx Subsystem
 ______________________________




                                                                   Bottom
 F3=Exit   F4=Prompt   F5=Refresh   F10=Additional parameters   F12=Cancel
 F13=How to use this display        F24=More keys
```

Figure L13-5: Create class.

c. While the subsystem is inactive, add a routing entry, as shown in Figure L13-6.

```
                        Add Routing Entry (ADDRTGE)

Type choices, press Enter.

Subsystem description . . . . .   NEWSUBxx        Name
  Library . . . . . . . . . . .     userid         Name, *LIBL, *CURLIB
Routing entry sequence number  .   9999            1-9999
Comparison data:
  Compare value . . . . . . . .    *ANY

  Starting position . . . . . .    1               1-80
Program to call . . . . . . . .    QCMD            Name, *RTGDTA
  Library . . . . . . . . . . .      QSYS          Name, *LIBL, *CURLIB
Class . . . . . . . . . . . . .    userid          Name, *SBSD
  Library . . . . . . . . . . .                    Name, *LIBL, *CURLIB
Maximum active routing steps . .   *NOMAX          0-1000, *NOMAX
Storage pool identifier . . . .    2               1-10



                                                                    Bottom
F3=Exit   F4=Prompt   F5=Refresh   F12=Cancel   F13=How to use this display
F24=More keys
```

Figure L13-6: Add routing entry.

d. Start the subsystem. Using the WRKSYSSTS command, press the F11 function key (twice), until the name of your subsystem is listed. Screen print the screen showing this subsystem is active. Attach screen print of this screen.

e. What pool identifier was assigned to your subsystem? ____________

f. Use the `Work with Active Jobs` to find your subsystem.

g. On the WRKSYSSTS screen, press F14 (Work with Subsystems) to see that your subsystem is listed and active. Attach a screen print of this screen.

h. Now it is time to do cleanup. You need to do the following:

   1. End NEWSUBXX subsystem immediately.

   2. Delete the class and subsystem you created. Remember they are stored in your library.

      i. Have your instructor verify that you have completed all the steps of this section.

END-OF-CHAPTER AIDS

CHAPTER SUMMARY

Subsystems create the environment, kind of the computer-within-a-computer, in which jobs can run. Each subsystem has its own allocation of computer resources. It is up to the system operator to ensure that each subsystem has the resources it needs to get the job done as it needs to at the time.

This means that during the day, when users are doing data entry, the interactive type jobs need to get the lion's share of machine resources. We do not want users waiting for screens. But at night, after the users go home, most computers start to run large batch processing jobs. Again, it is up to the system operator to take away resources from the interactive subsystems and reassign them to the batch subsystems to favor this nighttime processing.

Through subsystems, the AS/400 can support a wide variety of job types in ways that vary according to changing needs and priorities.

KEY TERMS

activity levels	pool	special shared pools
*BASE	pool identifier	storage pool
batch job	private pools	storage size
faulting	routing	subsystem
general shared pools	routing data	thrashing
*MACHINE	routing entry	time slice
paging	shared pools	

CHAPTER SELF-TEST

Solutions to these self-test questions are in appendix D.

True-False Questions

___ 1. If you have only *MACHINE and *BASE pool, interactive and batch jobs compete for memory resources.

___ 2. An AS/400 can have a total of 48 pools.

___ 3. Private pools can only support a single subsystem, while shared pools may support multiple subsystems.

___ 4. To increase the throughput of any subsystem, you can adjust the activity level. All the memory pools allow you the capability to adjust the activity level to improve performance.

___ 5. A subsystem can be assigned more than one storage pool.

___ 6. The WRKSHRPOOL command can be used to work with all pools.

___ 7. Jobs always run in subsystems.

___ 8. For a job to enter the subsystem, it requires a work entry in the subsystem description. Interactive jobs can enter the interactive subsystem through a workstation entry.

___ 9. Job descriptions give a job its runtime attributes.

Fill in the Blanks

1. The minimum size for the machine memory pool should never fall below ________________.

2. The system value that defines the size of the machine pool is ______________________, and minimum size of the base pool is ______________________.

3. The ______________________ determines the number of jobs active in a subsystem that the system will work on at the same time.

4. The ______________________ gives the subsystem a place to find the job's runtime attributes.

5. When a job enters the system, it gets its routing data from its ______________________. This data is compared with the values in the ____________________________ until a match is found. The match associates the job with a _________________ to determine what the runtime attributes are.

6. The AS/400 has a Command Processing Program that calls __________________ to execute commands.

Chapter Review Questions

1. Explain the following terms:
   a. Job description.
   b. Job class.
   c. Subsystem.
   d. Storage pool.
   e. Routing entry.
   f. Time slice.
   g. Paging.

2. What are the differences between shared and private pools? Why should you have both types of pools?

3. For best performance, how would you allocate memory to the batch and interactive subsystem pools?

4. What is the difference between Maximum Active Jobs and Maximum Activity Level?

14

Work Management and Performance

Chapter Objectives

Upon completion of this chapter, you should be able to:

- Describe the three states of a job and state transition.
- Identify and explain the system values related to jobs and work management.
- Explain performance management.
- Explain the use of the Work with System Status and Work with System Activity commands.
- Demonstrate the use of Performance Monitor/400 (PM/400).

Overview

Chapters 7 (Managing Devices), 12 (Working with Jobs), and 13 (Subsystems) discuss many individual pieces of the AS/400, and how to create and use those pieces. This chapter explains how the AS/400 uses all those pieces to run programs. If any piece seems hazy, do not hesitate to review it in one of those chapters.

When we understand how the pieces work together, we will be able to do advanced functions on the AS/400, like *performance tuning*. This chapter also presents an overview of performance-tuning techniques for the AS/400. This overview will provide a practical example of using the pieces and the knowledge of their interrelationships to really make the AS/400 run well.

THINGS THAT MAKE JOBS RUN

There have to be six things for any AS/400 job to run:

- Devices (workstations, printers, communications lines, etc.).
- Job descriptions.
- Job classes.
- Job queues.
- Subsystems with:
  - Routing entry(s).
  - Job queue entries—for batch subsystems only.
  - Workstation entry(s)—for interactive subsystems only.
  - Communication entry(s)—for communication subsystems only.
- A valid user ID or password (see chapter 11).

HOW THE AS/400 RUNS

Interactive Jobs

An interactive job is a real-time job performed at a workstation. The job's name is the same as the workstation name that the user signs onto. To start an interactive subsystem, the AS/400 needs:

- A workstation device known to the system (probably courtesy of auto configuration).
- A valid user identification and password (see chapter 11).
- A subsystem (default QINTER) that has:
  - A job description (default QGPL/QDFTJOBD will do).
  - A job class (default classes have the same name as the default subsystems: QINTER).

In addition to those objects, the system needs some "glue" to connect them:

- One or more Workstation Entries (WSE) in the subsystem. These connect the subsystem with a specific terminal device and, when a user signs on, the job with a job description.
- One or more routing entries in the subsystem. When a match is found between the job description's routing data to one of these entries, the job is connected to a class and an initial program (usually QSYS/QCMD).
- A routing entry with *ANY for CMPVAL, or a match with the data in the routing data in the job description. The routing entry should have:
  - Reference to a job class or *SBSD.
  - An initial program to call:
    - Use QSYS/QCMD for a general AS/400 main menu.
    - Specify a program or application for users.

The system runs interactive jobs through interactive subsystems. Interactive subsystems, through their workstation entries (WSE), do double duty:

- They project the sign-on screen to the workstation.
- After the user signs on, they receive the sign-on screen and start the subsystem's job initiation.

When the user signs on, his or her authority is checked before the incoming screen gets to the subsystem. Assuming the user passes the authority check, the AS/400 goes first to the subsystem's workstation entry for the job name (the name of the workstation). It needs to know the runtime attributes of the job.

Runtime attributes are the attributes it will have while it is active in the subsystem. Once the subsystem has the job description, it has the job attributes it needs. The job description's routing data also gives the subsystem a key to a job class. The subsystem retrieves the job class to get the runtime attributes to assign to the job.

The subsystem uses the job description routing data to find a match in the subsystem's routing entries. When it finds a match, it knows which program will support the job. Almost always, this is QSYS/QCMD. (This is familiar—it presents the AS/400 main menu.) It also checks in what memory pool it is to run.

At this point, the interactive job begins. There is just one last loose end, and that is what happens when the user ends the job. If the program that the routing entry specified to run the job is a nonsystem program (an application menu, for example), when the user ends the job, he/she will be automatically signed off. If the supporting program was QSYS/QCMD, when the job ends, the AS/400 main menu is presented to the user and he or she must sign off to end the job.

Interactive jobs do not end until the user signs off. When the user signs off, the workstation entry resumes displaying a sign-on screen.

Batch Jobs

A batch job runs in the background; in other words, it does not tie up a workstation. Batch jobs are started in one of four ways:

- A user or program issues the Submit Job (SBMJOB) command.
- A user issues a communication program start request.
- A subsystem is started and it has been told to start one or more autostart jobs.
- A subsystem is started and it starts one or more preliminary or prestart jobs.

Autostart jobs and *prestart jobs* are jobs that have been added to the subsystem description with the Add Autostart Job Entry (ADDAJE) or Add Prestarted Job Entry (ADDPJE) command.

Prestarted jobs start right away within the subsystem, but they take no resources until they are activated. For more information, refer to Prestart Jobs in the *OS/400 Work Management V4R4*.

Autostart jobs and jobs submitted by users or programs must go into a job queue before entering a subsystem to run. They might have to wait for other jobs to complete before they can enter the subsystem or they can fall right through, but they have to enter a job queue before they can enter a subsystem.

These two items are provided by the user, then the system needs to build or use the defaulted objects for:

- A job description (default QDFTJOBD).
- A job queue (default job queues supplied with the same names as the default subsystems they serve, e.g., QBATCH for the QBATCH subsystem).
- A subsystem (probably called QBATCH, another default). The job description is obtained from one of several places in this order:
  - Specified on the SBMJOB command itself.
  - The job description named on either the:
    - Profile of the user submitting the job.
    - The job description of the program submitting this job.
    - The default job description named on the subsystem.

The job description provides job attributes and, through routing data, the key for the subsystem to get the job class that provides the runtime attributes. After the job descriptions are available, the system needs some "glue" to connect them, like:

- One or more routing entries in the subsystem. When a match is found between the job description's routing data and one of these entries, the job is connected to a class and an initial program (usually QSYS/QCMD).
- One or more attached job queues. Job queues get attached to the subsystem through the Add Job Queue Entry (ADDJOBQE) command.
- Additionally, the target subsystem should have a routing entry of one or more of the following:
  - *ANY.
  - A match with the routing data from the job description.
  - A match with the routing data from the SBMJOB command.
  - Enough memory to run the job.

The subsystem takes the routing data from the job description and the job to make a match with the subsystem's routing entries. A routing entry produces:

- Supporting program to run.
- Storage pool to run in.
- Job class.

From the last item, the job class, the subsystem gets the job's runtime attributes. At this point, the system has enough information to start the job.

Communication Jobs

Think of a *communication job* as a hybrid between interactive and batch. It is a job started on one system by another system. The remote system needs to send a program start request down an established communication link; the target system does the rest.

The program start request is a string of routing data. Position 29 of this string must contain the value PGMEVOKE. Position 37 of the routing data must contain the name of the supporting program the subsystem is to start if one is to be used. The library of that supporting program can be specified starting in position 47.

The subsystem knows to look for these kinds of requests only if it has an appropriate *communications entry*. These communications entries are part of the interactive subsystem, but are not put in when the subsystem is created; they are put in later through the Add Communications Entries (ADDCMNE) command. The communications entry can specify the job description so the subsystem can get job attributes, but it does not have to—the system can search for it like it would with any interactive job.

The subsystem must have one or more routing entries for the job so it can assign runtime attributes. Subsystems with communication entries receive the incoming request and attempt to route it using the routing data. Usually only one subsystem handles communication jobs.

When the subsystem has the request and it matches the routing data to its internal routing entry, it can retrieve the job's runtime attributes. Like batch subsystems, it gets the job class and pool to run in; however, the supporting program to run and its library are specified in positions starting at 37 and 47 of the program start request (used as routing data).

Communication jobs have a unique twist over batch jobs, however. If the supporting program is to run in a special environment, this should be done through another, dedicated routing entry in the subsystem description. Routing entries are sequentially numbered—just number the routing entry for the supporting program lower than the routing entry that matches PGMEVOKE. Yes, they both have to be present. With that special environment tool, the supporting program still runs in the subsystem, but it runs with its own class and storage pool.

NEW SYSTEMS—WHERE TO NOW?

We have discussed the building blocks that make up job control and job environments on the AS/400, as well as the internal interactive and batch work management. The AS/400 comes with two subsystems up and running: QBASE and QCTL. As a minimum, the system operator should also configure and start the following subsystems:

- QCMN to handle communication jobs. If the network is LAN-based, the terminals will come in through this subsystem before being handed off to QINTER.
- QINTER subsystem for interactive jobs.
- QBATCH subsystem for batch jobs.
- QSPL subsystem for printing jobs.

Review these subsystems. Also, review the generic job descriptions, classes, queues, and so on that came with the machine. Add some memory and routing information to the subsystems. Add some WSE to the QINTER subsystem description, then start the subsystems.

Start by configuring the system using as many of the default pieces supplied by IBM. As users are allowed on-line, the jobs they run will be pretty much as they should be. Later, as the operations staff gets used to the AS/400, they will make changes to most of this. They will be cloning new subsystems from the AS/400-supplied ones and using their knowledge to create sophicated configurations. First time out, though, just use the default values to build a basic configuration.

PERFORMANCE

The AS/400 has the ability to constantly "tune" or reassign resources dynamically, while jobs are running. These keep the AS/400 running at a generally optimal level.

Another set of tools (and many of the commands we have already discussed) allows the system operator to instantly solve problems such as slow-running programs or programs that are taking up too many system resources.

The system operator can also use these tools to expedite important programs, ensuring they get the lion's share of resources with which to run.

Although we have seen near miracles occur through clever performance tuning, one caveat to keep in mind is that if the AS/400 is out of capacity, no amount of tuning will help. But by doing everything the system operator can and documenting those efforts, his own data can help make the case for an AS/400 upgrade.

PERFORMANCE COMPONENTS

References to AS/400 performance implies any or all of six major areas:

- Emergencies. The performance just degrades for some reason.
- Tuning. Is the AS/400 optimally set up for your job mix?
- Monitoring. The ongoing capture of performance data.
- Analysis. Periodic reporting from captured performance data.
- Capacity planning. Measuring the health of the AS/400 and predicting what it will be in the future.
- Stress tests and individual program and application measurements.

All these areas come together eventually. A properly tuned AS/400 will encounter fewer emergencies. Adequate *monitoring* and *reporting* will avoid waking up one day to find the AS/400 out of capacity. Finally, testing applications for resource impact before they go into production will avoid performance emergencies.

The AS/400 has tools that automate the performance-tuning process. It is a good idea to use them. When configuring a new AS/400, use the Work with System Values (WRKSYSVAL) command to set two system values:

- QDYNPTYSCD set to 1 to turn on *dynamic priority scheduling.*
  - QDYNPTYADJ allows a *dynamic priority adjustment.* This allows the few interactive jobs that may be attached to the server to keep their priorities intact (value 0) or be changed with the rest of the system (value 1). Of course, this system value is in effect only if QDYNPTYSCD is set to 1.
- QPFRADJ set to 1, 2, or 3 to turn on *performance adjustment.* This manages pool memory allocations automatically while the AS/400 is processing.

Dynamic priority scheduling prevents a single program from gobbling up all of the system resources. The classic case here is the user (or programmer) that starts a large, complex interactive query. Count on that job taking 40 percent or more of the CPU. Dynamic priority scheduling senses what is happening and knocks the job's priority back, allowing other jobs to get some system resources.

In a similar vein, it also is sensitive to jobs that have been waiting for a period of time without getting any system resources; these get a boost in priority. The two approaches combine to make a powerful tool that takes CPU resources away from hogging programs and gives them to languishing programs.

Although these tools are very good, there is still a need for some manual monitoring for a couple reasons. Although dynamic priority scheduling does a terrific job, it is quick to reset changed priorities after they have been lowered. This is good because the earlier versions of priority-adjusting tuners changed priorities and left them there. The result was often a topsy-turvy system with interactive users having very low priorities and batch jobs having very high priorities. The new way is better but if there really is a system-hogging program, the system operator may want to go in and change its runtime priority so it will stay low throughout its run. Another example: Sometimes during month-end processing, only one or two programs are running on the AS/400. The system operator may want these critical-path programs to be hogs so they will get done quickly. In that case, he/she does not want dynamic priority scheduling in effect.

In another vein, the system operator may not want performance adjustment changing the system's memory sizes. Like the dynamic priority-scheduling tool, this has been improved to the point that it is pretty good. However, some situations dictate that memory pools be set and simply not changed. In that case, turn off the automatic adjustment through the system value.

One thing a new AS/400 customer may want to do is set system value QPFRADJ to 1 (set memory sizes at IPL time), start the machine, and then see to what sizes the AS/400 sets the pools. Or, set the system value to 2 and run the machine for a while. Then check the memory *pool sizes* in the middle of the day when things are busy. A system operator may want to accept the system values at this point, turn off the system value, and set the pools sizes within the subsystem descriptions (refer to chapter 13, Subsystems) according to the sizes the adjuster came up with.

AS/400 priorities are expressed in numbers from 00 through 99; the higher the number, the lower the priority or the less important the program. This can be confusing, so be aware of it. When seeing that a priority number has been lowered, interpret that to mean the priority was raised. When a priority number is raised, that means the priority was lowered.

Most reported performance problems have to do with interactive jobs. After all, it is the users at the workstations who are the most "tuned" to system fluctuations. So set up the interactive subsystem wisely to begin with. Give it plenty of memory and do not allow it to support more than 200–300 workstations at one time. Through the use of workstation names and generic workstation entries

(WSE) on the subsystem, keep the supported workstations limited to between 200 and 300. The default name for an interactive subsystem, and the one most used, is QINTER. If a second subsystem is needed, just name it QINTER2 to make it unique. A common practice in such large IT departments is to split interactive workstations into subsystems by department. That way, if one department needs more horsepower than another does, it is easy to raise all priorities for its workstations.

Emergencies

Computers spoil people. The satisfaction of quick response times decays too soon. After that, there is an underlying feeling that the computer is slow. That feeling gets prodded every once in a while when an errant program suddenly gobbles up too much of the computer's resources and it really does experience a sharp increase in response time.

It is now common practice to have all AS/400 workstations attached to a LAN, not directly into the AS/400. Too often, response-time emergencies are caused by a problem on the LAN. This book deals with the AS/400, although we will mention LAN performance problems in this chapter because they are part of the big picture of providing good user service. We will not go into any depth because they are often things apart from the AS/400.

Sometimes users' response-time complaints are due to simple transmission time across a busy or large LAN. The AS/400 may be working fine, but communication is being bogged down on the LAN. Unfortunately, AS/400 performance tools do not address this activity because it takes place outside the AS/400. Many IT departments address this problem by incorporating a LAN management system to determine the amount of transmission delays going on.

Quite often, AS/400 performance emergencies are transitory, but the smart system operator really will not make that assumption. Look into the system on the chance that the initial symptom (slow response time) is not going to suddenly escalate into an overflowed ASP or a locked CPU.

TIP:

Although anyone on the MIS staff can look into a performance problem, we prefer to have one person do the investigation on the system console. The console is set to run at a very high priority (10), so it is better able than other workstations to grab system resources from a runaway program. Also, multiple people executing the same system commands discussed in this chapter will further bog the system down.

The primary command to isolate an emergency is Work with Active Jobs (WRKACTJOB). Figure 14-1 shows a sample screen from that command.

```
                  Work with Active Jobs                       BIGBLUE
                                                    07/05/99  15:03:35
CPU  %:    99.9   Elapsed time:    00:00:09     Active jobs:    248

Type options, press Enter.
  2=Change    3=Hold    4=End    5=Work with    6=Release    7=Display message
  8=Work with spooled files     13=Disconnect ...

Opt  Subsystem/Job   User        Type       CPU %  Function          Status
 _   QINTER          QSYS        SBS           .0                     DEQW
 _     QPADEV0004    DAWSON#M    INT           .0  CMD-WRKACTJOB      RUN
 _     DSP01         SMITH#J     INT         16.9  PGM-DMZ199Z        RUN
 _     DSP02         JONES#R     INT           .0  PGM-CHG110         RUN
 _     DSP23         OPSOP       INT           .0  PGM-JOB002         RUN
 _   QBATCH          QSYS        SBS           .0                     DEQW
 _     RPGRPT        USER10      JOB           .0  PRG-RPGRPG1        RUN
 _   QPGMR           QSYS        SBS           .0                     DEQW
 _   QSERVER         QSYS        SBS           .0                     DEQW
                                                                         More...
Parameters or command
===>____________________________________________________________

F3=Exit   F5=Refresh        F7=Find       F10=Restart statistics
F11=Display elapsed data    F12=Cancel    F23=More options    F24=More keys
```

Figure 14-1: Display screen for the Work with Active Jobs (WRKACTJOB) command.

On the first pass at an emergency, the operator should be most interested in two areas. First, he should know the overall CPU percentage that is indicated in the upper-left corner. Second, he should know the CPU percentages for the individual jobs. These are listed in the middle of the screen. Those areas are highlighted in Figure 14-1. The CPU percentage may often be around 99.9 percent (perhaps even over 100%, which is indicated by the symbol ++++). Check this percentage figure first. Primarily, this number provides a quick look at the overall health of the system. The CPU can be high for three reasons:

- Programs are complex (and not doing much disk IO or user interfacing).
- Page faulting is causing a lot of extra disk IO.
- Overall load on the system (number of jobs) is too high.

Although IBM recommends that CPU usage percentage be kept below 70 percent (for single-processor systems), and 81 percent (for a four-way processor), in real life, even AS/400s without noticeable performance problems may show CPU usage in the 90-percent range all the time. That is the reality but do keep this in mind: any CPU utilization running over 90 percent is getting hammered from excessive seize/lock conflicts.

When searching for a performance problem, if the CPU percentage is over 90 percent—even if it is most of the time—continue looking for a problem within the AS/400. If the percentage indicated is lower, say 75 percent, it might be a good indication that the hang-up is due to a lost device on the LAN. For example, if a gateway goes down and strands its users, the users will still have their screens up and will be getting tired of waiting. The AS/400 is happily cruising because it just lost one hundred or so users. If you are having a response-time problem and seeing a low CPU percentage, immediately suspect the LAN.

Work with Active Jobs

If the operator checks the overall CPU percentage and finds it high, the operator should quickly figure out who is using the largest CPU percentage. A nice feature of the Work with Active Jobs command is that the jobs can be reorganized in the order of CPU percent usage. Place the cursor onto the CPU percentage column and press the F16 (Shift + F4) key. Figure 14-2 shows a sample of the resulting screen.

```
                    Work with Active Jobs                         BIGBLUE
                                                     07/05/99  15:03:35
CPU %:    99.9      Elapsed time:    00:07:09     Active jobs:    248

Type options, press Enter.
  2=Change    3=Hold    4=End    5=Work with    6=Release    7=Display message
  8=Work with spooled files     13=Disconnect ...

Opt  Subsystem/Job  User          Type  CPU %  Function          Status
 _     SQLEXEC      PGMABC        INT    35.5  CMD-EXECUT        RUN
 _     BRM_MAINT    OPC           BCH    23.2  PGM-RBT164        RUN
 _     ESFR1766     PGMDEF        BCH    11.4  PGM-DMZ199Z       RUN
 _     ROSE05V1     PGMDEF        BCH    10.9  PGM-RBT096        RUN
 _     SQLEXEC      USRRGC        BCH     7.1  CMD-EXECUTE       RUN
 _     MIMIXAPYC    OPSOP         BCH     5.6  PGM-DM2110C       RUN
 _     XTRA0202     QUSER         EVK     3.3                    ICFW
 _     SQLEXEC      PGMXYZ        BCH     3.1  CMD-EXECUTE       RUN
 _     SERVICE      QSVCDRCTR     BCH     3.0  PGM-ANCONTROL     RUN
                                                                      More...
Parameters or command
===>_____________________________________________________________________
F3=Exit    F5=Refresh          F7=Find          F10=Restart statistics
F11=Display elapsed data    F12=Cancel    F23=More options    F24=More keys
```

Figure 14-2: Display screen for Work with Active Jobs command after the display has been sorted by using the cursor and the F16 key.

There are some jobs that do not run all the time, but when they do run, they take a lot of resources until they are complete. In the example in the figure, IBM product BRMS (Backup and Recovery Media Services) runs a job called BRM_MAINT, which takes a lot of CPU. There is little the operator can do about this job because it is a function that has to run. Not all AS/400s have BRMS, but the point is, packaged software and some system programs can just take a lot of horsepower to run.

Figure 14-2 reveals that user PGMABC is running a structured query language (SQL) and taking 35 percent of the CPU. When a program or a user is killing the system, it will appear at the top with a CPU percentage of 30 percent or higher—after the jobs are sorted with the F16 key. This program is definitely a problem on this system. Notice the type program it is: INT, or interactive. Running queries or SQLs from an interactive session is generally frowned on for the reason we see here. By their nature, queries and SQLs are batch programs and should be submitted to run in batch, not interactive. The result is often that they eat up more than their share of CPU resources, like we see in Figure 14-2.

There are as many ways of handling a performance problem as there are performance problems. We will walk through one way to handle a system similar to that shown in Figure 14-2 for an example of the process.

Once a problem program like the SQL has been identified, we would put it on hold by putting a 3 on the Option line to the left of the job. Putting it on hold right away frees system resources for other jobs, providing immediate relief for the users.

After holding the job, enter 5 on the Option line to show what program it is running and what files it is updating. Option 5 will also display any system messages the job has encountered. We recommend noting the program, any open files, and any messages. Next, call the user or programmer responsible (preferably the programmer) to confer. While this is going on, the emergency is fading away because the offending program is being held.

If the job's user or programmer confirms that the job must run, it can be released from hold by entering 6 on the Option line. Then, use option 2 (Change) to lower the program's priority (remember, raise the number to lower the priority). This allows the program to continue, but at a lower priority so other jobs do not get starved for resources. What priority would you set it at? Well, even though it is an interactive job, it should be running in batch—we would set it at a batch priority of 50; the normal interactive priority is 20.

To lower it from the screen displayed in Figure 14-2, enter 2 (Change) on the Option line and press Enter. The CHGJOB job command will appear in a screen similar to the one shown in Figure 14-3.

```
                         Change Job (CHGJOB)

Type choices, press Enter.

Job name . . . . . . . . . . . . > SQLEXEC       Name, *
  User . . . . . . . . . . . . . >   PGMABC      Name
  Number . . . . . . . . . . . . >   905191      000000-999999
Job priority (on JOBQ) . . . . .   *SAME         0-9, *SAME
Output priority (on OUTQ)  . . .   5             1-9, *SAME
Print device . . . . . . . . . .   PRT01         Name, *SAME, *USRPRF...
Output queue . . . . . . . . . .   FACOUTQ       Name, *SAME, *USRPRF, *DEV...
  Library  . . . . . . . . . . .     QGPL        Name, *LIBL, *CURLIB
Run priority . . . . . . . . . .   50            1-99, *SAME






                                                                      Bottom
F3=Exit   F4=Prompt   F5=Refresh   F10=Additional parameters   F12=Cancel
F13=How to use this display        F24=More keys
```

Figure 14-3: Screen to change a job's priority—overwrite the value in the Run Priority parameter.

Changing the job's priority is as simple as putting the 50 (its new priority) on the last parameter, Run Priority. After changing a priority like that, give the job 10 to 20 minutes to give up its hold on the system. These guaranteed delays are one reason to react quickly to performance situations.

This example has a clear offender, an interactive SQL, which is probably causing a response-time problem. If changing the SQL's priority does not return the system to normal or if that job had not been there, try looking further down the list of jobs. In this example, we would focus on the third and fourth jobs in the list shown in Figure 14-2.

Although both jobs are taking only about 11 and 10 percent respectively, together they are taking 22.3 percent, and they both belong to the same user. Cases like these—two programs fired off by the same user—often will require the same resources and will be in constant conflict for those resources (for example, two queries running together, looking for different things, but running against the same file). Conflicts cause seize/lock waits and degrade the system. The solution could be to hold one of the programs until the other finishes, then release the held program. The result probably will be that both programs finish faster and cause less damage to the rest of the system in the process.

Sometimes the WRKACTJOB command will not show any jobs taking high CPU percentages and the system operator has to look elsewhere. The next items to look for are unusually low (powerful) priorities where they should not be. Like the CPU percentages, sort the display from Figure 14-2 by placing the cursor on the Priority column and pressing the F16 key. Figure 14-4 shows a sample of sorted priorities.

```
                    Work with Active Jobs                           BIGBLUE
                                                        07/05/99  15:03:35
CPU %:    99.9      Elapsed time:    00:07:09       Active jobs:    248

Type options, press Enter.
  2=Change    3=Hold    4=End    5=Work with    6=Release    7=Display message
  8=Work with spooled files     13=Disconnect ...

                                                   ----Elapsed-----
Opt  Subsystem/Job  Type  Pool  Pty       CPU  Int     Rsp  AuxIO   CPU %
 _     MONJRN       BCH     2   10         .1                   0      .0
 _     MONSYSSTS    BCH     2   10       30.1                   2      .0
 _     MONTAPSTSD   BCH     2   10       40.6                  18      .0
 _     QBRMRCY      BCH     2   10         .5                   0      .0
 _     QSYSSCD      BCH     2   10        1.0                   0      .0
 _     QMLMAIN      PJ      2   11       68.1                   0      .0
 _     QMLRS232     PJ      2   11       35.0                   0      .0
 _     QMLTRACE     PJ      2   11      165.2                   0      .0
 _     RBCMANAGER   BCH     2   11      568.8                  37      .0
                                                                   More...
Parameters or command
===>______________________________________________________________
F3=Exit    F5=Refresh          F7=Find        F10=Restart statistics
F11=Display elapsed data       F12=Cancel     F23=More options    F24=More keys
```

Figure 14-4: Display screen for WRKACTJOB command after using the cursor position and the F16 key to sort by priorities.

The system operator should have an idea about which jobs have legitimate high priorities. Scan this list for examples of high priorities that do not belong. Remember, users or programmers have special authority for job control in their user profile. For additional information, see chapter 11. These folks could have given themselves extra priority to boost their jobs through the system.

If there are not any jobs taking large CPU percentages or that have low priorities, try checking the DASD activity—very high activity can cause a performance problem. Do this by pressing the F11 key. Figure 14-5 shows the same set of jobs from Figure 14-2 after F11 has been pressed.

```
                    Work with Active Jobs                      BIGBLUE
                                                     07/05/99  15:03:35
CPU %:    99.9      Elapsed time:    00:07:09     Active jobs:   248

Type options, press Enter.
  2=Change   3=Hold   4=End   5=Work with   6=Release   7=Display message
  8=Work with spooled files   13=Disconnect ...

                                               ----Elapsed-----
Opt  Subsystem/Job  Type  Pool  Pty     CPU  Int    Rsp  AuxIO  CPU %
 _     SQLEXEC      INT     4   20   3120.0                 238   35.5
 _     BRM_MAINT    BCH     4   40    892.9                3540   23.2
 _     ESFR1766     BCH     4   50    718.9                5268   11.4
 _     ROSE05V1     BCH     4   50   2097.0                  77   10.9
 _     SQLEXEC      BCH    10   50    345.3                3312    7.1
 _     MIMIXAPYC    BCH     9   25   9162.1                5593    5.6
 _     XTRA0202     EVK     5   19     29.3                 112    3.3
 _     SQLEXEC      BCH     4   50     88.0               21386    3.1
 _     SERVICE      BCH     2   51    221.3                   0    3.0
                                                                More...
Parameters or command
===>
F3=Exit   F5=Refresh        F7=Find       F10=Restart statistics
F11=Display elapsed data    F12=Cancel    F23=More options    F24=More keys
```

Figure 14-5: Display screen for Work with Active Jobs command after the F11 key has been pressed.

If a job shows extremely high DASD activity, there may be nothing that can be done other than to hold it or lower its priority.

At this point, if the problem still exists, look deeper into the system using the command Work with System Activity (WRKSYSACT). Figure 14-6 shows an example of that command's display.

```
                   Work with System Activity                    BIGBLUE
                                                       07/05/99  16:49:42
Automatic refresh in seconds . . . . . . . . . . . . . . . . .        5
Elapsed time . . . . :   00:00:02        Overall CPU util . . : 99.9
                                      CPU 1 util  . . . . . . : 99.9
                                      CPU 2 util  . . . . . . : 99.9

Type options, press Enter.
  1=Monitor job   5=Work with job
                                                       Total  Total
     Job or                                        CPU   Sync  Async    PAG
Opt  Task        User       Number  Thread    Pty  Util   I/O    I/O  Fault
 _   QBRMNET     QPGMR      161530  0000002F   30  30.6   827    452     68
 _   HAL25V6     PGMDEF     161609  0000005B   50  15.3    48    154      0
 _   SQLEXEC     PGMABC     161585  00000013   50  13.9     2    219      0
 _   ESFR176     PGMDEF     161460  0000001B   50   9.6    70     16      0
 _   TSFR680     OPC        161604  0000007F   50   8.7    32     32      0
 _   ROSE05V1    PGMDEF     161255  0000005A   50   8.6     0    222      0
 _   ISLWES4     PGMGHI     161495  0000004C   20   1.2     7      1      2
 _   SERVICE     QSCVDRCTR  161488  00000023   51    .3     0      0      0
                                                                   Bottom
F3=Exit   F10=Update list   F11=View 2   F12=Cancel   F19=Automatic refresh
F24=More keys
(C) COPYRIGHT IBM CORP. 1981, 1998.
```

Figure 14-6: Work with System Activity screen.

This screen refreshes itself every five seconds. That is the default value; the user of this command can override it. If he/she is investigating a performance problem, he/she probably should make it twenty seconds; otherwise, the frequency of refreshing this command may cause more degradation to the system he/she is trying to fix. Thanks to the constant refresh, this command will monitor transitory problems. Another benefit is that this command will show system tasks and their CPU percentages (which do not normally appear on the WRKACTJOB display). System tasks will have the user identification label "SYS" (notice the second column, User). These are examples of the system jobs we have mentioned.

Any AS/400 job can have two components: a user component and a system component. The user component is what WRKACTJOB displays. System components do not appear there because they have a very high priority and are very transitory (lasting less than a second); however, any system-intensive job can have a long system component that consumes the CPU. This is known as a *transparent problem* and is almost impossible to figure out without an extremely in-depth knowledge of jobs and their system components. WRKSYSACT shows the system jobs along with user jobs.

A prime example of such a problem is a large library save started during the day. The command (and user portion) is SAVLIB, which will show to be taking 0-3 percent CPU utilization. Yet the system will be pegged. Looking at the WRKSYSACT screen, the operator will see user SYS (that owns the system portion) taking 40 percent of the CPU. And talk about abnormally high priorities, user SYS's task will run at a priority of one! It takes some creativity and a lot of experience to associate a high-percentage SYS task with its user portion. Once the two are paired, the solution to such a problem could be twofold:

- Cancel the user job (the system task will go with it).
- Institute a rule that the user job (like a large save library) will not be started during the production day unless an unusual situation exists.

Emergency Aftermath

The recovery period following an emergency has the potential to cause worse damage than the original event. Changing almost anything in the system at a time when the system is getting hit hard can really cause it to flop. When a runaway job's priority is changed to 55 in order to minimize its impact, the first thing the system seems to do is start running at about 150 percent. Depending on how deep the program was into the system, sometimes even a simple hold will be delayed for thirty or more minutes. New priorities always require time to take effect. Meanwhile, the system performance degrades further. All anyone can do during this time is wait.

Earlier, we mentioned the potential for a LAN problem. The way LANs go down (and come back up) on an AS/400 can cause a performance "emergency." As an example, consider a gateway or a bridge that supports one hundred workstations that suddenly fails: probably the only way anyone knows there is a problem is that one hundred users are stuck on a single screen.

When the AS/400 fails to see the failed hardware device, it will disconnect all users who were attached to that device. This can be a major problem on the AS/400 with one hundred-plus sessions dumping logs to disk and cleaning up after themselves.

Another problem happens when the device comes back on-line and all one hundred users are told (usually through an overhead announcement) to sign back on again. Even a powerful AS/400 will see performance die for fifteen to forty-five minutes as it handles one hundred new sign-ons, and there is nothing anyone can do about it. Particularly large companies have the help desk selectively bring up groups of users at a time to minimize this hit.

TIP:

Another problem with LANs and AS/400s is that LANs tend to be a little flaky. Rather than have workstations dropping on and off all the time, many customers customize their AS/400s slightly to accommodate that instability. They modify system value QDSCJOBITV (Disconnect Job Interval) to keep LAN-connected interactive jobs active until ten or fifteen minutes of no communication has elapsed.

Every AS/400 customer needs to develop guidelines for performance emergencies. Depending on the job mix and LAN usage, those procedures should include the following:

- First indications of problems (calls from users, monitoring programs, etc.).
- Initial steps to identify the type of problem:
    - Who takes what action? Assign one person, usually someone with ready access to the system console.
    - What to look for.
    - Specific things to do.
- Problem identification:
    - Action taken:
        - Hold programs.
        - Contact developers.
        - Change job priorities.
        - Cancel jobs.
        - Get hardware back up.
    - Who must be notified:
        - LAN administration.
        - Programming.
        - Management.
- Recovery:
    - What is the status of the AS/400?
        - Is the AS/400 suffering from heavy-user disconnections?
        - Have all job changes taken effect?
        - Have high-hitting jobs released their holds on the system?
    - Are users to sign off and then sign on or just be patient?

Performance Tuning

While an emergency can happen to any AS/400, getting an AS/400 into tune and keeping it there will allow any company to generally have fewer emergencies. Performance tuning an AS/400 is almost a lost art. It's too bad no one really bothers anymore. Most AS/400s being considered for upgrade only need a good tune-up.

There really are not too many specific tasks to tuning, and there is a definite lack of what is right for any particular system. The problem is that the AS/400 gets tuned to support a job mix. As the mix changes, the tuning requirements change. Because the mix is always changing, customers try to strike a happy medium—defining that happy medium is the challenge.

A lightly loaded AS/400 always runs well and looks relatively healthy. Do not waste time doing performance tuning during those times. Always monitor AS/400s during the busiest time for any job mix. Take note of what we are saying here. The busiest time for a set of interactive jobs tends to be from 10 A.M. to 2 P.M. (excluding lunch hour). The busiest time for a batch job mix is generally during nightly processing. Some twenty-four-hour companies are even more complex. For example, the job mix might not completely change from interactive to batch, but the emphasis on either could change.

There are two performance-tuning tasks: monitoring and modifying. Monitoring tasks should be done during the busy, stressful times mentioned above. Modifying system parameters—such as changing memory or *activity levels*—should be done during less busy times, if possible.

Monitoring Tasks

So what values should be monitored to check the health of an AS/400? Well, it is not the CPU percentage alone. That is like diagnosing a mechanical problem with a car by measuring how fast its engine is running. "It is always running very fast; we need another car." Not true. Like car engines, computer CPUs are sometimes supposed to run fast, sometimes idle. When the CPU shows a 99.9 percent utilization, it may or may not have a serious problem; the percentage alone is not enough to draw that conclusion.

In addition to CPU percentage, there are two AS/400 monitoring issues of concern to us.

- Wait-to-ineligible ratio.
- Nondatabase faults:
  - Nonmachine pool.
  - Machine pool.
  - All pools.

Wait-to-Ineligible Ratio

The wait-to-ineligible ratio is the primary factor to use when considering the AS/400's current state. Jobs have three run states:

- Active—currently running.
- Wait—waiting for something, either:
  - A disk access, which could be a page retrieval or some record retrieval.

    - A user's response to a screen.

- Ineligible—the job is ready to run and waiting for the system to allocate resources to it.

From these three states, IBM defines six transition states (or the act of a job going from one state to another):

- Active-to-wait.
- Active-to-ineligible.
- Wait-to-ineligible.
- Ineligible-to-active.
- Wait-to-active.
- Ineligible-to-wait.

The most significant of these to us is the wait-to-ineligible. The AS/400 uses transition state numbers as ratios to each other. Such a ratio would be the number of one type of transition to the number of another type of transition as measured within a period (like a minute). Transition ratios are used to define what a healthy system looks like; valid ratios are available for each AS/400 model and each version of the operating system. The ratios are found in appendix A of the IBM redbook, *AS/400 Performance Management*.

Keep in mind that the text and examples in this chapter all use acceptable values for an AS/400, but that the values will vary widely from model to model. The actual values for a particular model can be found in the work management manual.

For this example, the primary transition ratio is the wait-to-ineligible to active-to-wait. Expect the ratio to be around 10 percent. In other words, 10 percent of the number of jobs going from active-to-wait go from wait-to-ineligible.

Let us spend a little more time on this. If, in a one-minute period, one hundred jobs—they do not have to be one hundred unique jobs, sometimes the same job can make a state change in the same time period—are active and go to a wait state, they wait either for user input or for a disk read or write. In the same period, 10 percent of that number, or ten jobs, that were in a wait status, completed waiting and tried to go active but were unable to because the system was busy servicing other jobs. If the target for this model AS/400 were a 10 percent ratio of active-to-wait to wait-to-ineligible, this would be considered a correctly tuned AS/400.

To understand why the preceding 10 percent is a good situation, consider what happens when there aren't any jobs waiting to run. When there aren't any jobs ineligible, it is an indication that not too much is running on the system or that it is an overtuned system. In other words, so many system resources are allocated that no jobs ever have to become ineligible. That's great for individual jobs and it's usually the way new customers to the AS/400 tune their machines. Nevertheless, overtuned systems experience random jobs that just degrade for no reason.

The monitoring command for these ratios is Work with System Status (WRKSYSSTS). Figure 14-7 shows a sample.

```
                      Work with System Status                        BIGBLUE
                                                           07/05/99  18:50:23
% CPU used . . . . . . . :          1.0  Auxiliary storage:
Elapsed time . . . . . . :     00:00:01    System ASP . . . . . . :     29.36 G
Jobs in system . . . . . :          984    % system ASP used  . . :     15.3099
% addresses used:                          Total  . . . . . . . . :     29.36 G
  Permanent  . . . . . . :         .007    Current unprotect used :       333 M
  Temporary  . . . . . . :         .013    Maximum unprotect  . . :       359 M

Type changes (if allowed), press Enter.

System     Pool    Reserved    Max   Active->  Wait->  Active->
 Pool   Size (K)  Size (K)  Active    Wait     Inel     Inel
   1       39312     53108   +++++      .0       .0       .0
   2       60940         0      18    18.0      2.0       .0
   3        1308         0       1      .0       .0       .0
   4       29512         0       0      .0       .0       .0
                                                                      Bottom
Command
===>
F3=Exit   F4=Prompt     F5=Refresh    F9=Retrieve    F10=Restart
F11=Display pool data  F12=Cancel   F14=Work with subsystems    F24=More keys
```

Figure 14-7: Work with System Status screen.

To transition monitoring, focus on two columns: Active-to-Wait and Wait-to-Ineligible. If the performance manual tables told us to expect Wait-to-Ineligible to be approximately 10 percent or less (but not equal to 0 percent) of the Active-to-Wait value, this system would be healthy.

If the results of monitoring suggest changes, the next step is to *modify* parameters. The only way to make the Wait-to-Ineligible column change up or down is to change the MAX ACT figure shown on the screen. Lower the figure in increments of two, waiting approximately twenty minutes between each adjustment, then recheck. Continue this until the Wait-to-Ineligible number drops to almost zero, and then increase the figure by 2 one time.

Pool Sizes can be changed from this screen by positioning the cursor on the appropriate `Pool Size` field and enter in the new figure.

Non-Database Faults (Non-Machine Pool)

Although it is not obvious, Figure 14-7 actually shows three types of memory pools:

- System Pool 1. This is called the *machine pool.* It is always present on any functioning AS/400, and it is where the system does its system tasks.
- System Pool 2. This is called the *base pool,* because it is often written as *BASE—it may be referred to as "star-base." This is the repository for all memory not otherwise assigned to System Pool 1 or System Pools 3-16.
- System Pools 3 through 16. These are optional; you do not have to have any. They are the *user-defined pools.*

Nondatabase faults are another crucial point to monitor for appropriate system tuning. Database faults can be application issues, but nondatabase faults are a way of saying that there is not enough memory to adequately support the program.

Monitor the nondatabase (NON-DB) fault value on the screen as shown in Figure 14-7. Make the fault rate change by changing the Pool Size value. Raising the Pool Size makes more memory available and lowers the nondatabase faulting rate.

These pools should have nondatabase faults of between ten and twenty pages per minute. In the example shown in Figure 14-7, the below-10 faults are for noninteractive jobs that are lightly loaded during the day; in fact, none may be running on the system this example was taken from. In this case, the fault rate for noninteractive jobs would be low. If a pool supporting interactive jobs needed some extra memory, however, it could come from one of these batch pools.

Non-Database Faults (Machine Pool)

Pool 1, the machine pool, should have a nondatabase fault rate between three and five pages per minute and can be adjusted by changing the memory assigned to Pool 1 until that rate is achieved.

Nondatabase Faults (All Pools)

Another activity to monitor is the total nondatabase faults for all pools (including the machine pool). The value for this specific AS/400 should be between 180 and 300.

If the value is not between 180 and 300, it could mean that one or more pools are seriously out of tune. If all pools are tuned and there are no further steps to take (such as no inactive pools from which to draw memory), only then can one say that the AS/400 could be out of capacity and in need of an upgrade.

When to Monitor

Beware of zeroes at key monitoring points. If the AS/400 is lightly loaded, this is what it should produce. If it is out of tune, it may also produce them. If the system operator miscalled this and made adjustments based on those values, the AS/400 would not function well when any serious workload hits it. Always monitor when the AS/400 is getting hammered, then zero-values will indicate tuning is necessary.

Take several monitor samples and do not worry about reacting to every little thing. The best-tuned AS/400s will produce periods where the monitored values are not good. Constant, effective monitoring produces a trend indicating that the system settings are acceptable most of the time.

A company that closely monitors for this trend may develop several trends, one for each job mix. Remember, any AS/400 can be tuned for any job mix. The choice is to tune the machine for each job mix using predetermined settings, or to tune it for generally all job mixes.

Approach performance monitoring like stockbrokers advise approaching investing. Establish a long-term goal and try to reach that without flipping out over every little glitch. As with investing in the stock market, do not check performance hourly or daily, focus instead on the big picture. Do not seriously consider every individual monitoring sample until several of them indicate a trend.

When to Modify

When change are made to either the memory level or the activity level, the system must go through a fairly intensive rearranging of the jobs in those pools. This can get intensive when taking memory from one or more pools and putting it into one or more other pools. When the changes are made, the CPU activity light goes steady for anywhere from several seconds to several minutes, indicating the system is pegged. For this reason, do not make modifications when the system is heavily loaded.

When changing an activity level in response to a performance emergency, do not expect dramatic changes to happen right away. It can take several minutes for the system to settle in and reflect the benefits of a better activity level.

Performance Tuning Summary

Performance tuning must be an ongoing activity. It is not a good idea to start doing it when the system is crashing. Remember the rules:

- Monitor when the system is at its busiest (for the job mix).
- Modify when the system is at its lightest.
- When reassigning memory among pools, do so in the following order:
    - Decrease memory in all pools.
    - Increase memory in all pools.

Also, remember that monitoring is an ongoing process. It is tedious, but if the system operator has the AS/400 properly tuned, chances are, it will not have a performance emergency.

Performance Monitoring and Analysis

Under the umbrella of *Performance Tools/400*, the AS/400 has some powerful data-collecting and reporting tools:

- Performance Data Monitor will collect and report performance data. Start it with the Start Performance Monitor (STRPFRMON) command.
- Automatic data collection can also be started with the Add Performance Collection (ADDPFRCOL) command.
- Performance trend analysis can be done automatically every month with the Automated Performance Management Tool. Start this with the Analyze Performance Data (ANZPFRDTA) command, but this is a CPU hog, so run it during off-hours.
- The Performance Tools Advisor provides an overall analysis of the performance settings within your AS/400. Optionally, the Advisor will ask before it implements its recommendations. If the operator answers affirmative, it will make the changes. *Note*: Set QPFRADJ to zero to run this program.

TIP:

Try this: Set QPFRADJ to 2 or 3 to have the AS/400 self-tune itself. Later, run it off and run Performance Tools Advisor and see how the AS/400 scores its own attempts at tuning.

- Print Transaction Report (PRTTNSRPT) will help locate "hot spots" of suspect jobs. To run this command, Performance Monitor (STRPFRMON) must have been started with the parameter TRACE(*ALL).

On a new AS/400, use automatic tuning once and use its settings as guidelines. Then set the system up according to those guidelines, capture performance data, and periodically run an analysis report or two. Actually, this can be a nice alternative to using the tables in the performance book—let the system come up with the starting values for you.

Print Transaction Report will help locate stubborn performance problems. For example, users may complain that the system runs terribly for a period of fifteen to thirty minutes some mornings (but not all mornings). Maybe the system operator has checked Work with System Status (WRKSYSSTS) and Work with Active Jobs (WRKACTJOB) and has not found anything wrong. Print Transaction Report will focus on a particular job.

When CPU usage goes over 90 percent, seize/lock conditions increase, degrading performance. During slow periods, run the Print Transaction report, asking for an analysis of seize/locks for a previous busy time. Limit the time of the seize/locks to greater than fifty milliseconds and use the time of day (TOD) to limit the analysis to a time of day. The program will print a report isolating the seize/locks that occurred when the CPU percentage hit the roof. From these, the operator can get a list of the programs that caused the most trouble during the period.

This product writes thousands of records to hundreds of files. There is more information here than anyone could ever want or use. IBM has a subscription service that takes this data monthly and produces more reports than you could ever use. Once armed with a suspect program, try the last (and our favorite) AS/400 performance tool, Performance Explorer. This tool asks for a set of programs or jobs to analyze and print a report that describes them in incredible detail.

Capacity Planning

The AS/400 comes with a built-in capacity-planning product called BEST/1. Unfortunately, we have never had it tell us anything other than "buy more hardware."

That is not to say the conclusion is invalid. Most people do not run it when they have a lot of capacity; therefore, the conclusion is probably valid. Given just that conclusion, we would have to do a lot of support work before using it alone to make a board-level recommendation for a major upgrade.

Look at capacity planning as the ultimate culmination of the other techniques discussed in this chapter. Performance activities and measuring must ultimately result in capacity planning information. Before a proposal for an upgrade can be seriously made, it must be backed up with evidence that the system operations staff has done all that is reasonably possible to improve the system. This record must include:

- Performance tuning :
  - What was monitored?

- What was modified?
- Why will continued modification not work?

- Monthly trends of key AS/400 items used should reflect a steadily growing trend:
  - Response times.
  - CPU utilization.
  - DASD utilization.
- The staff handles emergencies as efficiently as anyone. At some point, it needs to be able to demonstrate:
  - Performance-related emergencies have grown in number and frequency.
  - The emergencies are caused by:
    - Growth in applications on the system.
    - Growth in the number of users on the system.
    - Growth in transaction levels.

With the preceding, capacity issues are easy to spot and easy to document. That data works very nicely to support BEST/1 findings.

When considering a model upgrade, the big consideration will be the amount of power gain the different AS/400 models will produce. There are two measurements of this power: *Relative Performance Rating* (*RPR*) and the newer *Commercial Processing Workload* (*CPW*).

RPR has been around since the birth of the AS/400 and is based on how many times faster any particular configuration is than the original, smallest AS/400—a model B10. The testing standard this was based on was IBM-developed and called *RAMP-C*. The problem with this is that the transactions pumped through were too simple. As disk IO got better and AS/400 memory got big enough that entire files could be cached, the measurement became meaningless.

The more sophisticated replacement is CPW. CPW uses order-entry transactions that access and update many database files. Where RPR counted transactions completed when the CPU usage percentage was at 70 percent, CPW disregards CPU percentage—it counts the number of transactions the system can complete while delivering 90 percent of those transactions at less than five-seconds response time. This measurement (and its more complex transaction structure) guarantees a more realistic measurement guideline.

PERFORMANCE TIPS

Here are some miscellaneous functions anyone can do to improve AS/400 performance without doing any analysis.

Use the Set Object Access (SETOBJACC) command to preload entire files into their own dedicated storage pool for certain kinds of processing. We like to use this for critical batch programs that are run during off-hours. Assign a lot of memory to a storage pool and load a physical file or logical file into it, then kick off the job. It will run very fast. On the subsystem description, assign the normal system pool 2 (*BASE), one user pool for the program and other files, then one or more pools dedicated to the largest and busiest of the files the program will access. Before using the SETOBJACC command:

- Set system value QPFRADJ to zero (turn it off).
- Issue the CLRPOOL command to clear the pool.

Keep in mind that most applications are disk-bound, not CPU-bound, and that disk-intensive operations cost dearly. These operations are journaling, commitment control, and (to a lesser extent), RAID-5, and mirroring. The trade-off is database security for speed. RAID-5 and mirroring have become so fast over the years, we do not worry about them anymore. But journaling and commitment control will still make their sting felt. When the shop needs either or both, go for it; but do it with appropriate planning. Do not fall into the trap that many do and just turn on journaling for a whole library; think and plan through the journaling/commitment control strategy.

Disk accessing technology is one that has increasingly improved over the years. In fact, the improvement of fast access and controller-based caching has been exponential. One result of this to keep in mind when looking at the big picture (the applications and the AS/400) is that, as the DASD block is removed, the CPU becomes the next blockage. Read it this way—as you replace older DASD with new, watch your CPU usage percent increase.

Implementing ILE High Level Languages (HLL) properly will significantly enhance the performance of an AS/400, especially in applications that rely on frequent calling of external programs. ILE allows those programs to be *bound modules* of a single program. If an organization is using ILE, however, *activation groups* should be kept to a minimum or some of those performance gains will start to disappear.

The AS/400 Server

AS/400s sold as servers are tuned to favor batch processing. Leave them as servers! The temptation is to look at the hardware packed in one of those servers, see how fast it runs, and think it may be a nice platform for some interactive workstations.

Two things we will promise: One, the few workstations will run terribly. Two, if more than a few are attached (enough to make the interactive CPU percentage go up to 10 percent of the machine), nothing will run well—neither batch nor interactive. Plan to limit the access to the server machine to the minimum interactive. IBM recommends less than 2 percent of the interactive CPU percentage.

Sometimes the definition of what is an interactive job is in doubt. If an interactive job collects input parameters then starts a batch-reporting job, that job may or may not be interactive, depending on how it was started. When applications problems are suspected on an AS/400 server, use the Work with Active Job (WRKACTJOB) command and look in the Type column. Interactive jobs will be identified with an INT; all others are noninteractive jobs.

Finally, the system will do dynamic prioritizing on server AS/400, but limit it to only adjusting the priorities of batch jobs. This is assuming that the one or two interactive jobs running on the system may be critical to its being. If the AS/400 is running dynamic prioritizing, and you do not want interactive jobs' priorities changed, set system value QDYNPTYADJ to 0. If interactive jobs' priorities are to be changed, set it to 1.

LAB #14: WORK MANAGEMENT AND PERFORMANCE

Upon completion of this lab, you should be able to:

- Explore the job/work load on your system.
- Explore the system pool allocation on the AS/400.
- Demonstrate the ability to work with subsets of active jobs.
- Demonstrate the ability to determine the vital system statistics available on the AS/400.
- Explore performance-related system values.

NAMING CONVENTIONS FOR THIS LAB

During the lab, every time you encounter one of the lab names that contains xx, replace the xx with the number that has been assigned. As you complete the lab assignment, create and modify your environment to reflect your specific assigned names (Figure L14-1).

	Lab Name: Identified in Commands as:	Your Assigned Name:
Profile (User ID)	USERID	
Library Name	USERID	
Output Queue	USEROUTQ	

Figure L14-1: Naming conventions.

INTRODUCTION

The previous two chapters laid out the groundwork for an understanding of how work is processed on an AS/400. Jobs and subsystems were discussed, as well as their relationship. In this section, you will continue to explore the concepts of how work is processed and how you can the get the most out of your AS/400. This section discusses more commands that let you get a handle on your system.

JOBS ON YOUR SYSTEM

To start getting the idea of the workload on your system, let's determine which jobs are active in the subsystems of your system.

- Enter WRKSBSJOB on the command line.
- Press F4 (Prompt).
- What is the default value for the subsystem parameter? ________________
- Press Enter.

This will bring up the first subsystem alphabetically on your system. If you press Enter, you will go to the next subsystem, and so on, and so on. You will go through the active subsystems on your system to look at the jobs that are active.

- Determine the number of jobs active in each of the subsystems at this time. Place this information in the chart shown in Figure L14-2.

Subsystem	Number of Active Jobs
QBATCH	
QCMN	
QCTL	
QINTER	
QSNADS	
QSPL	
QSYSWRK	
QYFPCS	

Figure L14-2: Active jobs in each subsystem.

WORKING WITH YOUR SYSTEM'S STATUS

One of the more important commands on your system allows you to view the workflow. This important command is Work with System Status. Let us now explore the type of information that is available with this command.

- Enter WRKSYSSTS on the command line.
- Press Enter.
- From the information on this screen, complete the following questions:
  What is the current CPU usage? ________________________________
  How many jobs are on your system?________________________________
  What percentage of your auxiliary storage (disk) is currently being used?
  ____
  How much disk space is available on your system? ___________________
- Press F11 (Display Transition Data).
- Which system pool has the highest Active-to-Wait value? _____________
  What value is displayed? ______________________________________
  Using help, what does Active-to-Wait tell you? ____________________

- Press F11 (Display Pool Data).
- What pool names do the system pool numbers correspond to?
  System Pool 1 ______________________________
  System Pool 2 ______________________________
  System Pool 3 ______________________________
  System Pool 4 ______________________________
- Press F14 (Work with Subsystems).
- Which subsystems have more than one subsystem pool defined? What system pool number are they using? ______________________________
  ____
  ____

All memory that is not allocated to specific subsystems is located in the *BASE pool. All active subsystems on your system share access to the memory in the *BASE pool. In order to have memory set aside for a specific subsystem, additional pools are allocated to the subsystem. Now you will determine which pools have been allocated to the above subsystems.

- Place option 5 (Display Subsystem Description) to the left of the first subsystem with multiple pools.
- Press Enter.
- Enter 2 (Pool Definitions).
- Press Enter.
- As shown in Figure L14-3, complete the chart for the subsystems with multiple storage pool allocations.

Subsystem	Second Storage Pool Name
QINTER	
QSPL	

Figure L14-3: Subsystems with multiple storage pool allocations.

The Work with Subsystems screen has more information available than just memory pools allocated to a subsystem. It will also provide information about the number of active jobs on the system. The Work with System Status screen allows you to monitor the disk usage as well as the active jobs on your system.

- Press F11 (Display System Data).
- What are the two subsystems with the greatest number of active jobs? ____
____
- Press F12 (Cancel). This will return you to the `Work with System Status` screen.
- Press F16 (Work with Disk Status).
- How many disk units are on your system? ____________________________
What is the percentage of disk utilization on unit one and on the other units? ____
- Press F12 (Cancel).
- Press F15 (Work with Active Jobs).
- Press F20 (Subset).

This will bring up the Subset Active Jobs screen. On this screen, you can change the sequence of the display—you can view the active jobs by auxiliary storage, CPU usage, name, pool priority, and users, among other options. You can also view a subset of the jobs that have a CPU usage over a certain value. Being able to re-sequence this screen helps you view the active jobs using the highest percentage of CPU usage on the system. Now it is time for you to try some of the parameters.

- Change the `Sequence` parameter to *CPU.
- Press Enter.
- Screen print the revised `Work with Active Jobs` screen.
- Print and attach to your submission sheet.
- Label it printout #1.
- Press F20 (Subset).
- Change the `Sequence` parameter to *SBS.
- Change the `CPU Percent Limit` parameter to 0.5.
- Press Enter.
- Screen print the revised `Work with Active Jobs` screen.
- Print and attach to your submission sheet.
- Label it printout #2.

Also, notice that you can set the Work Active Job screen to dynamically refresh the screen. This uses CPU time and can affect the system's performance if several members of the class were to use this function at a given time.

PERFORMANCE SYSTEM VALUES

There are a series of system values that are related to subsystems and work management on the AS/400. Now is the time to explore these values.

- Enter the command to `Display System Values` on the command line.
- Press Enter.
- As shown in Figure L14-4, complete the chart for the system values that affect work management on your system.

System Value	Description of Value	Current Value	Available Values
QCTLSBSD			
QPFRADJ			
QDYNPTYSCD			
QDYNPTYADJ			
QMAXACTLVL			
QTSEPOOL			

Figure L14-4: System values that affect work management.

END-OF-CHAPTER AIDS

CHAPTER SUMMARY

Work management is the understanding of how the AS/400 manages jobs. Knowing it well is crucial to understanding the many pieces that go into an AS/400 system. From that knowledge comes the knowledge of how to "tune" an AS/400 for optimum performance given a wide range of requirements. And the knowledge that comes from performance analysis is crucial to making convincing arguments when the time comes to pry more money out of the company for AS/400 hardware.

It all fits together.

KEY TERMS

activation groups
activity levels
Add Job Queue Entry (ADDJOBQE)
autostart job
base pool
bound modules
Commercial Processing Workload (CPW)
communication job
communications entry
dynamic priority adjustment
dynamic priority scheduling
machine pool
modify
monitoring
performance adjustment
Performance Tools/400
performance tuning
pool sizes
prestart jobs
Relative Performance Rating (RPR)
reporting
transparent problem
User-defined pools
Work with Active Jobs (WRKACTJOB)
Work with System Activity (WRKSYSACT)
Work with System Status (WRKSYSSTS)

CHAPTER SELF-TEST

Solutions to these self-test questions are in appendix D.

True-False Questions

___ 1. The job class determines job attributes.

___ 2. Once a user submits a job to batch, the user can log off and go home for the day. The results of the batch job will be available upon the user's return.

___ 3. When a user logs onto the system, an interactive job begins. That job ends when the user logs off.

___ 4. A job that starts when a subsystem is started is called an autostart job.

___ 5. Jobs can enter a subsystem from job queues, workstations, communication, or as prestart or autostart jobs.

___ 6. All subsystems handle communication jobs as a normal practice.

___ 7. Performance adjustment prevents a single program from using up all the system resources.

___ 8. To raise a job priority, you would lower the priority number.

___ 9. The system component of a job is displayed through the Work with Active Job command.

___ 10. To see a transparent problem, you would use the WRKSYSACT command.

___ 11. The more memory a set of jobs has, the faster they will run.

Fill in the Blanks

1. An interactive job is started from a ________________, and a batch job is started from a __________________.

2. The operator establishes a new job queue called Payroll. He/she wants to be able to submit jobs to it and have them execute. He/she needs to attach the Payroll job queue to

the QBATCH subsystem. He/she would use the _____________ command to accomplish this task.

3. While logged onto an AS/400, you want to start a job on another AS/400. This is an example of a ______________ job.

4. For communication jobs to be processed by a subsystem, there must be a communication entry in the subsystem description. After the subsystem exists, you would use the ____________ command to define the entry to the system.

5. An AS/400 ships with the ____________ and ____________ subsystems up and running.

6. To determine if you have a runaway job, you would use the ____________________ command to find and end the job.

7. On the Work with Active Job command, if you want to display the jobs in order of their CPU usage, you would use the ___________ key.

8. Normally, batch jobs run at a priority of __________ , while interactive jobs run at a priority of ______________.

9. AS/400 jobs have two components: a __________ component and a __________ component.

10. The ______________ pool contains all memory not allocated to the machine or user-defined pools.

11. To change the Wait-to-Ineligible ratio on your system, you would change the ________________ value.

12. To modify the nondatabase faults on your system, you would change the __________________ value.

13. When you increase memory in the interactive pool, the memory is decreased in the ____________ pool.

Chapter Review Questions

1. Explain the following terms:
   a. Job attributes.
   b. Runtime attributes.
   c. Prestart jobs.
   d. Autostart jobs.
   e. Communication jobs.
   f. Dynamic priority scheduling.
   g. Activity level.

   h. Relative Performance Rating (RPR).

   i. Commercial Processing Workload (CPW).

2. How can a user submit a job to batch? List methods.

3. Identify the major components for system performance.

4. When users call you to complain about a performance problem (they are waiting too long for a job to process), what command do you use to find the problem? What values do you look at to determine the problem? What type of problem can occur and what are the indications for each?

5. What is meant by a "transparent problem"?

6. What method would you use to get starting values for system tuning?

7. What types of activities are disk-intensive?

15

MESSAGES, LOGS, AND CLEANUP

CHAPTER OBJECTIVES

Upon completion of this chapter, you should be able to:

- Describe messages, their purpose, and construction.
- Describe how messages become logs.
- Describe how to work with messages and logs.
- Describe the types of logs on an AS/400 and how to use them.
- Describe how to perform cleanup tasks on the AS/400.
- Describe the AS/400 system reply list, what it is, and how to use it.
- Demonstrate how to display a job log.
- Demonstrate how to set up and use job accounting.
- Describe the system values that affect security auditing.
- Demonstrate system cleanup.

OVERVIEW

A message is a unit of communication within the AS/400. It is used to cause things to happen, to send information, and to request information. The AS/400 uses a lot of messages to communicate between every piece of hardware within the system and between every executing job.

Messages are not automatically deleted; they are stored in logs to create evidence of what the AS/400 did. For this reason, messages are not destroyed; they are kept in collections called *logs*. The log provides a convenient way to retrieve old messages and take some action with them. A lot of audit, recovery, and analysis activity can be performed using logs.

The typical AS/400 produces thousands of messages every hour. There is a point after which it is impractical to keep all those messages. At that point, old logs should be deleted. Many IT departments forget to do that, and because logs are stored on disk, pay a high price for that carelessness. The activity of keeping old logs around long enough to be available if they are needed, but not long enough to cause a storage problem is called *cleanup*.

The AS/400 keeps four types of logs; that is, four collections of messages. Some are automatic—they are just there for the customer to use—others have to be started. The four logs and a brief description of how automatic they are and where they kept include:

- History (QHST):
  - Automatic.
  - Is kept in a physical file.
- Job:
  - Automatic, but what is logged can be changed.
  - Is kept within active jobs or in spooled output files for completed jobs.
- Job accounting:
  - Not automatic; requires manual start.
  - Is kept in a journal.
- Security audit:
  - Not automatic; requires manual start.
  - Is kept in a journal.

MESSAGES

History, *job log*, and security-audit journal entries all start life as mere messages. This section stays away from the esoteric, under-the-covers messages and just focuses on those that mean something to us humans. Messages can be informational (require no answer) or inquiry (require an answer).

Messages are not sent directly to addressees; they are first sent to queues called message queues. Every user currently signed onto the system, every active job, many objects, and most hardware devices have their own message queues. User message queues are usually the same name as the user profile.

When a user signs off, his message queue goes away. Each workstation device, on the other hand, also has a message queue that is always active. The difference between the two is illustrated in a common AS/400 scenario. Messages that appear on a workstation screen come from one of two message queues: the workstation's queue or the user's queue. When the night system operator wants to bring down the computer, he sends a message asking the users to please sign off in five minutes. If he sends the message to *ALL user queues, only those users currently signed on will see it. If he sends it to *ALL workstation queues, all users will see it. In addition, when other users sign on in the morning, they will get the message, "System coming down, please sign off in five minutes." This can be confusing to say the least.

One very important message queue on every AS/400 is the generic one reserved for the system operator called QSYSOPR. Messages can be sent to the system operator by directing them to the system operator message queue. The nice thing here is that a system operator also has a user profile and a message queue with that name. But when the system operator is at work, he or she usually works only with the generic queue, QSYSOPR. That way, messages are sent to and handled from a common queue without having to worry about which particular operator is on duty at the time.

Programs running on the system have their own message queues, and other programs can send messages to them.

Lastly, anyone can create a message queue with the Create Message Queue (CRTMSGQ) command. Once created, messages can be sent to it and retrieved from it. In real life, we do not get a lot of messages from each other, but we get a lot from the system and programs running within the system.

MESSAGES TO USERS

The messages users receive while signed on an AS/400 workstation will be in one of three forms: break, notify, or program.

Break Messages

Break messages are hard to miss because they interrupt the workstation to display a full screen of just the MESSAGE. Specific messages can be sent as a break message by selecting a parameter on the SNDMSG or SNDBRKMSG commands. Or, the receiving workstations can be set up to treat all incoming messages as break messages, so the person at the workstation will never miss one.

Notify Messages

Notify messages are a little subtler; they only announce themselves via a small icon on the lower-left corner of the workstation screen. These icons vary in shape according to the terminal emulation and workstation manufacturer.

Notify messages are viewed by entering the Display Message (DSPMSG) command on any command line. The AS/400 will display what is known as the first-level message. For more information, go to the second-level message. Do this by positioning the cursor to the message itself and pressing the F1 (Help) key.

Program Messages

The third message type is a program message. It appears on the bottom line of the screen when a command or program completes. Like notify messages, it is only the first-level message. For more information, position the cursor on it and press the F1 (Help) key.

Program messages often come in sets. Get in the habit of looking for a small plus sign (+) on the far-right of the program messages. The plus sign indicates that there are more messages. Look at the other messages by putting the cursor on the message and pressing the Page Down key. Go back up the list by pressing the Page Up key. Press the F1 or Help key on any of them to get the second-level message.

MESSAGE CONSTRUCTIONS

Messages are kept in database tables called *message files.* The system comes with several message files, and developers often create others for their own use. To see what a message looks like, use the Work with Message Description (WRKMSGD) command like this:

```
WRKMSGD CPA4002
```

"CPA4002" is an example of a message key. This command will present a screen of several messages, in alphabetical order, with message CPA4002 at the top of the list. Use option 5 (Display Message) to get the system to produce a menu similar to the one shown in Figure 15-1.

```
                      Select Message Details to Display
                                                        System:   BIGBLUE
Message ID . . . . . . . . . :   CPA4002
Message file . . . . . . . . :   QCPFMSG
  Library  . . . . . . . . . :     QSYS
Message text . . . . . . . . :   Verify alignment on printer &3. (I G N R C)


Select one of the following:

     1. Display message text
     2. Display field data
     3. Display reply specifications
     4. Display special reply values
     5. Display message attributes

    30. All of the above


Selection __


F3=Exit   F12=Cancel
(C) COPYRIGHT IBM CORP. 1980, 1998.
```

Figure 15-1: Work with Message Descriptions (WRKMSGD) command menu.

The figure shows the menu of what can be done with message CPA4002. At the top of the screen, it also tells us that the message is kept in message file QCPFMSG in library QSYS. We also see a version of the short, or first-level, message text. If that is all we wanted to find out, we could just exit this screen. Take option 1 (`Display Message Text`) to see the message text. Figure 15-2 contains a sample.

```
                     Display Formatted Message Text
                                                        System:   BIGBLUE
Message ID . . . . . . . . . :   CPA4002
Message file . . . . . . . . :   QCPFMSG
  Library  . . . . . . . . . :     QSYS

Message . . . . :   Verify alignment on printer &3. (I G N R E C)
Cause . . . . . :   The forms may not be aligned correctly.  The first line
  for the file is &4.
Possible choices for replying to message . . . . . . . . . . . . . . . :
  I - To continue printing aligned forms starting with the next line of the
    file, type an I.
  G - To continue printing aligned forms skipping to the next form and
    printing the first line again, type a G.
  N - To print the first line again on the next form and to verify the
    alignment,
    1. Press Stop only if Start and Stop are two keys, or press Reset.
    2. Advance the paper to the next form by pressing Form Feed/New Page.
    3. Adjust the alignment with the forms adjust control.
                                                                   More...
Press Enter to continue.

F3=Exit   F11=Display unformatted message text   F12=Cancel
```

```
            Display Formatted Message Text
                                                   System:   BIGBLUE
Message ID . . . . . . . . . :   CPA4002
Message file . . . . . . . . :   QCPFMSG
  Library  . . . . . . . . . :     QSYS

    4. Press Ready, Start, or Start/Stop.
    5. Type an N.
R - To print the first line again on the current form and to verify    the
alignment if the forms are not aligned,
    1. Press Stop only if Start and Stop are two keys, or press Reset.
    2. Adjust the alignment with the forms adjust control.
    3. Press Ready, Start, or Start/Stop.
    4. Type an R.
  E - To eject a page and print the first line again,
    1. Press Stop only if Start and Stop are two keys, or press Reset.
    2. Adjust the alignment with the forms adjust control.
    3. Press Ready, Start, or Start/Stop.
    4. Type an E.

                                                 More...
Press Enter to continue.

F3=Exit   F11=Display unformatted message text   F12=Cancel
```

```
                    Display Formatted Message Text
                                                         System:   BIGBLUE
Message ID . . . . . . . . . :   CPA4002
Message file . . . . . . . . :   QCPFMSG
  Library  . . . . . . . . . :     QSYS

  C - To cancel processing, type a C.




                                                      Bottom
Press Enter to continue.

F3=Exit   F11=Display unformatted message text   F12=Cancel
```

Figure 15-2: Details of message text for message CPA4002 (screens 1-3).

This figure repeats the message text at the top and shows possible causes for the message, the possible replies to the message, and what each one means. There is more to it; if we page down, we also see the rest of the message details.

Messages can have variables in them. Variables are areas of data that are not filled in when the message is created. They are filled in when the message is displayed. The example message text for CPA4002 has a single variable, &3. The cause message also has a variable, &4.

Option 2 from the menu shown in Figure 15-1 shows all MSGDTA variables. Figure 15-3 contains a sample.

```
                         Display Field Data

Message ID . . . . . . . . . :   CPA4002
Message file . . . . . . . . :   QCPFMSG
  Library  . . . . . . . . . :     QSYS


                                    Decimal      Vary
Field     Data Type     Length     Positions    Length     Dump
 &1       *CHAR           10                               *NO
 &2       *CHAR           10                               *NO
 &3       *CHAR           10                               *NO
 &4       *BIN             2                               *NO
 &5       *CHAR           10                               *NO
 &6       *CHAR           10                               *NO
 &7       *CHAR            0                               *NO
 &8       *CHAR            0                               *NO
 &9       *CHAR            0                               *NO
 &10      *CHAR            0                               *NO
                                                                   More...
Press Enter to continue.

F3=Exit   F12=Cancel
```

Figure 15-3: Variables used in message CPA4002.

Later, we will see how to access a message's variables directly when creating entries in the system reply list.

With the variables supplied, the message in Figure 15-2 and 15-3 can come out looking like:

```
Verify alignment on printer ARPRT01. (I G N R E C)
```

SYSTEM OPERATOR MESSAGE QUEUE: QSYSOPR

In most AS/400 IT departments, the most important message queue comes with the AS/400 as a default and is called the *system operator message queue*. It is always named QSYSOPR. This is where all the really important system information goes. All batch jobs and any problems on the system, unless otherwise handled, go to message queue QSYSOPR. When the system itself feels the need to burp, it sends a message to QSYSOPR. There are two things to remember about this queue:

- Important things can get lost among many unimportant messages.
- Operators take lunch breaks and can miss time-critical messages.

The AS/400 has a way around these problems. One is to create a special message queue just for really hot system messages. Do this with this command:

```
CRTMSGQ QSYS/QSYSMSG TEXT('System operator really +important message queue')
```

The message queue must be named QSYSMSG and placed in the QSYS library. Once it is in existence, the AS/400 has a predetermined list of messages it will send to this queue instead of the QSYSOPR message queue. For a complete list of these messages and what they mean, see *OS/400 CL Programming V4R4*.

SYSTEM REPLY LIST

System inquiry messages require a reply and can start to get in the way when they come up constantly, hanging up programs until the operator responds. The response to these messages is almost always the same, so all they do is delay processing.

For these situations, the AS/400 has a *system reply list*, which is a list of inquiry-only messages that the system will respond to for us. An example would be a message to change forms on a laser printer. The problem would be that the printer only contains blank white stock paper (called the *form* in AS/400 parlance). The operator would not actually change forms on such a printer, he just responds to the message to have the system go ahead and resume printing. However, a line printer in the computer room will not be so predictable. It does take different forms, so the same message to it would require some action and a response from the operator.

With the system reply list, the operator can have the system automatically answer for him when the message appears. In the case of the two printers, the message can also be interpreted to determine which ones the system should respond to and which ones to pass on to the user or system operator.

The system reply list is not automatically used by all jobs. A job (or its job description) has to have the parameter INQMSGRPY(*SYSRPYL) specified or it will ignore this list. Most jobs do not have this set. The AS/400 comes with a basic system reply list that looks like Figure 15-4.

Sequence Number	Message Identifier	Compare Value	Reply	Dump
10	CPA0700	*NONE	D	*YES
20	RPG0000	*NONE	D	*YES
30	CBE0000	*NONE	D	*YES
40	PLI0000	*NONE	D	*YES

Figure 15-4: System reply list.

Figure 15-4 is a little difficult to decipher. The trailing (or right-most) zeroes of each message identifier are treated like wildcards. This means if any error starting with the error number's trailing zeros and going to the 9s in those spaces, or to another message number, will receive the response specified in the Reply column. We know that does not mean much, so try these examples:

- From the table, all messages CPA0700 through CPA0799 from any job with INQMSGRPY (*SYSRPYL) will be answered automatically with a "D" (causing a program dump).
- From the table, all messages RPG0000 through RPG9999 will be answered.
- If the table had an entry with Sequence 15 (putting it between Sequence Numbers 10 and 20), and that entry's message identifier was CPA0751, then all messages CPA0700 through CPA0751 will be answered.
- One last item, if the table had an entry with Sequence 15 (putting it between Sequence Numbers 10 and 20), with a message's identifier of CPA0750, then all messages CPA0700 through CPA0750 will be answered and all messages CPA0750 through CPA0759 will be answered.

Reply list entries are added to the list with the ADDRPYLE command.

To illustrate, let us walk through the Change Paper message discussed above. Assume this particular AS/400 has a line printer directly attached to the AS/400. The line printer has a device name of QSYSPRT. Also assume the AS/400 has any number of laser printers attached to it, each with its own name. We want the AS/400 to automatically respond when an align-forms message (which is CPA4002) is received for any printer except the line printer in the computer room. In other words:

- If the align-forms message is not for QSYSPRT, it must be for a laser printer and the system will just reply with an "I" for ignore.
- If the align-forms message is for QSYSPRT, it is for the line printer and the message will be passed through to the intended destination.

First look at the message construction to see where the printer name is. The command to do this is WRKMSGD CPA4002. Refer to Figures 15-1, 15-2, and 15-3 for details of the screen associated with this command.

Now, using the ADDRPYLE command, add two reply message entries to the system reply list shown in Figure 15-4—one for the laser printer that always gets an answer of "I," and one for the line printer that we want the user or system operator to see and respond to. Add message CPA4002 immediately after CPA0700.

We position new reply entries by the Sequence Number—CPA0700 is Sequence Number 10; and the next entry, RPG0000, is Sequence Number 20—so we will use any number in between. Let's try Sequence Number 12. Here is the command:

```
ADDRPYLE SEQNBR(12) MSGID(CPA4002) RPY(*RQD) +CMPDTA('QSYSPRT' 21)
```

Refer to 15-2 and 15-3. The message text on 15-2 has an &3 as the variable that contained the printer name. On 15-3, that variable is the third one in the list, and it starts on column 21 (the first two fields are 10 characters each, 10 + 10 is 20, the third field must start on 21). When the message is sent, column 21 will have the name of the printer, so that is where we specify the comparison for value QSYSPRT.

This reply list entry will take care of the requirement that the align-form messages destined for the system printer will be forwarded to an operator who will have to respond to it. Here is a reply list entry without the compare message to catch CPA4002's for the other printers:

```
ADDRPYLE SEQNBR(14) MSGID(CPA4002) RPY(G)
```

This entry makes no comparison for the printer device name. Of the two messages, the one for QSYSPRT had to be first, otherwise, the no-compare message would have passed anything (even QSYSPRT), and no message would have hit the reply for QSYSPRT. Figure 15-5 shows the system reply list after those changes.

Sequence Number	Message Identifier	Compare Value	Reply	Dump
10	CPA0700	*NONE	D	*YES
12	CPA4002	'QSYSPRT' 21	&RQD	*NO
14	CPA4002	*NONE	G	*NO
20	RPG0000	*NONE	D	*YES
30	CBE0000	*NONE	D	*YES
40	PLI0000	*NONE	D	*YES

Figure 15-5: System reply list after changes.

The reply to the reply list entry on sequence is *RQD, meaning that a reply is still required of the operator or user and so the message is just sent through. The operator/user still has to reply to it.

HISTORY LOGS (QHST)

History logs are:

- Automatic.
- Kept in a physical file.

Everything that the AS/400 does results in a message going somewhere around the system. In addition to their intended destinations, one place all high-level messages (system activities, job information, device status, operator messages, and more) go to is a history message queue named QHST.

A program receives those messages and writes them to a physical file that is called the *history log*. This history log is named QHSTYYJJJN:

- YY is the year on which the physical file was created.
- JJJ is the Julian date on which the physical file was created.
- N is a Sequence Number (0–9, A–Z).

The maximum number of records in this physical file is set in system value QHSTLOGSIZ. To find which history logs are on an AS/400, use the command:

```
WRKOBJ QSYS/QHST* *FILE
```

There may be many history logs on an AS/400, but only one can be current. The contents of this log can be displayed with the command:

```
DSPLOG
```

The nice thing about a log and its command is that it can quickly limit the messages displayed. For example, the search can be limited to messages issued during a specific time period, by a specific job, or certain message IDs. Figures 15-6 and 15-7 show the prompted version of the command DSPLOG.

```
                          Display Log (DSPLOG)

Type choices, press Enter.

Log . . . . . . . . . . . . . .   QHST          QHST
Time period for log output:
  Start time and date:
  Beginning time . . . . . . . .  *AVAIL        Time, *AVAIL
  Beginning date . . . . . . . .  *CURRENT      Date, *CURRENT, *BEGIN
  End time and date:
  Ending time  . . . . . . . . .  *AVAIL        Time, *AVAIL
  Ending date  . . . . . . . . .  *CURRENT      Date, *CURRENT, *END
Output . . . . . . . . . . . . .  *             *, *PRINT, *PRTWRAP




                                                                  Bottom
F3=Exit   F4=Prompt   F5=Refresh   F10=Additional parameters   F12=Cancel
F13=How to use this display        F24=More keys
```

Figure 15-6: Prompted version of DSPLOG command (part 1 of 2).

From this screen, press F10 (Additional Parameters), and then press the Page Down key to get more information as shown in Figure 15-7.

```
                        Display Log (DSPLOG)

 Type choices, press Enter.

                       Additional Parameters

 Jobs to display . . . . . . . .   *NONE        Name, *NONE
   User . . . . . . . . . . . . .               Name
   Number . . . . . . . . . . . .               000000-999999
               + for more values

 Message identifier . . . . . . .  *ALL         Name, *ALL
               + for more values

                                                              Bottom
 F3=Exit   F4=Prompt   F5=Refresh   F12=Cancel   F13=How to use this display
 F24=More keys
```

Figure 15-7: Prompted version of DSPLOG command (part 2 of 2).

From the screens shown in the figures, we can specify a beginning date and time to to display the messages. This is handy when researching a problem that the operator knows happened today, but is unsure of what time it happened. Or, if the operator knows a problem happened before a particular time, like before lunch, the operator can use the ENDING TIME and ENDING DATE parameters to specify these.

If the operator knows the user or the job number, the operator can specify these on the JOBS TO DISPLAY, USER, and NUMBER parameters. Note that most of the time, no one knows the job number, but we probably know the user. Also, these parameters can be added to by placing a plus sign on the + FOR MORE VALUES parameter and pressing Enter. That way, messages for several users can be displayed. Finally, if the operator knows the message identification, the operator can specify that on the MESSAGE IDENTIFIER parameter. Figure 15-8 shows a sample of a screen of history log data.

```
                         Display History Log Contents

Operating System/400 grace period expires in 67 days on 08/30/99.
Cleanup has started.
Job 187292/QPGMR/QCLNUSRMSG started on 06/25/99 at 02:00:02 in subsystem QCTL
Job 187293/QPGMR/QCLNSYSMSG started on 06/25/99 at 02:00:02 in subsystem QCTL
Job 187294/QPGMR/QCLNSYSPRT started on 06/25/99 at 02:00:02 in subsystem QCTL
Job 187295/QPGMR/QCLNSYSLOG started on 06/25/99 at 02:00:02 in subsystem QCTL
Job 187296/QPGMR/QCLNCALITM started on 06/25/99 at 02:00:02 in subsystem QCTL
Job 187297/QPGMR/QCLNUSRPGM started on 06/25/99 at 02:00:02 in subsystem QCTL
User cleanup program started.
User cleanup program successfully completed.
Cleanup of OfficeVision/400 calendar items started.
Cleanup of operator and work station messages started.
Cleanup of job logs and other system output started.
Job 187297/QPGMR/QCLNUSRPGM ended on 06/25/99 at 02:00:02; 1 seconds used; en
Cleanup of user messages started.
Cleanup of job logs and other system output successfully completed.
Job 187294/QPGMR/QCLNSYSPRT ended on 06/25/99 at 02:00:02; 1 seconds used; en
                                                                       More...
Press Enter to continue.

F3=Exit   F10=Display all   F12=Cancel
```

Figure 15-8: Results of DSPLOG command.

The messages in the figure are not shown with their message identifiers, although each has one. At first glance, it looks cryptic. There is a lot in the QHST file. Sometimes when things happen that do not get into other logs, like the job log, they end up here. However, placing the cursor over any line and pressing the F1 (Help) key can clear up message obscurity. Figure 15-9 shows an example of expanding one of the lines from Figure 15-8.

```
                       Additional Message Information

Message ID . . . . . . :   CPF1164       Severity . . . . . . . :   00
Message type . . . . . :   Completion
Date sent  . . . . . . :   06/25/99      Time sent  . . . . . . :   02:00:02

Message . . . . :   Job 187297/QPGMR/QCLNUSRPGM ended on 06/25/99 at 02:00:02;
  1 seconds used; end code 0

Cause . . . . . :   Job 187297/QPGMR/QCLNUSRPGM completed on 06/25/99 at
  02:00:02 after it used 1 seconds processing unit time.  The job had ending
  code 0. The job ended after 1 routing steps with a secondary ending code of
  0.  The job ending codes and their meanings are as follows:
     0 - The job completed normally.
    10 - The job completed normally during controlled ending or controlled
  subsystem ending.
    20 - The job exceeded end severity (ENDSEV job attribute).
                                                                       More...
Press Enter to continue.

F3=Exit   F6=Print   F9=Display message details   F12=Cancel
F21=Select assistance level
```

Figure 15-9: Expansion of the line marked on Figure 15-8 with cursor.

The operator who knows how to quickly wade through all those records can pull out a lot of information.

When one history file fills up, the system creates another one. It does not take much time for history logs to take up quite a bit of system space. The best way to keep them manageable is to have the system automatically clean them up (see the section on System Cleanup below).

It is particularly important to save and delete all noncurrent history files before doing a SAVSYS (Save System), particularly prior to installing a new release of the operating system (OS). Cleaning up old files will save a lot of time.

JOB LOGS

Job logs are:

- Automatic, but what is logged can be changed.
- Kept:
  - Within active jobs.
  - In spooled output files for completed jobs.

Every job that runs on the AS/400 collects messages into an internal log while it is running. When the job finishes, the contents of the job log are written to a spooled output file in queue QPJOBLOG or QEZJOBLOG.

The user or computer operator can change the types of messages that any job logs have. Job logs can even be turned off; however, that can be a risky practice.

If an AS/400 job terminates abnormally, the computer produces a job log even if logging is turned off. The danger comes in when a job completes "normally" as far as the operating system is concerned, but still had a problem—like it produces a report that does not balance. The job log is the only audit of what really occurred when the job was running.

Job logs come down to this: Most of the time they are not needed and take up valuable DASD space. The temptation is to not collect them. But the one time a crucial program fails, the only audit of what happened will probably be the job log. The system operator's task is to balance DASD space against the need for an audit trail.

A job may not produce a job log for any of several reasons. This is no big deal most of the time, but when a "problem" job completes without producing a job log, find out why by looking in the history log (refer to the section labeled History Logs [QHST]) for message CPF1164. The reason a log was not produced will be encoded in the message. The codes are listed in *OS/400 Work Management V4R4.*

LOGGING LEVEL

Specify what messages should be collected for any job by manipulating the job's *logging level.*

As a job becomes active on an AS/400, one of the characteristics obtained from the Job Description is the logging level of that job. Before the job starts, changing the job description with the Change

Job Description (CHGJOBD) or Work with Job Description (WRKJOBD) command can change the logging level.

After a job is active on the system, the logging level can be changed with the Change Job (CHGJOB) command. In any of these commands, the key parameter that controls the logging level is LOG. There are three parts to the LOG parameter. Figure 15-10 shows a representation of it.

```
Message logging:
   Level . . . . . . . . . . . . .   4          0-4, *SAME
   Severity . . . . . . . . . . .    00         0-99, *SAME
   Text . . . . . . . . . . . . .    *NOLIST     *SAME, *MSG, *SECLVL,
*NOLIST
```

Figure 15-10: Sample LOG parameter.

- Level accepts a numeric code from 0 to 4.

  0 Nothing is logged.

  1 Only messages sent to the job's external message queue that have a severity greater than or equal to that specified under Severity (discussed below). Examples are job start/stop time and its completion status.

  2 Level 1 messages plus:

  - Any requests/commands from a CL program that have a severity greater than or equal to that specified under Severity (discussed below). All messages associated with those requests/commands as long as the messages have a severity greater than or equal to that specified under Severity (discussed below).

  3 Level 1 messages plus:

  - Level 2 messages plus:
  - All requests/commands from a CL program. All messages associated with those requests/commands as long as the messages have a severity greater than or equal to that specified under Severity (discussed below).

  4 Level 1 messages plus:

  - Level 2 messages plus:
  - Level 3 messages plus:
  - Any message from anywhere with a severity greater than or equal to that specified under Severity.

- Severity specifies the Severity Level of the requests/commands/messages logged. On the AS/400, messages have *severities* that range from 00 to 99. The 00 messages are informational only. The 99 messages tend to be the last message before a program abnormally terminates. Most serious job messages are level 30 or higher. That means when a severity of 30 is specified, with a level greater than 0, and text other than *NOLIST, all messages of severity 30 through 99 will be captured.

- *Text* is the amount of message text to be written to the job log. All messages on the AS/400 have two levels:

- Level 1 is the short, eighty-bytes-or-less version.
- Level 2 is the long version for those new to the system or the particular message. This is sometimes referred to as the *second-level message.*

The possible values for text are:

- *MSG. Only the level 1 text of the message is written to the log.
- *SECLVL. Level 2, or second-level, messages are written to the log.
- *NOLIST. No messages are logged unless the program ends abnormally.

Most AS/400 IT departments specify a 4 for Level, and 0 for Severity. After that, *NOLIST is fairly standard for stable, established applications, and *MSG is used for others or for new applications. For AS/400-supplied job description objects, QCTL, QINTER, QBATCH, and QPGMR come with LOG(4 0 *NOLIST). An operator or user can create his/her own or change these with the CHGJOBD command.

There is one trap about message logging for interactive jobs. An interactive job ends only when the user signs off with the SIGNOFF command. A parameter on that command, LOG, can have a default of *NOLIST that allows no logging to occur no matter to what level the job-description logging level is set.

To get logging to occur according to the job description, the command's LOG parameter needs to be set to LOG(*LIST). Do so with the following command:

```
CHGCMDDFT SIGNOFF NEWDFT('LOG(*LIST)')
```

DISPLAYING THE JOB LOG

From time to time, the system operator will want to look at a job log. The log can be a part of a running job or on the spool file for a completed job. To display the job log from:

- A current interactive job, do any of the following:
  - Enter DSPJOBLOG on command line and press Enter, followed by F10.
  - Enter WRKJOB on command line, press Enter, select option 10, then press F10.
  - From the screen of any interactive job, press F10.
  - If a job is still active but from another user, do either:
    - WRKUSRJOB (if you know who the user is).
    - WRKACTJOB. Find the job and select option 5 (`Work with Job`), then select option 10 (`Display Job Log`).
  - Press System Request key, option 3 (`Display Current Job`). Select option 10 (`Display Job Log`) and press F10.
  - Sign off from the session, making sure LOG(*LIST) is set on the Sign-off command. Then sign onto a new session and browse the job log from QEZJOBLOG.
- For any other job, do either of the following:
  - If the job is no longer active in the system, do WRKUSRJOB, select option 8 (`Display Spooled File`), find last (which will be the latest) QPJOBLOG. Select option 5 (`Display Job Log`).

- WRKOUTQ QPJOBLOG (or QEZJOBLOG). The resulting list can be hundreds of screens long. Use F18 to quickly go to the bottom where the most current job logs are.

JOB ACCOUNTING

Job Accounting is:

- Not automatic; requires manual start.
- Data is kept in a journal receiver.

Job accounting captures information about jobs that reveal who uses what on the computer. It tracks usage of processing unit, printer, display stations, database, and communications functions.

A key distinction of job accounting is the use of the accounting code. A job's accounting code can be loaded into the job description or the user profiles. The accounting code is optional because it is only a grouping device; it is not necessary for anything else. The accounting code helps make job accounting more meaningful because it can be used to analyze computer resource usage not just by job, but by all jobs in a particular department (or by individual).

For example, if all the jobs accounting runs has ACC as an accounting code prefix and this is further separated into codes ACCAR for Accounts Receivable and ACCAP for Accounts Payable, very specific usage monitoring could occur. Accounting codes can be up to fifteen characters in length.

What is interesting about job accounting information is that it has basic information to monitor other things about the jobs on the system. It contains response time information, DASD IO information, user, and start/stop times. For this reason, it can monitor job performance without having to use Performance Monitoring tools. Or, if the AS/400 experienced sudden performance degradation and Performance Monitor was not on but job accounting was, that log can give a savvy operator a pretty good idea of what happened to cause the degradation.

SET UP JOB ACCOUNTING

Job accounting is really a kind of journaling. We include an overview of how to set it up but for more information on journaling, refer to Chapter 17, Journaling.

To set up job accounting, start by creating a *journal* and *journal receiver*. These will be in a library (logically enough), and it is a good idea to create a special library and receiver unique for job accounting. For performance reasons, it is a lot smarter to create a dedicated job accounting library. Create the library with this command:

```
CRTLIB <library name>
```

Create a journal receiver. Receiver names should be ten characters long (six alpha characters followed by four numeric, and generally start with 0001 as the numeric). This is an accounting journal; therefore, ACCJRN0001 would be a good name.

```
CRTJRNRCV JRNRCV(<library name>/ACCJRN001)
```

then create the journal. For job accounting, the operator has no choice about the library or journal name. Here is the command:

```
CRTJRN QSYS/QACGJRN
```

Set system value QACGLVL, which controls job accounting logging. Use the WRKSYSVAL command to reset its contents as needed to one of the following values:

- *NONE. Turns off job accounting.
- *JOB. Captures the performance portion of each job.
- *PRINT. Captures each job's printing information.
- *JOB*PRINT. Combines *JOB and *PRINT entries.

It may seem silly to have a value of *NONE, but one strategy for a company that does not intend to use job accounting all the time is to set up the journal and journal receiver and control data collection simply by changing this system value.

When a journal receiver fills up or if job accounting is to be used sporadically, change journals. Use the command:

```
CHGJRN  JRNRCV(*GEN)
```

DISPLAYING JOB ACCOUNTING JOURNAL

Because job accounting information is in a *job accounting journal*, there are two ways of getting to the data:

- Display Journal (DSPJRN). This captures many records from the journal. It is best to use this command's parameter, outfile(*OUTFILE) to collect the extracted records into a physical file. Then, the entries can be browsed there.
- Receive Journal Entry (RCVJRNE). For specific, real-time journal entries, rcvjrne is usually used by a programmer in a CL program he/she writes.

Journal entries have two sets of fields:

- Lots of fields that make up the header information.
- A big blank field for the original contents of the journaled data.

This level is getting pretty deep and the system operator does not necessarily have to be an expert on reading the contents of journals. If one were interested, they are best read with AS/400 Query. The AS/400 comes with two skeleton files and formats that contain the field layouts for these entries. They are known as the *field reference files* for the journal entries:

- QSYS/QAJBACG (Format QWTJAJBE).
- QSYS/QAPTACG (Format QSPJAPTE).

To read those journal entries (if you are a masochist), you could take the fields from those reference files and create a DDS for them. It is more realistic to just create duplicates of each (CRTDUPOBJ command) in your library. Name the duplicates whatever you like. Then, when you display the journal entries, use this command to extract job records:

```
DSPJRN JRN(QACGJRN) JRNCDE(A) ENTTYP(JB) + OUTPUT(*OUTFILE) +
OUTFILE(<your library>/<your job file (the duplicate)>)
```

That would extract the job records into your new physical file. From there, querying the file's contents will be very easy. Accounting journal entries appear in three formats identified by the journal entry code:

- JB for job-related records.
- DP for directly printed files.
- SP for spooled files.

There are not many direct print jobs on an AS/400; therefore, there will not be a lot of DP records. But there will be a lot of JB and SP records.

SECURITY AUDIT JOURNAL

The security audit journal is:

- Not automatic; requires manual start.
- Data is kept in a journal receiver.

While system history logs and job logs are always there, the *AS/400 Security Audit Journal* must be set up and activated before it can be used. The Security Audit Journal audits security-related activities. The operator sets what will be logged.

The Security Audit Journal focuses on activities of an individual user, a specific object, or one individual's contact with a specific object. It can monitor for both systemwide and user-specific activities.

Security auditing on the AS/400 is a powerful tool for detecting security problems, because it does not just log the successful completion of a function; it will log any attempt at a function. In other words, if an unauthorized user attempted to use System Service Tools (SST) to circumvent the AS/400 security, and that user was monitored just for *SERVICE, the log would show his unsuccessful attempts (and, hopefully, no successful ones).

Typically, security audit is turned on and off for relatively brief periods of time and focused on specific problems: user(s) or object(s). The reason is that security audit is a tightly focused problem-solving tool. An operator will turn it on for a day or two, turn it off, and review the results. It really does not need to be running all the time.

SET UP THE SYSTEM FOR SECURITY AUDITING

To set up security auditing:

- Create a library for the journal receiver with the CRTLIB command. Name it anything, but it should be a library dedicated to this journal. Do not use any production libraries.
- Create a journal receiver in this library. Use ten characters for its name (the first six of which are alpha characters and the last four are "0001." For example, SECAUD0001. Use this command:

```
CRTJRNRCV JRNRCV(<your library>/SECAUD001) + AUT(*EXCLUDE) +
TEXT('Security Auditing Journal Receiver')
```

- The security journal must be named QAUDJRN and it must reside in QSYS. Create the journal with the CRTJRN command (use the library/file names as indicated):

```
CRTJRN QSYS/QAUDJRN + JRNRCV(<your library>/SECAUD001) + AUT(*EXCLUDE) +
TEXT('Security Auditing Journal')
```

SET THE SYSTEM VALUES

There are four system values that affect security auditing. Use the WRKSYSVAL command to display or change them:

- QAUDCTL (Audit Control). This starts and stops security auditing. Change this to anything other than *NONE to start capturing security audit information. Change it back to *NONE to stop capturing security audit information.
- QAUDLVL (Audit Level). This specifies what actions on objects are audited. Because an audit level usually contains more than one value and there are many values, refer to appendix B in this book for a list of them, or refer to IBM manual *OS/400 Security- Reference V4R4, Planning the Auditing of Actions* for a description of all possible actions.
- QAUDFRCLVL (Audit Force Level). This is a performance function; it blocks the audit records before they are written to the journal. There is a trade-off here. For absolute protection so that no security journal records are lost in the event of a system failure, set this value to 1. However, performance can be degraded. Rather than try to figure out optimum blocking, use the value *SYS and the system will calculate some optimum value for this value. If the system goes down, a minimum (but some) number of records may be lost. Do not get too caught up with this system value; remember, no records are lost if the AS/400 does not go down abnormally.
- QAUDENDACN (Audit End Action). This tells the system what to do if it is unable to write an audit record to a journal. The default is *NOTIFY and the system just sends a message to the system operator. However, if the organization requires that the security audit be active in order for the AS/400 to even be up, specify *PWRDWNSYS. The instant the system is unable to write a record to the Security Audit Journal, it does a PWRDWNSYS *IMMED. Because it can wreak havoc with users, do not do this unless absolutely necessary. Also, if it is selected, ensure good journal change/backup/cleanup procedures are in place. There are two reasons security audit may not be able to write to a journal:
  - It is full and needs to be changed.
  - It is damaged. In most cases, an IPL is necessary to resume monitoring.

There are also two values, one on every object and one on every user profile, that affect what is audited.

- AUDLVL (Audit Level). This is a parameter on the user profile that specifies what actions are audited for that user. Here are the possible values:
  - *NONE. Turns off auditing this user.
  - *CMD. Logs all the commands used by this user.
  - *CREATE. Logs all objects created by this user.
  - *DELETE. Logs all objects deleted by this user.
  - *JOBDTA. Logs all job actions by this user.

- *OBJMGT. Logs all objects moved or renamed by this user.
- *OFCSRV. Logs some OfficeVision tasks by this user.
- *OPTICAL. Logs all optical tasks performed by this user.
- *PGMADP. Logs when this user runs programs that adopt authority.
- *SAVRST. Logs save/restore functions performed by this user.
- *SECURITY. Logs security functions performed by this user.
- *SERVICE. Logs attempts by this user to access SST or DST.
- *SPLFDTA. Logs spool file activity performed by this user.
- *SYSMGT. Logs system management tasks performed by this user.

- OBJAUD (Object Audit). This is a parameter on object descriptions that specify what actions are audited for that object. Here are the possible values:
  - *NONE. Turns off auditing for this object.
  - *USRPRF. Only reports the auditing information called for by the user profile parameter AUDLVL.
  - *CHANGE. Reports any changes (or change attempts) made to the object.
  - *ALL. Audits any attempts to change or even use the object.

SET SECURITY AUDITING ON OBJECTS/USERS

The AUDLVL and OBJAUD work together to provide an auditing picture. Although many scenarios are possible, the following sections contain three typical ones:

Specific File—Any User

- Use the CHGOBJAUD command to change the specific file object's OBJECT AUDITING VALUE (OBJAUD) to *CHANGE or *ALL.
- Ensure the system value, QAUDCTL, is set to *OBJAUD.

Many Files—One User

- Use the CHGOBJAUD command to change the file object's Object Auditing Value (OBJAUD) to *USRPRF. (*Note*: The CHGOBJAUD command accepts generic library and file names; use these to save time. However, do not use *ALL/*ALL, because it can take hours to implement. Also, carrying that much security auditing could degrade your system. It is better to specify any subset or *ALL files within a library.)
- Use the CHGUSRAUD command to set the user profile's OBJAUD value to *CHANGE or *ALL.
- Ensure the system value, QAUDCTL, is set to *OBJAUD.

One File—One User

Use the CHGOBJAUD command to change the specific file object's Object Auditing Value (OBJAUD) to *USRPRF.

Use the CHGUSRAUD command to set the user profile's Object Auditing Value (OBJAUD) to *CHANGE or *ALL.

Ensure the system value, QAUDCTL, is set to *OBJAUD.

MANAGING SECURITY AUDIT JOURNAL RECEIVERS

The Security Audit Journal is just a journal. For more information on the subject, refer to chapter 17, Journaling. Because of the extra security on it (through the AUT(*EXCLUDE) parameter on the CRTJRNRCV and CRTJRN commands), only the security officer or object owner can get to the information. Also, the system puts an exclusive lock on the journal while monitoring is taking place. Therefore, not everyone can get to the journal, and—even when the security officer can—many normal journal commands cannot be done because of this system lock.

For these reasons, only use this journal and its receivers to journal security audit records. Do not use it to do any regular database file journaling.

If the value specified in system value QAUDENDACN is *PWRDWNSYS, do not let this receiver fill up. Create a special message queue for audit messages and associate that queue with the QSYS/QAUDJRN journal. Then have a message-handling program written that monitors this queue. If it gets a "threshold reached" message, it should change receivers and pass the message on to the system operator. For normal operation, periodically:

- Change receivers: CHGJRN JRN(QAUDJRN) JRNRCV(*GEN).
- Save the receiver with the SAVOBJ command, specifying object type *JRNRCV.
- Delete the old receiver after it is saved with the DLTJRNRCV command.
- To look at the contents of a receiver when the current one is unknown, WRKJRNA QAUDJRN will display which receiver is currently attached.

VIEWING SECURITY AUDIT JOURNAL RECEIVERS

View or use the contents of the Security Audit Journal receivers by:

- Command DSPJRN QAUDJRN. This displays the contents of the journal receiver.
- Command DSPJRN QAUDJRN OUTPUT(*OUTFILE). Accesses the resulting outfile with a query or a program.

SECURITY AUDIT PLANNING

Many AS/400 companies make the same set of mistakes when implementing security auditing. They ask for too much data, so it becomes unusable. Or they set up elaborate auditing rules and never review the data. Security auditing is nice and it gets rave reviews from auditors, but don't use it without a need. There is a performance cost to using it and it uses up DASD. Plan very carefully what it is about security you want to monitor. Ask yourself:

- Who am I concerned about?
- What objects am I concerned about?
- What types of security failures would I like to know about?

Then implement only these and use the data. Unlike other logging, security audit journaling is sometimes activated for a short period of time just to monitor for a suspected problem. Then the monitor is turned off and the results are reviewed.

SYSTEM CLEANUP

If people cleaned their homes like they clean up their computers, we would buy new homes every year just to escape the clutter of the old one. Obviously, this would not work. However, that is how most computer installations approach cleanup. It is fortunate that computer garbage does not smell. The AS/400 has several tools available to help clean up old data—use them. A "clean" AS/400 IPLs faster, its overall performance is much better, and it does not require new DASD so often.

AUTOMATIC CLEANUP

The AS/400 comes with an automatic system cleanup program that works fairly well for keeping the amount of old messages and logs down to a manageable size. To get into the cleanup screen, enter:

```
GO CLEANUP
```

on the command line and select option 1 from the cleanup menu. The resulting screen is shown in Figure 15-11.

```
                         Change Cleanup Options                         BIGBLUE
                                                             06/25/99  08:23:43
 Type choices below, then press Enter.

 Allow automatic cleanup . . . . . . . . . . . .   Y               Y=Yes, N=No

 Time cleanup starts each day  . . . . . . . . .   01:00:00        00:00:00-
                                                                   23:59:59,
                                                                   *SCDPWROFF,
                                                                   *NONE

 Number of days to keep:
   User messages . . . . . . . . . . . . . . . .   7               1-366, *KEEP
   System and workstation messages . . . . . . .   4               1-366, *KEEP
   Job logs and other system output  . . . . . .   7               1-366, *KEEP
  System journals and system logs . . . . . . . .  15              1-366, *KEEP
   OfficeVision for AS/400 calendar items  . . . . 1               1-366, *KEEP


 F1=Help   F3=Exit   F5=Refresh   F12=Cancel
```

Figure 15-11: Automatic cleanup menu.

The first parameter, Allow Automatic Cleanup, accepts a Y or N and tells the system to do the cleanup automatically. Put a Y here to allow the system to do automatic cleanup. The Time Cleanup Starts Each Day tells the system when to do the cleanup. In the example, this customer wants the automatic cleanup to start at 1 A.M. every day. Because these times are in military time, that means 0100 (or 1:00 A.M.). The parameters under Number of Days to Keep are the really interesting items. To the right of each is a number for the days.

- User Messages. All old user messages are purged after the allowed time (in this case, after seven days). This does not clean up the system-operator messages or security-officer messages.
- System and Workstation Messages. All old messages that belong to the system operator or to any device-message queue are erased after the allowed time.
- Job Logs and Other System Output. All old job logs are purged after the allowed number of days.
- System Journals and System Logs. The system keeps journals to assist its many tasks. This parameter says they will be purged after the allowed number of days. Included in system logs are the history logs (QHST) and problem logs generated by the AS/400 self-diagnostics. Included in this category is PTF cleanup.
- OfficeVision/400 Calendar Items. Such items are purged after the allowed number of days.

CLEAN UP USER PROFILES

It is not uncommon for a company audit to find active user profiles on an AS/400 two years after the users had left the company—even when the person had been asked to leave. Forgotten user profiles can build up quickly. This is an audit issue as well as capacity and performance issue. To clean up old user profiles, enter:

```
GO SECTOOLS
```

on any command line and press the Enter key. Figure 15-12 has a sample of the resulting screen.

```
SECTOOLS                        Security Tools
                                                  System:   BIGBLUE
 Select one of the following:

   Work with profiles
      1. Analyze default passwords

      2. Display active profile list
      3. Change active profile list
      4. Analyze profile activity

      5. Display activation schedule
      6. Change activation schedule entry

      7. Display expiration schedule
      8. Change expiration schedule entry

      9. Print profile internals

                                                     More...
Selection or command
===>____________________________________________________

 F1=Help   F3=Exit   F4=Prompt   F9=Retrieve   F12=Cancel
```

Figure 15-12: SECTOOLS menu.

The Security Tools menu makes a wide variety of security activities easily possible. Select option 4 (`Analyze Profile Activity`) from that menu. Figure 15-13 shows a sample of the resulting screen.

```
                    Analyze Profile Activity (ANZPRFACT)

 Type choices, press Enter.

 Number of inactive days . . . . ______          1-366, *NOMAX
```

Figure 15-13: Screen to analyze user profiles' activity.

Enter the number of inactive days on this screen. This tells the analyzer how many days a profile can be unused before it is considered inactive. This cleanup is scheduled and will take effect as soon as the Enter key is pressed. The system will schedule a job to run once a month (starting at 1 A.M. the current day).

This program marks any profile that hasn't been used within the number of days specified as *DISABLED. This command runs automatically in the background. It produces a report of inactive profiles it found every time it runs and sends it to the system operator. From this report, the system operator can delete old user profiles. Use the Work with User Profiles (WRKUSRPRF) command, scroll to the user profile, and put a 4 on the option line. Press Enter and the profile disappears.

The AS/400 leaves the actual cleanup of old profiles up to the system operator because there may be people on sick leave who should be left on the system. Only a human can make those decisions. The system operator can select user profiles for omission from the inactive report. To do this, select option 3 from the menu shown in Figure 15-12. That option presents a screen that names profiles exempt from the inactive analysis. Figure 15-14 contains a sample of this object screen.

```
                  Change Active Profile List (CHGACTPRFL)

 Type choices, press Enter.

 User profile . . . . . . . . . .   __________     Name
               + for more values    __________
 Action . . . . . . . . . . . . .   *ADD______     *ADD, *REMOVE
```

Figure 15-14: Screen to add a user profile to be exempt from the inactive analysis.

On the screen shown in Figure 15-14, name the profile or put a plus sign (+) on the `+ For More Values` parameter to add more. The names entered can be added (Action *ADD) to the exempt list or removed (Action *REMOVE) from it.

When a user profile is deleted, any objects it owns stay on the system. As the profile is deleted, all objects' ownership changes to the default user by the system. There are many, many objects owned by this nonexistent person; the smart system operator will want to review the objects owned by a user before deleting the user from the system. Although a formal review process may be in order involving more people than the operator, the idea is to first display the objects owned by the soon-to-be-deleted user and delete those that are not needed.

From the Work with User Profile (WRKUSRPRF) command, enter 12 on the option line to the left of the user profile targeted for deletion (but do this before deleting the profile with an option 4). The system will display a list of objects owned by that user. Figure 15-15 contains a sample of objects owned by a hypothetical user.

```
                          Work with Objects by Owner

 User profile . . . . . . . :    A82997990

 Type options, press Enter.
   2=Edit authority       4=Delete    5=Display authority    7=Rename
   8=Display description  9=Change owner

 Opt  Object                Library       Type        Attribute
  _   AGTFM                 BIGLIB        *PGM        RPGLE
  _   BREPORT               BIGLIB        *PGM        RPGLE
  _   BREPORTTRY            BIGLIB        *PGM        RPGLE
  _   BRKFM                 BIGLIB        *PGM        RPGLE
  _   INQSUBP               BIGLIB        *PGM        RPGLE
  _   LSTFM                 BIGLIB        *PGM        RPGLE
  _   MAINTMENUP            BIGLIB        *PGM        CLP
  _   MENUPGM               BIGLIB        *PGM        CLP
  _   SUBMENUP              BIGLIB        *PGM        CLP
                                                                   More...
 Parameters or command
 ===> _______________________________________________________________
 F3=Exit      F4=Prompt    F5=Refresh    F9=Retrieve    F11=Display descriptions
 F12=Cancel   F17=Top      F18=Bottom
```

Figure 15-15: Partial list of the objects owned by user A82997990.

There are two options available to the system operator concerning owned objects:

- Change the object's ownership to another profile. To do this, enter 2 in the Option column.
- Delete the object. To do this, enter a 4 in the Option column.

The user can still own spool files. When the user is deleted, all spool files are deleted (instead of kept under new ownership like the objects). It may not be desirable to automatically delete all these, so a similar review should be done beforehand. Enter on any command line:

```
WRKSPLF SELECT(old user profile name)
```

Press the Enter key. On the Work with All Spooled Files display, Figure 15-16, save any important spool files by copying them to another user's output queue before deleting the user's profile.

```
                         Work with All Spooled Files

 Type options, press Enter.
   1=Send  2=Change   3=Hold   4=Delete   5=Display   6=Release   7=Messages
   8=Attributes        9=Work with printing status


                               Device or                         Total      Cur
 Opt File        User          Queue        User Data    Sts    Pages     Page  Copy
 _4  RPGTST3B    RPGT313       CPAOUTQ                   RDY      10               1
 __  QPRINT      RPGT313       CPAOUTQ      RPGTST3B     RDY       1               1
 __  RPGTST3B    RPGT313       CPAOUTQ                   RDY      10               1
 __  RPGTST3B    RPGT313       CPAOUTQ                   RDY      10               1
 __  RPGTST3B    RPGT313       CPAOUTQ                   RDY      10               1
 __  QPRINT      RPGT313       CPAOUTQ      RPGTST3A     RDY       1               1
 __  STDCRSLF    RPGT313       CPAOUTQ                   RDY       3               1
 __  RPGTST3BB   RPGT313       CPAOUTQ                   RDY      10               1
                                                                            More...
 Parameters for options 1, 2, 3 or command
 ===> _________________________________________________________________
 F3=Exit   F10=View 4   F11=View 2   F12=Cancel   F22=Printers   F24=More keys
```

Figure 15-16: Sample of the WRKSPLF command.

> **TIP:**
>
> When spool files are deleted, the space doesn't necessarily return to the system automatically. To retrieve the space, enter RCLSPLSTG on the command line and press the Enter key.

CLEAN UP LICENSED PROGRAMS

Sometimes licensed programs get loaded and forgotten about. We do this when programs are sent to us on a trial basis. To properly remove these, enter:

```
GO LICPGM
```

on the command line and press the Enter key.

Depending on the licensed program, it may need to be saved before deletion. Either select option 1 (Save) from the LICPGM menu or use the SAVLICPGM command to save the program.

To delete the program, enter a 4 (Delete) on the Option line and press the Enter key. As an alternative to the GO LICPGM menu, delete a licensed program directly with the DLTLICPGM command.

CLEAN UP OLD DEVICE DESCRIPTIONS

One thing AS/400 customers are really bad about is creating device descriptions then forgetting about them. To check them, use the command WRKHDWRSC *xxx, where xxx will be:

- CMN for communications devices.
- LWS for local workstation devices.
- STG for storage resources.

The resulting screen will show devices and their statuses. Focus on device descriptions with a status of Not Detected. First, verify that the device is really not on the system (as opposed to being on the system but sitting around in a closet). If it is not, enter 4 on the Option line to delete the description.

MISCELLANEOUS CLEANUP TASKS

There are a few other things that are simple to do and can return a lot of space to an AS/400. Here they are with caveats where necessary:

- If files or libraries are saved to a Save File prior to saving to tape, free up the space with the Clear Save File (CLRSAVF) command. Think about this one, though. Some customers leave the files intact and clear them immediately prior to the next save, thus ensuring enough DASD space is available for the save.
- Use the Display File Description (DSPFD) to determine files that have a large number of deleted records. Return the space these deleted records occupy to the system by issuing the RGZPFM or by saving/restoring them. *Note*: If a file relies on physical sequence of records for ordering, do not do a RGZPFM to reclaim deleted records. In fact, leave it alone until a program modifies it for a more positive sequencing strategy.

- When a message queue suddenly gets a lot of messages, it expands in increments. Although the messages get deleted, the increments still exist, taking DASD. Message queues do not get returned to their original size until the Clear Message Queue (CLRMSGQ) is issued.
- While journaling, delete the journal receivers as soon as they are saved. Refer to chapter 17.

LAB #15: MESSAGES, LOGS, AND CLEANUP

Upon completion of this lab, you should be able to:

- Explore the parameters for job logs.
- Use the history log.
- Explore the messages stored in the system operator's message queue.
- Explore automatic cleanup features on the AS/400.

NAMING CONVENTIONS FOR THIS LAB

During the lab, every time you encounter one of the lab names that contains xx, replace the xx with the number that has been assigned. As you complete the lab assignment, you will create and modify your environment to reflect your specific assigned names (Figure L15-1).

	Lab Name: Identified in Commands as:	Your Assigned Name:
Profile (User ID)	USERID	
Library Name	USERID	
Output Queue	USEROUTQ	

Figure L15-1: Naming conventions.

INTRODUCTION

The concept of cleanup is to keep only needed items on your system as long as they are needed, then delete them. One of the areas that require constant cleanup is the area of logs. They tend to fill up the DASD. Let us start out looking at the various logs available on your system.

JOB LOGS

During the execution of a program, messages are collected into an internal log while it is running. When the job finishes, the contents of the job log are written to the spooled output. What is written to the log is determined by the values of the logging level. You will execute the ADDRESS1 program that is located in the OPRLIB. This program will execute without error. Most companies set the logging level to not produce a job log for jobs that completed normally. However, there are times that you want a record of what happened during the execution of a program that completes normally. Thus, you need to change the values of the logging level. Let's explore the logs produced when the different values are used.

- Add the OPRLIB to your library list.
- Enter SBMJOB on the command line.
- Press F4 (Prompt).
- Press F10 (Additional Parameters).
- Enter `Call ADDRESS1` for the `Command to Run` parameter.
- Page down to the `Message Logging` parameter.
- Enter 1 for `Level`, 0 for `Severity`, and *MSG for `Text` parameters.
- Press Enter.
- Retrieve the QPJOBLOG file you just produced from your spool file.
- Attach it to the submission sheet and label it printout #1.
- Repeat the above sequence with 4 for `Level`, 0 for `Severity`, and *MSG for `Text` parameters.
- Retrieve and attach the QPJOBLOG file just produced to your submission sheet and label it printout #2.
- Repeat the above sequence with 1 for `Level`, 0 for `Severity`, and *SECLVL for `Text` parameters.
- Retrieve and attach the QPJOBLOG file just produced to your submission sheet and label it printout #3.
- Repeat the above sequence with 4 for `Level`, 0 for `Severity`, and *SECLVL for `Text` parameters.
- Retrieve and attach the QPJOBLOG file just produced to your submission sheet and label it printout #4.
- Repeat the above sequence with 4 for `Level`, 0 for `Severity`, and *NOLIST for `Text` parameters.
- What happens when you use the above values for the `Message Logging` parameter? ____________________

Compare the four printouts to see the effect of these values. Answer the following questions:

- Which of the conditions above included the CL command(s) in the job log? ____________________
- Which job log included complete error messages, including the second-level messages? ____________________

SYSTEM OPERATOR MESSAGE QUEUE: QSYSOPR

The system operator message queue is one of the most important message queues on the system. It contains information about various hardware messages as well as messages indicating that there is a problem. Let's look through the current messages in the system operator message queue.

- Enter DSPMSG on the command line.
- Press F4 (Prompt).
- Enter *SYSOPR for the `Message Queue` parameter.
- Press Enter.

You are now viewing the messages that are received automatically in the system operator's message queue. Look through the messages that are in this queue.

- Page through the system operator's message queue.
- Find a `System Status Message Type` message or a `Message Hardware/Device-Related` message.
- Print the screen containing the above message(s).
- Retrieve the spool file you just produced.
- Attach it to the submission sheet and label it as printout #5.

THE HISTORY LOG

The history log contains messages from the various other logs on the system. This then produces a central repository of systemwide messages. To determine how your system is doing and to research problems, the history log is a good starting point. To start, you need to become familiar with the history log. Remember, when you are viewing the log and find a message that requires further investigation, you can place your cursor on the message and press the Help key to see second-level messages.

- Enter DSPLOG on the command line.
- Press F4 (Prompt).
- Complete the parameters as follows: `Log` is QHST, `Starting Time` is 5 P.M. in military time, `Starting Date` is *CURRENT, `Ending Time` is *AVAIL, `Ending Date` is *CURRENT, `Output` is *PRINT. This prints a copy of the history to the spool file.
- Press Enter.
- The history log will be a multipage log in your spool file.

- Using the WRKSPLF command, place option 2 (Change) to the left of the QPDSPLOG spool file.
- Press F4 (Prompt).
- Press F10 (Additional Parameters).
- Page through the parameters until you find the starting page and end page.
- You want to print only three pages.
- Place the page numbers for the Start and End parameters.
- Do not print the entire document.
- Retrieve the three pages of the history log.
- Attach to the submission sheet and label as printout #6.

AUTOMATIC CLEANUP

As cleanup is a constant task and many of the same items need to be deleted on a regular basis, the automatic cleanup function is quite helpful. In the next section, you will be asked questions based on the automatic cleanup setting for your AS/400. You may not have the authority to actually go into this function. If you find that you don't have access, ask your instructor to print out the screens for you or use the screens in this chapter.

- Enter GO CLEANUP on the command line.
- Press Enter.
- Enter 1 (Change Cleanup Options).
- Press Enter.
- This will bring you to the Change Cleanup Options screen. (Figure 15-11 in the chapter.)
- Is Automatic Cleanup in use on your system? ________________________
- If you answered "yes" to the above question, what time does Automatic Cleanup run?
  ____
- List the five items that can be managed using the Automatic Cleanup function. Include the number of days these items are retained. ________________
  ____
  ____
  ____

END-OF-CHAPTER AIDS

CHAPTER SUMMARY

There is a lot of activity that flows through the AS/400. Most of it is kept, providing a uniquely complete record of every type of activity that happened on the system. It is left up to operations to decide when the collected information is obsolete and ready for discard versus when it is fresh and useful (at least potentially useful).

This task is pretty much left up to us humans, but the AS/400 makes the job easier with a fairly rich set of tools. Learn to use the tools, clean up regularly, and your AS/400 will hum like a new machine a lot longer.

KEY TERMS

AS/400 Security Audit Journal	job accounting journal	message files
cleanup	job log	message queue
field reference files	journal	second-level message
form	journal receiver	severities
history log	log	system reply list
job accounting	logging level	text

CHAPTER SELF-TEST

Solutions to these self-test questions are in appendix D.

True-False Questions

___ 1. Other users send the majority of the messages received by a user.

___ 2. Three dots (...) to the right of a message at the bottom of the screen indicate there are more messages.

___ 3. Each predefined message has a message identifier.

___ 4. The advantage of the system reply list is that all jobs that have frequently occurring inquiry messages with a consistent answer can be responded to by the system all the time and not bother the user or operators.

___ 5. For a job to use the system reply list to obtain a response to a message, the job must have the INQMSGPRY parameter set to *YES.

___ 6. To determine why a job log was not produced, check the history log for message CPF1164.

___ 7. Most serious messages have a severity of 30 or higher.

___ 8. Job accounting is really a form of journaling.

___ 9. Security auditing is a good function to run in the background all the time to maintain a secure system.

___ 10. When you delete spool files, all the space used by the spool files does not automatically return to the system.

Fill in the Blanks

1. Logs consist of a collection of old ________________.

2. Break messages are sent to ________________.

3. The complete message includes the ____________ level message.

4. The most important message queue supplied with your AS/400 is the ________________ message queue.

5. The name of the message queue for really important messages is ______________, and it is found in _________ library.

6. The system value ________________ determines the maximum number of records in the history log's physical file.

7. To display the contents of the current history log, you would use the ______________ command.

8. The logging level for an active job comes from the ________________________.

9. When setting up journaling, you first create the ____________; next, you create the ____________. If the system value ________________ has not been set, do so.

10. When using Automatic Cleanup to clean up user messages, the ______________ and ________________ messages are not deleted.

Chapter Review Questions

1. Explain the following terms:
   a. System reply list.
   b. Log.
   c. History log.
   d. Job log.
   e. Journal receiver.

2. What are the four types of message logs and what do they contain?

3. What type of information is stored in the history log?

4. What ways can you limit the contents displayed from a history log?

5. What are the component parts of the LOG parameter? What is the meaning of these components?

6. What is the difference between first- and second-level messages?
7. What information is collected when job accounting is started?
8. What information is logged when security audit journal is used?
9. Who can access security audit journals?
10. What are the advantages of a clean AS/400?
11. What happens when you run SECTOOLS to analyze a profile's activity and specify a number of inactive days?
12. What happens when a user profile is deleted?
13. When developing your company's AS/400 system cleanup plan, you should include what items?

16

Basic Troubleshooting, Problem Solving, and Using Electronic Customer Support

Chapter Objectives

Upon completion of this chapter, you should be able to:

- Identify various sources of system problems.
- Modify customer information.
- Analyze a problem using the commands available on the system.
- Explain how to report a problem.
- Use the ECS modem to send a problem analysis.
- Use Copy Screen commands in problem resolution.

Hardware

Never forget that computers are machines. They have no common sense and possess no trace of intelligence. Problem solving is done by humans. Programmers have their ways of solving problems; system operators have theirs. We will discuss the various tools and skills system operators have to use when problem solving. IBM has some automated diagnostic services built into the AS/400, some of which can be a big help; others are more helpful to those new to the AS/400.

Many of the techniques and commands in this chapter are things we have discussed in previous chapters. We present them here as "real-life" examples of how AS/400 tools are used together.

HARDWARE-RELATED PROBLEMS

Hardware problems can be severe or mild. We can define *severe hardware problems* as those that render the system nonoperational. *Mild hardware problems*, on the other hand, cause some minor inconvenience, like a printer failure. This would be a mild problem when one or more printers are available to take over. The same problem could be severe if the system only has one printer.

Every AS/400 comes with an Electronic Customer Support (ECS) modem. The connection this modem and its line make can save a lot of hardware problems. IBM will dial into the AS/400 periodically to check on the health of the system. If IBM notices anomalies in the problem logs, it may dispatch a serviceperson.

On the other hand, the AS/400 is continuously self-diagnosing itself; it may take the initiative and dial out without anyone being aware of it. This combination of proactive support via the modem has saved many IT departments needless hardware failure in the past.

Power Failure/Line Conditioning

The electrical supply from any power company can be very poor. Poor in the sense that it contains voltage spikes and can easily fluctuate several volts throughout the day. These irregularities can shorten the life of computer hardware. Many AS/400 IT departments install an uninterruptible power supply (UPS) between the raw power-company-supplied electricity and the AS/400.

The primary purpose of a UPS is to filter or smooth out the incoming power. It does so through a large bank of batteries. The incoming power continually charges the batteries while the AS/400 runs off the batteries. Batteries are not sensitive and can easily absorb very erratic input power.

When a power outage occurs, UPSs will keep the AS/400 up until the batteries' power drains. How long a time this is is determined by both how much battery power is available and how large the electrical draw from the AS/400. It can be as little as five minutes or up to several hours.

UPS power is very expensive, so many IT departments opt for a minimum uptime after power failure, 15 minutes being an average. The UPS connects into the AS/400 and, when the power available within the UPS drops to a certain level, it sends a signal to the AS/400 ordering a normal shutdown. This grace period is about all the IT department needs, especially in urban areas where complete power outages are rare.

IT departments that require 24-hour uptime, like police departments and hospitals, rely on diesel-powered generator equipment that starts automatically to run the computer and the rest of the facility. Although these generators start automatically and are very fast at doing so, this startup still takes about 15 seconds. The AS/400 would have come down in that time, so again, a UPS is used to fill the gap. The UPS only has to keep the AS/400 up for those 15 seconds until the generator kicks in.

Many AS/400 IT departments carry insurance covering data or hardware loss due to power problems. These IT departments should have a 24-hour power quality graphing mechanism. This is a mechanical device that attaches to the line providing power coming into the computer. A circular disk of graph paper makes one revolution every twenty-four hours, and a pen records the quality of the power. This is cheap evidence to support an insurance claim that a disk drive and some data were lost due to irregular power.

Finally, AS/400 IT departments should include some sort of lightning protection, especially when supporting LANs that rely on cabling outside the building or private microwave towers. The surge from a lightning strike, in those cases, will come in through the unprotected data lines, not the power supply.

But keep in mind the nature of lightning protectors—they are not what most people think they are. A lightning protection device is basically a staged bunch of fuses that are set to absorb lightning power into the ground and blow as they do so. They do not protect equipment—computers do not survive lightning strikes. What lightning protection does is keep someone in the computer room from getting killed.

GENERAL PROBLEM SOLVING

The AS/400 has more than enough built-in information to document unexpected problems and help the system operator diagnose them. Great sources of information are the logs we discussed in previous chapters. While the problem-solving tools cannot always fix your problems, they can help to diagnose what is wrong and provide possible solutions.

JOBS FAIL

Occasionally a job fails. The system operator is usually instructed to call in a programmer or, if the failing job is part of a purchased application, the support line for that application. But before (or even after) that call is made, some investigating should be done using the tools on the system.

- Look in the Job's Log. Remember the job log from chapter 12? Every job, depending on its logging level, may have a job log associated with it. This log may be the only way to determine what went wrong.

  While a job is active, use the Display Job Log (DSPJOBLOG) or Work with Jobs (WRKJOB) command to access the Work with Jobs menu, then select option 10 from the menu. For a job that is ended, use the Work with Spool File (WRKSPLF) command; or if not sure of the job log's name, use the Work with Output Queue (WRKOUTQ) command, specifying QPJOBLOG or QEZJOBLOG to find the job log that way.

- Look in the QSYSOPR Message Queue. We discussed message queues in chapter 15. Remember that QSYSOPR becomes the repository for most system messages. When there is a problem with a job or device, check this message queue for messages that come up during processing. Even if a job log was not kept, messages in QSYSOPR will be there.

  Many minor problems that come up during the day are due to a pending message in this queue, so give it a quick check first.

- Look in the History Log. Finally, do not forget to check the history log as we discussed in chapter 15. It summarizes job information, device status, system operator messages, and PTF activity. It is a little more cryptic to read, but it may reveal a lot of useful information.

SYSTEM REFERENCE CODES (SRCS)

Very rarely, the AS/400 will have a very serious internal problem that defies any effort to diagnose it. This is very rare. Our experience with this kind of "hard-down" is limited to occasionally installing buggy new releases (for which we had faithfully saved to the system prior to attempting to put them on, so we saved our butts).

When these happen, IBM support is going to want to know information found on the display panel of the AS/400 CPU. This is the small LCD screen on the front of the box, not a workstation. Refer to panel diagram in chapter 8. The information there is cryptic to most AS/400 customers but is what IBM will use to solve the problem.

This code is called the *System Reference Code* (*SRC*). An SRC is an eight-character alphanumeric code such as B900 3004.

Appendix A of the System Operators' Guide contains a list of SRCs and what actions may be possible when they appear. Try to follow the instructions listed there.

Most of the time, IBM Support notes the SRC then asks the system operator to do a manual IPL and call them back. We discussed manual IPLs in chapter 8, and here is the short version of it:

- Change the control panel to the Manual mode.
- Use the Select switch to display function 03.
- Press the Enter button on the control panel.

This time, though, the system operator should know there is a problem and should stay with the AS/400, noting the SRCs that appear. Many of them will appear and disappear too fast to record—do not worry about recording every one, just the ones that hang around long enough to note. Some SRC codes indicate normal activity, some do not—IBM Support will sort out which ones are which.

Copy Screen Function

User complaints are not always exactly accurate. They say they are doing something one way, when they are really doing something completely different. If "looking over the user's shoulder" would help, there is an AS/400 utility known as *Copy Screen*.

This function allows the system operator to monitor, at his/her workstation, what someone else is doing at their workstation in order to determine the cause of a problem which they are experiencing. Use the Start Copy Screen (STRCPYSCN) command. Figure 16-1 contains a sample of the prompted version of this command.

```
                    Start Copy Screen (STRCPYSCN)

Type choices, press Enter.

Source device . . . . . . . . .   APUSER01      Name, *REQUESTER
Output device . . . . . . . . .   *REQUESTER    Name, *REQUESTER, *NONE
Job queue . . . . . . . . . . .   QCTL          Name
  Library . . . . . . . . . . .     *LIBL       Name, *LIBL, *CURLIB
File to receive output . . . . .  *NONE         Name, *NONE
  Library . . . . . . . . . . .                 Name, *LIBL, *CURLIB
Output member options:
  Member to receive output . . .  *FIRST        Name, *FIRST
  Replace or add records . . . .  *REPLACE      *REPLACE, *ADD

                                                                   Bottom
F3=Exit   F4=Prompt   F5=Refresh   F12=Cancel   F13=How to use this display
F24=More keys
```

Figure 16-1: Start Copy Screen function display.

The system operator should specify the name of the display device to copy, the display device name from which the operator is monitoring (*REQUESTER is fine), and the job queue where the monitoring job should run (probably QCTL). Finally, if output to a database file is desired, specify the file and member to receive the output. Output to a database file builds a hard copy of the screens and activity. When ready, press Enter.

When the command is started, the user who will be copied will receive a message—he/she must respond, authorizing that the job may be viewed. Once that response has been made, the system operator can follow along while the user continues the job. The system operator's keyboard will be locked, and he/she will be one screen behind the user. Remember this, because if the user claims to have just put in something, that something will not appear on the monitoring screen until the user presses the Enter key.

> **TIP:**
>
> One way to force a screen over to the monitoring workstation is to have the user press the Print Screen key.

To end Copy Screen, either the user or the system operator can issue the End Copy Screen (ENDCPYSCN) command. If the user wants to end copying but is unable to enter the command, try pressing SHIFT + SYS ATTN. This will result in an input line displayed at the bottom of the screen where the ENDCPYSCN command can be entered.

TROUBLESHOOTING—TWO COMMON PROBLEMS

While no one can predict all the problems that can come up in a day and adequately cover all the solutions to those problems, here are two common ones that system operators experience and general steps they take to solve them.

A SYSTEM PRINTER THAT DOES NOT WORK

A system printer is a printer that is directly connected to the AS/400. Usually this is a twinax connection. Some of these considerations can be applied to any printer.

- Check the power cable to ensure that it is connected to the outlet on the wall.
- Check that the outlet has power.
- If the printer has power:
  - If its display panel is blank or displaying garbage, make a service call and plan to reroute any output to another printer until it is fixed.
  - If the display panel appears normal and there is an indication on the panel that the printer is on-line:
    - Check the printer status from any AS/400 workstation with the Work with Configuration Status (WRKCFGSTS) command, specify *DEV and *PRT for the first two parameters; this command will list all printers. Select option 8 (`Display Status`) for the system printer. Check that it is varied on—the Status column will have a value of VARIED ON. If it is not varied on, make it so with option 1.
    - Check that an active writer is attached to the printer. Use the Work with Writers (WRKWTR) command to verify that the printer writer is active— writers get cancelled quite often. The printer writers are named the same as the printers. Find the writer for the system printer and, if it is not started, start it with the option 1 (`Start`).
    - Check that the printer's output queues are not held with the Work with Output Queue (WRKOUTQ) command. Notice the statuses in the right-most column. They should say *RLS or Released. If it is held (status *HLD), release the output queue with option 6 (`Release`).
    - The printed output may have been directed to another printer or another output queue. Displaying all jobs for the user with the Work with User Jobs (WRKUSRJOB) command will show the status of the job, whether it has even been run, and if it has been, where the output is. If the output is in the wrong queue, direct it to the right queue with the Work with Output Queue (WRKOUTQ) command.
    - Check the printer's message queue for pending inquiry that may explain why the printer is not printing. Use the Work with Writers (WRKWTR) command, then option 7 (`Display Messages`) for the appropriate printer writer.

A TAPE DRIVE THAT DOES NOT WORK

- Check the power cable to make sure that it is still connected to the outlet on the wall.
- Check that the outlet has power.
- Check that a tape is mounted on the drive and that the drive is in a READY state.

- If the tape drive is doing a SAV or RST, be very careful. Tape drives often hang for several minutes after an initial movement while the system does housekeeping in the background. This may be a completely normal situation, but it might appear as though nothing is happening.

- Check that the tape drive is varied on (ready to go) with the WRKCFGSTS command, specifying *DEV and *TAP for the first two parameters. If it is varied on, the Status column will show VARIED ON. If it is not, vary it on with option 1.

- Check the system operator's message queue (QSYSOPR) for pending inquiry messages that may explain why the tape drive is not working.

- If an error occurs during the tape operation, the operation must be started over. But before doing so:

  - Think about the temperature of the tape relative to the computer room temperature. If it was just brought in from off-site, it may have to sit on a shelf for a half-hour to adjust. (Magnetic media expands when warm and contracts when cold.)

  - Clean the read/write head of the tape drive. This is a very shiny silver box that the tape travels over; it often gets dirty with magnetic residue. When it becomes dirty, the read/write head will not work.

  - Check that the tape is properly initialized. If the tape is not, initialize it with the Initialize Tape (INZTAP) command.

  - If writing to a tape, try a different one. Tapes can become damaged or they can wear out after use. If a new one works where an older one failed several times, throw away the old one.

USING ECS FOR PROBLEM SOLVING

We mentioned at the top of this chapter that the ECS modem allows IBM to do some simple hardware-problem monitoring of the AS/400, and allows the AS/400 to contact IBM for service. However, the ECS modem has other uses in problem solving.

In order to make ECS possible, the IBM technician who installs the system creates line, controller, and device descriptions that should be left unchanged. The installer also enters the initial values for the telephone numbers to use to get in touch with IBM. Each IBM contact through the ECS modem automatically identifies the customer by company, AS/400 serial number, and contact person.

When this information changes, it should be updated in the AS/400's records. To do so, first go to the second problem menu by typing:

```
GO PROBLEM2
```

on the command line. Figure 16-2 contains a sample of that menu.

```
PROBLEM2                    Problem Handling
                                                          System:   BIGBLUE
 Select one of the following:

      1. Program temporary fix
      2. Work with alerts
      3. Performance tools
      4. Programming language debug
      5. Work with support contact information
      6. Copy screen image
      7. Work with alert descriptions

     70. Related commands




 Selection or command
 ===>5

 F3=Exit   F4=Prompt   F9=Retrieve   F12=Cancel   F13=Information Assistant
 F16=AS/400 Main menu
 (C) COPYRIGHT IBM CORP. 1980, 1998.
```

Figure 16-2:Contact information is changed from PROBLEM2 menu.

From the menu shown in Figure 16-3, select option 5 (Work with Support Contact Information). Figure 16-3 shows the menu that will result.

```
                          Work with Support Contact Information
                                                          System:   BIGBLUE
 Select one of the following:

      1. Work with question and answer (Q & A) database
      2. Work with local service information
      3. Work with IBM product information
      4. Work with technical information exchange (TIE)
      5. Work with upgrade order information
      6. Work with service providers





 Selection or command
 ===> 2

 F3=Exit   F4=Prompt   F9=Retrieve   F12=Cancel
 (C) COPYRIGHT IBM CORP. 1980, 1998.
```

Figure 16-3: Work with Support Contact Information menu.

From the menu shown in Figure 16-3, select option 2 (`Work with Local Service Information`). Figure 16-4 contains a sample of that screen.

```
                    Work with Local Service Information
                                                    System:   BIGBLUE
Select one of the following:

     1. Display service contact information
     2. Change service contact information










Selection
   2__

F3=Exit   F12=Cancel
```

Figure 16-4: Work with Local Service Information menu.

From this screen, select either option 1 (`Display Service Contact Information`) to display the contact information, or option 2 (`Change Service Contact Information`) to change it. Figure 16-5 contains a sample of a change screen.

```
                    Change Upgrade Contact Information
                                                System:   BIGBLUE
Type changes, press Enter.

Mailing address:
  Company name . . . . . . . .   World Wide Widgets
  Contact name . . . . . . . .   Mike Dawson
  Street address . . . . . . .   1234 E. Main St.
                                 ______________________________

  City/State . . . . . . . . .   Phoenix, AZ
  Country  . . . . . . . . . .   ____________________
  Zip code . . . . . . . . . .   85032

Telephone number . . . . . . .   (602) 555-1234

Fax number . . . . . . . . . .   (602) 555-5678




F3=Exit   F5=Refresh   F12=Cancel
```

Figure 16-5: Change Upgrade Contact Information screen.

To change anything, position the cursor and type over the values there. For an explanation of any of the fields shown, press the Help key. When done, press Enter.

USES OF ECS

ECS can be used to contact IBM in two ways. Each way requires a different command:

- ANZPRB. Use the Analyze Problem (ANZPRB) command to report hardware or software problems encountered.
- SNDPTFORD. Use the Send PTF Order (SNDPTFORD) command to place an order for PTFs. This can be ordered either individually or in cumulative packages. SNDPTFORD can also be used to obtain information about PTFs. The SNDPTFORD command is described in chapter 9.

ECS uses an ordinary modem and telecommunications setup. The ECS equipment can be set up to connect with other computer systems as well, although this should be done so sparingly. If the ECS modem is disconnected or reconnected to another line, it should be reset as soon as possible afterward. Here are some examples of other uses of the ECS modem:

- Non-IBM application support. ECS is so successful, many other vendors count on the ECS line for their use as well.
- Some customers are using the ECS modem to do *Electronic Data Interchange (EDI)*.
- The ECS modem can also be used for low-speed transfers between two systems.
- The ECS setup can be used to contact bulletin board services (BBS) that cater to IBM midrange professionals.

TIP:

Use the ECS modem for other uses wisely. If the configuration or physical line connection requires changing, do so temporarily. Ensure that after the other task is complete, the ECS is reset to its former condition.

Reporting Problems over ECS

Problems can be reported to IBM through the ECS. The command to do this is Analyze Problem (ANZPRB). The Analyze Problem, when submitted, will dial IBM and report the problem. Sometime later, the requester (probably the system operator) will either receive a PTF that addresses the problem or instructions to contact the technical support provider.

The ANZPRB command is how problem reporting begins. When a problem is suspected, the operator could use ANZPRB to report it to IBM. To do so, enter:

```
ANZPRB
```

on the command line and press F4.

This command will take the operator through sixteen screens to report a problem. In real life, the whole ANZPRB is more marketing hype than real substance. Only the simplest problems get real answers. The rest come back with instructions to contact the company that provides the support—IBM or the local VAR (Value-Added Retailer).

Any problem that is not simple requires much faster response time; so most customers just pick up the phone and call Support.

WORKING WITH PROBLEM LOGS

The AS/400 tracks all hardware and software problems encountered in a problem log. The Work with Problems (WRKPRB) command produces a list of these logs.

The WRKPRB command has a number of parameters to select where problem logs are to be displayed. If no parameter values are entered, WRKPRB presents all problem logs by default. Figure 16-6 contains a sample of that screen.

```
                              Work with Problems
                                                          System:   BIGBLUE
Position to . . . . . . .                   Problem ID

Type options, press Enter.
  2=Change   4=Delete   5=Display details    6=Print details
  8=Work with problem   9=Work with alerts   12=Enter text


Opt  Problem ID  Status          Problem Description
___  9919611334  PREPARED        WRKOUTQ command ended abnormally
___  9919610939  READY           WRKr detected a software problem on this AS/40
___  9918648822  READY           Software problem data for QTMTWSG has been log






                                                                        Bottom
F3=Exit      F5=Refresh   F6=Print list      F11=Display dates and times
F12=Cancel   F16=Report prepared problems    F24=More keys
```

Figure 16-6: Work with Problems screen.

If the system operator had used the ANZPBM command, those reported problems would occur on this screen as their own problem log. In this case, the first problem log would be an example of that. The other problem logs shown in the figure were generated by the system, presumably during save/restore operations that failed.

From this panel, the operator can edit problem logs by entering option numbers and pressing the Enter key. For example, using option 12 would let him/her enter or change the notes associated with a particular problem.

Like ANZPRB, this is another feature rarely used in real life, although it is nice to browse to see if the system is encountering problems that the system operator is unaware of.

DELETING OLD PROBLEM LOGS

Problem logs tend to use up disk space, so clean them up regularly. Delete them individually by selecting option 4 from the panel shown above in Figure 16-6. Or run the Delete Problem (DLTPRB) command, as follows:

```
DLTPRB PRBID(*ALL) STATUS(*VERIFIED *CLOSED) DAYS(7)
```

This command deletes all problem logs that are at least seven days old and have a status of *VERIFIED or *CLOSED (resolved problems). No matter what command is used, some problem logs may be undeletable. There is a system value (QPRBHLDITV) that determines how long a problem log must be held on the system before deletion is possible. This system value can be changed to a lower value (even zero) to give the system operator absolute control over which problem logs are deleted.

LAB #16: BASIC TROUBLESHOOTING, PROBLEM SOLVING, AND USING ECS

Upon completion of this lab, you should be able to:

- Use Copy Screen commands in problem resolution.
- Explore working with a problem.
- Print a system activity report.

NAMING CONVENTIONS FOR THIS LAB

During the lab, every time you encounter one of the lab names that begin with OPR, substitute it with your assigned name (Figure L16-1). You should note that the convention adopted in this text is to have your user ID match your user library. As you complete the lab assignment, you will explore using commands on the system.

	Lab Name: Identified in Commands as:	Your Assigned Name:
Profile (User ID)	OPRID	
Library Name	OPRID	
Output Queue	OPROUTQ	
Printer	PRT01	

Figure L16-1: Naming conventions.

INTRODUCTION

Troubleshooting a problem on any computer system is always a challenge. When problems occur often, there is frustration until the problems are resolved. Some of the techniques you need have been explored in previous labs. For example, you used the ECS modem to request a PTF order that could be used to solve a software problem. The ECS modem is also used to report problems when you are trying to solve them. You have also looked at the system operator's message queue and the history log. These receive messages related to problems.

One of the other challenges is to help a user that is remote resolve a difficulty they are having. Sometimes the Copy Screen function can be very helpful.

COPY SCREEN FUNCTION

Often, a user does not always report a problem accurately. They are not always aware of how they got into a difficult position. The Copy Screen function allows the user's screen to be displayed to the operator while the operator is walking a user through a problem/solution.

To demonstrate the Copy Screen function, you will need to work in pairs. You should do this section twice, once as the operator and once as the user. You will both need to be logged on to the same system.

The first thing each member of the pair needs to determine is the name of the workstation you are signed onto.

- Enter WRKACTJOB on the command line.
- Press Enter.
- Page through the active jobs and find your job in the QINTER subsystem.
- Write down the workstation/job name here. This name is found in the Column `Subsystem/Job` to the left of your user ID. ____________________________
- User One—Enter STRCPYSCN on the command line.
- Press F4 (Prompt).
- Enter the workstation/session name of User Two for the `Source File` parameter.
- Enter *REQUESTER for the `To Device` parameter.
- See Figure L16-2.
- Press Enter.
- User Two should answer `G` to grant permission to copy his/her screen to User One's terminal.
- User Two—press Enter.

```
                         Start Copy Screen (STRCPYSCN)

 Type choices, press Enter.

 Source device . . . . . . . . .   QPADEV00XX    Name, *REQUESTER
 Output device . . . . . . . . .   *REQUESTER    Name, *REQUESTER, *NONE
 Job queue . . . . . . . . . . .   QCTL          Name
   Library . . . . . . . . . . .     *LIBL       Name, *LIBL, *CURLIB
 File to receive output . . . . .  *NONE         Name, *NONE
   Library . . . . . . . . . . .                 Name, *LIBL, *CURLIB
 Output member options:
   Member to receive output . . .  *FIRST        Name, *FIRST
   Replace or add records . . . .  *REPLACE      *REPLACE, *ADD

                                                                      Bottom
 F3=Exit   F4=Prompt   F5=Refresh   F12=Cancel   F13=How to use this display
 F24=More keys
```

Figure L16-2: Start Copy Screen function to user on QPADEV00XX workstation.

Once you have started a Copy Screen session, the operator (User One) will not have control of his/her workstation display. User Two (the user) needs to enter commands and press Enter repeatedly. Each time User Two presses Enter, the screen is sent to User One. User Two can force a screen to User One by just pressing Enter again. User One's screen is always one screen behind User Two's. User Two should type some good and some bad commands in this exercise.

- User Two should issue some commands.
- Press Enter after each command. Repeat this for all commands.
- Then, press Enter.
- For example: WRKSPLF, DSPMSG, CPYF XXX *PRINT, WRKACTJOB, etc.

Once User Two has issued several commands, you are ready to end the session through the use of the End Copy Screen command. As User Two is in control, User Two needs to end the session. Remember, User One can always terminate a job from the System Request menu if needed.

- To end the Copy Screen operation, User Two enters ENDCPYSCN on the command line.
- Press Enter.
- Now control is returned to User One's screen.
- Reverse roles and repeat the above procedure.
- After both of you have successfully copied the screens of the other, initial each other's submission sheets to verify your success.
- Completed Copy Screen ______________________________

WORKING WITH PROBLEMS

Problem handling is made easier through the use of the Problem Handling menu(s). You are now going to explore some of the options on these menus.

- Enter `GO PROBLEM` on the command line.
- Press Enter.

There are several menu options on this screen that we have explored previously. In earlier chapters, the importance of the system operator's message queue in problem resolution was stressed, as well as the logs on the system. We will not include these in this lab.

With adequate authority, you can use menu option 2 (`Work with Problems`). If you take menu option 60, you will go to the PROBLEM2 menu.

- Enter `60` from the Problem menu or Enter `GO PROBLEM2` on the command line.
- lPress Enter.
- Enter menu option `3` (`Performance Tools`) on the command line.
- Press Enter.

The Performance Tools menu allows you to monitor the performance of your system. The performance may show changes due to problems. If performance monitoring is implemented at your site, you will be able to print out a System Activity Report.

- Enter menu option `8` (`System Activity`) on the command line.
- Press Enter.
- Next, Enter `2` (`Print Activity Report`).
- Press Enter.
- Print and attach the `Activity Report` to your submission sheet.
- Label it printout #1.
- Return to the `Problem Handling` menu.

Most of the other troubleshooting functions require additional authority to perform. Your instructor might demonstrate these for you.

ADDITIONAL ASSIGNMENTS

The remaining additional assignments will require additional authority or should be done with the supervision authority of your instructor.

1. Select the `Work with Problems` option on the PROBLEM menu. Lists of known problem on your system will be displayed. You will use one of these problems to do analysis.
   a. Next, select the `Analyze the Problem` option on `Work with Problems` screen.
   b. A problem analysis is run. Select the option to `Display the Detailed Report`. Screen-print the analysis.
   c. Print and attach to your lab.

END-OF-CHAPTER AIDS

CHAPTER SUMMARY

Problem solving is one area where all that we have discussed up till now comes into play. The operator uses commands to quickly investigate what is going on in the system. But even a good knowledge of commands accomplishes little unless combined with an equal knowledge of AS/400 concepts. The operator must have a sense of what users, queues, jobs, and objects are and how they relate.

KEY TERMS

Copy Screen
Electronic Data Interchange (EDI)
mild hardware problems
Send PTF Order (SNDPTFORD)
severe hardware problems
System Reference Code (SRC)

CHAPTER SELF-TEST

Solutions to these self-test questions are in appendix D.

True-False Questions

___ 1. An HP laser printer connected through an Ethernet connection is an example of a system printer.

___ 2. To check the status of a system printer, you would use the WRKCFGSTS command.

___ 3. On your AS/400, the printer and tape drive are the two most common problem areas.

___ 4. When troubleshooting any device problem, you should always check the QSYSOPR message queue for device-related messages.

___ 5. While attempting to do a Save operation, the operator found that the new tape he/she placed in the tape drive had not been previously used. The operator receives a message indicating that the tape had not been properly prepared. His/her next step would be to issue the DSPTAP TAP01 command to correct this problem.

___ 6. The job log can often help you find out why a job failed.

___ 7. The system operator can remotely walk a user through the solution of a problem by using the Copy Screen system utility.

___ 8. The AS/400 keeps a record of all hardware and software problems in the job log.

___ 9. When initially attempting to solve any problem, the first place to check is the SRCs on the system's control panel. The operator then looks up the SRC to determine the action needed.

Fill in the Blanks

1. In a power outage, a ________________ will keep the AS/400 running and allow the operator to power the system down. In fact, it will initiate a system power-down.

2. When using the Work with Configuration Status command to check the status of a system printer, a printer with a status of ________________ is available for use.

3. You would use the ____________________ command to determine if the printer writer is active.

4. To check that a device is ready for use, you would use the ______________________ command.

5. When attempting to determine the cause of a system problem, the system operator would want to review the messages in the ____________________ queue and/or the ___________________ log.

6. To report problems to IBM over your ECS modem, you would use the ________________ command.

Chapter Review Questions

1. Explain the following terms:
   a. Severe problem.
   b. System printer.
   c. ANZPRB.
   d. UPS.

2. What is the purpose for a UPS? List reasons for its use.

3. What are the considerations and concerns in protecting your system from lightning strikes?

4. How would you go about determining why a job failed?

5. Identify several uses for the ECS modem.

17

JOURNALING

CHAPTER OBJECTIVES

Upon completion of this chapter, you should be able to:

- Describe what journaling is.
- Describe what journal receivers are and how they are used.
- Describe what commitment control is and how it is used.
- Identify and explain the system values related to auditing and journaling.

OVERVIEW

Journaling is a facility that extends the AS/400 recovery capabilities beyond what can be obtained through backup or restore commands (see chapter 10, Backup and Recovery). The best one can hope for from an adequate backup strategy that doesn't include journaling, is a crashed system restored to the last save (which was probably the prior evening). Combine journaling with the same backup strategy, and a system can be restored to the same condition it was at the moment it was lost.

Journaling can be useful in nondisaster scenarios, too. For example, consider the nightly batch process that ran with the wrong posting date supplied. If its files were journaled, the system operator could have the system reverse every update the program made to the files with a single command. Or, if a data-entry operator made a gross error, with a simple command, he/she could remove all the updating he or she did to any files.

Finally, one thing that really stands out about the data held in the journal receiver—no one can ever change it. No programmer, not even the system operator, can change one byte of data inside a *journal*. For this reason, the information inside a journal becomes absolute law about what went on, who did it, and when.

Journaling has indirect benefits as well. It enables files to be backed up while in use. Journaling also makes commitment control possible.

The two main objects in journaling are the journal (object type *JRN) and the journal receiver (object type *JRNRCV). The journal contains the logic for capturing and storing receiver records. Another way to say it is that the journal contains all the information about what is journaled, but no real data. The journal places the data into the journal receiver.

Both objects must be named, and there is no need to get exotic in this area. A simple rule will suffice: unless the IT department has more than one journal and receiver set going, just use the name JOURNAL for the journal, and call the receiver RECEIV0001. That way, they are easy to remember and, when the system changes receivers late at night, it will calculate a new name for the receiver (RECEIV0002, then RECEIV0003, and so on). If dual receivers are used, name them something slightly different, for example, RCVRA0001 and RCVRB0001.

Journaling is usually done to all database files within a library, but it is not done to all libraries.

JOURNAL RECEIVER

The journal receiver is the central repository for images of transactions made against the database files the journal is journaling.

The journal receiver is an interesting object in itself when compared to database files. AS/400 database files are always in a current state. For example, one record's CUSNUM field may be equal to 123456 and the AMTDUE field is equal to 100.00. If someone looked at the file after a program changed either or both of those fields, they would only see the current value at the time. They could not see the previous value or the amount either field was changed by. That is because database files' fields are always in what is known as a *static condition*. A journal receiver, on the other hand, has every transaction that made changes to the database file. If someone looked at the same record through the journal receiver, he/she would see the starting value of the fields and every changed value. Not only that, he/she would see when the change was made and who made it.

That is complex enough, but add to it that the journal receiver contains all updating transactions for all the files it is journaling, plus a whole lot of system information, and one starts to get an idea of how powerful these can be.

Journal receivers get filled like bags of potato chips at a factory. The journal is the machine filling the bags. The chips are database records. One bag moves along a conveyor belt and stops under the journal. The journal drops chips in the bag until it is full or something tells it to stop, and then the bag moves on and is replaced with another empty bag.

Journal receivers should be changed as soon as they fill up. Receivers have their own maximum size that cannot be changed, but the operator can set a percentage of that size, called the *threshold.* When the receiver reaches the threshold, the system changes receivers.

Even if the journal receiver does not reach its threshold percentage, it should be changed once a day. Most AS/400 shops do this daily at midnight.

Changes to several physical files can be written to one journal; however, changes for one physical file can be written to only one journal at a time.

Journal receiver records contain their own fields related to journaling, but the database records they collect are held in a single, large, undefined field. To decipher the contents of a database record held in a journal receiver, the program, system, or operator has to retrieve its field definitions from its data description specifications (DDS).

Journal records show the updating activity to each record by storing the after-image of that record. Optionally, the operator can have the journal store the record's before-image as well. In addition to file updating activities, journal receivers also contain a great deal of file- and system-related information. For example, every time a file is opened or closed, a journal receiver record will be created. Or, if the system gets IPLed, a record will be created. The following is a list of the information the receiver can contain:

- Transactions (record level). Adds, changes, or deletes:
  - The before-image (optional).
  - The after-image.
- File information. Every time a file is:
  - Opened.
  - Closed.
  - Saved.
  - Restored.
  - Renamed.
  - Moved.
- File access path information.
- File member information. Every time a file member is:
  - Cleared.
  - Added.
  - Removed.
- System information. Every time the system is:
  - IPLed.
  - To perform dynamic tuning (per the QPFRADJ system value) for every change the system makes.

- Improvised information. Programmers can write their own records to the journal receiver. For example, users may want to record account balances, or programmers may want to place records that define application boundaries. The system operator may want to insert a notation into the journal as a record of some important event. The command to do this is the Send Journal Entry (SNDJRNE).

Each entry in the journal receiver is sequentially numbered. When a physical file is journaled, adds, changes, or deletes made to that physical file are journaled. This is true even when physical file changes are made through attached logical files. For example, consider a physical file, SWXP010, with an attached logical file named SWXP010L1. Changes are made to the physical file directly and indirectly through the logical file. If SWXP010 is journaled, all changes to that file are journaled. Even changes that are done through the logical file are recorded as changes to the physical file.

Optionally, access paths can be journaled—that means the physical file's key as well as all logical files (which, to the AS/400, are just access paths of the physical file). Always take that option. While it will increase the amount of data journaled, it will greatly reduce the recovery time if the system must rebuild.

Journaling, like anything on a computer, comes with a cost. Sometimes it impacts the machine enough that more DASD must be added to support journaling. Those costs must be weighed against journaling's benefits.

Along with this weighing, even a minimum journaling strategy can lower the cost. For example, when first considering journaling, the temptation is often to journal all the files in a production library. But when one considers the hundreds or thousands of files that the production system relies on, and then thinks about which ones are really dynamic, one quickly sees that many of those files are for support and are quite static. They probably do not need journaling; a weekly save may provide sufficient protection.

But the job of coming up with backup and journaling strategies that produce up-to-the-minute data protection, yet require the least computer impact is no small balancing act.

SETTING UP JOURNALING

Setting up journaling and maintaining journaling is really very simple. Actually, we will soon see that as complex and powerful as journaling is, doing it is fairly easy.

We will start with setting up journaling on a typical AS/400. All the system operator has to do is:

- Create a Journal Receiver (CRTJRNRCV).
- Create a Journal (CRTJRN).
- Start Journaling of the Physical Files (STRJRNPF).
- Start Journaling of the Access Paths (STRJRNAP).

Create a Journal Receiver (CRTJRNRCV)

Journal receivers are created with the Create Journal Receiver (CRTJRNRCV) command. Figure 17-1 shows the prompted version of it.

```
                  Create Journal Receiver (CRTJRNRCV)

Type choices, press Enter.

Journal receiver . . . . . . . .   RECEIV0001     Name
  Library  . . . . . . . . . . .    RCVLIB        Name, *CURLIB
Auxiliary storage pool ID  . . .   *LIBASP        1-16, *LIBASP
Journal receiver threshold . . .   *NONE          1-1919999, *NONE
Text 'description' . . . . . . .   Sample Receiver create


                         Additional Parameters

Preferred storage unit . . . . .   *ANY           1-255, *ANY
Authority  . . . . . . . . . . .   *LIBCRTAUT     Name, *LIBCRTAUT, *CHANGE...




                                                                    Bottom
F3=Exit   F4=Prompt   F5=Refresh   F12=Cancel   F13=How to use this display
F24=More keys
```

Figure 17-1: Prompted version of CRTJRNRCV command.

The option `Auxiliary Storage Pool ID` allows the system operator to specify a user ASP where the journal receivers will live (refer to Chapter 7, Managing Devices, for more information on ASPs). In this figure, it will just reside in the same ASP the library is in.

Option `Journal Receiver Threshold` specifies the threshold level of the receiver. Although this is optional, it should be set; and if MNGRCV(*SYSTEM) is set on the Create Journal (CRTJRN) command (see Create Journal [CRTJRN] next), this must be set to a value greater than or equal to 5,000. The system will send a message when the receiver becomes this size. The message will either go to the System Operator Message Queue (QSYSOPR) or to a special message queue. The desired queue is specified on the Create Journal (CRTJRN) command.

The threshold level should be set so that it is rarely encountered between daily receiver changes. However, if something unusual happens on the system that causes an abnormal number of entries to go to the receiver, the threshold message alerts the system operator to it. *Note*: This exceeded threshold alert could really be an alert to another abnormal situation that requires someone's attention; for example, a runaway program. Journal receivers will continue to accept journal entries way past their threshold point, but the system operator needs to determine why the system is generating so many file updates.

One journal can support *dual journal receivers*, creating the ultimate in crash protection. To start dual journal receivers, create them both by using the Create Journal Receiver (CRTJRNRCV) command. Make their names different and attach them both to the same journal.

Create a Journal (CRTJRN)

When at least one journal receiver is created, create the journal itself with the CRTJRN (Create Journal) command. Figure 17-2 shows a sample of it in prompted form.

```
                      Create Journal (CRTJRN)

Type choices, press Enter.

Journal . . . . . . . . . . . . .   JOURNAL      Name
  Library . . . . . . . . . . .     JRNLIB       Name, *CURLIB
Journal receiver . . . . . . . .    RECEIV0001   Name
  Library . . . . . . . . . . .     RCVLIB       Name, *LIBL, *CURLIB



Auxiliary storage pool ID . . .   *LIBASP      1-16, *LIBASP
Journal message queue . . . . .   QSYSOPR      Name
  Library . . . . . . . . . . .     *LIBL      Name, *LIBL, *CURLIB
Manage receivers . . . . . . . .  *USER        *USER, *SYSTEM
Delete receivers . . . . . . . .  *NO          *NO, *YES
Receiver size options . . . . .   *NONE        *NONE, *RMVINTENT, *MINFIXLEN

Text 'description' . . . . . . .  Sample Journal Create


                                                                    Bottom
F3=Exit   F4=Prompt   F5=Refresh   F10=Additional parameters   F12=Cancel
F13=How to use this display        F24=More keys
```

Figure 17-2: Prompted version of CRTJRN command.

Note the space for specifying dual journal receivers (the two input lines under the single journal receiver and its library) and specifying an ASP number. For single receivers (like most AS/400 IT departments), only specify the initial receiver. Do not worry about the receiver after the initial one. The system will take care of those. Because we specify at journal creation what receiver(s) it is to use, we will have created the receivers first. That is why we create journal receivers prior to creating journals.

Set the parameter MNGRCV to *SYSTEM. This automates much of the journal receiver maintenance.

Start Journaling (STRJRNPF and STRJRNAP)

After the journal and receiver(s) are created, journaling can start. There are two commands to do this. Start Journal Physical File (STRJRNPF) starts journaling of physical files and Start Journal Access Path (STRJRNAP) starts journaling of access paths.

Journaling access paths is optional but should always be done. Although it costs more as far as disk space goes, it will greatly reduce the time it takes to rebuild a system.

STRJRNPF starts journaling on one or more specified files in a library. Although files in several different libraries can be journaled together, the common practice is to journal all files in a particular library. Figure 17-3 shows a prompted version of the STRJRNPF command.

```
                    Start Journal Physical File (STRJRNPF)

 Type choices, press Enter.

 Physical file to be journaled  .   MASTFLE       Name
   Library  . . . . . . . . . . .     MSTLIB       Name, *LIBL, *CURLIB
              + for more values     ________
                                      *LIBL
 Journal  . . . . . . . . . . . .   JOURNAL        Name
   Library  . . . . . . . . . . .     JRNLIB       Name, *LIBL, *CURLIB
 Record images  . . . . . . . . .   *AFTER         *AFTER, *BOTH
 Journal entries to be omitted  .   *NONE          *NONE, *OPNCLO




                                                                    Bottom
 F3=Exit   F4=Prompt   F5=Refresh   F12=Cancel   F13=How to use this display
 F24=More keys
```

Figure 17-3: Prompted version of the STRJRNPF command.

Two STRJRNPF parameters will dramatically affect how much data is journaled and the resulting size of the journal receivers. They are Journal Entries to be Omitted (OMTJRNE) and Record Images (Images).

OMTJRNE(*OPNCLO) omits journaling the fact that each file is opened and closed (potentially, a great many entries). IMAGES(*BOTH) journals the before-images as well as the after-images. This method provides great recovery, but it doubles the amount of DASD space the receivers will take—that is the cost. Saving before-images gains the IT department recoverability of deleted records if it has to.

Access paths are the key paths for physical and logical files. Recreating all the access paths during recovery can take quite a while. Journaling access paths will reduce this time and hasten recovery after a system crash. The system is faster at recovering an access path from the journal than it is at rebuilding the same path from scratch.

Keep in mind that access paths cannot be journaled unless the related physical files are also journaled. Always start journaling in this order: STRJRNPF followed by STRJRNAP. Figure 17-4 shows a prompted version of the STRJRNAP (Start Journal Access Path) command.

```
                       Start Journal Access Path (STRJRNAP)

 Type choices, press Enter.

 Journaled file . . . . . . . . .   MASTFLE        Name
   Library  . . . . . . . . . . .     MSTLIB       Name, *LIBL, *CURLIB
              + for more values
                                      *LIBL
 Journal  . . . . . . . . . . . .   JOURNAL        Name
   Library  . . . . . . . . . . .     JRNLIB       Name, *LIBL, *CURLIB

                                                                         Bottom
 F3=Exit   F4=Prompt   F5=Refresh   F12=Cancel   F13=How to use this display
 F24=More keys
```

Figure 17-4: Prompted version of the STRJRNAP command.

When the two commands shown in Figures 17-3 and 17-4 are issued, journaling is in effect.

Save the Journaled Files (SAVOBJ)

Immediately after you start journaling, save the journaled database files with the Save Object (SAVOBJ) command. This is probably the most crucial step, because without it, the journaling may be useless. The reason is that, after journaling is started (and any time a new member is added to a journaled file), the fact that the file is being journaled is embedded on the file's file description. Prove this by using the Display File Description (DSPFD) command on a journaled and a nonjournaled file. On the first screen of that command, the file that is journaled has attached journal information.

If journaling is to be used to recover a damaged or lost file, the first step is to restore the file from the last good backup. The second step is to restore the journal receiver in effect at that time and start *applying journal entries* forward until the file's data is brought up to the time it was lost. The fly in the ointment is that one cannot apply journal entries to a file that was not journaled. So if the restored file was from a save taken before journaling was started, the file's description says it is not being journaled (because it was not at the time), and the system will never apply journal entries to that file.

This piece of data is called the *journal identifier* and is actually associated with each member of the file, not the file as a whole. So when journaling a multiple-member file, make sure this save happens every time a new member is added.

At this point, journaling should be well underway. But the system operator should perform one last task: verify one last time that the files that are meant to be journaled are actually being journaled. Look at each file's description (using the DSPFD command), and double-check using the journal's description of which files it is journaling. Check the files that the journal thinks it has with the Work with Journal Attributes (WRKJRNA) command:

```
WRKJRNA JRN(<library/journal name>)
```

If a lot of files are to be journaled, it helps to direct this command's output to a printer (OUTPUT[*PRINT]) and work from the hardcopy.

The check and double-checks are important, because too many IT departments go along under the false impression that everything they need is in the receivers.

Be particularly careful adding new files to an application and including them in the journaling mix. The STRJRNPF will not always fail with a nice error message; sometimes it just goes on even though it did not take. If a file is on the list as being journaled and, in fact, it is not, see if the new file is in a different library and/or ASP from the rest of the files. That is the most common reason files fail to get journaled.

MAINTAINING JOURNALS

After journaling is running and the journaled files are verified, the operator only has to do daily (and sometimes more frequently if there is a problem) maintenance. If the operator is smart and set the MNGRCV parameter to *SYSTEM when the journal was created, the system will automatically change journal receivers whenever they are full. The steps to maintain journals are:

- Change receivers periodically (once a day or when their threshold is reached).
- Save the filled receivers.
- Optionally, delete the filled receivers from the system.

Change Receivers

There are three times when an operator has to change receivers:

- On a regular (preferably daily) basis.
- When the receiver exceeds its threshold and the journal's MNGRCV parameter is not set to *SYSTEM.
- To reset the receiver's Sequence Number to 1, or change its threshold limit.

The command is Change Journal (CHGJRN). Figure 17-5 shows the prompted form.

The command shown in Figure 17-5 looks more complex than it is. Most of the time, the system operator will just specify the journal name and the Generate (*GEN) keyword on the parameter `Journal Receiver`. As long as the receivers are named so that they have trailing four digits, the system is able to create the new receivers it will change to.

The command to change receivers can be given at any time (even while journaling is active). The old journal receiver will be detached, the new receiver will be attached, and journaling will just continue.

The only other thing to watch for are the journal entry sequence numbers. They start with one and continue on. When journal receivers are changed and the Sequence Option parameter is not changed from the default *CONT (continue) to one, the sequence numbers for the next receiver will just continue from the last number in the old receiver. Normally, this is all right and the way most AS/400 IT departments run their journaling.

```
                         Change Journal (CHGJRN)

Type choices, press Enter.

Journal . . . . . . . . . . . .   JOURNAL       Name
  Library . . . . . . . . . . .     JRNLIB      Name, *LIBL, *CURLIB
Journal receiver:
  Journal receiver . . . . . . .  *SAME         Name, *SAME, *GEN
    Library . . . . . . . . . .     ________    Name, *LIBL, *CURLIB
  Journal receiver . . . . . . .  ________      Name, *GEN
    Library . . . . . . . . . .     ________    Name, *LIBL, *CURLIB
Sequence option . . . . . . . .   *CONT         *RESET, *CONT
Journal message queue . . . . .   *SAME         Name, *SAME
  Library . . . . . . . . . . .     ________    Name, *LIBL, *CURLIB
Manage receivers . . . . . . . .  *SAME         *SAME, *USER, *SYSTEM
Delete receivers . . . . . . . .  *SAME         *SAME, *NO, *YES
Receiver size options . . . . .   *SAME         *SAME, *NONE, *RMVINTENT...

Journal state . . . . . . . . .   *SAME         *SAME, *ACTIVE, *INACTIVE

                                                                 More...
F9=All parameters   F11=Keywords   F14=Command string   F24=More keys
```

Figure 17-5: Prompted version of the CHGJRN command.

This is not a problem until the number reaches 2,147,483,136. When it gets that high, journaling will stop. When the number reaches 2,147,000,000, the system operator will get a warning message to reset the sequence numbers.

If the journal was created with MNGRCV(*SYSTEM), this sequence number is reset to one every time the system is re-IPLed. It's another reason to let the system manage things. This sequence number thing is not a big deal. Even large systems take a long time to collect the maximum number of sequence numbers.

Saving Receivers

Save receivers as soon as possible after they have been detached. This is done with one of several Save commands:

- SAVLIB.
- SAVOBJ.
- SAVCHGOBJ.

Just remember that the receiver's object type is *JRNRCV.
Although it is possible to save receivers currently attached to journals, the saved version will be a partial version. It is labeled as such and that limits its usefulness when recovering.

When journal receivers are saved, they can be optionally saved with *freed storage*. The option and keyword is STG(*FREE). As soon as the save is complete, the storage taken up by the receiver's data (but not its description) is freed (the records are cleared). The (*FREE) option cannot be used on currently attached journal receivers.

Deleting Receivers

Journal receivers are deleted with the Delete Journal Receiver (DLTJRNRCV) command. This is always done after the receiver has been saved, never before. A journal receiver in use by a journal cannot be deleted. Figure 17-6 contains a prompted version of that command.

```
                    Delete Journal Receiver (DLTJRNRCV)

Type choices, press Enter.

Journal receiver . . . . . . . .   RECEIV0001    Name, generic*
  Library  . . . . . . . . . . .    RCVLIB       Name, *LIBL, *CURLIB...
Option . . . . . . . . . . . . .   *NONE         *NONE, *IGNINQMSG...
               + for more values   __________









                                                                  Bottom
F3=Exit   F4=Prompt   F5=Refresh   F12=Cancel   F13=How to use this display
F24=More keys
```

Figure 17-6: Prompted version of the DLTJRNRCV command.

Because of the importance of receiver chains, receivers can only be deleted in the order in which they were attached to the journal. The exception to this is when a receiver is designated as damaged. They can be deleted at any time after it is detached from the journal, or delete a receiver anytime when using dual receivers on a journal and its mate still exists on the system.

While the system will allow it, it's a very bad idea to delete a journal receiver that hasn't been saved first. The system will issue warning message CPF7025 if a receiver hasn't been saved. The operator can get past it by taking an I (Ignore) response.

The DLTJRNRCV has a parameter to override some of its internal protections. That parameter is DLTOPT (Delete Option). It has three valid values:

- *IGNEXITPGM—Ignores any messages from an attached user program that the receiver is in use.
- *IGNTGTRCV—Ignores the target system. This is used when deleting a journal receiver used in remote journaling. The value disables the system verification that the receiver has a full copy on a remote system prior to being removed.
- *IGNINQMSG—Ignores the warning message CPF7025 mentioned above. The system assumes you wanted to respond to it with I (Ignore) and continues processing.

Think twice (or three times) before taking any of these overrides.

RECEIVER CHAINS

Except for the first receiver attached to a journal when journaling started, every receiver has a predecessor. Also, every receiver except for the current one has a next receiver. These entries are made on the receivers when they are attached to and detached from journals. The sequence of predecessor/next creates what is known as a *receiver chain*. When receivers are used to recover data, the system operator needs to make sure the complete chain is on-line. In that way, when the system applies changes, it will go from the starting receiver right through the other ones.

For example, consider an IT department that changes receivers every day and loses a database file on Thursday. That IT department would restore the last saved version of the file. Let us presume it was made on Sunday and that the journal receiver in effect on Sunday was RECEIV0010.

The system operator would start applying journal entries with the RECEIV0010 receiver. But before starting, RECEIV0010 must be on the system as well as RECEIV0011 through RECEIV0014. The system will walk through consecutive receivers until it gets current.

On the other hand, if the system operator were restoring receivers and could not find RECEIV0011, he would have a problem. Not only would he have lost the changes for Thursday, but the system could not apply changes after RECEIV0010 (at least not automatically; the operator could re-request the apply starting with RECEIV0012 after RECEIV0010 completes).

> **TIP:**
>
> Good journal management includes good physical handling of the saved receivers and journals.

That missing RECEIV0011 is one example of what is referred to as a *broken chain*. Another broken chain can occur when a receiver is backed up while it is still attached to the journal. While this is theoretically possible, what actually happens is the receiver is only partially saved and, therefore, does not complete the restore. Aside from broken chains, other causes of journal chain problems are:

- Restoring a receiver from another system.
- Restoring a receiver that has not had its storage freed by a save operation.
- Saving or freeing a receiver and then trying to use it without restoring it.

MISCELLANEOUS JOURNALING FUNCTIONS

There are journaling functions that are not done very often and are not really categorized nicely anywhere else. They are:

- End journaling.
- Deleting journals (not to be confused with deleting receivers mentioned in the section labeled Deleting Receivers).

End Journaling

Journaling is rarely ended; it essentially goes on and on. If the IT department needs to end journaling for any reason, use the End Journal Physical File (ENDJRNPF) and the End Journal Access Path (ENDJRNAP) commands.

Because access paths cannot be journaled if the associated physical files are not also journaled, the system operator cannot end journaling on physical files if their access paths are still being journaled. The sequence for ending journaling is ENDJRNAP followed by ENDJRNPF. Figure 17-7 shows the prompted format of the ENDJRNAP command and Figure 17-8 shows the prompted version of the ENDJRNPF command.

```
                  End Journal Access Path (ENDJRNAP)

 Type choices, press Enter.

 Journaled file . . . . . . . . .   MSTFLE        Name, *ALL
   Library  . . . . . . . . . . .     MSTLIB      Name, *LIBL, *CURLIB
               + for more values    
                                      *LIBL
 Journal  . . . . . . . . . . . .   JOURNAL       Name, *FILE
   Library  . . . . . . . . . . .     JRNLIB      Name, *LIBL, *CURLIB




                                                                  Bottom
 F3=Exit   F4=Prompt   F5=Refresh   F12=Cancel   F13=How to use this display
 F24=More keys
```

Figure 17-7: Prompted version of the ENDJRNAP command.

```
                 End Journaling PF Changes (ENDJRNPF)

 Type choices, press Enter.

 Journaled physical file  . . . .   MSTFLE        Name, *ALL
   Library  . . . . . . . . . . .     MSTLIB      Name, *LIBL, *CURLIB
               + for more values    
                                      *LIBL
 Journal  . . . . . . . . . . . .   JOURNAL       Name, *FILE
   Library  . . . . . . . . . . .     JRNLIB      Name, *LIBL, *CURLIB




                                                                  Bottom
 F3=Exit   F4=Prompt   F5=Refresh   F12=Cancel   F13=How to use this display
 F24=More keys
```

Figure 17-8: Prompted version of the ENDJRNPF command.

Deleting Journals

When the rare moment comes when a journal has to be deleted, do so with the Delete Journal (DLTJRN) command. A journal cannot be deleted while it is journaling files. To get an active journal and its receivers off the system, here is the sequence:

- End journaling of all logical files with the End Journal Access Path (ENDJRNAP) command.
- End journaling of all files associated with the journal using the End Journal Physical File (ENDJRNPF) command.
- If commitment control is active and the journal is associated with it, end it with the End Commitment Control (ENDCMTCTL) command.
- Save/delete the journal using a Save command and Delete Journal (DLTJRN) command.
- Save/delete the journal receiver using a Save command and the Delete Journal Receiver (DLTJRNRCV) command.

USING JOURNALS

Eventually, every customer needs to use the journal information that has been collected. When this happens, the customers who set up journaling correctly always have the same reaction: "Journaling?"

The AS/400 handles journaling so smoothly that most IT departments forget all about it. Even if they remember having it, they certainly do not remember how to restore and apply journal entries.

Restoring Journals and Receivers

It is hard to say what a customer would need to restore prior to applying journal entries. If everything were on the system, unsaved, they would not have to restore anything. If the customer is recovering from a bad system, everything will have to be restored. Just in case, this section will discuss the worst case—where everything has been saved and needs to be restored.

Journals, receivers, and database files must be restored in order. If these items all resided on one library and were saved with a SAVLIB (Save Library) command, there is no problem. The system will ensure that all elements are restored in order when the RSTLIB (Restore Library) command is used.

If the objects were in different libraries (typically, database files and journals in one library; receivers in another), the system cannot determine the order no matter what commands saved them.

If the system cannot determine the correct order, it is the operator's responsibility. Restore these items in this order:

1. Journals.
2. Physical files.
3. Logical files.
4. Journal receivers (newest to oldest).

Needless to say, this can be a painful process. Many IT departments just do not deal with it. They lump all elements into one library and let the system sort them out.

That may be fine for them, but they pay a performance penalty the entire time journaling goes on. By using the alternative and distributing receivers to other libraries/ASPs, the long-term system degradation due to journaling is reduced. The cost is on the restore. The customer must take on the responsibility of restoring all elements in their proper order. Like a lot of computer issues, it is a trade-off of cost versus functionality.

Applying and Removing Journal Entries

Applying and *removing journal entries* to a database file are two ways of using journaled changes to fix corrupted files:

- Applying journal entries (sometimes referred to as "going forward").
- Removing journal entries (sometimes referred to as "going backward").

To remove journaled changes from a file, the journal must have been journaling both before-images and after-images on the physical file.

If a database file gets corrupted in the system sense (something like a disk going bad), whatever is on the disk will not be usable. To recover, the system operator will have to restore the last good version of the file, ensure that the receiver chain is present, then apply changes from that last date forward.

However, if a database file was corrupted in a nonsystem way, like a program or human error, the system operator could use a different method. For example, a file can be damaged because of a programming bug. The database file is not damaged in the system sense, but several thousand records could be bad. Because the system operator knows specifically which program and during which time period those records were corrupted, he/she does not have to go back to old versions of the file. He/she can just remove the changes made to the file by the bad program using the current journal receiver. In this case, he or she would start at the current time and remove journal entries (going backward) until the start of the bad program.

Applying Journal Changes

Journal changes are applied from a start date forward. The implication is that a file restore must have taken place for the IT department to end up with an old version of the file and more current journal entries. Here are the processes the system operator must do to apply journal changes:

- Restore the latest uncorrupted version of the file.
- Restore all the journal receivers that were used from the date/time of that save and are currently not on the system or were saved with their storage freed. Do this restore in order from the newest (today) back to the oldest (the date of the save).
- Ensure that the operator has exclusive use of the database file and the receivers (use the Allocate Object [ALCOBJ] command).
- Use the Apply Journaled Changes (APYJRNCHG) command. Specify the journal receiver from which the system should start applying. This journal receiver should be the one that was in effect when the database file was saved. *Note*: The starting time within the receiver's records can be specified, and the system will start applying changes at that point. Or, the system operator may even have to find a starting sequence number and specify that as a starting place.

Figure 17-9 shows the prompted version of the APYJRNCHG command.

```
                    Apply Journaled Changes (APYJRNCHG)

Type choices, press Enter.

Journal . . . . . . . . . . . .   JOURNAL       Name
  Library . . . . . . . . . . .     JRNLIB      Name, *LIBL, *CURLIB
Journaled physical file:
  Journaled physical file . . .   MSTFLE        Name, *ALL
    Library . . . . . . . . . .     MSTLIB      Name, *LIBL, *CURLIB
  Member . . . . . . . . . . . .  *FIRST        Name, *FIRST, *ALL
              + for more values     
Range of journal receivers:
  Starting journal receiver . .   *LASTSAVE     Name, *LASTSAVE, *CURRENT
    Library . . . . . . . . . .                 Name, *LIBL, *CURLIB
  Ending journal receiver . . .                 Name, *CURRENT
    Library . . . . . . . . . .                 Name, *LIBL, *CURLIB
Starting sequence number . . . .  *LASTSAVE     Number, *LASTSAVE, *FIRST
Ending sequence number . . . . .  *LASTRST      Number, *LASTRST, *LAST


                                                                More...
F3=Exit   F4=Prompt   F5=Refresh   F12=Cancel   F13=How to use this display
F24=More keys
```

```
                    Apply Journaled Changes (APYJRNCHG)

Type choices, press Enter.

Ending date and time:
  Ending date . . . . . . . . .                 Date
  Ending time . . . . . . . . .                 Time
Fully qualified job name . . . .                Name
  User . . . . . . . . . . . . .                Name
  Number . . . . . . . . . . . .                000000-999999
Fully qualified job name . . . .                Name
  User . . . . . . . . . . . . .                Name
  Number . . . . . . . . . . . .                000000-999999
Commitment boundary . . . . . .   *NO           *NO, *YES





                                                                 Bottom
F3=Exit   F4=Prompt   F5=Refresh   F12=Cancel   F13=How to use this display
F24=More keys
```

Figure 17-9: Prompted version of the APYJRNCHG command (parts 1 and 2).

This command requests the qualified journal name that is the source of journal entries. The next set of parameters wants to know to which file it should apply journals. This parameter is used to specify a file, multiple files, or the generic *ALL.

The next parameter, Range of Journal Receivers, specifies the receiver to start. The system operator could tell the system where the receiver should end. However, common practice is to start with the first journal receiver after the last save of the file and continue through the receiver chain until applying the current receiver's changes.

If the operator only wants to restore the changes within a range of entry sequence numbers, the start and end numbers can be specified in the Starting Sequence Number and Ending Sequence Number parameters. If these numbers are not known, they can be found by using the Display Journal (DSPJRN) command. For additional information, see the IBM manual *OS/400 Backup and Recovery V4R4.*

If he or she does not want to apply all journal changes from all receivers, he/she probably wants to apply journal changes for a specific time period. In that case, the date and time range can be specified.

If the specific job user or job number to apply changes from is known, they can be specified. If files are updated with programs that use commitment control, the option of adhering to those boundaries or not is available. If the IT department is recovering from a system crash and it uses commitment control, the operator probably will want to adhere to those boundaries. When the system applies journaled changes, it applies them in order from oldest to most current. For additional information, see the IBM manual *OS/400 Backup and RecoveryV4R4.*

Removing Journal Changes

Depending on the operator's journaling skill, strategy, and the nature of the problem he/she is trying to recover from, it might be easier to remove journaled changes than try to restore the file and apply a lot of changes. There are three advantages to removing journal changes rather than applying journal changes:

- The operator does not have to reload the last saved version of the damaged file.
- Generally, the operator does not have to reload receivers; the current one is sufficient.
- Removing changes uses considerably fewer records and goes faster.

There are details in removing journal entries that the operator must be concerned about that are not a concern when applying journal changes:

- Journaling must have included before-images and after-images of changed records.
- When specifying where the system should stop removing journaled changes, the operator cannot specify a certain time (such as 7:30 A.M.). He/she must specify the sequence number. That is an extra step. To stop journaling from removing entries at 7:30 A.M., he/she has to use the Display Journal (DSPJRN) command to determine what sequence number was in effect at that time.
- The current receiver is generally far enough back in the sequence, but the operator should check to see if the current receiver goes back to the time where he/she wants to stop removing entries. If it does not go back far enough (in the example, receivers were changed sometime between 7:30 A.M. and the current time), he/she must make sure the previous receiver is on the system.
- When the system removes journaled changes, it removes them from the most current to oldest.

- This command cannot be used to rebuild a database file damaged from a system problem. The command works on files corrupted by a bad program or a crazed user.

Figure 17-10 shows the prompted Remove Journaled Changes (RMVJRNCHG) command.

```
                      Remove Journaled Changes (RMVJRNCHG)

Type choices, press Enter.

Journal . . . . . . . . . . . .   JOURNAL       Name
  Library . . . . . . . . . . .     JRNLIB      Name, *LIBL, *CURLIB
Journaled file identification:
  Journaled physical file . . .   MSTFLE        Name, *ALL
    Library . . . . . . . . . .     MSTLIB      Name, *LIBL, *CURLIB
  Member . . . . . . . . . . . .  *FIRST        Name, *FIRST, *ALL
             + for more values      
Range of journal receivers:
  Starting journal receiver . .   *CURRENT      Name, *CURRENT
    Library . . . . . . . . . .                 Name, *LIBL, *CURLIB
  Ending journal receiver . . .                 Name
    Library . . . . . . . . . .                 Name, *LIBL, *CURLIB
Starting sequence number . . . .  *LAST         Number, *LAST, *LASTSAVE
Ending sequence number . . . . .  *FIRST        Number, *FIRST


                                                                  More...
F3=Exit   F4=Prompt   F5=Refresh   F12=Cancel   F13=How to use this display
F24=More keys
```

```
                      Remove Journaled Changes (RMVJRNCHG)

Type choices, press Enter.

Fully qualified job name . . . .                Name
  User . . . . . . . . . . . . .                Name
  Number . . . . . . . . . . . .                000000-999999
Commitment boundary . . . . . .   *NO           *NO, *YES











                                                                   Bottom
F3=Exit   F4=Prompt   F5=Refresh   F12=Cancel   F13=How to use this display
F24=More keys
```

Figure 17-10: Prompted version of the RMVJRNCHG command (parts 1 and 2).

Specify *CURRENT as the value for the Starting Journal Receiver parameter (as opposed to LASTSAV). The sequence numbers are from the LAST to the FIRST. Note: If these parameters are left as defaulted (*LAST/*FIRST), the system will apply all changes in the current receiver only.

JOURNALING PERFORMANCE CONSIDERATIONS

The bad news is that journaling costs in terms of DASD utilization and system performance. The good news is that the system helps speed up journaling activities, and there is one thing the system operator can do to improve performance. The system will save before- and after-images and write them to DASD in one operation rather than two. It will also analyze the write arms within the receiver ASP and try to use the fastest ten. It will also distribute the workload evenly over these ten so as soon as one is busy, it will use the next, then the next and so on.

To make journaling less expensive on the performance side, the system operator can isolate journal receivers into their own user ASP (but, remember, the cost of this is incurred during a restore).

JOURNALING STRATEGY

There are many parts to journaling strategy. Unlike saves (except saves to a Save File), journaling uses a lot of disk space. One strategy consideration will be that the journaling use minimal disk space. One way of conserving disk space is to limit what is journaled; an element of the strategy may be to not journal access paths, for example. However, the recovery from that journal would take a very long time while a recovery from a more complete journal would take a lot less time. For that matter, how often does the IT department expect to need to recover from journals? Many IT departments run years and never go to their journals. Yet, on the other hand, if the AS/400 was down so hard that complete recovery from journal was necessary, how long can the downtime be? Do seconds count, or will the company feel that if they are down that hard, a couple extra hours will not matter? Suddenly, the simple equation of disk space versus recovery time has many variables. This is the kind of analysis that needs to go into developing a journaling strategy.

Here are some basic options for setting up journaling that every journal strategy writer should consider:

- Everything—database files, journals, and receivers—goes into the same library and the same ASP. While this is the simplest and most common method of journaling, it's not the most efficient for performance.
- Files and journals in one library, receivers in another, but both in the same ASP—a little better for performance and managing backup and recovery.
- Files and journals in the system ASP, receivers in a library user ASP—preferably one with its own input/output bus. This provides the best performance and maximum protection of journal entries.
- Journal receivers in a nonlibrary user ASP, files in the system ASP, and journals in either the system ASP or the same nonlibrary user ASP as the journal receivers.

At the end of the day, no matter what decisions were made about journal object placement, run a CL program that will:

- Change journal receivers.
- Save the library with the SAVLIB command.

- Save changed objects with the SAVCHGOBJ command, excluding journaled files and attached receivers.
- Save the old receivers and then delete them. If you have the disk space, try to leave the last several receivers on the system.

This is a simple CL program that is found in many AS/400 IT departments. An operator or developer familiar with CL programming must write it. CL programming language is beyond the scope of this book; for an example of such a program, refer to the IBM manual, *OS/400 CL Programming.*

JOURNALING TO A REMOTE AS/400

Remote journaling is the capability for the AS/400 to journal to another AS/400. There are some considerations for remote journaling:

- Local journaling has to be in effect for remote journaling to work.
- Remote journaling will not improve performance while journaling. If anything, it will degrade performance to some degree.

With that out of the way, here is what remote journaling will do:

- By replicating journals and journal receivers on another platform, the customer gets better data protection from a hardware failure.
- Although complete synchronization of the two machines is not part of remote journaling, it at least builds the basis for a future hot backup site.

Remote journaling consists of a local AS/400 with a local database being updated, and those update activities being journaled. Through that local journal, a remote journal and receiver are created and activated on a remote AS/400. The local database may or may not exist on the remote AS/400; the focus at this time is primarily on the journaling. All entries that go into the local journal are automatically sent to the remote platform and inserted into the remote journal receiver.

Remote journals can be configured in two ways:

- *Broadcast*. This is the simplest way. The journal and receiver on machine A are replicated on machine B.
- *Cascade*. The journal and receiver on machine A are replicated on machine B, from machine B to machine C, and so on, to a maximum of 255 AS/400s replicating the same journal. Note, though, the names and nature of cascade—
  journal entries must flow from machine A to machine B and from machine B to machine C. Journal entries cannot flow from machine A directly to both machines B and C.

Although remote journals and their receivers are merely journals and receivers, there are some differences. Here are some considerations for them:

- Remote journals can only receive entries from a local journal. They cannot directly journal database files on their AS/400, nor can an application running on the remote platform force an entry into them.
- Some of the characteristics of the remote journals and receivers cannot be set or changed directly. They can only be set or changed by altering those same characteristics on the local journals/receivers.

- All AS/400s meant to support remote journaling (the source and target platforms) must be on V4R2 or later.
- Once a remote journal is added to a local journal, local receivers cannot be deleted if all entries have not been updated to the remote journal. Yes, the local journal knows the current status of the remote journal at all times.
- Because of built-in delays (different sizes or workloads of the two platforms, communication delays, etc.), a big consideration for remote journaling is the synchronization of the two journal receivers.
- The remote journal can never be ahead of the local journal.
- The remote journal can be at the same status as the local journal. That is, both receivers contain the same entries; there are no unposted entries in the queue for the remote journal. This condition is referred to as *caught-up*.
- The remote journal can have fewer entries than the local journal. The missing entries either have not gotten to the remote system yet or are in a posting queue, waiting to be placed in the remote receivers. This can simply happen when the local journal is journaling, but the remote has just been activated.
- Remote journals have the same directories and receiver chains as the local journals, however:
  - A remote journal does not have an attached receiver until it is activated. (A local journal can have an attached receiver even when it is not journaling anything.)
  - If a remote journal is in catch-up mode, it can have a receiver attached to it that is different than the local journal's receiver.
  - A remote journal in caught-up mode will have the same receiver attached as the local journal's receiver.
- Journal management functions are also replicated across platforms. When the local platform changes a receiver and/or resets the sequence number, those changes take place automatically on the remote platform.
- Use careful monitoring of remote journals. If a change on the remote system fails, remote journaling may just end. Monitor by watching for messages on both the journal message queue and the system operator's message queue (QSYSOPR).
- Most of the commands to work with remote journals are APIs. Refer to IBM manual *OS/400 Journal & Commit APIs V4R4* for more information.

Setting up Remote Journaling

Here are the steps to set up and start remote journaling:

- Ensure all libraries are on the remote system—that means the database libraries, local journals, and receivers reside on the local platform. These must be duplicated on the remote system. The exception to this is if *redirection* is used. Redirection allows the journals and receivers to exist in different libraries on the two systems.
- Ensure the user profile that manages journaling on the local system exists (and has the same authorities) on the remote system.

- If the journal name already exists on the remote system, it will be used, if possible. If not, it will be created. There are three conditions that, if they exist, will prevent the duplicated journal from being used:
    - The name is not the name of a remote journal.
    - The name is of a remote journal but one that was not previously associated with the local journal.
    - The type of journal does not match the type required.
- Start communication and verify both AS/400s are up. There are three communications protocols, and their drivers, supported by remote journaling that must be active on both the local and remote systems:
    - OptiConnect/400—This must have subsystem QSOC active.
    - SNA.
    - Vary on line/controller/device.
- Subsystem QCMN must be active.
- TCP/IP—STRTCP and DDM servers must be active.
- Create the *relational database* (*RDB*) entry (refer to the following text section on RDB entries below). This entry names the remote AS/400 and specifies the communications protocol that will be used.
- From the local platform, add remote journal with the Add Remote Journal (ADDRMTJRN) command. Make the journal status (*INACTIVE).
- From the local platform, activate remote journaling with the Change Remote Journal (CHGRMTJRN) command. On this command, specify the starting point. This specification can be in the form of:
    - *ATTACHED—the starting point is the starting point of the receiver currently attached to the remote journal. If no receiver is attached, journaling will just start.
    - *SRCSYS—journal entries on the remote system will start with the earliest entries in the earliest journal receivers currently attached to the local system. Note: This can cause a long time in catch-up mode.
    - <LIBR/LOCAL RCVR>—specify the library and name of the local journal receiver from which to start taking entries to the remote system.

Remote journaling can be activated or inactivated at any time at the local level with the Change Journal (CHGJRN) command.

To remove a remote journal, inactivate it first with the Change Journal (CHGJRN) command, then remove it with the Remove Remote Journal (RMVRMTJRN) command. Add it back again with the Add Remote Journal (ADDRMTJRN) command.

When activating remote journaling in a cascade situation, make sure all downstream platforms' remote journaling are inactivated first. Then activate the systems sequentially starting from the local and moving outward, following the journal entries.

Asynchronous Versus Synchronous Remote Journaling

When remote journaling is activated, the system has the option of activating it asynchronously or synchronously. Both deserve careful consideration.

In an *asynchronous update mode* the journal entries bound for the remote journal are sent off in that direction and control immediately returns to the application. We just assume the entry made it to the remote journal. This is the fastest method of remote journaling. On a large, active file, a synch update may be the only way to go.

In a *synchronous update mode*, the journal entries bound for the remote journal are sent off in that direction, and the local application waits until it receives notice of a successful receipt of the entry. This is very high reliability and security, but it has a huge cost in application wait time. Users may find their interactive response time unacceptable. On the other hand, in normal use, remote journals with synchronous update rarely have catch-up to do. They are always caught up, so the local and remote platforms are always in perfect synch.

These two update modes also affect how the remote journal statuses appear. For the most part, those statuses will either be *SYNC or *ASYNC. When the remote journal's mode is changed, it will just change. However, if it was *ASYNC and is changing to *SYNC, its status may become *SYNCPEND until all pending entries are posted. Although there is an *ASYNCPEND, we rarely see it. When changing from *SYNC to *ASYNC, we can generally assume there are no pending entries (because of the nature of *SYNC), and the change just happens.

When a remote journal's status is set to inactive and it is updating asynchronously, the user will often see a status of *INACTPEND in between *ACTIVE and *INACTIVE.

RDB Entries

Relational database (RDB) entries are one of those things IBM gives us just to test our sense of humor. RDB makes better sense when we think of it as *remote database*. Its reason for being is to allow us to specify the name of the relational database our applications will be addressing. That is nice, however, every AS/400 comes with one and only one relational database and we cannot avoid using it. What the RDB does is names a relational database on another AS/400 that applications will access. To simplify this concept even further, when naming the remote relational database, just name it the same name as the remote AS/400 is named on the network.

Forget for now what RDB stands for and think of it as meaning the name of a remote AS/400 whose files will be accessed. Every AS/400 has exactly one *RDB directory*. The RDB directory holds all the names of the relational databases the operator has entered into it. When working with a database shared between a local and remote AS/400, the operator must create an *RDB directory entry*. Do so with the Add Relational Database Directory Entry (ADDRDBDIRE) command. Figure 17-11 contains a sample of the prompted version of that command.

This command has three parameters, one of which is a Text field. The other two are:

- RDB—The name of the AS/400 that the directory entry is being made for.
- RMTLOCNAME—Names the other AS/400 that the directory entry is being made for.

```
                     Add RDB Directory Entry (ADDRDBDIRE)

Type choices, press Enter.

Relational database . . . . . .   ____________________
Remote location:
  Name or address . . . . . . .   ________________________________________
  ________________________________________________________________
  ________________________________________________________________

  Type . . . . . . . . . . . . .   *SNA           *SNA, *IP
Text . . . . . . . . . . . . . .   *BLANK________________________________________







                                                                        Bottom
F3=Exit   F4=Prompt   F5=Refresh   F12=Cancel   F13=How to use this display
F24=More keys
```

Figure 17-11: Prompted version of ADDRDBDIRE command.

Each AS/400 on the network (or, for remote journaling, both the local and remote AS/400s) must have RDB directory entries for the other. Here is an example of the RDB directory entries for machine A and machine B. (Assume machine A is our local and machine B is remote.):

- On machine A:
  - `addrdbdire rdb(macha) rmtlocname(*local) text('.....')`
  - `addrdbdire rdb(machb) rmtlocname(machb) text('.....')`
- On machine B:
  - `addrdbdire rdb(machb) rmtlocname(*local) text('.....')`
  - `addrdbdire rdb(macha) rmtlocname(macha) text('.....')`

If you do not know the name of the attached AS/400, use the Display Network Attributes (DSPNETA) command.

The RDB entry does double duty—it also is where the communications protocol is specified for remote journaling.

Remote Journaling Performance Considerations

Remote journaling costs even more in performance than local journaling. There is not a nice way to put it. However, here are some things the system operator can do to ameliorate the impact:

- Isolate the remote journal to its own communication hardware and protocol. Do not use the communications link for other functions.

- Use the fastest communications protocol available. If possible, use the OptiConnect/400 bus transport.
- Select asynchronous update mode. This is many times faster than synchronous; however, the local and remote databases are not always in synch with this method. That may be unacceptable for some customers' needs.
- Reduce the amount of information journaled. Do this at the local journal level. Journal only after-images, and do not journal file open and close events.
- The RDB entry at the time of remote journal activation determines the communication protocol in use. To change the RDB entry, the operator must stop and restart remote journaling for the change to go into effect.
- The more receivers present (in a cascade), the longer each file update is going to take. This is simple: three receivers will take three times longer to process every database update than one receiver will.
- Add memory to *BASE to increase performance on either the local or remote platform.

COMMITMENT CONTROL

Commitment control is a process that wraps complex transaction pieces together so nothing gets lost. Unlike many of the subjects in this textbook, enabling commitment control is a process shared by programmers and operators. Usually, neither group has the whole picture. Not only is the process shared, it should be reviewed by both sides to ensure that commitment control is really happening, because it may not be and the system will not give any errors or warnings.

To understand commitment control, imagine a large, complex transaction, like order entry. When an order is taken, many files have to be changed—inventory has to be decreased; the customer's financial records have to have the amount of the order added to it; a record has to be added to the shipping file or it will not get shipped; if the order takes the inventory below a certain level, a replenishment order may be automatically created; etc. Order entry usually touches every piece of a business—it is not uncommon for a single order to cause fifty files to be updated.

Now the AS/400 is very reliable and never goes down, but what if it did halfway through an order? Some number of those fifty files (we do not know what number) would be updated and some other number would not. The database tables would be *out of synch*; the recovery from which is almost impossible. Even by applying journal entries, we would bring the tables up to the point of failure accurately, but we still would not know which files were updated and which ones were not at the second the machine went down.

The solution is commitment control, and it allows the programmer to bundle together all file updates for one transaction. The updates to the files only sort of happen (actually, they are stored in journal receivers). No files are actually updated until the program is sure the transaction is complete. When the transaction is complete, all files are *committed* or their changes are locked in. If the system were to go down at any time, the file updates that would have been made on the system would only be those up to the last commit; any updates since that point would not have been made.

Commitment control ensures that, when a system goes down hard, those recovering the system can always be assured that the database tables are in synch. By the way, there is another programmer's piece to commitment control and that is *rollback.* If the system stayed up but the application detected an error while updating the last file, the RPG program would issue the rollback operation and all previous file updates up to the last commit would be undone.

The programmer needs to insert the Commit and Rollback operations in the RPG or COBOL program; the operator needs to ensure the infrastructure is in place to support commitment control. Also, they should both double-check to ensure that the files that are intended to be committed are. This check should ensure:

- All files that are committed are also journaled and being done so to the same journal.
- All files that are committed are in the same library.

After making sure that journaling is going on, the operator starts commitment control by issuing the Start Commitment Control (STRCMTCTL) command. Figure 17-12 contains a prompted version of that command.

```
                         Start Commitment Control (STRCMTCTL)

 Type choices, press Enter.

 Lock level . . . . . . . . . . .   *CHG          *CHG, *CS, *ALL
 Notify object:
   Object . . . . . . . . . . . .   *NONE          Name, *NONE
     Library  . . . . . . . . . .                  Name, *LIBL, *CURLIB
   Object type:
   (*MSGQ *DTAARA or *FILE) . . .                  *MSGQ, *DTAARA, *FILE
   Member, if *FILE . . . . . . .                  Name, *FIRST
 Commitment definition scope  . .   *ACTGRP        *ACTGRP, *JOB
 Text 'description' . . . . . . .   *DFTTEXT

 Journal  . . . . . . . . . . . .   *NONE          Name, *NONE
   Library  . . . . . . . . . . .                  Name, *LIBL, *CURLIB
 Journal entries to be omitted  .   *NONE          *NONE, *LUWID


                                                                    Bottom
 F3=Exit   F4=Prompt   F5=Refresh   F12=Cancel   F13=How to use this display
 F24=More keys
```

Figure 17-12: Prompted version of the STRCMTCTL command.

The only required parameter is Lock Level (LCKLVL). It controls which records are locked, and for how long, when commitment control is in effect. Possible values are:

- *CHG—Records accessed for change or deletion are locked. Records opened for update or delete but released (within the program) without any action are then unlocked. Otherwise, records stay locked until they are committed or rolled back.
- *CS—Every record accessed is locked. Even records that are read and will not be changed are locked. If another record is read (for no update) from the same file, the original locked read record is unlocked. Otherwise, records stay locked until they are committed or rolled back.
- *ALL—Every record accessed for any reason is locked until all records are committed or rolled back.

End commitment control with the ENDCMTCTL command. There are no parameters for this command, just enter it on the command line and press Enter.

END-OF-CHAPTER AIDS

CHAPTER SUMMARY

Journaling begins life as an extension of the AS/400 backup and recovery functions. Where backup/recovery provide data protection up to the date/time of the last backup, journaling provides protection up to the minute of system failure. But journaling goes way beyond where it starts. It provides an absolute audit of what went on the system. This audit can be used to trace problems due to the program and user. It can answer the universal computer question, "What happened?"

Journaling can selectively remove unwanted transactions that would be impossible from simple backup media. Just the existence of journaling makes commitment control possible. Commitment control brings that data protection down to the fractional transaction level. With all these tools, it is no wonder that AS/400 data integrity is the highest in the industry.

KEY TERMS

applying journal entries
asynchronous update mode
broadcast
broken chain
cascade
caught-up
commitment control
committed
dual journal receivers
freed storage
journal
journal identifier
journal receiver
journaling
out of synch
RDB directory
RDB directory entry
receiver chain
redirection
relational database (RDB)
remote database
remote journaling
removing journal entries
rollback
static condition
synchronous update mode
threshold

CHAPTER SELF-TEST

Solutions to these self-test questions are in appendix D.

True-False Questions

___ 1. The journal receiver contains the information about what is to be journaled.

___ 2. Journaling is generally done on important database files within a library.

___ 3. When journaling the system, you always store both before- and after-images of a database record.

___ 4. The Send Journal Entry command allows the programmer or system operator, for example, to enter information in the journal receiver.

___ 5. When journaling the changes made to a physical file through a logical file, the journal shows the data as a logical file data change.

___ 6. Access paths are never journaled.

___ 7. When setting up a journal receiver, you should specify a threshold value. The value for the Threshold parameter should be set so that normal daily operations do not exceed this value.

___ 8. You can journal together the physical files in multiple libraries; however, the normal procedure is to confine your journaling to the physical files in a single library.

___ 9. Since journaling access paths markedly improves your ability to restore your company's system, it is recommended that you always journal access paths whether you journal the physical files or not.

___ 10. To end journaling, you first end journaling of the physical files followed by access paths.

___ 11. For very good protection, a company may choose to have multiple copies of their journals created. When these copies of the journals are produced on more than one machine at the same time, this is referred to as remote journaling.

___ 12. Commitment control and journaling are two terms for the same process.

Fill in the Blanks

1. In order to do journaling, you need both a ____________________ and a ____________________.
2. The system changes to a new receiver when the ________________ is reached.
3. The three SAVE commands that can be used to save journal receivers are ________________, ______________ or ____________________.
4. When doing journaling, you need to create first the ________________, then the ________________.
5. To simplify journaling, set the __________________________ parameter to ________________________. This will automate much of the journal receiver maintenance.
6. The amount of data journaled and the size of the journal receiver are greatly affected by the ______________________ and ______________________ parameters.
7. When starting journaling, you must start journaling the ____________________ before you start journaling the __________________.
8. To verify the files being journaled, you would use the __________________ command to list the journaled files. This list should be checked to make sure that what is being journaled is what you planned.
9. The journal receivers keep track of the previous and next receiver in order. This is referred to as the ____________________.
10. Remote journaling became available with the __________________ release of the operating system.

Chapter Review Questions

1. Explain the following terms:
   a. Journal.
   b. Journal receiver.
   c. Threshold.

   d. Freed storage.

   e. Receiver chain.

   f. Redirection.

   g. Commitment control.

2. Why would a company want to use journaling? List reasons.

3. What is the difference in the data stored in a database file compared to a journal receiver?

4. Identify some types of information that can be stored in a journal receiver.

5. Why should you journal both physical files and access paths? What are the advantages and disadvantages?

6. Why would a company want to use both before- and after-imaging? What are the advantages and disadvantages?

7. Why is it critical to save the journaled files prior to starting the journaling process?

8. What is the process for restoring a journaled file? What are the limitations to the process?

9. What are the steps for deleting a journal receiver?

10. Identify possible broken chain problems with journal receivers.

11. Identify the steps needed to restore journals and journal receivers.

12. What are the considerations in a journaling strategy?

13. What is the difference between synchronous and asynchronous update mode in remote journaling?

14. What is meant by caught-up in remote journaling?

15. Why would you use an RDB directory?

16. What is the role of the programmer in implementing commitment control?

18

COMMUNICATIONS: SNA, APPC, AND APPN

CHAPTER OBJECTIVES

Upon completion of this chapter, you should be able to:

- Describe the APPC (Advanced Peer-to-Peer Communications) functions.
- Explain Systems Network Architecture (SNA) protocol.
- Describe the Advanced Peer-to-Peer Networking (APPN).
- Explain APPC/APPN configuration of line, controller, and devices.
- Set up SNA distribution services.
- Use pass-through to remote systems.

OVERVIEW

We have all heard of networks with a host of names like *Ethernet*, *Token-Ring*, *X.25*, frame relay, ISDN, and so on. These are called the communication protocols of the particular network.

A *communication protocol* is a set of rules that govern how two or more devices will communicate over a network. If you connected a PC with your friend's PC via a simple wire on the two communication ports and did nothing else, conceivably you could start to write your own communication protocol. You could start with a rule that says: When one of us sends something, we will end it by sending, "over." Add to that another rule that says: When one of us receives the word "over," if we have just received and understood a message, we will acknowledge that fact with the reply, "OK."

But add to those two rules a rule for how one station will listen before starting to send—to make sure the line is clear. Add another rule that says: Just to make sure that you know it is me sending the message, here is a secret password only the two of us know. You might wonder how the receiving station knows it received the complete message. Add to that a rule that says that the sending station will count the number of words in a message and send that number with the "over" word. And another rule that the receiving station will count the message words as it receives them, verify its count with the count received with the "over," and only if the two numbers agree will it acknowledge the message with the "OK."

See how easy it is to quickly come up with a fairly complex set of rules for a simple two-station network? Add a third or fourth station, and the complexity really goes up. Now you have addressing issues. Also, the issue of whether each message is directed only to the addressee or is directed down the wire; all stations receive it but only the one it is addressed to will acknowledge it. Or, what if one station can receive a message and forward it to another workstation? That begs another rule.

Basically, that is kind of the scenario all protocols are developed under. As the rules for one protocol grow, they basically form the protocol into a fairly dedicated application. Then, when someone needs a network that has a different set of strengths, a new protocol evolves. Each one has its own personality, strengths, and weaknesses. That is why we have Ethernet—fast and cheap; and Token-Ring—just as fast, more reliable, and better able to handle high message loading. Companies with very remote locations might use frame relay for fast, cheap, reliable coast-to-coast communications. X.25 is also coast-to-coast, plus it features the ability to receive and deliver different protocols—so a message following the Ethernet rules can come in at one, and a message following the Token-Ring rules can come out the other.

Probably the oldest protocol is *asynchronous*. Asynchronous was certainly the simplest. Every time there was anything to send to the computer, it was sent. The nice thing about an asynchronous protocol was (and is, by the way) that its rule set is so small, a noncomputer device—like a keyboard or a weighing machine—could be connected to a computer. The word asynchronous has evolved into having two meanings. On the one hand, it is a communication protocol; on the other hand, it describes how messages or tasks within a computer are processed. Simply, if a task is fired off asynchronously, that means the job or task that started it issues the start command, then goes on with its work. It does not see if the new job is able to start, and it certainly does not wait to see if the new job is completed successfully. When something is said to happen asynchronously in a computer, that means it was just thrown in and left to run or not on its own.

In the AS/400's beginning, there were only two communication protocols: *5250* (also referred to as *twinax* because of the unique cabling it required) and asynchronous. 5250 was for the IBM-compatible devices connected directly to the AS/400; asynchronous was for all others.

Although 5250 was ahead of its time, over the years, IBM allowed it to be eclipsed by the rest of the world. In its place, IBM improved the AS/400's connectivity to the point that, today, it offers native support for all existing protocols.

However, the AS/400 owes its roots to 5250. Deep in its heart, all AS/400 communications are still based on *System Network Architecture (SNA)* and its host-to-host architectures: *Advanced*

Peer-to-Peer Communications (APPC) and *Advanced Peer-to-Peer Networking* (*APPN*). APPC enables two AS/400s to connect and work together. APPN is an extension of APPC, offering the same but supporting multiple AS/400s to connect and work together in a network.

This chapter explores 5250, APPC, and APPN. Chapter 19 will address specifically six industrywide protocols that the AS/400 supports.

When the AS/400 supports a new protocol, it first does so in an *emulation mode*. Emulation mode means that the protocol exists over an existing, more reliable one; for example, if the AS/400 could only support 5250 (that is not true; it supports others—just bear with us here for the example) and it was going to offer Ethernet. The first Ethernet may be offered in emulation mode, meaning that the operator would configure a line to run under Ethernet, then the AS/400 would bring up that set of protocol rules. When messages came in or went out over the line, they would be in Ethernet format, but when they reached the communication controller inside the AS/400, they would have been reformatted to match the 5250 protocol rules. Emulation mode has a cost in performance to it, but it is a safe way to introduce a new protocol—under the "sheets;" the older, reliable protocol is actually doing all the work. As the new protocol stabilizes, it becomes *native*; that is, it runs at the same low level as the older protocol (in our case, 5250). Performance gains of 1,000 percent can be realized when a new protocol goes from emulation to native. Native versus emulation does not mean much to the average customer—how the product is used does not change, although it may become easier due to new features. The difference is in the speed of the protocol.

The whole subject of communications on any platform is very complex. As a textbook, this book describes the high points. If, while studying the subject, you get overwhelmed (and you probably will), remember that just by relying on IBM-supplied defaults and automatic configuration, anyone can do a pretty fair job of bringing up a network. If you are interested in more detail on any of the specific areas, refer to the IBM manuals referenced throughout this chapter.

SYSTEMS NETWORK ARCHITECTURE (SNA)

SNA is at the highest level of IBM communication. SNA is not as simple as a protocol. SNA is a collection of descriptions of logical structures, protocols, and instruction sequences that handle all parts of IBM communications.

SNA is omnipresent over all IBM platforms, including mainframes. But it is relatively unknown in the LAN world. Exceptions are the PC-based servers designed specifically for SNA communications.

ADVANCED PEER-TO-PEER COMMUNICATIONS (APPC)

Under SNA, APPC handles AS/400 communications. Another way to put it is that APPC uses what it needs from SNA's library to support AS/400 communications. For students so inclined, it does so as an implementation of SNA logical unit 6.2 and node type 2.1 architectures.

All of what we say about APPC in this section also holds true for APPN in the next section, because APPN is an extension of APPC.

A key thing to remember about APPC is that it is a peer-to-peer architecture. One platform can act as the master to the other platforms if desired, but that is not required. Multiple hosts can exist as equal partners on the network. One other thing: APPC is not a protocol; it supports protocols.

APPC Functions

Most AS/400 customers' direct contact with APPC is through the following functions that it offers. For all the functions, APPC or APPN must be in effect to use them.

- *Distributed data management (DDM).* Allows a program or user on one system to access database files on another system. See the section on Distributed Data Management.
- *SNA Distribution Services (SNADS).* Allows electronic mail and files to be sent to another system. See the section on SNA Distribution Services.
- *Display station pass-through.* Allows a user signed onto one AS/400 to pass through it into another AS/400 and sign on there as a "local" workstation. See the section on Display Station Pass-Through.
- *OptiConnect/400.* This is a combination hardware and software that provides very high-speed communications between host AS/400s. See the section on OptiConnect/400.
- *Electronic Customer Support (ECS).* Allows a customer to access question-and-answer and problem-solving databases at IBM. Also, a customer can use ECS to order OS releases and PTFs. PTFs also can be delivered via ECS. See the section on Electronic Customer Support.
- *SNA pass-through.* Allows SNA data to be passed between applications.
- *File transfer support.* Moves file members from one system to another.
- *Client Access/400.* Provides system access and functions to an attached personal computer.
- *Alert support.* When a problem or impending problem is detected by the system, it alerts the operator.
- *CICS/400.* Allows developers to write programs to process workstation transactions.

Communication Lines Support

All AS/400 communications lines are under APPC. Each line can be one of the following types of communications (a line adapter for each must be installed on the AS/400):

- Distributed data interface (DDI).
- Frame-relay network (FR).
- ISDN data line control (IDLC).
  - Switched.
  - Nonswitched.
- Synchronous data link (SDLC).
  - Point-to-point switched.
  - Point-to-point nonswitched.
  - Multiple-point nonswitched.

- X.25.
- Token-Ring.
- Ethernet.
- Wireless.

ADVANCED PEER-TO-PEER NETWORKING (APPN)

APPN is an enhanced APPC. Whereas APPC is concerned with two AS/400s connected by a single line; APPN is concerned with multiple AS/400s, multiple lines, and even multiple APPN networks. APPN is an extension of APPC. That is, it has APPC as its core; it just adds its own functionality on top.

> **TIP:**
>
> APPN offers enough added functionality that many AS/400 customers use APPN to support a simple, two-AS/400 network instead of APPC.

Although a customer could support a network of AS/400s solely with APPC, the work would be prohibitive. On the other hand, APPN takes on the network-support chores such as:

- Working with distributed directories.
- Selecting routes dynamically.
- Creating and starting remote locations automatically.
- Prioritizing data routing.

APPN will control transmissions in complex networks where multiple AS/400s are attached. Not all AS/400s have direct routes between them. APPN automatically will choose AS/400s (or nodes) it can use as intermediate systems to get to a target AS/400. If all systems and lines are under APPN control, no operator on the system has to worry about how a transmission will get to its destination. An APPN network can consist of any mixture of these devices:

- Personal computer.
- IBM midrange computers.
- S/36.
- S/38.
- RISC System 6000.
- The following mainframe hosts:
  - S/370.
  - S/390.
  - 30xx.
  - 43xx.
  - 9370.

In addition to the APPC functions already discussed, APPN provides:

- Distributed directory services. APPN, given a remote system name, will search the network to locate that system.
- Dynamic route selection based on user-defined rules. APPN will determine the best route to take to send a transmission to a remote system. The system operator defines the parameters it will use. For example, rules can be set up to specify that either the lowest cost or fastest routing be obtained.
- Intermediate session routing. Any AS/400 can be used as an intermediate station for routing objects to a final destination.
- Automatic creation and vary on of APPN controller descriptions on Token-Ring or Ethernet networks. APPN dynamically determines the remote system's LAN address.
- Automatic creation and starting of remote device descriptions necessary to complete a network transmission.

NODES, CONTROL POINTS, AND CLASS-OF-SERVICE

Each device on APPN is referred to as a *node*. There are basically two types of nodes:

- *Network node*. This is a network device running APPN and fully participating by providing intermediate session routing, route selection services, and distributed directory services. This is a network link between other nodes.
- *End node*, sometimes called peripheral node. This is a network device on the end of a network line connected to a single network node. End nodes can also be:
  - Low-entry networking node. Basically, this is a network device on an APPN network, but it only runs APPC.
  - APPN end node. This is a network device on an APPN network, running APPN, but it can receive some additional automatic configuration benefits from APPN.

Although an end node is on the periphery of a network, it can also be an end node on another network.

When end nodes are attached to network nodes, the network node must be configured as a *network server node.* APPN can support up to five network server nodes per APPN network. They are created within the Change Network Attributes (CHGNETA) command (refer to the section on Network Attributes for more information). These servers provide services for the attached end nodes:

- Directory searches.
- Route calculations.
- Remote locations do not have to be configured on the end nodes; the network node servers will do that.
- The end nodes are able to inform the network server node of all their local locations. That information stays within the network server node for its use in routing transmissions.

Note that the designations of the nodes have nothing to do with the quality or type of those nodes. They are only configuration decisions. However, network nodes require significantly more computer resources than end nodes.

When APPN is up, *control points* (*CP*) are established. A simple control point is the directory and route information between two nodes. Network nodes build control-point information about themselves and all attached nodes.

End node control points only contain their own information, and that comes from the control point on the attached network server node. Once the connection is established and this information is obtained, it becomes part of the *network topology database* that is kept on each network node (but not end nodes). Each network node always contains complete system information. It uses the information to route transmissions.

When a network link goes down, the adjacent control points reconfigure themselves and update all nodes' network topology databases so each network node is aware that the network configuration has changed. Each network node always has a real-time network topology with which to work.

Any network node knows (from its network topology database) all the links and nodes between it and the destination node. This information is referred to as the *transmission group* (*TG*). The transmission group contains:

- Communication speed.
- Security.
- Cost factor desired:
  - By connect time.
  - By the byte transmitted.
- Propagation delay. How much time will elapse between sending and receiving the transmission based on optimum conditions? This is not always significant, but it can be. For example, a transmission from San Francisco to London will have a propagation delay. If APPN had a choice of going via satellite or landline, the propagation delay difference between the two could be significant.

The network configuration also has some influence into the potential traffic routing through two parameters on the Change Network Attributes (CHGNETA) or Create Network Attributes (CRTNETA) command (refer to the section on Network Attributes for more information):

- Route Addition Resistance (RAR). This is a number from zero through 255 that describes how the operator feels about using a node for intermediate routing to other nodes. The higher the number, the more resistant the network nodes will be to use that node for intermediate routing.
- Route Congestion. This parameter allows the operator to set a percentage regarding a node's availability to do intermediate routing. The default is 90 percent. If a node's utilization is 90 percent or above, the network will try not to use it for intermediate routing. If it is below 90 percent, the network will use it, but it will take into consideration any RAR value the customer has set.

APPN uses something called a *class-of-service (COS)* to determine the best routing (by the operator's definition) for a transmission. The class-of-service uses the network node attributes and the transmission group characteristics together to come up with an optimum routing plan. Note that class-of-service does this for every transmission, so APPN's routing is considered *dynamic routing* and is, therefore, always optimum.

Class-of-service is created with the Create Class-of-Service Description (CRTCOSD) command. The APPN session locates the class-of-service through the mode description specified on each session initiation. For additional information, see the section about Create Mode Descriptions.

APPC/APPN CONFIGURATION

The user configuring for APPC or APPN must have *IOSYSCFG in his or her user profile. That is a special authority; refer to chapter 11 for more information.

Each AS/400 pair and the line between them make an APPC configuration. There can be more than one APPC configuration up at a time, but each must have a unique name. Several AS/400 objects have to be configured at the same time to make one APPC configuration. Do not get confused by the double meaning of the word *configuration*. Another way to say it is, we will create and/or change several AS/400 objects to make a single configuration or network link. Here are the items and the order in which they must be created:

- Location/configuration list (for APPN only).
- Connection list (for ISDN only).
- Network interface (for ISDN or frame-relay only).
- Lines:
  - SNA pass-through requires two lines (one to send and one to receive).
  - Non-SNA pass-through only requires one line.
- Controller:
  - SNA pass-through requires two controllers (one for each line).
  - Non-SNA pass-through only requires one controller.
- Device:
  - SNA pass-through requires type *SNPT.
  - Mode description.

CREATING LOCATION/CONFIGURATION LISTS (APPN ONLY)

Location lists or *configuration lists* contain the local and remote names of all the systems APPN is to support. Location lists are optional, but their use is recommended because they save time later administering the network. However, they have a weak spot that must be considered. Many of the parameters of the create/change commands for location lists use a default of *NETATR or Network Attribute. Logically enough, *NETATR takes information from the network itself. However, if any network attribute is changed (through the CHGNETA) after the location list is prepared, those changes will not be reflected in the location list. If location lists are used and *NETATR is taken for any parameters, when any changes are made to the network attributes, the location entry must be deleted and re-added before the new attribute takes effect.

Local and remote locations are kept on separate location lists for APPN networks. A local list contains names of the locations defined on the local system. This sounds very complex, but it isn't—just enter the name of the local system. Figure 18-1 shows a prompted version of the Create Configuration List (CRTCFGL) command.

```
                    Create Configuration List (CRTCFGL)

Type choices, press Enter.

Configuration list type  . . . . > *APPNLCL      *APPNDIR, *APPNLCL...
Configuration list . . . . . . . > *QAPPNLCL     Name
Default filter action  . . . . .   *REJECT
APPN remote CFGL filter  . . . .   *ACCEPT
Text 'description' . . . . . . . > 'Configuration List QAPPNLCL'
________

                         Additional Parameters

APPN local location entry:       _
  Local location name  . . . . .   *PROMPT       Name, *PROMPT
  Entry 'description'  . . . . .   _________________________
               + for more values _

                                                                More...
F3=Exit   F4=Prompt   F5=Refresh   F12=Cancel   F13=How to use this display
F24=More keys
```

Figure 18-1: Prompted version of the CRTCFGL command.

There are a lot of parameters to this command, but for creating a local list, keep it simple. Enter *APPNLCL as the type of list. The list name, QAPPNLCL, is supplied by the system and is mandatory. Any AS/400 can only have one location/configuration list, and it must be named QAPPNLCL.

The Local Location Name can be the name of the system plus the names of any other systems it is supposed to respond to. For example, consider two AS/400s named PHX01 and PHX02. If PHX02 went down and both systems were named on PHX01's local location list, it would receive messages for both systems. This parameter can contain up to 476 local names.

Optionally, the operator could enter *PROMPT on this parameter. In that case, every time APPN came up on that machine, the operator would have a change to put in from one to 476 local system names. This can be a nice feature, just keep in mind that this can be a lot of manual keying.

Give a brief description of the list on the Entry 'Description' parameter. Then enter the local system name(s) as the APPN Local Location Entry.

Similarly, location names remote to the local system need to be defined in lists. The same command (CRTCFGL) is used, but the list type must be *APPNRMT. Instead of entering the local system name, the operator enters three things:

- Remote location name. The remote location name can be the actual name of the remote system, a generic name, or the generic *ALL. The following are valid values:
  - PHX02—only for an AS/400 named PHX02.
  - PHX*—for all AS/400s with a name starting with "PHX."
  - *ALL—for all AS/400s connected.

- Network ID. The name of the network that the remote location resides on is the network identification.
- Local location name. The location name of the local AS/400. APPN links the local and remote location names to make a unique pair name.

That is all that is needed for identifying remote locations. If using directory entries, the system operator also should enter the:

- Control-point name. The name of the control point that provides network functions for the remote location.
- Control-point network ID. The name of the network on which the control point resides.

If the remote location is going to provide transparent access, the password to that system must be defined on a remote location list. To do that, enter the:

- Location password.
- Secure location. The secure location determines where password verification occurs. If a *YES is specified and a remote location wants to start a program on the local location, it can verify the password before starting the program. If *NO (the default) is specified, the remote location may not verify the password. The local location must verify the password.

When defining a single-session connection, enter the:

- Single session location. The option is *YES.
- Locally controlled location. For this local and remote pair network, is the session controlled locally? Options are *YES and *NO (with *NO being the default—take the default).
- Preestablished session. Will the session be automatically started when the node is started between the two systems? Options are *YES and *NO (with *NO being the default—take the default).
- Number of conversations. How many conversations will be allowed? Valid values are 1 through 512 (with the default being 10).

Creating a Connection List (ISDN Only)

The ISDN lines and controllers can refer to entries on the *connection list* to obtain information on managing calls sent or received across the network. First, create the list and then manage the entries in it. The commands to work with the list are:

- WRKCNNL (Work with Connection Lists).
- CRTCNNL (Create Connection List).
- CHGCNNL (Change Connection List).
- DSPCNNL (Display Connection List).
- DLTCNNL (Delete Connection List).

The commands to work with communications list entries are:

- WRKCNNLE (Work with Connection List Entries).
- ADDCNNLE (Add Connection List Entries).

- CHGCNNLE (Change Connection List Entries).
- RNMCNNLE (Rename Connection List Entries).
- RMVCNNLE (Remove Connection List Entries).

Creating a Network Interface Description (ISDN or Frame Relay Only)

The network interface description is an object the system will refer to when it needs information about how the AS/400 and the network should interface. The commands to work with the description are:

- WRKNWID (Work with Network Interface Description).
- CRTNWIxxxx (Create Network Interface Description).
- CHGNWIxxxx (Change Network Interface Description).
- DSPNWID (Display Network Interface Description).
- DLTNWID (Delete Network Interface Description).

Some of these commands are specific to ISDN networks and some are specific to frame relay. Where the commands have xxxx, substitute:

- ISDN for ISDN.
- FR for frame relay.

Creating a Line Description

The line description will describe to the system the physical line connection and the data link protocol to be used between the AS/400 and the network. The commands to work with lines are:

- WRKLNID (Work with Line Description).
- CRTLINxxxx (Create Line Description).
- CHGLINxxxx (Change Line Description).

Some of these commands are particular to specific line types. Where the commands have xxxx, substitute:

- DDI for DDI.
- ETH for Ethernet.
- FR for frame relay.
- IDLC for IDLC.
- SDLC for SDLC.
- TRN for Token-Ring.
- X25 for X.25.
- WLS for wireless.

When configuring an APPC line, there is not much more to do than the basic commands we have already discussed. However, when configuring an APPN line, other command parameters deserve some attention:

- *Link Speed* (LINKSPEED). The speed of the link. The default is *INTERFACE, and it provides automatic speed setting. In most cases, just use this default. Often, the speed of the line is known (from the line provider). If this is the case, enter that speed here.
- *Cost Per Connect Time* (COSTCNN). Cost per connect time is the relative (not actual) cost of being connected on the line. The default *CNN bases relative cost on the type of connection. Override this with any number from 0 through 255. The lower numbers represent lower costs.
- *Cost Per Byte* (COSTBYTE). Cost per byte is the relative (not actual) cost per byte of being connected on the line. The default *CNN bases relative cost on the connection type. Override this with any number from 0 through 255. The lower numbers represent lower costs.
- *Security Used on the Line* (SECURITY). Security on the line does not apply to AS/400 user identification, passwords, or object security. This parameter's possible values are:
  - *NONSECURE—No security.
  - *PKTSWTNET—Packet-switched network. Security is through packets' random routing through the network.
  - *UNDGRDCBL—Underground cable in secured conduit.
  - *SECURECND—Secured conduit; not guarded.
  - *GUARDCND—Guarded conduit; protected against physical tampering.
  - *ENCRYPTED—Data flowing on line is encrypted.
  - *MAX—Guarded conduit; protected against physical tampering and radiation tapping.
- *Propagation Delay* (PRPDLY). Propagation delay is the expected time a transmission takes to travel from one end of a link to another. Possible values are:
  - *MIN—Minimum delay.
  - *LAN—Less than .48 milliseconds. Specifies local area network delay.
  - *TELEPHONE—From .48 milliseconds to 49.152 milliseconds. Specifies telephone network delay.
  - *PKTSWTNET—From .49.152 milliseconds to 245.76 milliseconds. Specifies packet-switched network delay.
  - *SATELLITE—Greater than 245.76 milliseconds. Specifies satellite network delay.
  - *MAX—Maximum delay.
- *User-Defined Value* 1, 2, 3 (USRDFN1, USRDFN2, USRDFN3). Specify a numeric value from 0 through 255. The default is 128. The values can be changed during operations to indicate various activities on the network.
- *Automatically Create Controller* (AUTOCRTCTL). Specifies whether the system is to automatically create controller descriptions when incoming calls are received. Possible values are *YES and *NO (with *NO being the default).

- *Automatically Delete Controller* (AUTODLTCTL). Specifies whether and for how long the APPC controller can remain idle (status varied on pending) before the controller description is varied off and deleted. These values are the number of minutes. The default is 1,440 (twenty-four hours). However, any value from 1 to 10,000 can be used.

Creating an APPC/APPN Controller Description

A controller defines the network node. A lot of the controller information on a local machine is actually used more by the adjacent nodes than the one it is on.

Start with the Work with Controller Descriptions (WRKCTLD) command. From there, it is easy: Select option 1 (Create) to get to the Create Controller APPC (CRTCTLAPPC) command. This command creates an APPC controller, and it has a parameter (APPN-CAPABLE) that, when specifying *YES, turns it into an APPN controller. Figure 18-2 shows the prompted version of the WRKCTLD command.

```
                      Work with Controller Descriptions
                                                           System:   BIGBLUE
Position to  . . . . . ____________       Starting characters

Type options, press Enter.
  2=Change   3=Copy    4=Delete   5=Display   6=Print   7=Rename
  8=Work with status   9=Retrieve source      12=Print device addresses

Opt  Controller  Type       Text
__   CTL01       6A59       CREATED BY AUTO-CONFIGURATION
__   ETHLINET    *NET       CREATED BY AUTO-CONFIGURATION
__   QCTL        6A59       Controller description created during IPL.
__   CTRA01      *APPC      SYS01 on Tokenring1
__   CTRA02      *APPC      SYS02 on Tokenring2
__   GE20S03     *APPC      Gateway 20 Tokenring2 GE20S03 50000E2020222
__   QESCTL      *HOST
__   QILANM3601  *APPC      SYSTEM SUPPLIED ILAN CONTROLLER DESCRIPTION
__   QPACTL01    *VWS       Controller created for S102HZ5M.
__   QVIRCD0001  *VWS       Controller created for BIGBLUE.
__   VISACTL     *BSC
                                                                 Bottom
Parameters or command
===>__________________________________________________________________
F3=Exit   F4=Prompt   F5=Refresh   F6=Create   F9=Retrieve   F12=Cancel
F14=Work with status
```

Figure 18-2: Prompted version of the WRKCTLD command.

This is the list of all the controllers on a sample system. By pressing F6 (Create), the command to create a new controller description comes up. Figure 18-3 shows the prompted version of that screen:

```
                      Create Controller Description

Type choices, press Enter.

  New controller
    description  . . . . > TESTNODE__    Name

  Controller type/class    ______        F4 for list
```

Figure 18-3: The screen after pressing F6 (Create) from the WRKCTLD command.

Notice that the description starts off simply with just two parameters. Enter the controller name, in this case TESTNODE, and the type/class of the controller. By positioning the cursor on this parameter and pressing F4, the system will provide all possible values for the type/class:

- *APPC (Advanced program-to-program communications).
- *ASYNC (Asynchronous communications).
- *BSC (Binary synchronous communications).
- *FNC (Finance).
- *HOST (SNA host).
- *LWS (Local workstation).
- *NET (Network).
- *RTL (Retail).
- *RWS (Remote workstation).
- *TAP (Tape).
- *VWS (Virtual workstation).

As shown in Figure 18-3, we selected *APPC as the type of controller. When we press Enter, we get a new command, CRTCTLAPPC, with the controller name and type/class filled in, but with new, specific APPC parameters added. See Figure 18-4.

```
                    Create Ctl Desc (APPC) (CRTCTLAPPC)

Type choices, press Enter.

Controller description . . . . . > TESTNODE      Name
Link type  . . . . . . . . . . .   ______        *ANYNW, *FAX, *FR, *IDLC...
Online at IPL  . . . . . . . . .   *YES          *YES, *NO
Switched connection  . . . . . .   *NO           *NO, *YES
```

Figure 18-4: Prompted version of the CRTCTLAPPC command.

This command has a couple of presentations. The first one, displayed in Figure 18-4, requests four bits of information:

- The name of the controller (already provided; it was carried over).
- The link type.
- Whether the controller will be automatically online anytime the AS/400 IPLs.
- Whether the controller will be connected to a switched or nonswitched line.

Let us focus on the link type. Place the cursor on the parameter and press F4 to get a list of valid link types:

- *ANYNW.
- *FAX.
- *FR.
- *IDLC.
- *ILAN.
- *LAN.
- *LOCAL.
- *SDLC.
- *TDLC.
- *X25.

To define a controller for an ISDN link, specify either *IDLC or *X25 for the link type. We selected the *LAN link type. Press the Enter key, and the command will expand as shown in Figure 18-5.

```
                    Create Ctl Desc (APPC) (CRTCTLAPPC)

 Type choices, press Enter.

 Controller description . . . . . > TESTNODE      Name
 Link type  . . . . . . . . . . . > *LAN          *ANYNW, *FAX, *FR, *IDLC...
 Online at IPL  . . . . . . . . .   *YES          *YES, *NO
 APPN-capable . . . . . . . . . .   *YES          *YES, *NO
 Switched line list . . . . . . .   __________    Name
               + for more values    __________
 Maximum frame size . . . . . . .   *LINKTYPE     265-16393, 256, 265, 512...
 Remote network identifier  . . .   *NETATR       Name, *NETATR, *NONE, *ANY
 Remote control point . . . . . .   ________      Name, *ANY
 Exchange identifier  . . . . . .   ________      00000000-FFFFFFFF
 Initial connection . . . . . . .   *DIAL         *DIAL, *ANS

                                                                    Bottom
 F3=Exit   F4=Prompt   F5=Refresh   F10=Additional parameters   F12=Cancel
 F13=How to use this display        F24=More keys
```

Figure 18-5: Prompted version of the CRTCTLAPPC command.

The significant parameter for this is APPN-CAPABLE. The default is *YES. This is what differentiates a controller as APPC or APPN. By using the default and pressing Enter, the command will again expand as shown in Figure 18-6.

```
                    Create Ctl Desc (APPC) (CRTCTLAPPC)

 Type choices, press Enter.

 Controller description . . . . . > TESTNODE      Name
 Link type  . . . . . . . . . . . > *LAN          *ANYNW, *FAX, *FR, *IDLC...
 Online at IPL  . . . . . . . . .   *YES          *YES, *NO
 APPN-capable . . . . . . . . . .   *YES          *YES, *NO
 Switched line list . . . . . . .   __________    Name
               + for more values    __________
 Maximum frame size . . . . . . .   *LINKTYPE     265-16393, 256, 265, 512...
 Remote network identifier  . . .   *NETATR       Name, *NETATR, *NONE, *ANY
 Remote control point . . . . . .   ________      Name, *ANY
 Exchange identifier  . . . . . .   ________      00000000-FFFFFFFF
 Initial connection . . . . . . .   *DIAL         *DIAL, *ANS
 Dial initiation  . . . . . . . .   *LINKTYPE     *LINKTYPE, *IMMED, *DELAY
 LAN remote adapter address . . .   ____________  000000000001-FFFFFFFFFFFF
 LAN DSAP . . . . . . . . . . . .   04            04, 08, 0C, 10, 14, 18, 1C...
 LAN SSAP . . . . . . . . . . . .   04            04, 08, 0C, 10, 14, 18, 1C...
 APPN CP session support  . . . .   *YES          *YES, *NO
                                                                Bottom
 F3=Exit   F4=Prompt   F5=Refresh   F10=Additional parameters   F12=Cancel
 F13=How to use this display        F24=More keys
```

Figure 18-6: CRTCTLAPPC expanded for APPC information.

The last parameter in Figure 18-6, APPC CP Session Support, defines the node as capable of being a control point on the network. The command has now expanded to the point where it continues onto a second screen. See Figure 18-7.

```
                        Create Ctl Desc (APPC) (CRTCTLAPPC)

Type choices, press Enter.

APPN node type . . . . . . . . .   *ENDNODE        *ENDNODE, *LENNODE...
APPN/HPR capable . . . . . . . .   *YES            *YES, *NO
HPR path switching . . . . . . .   *NO             *NO, *YES
APPN transmission group number     1               1-20, *CALC
APPN minimum switched status . .   *VRYONPND       *VRYONPND, *VRYON
Autocreate device  . . . . . . .   *ALL            *ALL, *NONE
Autodelete device  . . . . . . .   1440            1-10000, *NO
User-defined 1 . . . . . . . . .   *LIND           0-255, *LIND
User-defined 2 . . . . . . . . .   *LIND           0-255, *LIND
User-defined 3 . . . . . . . . .   *LIND           0-255, *LIND
Model controller description . .   *NO             *NO, *YES




                                                                       Bottom
F3=Exit   F4=Prompt   F5=Refresh   F10=Additional parameters   F12=Cancel
F13=How to use this display        F24=More keys
```

Figure 18-7: Second screen of the CRTCTLAPPC command.

APPN NODE TYPE parameter is where the node is designated as an end node or a network node. For more detailed descriptions of the controller description parameters, see IBM manual *OS/400 APPN Support V4R4.*

Create APPC/APPN Device Descriptions

The device description tells the networked nodes something about the logical (not the physical) connection between them. Each pair of nodes has a connection and must have a device description describing that connection. The command, Create Device Description for APPC (CRTDEVAPPC), creates a description for an APPC device. Figure 18-8 shows a prompted version of that command.

The parameter, Remote Location Name (RMTLOCNAME), is the name of the remote AS/400. This name can be:

- The LCLLOCNAME of the remote AS/400 (APPC only).
- A name specified in the local location list (refer to Creating Location/Configuration Lists [APPN] for more about these) of the remote AS/400 (APPN only).
- The local location name specified on the remote AS/400's network attributes (controlled through the CHGNETA command [APPN only]).
- The local control-point name (APPN only).

```
                  Create Device Desc (APPC) (CRTDEVAPPC)

Type choices, press Enter.

Device description . . . . . . .   __________   Name
Remote location  . . . . . . . .   ________     Name
Online at IPL  . . . . . . . . .   *YES         *YES, *NO
Local location . . . . . . . . .   *NETATR      Name, *NETATR
Remote network identifier  . . .   *NETATR      Name, *NETATR, *NONE
Attached controller  . . . . . .   __________   Name
Mode . . . . . . . . . . . . . .   *NETATR      Name, *NETATR
               + for more values   ________
Message queue  . . . . . . . . .   QSYSOPR      Name, QSYSOPR
  Library  . . . . . . . . . . .     *LIBL      Name, *LIBL, *CURLIB
APPN-capable . . . . . . . . . .   *YES         *YES, *NO
Single session:
  Single session capable . . . .   *NO          *NO, *YES
  Number of conversations  . . .   ______       1-512

                                                                   Bottom
F3=Exit   F4=Prompt   F5=Refresh   F10=Additional parameters   F12=Cancel
F13=How to use this display        F24=More keys
```

Figure 18-8: Prompted version of the CRTDEVAPPC command.

The Local Location Name (LCLLOCNAME) is the name of the local AS/400. The default *NETATR tells APPC to take the local name from the network attributes. Alternatively, the operator can specify the local network name.

The Remote Network Identifier (RMTNETID) is the name of the remote network where the location resides. The default *NETATR tells APPC to take the name from the network attributes.

The network node servers take this information and find matches to consider a link valid. If an AS/400 is paired with several other AS/400s, there must be a device description for each pair. The network server node must detect matching remote name/remote ID and local name/local ID information on two AS/400s for the link to be recognized.

For example, SYS01 is connected to SYS02 and SYS03. Conversely, SYS02 is connected to SYS01 and SYS03 is connected to SYS01. The network server node must find a device description on SYS01 with this combination:

SYS01 Device Description

RMTLOCNAME = SYS02

RMTNETID = SYS02's network ID

LCLLOCNAME = SYS01

SYS02 Device Description

RMTLOCNAME = SYS01

RMTNETID = SYS01's network ID

LCLLOCNAME = SYS02

Only when the network server node finds this combination will it consider the connection valid.

Mode Name (MODE) tells both ends of the network which mode to use. Unless the Single Session Location (SNGSSNLOC) is set to 1, a maximum of fourteen modes is allowed. If the Single Session Location is set to one, only 1 mode may be specified.

The Use APPN Function (APPN) specifies whether or not the device (the AS/400) will be used on an APPN network. Take the default, *YES.

The Single Session Location (SNGSSNLOC) allows the operator to specify that the communications over the network will be limited to one session or more. Valid values are *YES (only one session will be allowed) and *NO (multiple sessions will be allowed).

For more detailed information on the other parameters, see IBM manual *OS/400 APPN Support V4R4.*

Create Mode Descriptions

Mode descriptions describe the session characteristics and numbers of communications sessions that will be allowed between network nodes. When considering a mode in the device or network description, remember that a mode of the same name must exist on both local and remote AS/400s in order for a session to happen. The mode does not need to exist on an intermediate session because the communication is being routed to another network. When low-entry networking nodes are remote locations, their modes must exist on the network node server that services them. To help configure this, every AS/400 comes shipped with five predefined modes:

- BLANK. The name really is blank; there is no name. When this name (BLANK) is specified, APPN will look for the default mode named with eight blank characters.
- #BATCH. A mode tailored for batch communications.
- #BATCHSC. The same as #BATCH except it has security built in for packets (*PKTSWTNET).
- #INTER. A mode tailored for interactive communications.
- #INTERSC. The same as #INTEr except it has security built in for packets (*PKTSWTNET).

Use one of the preceding modes. Even in a shop that needs to create its own modes, at least display these first to see how IBM has set up the mode parameters. For a detailed description of the IBM-supplied modes, see IBM manual *OS/400 APPN Support V4R4.* Create new modes with the Create Mode Description (CRTMODD) command. Figure 18-9 shows a prompted version of that command.

Put the name of the mode in the Mode Description Name (MODD) parameter. Maximum Number of Sessions (MAXSSN) specifies how many sessions can be active at one time through the mode. The maximum in this parameter is 512, and the default is 8. The value for this parameter should be equal to the number specified for the Locally Controlled Sessions (LCLCTLSSN) parameter on the local system, plus the value specified for the remote system.

The Maximum Number of Conversations (MAXCNV) specifies how many conversations can be active at one time over this mode. The maximum is 512, and the default is 8. Conversations are temporary transmissions sent over a session while the session is active. For an APPC AS/400, the maximum total conversations for all modes cannot exceed 512.

```
                    Create Mode Description (CRTMODD)

Type choices, press Enter.

Mode description . . . . . . .   __________   Name
Maximum sessions . . . . . . .   8_____       1-512
Maximum conversations  . . . .   8_____       1-512
Locally controlled sessions  .   4_____       0-512
Pre-established sessions . . .   0_____       0-512
Maximum inbound pacing value .   *CALC_____   1-32767, *CALC
Inbound pacing value . . . . .   7____        0-63
Outbound pacing value  . . . .   7____        0-63
Maximum length of request unit   *CALC______  241-32767, *CALC
Data compression . . . . . . .   *NETATR____  1-2147483647, *NETATR...
Inbound data compression . . .   *RLE__       *RLE, *LZ9, *LZ10, *LZ12...
Outbound data compression  . .   *RLE__       *RLE, *LZ9, *LZ10, *LZ12...
Session level encryption . . .   *NONE        *NONE, *ALL
Text 'description' . . . . . .   ______________________________________
______
                                                                More...
F3=Exit   F4=Prompt   F5=Refresh   F12=Cancel   F13=How to use this display
F24=More keys
```

```
                    Create Mode Description (CRTMODD)

Type choices, press Enter.

                         Additional Parameters

Class-of-service . . . . . . .   #CONNECT     Name, #CONNECT, #BATCH...
Authority  . . . . . . . . . .   *LIBCRTAUT   Name, *LIBCRTAUT, *CHANGE...
```

Figure 18-9: Prompted version of the CRTMODD command (parts 1 and 2).

The Locally Controlled Sessions (LCLCTLSSN) parameter specifies the minimum number of sessions this local AS/400 will establish and control. The Preestablished Sessions (PREESTSSN) parameter specifies the number of concurrent sessions that will be established automatically when the mode is started. Others can be established after the mode is started (as they are needed) so long as their number does not exceed the number specified in the MAXSSN parameter. Specify the class of service of the mode in the Class-of-Service (COS) parameter. Possible values are:

- #CONNECT—The default.
- #BATCH.
- #INTER.
- #BATCHSC.
- #INTERSC.
- Class-of-service name.

The class of service is only required for APPN configurations; do not worry about it for APPC. However, if the class of service for an APPN configuration is named, a class of service by that name must already exist on the system. Refer to the section on Create Class-of-Service Descriptions for more information.

For more detailed information on the other parameters, refer to IBM manual *APPN Support V4R4*.

Create Class-of-Service Descriptions

Class-of-service descriptions are used to select the nodes and groups to be included in the APPC/APPN session routes. For small two- or three-node networks, do not worry too much about class of service. Just use one of the IBM-supplied descriptions. But large and complex networks—especially international networks supporting multinational telephone regulations—should have the class of service thoroughly analyzed before creating new classes of service. Every AS/400 comes with five classes of service already configured by IBM. They are:

- #CONNECT—The default.
- #BATCH—A class of service for batch communications.
- #BATCHSC—The same as #BATCH except that it has data link security for switched packets (*PKTSWTNWK).
- #INTER—A class of service for interactive communications.
- #INTERSC—The same as #INTER except that it has data link security for switched packets (*PKTSWTNWK).

Create classes of service with the Create Class-of-Service Description (CRTCOSD) command. It allows the system operator to dictate many routing rules for communicating by APPN. With these rules, APPN can save communications dollars and maximize communications throughput.

When creating classes of service without using IBM's defaults, specify all the classes of service on all networks. Through class of service, the operator can specify routing rules to reflect:

- Link speed.
- Cost per connect time.
- Cost per byte.
- Line performance.
- Security.

Preferences on classes of service are indicated through weighting factors. The lower the weighting factor, the more desirable the factor. Each class of service has eight rows in order of weight (one is the smallest weight, and eight is the largest). Therefore, what is specified in row one should be more desirable than what is specified in row two (which would be more desirable than what is in row three, and so on).

When specifying link speed and security, the higher speeds should be near the bottom rows because higher is better. When specifying link costs, the higher costs should be near the higher rows because higher costs are less desirable. The person creating (or changing) the class of service does not have to go crazy trying to come up with eight rules for every item. Most people only specify one or two values in the tables. However, putting those one or two in rows 1 or 2 or in rows 7 or 8 will weight the overall result when that decision table is compared to other tables.

Use the Create Class-of-Service Description (CRTCOSD) command to create a class of service. Figure 18-10 shows a prompted version of the command.

```
Create Class-of-Service Desc (CRTCOSD)

 Type choices, press Enter.

 Class-of-service description . . > TESTCLS      Name
 Transmission priority  . . . . .   *MED          *LOW, *MED, *HIGH
```

```
                    Create Class-of-Service Desc (CRTCOSD)

 Type choices, press Enter.

 Row 1 for lines:
   Line row weight  . . . . . . .   30          0-255
   Minimum link speed . . . . . .   4M          *MIN, 1200, 2400, 4800...
   Maximum link speed . . . . . .   *MAX        *MIN, 1200, 2400, 4800...
   Minimum cost/connect time  . .   0           0-255
   Maximum cost/connect time  . .   0           0-255
   Minimum cost/byte  . . . . . .   0           0-255
   Maximum cost/byte  . . . . . .   0           0-255
   Minimum security for line  . .   *NONSECURE  *NONSECURE, *PKTSWTNET...
   Maximum security for line  . .   *MAX        *NONSECURE, *PKTSWTNET...
   Minimum propagation delay  . .   *MIN        *MIN, *LAN, *TELEPHONE...
   Maximum propagation delay  . .   *LAN        *MIN, *LAN, *TELEPHONE...
   Minimum user-defined 1 . . . .   0           0-255
   Maximum user-defined 1 . . . .   255         0-255
   Minimum user-defined 2 . . . .   0           0-255

                                                                    More...
 F3=Exit   F4=Prompt   F5=Refresh   F12=Cancel   F13=How to use this display
 F24=More keys
```

```
                    Create Class-of-Service Desc (CRTCOSD)

 Type choices, press Enter.

   Maximum user-defined 2 . . . .   255         0-255
   Minimum user-defined 3 . . . .   0           0-255
   Maximum user-defined 3 . . . .   255         0-255
 Row 1 for nodes:
   Node row weight  . . . . . . .   5           0-255
   Min route addition resistance    0           0-255
   Max route addition resistance    31          0-255
   Minimum congestion for node  .   *LOW        *LOW, *HIGH
   Maximum congestion for node  .   *LOW        *LOW, *HIGH
```

```
                 Create Class-of-Service Desc (CRTCOSD)

Type choices, press Enter.

Row 2 for lines:
  Line row weight . . . . . . .   60           0-255
  Minimum link speed . . . . . .  56000        *MIN, 1200, 2400, 4800...
  Maximum link speed . . . . . .  *MAX         *MIN, 1200, 2400, 4800...
  Minimum cost/connect time  . .  0            0-255
  Maximum cost/connect time  . .  0            0-255
  Minimum cost/byte  . . . . . .  0            0-255
  Maximum cost/byte  . . . . . .  0            0-255
  Minimum security for line  . .  *NONSECURE   *NONSECURE, *PKTSWTNET...
  Maximum security for line  . .  *MAX         *NONSECURE, *PKTSWTNET...
  Minimum propagation delay  . .  *MIN         *MIN, *LAN, *TELEPHONE...
  Maximum propagation delay  . .  *TELEPHONE   *MIN, *LAN, *TELEPHONE...
  Minimum user-defined 1 . . . .  0            0-255
  Maximum user-defined 1 . . . .  255          0-255
  Minimum user-defined 2 . . . .  0            0-255
```

```
                 Create Class-of-Service Desc (CRTCOSD)

Type choices, press Enter.

  Maximum user-defined 2 . . . .  255          0-255
  Minimum user-defined 3 . . . .  0            0-255
  Maximum user-defined 3 . . . .  255          0-255
Row 8 for nodes:
  Node row weight  . . . . . . .  10           0-255
  Min route addition resistance   0            0-255
  Max route addition resistance   63           0-255
  Minimum congestion for node  .  *LOW         *LOW, *HIGH
  Maximum congestion for node  .  *LOW         *LOW, *HIGH
Text 'description' . . . . . . .  *BLANK

                        Additional Parameters

  Authority  . . . . . . . . . .  *LIBRCRTAUT  Name, *LIBRCRTAUT, *CHANGE
```

Figure 18-10: Prompted version of the CRTCOSD command (parts 1-5).

Name the class of service on the Class-of-Service Description Name (COSD) parameter. On the Transmission Priority (TMSPY) parameter, specify the priority any transmission under this class of service will have. Possible values are:

- *LOW.
- *MED—The default.
- *HIGH.

Things get interesting on the Row 1 For Lines (ROW 1 LINE through ROW 8 LINE) parameters. The system operator cannot see the table being built. The idea is to create a mental image (or sketch one on a piece of paper), and only use these parameters to enter data into the appropriate row within the table. When putting in values for multiple rows, specify them in ascending sequence: Row one first, row eight last. Most rows have minimum and maximum values. When they do have values, the minimum value entered cannot be greater than the maximum value. Additionally, the maximum values cannot be less than the minimum value.

NETWORK ATTRIBUTES

AS/400s come with IBM-supplied values for AS/400 network attributes. Most of the time, these defaults are adequate, but any system operator ought to know what they are. Take a look at them with the Display Network Attributes (DSPNETA) command.

Although changes are usually necessary, if any are desired, make them through the Change Network Attributes (CHGNETA) command. Unfortunately, Network Attributes cannot be both displayed and changed from the same command. The CHGNETA command just shows *SAME for all the network attributes, hiding the current values. Therefore, use DSPNETA to get an idea of the current values before changing anything.

An important network attribute is the base level of *high-performance routing (HPR).* This is an enhancement to APPN to improve data routing performance and reliability over high-speed links such as (but not limited to) OptiConnect/400.

HPR takes intermediate node traffic switching functions down below the MI layer. Beyond that, it uses its own routing algorithms and can accomplish the same switching with less storage and processing requirements than traditional APPN.

Closely related to the HPR is the *HPR Tower RTP (Rapid Transport Protocol*) function. This is another speed enhancement. For a node to support HPR Tower RTP, at least one other node must have the same RTP support.

Controlling network attributes is something common to both APPC and APPN networks. There are only four parameters that can be changed on APPC-only networks:

- Local network ID (LCLNETID).
- Local control-point name (LCLCPNAME).
- Default local location name (LCLLOCNAME).
- Default mode name (DFTMODE).

On APPN networks, the CHGNETA command can also change:

- Local Network ID (LCLNETID). IBM supplies APPN for this value, but it should be changed to a network ID that is really on the system. If the APPN network is large (or becomes large), management and configuration will be easier. It is a good idea to create a name here that is unique in the world, not just unique to the organization. IBM maintains a registry of such names. Contact the IBM branch about how to contact IBM's SNA Network Registry.
- Local Control-Point Name. IBM supplies Snnnnnnn where nnnnnnn is the serial number of the local machine. Override this value, if desired, but it is not necessary. Make note of this name. When the connected remote AS/400's controller descriptions are configured, this name must be entered as the remote control-point name (RMTCPNAME).
- Default Local Location Name. IBM supplies *Snnnnnnn* where *nnnnnnn* is the serial number of the AS/400. This is adequate; just leave it intact.

- Default Mode. The IBM default is a mode called BLANK. This mode is also supplied by IBM. To specify a locally created mode, that mode must have been first defined with the Create Mode (CRTMOD) command.

- APPN Node Type. The APPN node specifies whether the local system is an End Node (*ENDNODE) or a Network Node (*NETNODE). This must agree with the APPN Node Type parameter of the CRTCTLAPPC command used to create the APPC/APPN controller.

- Maximum Number of Intermediate Sessions Allowed. Only used for APPN network nodes, intermediate sessions determine the congestion level for the node. Intermediate sessions are APPN sessions that have started to receive or resend network traffic not addressed to the local AS/400. The valid values for this parameter are 0–9999. The IBM-supplied default is 200. When the number of intermediate sessions reaches 90 percent of the number in this parameter, APPN considers the node congested and starts routing traffic around it until its number of intermediate sessions falls below 80 percent of this value.

- Route Addition Resistance (RAR). Only used for APPN network nodes, a RAR is a relative number between 0 and 255 indicating how desirable the node is as an intermediate traffic handler. The default from IBM is 128. Increase the number on a node, and it becomes less desirable. Decrease the number on a node, and it is more desirable.

- Network Node Service Provider List. Only used for end nodes, the list contains the names of up to five network node servers. Each name is a combination network ID and control-point name of each network node server. IBM supplies *LCLNETID and *ANY. These generic values give the most flexibility, and they should suffice.

- Allow HPR Transport Tower Support (ALWHPRTWR). Specifies the network attribute that allows the use of HPR transport tower support for APPN session traffic. Possible values are *YES or *NO.

- HPR Path Switch Timers (HPRPTHTMR). Specifies the amount of time in minutes to allow for a path switch attempt of an RTP connection. Four categories of priorities can be specified to control the time allowed:

    a. Element One: Network Priority. Possible values are:

        i. Transmission Priority. Default value of one minute.

        ii. *NONE. No path switch is allowed.

        iii. Network Priority. Specify the amount of minutes for the system to attempt to switch paths in an RTP connection that has network transmission priority. Valid values range from 1 through 10,000.

    b. Element Two: High Priority. Possible values are:

        i. Transmission Priority. Default value of two minutes.

        ii. *NONE. No path switch is allowed.

        iii. High Priority. Specify the amount of minutes for the system to attempt to switch paths in an RTP connection that has high priority. Valid values range from 1 through 10,000.

    c. Element Three: Medium Priority. Possible values are:

        i. *NONE. No path switch is allowed.

   ii. Medium Priority. Specify the amount of minutes for the system to attempt to switch paths in an RTP connection that has medium priority. Valid values range from 1 through 10,000.

d. Element Four: Low Priority. Possible values are:

   i. *NONE. No path switch is allowed.

   ii. Low Priority. Specify the amount of minutes for the system to attempt to switch paths in an RTP connection that has low priority. Valid values range from 1 through 10,000.

There are a couple of considerations before changing any APPN values:

- Any APPN controllers (which are controller descriptions with APPN[*YES]) must be varied off before making changes.
- The values for parameters Local Network ID, Local Control-Point Name, and Default Local Location Name cannot be changed to any values that cause a combined name similar to one used on a location list for any remote AS/400.

CL COMMANDS FOR COMMUNICATIONS

There are a lot of CL commands for controlling communications, but CL's construction makes them easy to remember:

- Lines:
  - Can be created or changed with the CRT or CHG prefix attached to the noun LIN (CHGLIN..., CRTLIN...).
  - Both commands must have a suffix of one of the following:
  - DDI (DDI).
  - ETH (Ethernet).
  - FR (frame relay).
  - IDLC (IDLC).
  - NET (network).
  - SDLC (SDLC).
  - TDLC (TDLC).
  - TRN (Token-Ring network).
  - X25 (X.25).
- Controllers:
  - Can be created or changed with the CRT or CHG prefix attached to the noun CTL (CHGCTL..., CRTCTL...).
  - Both commands must have a suffix of one of the following:
    - APPC (for APPC or APPN).
    - HOST.

- Device descriptions:
  - Can be created or changed with the CRT or CHG prefix attached to the noun DEV (CHGDEV..., CRTDEV...).
  - Both commands must have a suffix of one of the following:
    - DDI (DDI).
    - ETH (Ethernet).
    - FR (frame relay).
    - IDLC (IDLC).
    - NET (network).
    - SDLC (SDLC).
    - TDLC (TDLC).
    - TRN (Token-Ring network).
    - X25 (X.25).
- Mode descriptions:
  - Can be created or changed with the CRT or CHG prefix attached to the noun MOD (CHGMOD, CRTMODD).
- Class-of-Service (COS) Descriptions:
  - Can be created or changed with the CRT or CHG prefix attached to the abbreviation COS (CHGCOSD, CRTCOSD).

USING APPC/APPN

After all that configuration effort, using the APPC/APPN network is simple. The operator only has to:

- Vary the configuration on and off.
- Control modes.

For those unfamiliar with IBM terminology, read "vary" as "turn." To vary on a device is to turn the device on. Well, it is already on as far as power goes. The vary-on command turns it on logically, or makes it come to life as far as the AS/400 is concerned.

The Vary Configuration (VRYCFG) command works on all those communications devices that go with a network. Figure 18-11 has a prompted version of the command.

```
                    Vary Configuration (VRYCFG)

Type choices, press Enter.

Configuration object . . . . . . > APPNDEV       Name
               + for more values
Type . . . . . . . . . . . . . . > *NWI          *NWS, *NWI, *LIN, *CTL...
Status . . . . . . . . . . . . . > *ON           *ON, *OFF, *RESET...
Range  . . . . . . . . . . . . .   *NET          *NET, *OBJ
Vary on wait . . . . . . . . . .   *CFGOBJ       *CFGOBJ, *NOWAIT, 15-180 (sec)
Reset  . . . . . . . . . . . . .   *NO            *NO, *YES
```

Figure 18-11: Prompted version of the VRYCFG command—used to start/stop APPC and APPN networks.

The Status (STATUS) parameter actually turns the network on and off. The values *YES and *NO signify an on or off operation. Specify the name of the object that is to be varied with the CFGOBJ parameter.

Specify the type of object that is being varied on or off on the CFGTYPE parameter. The five possible values for the CFGTYPE parameter are:

- *NWS (Network server).
- *NWI (Network interface).
- *LIN (Line).
- *CTL (Controller).
- *DEV (Device).

There are a lot of objects that make up an APPC/APPN network—that should be obvious; we have been discussing all of them. They do not have to be all varied on or off individually. Most of these vary commands have a parameter, RANGE(*NET), that will automatically vary on all objects downstream from the one description specified. When starting the network, specify *NWS or *NWI for the CFGTYPE parameter and all devices connected to the CFGOBJ will be varied on or off together.

After the APPC/APPN configuration is varied on, a mode must be started. Modes are specified on the device descriptions (refer to the section Create Device Descriptions and the section Create Mode Descriptions). There can be many modes for one configuration. Once the mode is started, individual sessions can be established between locations. Modes get started in four ways:

- For device descriptions automatically created by APPN, a mode is started when a request to start a session is received.
- For device descriptions created with APPN(*YES), a mode is started when a request to start a session is received.
- For device descriptions manually created with APPN(*NO), a mode is started when the device description is varied on.
- Start a mode with the Start Mode (STRMOD) command.

Once a mode is started (with the command or automatically), end it with the End Mode (ENDMOD) command. Check on any mode with the Display Mode Status (DSPMODSTS) command.

Occasionally, sessions will fail to be established. When this happens, look at the number of sessions on a mode as well as its maximum number of sessions value. Often the maximum number of sessions is set equal to the number of sessions already running. To correct this (and allow the new session to start), use the Change Sessions Maximum (CHGSSNMAX) command to increase the number of sessions that may be active over an individual mode.

Using APPC Functions

In a section at the beginning of this chapter, we introduced ten of the more significant interconnectivity functions that come with APPC. Remember, APPN is an extension of APPC, so although these functions are part of APPC, APPN networks share them as well. Here is a more in-depth discussion of each.

Distributed Data Management

Distributed data management is a way for a program or user on one system to access database files on another system. Through DDM, the operator can also submit a command from a local machine to do something to a file on a remote machine.

DDM is for accessing the file's records to read, add, change, or delete them. Although it can be used to move files from one system to another, it is better to use SNADS to move files. See the section, SNA Distribution Services. The five commands to work with DDM files are:

- WRKDDMF (Work with DDM Files)—an easy way to get to the other DDM commands.
- CRTDDMF (Create DDM File).
- CHGDDMF (Change DDM File).
- DSPDDMF (Display DDM File).
- DLTF (Delete DDM File).

The prompted versions of the commands (except DLTF) are similar. We will go through the CRTDDMF to explain the parameters. Figure 18-12 shows the prompted version.

```
                          Create DDM File (CRTDDMF)

 Type choices, press Enter.

 DDM file . . . . . . . . . . . .   _________     Name
   Library  . . . . . . . . . . .     *CURLIB     Name, *CURLIB
 Remote file:
   File . . . . . . . . . . . . .   _________     Name, *NONSTD
     Library  . . . . . . . . . .     _______     Name, *LIBL, *CURLIB
   Nonstandard file 'name'  . . .   ________________________________


 Remote location  . . . . . . . .   _________     Name
 Text 'description' . . . . . . .   *BLANK
```

```
                         Create DDM File (CRTDDMF)

 Type choices, press Enter.

                          Additional Parameters

 Device:
   APPC device description . . .   *LOC          Name, *LOC
 Local location . . . . . . . . .   *LOC          Name, *LOC, *NETATR
 Mode . . . . . . . . . . . . . .   *NETATR       Name, *NETATR
 Remote network identifier . . .   *LOC          Name, *LOC, *NETATR, *NONE
 Access method:
   Remote file attribute . . . .   *RMTFILE      *RMTFILE, *COMBINED...
   Local access method . . . . .   ____________  *BOTH, *RANDOM, *SEQUENTIAL
 Share open data path . . . . . .   *NO           *NO, *YES
 Protected conversation . . . . .   *NO           *NO, *YES
 Record format level check . . .   *RMTFILE      *RMTFILE, *NO
 Authority . . . . . . . . . . .   *LIBCRTAUT    Name, *LIBCRTAUT, *ALL...
 Replace file . . . . . . . . . .   *YES          *YES, *NO
                                                                      Bottom
 F3=Exit   F4=Prompt   F5=Refresh   F12=Cancel   F13=How to use this display
 F24=More keys
```

Figure 18-12: Prompted version of the CRTDDM command (parts 1 and 2).

It is a common (but not required) practice to create a special library named DDMLIB on the source computer for DDM files.

The DDM FILE parameter is the local name used to refer to the file. That does not have to be the real name of the file. The Remote File parameter is the actual library and name of the file on the remote system.

To access an AS/400 file, enter its file and library name on the REMOTE FILE parameter. To access an S/38 or S/36 file or just one member of an AS/400 file, enter *NONSTD as the remote file name and the name of the remote file (enclosed in single apostrophes) on the NONSTANDARD FILE 'NAME' parameter.

For example, the System/38's naming convention would require a library and file name in this form: 'MASTFILE.LIBRNAME'.

The Remote Location Name parameter is the name of the remote system on which the file resides.

The additional parameter screen has a couple of interesting items in it. The device, location, and mode are APPC-related and are usually left to *LOC (or the values used when APPC is set up). The record format level check parameter allows AS/400 normal level checking to occur on the remote file. A value of *NO will disable level checking. This parameter provides some latitude on level checks when accessing DDM files. But be careful—level checks are there for a reason; turning them off may result in programs accessing out-of-date files.

DDM files are extremely simple. Once one is created, it is available for use right away. Think of DDM files as files on the local system. Not only are they easily accessible by application programs, almost any database file-related CL command can be run against them, and CL commands that allow output to OUTFILES can be directed to them. For all practical purposes, DDM files in use are treated as local files.

The command to submit other commands to a remote system is the Submit Remote Command (SBMRMTCMD). It is similar to the Submit Job (SBMJOB) command in that it contains a command embedded within it. The embedded command can be an OS/400 command, a locally created command, or a CALL to start a program running.

For more information, refer to IBM manual *Distributed Data Management V4R4*.

OptiConnect/400

OptiConnect/400 is a high-speed, high-availability optical bus between two or more AS/400s. It is a combination of hardware (referred to as OptiConnect), software support from APPC (referred to as OptiConnect/400), and APIs.

The addition of special APIs for the product is nice because, not only is the optical bus extremely fast, savvy developers and business partners can write programs to access records or move entire files by using them. And APIs run under the MI level, yielding even faster throughput.

OptiConnect/400 is only currently available for high-end AS/400s. OptiConnect does not replace DDM (refer to section above) or SNADS (refer to the section on SNA Distribution Services); it enhances their performance. It also provides a fast path for remote backup and recovery and remote journaling.

We have been discussing two systems as local and remote. In OptiConnect/400 parlance, these become *hub* and *satellite*. An OptiConnect network can consist of one hub and up to thirteen satellites.

OptiConnect comes with its own library (QSOC), subsystem description (QSOC), pre-startable management job, and job description. The customer does not have to create any of this. To start OptiConnect, use the Start Subsystem (STRSBS) command:

```
STRSBS QSOC/QSOC
```

To end OptiConnect, use the End Subsystem (ENDSBS) command:

```
ENDSBS QSOC/QSOC *IMMED
```

OptiConnect comes with its own commands:

- Verify Optical Connection (VFYOPTCNN). Verifies the optical connection. The results of this verify end up in a job log. Run the command from any command line, then use the Display Job Log (DSPJOBLOG) when it completes.
- Work with OptiConnect Activity (WRKOPCACT). Checks the OptiConnect activity on the systems (the hub and all satellites).

Do not forget these commands come with the product, so they are found in the QSOC library. OptiConnect/400 can be configured in two ways:

- STANDARD. Just specify the keyword, QYCTSOC, on the Device Description parameter on the DDM file when it is created (CRTDDM) or changed (CHGDDM). Refer to the section on Distributed Data Management. This method works fine except it does not support SNADS (see the next section for more information on SNADS).
- *OPC CONTROLLER AND DEVICE. This method requires a special controller and device be created for OptiConnect/400. In this configuration, OptiConnect supports SNADS.

To create the *OPC controller, use the same Create Controller (CRTCTLAPPC) we discussed before. Figure 18-13 contains a prompted example of that command.

```
                   Create Ctl Desc (APPC) (CRTCTLAPPC)

Type choices, press Enter.

Controller description . . . . . > OPTICTL       Name
Link type  . . . . . . . . . . . > *OPC          *ANYNW, *FAX, *FR, *IDLC...
Remote System Name . . . . . . .   RMTSYS        Character value
Data link role . . . . . . . . .   *NEG          *NEG, *PRI, *SEC
```

Figure 18-13: Example of CRTCTLAPPC for an OptiConnect controller.

Create a controller on each system, the hub, and all satellites. The Data Link Role parameter must be *PRI (Primary) for the hub, and *SEC (Secondary) for the satellites.

The DSAP value can be 04, 08, 0C, 10, 14, 78, or 7C but they must be the same on paired systems' controllers.

Next, create devices on both systems. Use the Create Device Description (CRTDEVD) command. A sample is shown in Figure 18-14.

```
                   Create Device Desc (APPC) (CRTDEVAPPC)

Type choices, press Enter.

Device description . . . . . . . > OPTDEV        Name
Remote location  . . . . . . . . > RMTSYS        Name
Online at IPL  . . . . . . . . . > *NO           *YES, *NO
Local location . . . . . . . . .   *NETATR       Name, *NETATR
Remote network identifier  . . .   *NETATR       Name, *NETATR, *NONE
Attached controller  . . . . . . > OPTCTL        Name
Mode . . . . . . . . . . . . . .   *NETATR       Name, *NETATR
               + for more values   
Message queue  . . . . . . . . .   QSYSOPR       Name, QSYSOPR
  Library  . . . . . . . . . . .     *LIBL       Name, *LIBL, *CURLIB
APPN-capable . . . . . . . . . .   *YES          *YES, *NO
Single session:
  Single session capable . . . .   *NO           *NO, *YES
  Number of conversations  . . .   ____          1-512


                                                                   Bottom
F3=Exit   F4=Prompt   F5=Refresh   F10=Additional parameters   F12=Cancel
F13=How to use this display        F24=More keys
```

Figure 18-14: Example of an OptiConnect device created with the CRTDEVD command.

Note that the APPN and Online at IPL parameters must both be set to NO. After the controller and device are created on both systems, start OptiConnect by varying on the controller and specifying Range(*NET). Here is an example:

```
VRYCFG CFGOBJ(<controller name>) CFGTYPE(*CTL) STATUS(*ON)
```

For more information, refer to IBM manual *OptiConnect for OS/400.*

SNA Distribution Services

Systems Network Architecture Distribution Services (SNADS) is a method to distribute objects to other systems. It can distribute documents, files, input streams, and messages. Along with distribution (sending and receiving objects), SNADS also performs the routing of those objects. The objects to be distributed can be done so immediately or held until a later time. Think of SNADS as an application program that runs on both the local and remote AS/400s that are connected with APPC or APPN.

The SNADS program features are dependent on the APPC device's description, plus three other system objects. Fortunately, every AS/400 comes loaded with one of each of these objects, and they are all named the same:

- QSNADS subsystem. The subsystem comes with an autostart job entry of QZDSTART. For more information on autostart jobs, see chapter 7.
- QSNADS job queue.
- QSNADS user ID.

Along with the three system objects, the system needs three SNADS objects:

- System Distribution Directory:
  - User ID/Address. The user identification and address are used as a pair to create a unique name. The address is the name of the remote system. This combined pair will make a match on the System Distribution Directory of the remote system.
  - System Name/Group. The system name is the name of the remote system. The system name and group are used as a pair to create a unique name. Group is optional and can be left off. This pair is used to make a match on the System Distribution Routing Table.
- System Distribution Routing Table containing:
  - System Name/Group. The system name is the name of the remote system. The system name and group are used as a pair to create a unique name. Group is optional and can be left off. This pair is used to make a match on the System Distribution Queue.
- System Distribution Queue. The following four items are used together to locate an APPC device configuration:
  - Remote location name.
  - Mode.
  - Remote network ID.
  - Local location name. *Note*: This is the first time in these three items that we have specified the local system.

The System Distribution Directory must be in place on both the local and remote AS/400s. The requesting user's identification and address is sent with the objects being transmitted and the remote machine uses that to find a match in its own System Distribution Directory. From that match, it assigns a local (to it) user ID. That user ID is a valid user on the remote system who will receive the object.

Note that if two machines can both send and receive each other's objects, each directory must contain two entries for each user ID: user ID/local system name and user ID/remote system name. One entry will be used when the machine is sending and the other when it is receiving.

The remote location name of the System Distribution Queue is used to find a matching APPC Device Description on the local AS/400. That, in turn, is used by APPC to find the correct remote AS/400. Therefore, the APPC device description must exist on both the local and remote systems.

When a SNADS application receives an object, it does not presume that object is for its AS/400. SNADS first tries to match the object's destination user ID/address to one in its own System Distribution Directory. If the address is for another AS/400 it is communicating with, SNADS merely forwards the object on. If it finds a match and the local user ID has a local address, it completes the transaction by receiving the object for the user. The commands to work with these SNADS items are:

- System Distribution Directory:
  - WRKDIR (Work with Directory).
- System Distribution Routing Table:
  - ADDDSTRTE (Adds an Entry).
  - CHGDSTRTE (Changes an Entry).
  - RMVDSTRTE (Removes an Entry).
- System Distribution Queue:
  - ADDDSTQ (Adds an Entry).
  - CHGDSTQ (Changes an Entry).
  - HLDDSTQ (Holds the Distribution Queue).
  - INZDSTQ (Initializes the Distribution Queue)—optionally deleting entries.
  - RLSDSTQ (Releases the Distribution Queue).
  - RMVDSTQ (Removes an Entry).
  - SNDDSTQ (Sends an Entry).
  - WRKDSTQ (Work with Distribution Queues or Entries)—allows the operator to check the status of distribution.
- All items:
  - CFGDSTSRV. Adds, changes, removes, and displays distribution-queue or routing-table entries. This command has one parameter (OPTION) that controls its navigation. Possible values are:
    - *SELECT. This causes a menu to display.

- Bypass the menu and work on distribution queues.
- Bypass the menu and work on the routing table.
- Bypass the menu and work on the secondary system name table.

- DSPDSTSRV. Displays the distribution queues and routing tables.

SNADS is basically an application of several programs. Four of these are called router, sender, receiver, and arriver.

- Router. The program name for router is QROUTR. Only one router program is used in a SNADS subsystem. Router should be an autostart job so it will start when the subsystem starts. If the router fails, SNADS communication is impossible and error CPC8803 is sent to the operator. The router performs three tasks:
  - Delivers objects.
  - Forwards objects to other users on other systems.
  - Redirects objects to users who may have once been on the local system but who have moved.
- Sender. This program sends objects from the distribution queue to the remote system. It can send objects immediately or schedule them for later. It recognizes objects' delivery priorities, and it will attempt to retry a delivery that failed for any reason. While the program name varies, it assumes the RMTLOCNAME specified on the distribution queue. Sender is active as long as the SNADS subsystem is active. If problems are suspected, check for them with the Work with Distribution Queues (WRKDSTQ) command.
- Receiver. This program receives incoming objects. The program name is determined by the device used to connect to the remote system. This job starts as soon as the APPC/APPN conversation is started and stays up until the conversation is ended or an error occurs.
- Arriver. This program delivers mail intended for users on the local system.

Setting up SNADS

Here are the steps for bringing up SNADS on the system:

1. Have APPC or APPN active.
2. Make sure the IBM-supplied subsystem, QCMN, is active. It has one communications entry and SNADS will use it.
3. Start the QSNADS subsystem. This is another supplied by IBM.
4. To use SNADS to distribute mail, start the mail server framework with the STRMSF command.
5. With the Configure Distribution Services (CFGDSTSRV) command:
   a. Define the distribution queue(s). Use parameter OPTION(1). A distribution queue with the appropriate name must exist. If one does not, it can be added with the Add Distribution Queue (ADDDSTQ) command.

b. Define the routing table. Use parameter OPTION(2). A routing table must already exist. If one does not, add one with the Add Distribution Routing Entry (ADDDSTRTE) command.

6. With the Work with Directory (WRKDIR) command, enroll network users in the System Distribution Directory.

7. With the Work with Distribution Lists (WRKDSTL) command, set up distribution lists.

8. Save the SNADS configuration. Saving the configuration now will make it easy to restore later.

When working with the configuration directory, we can gain more flexibility with user IDs by specifying *ANY. Any transmission bound for that AS/400 would be received and routed. *ANY can be combined with legitimate user IDs. Include it at the bottom of the distribution directory for incoming objects or mail for anyone (such as visitors from other locations) not on the list. For more information, refer to IBM manual *SNA Distribution Services V4R4.*

Routing SNADS over OptiConnect

To get SNADS to run over OptiConnect, first be familiar with OptiConnect material presented earlier in this chapter. Configure the OptiConnect/400 controller and device then configure SNADS. Then:

1. Add a Directory Entry (ADDDIRE).

   a.
   ```
   ADDDIRE USRID(<address of remote system>/*ANY)  + usrd(description) +
   sysname(<name of remote system>)
   ```

2. Add a Distribution Queue (ADDDSTQ).

   a.
   ```
   ADDDSTQ DSTQ(<name of queue>) RMTLOCNAME(<name-must be same name from+
   appc dev desc>) DSTQTYPE(*SNADS) MODE(*NETATR) RMTNETID(*NONE) +
   LCLLOCNAME(<name-must be same name from appc dev desc>)ADDDSTRTE
   ```

3. Add a Distribution Routing Entry (ADDDSTRTE).

   a.
   ```
   SYSNAME(<name of system>) FAST(<fast data queue name>) +
   STATUS(<status data queue name>) DATAHIGH(<datahigh data queue name>)+
   DATALOW(<datalow data queue name>)
   ```

Display Station Pass-Through

Display station pass-through is a method of signing onto a remote AS/400 through a workstation connected to a local AS/400. Though this sounds like access to multiple AS/400s via a network, it really is not. In this case, the workstation itself has no direct connection to the remote AS/400, although the two AS/400s are connected. To make the pass-through happen, the user must be signed on to the local AS/400 at the time.

Display station pass-through gets really interesting when it is done over an APPN network with lots of AS/400s and routing entries. With pass-through, users can sign onto any remote AS/400 from their workstation, going through the local AS/400. Depending on the number of sessions allowed at one time on the workstation, users can even pass through to other remote AS/400s at the same time.

One important capacity point with display station pass-through: Every pass-through takes up one session.

Start the display station pass-through function with the Start Pass-Through (STRPASTHR) command. Figure 18-15 shows the prompted form.

```
                       Start Pass-Through (STRPASTHR)

Type choices, press Enter.

Remote location . . . . . . . .   __________   Name, *CNNDEV
APPC device . . . . . . . . . .   *LOC         Name, *LOC
              + for more values   __________
Virtual controller . . . . . . .  *NONE        Name, *NONE
Virtual display device . . . . .  *NONE        Name, *NONE
              + for more values   __________
Mode . . . . . . . . . . . . . .  *NETATR      Name, *NETATR
Local location . . . . . . . . .  *LOC         Name, *LOC, *NETATR
Remote network identifier  . . .  *LOC         Name, *LOC, *NETATR, *NONE
System request program . . . . .  *SRQMNU      Name, *SRQMNU
  Library  . . . . . . . . . . .    ________   Name, *LIBL, *CURLIB

                         Additional Parameters

User profile . . . . . . . . . .  *NONE        Character value, *NONE...
User password  . . . . . . . . .  *NONE        Character value, *NONE
                                                                   More...
F3=Exit   F4=Prompt   F5=Refresh   F12=Cancel   F13=How to use this display
F24=More keys
```

```
                       Start Pass-Through (STRPASTHR)

Type choices, press Enter.

Initial program to call  . . . .  *RMTUSRPRF   Name, *RMTUSRPRF, *NONE
Initial menu . . . . . . . . . .  *RMTUSRPRF   Name, *RMTUSRPRF, *SIGNOFF
Current library  . . . . . . . .  *RMTUSRPRF   Name, *RMTUSRPRF
Display option . . . . . . . . .  *YES         Character value, *YES, *NO
```

Figure 18-15: Prompted version of the STRPASTHR command (parts 1 and 2).

Most of the time, the operator can just specify the remote AS/400 name on the RMTLOCNAME parameter. This will suffice in every case except for the case when running APPN and supporting multiple APPN networks. Then the operator also needs to specify the network ID on the Remote Network Identifier (RMTNETID) parameter.

What constitutes a system name can be confusing—it is the local name of the remote system. As such, the system name can be one of these three choices:

- As defined on the remote system's APPN configuration list (as a local location).

- The local location name of the remote system.
- Local control-point name (APPN only).

If the system name is not clear, use one of the following commands at the remote system to determine what location names are valid:

- WRKCFGL (Work with Configuration List).
- DSPNETA (Display Network Attributes).
- DSPAPPNINF (Display APPN Information).

Most of the time, the system operator will use the remote system's name and his or her own user ID/password. The next thing the operator will see is a logon menu from the remote system. He should sign on and continue as if it were his primary machine. To go back to the original (or local) AS/400, use the Transfer Pass-Through (TRFPASTHR) command or one of these command keys:

- While on the target AS/400:
    - System Request, option 10.
    - System Request, option 13.
    - System Request, option 14.
- While on the local AS/400:
    - System Request Menu, F3.
    - System Request, option 15.

When through, terminate the session with the End Pass-Through (ENDPASTHR) command.

Configuring Display Station Pass-Through

The APPC/APPN controller and device configurations are enough for display station pass-through. But there two areas to think about:

- Whether to have the remote system configure its controller automatically or configure it manually.
- Whether to allow remote sign-on capability.

AUTOMATIC OR MANUAL CONFIGURATION

Although the remote system has its own physical devices and controllers for its communications, it needs a logical configuration in order to support communication. The remote system can be set to configure devices automatically or the customer can do them manually.

If automatic configuration is desired, these devices and controllers so configured are referred to as *virtual devices*. They will be controlled by the QAUTOVRT system value, which can contain any number between 0 and 9999. If QAUTOVRT is set to any non-zero number, autoconfig is on until the system has configured as many devices as specified in the system value. To get started, use the Change System Value (CHGSYSVAL) command to set QAUTOVRT to 10.

If relying on autoconfig (no devices or controllers have been configured manually) and either QAUTOVRT is set to 0 or it has already configured the number of devices specified on the system value, display station pass-through will fail.

Even a 10-device limit is not as limiting as it may sound. Autoconfigured devices stay on the system until they are deleted.

By the way, consider this for security purposes: When the system automatically creates devices, the user who is signing on becomes their owner.

Controllers can support many devices, and automatic configuration will create one controller for every 250 devices. It will not create a second controller until it needs to attach device 251.

This might seem like a lot of devices on a controller, but everything is virtual. Therefore, it is really no big deal. However, from a management perspective, 250 devices on one controller does not help when there are system problems. The main reason for manually configuring controllers and devices is that smaller numbers of devices can be grouped to individual controllers.

If QAUTOVRT is set to 0, automatic configuration for virtual devices is turned off, and all controllers and devices must already exist on the target system before pass-through can occur.

Create device and controller descriptions manually with the Create Device Description (CRTDEVD) and Create Controller Description (Virtual Workstation) (CRTCTLVWS) commands. We have discussed creating device descriptions in the section on Create Device Descriptions. Figure 18-16 shows the prompted version of the CRTCTLVWS command.

```
                     Create Ctl Desc (Virtual WS) (CRTCTLVWS)

 Type choices, press Enter.

 Controller description . . . . .   __________   Name
 Online at IPL  . . . . . . . . .   *YES         *YES, *NO
 Text 'description' . . . . . . .   *BLANK
 

                            Additional Parameters

 Attached devices . . . . . . . .   __________   Name
               + for more values    __________
 Authority  . . . . . . . . . . .   *LIBCRTAUT   Name, *LIBCRTAUT, *CHANGE...





                                                                        Bottom
 F3=Exit   F4=Prompt   F5=Refresh   F12=Cancel   F13=How to use this display
 F24=More keys
```

Figure 18-16: Prompted version of the CRTCTLVWS command.

Devices must be created before controllers are created. Virtual controllers and devices on the remote system must match physical devices on the local system. If a like device is not available, an alternate virtual device can be used, but the VRTDEV parameter must have been specified on the

STRPASTHR command. For a chart of matching displays and acceptable alternatives, see the IBM manual, *OS/400 Remote Work Station Support V4R4.*

User Profile Configuration

User profiles must exist on the remote system for users who are passing through. Use the Create User Profile (CRTUSRPRF) command to create the pass-through profiles.

When display station pass-through is initially set up, relax security long enough to work out connection issues without getting confused by those security issues. But when pass-through is live, seriously consider security. A user entering a system from another AS/400 is not "local" and should probably have limited access.

The automatic creation of controllers and devices is a weak point in security for display station pass-through. When an unknown user attempts to sign on to the remote system, the system will create the devices for him. There is a system value, QMAXSIGN, that is supposed to limit the number of failed sign-on attempts. It does very well for controllers and devices that are manually configured (and no automatic configuration is allowed). However, all it does with automatic configuration is set the newly configured controller/device to inactive after the number of failed sign-on attempts; then the system will automatically create new controllers/devices.

There are two things about display station pass-through that somewhat ameliorate this issue:

- The incoming user was at least a valid user on another connected AS/400, so it may not be that big of a problem, but it bears thinking about.
- The Create Line Description commands now have a parameter, Autodelete Controller (it follows the Autocreate Controller parameter), where the operator can specify after how many idle minutes the system is to delete the controller automatically.

Beyond that, there is another issue to consider. That issue is: when a user starts a passthrough session, will he/she be presented with a sign-on screen or will the access to the remote system be transparent (automatic sign on)? The same decision with a new twist must be made when a program (or menu option) automatically starts pass-through for its own use; the operator could allow automatic sign-on capability, but then should also specify that the pass-through program automatically signs off when its job ends.

To make a sign-on screen appear, use the Change System Value (CHGSYSVAL) command to change system value QRMTSIGN to *FRCSIGNON. Set it to *SAMEPRF to bypass the sign-on screen, making the process automatic. It is easier to use *FRCSIGNON when setting up a pass-through. Change it after the connection is established and stable (meaning it works every time).

With system value QRMTSIGN set to *SAMEPRF (transparent sign on), the system will take the user profile and password from the parameters of the STRPASTHR command. Even with automatic sign on, the user will see system messages as the pass-through is accomplished. If these are seen as distracting, they can be suppressed from the user's screen by specifying PASTHRSCN(*NO) on the STRPASTHR command.

For more information on display station pass-through, refer to the IBM manual, *OS/400 Remote Work Station Support V4R4.*

Electronic Customer Support (ECS)

Electronic Customer Support (ECS) comes with every AS/400. The ECS feature allows the customer to contact IBM directly and inquire about current PTFs, log problems, and even order PTFs or operating system upgrades.

Also, when the AS/400's internal self-diagnostics sense a problem developing, the AS/400 will use the ECS line to initiate a service call to IBM. Or the operator can use this connection to contact IBM for question/answer support.

All AS/400s come with an ECS modem installed, and it should have been connected to an outside phone line when installed. The ECS lines, controllers, and device are already configured. Most customers just use the equipment as delivered. The lines and controllers IBM defined for ECS are:

- For non-service-related issues (problems, PTFs, OS/400, and product information):
  - QTILINE (Line).
  - QTICTL (Controller).
  - QTIDA (Device).
- For IBM service:
  - QESLINE (Line).
  - QESCTL (Controller).
  - QESPAP (Device).

Although it has never happened yet, the phone number for the IBM Service Department may someday have to be changed. If that day comes, type either CALL QESPHONE or CALL QTIPHONE on any command and press Enter. A screen will appear on which the phone number can be changed.

The AS/400 itself contains contact information about products, service, and PTFs. IBM uses this information, so it needs to be kept updated. Do so from the AS/400 Main Menu, select option 7 (`Define or Change the System`), and then select option 4 (`Work with Support Contact Information`). The operator will have an opportunity to change one of six contact areas:

- Q & A database.
- Local service.
- IBM product.
- Technical information exchange.
- Upgrade order.
- Service providers.

For more information on the ECS, refer to IBM manuals *OS/400 Communication Configuration V4R4* and *AS/400 System Operations V4R4*.

END-OF-CHAPTER AIDS

CHAPTER SUMMARY

This chapter covered the basic "out-of-the-box" skills that form the foundation for understanding all AS/400 communications. Although there was a lot of material presented, the process is really quite simple. Setting up a new communication line is a matter that requires a simple subset of the material. Even if you are faced with the challenge of setting up all communications for an AS/400 at one time, take it one line at a time and it will be easy.

Keep in mind when reading the next chapter about LAN communications that they actually run under these three basic building blocks. All AS/400 activity to devices like workstations, printers, and modems must go through SNA and either APPC or APPN.

KEY TERMS

5250
Advanced Peer-to-Peer Communications (APPC)
Advanced Peer-to-Peer Networking (APPN)
alert support
APPN NODE TYPE parameter
asynchronous
CA/400
CICS/400
class-of-service (COS)
class-of-service descriptions
communication protocol
configuration
configuration lists
connection list
control points (CP)
display station pass-through
distributed data interface (DDI)
distributed data management (DDM)
dynamic routing
emulation mode
end mode command
Ethernet
file transfer support
frame-relay network (FR)
high-performance routing (HPR)
HPR Tower RTP (rapid transport protocol)
hub
ISDN data line control (IDLC)
location lists
native
network node
network server node
network topology database
node
OptiConnect/400
satellite
SNA pass-through
synchronous data link (SDLC)
System Network Architecture (SNA)
Systems Network Architecture Distribution Services (SNADS)
Token-Ring
transmission group (TG)
twinax
virtual devices
wireless
X.25

CHAPTER SELF-TEST

Solutions to these self-test questions are in appendix D.

True-False Questions

___ 1. The AS/400 does not support the asynchronous communication protocol.

___ 2. Before a network node can support end nodes, it must be configured as a network node server.

___ 3. Configuration lists must be named *APPNLCL.

___ 4. A network node is defined to a local AS/400 in a controller.

___ 5. To define a node as either an end node or a network node is done via the APPN Node Type parameter of the CRTCTLAPPC command.

___ 6. When configuring an APPC or an APPN connection, the maximum number of sessions it can support is 256.

___ 7. When creating a class-of-service, there is an internal table containing one to eight rows of various communication preference values.

___ 8. To "vary" a device on or off is the equivalent of making the device "on-line" or ready to communicate with the host.

___ 9. When setting up DDM, it is a common practice to create a special library named DDMLIB.

___ 10. When an AS/400 running SNADs receives a message, it assumes it is the addressee and tries to process the message.

Fill in the Blanks

1. The original communications protocol the AS/400 was known for was ________________.

2. A network device at the end of an APPN network line is referred to as a(n) ____________________________.

3. The overall rule-set that governs all AS/400 communications is contained in __________________________.

4. The APPC function that allows one AS/400 to access the database of another AS/400 is ______________.

5. An IBM product that facilitates connection of personal computer workstations to an AS/400 is ________________.

6. When a transmission is timed from one link end to another, it always experiences some amount of delay or slowdown. This delay is called ________________.

7. The ________________ tells the networked nodes something about the logical connection between them.

8. To view the attributes of a network, use the ______________ command.

9. After an APPC/APPN network is configured, the operation must __________ _______ _______ to activate it.

10. ____________ is a high-speed, high-availability bus between two or more AS/400s.

Chapter Review Questions

1. Explain the following terms:
   a. Twinax.
   b. Display station pass-through.
   c. APPN.
   d. Controller.
2. How is SNA different from APPN or APPC?
3. Name and describe five of the ten APPC functions.
4. What two types of nodes are found on an APPN network?
5. What does the class-of-service provide to the APPN network?
6. What are the six objects that must be created for an APPC configuration?
7. Name six of the eight communications types that AS/400 lines can support.
8. To have a switched controller that is automatically on when the AS/400 IPLs, what two parameters of the CRTCTLAPPC command must be utilized?
9. On what object of an APPC or APPN network is the link speed specified?
10. What is the first task to perform when setting up a distributed data management file?

19

COMMUNICATIONS: LANS AND TCP/IP

CHAPTER OBJECTIVES

Upon completion of this chapter, you should be able to:

- List the different LAN protocols that the AS/400 supports.
- Explain and configure the following protocols:
  - Ethernet.
  - Token-Ring.
  - Wireless.
  - DDI.
  - Frame Relay.
  - ATM.
- Explain and configure the TCP/IP protocol.
- Have a working knowledge of the TCP/IP applications:
  - Telnet.
  - FTP.
  - SMTP.
  - POP.

    - REXEC.
    - LPR/LPD.
    - SNMP.
    - WSG.
- Demonstrate how the AS/400 is configured for Internet access.

OVERVIEW

Although SNA, APPC, and APPN provide the basis for all AS/400 connectivity and provide functionality that other platforms only dream about, the actual communication connection is usually done through industry-standard protocols.

From this chapter forward, we will walk through the LAN "stack" similar to how it is implemented on the AS/400. The LAN stack is composed of several physical *layers*. These layers separate the protocol software from the hardware that carries out the work. The more layers, the more the protocol is removed from the hardware, and the slower it runs. The smaller number of layers brings the protocol closer to the hardware, so the protocol runs faster and is considered more "native."

This chapter discusses *physical network layer* protocols. The focus is on the system operator. Supporting basic 5250 workstations on one or more AS/400s via APPC can be done with the information in chapter 18. Supporting an in-house LAN or LANs and doing business on the Internet requires the information in this chapter.

The protocols in this chapter provide AS/400 access via personal computers and over LANs and, in the case of frame relay and ATM, WANs. This chapter explains how AS/400s and LANs connect.

Networks used to refer to connecting a handful of departmental PCs. They have come to mean connecting thousands of workstations all coming together for sharing of resources, data, and general communication. In other words, with the AS/400, we are talking about infrastructure of most organizations. Even the term "network" has expanded from those handfuls of PCs connected together to several networks networked together. Each separate network is called a *network segment* of the larger network. Yes, things have become complicated.

Networks are linked together through common nodes that can route data *packets* from one network to other. These common connecting nodes are referred to as:

- *IP routers* or simply as *routers*.
- Gateways.
- Bridges.

A router is not anything magical; it is a dedicated PC that connects two or more networks and routes packets from one to the other. The connected networks can have the same or different protocols. For example, an Ethernet network can connect with a Token-Ring network through a router.

The term *gateway* is often used in place of router, and while they are pretty much interchangeable in use, there are important distinctions. Both do data routing and transferring, but a device called a gateway often offers specialized functions. For example, in the AS/400 arena, gateways are available to convert green-screens on the fly into HTML Internet-friendly screens. These help make the AS/400 Internet-ready without converting application coding. Other gateways specialize in providing a *firewall*, or extra layer of security dedicated to securing Internet-bound data.

A *bridge* can also connect networks. Again, a bridge is pretty much the same as a router, except a bridge uses physical addresses instead of IP addresses. A bridge does not have an assigned IP address like an IP router. A bridge is transparent in the *TCP/IP* (Transmission Control Protocol/Internet Protocol) network. A set of bridged networks (or segments) appears and acts as a single physical network.

A network physically connected to an AS/400 is a *local network* for that system. A network that a system can reach only after passing through one or more IP routers is a *remote network* to the AS/400. On the other hand, consider two networks connected by a node, each of which has an AS/400—one AS/400's local network is the other's remote network and vice versa.

PROTOCOLS

The LAN protocols for the AS/400 supports are:

- Token-Ring.
- Ethernet.
  - IEEE 802.3.
  - Version 2.
- Wireless (not really a protocol, runs over Ethernet).
- DDI.
- Frame relay.
- Asynchronous transfer mode (ATM).

Wireless communications actually uses Ethernet's frame protocol. However, we discuss it in this chapter because it is growing in popularity and requires some additional steps for configuration.

Of the listed protocols, Ethernet Version 2 is the most "native." It has a single layer, the *medium access control (MAC)*, between the hardware and the network. The others have two layers:

- MAC is the layer closest to the hardware. It provides the *adapter address*. Sometimes this address is simply referred to as the MAC address. The MAC layer does frame transmission and reception, recognition, and error detection.
- The *logical link control (LLC)* provides logical connection, disconnection, flow control, and error handling.

AS/400 LAN OVERVIEW

Protocol support for the AS/400 LAN falls into two broad categories:

- *Acknowledged support*—provides better error-handling capability but must run under SNA. Most AS/400 communications are acknowledged.

- *Unacknowledged support*—provides data transfer without SNA, but error handling is minimal.

The LAN devices attached to an AS/400 are logically switched. That is a little confusing at first because a dial-up remote device is considered switched. In this case, *switched* simply means that a workstation can connect to the AS/400 and expect that a communication session will be started for it, then disconnect (the session will be ended), and again reconnect.

Connecting any device to a LAN requires a LAN adapter card. Introducing an AS/400 to a LAN is no exception. To connect to a LAN, the AS/400 needs one or more adapter cards, and each of those cards supports a specific number of SNA connections.

AS/400 support of PC LANs can be treated with one of two strategies. With the first option, the AS/400 supports all devices directly. This requires a device configuration for each personal computer. Configuring each PC can be a pain, but the nice part is that LAN support is under the AS/400 umbrella. The other option is to separate the PC LAN from the AS/400 with a gateway. Using a gateway can be advantageous in a large shop where the AS/400 staff does not do LAN work, and the LAN staff does not do AS/400 tasks. Those shops would be best set up with the AS/400(s) supporting a small network and a few gateways as nodes. Each gateway will support its own section of a much larger LAN.

Bridges connect dissimilar LANs. Shops that use bridges need to be especially aware of addressing issues because bridges rely on device addressing, not the more hardware-independent IP addressing (which we discuss in-depth later). The addresses of Ethernet devices are slightly different from Token-Ring and DDI device addresses. Dissimilar addresses can be corrupted passing through a bridge. For more information about this configuration, see IBM manual *OS/400 LAN, Frame-Relay, and ATM Support V4R4,* appendix D.

One term used over and over when configuring LAN objects is *resource name*. This term indicates a concatenation of the adapter and *port* of that adapter the object will use. Use the Work with Hardware Resources (WRKHDWRSC) command (with *CMN specified as its only parameter) to find the input/output adapter (IOA) and the port number in use. Concatenate the port number onto the IOA name to create a resource name. For example, if the IOA name is LIN01, and the LAN is using the second port on the adapter, the resource name is LIN012.

LAN Addresses

Every device on the LAN, including AS/400s, requires a LAN adapter card. The adapter address, or MAC address, can be found on that card. While the MAC address is a 6-byte address, it is more frequently known by the 12 hexadecimal characters that make up the 6 bytes. Although many AS/400 customers think of the MAC address as a 12-character address, it has only 6 bytes. While the technically correct name for this is the MAC address, most AS/400 customers refer to it as the *adapter address*.

Every AS/400 adapter comes from the factory with a unique address called the *preset address*. System operators can assign their own additional address when they configure the line description. This is not required, but it is a good idea for later LAN maintenance. If the adapter card has to be replaced and the network relies on the preset address only, someone will have to assign the old preset address as the additional address anyway. On the other hand, if the operator relied on an additional address from the start, the operator only has to invoke the same additional address on the new adapter.

A frame-relay network adapter does not come with a preset address. When configuring a *bridged frame-relay environment* (see section on Frame Relay) that will connect to a remote Token-Ring, Ethernet, or DDI LAN through a network processor, the operator must assign an adapter address for each line description created.

When working with LAN devices, the system operator will often need to know adapter addresses. To quickly find them for all devices on a varied-on line, use the Display Line Description (dsplind) command.

Another set of addresses associated with adapters are *service access points (SAPs)* that come in pairs: the source SAP (SSAP) and the destination SAP (DSAP). LAN communication flows from a SSAP address on one device to a DSAP address on another device. SSAP and DSAP addresses must be the same for a communication direction and destination to be established. The AS/400 provides default SAP addresses, and most customers just accept them.

For those operators brave enough to define their own SAP addresses, they can define up to 24 SSAPs per Token-Ring or Ethernet adapter. Acknowledged services require that the addresses have SAP addresses in the range of hex 04 to hex 9C. The ones we specify must end in a 0, 4, 8, or C. For TCP/IP, just use hex AA as a SAP. Unacknowledged services can use any address from hex 02 through hex FE (as long as it is divisible by 2).

General Notes on Configuring LANs

Before attempting to use any configuration commands, make sure the user profile has *IOSYSCFG special authority. Many of the configuration commands are restricted from anyone without this authority.

We will walk through configuring the line descriptions and controller descriptions on each LAN type. In reality, many shops let the AS/400 do most of the work by accepting the default values and using autoconfiguration. Other shops worry about security with autoconfiguration. For the customer completely new to AS/400s and LANs, we suggest bringing up a LAN using autoconfiguration, then checking all those autoconfigured devices to see what the AS/400 used for parameter values. That will quickly give you an idea of what works. Then, if the organization wants more security, delete the autoconfigured devices and manually create new ones—at least you have a rough idea of a configuration that will work on which to build.

The only thing the customer must create is the line description (with the CRTLIND command). Optionally, the AS/400 will automatically configure the controller and device descriptions.

The command parameters of CRTLIND that turn on automatic configuration are APPC Controllers Created Automatically (AUTOCRTCTL[*YES]) and Create Device Descriptions (AUTOCRTDEV[*YES]). These parameters are also on the Change Line Description (CHGLIND), but they do not appear when you display the line description through the DSPLIND command.

With automatic configuration on, when a workstation attempts to connect and a controller or device does not exist, the system will create one. Even if only the (AUTOCRTCTL[*YES]) was specified (that is only the controller), if the device does not exist, the system will create one.

To accommodate logically switched devices, the description for the LAN controller on an AS/400 always has the Initial Connection (INLCNN) parameter set to *DIAL. The setting is to *DIAL even if *APPN automatically creates the controller descriptions. This parameter has more to do with when *polling* occurs than when anything is physically dialed.

Another parameter, Dial Initiation (DIALINIT), can be set to *IMMED to initiate polling as soon as the controller is varied on. Or it can be set to *DELAY to delay polling until the first program attempts to access the link. A better suggestion is to just use the default *LINKTYPE.

A parameter that really should be left alone is the Data Link Role (ROLE). Its default is negotiable (*NEG) and that is the best setting for most shops. The *NEG value allows the AS/400 to determine what stations are primary and secondary for communications.

TOKEN-RING

A Token-Ring LAN supports the IEEE 802.5 standard. It uses a token to pass data. Using a ring topology—tokens go around the ring and pass through every workstation—each workstation either passes the token on (if it is not the addressee) or receives it.

Several workstations on a Token-Ring can be attached to a concentrator called a *multistation access unit (MAU)*. IBM's 8228 MAU supports seven workstations. A Token-Ring LAN supports two transmission speeds: 4 megabytes per second (MBps) and 16 MBps. A Token-Ring LAN uses shielded twisted-pair (STP) cabling.

Although Token-Ring was a giant step forward in speed for the AS/400 (it was the first to break past the 1 MBps of 5250), computing demands have also made it too slow. There is a workaround, however, and that is to use a concentrator in place of the MAU. IBM's 8272 Controller works just fine. This device creates a star topology, receives all tokens, and routes them directly to their destination. OK, it is not a ring, and some say it is not even a token anymore—but, although speeds stay the same, performance is dramatically higher and the network gets a higher bandwidth.

When a Token-Ring relies on an MAU, it is considered a *half-duplex Token-Ring*. When it relies on the controller, it is considered a *full-duplex Token-Ring*.

Token-Ring Adapter Addressing

The Token-Ring adapter address is a 6-byte or 48-bit address. Read it like it is transmitted: from bit0/byte0 to bit7/byte5. There are two of these addresses—the destination address and the source address—on a token. Figure 19-1 shows the destination address. Note that three bits are reserved.

- IG—Individual/group:
  - The 0 means the address is an individual address or one associated with a particular station on the network.
  - The 1 means the address is a group address or that it is destined for more than one destination.
- UL—Universal/local:
  - The 0 means the address is universally administered.
  - The 1 means the address is locally administered.

- FAI—Only refers to locally administered group addresses:
  - The 0 means the locally administered address is a functional address.
  - The 1 means the locally administered address is a group address.

Figure 19-2 shows the Token-Ring source address (two bits reserved).

Byte 0							
0	1	2	3	4	5	6	7
IG	UL						
Byte 1							
0	1	2	3	4	5	6	7
FAI							
Byte 2							
0	1	2	3	4	5	6	7
Byte 5							
0	1	2	3	4	5	6	7

Figure 19-1: Token-Ring destination address.

Byte 0							
0	1	2	3	4	5	6	7
U	UL						
Byte 1							
0	1	2	3	4	5	6	7
Byte 2							
0	1	2	3	4	5	6	7
Byte 5							
0	1	2	3	4	5	6	7

Figure 19-2: Token-Ring source address.

- U:
  - The 0 means routing information is not present in the frame.
  - The 1 means routing information is present in the frame.
  - UL—Universal/local:
  - The 0 means the address is universally administered.
  - The 1 means the address is locally administered.

These bits must be considered when assigning or working with Token-Ring addresses because their use limits the range of numbers available for addressing.

- Bit0/byte0 has two implications:
  - Destination addresses:
    - Individual adapter addresses can be 000000000000 through 7FFFFFFFFFFF.
    - Group addresses can be 800000000000 through FFFFFFFFFFFF.

- Source addresses:
  - Routing information present. The range of Token-Ring addresses will be 800000000000 through FFFFFFFFFFFF.
  - No routing information present. Token-Ring addresses will be in the range 000000000000 through 7FFFFFFFFFFF.
  - Bit1/byte0. If the address (destination or source) is locally administered, the range is limited to 400000000000 through 7FFFFFFFFFFF.
  - If the address is locally administered, bit0/byte1 further limits the address.
  - Group address. The adapter's address range is limited to the range 400080000000 through 7FFFFFFFFFFF.
  - Functional address. The adapter's address range is limited to the range C00000000000 through C00040000000. There are some dedicated functional addresses and some that can be user-defined.

Heterogeneous LANs using bridges must pay particular attention to Token-Ring addressing. If this description fits your shop, see IBM manual *AS/400 LAN, Frame-Relay, and ATM Support V4R4*.

Token-Ring Considerations

A Token-Ring network requires a Token-Ring adapter card on each device (AS/400 and workstations), and every device's adapter card must connect to an MAU or concentrator. There are two factors to plan for before starting to configure a Token-Ring network:

- Speed.
- Maximum frame size.

Token-Ring networks have the option to run at two speeds: 4 MBps or 16 MBps. Once the choice is made, all Token-Ring adapter cards must be set to the same speed.

Token-Ring data is stored in the token as a *frame*. A frame can be from 265 through 16,393 bytes, and this is called the *frame size*. The larger the frame size, the more efficiently data can be moved. Following are the areas where the frame size is determined:

- The Maximum Frame Size (MAXFRAME) parameter on the Create Token-Ring Line Description (CRTLINTRN) command.
- The Maximum Frame Size (MAXFRAME) parameter on the Create Token-Ring Controller Description (CRTCTLTRN) command.

The system may override the selected frame size at any time with the smallest of the large frame sizes any individual adapter can handle. If most of the adapters on a network can handle a 16,393-byte frame size (and that is what was specified on one of the MAXFRAME parameter fields), but one adapter can only handle a 4,096-byte frame size, the system will only use the 4,096-byte frame size.

If a Token-Ring network passes its frames across a bridge, the maximum size that the bridge can handle must be taken into consideration in the frame-size calculation. If the frame size is described as too large for the bridge, that frame will be discarded when the network tries to send it through. Unfortunately, the network does not automatically incorporate the bridge frame size in its calculations. The system operator must do that calculation. Just ensure that the bridge size is at least as large as the smallest of one of the three frame sizes listed in the preceding description.

Configuring a Token-Ring Network

Before configuring a Token-Ring network, several decisions need to be made:

- Resource name. For a discussion of how to determine the resource name, see section on LAN Overview. This is the second parameter of the crtlintrn command.
- Adapter address. The adapter address must have twelve characters and start with 40000.
- Speed.
- Frame size.

After determining the preceding four items, perform the following commands in sequence:

- CRTLINTRN (Create Line Description).
- CRTCTLAPPC (Create Controller Description)—optional.
- CRTDEVAPPC (Create Device Description)—optional.

Create Line Description (Token-Ring) (CRTLINTRN)

One thing about using these commands is they unfold in response to the entries—they do not just appear all at once as have others in this book. Each one is tailored according to the values specified for the parameters, so the parameters are customized to the line, controller, or device being created. The resource name in Figure 19-3 must be the adapter name.

```
                   Create Line Desc (Token-Ring) (CRTLINTRN)

 Type choices, press Enter.

 Line description . . . . . . . . > TOKENRING1    Name
 Resource name  . . . . . . . . . > IPCSNOTE00    Name, *NWID, *NWSD
 NWI type . . . . . . . . . . . .   *FR           *FR, *ATM
 Online at IPL  . . . . . . . . .   *YES          *YES, *NO
 Vary on wait . . . . . . . . . .   *NOWAIT       *NOWAIT, 15-180 seconds
 Maximum controllers  . . . . . .   40            1-256
 Line speed . . . . . . . . . . . > 16M           4M, 16M, *NWI
 Duplex . . . . . . . . . . . . .   *HALF         Character value, *HALF, *FULL
 Maximum frame size . . . . . . . > 16373         265-16393, 265, 521, 1033...
 Local adapter address  . . . . . > 40000A010111  400000000000-7FFFFFFFFFFF...
 Exchange identifier  . . . . . .   *SYSGEN       05600000-056FFFFF, *SYSGEN
 SSAP list:                         _
   Source service access point  .   *SYSGEN       02-FE, *SYSGEN
   SSAP maximum frame . . . . . .   ________      *MAXFRAME, 265-16393
   SSAP type  . . . . . . . . . .   ________      *CALC, *NONSNA, *SNA, *HPR
              + for more values     _
                                                                        More...
 F3=Exit   F4=Prompt   F5=Refresh   F12=Cancel   F13=How to use this display
 F24=More keys
```

```
                Create Line Desc (Token-Ring) (CRTLINTRN)

Type choices, press Enter.

Text 'description' . . . . . . . > 'TOKEN RING 1 LINE DESCRIPTION'


                     Additional Parameters

Network controller . . . . . . .  __________     Name
Activate LAN manager . . . . . .  *YES           *YES, *NO
TRLAN manager logging level  . .  *OFF           *OFF, *MIN, *MED, *MAX
TRLAN manager mode . . . . . . .  *OBSERVING     *OBSERVING, *CONTROLLING
Log configuration changes  . . .  *LOG           *LOG, *NOLOG
Token-ring inform of beacon  . .  *YES           *YES, *NO
Functional address . . . . . . .  *NONE          *NONE, C00000000001...
               + for more values  _
Early token release  . . . . . .  *LINESPEED     *YES, *NO, *LINESPEED
Error threshold level  . . . . .  *OFF           *OFF, *MIN, *MED, *MAX
Link speed . . . . . . . . . . . > 16M
                                                                 More...
F3=Exit   F4=Prompt   F5=Refresh   F12=Cancel   F13=How to use this display
F24=More keys
```

```
                Create Line Desc (Token-Ring) (CRTLINTRN)

Type choices, press Enter.

Cost/connect time  . . . . . . .  0              0-255
Cost/byte  . . . . . . . . . . .  0              0-255
Security for line  . . . . . . .  *NONSECURE     *NONSECURE, *PKTSWTNET...
Propagation delay  . . . . . . .  *LAN           *MIN, *LAN, *TELEPHONE...
User-defined 1 . . . . . . . . .  128            0-255
User-defined 2 . . . . . . . . .  128            0-255
User-defined 3 . . . . . . . . .  128            0-255
Autocreate controller  . . . . . > *YES          *YES, *NO
Autodelete controller  . . . . .  1440           1-10000 (minutes), *NONE
Recovery limits:
  Count limit  . . . . . . . . .  2              0-99, *SYSVAL
  Time interval  . . . . . . . .  5              0-120 minutes
Authority  . . . . . . . . . . .  *LIBCRTAUT     Name, *LIBCRTAUT, *CHANGE...



                                                                  Bottom
F3=Exit   F4=Prompt   F5=Refresh   F12=Cancel   F13=How to use this display
F24=More keys
```

Figure 19-3: Create Line Description for Token-Ring network (parts 1, 2, and 3).

There is a parameter on this command that refers to the word *duplex*. Duplex refers to how communication messages can flow over the lines. Consider a network of just two stations. If the network is full-duplex, each can send or receive at the same time, regardless of the other. If the stations are half-duplex, one station can only send when the other is ready to receive. Communication only flows in one direction.

The Duplex parameter refers to the hardware making the Token-Ring connection. The traditional 8228 MAU makes a half-duplex Token-Ring while an 8272 controller makes a full-duplex Token-Ring.

The Autodelete Controller parameter allows the system to automatically delete any automatically created controller after it has been idle for so many minutes. The default, 1,440 minutes is twenty-four hours. This is a nice feature and should be used any time controllers are automatically created.

Create Controller Description for APPC (CRTCTLAPPC) (Optional)

If the Autocreate Controller parameter is specified on the line description as *YES, this section can be skipped (but read it anyway). When attempting to establish a communication session, the line will create the controller. By also specifying AUTOCREATE DEVICE(*YES), the system will also automatically create any needed device descriptions.

Note the relationship of the autocreates. The first object created was the line description, and it had the option of specifying that the controller (the next item to create) could be done so automatically. The controller is the second object to be created, and it has the optional parameter to autocreate a device. But if a user requested that the controller be autocreated, he has no choice over whether the device will also be autocreated—it just will. The rule is this: If the controller is to be autocreated, the device is also autocreated.

If the option to autocreate the controller was not selected when the line was created, the controller has to be created. For an AS/400-to-AS/400 network, use the Create Controller—APPC (CRTCTLAPPC) command. See Figure19-4 for a sample of that command.

```
                     Create Ctl Desc (APPC) (CRTCTLAPPC)

 Type choices, press Enter.

 Controller description . . . . . > TRAS400       Name
 Link type  . . . . . . . . . . . > *LAN          *ANYNW, *FAX, *FR, *IDLC...
 Online at IPL  . . . . . . . . .   *YES          *YES, *NO
 APPN-capable . . . . . . . . . .   *YES          *YES, *NO
 Switched line list . . . . . . . > TOKENRING1    Name
                + for more values
 Maximum frame size . . . . . . .   *LINKTYPE     265-16393, 256, 265, 512...
 Remote network identifier  . . .   *NETATR       Name, *NETATR, *NONE, *ANY
 Remote control point . . . . . . > LANAPPN       Name, *ANY
 Exchange identifier  . . . . . .                 00000000-FFFFFFFF
 Initial connection . . . . . . .   *DIAL         *DIAL, *ANS
 Dial initiation  . . . . . . . .   *LINKTYPE     *LINKTYPE, *IMMED, *DELAY
 LAN remote adapter address . . . > 40000A020222  000000000001-FFFFFFFFFFFF
 LAN DSAP . . . . . . . . . . . .   04            04, 08, 0C, 10, 14, 18, 1C...
 LAN SSAP . . . . . . . . . . . . > 08            04, 08, 0C, 10, 14, 18, 1C...
 APPN CP session support  . . . .   *YES          *YES, *NO
                                                                        More...
 F3=Exit   F4=Prompt   F5=Refresh   F12=Cancel   F13=How to use this display
 F24=More keys
```

```
                    Create Ctl Desc (APPC) (CRTCTLAPPC)

Type choices, press Enter.

APPN node type . . . . . . . . .  *ENDNODE      *ENDNODE, *LENNODE...
APPN/HPR capable . . . . . . . .  *YES          *YES, *NO
HPR path switching . . . . . . .  *NO           *NO, *YES
APPN transmission group number    1             1-20, *CALC
APPN minimum switched status . .  *VRYONPND     *VRYONPND, *VRYON
Autocreate device  . . . . . . .  *ALL          *ALL, *NONE
Autodelete device  . . . . . . .  1440          1-10000, *NO
User-defined 1 . . . . . . . . .  *LIND         0-255, *LIND
User-defined 2 . . . . . . . . .  *LIND         0-255, *LIND
User-defined 3 . . . . . . . . .  *LIND         0-255, *LIND
Model controller description . .  *NO           *NO, *YES

                                                                   Bottom
F3=Exit   F4=Prompt   F5=Refresh   F10=Additional parameters   F12=Cancel
F13=How to use this display        F24=More keys
```

Figure 19-4: Create Controller Description screen for AS/400-to-AS/400 Token-Ring network (parts 1 and 2).

The Remote Control Point, LAN DSAP, and LAN SSAP parameters must agree between the local and remote AS/400s' controllers. Do not make the mistake of making them agree between controller and line—lines agree with lines, controllers with controllers.

Also, by agree, we mean that the DSAP on the local machine must be the same as the SSAP on the connected machine, and the SSAP on one must be the same as the DSAP on the connected. If there is any doubt of the value of any of these, use the Display Network Attribute (DSPNETA) command on the remote machine to check them. The Adapter Address is the address of the adapter on the remote AS/400.

For an AS/400-to-PC network, use the same Create Controller—APPC (CRTCTLAPPC) command. See Figure 19-5 for a sample of that command.

The remote control point is the name assigned to the remote PC. The system operator should have a naming convention for this to make device status checks easy. For example, every device could be named something starting with the letters PC. Then, when running the Work with Configuration Status (WRKCFGSTS) command, he/she could specify the generic name PC* and isolate devices to just personal computers. He could go one step further and follow the PC label with some kind of designation for the department or location. An example would be the phone extension where the device is located.

```
                 Create Ctl Desc (APPC) (CRTCTLAPPC)

Type choices, press Enter.

Controller description . . . . . > TRLAN01       Name
Link type  . . . . . . . . . . . > *LAN          *ANYNW, *FAX, *FR, *IDLC...
Online at IPL  . . . . . . . . .   *YES          *YES, *NO
APPN-capable . . . . . . . . . .   *YES          *YES, *NO
Switched line list . . . . . . . > TOKENRING1    Name
               + for more values   _
Maximum frame size . . . . . . .   *LINKTYPE     265-16393, 256, 265, 512...
Remote network identifier  . . .   *NETATR       Name, *NETATR, *NONE, *ANY
Remote control point . . . . . . > GE01S01       Name, *ANY
Exchange identifier  . . . . . .                 00000000-FFFFFFFF
Initial connection . . . . . . .   *DIAL         *DIAL, *ANS
Dial initiation  . . . . . . . .   *LINKTYPE     *LINKTYPE, *IMMED, *DELAY
LAN remote adapter address . . . > 10004100512B  000000000001-FFFFFFFFFFFF
LAN DSAP . . . . . . . . . . . .   04            04, 08, 0C, 10, 14, 18, 1C...
LAN SSAP . . . . . . . . . . . .   04            04, 08, 0C, 10, 14, 18, 1C...
APPN CP session support  . . . . > *NO           *YES, *NO
                                                                        More...
F3=Exit   F4=Prompt   F5=Refresh   F10=Additional parameters   F12=Cancel
F13=How to use this display        F24=More keys
```

```
                 Create Ctl Desc (APPC) (CRTCTLAPPC)

Type choices, press Enter.

APPN node type . . . . . . . . .   *ENDNODE      *ENDNODE, *LENNODE...
APPN/HPR capable . . . . . . . .   *YES          *YES, *NO
HPR path switching . . . . . . .   *NO           *NO, *YES
APPN transmission group number     1             1-20, *CALC
APPN minimum switched status . .   *VRYONPND     *VRYONPND, *VRYON
Autocreate device  . . . . . . .   *ALL          *ALL, *NONE
Autodelete device  . . . . . . .   1440          1-10000, *NO
User-defined 1 . . . . . . . . .   *LIND         0-255, *LIND
User-defined 2 . . . . . . . . .   *LIND         0-255, *LIND
User-defined 3 . . . . . . . . .   *LIND         0-255, *LIND
Model controller description . .   *NO            *NO, *YES




                                                                         Bottom
F3=Exit   F4=Prompt   F5=Refresh   F10=Additional parameters   F12=Cancel
F13=How to use this display        F24=More keys
```

Figure 19-5: Create Controller Description screen for AS/400-to-PC Token-Ring network (parts 1 and 2).

The Adapter Address parameter is the manufacturer's address of the adapter on the PC.

Create Device Description for APPC (CRTDEVAPPC) (Optional)

If devices are not to be autocreated by the system, use the Create Device Description for APPC (CRTDEVAPPC) command. Figure 19-6 contains a sample of this command.

```
                 Create Device Desc (APPC) (CRTDEVAPPC)

Type choices, press Enter.

Device description . . . . . . . > TR400HOST      Name
Remote location  . . . . . . . . > TST4001        Name
Online at IPL  . . . . . . . . .   *YES           *YES, *NO
Local location . . . . . . . . . > TEST4002       Name, *NETATR
Remote network identifier  . . .   *NETATR        Name, *NETATR, *NONE
Attached controller  . . . . . . > TRAS400        Name
Mode . . . . . . . . . . . . . . > BLANK          Name, *NETATR
               + for more values   _
Message queue  . . . . . . . . .   QSYSOPR        Name, QSYSOPR
  Library  . . . . . . . . . . .     *LIBL        Name, *LIBL, *CURLIB
APPN-capable . . . . . . . . . .   *YES           *YES, *NO
Single session:
  Single session capable . . . .   *NO            *NO, *YES
  Number of conversations  . . .   ____           1-512


                                                                   Bottom
F3=Exit   F4=Prompt   F5=Refresh   F10=Additional parameters   F12=Cancel
F13=How to use this display        F24=More keys
```

Figure 19-6: Create Device Description screen for a Token-Ring network..

If the Autocreate Device parameter was set to *ALL on the controller description (Figure 19-5), the system creates the device description automatically and this step can be omitted.

If Autocreate Controller(*YES) was specified on the line description and the line description creates the controller description, it creates it with Autocreate Device(*ALL) and this step can still be skipped. The parameters we changed on the figure are marked with a > symbol.

Token-Ring LAN CL Commands

To work with the Token-Ring LAN adapters, use the WRKHDWRSC command with *TRN as the second parameter. Figure 19-7 shows how it looks.

```
                 Work with Hardware Resources (WRKHDWRSC)

Type choices, press Enter.

Type . . . . . . . . . . . . . . > *LAN           *CMN, *CSA, *LAN, *LWS...
Line type  . . . . . . . . . . . > *TRN           *ALL, *DDI, *TRN
```

Figure 19-7: WRKHDWRSC command for Token-Ring adapters.

Pressing the Enter key causes the system to display the screen shown in Figure 19-8.

```
                         Work with LAN Adapter Information
                                                           System:   BIGBLUE
 Type options, press Enter.
   1=Add entry   2=Change   4=Remove entry   7=Rename


                                    Line
 Opt  Address       Name           Type  Description
 __   ____________
 __   50000E919111  GE91S01        *TRN  E/400 GATEWAY 91
 __   40000A010111  TOKENRING1     *TRN  SYS01 - TOKEN RING 1
 __   40000A020211  TOKENRING2     *TRN  SYS02 - TOKEN RING 2
 __   50000E909111  GE90S01        *TRN  E/400 GATEWAY 90
 __   50000E171711  GE17S02        *TRN  E/400 GATEWAY 17
 __   50000E131311  GE13S02        *TRN  E/400 GATEWAY 13
 __   50000E111111  GE11S02        *TRN  E/400 GATEWAY 11
 __   50000E010122  GE01S01        *TRN  E/400 GATEWAY 01







                                                                     Bottom
 Command
 ===>__________________________________________________________________________
 F3=Exit   F4=Prompt    F5=Refresh   F6=Print   F9=Retrieve
 F11=Display full text   F12=Cancel   F17=Position to
```

Figure 19-8: Formatted version of the WRKHDWRSC command used for Token-Ring adapters.

This screen displays information about an adapter. The user can then remove, add, or change an adapter. This is a somewhat limited command for working with adapters although it is great for the user that has not memorized all the adapters.

If the specific adapter is known, a more potent alternative is the Work with LAN Adapters (WRKLANADPT) command. Figure 19-9 shows the prompted version of the WRKLANADPT command.

```
                      Work With LAN Adapters (WRKLANADPT)

 Type choices, press Enter.

 Line description . . . . . . . . > TOKENRING1    Name
 Output . . . . . . . . . . . . .   *_________    *, *PRINT
```

Figure 19-9: WRKLANADPT command setup.

By pressing the Enter key from the screen shown in Figure 19-9, the operator obtains detailed information about line TOKENRING1. From the screen shown in Figure 19-10, the operator can do several things. Putting a 5 on the option line to the left of adapter TOKENRING1 will produce a description of the LAN adapter profile as shown in Figure 19-11.

```
                         Work with LAN Adapters
                                                         System:   BIGBLUE
  Line description . . . . . . . . :   TOKENRING1
  Line type  . . . . . . . . . . . :   *TRN

Type options, press Enter.
  1=Add entry   2=Change   4=Remove entry   5=Display profile   6=Print
  7=Rename

Opt  Address       Name                 Status  Description
___  ____________
_5   40000A010111  TOKENRING1           Active  SYS01 - Token Ring 1
__   0002BA0200A6  D2BA0200A6           Active
__   40000A020211  TOKENRING2           Active  SYS02 - Token Ring 2
__   50000E131311  GE13S02              Active  E/400 - Gateway 13
__   50000E010122  GE01S01              Active  E/400 - Gateway 01
__   0000F61B9EE0  D0F61B9EE0           Active
__   50000E919111  GE91S01              Active  E/400 - Gateway 91

                                                                     Bottom
Command
===>____________________________________________________________________
F3=Exit   F4=Prompt    F5=Refresh   F6=Print   F9=Retrieve
F11=Display full text  F12=Cancel   F17=Position to
```

Figure 19-10: WRKLANADPP command for adapter TOKENRING1.

```
                         Display Adaptor Profile
                                                    System:    BIGBLUE
  Product ID . . . . . . . . . . . . . . :   0000000000000000000000000000000000
  Licensed internal code . . . . . . . . :   F0F0F0F8F4F4F0F4F940
  Group address  . . . . . . . . . . . . :   C00080000000
  Adaptor address. . . . . . . . . . . . :   40000A010111
  Adaptor name . . . . . . . . . . . . . :   TOKENRING1
  Adaptor Description. . . . . . . . . . :


                                                         Functional
  Function                                               Address
  Ring Error Monitor                                     C00000000008
  Configuration Report Server                            C00000000010
```

Figure 19-11: LAN adapter profile for TOKENRING1.

This displays the LAN adapter information as well as the next LAN adapter from it on the network (in the NAUN ADDRESS parameter). This can help troubleshoot a Token-Ring problem by identifying the next adapter to check.

Note something here: the line and the adapter are both named TOKENRING1. This is common practice, and it helps the operator quickly locate all the pieces of a communication point.

The F10 key from Figure 19-11 produces the status of the adapter. A sample is shown in Figure 19-12.

```
                              Display LAN Status
                                                          System:    BIGBLUE
    Line description . . . . . . . . . . . :     TOKENRING1
    Ring status. . . . . . . . . . . . . . :     Normal
```

Figure 19-12: Status of adapter TOKENRING1.

We see that the adapter's status is NORMAL.

ETHERNET

An Ethernet LAN supports one of two standards: Ethernet Version 2 and the IEEE 802.3 standard. It is better to use the IEEE 802.3 standard on the AS/400 because it is acknowledged; Version 2 is unacknowledged. Unacknowledged service is faster, but error checking is minimal. Using Ethernet with reduced error checking is risky.

Ethernet uses the *Carrier Sense Multiple Access with Collision Detection (CSMA/CD) protocol*. Basically, when a station has something to transmit, it checks to see if the line is busy. If the line is not busy, the station transmits and monitors the line while transmitting, in case another station also transmits. If another station does transmit, that causes a collision, and both stations first will stop transmitting, then wait some random amount of time, then try again.

Standard Ethernet uses a *bus topology*. That is, cable is laid and individual nodes are *dropped* along its path. That method worked for small networks but ultimately led to problems in large networks. A solution was to connect Ethernet nodes to a central switch in a star topology. IBM's switch is the 8271 Ethernet switch. Generically, this device is referred to as a *switching hub*. Similar to the introduction of star topology in Token-Ring networks, this results in a nontraditional network but one that is faster and more reliable.

Today, large Ethernet LANs reduce their errors (and increase throughput) by isolating network segments. Straight buses are isolated by the use of *repeating hubs*, while star topologies are isolated by the use of several switching hubs.

Ethernet networks can be tricky because they really do not have much traffic management capability. Therefore, a lot of transmissions on the line cause many collisions (and then retries) to occur, and performance can rapidly decay. Part of setting up and maintaining an efficient Ethernet network is knowing exactly what transmission level is acceptable and what the level will be on any given line. *Note*: Transmission activity level is independent of the number of workstations on the line.

Traditional Ethernet transmits data at 10 MBps, *fast Ethernet* transmits data at 100 MBps. An Ethernet network uses a coaxial cable. AS/400s connect to Ethernet networks through an Ethernet controller card on the AS/400, a *transceiver* that is attached to or built into the network coaxial cable, and a cable to connect the controller card and transceiver. The controller must come from IBM, but the plug, cable, transceiver, and coaxial cable can come from any vendor.

Ethernet Adapter Addressing

The Ethernet adapter address is a 6-byte or 48-bit address. Read the bytes in the same order they are transmitted—from bit0/byte0 to bit7/byte5. Figure 19-13 is a sample address. Note that two bits are reserved.

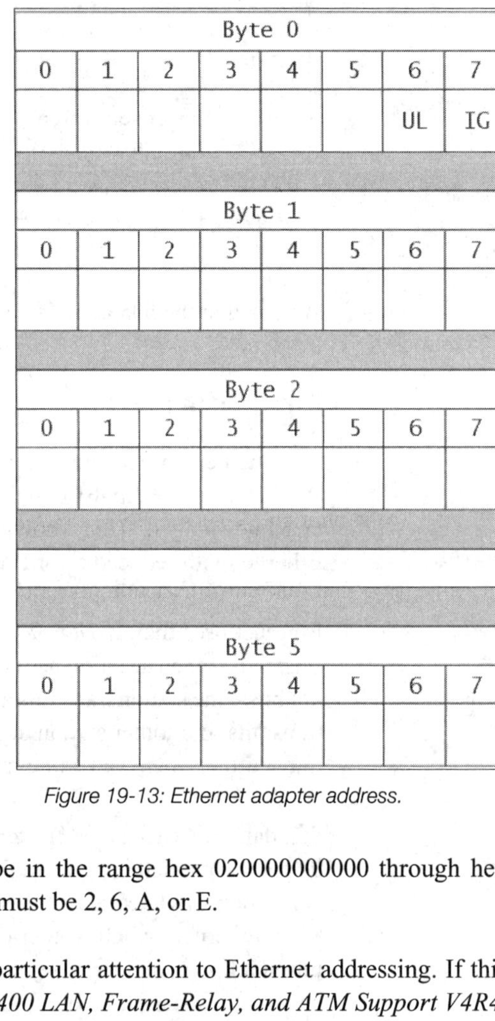

Figure 19-13: Ethernet adapter address.

- UL—Universal/local:
  - The 0 means the address is universally administered.
  - The 1 means the address is locally administered.
- IG—Individual/group:
  - The 0 means the address is an individual address or one associated with a particular station on the network.
  - The 1 means the address is a group address or that it is destined for more than one destination.

The range of valid adapter addresses are hex 000000000000 through hex FFFFFFFFFFFF. However, the implications of the two reserved bits on possible valid addresses are:

- If bit7/byte0 = 0, then byte 0 must be an even number.
- If bit6/byte0 = 1, then byte 0 must be in the range hex 020000000000 through hex FEFFFFFFFFFF and the second digit must be 2, 6, A, or E.

Heterogeneous LANs using bridges must pay particular attention to Ethernet addressing. If this description fits your shop, see IBM manual *AS/400 LAN, Frame-Relay, and ATM Support V4R4*, section 2.1.2.

Ethernet Configuration

Ethernet line descriptions default to a maximum frame size of somewhere around 1,500 (computed by the AS/400). The range is narrow—from 1,493 to 1,500—that is the maximum frame size. The minimum, including addressing bytes and one byte of data, is twenty. Optionally, the system operator can specify a maximum frame size in two places:

- On the line description, at the SSAP parameter.
- On the controller description.

When Ethernet connects, the frame size will be the smallest of these values:

- Default line description maximum frame size (around 1,500—which cannot be specified on the line description).
- SSAP MAXFRAME parameter value.
- Controller MAXFRAME parameter value.

If an Ethernet network passes its frames across a bridge, the maximum frame size of the bridge must be taken into consideration in the frame-size calculation. If the specified frame size is larger than the frame size of the bridge, that frame will be discarded when the network tries to send it through the bridge. Unfortunately, the network does not automatically incorporate the bridge frame size in its calculations. The system operator must do the calculation. Make certain all specified frame sizes are no larger than any of the frame sizes of the network's bridges.

After determining the preceding items, do the following commands in sequence:

- CRTLINTRN (Create Line Description).
- CRTCTLAPPC (Create Controller Description)—optional.
- CRTDEVAPPC (Create Device Description)—optional.

Create Line Description (Ethernet) (CRTLINETH)

Create a line description for an Ethernet LAN with the Create Line Description—Ethernet (CRTLINETH) command. Figure 19-14 shows a prompted version of that command.

```
                    Create Line Desc (Ethernet) (CRTLINETH)

 Type choices, press Enter.

 Line description . . . . . . . . > ETHLINE1      Name
 Resource name  . . . . . . . . . > LIN121        Name, *NWID, *NWSD
 Online at IPL  . . . . . . . . .   *YES          *YES, *NO
 Vary on wait . . . . . . . . . .   *NOWAIT       *NOWAIT, 15-180 seconds
 Local adapter address  . . . . . > 020055010111  020000000000-7EFFFFFFFFFF...
 Exchange identifier  . . . . . .   *SYSGEN       05600000-056FFFFF, *SYSGEN
 Ethernet standard  . . . . . . .   *ALL          *ETHV2, *IEEE8023, *ALL
 Line speed . . . . . . . . . . .   10M           Character value, 10M, 100M...
 Duplex . . . . . . . . . . . . .   *HALF         Character value, *HALF...
 SSAP list:
   Source service access point  . > 04            02-FE, *SYSGEN
   SSAP maximum frame . . . . . . > *MAXFRAME     *MAXFRAME, 265-1496, 265...
   SSAP type  . . . . . . . . . . > *CALC         *CALC, *NONSNA, *SNA, *HPR
              + for more values
 Text 'description' . . . . . . . > 'Ethernet Line 1 Description'

                                                                     More...
 F3=Exit   F4=Prompt   F5=Refresh   F12=Cancel   F13=How to use this display
 F24=More keys
```

Figure 19-14: Create Line Description screen for AS/400 Ethernet network.

Note the local adapter address because any remote nodes will have to use this address to communicate to this node. In this case, we made up an address, but we could have used the adapter's preset address.

The Ethernet Standard (ETHSTD) parameter determines what type of Ethernet is to be supported and, by implication, what the maximum frame size will be. The ETHSTD parameter cannot be changed after the line description has been created. Possible values for ETHSTD and their possible maximum frame sizes are:

- *ALL (the default). Either Ethernet version will be supported; maximum frame size will match the version.
- *IEEE8023. Ethernet version IEEE 802.3; maximum frame size—1,496.
- *ETHV2. Ethernet version 2; maximum frame size:
  - SNA support—1,493.
  - Non-SNA support—1,500.

There is a Line Speed parameter on the Create Line Description (Ethernet) screen, which determines whether the line will use Ethernet at 10MBps or 100MBps. The Duplex parameter determines whether the data on the Ethernet line will be sent half-duplex or full duplex. Half-duplex means that only one line is used, and the network can either send or receive at any time. Full duplex requires two lines and a controller and means that the network can send and receive simultaneously.

If Autocreate Controller (*YES) is specified on the last screen, any controllers the system needs but doesn't have are created automatically when a communication event starts. If this parameter contains *YES and the device that should be attached to the controller also does not exist, that, too, will be created automatically.

Create Controller Description for APPC (CRTCTLAPPC) (Optional)

This step is optional. It is only necessary if the controller does not exist and Autocreate Controller on the Create Line Description command was set to *NO.

Figure 19-15 shows a prompted version of the Create Controller Description APPC (CRTCTLAPPC) command.

```
                        Create Ctl Desc (APPC) (CRTCTLAPPC)

Type choices, press Enter.

Controller description . . . . . > APPCETH1      Name
Link type  . . . . . . . . . . . > *LAN          *ANYNW, *FAX, *FR, *IDLC...
Online at IPL  . . . . . . . . .   *YES          *YES, *NO
APPN-capable . . . . . . . . . . > *NO           *YES, *NO
Controller type  . . . . . . . .   *BLANK        *BLANK, *FBSS, 3174, 3274...
Switched line list . . . . . . . > ETHLINE1      Name
               + for more values   _
Maximum frame size . . . . . . .   *LINKTYPE     265-16393, 256, 265, 512...
Remote network identifier  . . .   *NETATR       Name, *NETATR, *NONE, *ANY
Remote control point . . . . . .   ________      Name, *ANY
Exchange identifier  . . . . . .   ________      00000000-FFFFFFFF
Initial connection . . . . . . .   *DIAL         *DIAL, *ANS
Dial initiation  . . . . . . . .   *LINKTYPE     *LINKTYPE, *IMMED, *DELAY
LAN remote adapter address . . . > 020055010222  000000000001-FFFFFFFFFFFF
LAN DSAP . . . . . . . . . . . .   04            04, 08, 0C, 10, 14, 18, 1C...
LAN SSAP . . . . . . . . . . . . > 08            04, 08, 0C, 10, 14, 18, 1C...
                                                                       More...
F3=Exit   F4=Prompt   F5=Refresh   F10=Additional parameters   F12=Cancel
F13=How to use this display        F24=More keys
```

```
                    Create Ctl Desc (APPC) (CRTCTLAPPC)

 Type choices, press Enter.

 HPR path switching . . . . . . .   *NO             *NO, *YES
 Autocreate device  . . . . . . .   *ALL            *ALL, *NONE
 Text 'description' . . . . . . . > 'Ethernet controller APPCETH1-line ETHLINE1'









                                                                         Bottom
 F3=Exit   F4=Prompt   F5=Refresh   F10=Additional parameters   F12=Cancel
 F13=How to use this display        F24=More keys
```

Figure 19-15: Create Controller Description screen for AS/400 Ethernet network (parts 1 and 2).

Note that the switched-line list is the name of the line created in Figure 19-14. The line must exist before it is named on the CRTCTLAPPC command. More than one line can be listed here (just put a plus sign [+] on the `+ For More Values` parameter), but they all must exist before they can be listed.

The LAN Remote Adapter Address must be the address of the remote adapter (not the local).

The Autocreate Device (*ALL) parameter and value on the second screen tells the AS/400 to go ahead and automatically create a device description when one does not exist when a communications event starts.

Create Device Description for APPC (CRTDEVAPPC) (Optional)

This step is optional. It is only necessary when the device does not exist and the Autocreate Device and Autocreate Controller parameters were specified as *NO on previous commands. Figure 19-16 shows a prompted version of the Create Device Description APPC (CRTDEVAPPC) command.

```
                  Create Device Desc (APPC) (CRTDEVAPPC)

 Type choices, press Enter.

 Device description . . . . . . . > APPCETH1      Name
 Remote location  . . . . . . . . > APPCETH2      Name
 Online at IPL  . . . . . . . . .   *YES          *YES, *NO
 Local location . . . . . . . . .   *NETATR       Name, *NETATR
 Remote network identifier  . . .   *NETATR       Name, *NETATR, *NONE
 Attached controller  . . . . . . > APPCETH1      Name
 Mode . . . . . . . . . . . . . .   *NETATR       Name, *NETATR
                + for more values   _______
 Message queue  . . . . . . . . .   QSYSOPR       Name, QSYSOPR
   Library  . . . . . . . . . . .     *LIBL       Name, *LIBL, *CURLIB
 APPN-capable . . . . . . . . . . > *NO           *YES, *NO
 Single session:
   Single session capable . . . .   *NO            *NO, *YES
   Number of conversations  . . .   ____          1-512



                                                                         Bottom
 F3=Exit   F4=Prompt   F5=Refresh   F10=Additional parameters   F12=Cancel
 F13=How to use this display        F24=More keys
```

Figure 19-16: Create Device Description screen for Ethernet connection.

The Attached Controller parameter must be an Ethernet controller that already exists. If you are following this sequence, it is the name of the controller created in the previous section.

WIRELESS

Wireless communication with the AS/400 supports mobile and stationary communication devices that connect to the AS/400 via radio frequency (RF) rather than cabling.

Wireless is found mostly in the retail and warehousing industries where users routinely work with handheld computing devices called *Portable Transaction Computers (PTCs)*. Wireless communications with the AS/400 can support PTCs, bar code readers, and stationary desktop computers.

Wireless communications' networks are defined as being single- or multiple-cell networks. A *cell* is the sphere of sensitivity surrounding an antenna. A single-cell network has one antenna mounted on one *access point*. Wireless devices (each with its own antenna) access the AS/400 through that access point.

A multiple-cell network has several access points. The access points are generally connected to each other, so they can share communication responsibilities as mobile PTCs move from one sphere to another. Access points can, themselves, connect to the AS/400 through RF. Multiple-cell networks allow users more consistent coverage while mobile. Hardware requirements to wireless LANs on the AS/400 are:

- An IBM 2668 Wireless LAN adapter on the AS/400. This adapter card has a coaxial connector for an antenna and an RS-485 port to connect cabled access points. Both can be used simultaneously.
- A 266A Virtual Workstation Controller built into the 2480 adapter. Remember this because as the wireless network is configured, the line configures to the 2480 adapter, and the controller configures to the 266A Virtual Workstation Controller. Trust us: Remember these two pieces of hardware.
- Each access point is an IBM 2480 Model RS Access Point. It communicates to PTCs through an antenna, of course, but it can communicate to the AS/400 either through RF or through an RS-485 cable.

Wireless is not a communications protocol; it is merely another way of connecting a LAN. Think of it as a cableless Ethernet.

Wireless LAN speeds are either 1 MBps or 2 MBps. Either is OK, but the same speed must be set consistently across all network devices.

Wireless Adapter Addressing

Wireless adapter addressing is identical to Ethernet addressing. For more information, refer to the Ethernet Adapter Addressing section.

However, wireless addressing has some additional complexity. The 2668 Wireless LAN Adapter has two 6-byte hexadecimal addresses in it. Also, the 266A Virtual Workstation Controller incorporated on the adapter carries two addresses. These addresses and where they are located are:

- Adapter Address—located on the 2668 Wireless LAN Adapter. This is specified on the ADPTADR parameter on the Create Line Description (Wireless) (CRTLINWLS) command.
- Hop ID—located on the 2668 Wireless LAN Adapter. This is the access point address. It's specified on the HOPID parameter on the Add Extended Wireless Line Member (ADDEWLM) command.
- Destination ID—located on the 266A Virtual Workstation Controller. This is the local destination ID (transport address) that the PTC will connect to at emulation startup time. This is the TXPADR parameter on the Add Extended Wireless Line Member (ADDEWCM) command.
- Transport Port—located on the 266A Virtual Workstation Controller. This is the local destination ID (transport address) that the PTC will connect to at emulation startup time. This is the TXPPORT parameter on the Add Extended Wireless Line Member (ADDEWCM) command.

Valid address ranges for the four addresses are:

- Adapter address—020000000000 through FEFFFFFFFFFF, where the second character from the left must be 2, 6, A, or E.
- Hop ID—020000000000 through FEFFFFFFFFFF, where the second character from the left must be 2, 6, A, or E.
- Destination ID—4001 through 4FFE. This value must match the destination ID specified for the PTC or barcode device.
- Transport port—0 through 15.

Wireless Configuration

When configuring wireless devices, the configuring commands are similar to other configuring commands. In fact, the line/controller/device are the same as Ethernet, so in addition to the material presented here, be familiar with the material presented in the Ethernet Configuration section.

Wireless devices require more information to configure and this is entered through *extended commands*.

That is not enough; the extended information is stored as source in a file member and retrieved and downloaded when a remote device or the line is varied on. (*Varying on a line and device* is how communications are established on the AS/400.) To configure a wireless network, follow these steps in this order:

- CRTLINWLS (Create Line Description—Wireless).
- ADDEWLM (Add Extended Wireless Line Member).
- CRTCTLLWS (Create Controller Description—Local Workstation).
- ADDEWCM (Add Extended Wireless Controller Member).
- ADDEWCPTCE (Add Extended Wireless Controller PTC Entry)—for PTC devices, but not for bar-coding devices.
- ADDEWCBCDE (Add Extended Wireless Controller Barcode Entry)—for bar-coding devices only.

That seems like a lot more than the line, controller, and device we are used to configuring, but it really is not. Remember, we need more data to configure wireless networks, so first we create a line description (CRTLINWLS), then we add wireless-specific information to it (ADDEWLM), and store that information as source in a file member.

The controller is next, so we create the controller (CRTCTLLWS), then add wireless-specific data to its member (ADDEWCM), and store that information as source in a file. Then we need to add a little more information about the devices that the controller will have to support, so we add that data with either the ADDEWCPTCE or ADDEWCBCDE commands.

Both the line and controller descriptions require a resource name (parameter RSRCNAME). There are two resource names on the system to use and many customers mix these up. Use the Work with Hardware Resources (WRKHDWRSC) command to determine the correct resource names, but use the command like this:

- Line description resource name—WRKHDWRSC *CMN—the resource name will be in the form LINxxx, where xxx are three numeric digits. The resource name to use will be the one associated with the 2668 Wireless Connection.
- Controller description resource name—WRKHDWRSC *LWS—the resource name will be in the form CTLxx where xx are two numeric digits. The resource name to use will be the one associated with the 266A Virtual Controller.

When configuring a wireless network, all the configuration data, normal and enhanced, is stored in two files:

- QGPL/QEWLSRC—contains line configuration data.
- QGPL/QEWCSRC—contains controller configuration data.

The person configuring the network can put each network segment's configuration data in unique file members in these files. All configuration data gets into these files—the normal and the enhanced data. When the line is varied on, the data from QEWLSRC is sent to the line and the data from QEWCSRC to the controller.

We have been ignoring Creating Device Description. After doing the line, controller, and all enhanced configuring, the system has more than enough to automatically configure the devices. This configuration happens when the communications is established.

For anyone who really wants to, the devices can be created manually with the Create Device Description (CRTDEVD) command. These devices are created with the TYPE 3476 and a DEVICE CLASS as *LCL.

Create Line Description (Wireless) (CRTLINWLS)

Here is an example of configuring a wireless network. First, create the line description (CRTLINWLS); Figure 19-17 has a sample of that command.

```
                    Create Line Desc (Wireless) (CRTLINWLS)

 Type choices, press Enter.

 Line description . . . . . . . . > WLSLIN       Name
 Resource name  . . . . . . . . . > LIN011       Name
 Online at IPL  . . . . . . . . .   *YES         *YES, *NO
 Vary on wait . . . . . . . . . .   *NOWAIT      *NOWAIT, 15-180 seconds
 Local adapter address  . . . . .   *ADPT        020000000000-FEFFFFFFFFFF...
 Exchange identifier  . . . . . .   *SYSGEN      05600000-056FFFFF, *SYSGEN
 Ethernet standard  . . . . . . .   *ALL         *ETHV2, *IEEE8023, *ALL
 SSAP list:
   Source service access point  .   *SYSGEN      02-FE, *SYSGEN
   SSAP maximum frame . . . . . . Create Line Desc (Wireless) (CRTLINWLS)

 Type choices, press Enter.

 Line description . . . . . . . . > WLSLIN       Name
 Resource name  . . . . . . . . . > LIN011       Name
 Online at IPL  . . . . . . . . .   *YES         *YES, *NO
 Vary on wait . . . . . . . . . .   *NOWAIT      *NOWAIT, 15-180 seconds
 Local adapter address  . . . . .   *ADPT        020000000000-FEFFFFFFFFFF...
 Exchange identifier  . . . . . .   *SYSGEN      05600000-056FFFFF, *SYSGEN
 Ethernet standard  . . . . . . .   *ALL         *ETHV2, *IEEE8023, *ALL
 SSAP list:                         _
   Source service access point  .   *SYSGEN      02-FE, *SYSGEN
   SSAP maximum frame . . . . . .   __________   *MAXFRAME, 265-1496, 265...
   SSAP type  . . . . . . . . . .   _______      *CALC, *NONSNA, *SNA
                 + for more values _
 Initialization source file . . . > QEWLSRC      Name, *NONE
   Library  . . . . . . . . . . . >   QGPL       Name, *LIBL, *CURLIB
 Initialization source member . . > WLS001       Name, *NONE

                                                                      More...
 F3=Exit   F4=Prompt   F5=Refresh   F10=Additional parameters   F12=Cancel
 F13=How to use this display        F24=More keys
```

```
                    Create Line Desc (Wireless) (CRTLINWLS)


 Type choices, press Enter.


 Initialization program . . . . > QZXCINZ      Name, *NONE
   Library  . . . . . . . . . .     *LIBL      Name, *LIBL, *CURLIB
 Text 'description' . . . . . . > 'Create Line Description for wireless network
```

Figure 19-17: Prompted version of the Create Line Description (Wireless) (CRTLINWLS) command (parts 1 and 2).

The screen shown in Figure 19-17 is defining a line named WLSLIN, which is attached to resource name LIN011. The resource name was obtained by using the WRKHDWRSC *CMN and seeing what resource was attached to the 2668 wireless adapter. At the bottom of the screen, note the initialization source file specified as QGPL/QEWLSRC. This configuration is to be stored in member WLS001 of that file.

The second screen of the command shows the initialization program QZXCINZ named. This program is invoked when the user presses the Enter key. It, in turn, invokes the related command, ADDEWLM. A sample is shown in Figure 19-18.

```
                    Add Wireless Line Member (ADDEWLM)

 Type choices, press Enter.

 Initialization source member . . > WSL001        Name

                              Additional Parameters

 Initialization source file . . . > QEWLSRC       Name, QEWLSRC
   Library . . . . . . . . . . . >   QGPL         Name, *LIBL, *CURLIB
 Adapter configuration . . . . .    *ALL          *ALL, *RADIO, *WIRED
 Hop identifier . . . . . . . . .   *ADPT         020000000000-FEFFFFFFFFFF...
 Root cell . . . . . . . . . . .    *YES          *YES, *NO
 Frequency . . . . . . . . . . .    1             1, 2, 3, 4, 5
 Data rate . . . . . . . . . . .    2M            2M, 1M
 Radio system identifier . . . .    000002        000002-FFFFFE
 Text 'description' . . . . . . . > 'Automatically called ADDEWLM'

                                                                        Bottom
 F3=Exit   F4=Prompt   F5=Refresh   F12=Cancel   F13=How to use this display
 F24=More keys
```

Figure 19-18: Command ADDEWLM automatically called by the program named on the command in Figure 19-17.

This command came up with the initialize source member, file, and library already filled in. The rest of the parameters were all right, too. In this simple example, the AS/400 only had one adapter, so the Hop Identifier did not need to be changed. As a result, the default *ADPT was sufficient. Pressing the Enter key from the screen in Figure 19-18 creates the line description. Actually, it copies the line configuration data into file QGPL/QEWLSRC, member WLS001.

Create Controller Description (Wireless) (CRTCTLLWS)

After the line, configure the controller. Figure 19-19 contains a sample of the Create Controller Description (Local Wireless) (CRTCTLLWS) command.

```
                     Create Ctl Desc (Local WS) (CRTCTLLWS)

 Type choices, press Enter.

 Controller description . . . . . > WLSCTL        Name
 Controller type . . . . . . . . . > 266A          2637, 2638, 2661, 6040...
 Controller model . . . . . . . . > 1             1, 0001, 2, 0002
 Resource name . . . . . . . . . . > CTL11         Name
 Online at IPL . . . . . . . . .    *YES          *YES, *NO
 Initialization source file . . . > QEWCSRC       Name, *NONE
   Library . . . . . . . . . . . >   QGPL         Name, *LIBL, *CURLIB
 Initialization source member . . > WLS001        Name, *NONE
 Initialization program . . . . . > QZXCINZ       Name, *NONE
   Library . . . . . . . . . . .      *LIBL        Name, *LIBL, *CURLIB
 Text 'description' . . . . . . . > 'Create controller for wireless network'

                                                                        Bottom
 F3=Exit   F4=Prompt   F5=Refresh   F10=Additional parameters   F12=Cancel
 F13=How to use this display        F24=More keys
```

Figure 19-19: Prompted version of the Create Controller Description (CRTCTLLWS) command.

This screen creates a wireless controller named WLSCTL, type 266A. Resource name CTL11 was obtained through the WRKHDWRSC *LWS and seeing which resource was attached to the 266A Virtual Workstation Controller.

The initialization source file, library, and member are specified as QGPL/QEWCSRC, member WLS001. Note that the member can be named the same as the member in the line description because they are members of different physical files.

Finally, initialization program QZXCINZ is named, and it calls the related command, Add Extended Wireless Controller Member (ADDEWCM). Refer to Figure 19-20 for a sample of that command.

```
                    Add Wireless Ctl Member (ADDEWCM)

Type choices, press Enter.

Initialization source member . . > WLS001        Name

                         Additional Parameters

Initialization source file . . . > QEWCSRC       Name, QEWCSRC
  Library . . . . . . . . . . . >   QGPL         Name, *LIBL, *CURLIB
Destination ID . . . . . . . . .   4001          4001-4FFE
Transport port . . . . . . . . .   0             0-15
Text 'description' . . . . . . . > 'Automatically called command ADDEWCM'
Keyboard remap source member . .   *NONE         Name, *NONE
Screen reformat rules member . .   *NONE         Name, *NONE
Keyboard remapping source file     QEWCKBDMAP    Name, QEWCKBDMAP
  Library . . . . . . . . . . .     QGPL         Name, QGPL
Screen reformatting rules file     QEWCSCNFMT    Name, QEWCSCNFMT
  Library . . . . . . . . . . .     QGPL         Name, QGPL
                                                                     Bottom
F3=Exit   F4=Prompt   F5=Refresh   F12=Cancel   F13=How to use this display
F24=More keys
```

Figure 19-20: Prompted version of the ADDEWCM command.

In this case, like the previous, we just accepted the defaults. Complete the controller configuration with either the Add Extended Wireless Controller PTC Entry (ADDEWCPTCE) or the Add Extended Wireless Controller Barcode Entry (ADDEWCBCDE). Neither of these commands will start automatically; the configurator must start them on the command line.

Figure 19-21 has a prompted version of the Add Extended Wireless Controller PTC Entry (ADDEWCPTCE) command.

```
                    Add EWC PTC Entry (ADDEWCPTCE)

Type choices, press Enter.

PTC group . . . . . . . . . . . . > PTC001
Initialization source member . . > WLS001        Name

                        Additional Parameters

Initialization source file . . .   QEWCSRC      Name, QEWCSRC
  Library . . . . . . . . . . .      *LIBL      Name, *LIBL
PTC ID range:
  Begin ID . . . . . . . . . . .   0001         0001-1022
  End ID . . . . . . . . . . . .   1022         0001-1022
Intensity . . . . . . . . . . .    *NORMAL       *NORMAL, *INVERSE
Status line . . . . . . . . . .    *YES         *YES, *NO
Cursor type . . . . . . . . . .    *UNDERLINE   *UNDERLINE, *BLOCK
Inactivity timer . . . . . . . .   *DEV         0-9999, *DEV
Backlight timer . . . . . . . .    *DEV         0-9999, *DEV
Backlight key . . . . . . . . .    *ON          *ON, *OFF
                                                              More...
F3=Exit   F4=Prompt   F5=Refresh   F12=Cancel   F13=How to use this display
F24=More keys
```

```
                    Add EWC PTC Entry (ADDEWCPTCE)

Type choices, press Enter.

Bypass exit . . . . . . . . . .    *YES         *YES, *NO
Automatic run . . . . . . . . .    *YES         *YES, *NO
Printer . . . . . . . . . . . .    *SYSTEM      *SYSTEM, *PTC
Wand type . . . . . . . . . . .    *NONE        *NONE, *PENCIL, *LASER...
Wand pecking rate . . . . . . .    *DEV         *DEV, 2, 4, 8, 16, 32, 48
Laser read timer . . . . . . . .   *DEV         *DEV, 1440, 2880, 4320, 5760
Barcode function keys . . . . .    *OFF         *OFF, *ON
Auto Enter . . . . . . . . . . .   *OFF         *OFF, *ON
Cursor location . . . . . . . .    *HOLD        *HOLD, *FIRST
Short scan . . . . . . . . . . .   *YES         *YES, *NO
Scan end of file . . . . . . . .   *YES         *YES, *NO
Fast poll interval . . . . . . . > 125          0-9999, *DEV
Fast poll delay . . . . . . . . > 0            0-9999, *DEV
Fast poll decay . . . . . . . . > 2            0-255, *DEV
Slow poll interval . . . . . . . > 200          0-99999, *DEV

                                                              More...
F3=Exit   F4=Prompt   F5=Refresh   F12=Cancel   F13=How to use this display
F24=More keys
```

```
                     Add EWC PTC Entry (ADDEWCPTCE)

 Type choices, press Enter.

 Destination hop:
   Destination ID . . . . . .   *NONE          4001-4FFE, *NONE
   Frequency  . . . . . . . .   ____           1, 2, 3, 4, 5, 900, 901...
   Data rate  . . . . . . . .   _____          *NONE, 1M, 2M
   Radio system identifier  .   ________       000002-FFFFFE
             + for more values
 Barcode group  . . . . . . .   *NONE
             + for more values  ______________
 Text 'description' . . . . . > 'Enhanced Controller configuration data for PTC'
 Enable keyboard remapping  .   *NO            *NO, *YES
 Enable screen reformatting .   *NO            *NO, *YES
 Device name prefix . . . . .   QWLS______     Name



                                                                         Bottom
 F3=Exit   F4=Prompt   F5=Refresh   F12=Cancel   F13=How to use this display
 F24=More keys
```

Figure 19-21: Prompted version of the ADDEWCPTCE command (parts 1 through 3).

This protocol uses another piece of communication control referred to as *polling*. The *host* goes through all devices, polling (or asking) each device if it is still there and/or does it have any messages. Sometimes, some devices are very busy communicating while others are idle. To continually poll all devices would take valuable computer resources from the devices that are busy. To compromise, the AS/400 uses complex formulas to "guess" which devices are going to be idle and which are busy. The idle devices get left off of several polling cycles. The longer a device stays idle, the more it is bypassed in polling.

The PTC devices (but not the bar-code readers) have some interesting *polling parameters.* There are four of them at the bottom of the second screen in Figure 19-21. In the example, we entered the default values to make the explanation clearer. The four refer to polling sequences. Polling is a piece of LAN protocol where the one device just makes sure another is still there. It is an "Are you there?" query issued at regular periods of time. If the receiving device does not answer, it may be taken offline as inactive. Both the AS/400 and each PTC unit poll each other. Sometimes it is the AS/400 polling the PTC, sometimes the PTC polls the AS/400. They both need to know the other is there. The poll-related parameters refer to the PTC polling of the AS/400 and are intended to exert enough control to conserve battery power. Here is a description of the four poll parameters:

- POLL. This sets the fast poll interval for the PTC. The default, 125ms, means that the PTC will poll the host every 125 milliseconds.

- POLLDLY. This is the amount of time polling is suspended following the start of a transmission in either direction (to the host or from the host).

- POLLDECAY. This is the number of PTC polls before the poll rate is cut in half. Polling proceeds rapidly at first, at the rate specified in the poll parameter, then halves its rate. If the fast poll was 125ms, after two such polls (the default is two), the new rate could be every 250ms.

- SLOWPOLL. The slowest rate at which polling will occur. This is the slowest rate the poll can get to through poll decay.

Figure 19-22 has a prompted version of the Add Extended Wireless Controller Barcode Entry (ADDEWCBCDE) command.

```
                     Add EWC Barcode Entry (ADDEWCBCDE)

 Type choices, press Enter.

 Barcode group  . . . . . . . . . > BCD001
 Initialization source member . . > WLS001       Name

                            Additional Parameters

 Initialization source file . . .   QEWCSRC      Name, QEWCSRC
   Library  . . . . . . . . . . .     *LIBL      Name, *LIBL, *CURLIB
 Barcode type . . . . . . . . . .   *UPC
 Label length . . . . . . . . . .   0            0-64
 First check digit  . . . . . . .   *NO          *NO, *YES
 Second check digit . . . . . . .   *NO          *NO, *YES
 All zeros  . . . . . . . . . . .   *NO          *NO, *YES
 Alpha display  . . . . . . . . .   *NO          *NO, *YES
 Add on 2 . . . . . . . . . . . .   *NO          *NO, *YES
 Add on 5 . . . . . . . . . . . .   *NO          *NO, *YES
 System 1 UPC-E . . . . . . . . .   *NO          *NO, *YES
                                                                  More...
 F3=Exit   F4=Prompt   F5=Refresh   F12=Cancel   F13=How to use this display
 F24=More keys
```

```
                     Add EWC Barcode Entry (ADDEWCBCDE)

 Type choices, press Enter.

 System 0 UPC-E . . . . . .   *NO           *NO, *YES
 UPC-E  . . . . . . . . . .   *NO           *NO, *YES
 EAN 13 . . . . . . . . . .   *NO           *NO, *YES
 Extended Character Set . .   *NO           *NO, *YES
 Add on . . . . . . . . . .   *BIDIRECTIONAL
 Drop begin . . . . . . . .   0             0-64
 Drop end . . . . . . . . .   0             0-64
 Text 'description' . . . . > 'Sample bar code device controller configuration'




                                                                   Bottom
 F3=Exit   F4=Prompt   F5=Refresh   F12=Cancel   F13=How to use this display
 F24=More keys
```

Figure 19-22: Prompted version of the ADDEWCBCDE command (parts 1 and 2).

When the customer varies on the line, a sequence of events should start that end up with the remote devices communicating with the AS/400. Normally, we let device descriptions be created automatically by the system. However, Figure 19-23 contains a sample of the command, Create Display Device Description (CRTDEVDSP).

```
                 Create Device Desc (Display) (CRTDEVDSP)

 Type choices, press Enter.

 Device description . . . . . . . > WLSDEV1       Name
 Device class . . . . . . . . . . > *LCL          *LCL, *RMT, *VRT, *SNPT
 Device type  . . . . . . . . . . > 3476          3101, 3151, 3161, 3162...
 Device model . . . . . . . . . . > 1             0, 1, 2, 3, 4, 5, 12, 23...
 Port number  . . . . . . . . . . > 0             0-17
 Switch setting . . . . . . . . .   __            0, 1, 2, 3, 4, 5, 6
 Online at IPL  . . . . . . . . .   *YES          *YES, *NO
 Attached controller  . . . . . . > WLSCTL        Name
 Keyboard language type . . . . .   *SYSVAL       *SYSVAL, AGB, AGE, AGI...
 Allow blinking cursor  . . . . .   *YES          *YES, *NO
 Text 'description' . . . . . . . > 'Sample Wireless device'

                                                                      Bottom
 F3=Exit   F4=Prompt   F5=Refresh   F10=Additional parameters   F12=Cancel
 F13=How to use this display        F24=More keys
```

Figure 19-23: Prompted version of the CRTDEVDSP command.

DISTRIBUTED DATA INTERFACE (DDI)

Distributed data interface (DDI) is a LAN that supports the ANSI X3T9.5 standard. DDI devices are attached on two counter-rotating rings that run at 100 MBps. One ring is designated the *primary ring* and is active most of the time. The other, the *secondary ring*, can maintain the network if a device becomes inactive. On the AS/400, DDI is commonly referred to as *FDDI (fiber optic DDI)* or *SDDI (shielded twisted-pair DDI)*. It is very common to use DDI to connect multiple AS/400s for superior file-transfer speeds. DDI networks consider all devices as members of one of two classes:

- Class A. Devices directly attached to both rings.
- Class B. Devices attached to only one ring or attached to the ring through a *concentrator*.

DDI is normally used to connect two or more AS/400s over a high-speed network. As such, all the network needs are the ring media (the cables) and the appropriate adapters in the AS/400s. Unless the intention is to connect LAN devices to a DDI ring (something not usually done), the other hardware is not necessary.

Connecting a LAN device, like a personal computer, to a DDI ring requires a concentrator (IBM's is the 8240 FDDI Concentrator). One side of this concentrator attaches to the DDI rings. The concentrator contains one or more (up to a maximum of six) *device attachment (DA) cards*. These cards connect to the personal computers. DA cards are manufactured specifically to support fiber or copper connections. Each DA card can support up to four devices.

The DDI adapter uses the same 48-bit adapter address as the Token-Ring adapters. Frame-size considerations are the same as those for Token-Ring frame sizes. On a DDI network, valid frame sizes range from 265 through 4,444 (default is 4,105).

Sometimes, DDI networking people refer to frame sizes in *symbols* (with two symbols representing one byte). Therefore, a DDI network supporting a frame size of 8,210 symbols is, in other words, the same as saying it supports a 4,105-byte frame size.

DDI Configuration

To configure a DDI network over two AS/400s, create these objects in the following sequence:

- CRTLINDDI (Create Line Description).
- CRTCTLAPPC (Create Controller Description)—Optional.

Create Line Description (DDI) (CRTLINDDI)

Create the DDI line with the Create Line Description (DDI) (CRTLINDDI) command. Figure 19-24 has a sample of it.

```
                    Create Line Desc (DDI) (CRTLINDDI)

 Type choices, press Enter.

 Line description . . . . . . . . > DDILIN1       Name
 Resource name  . . . . . . . . . > LIN441        Name, *NWID
 Online at IPL  . . . . . . . . .   *YES          *YES, *NO
 Vary on wait . . . . . . . . . .   *NOWAIT       *NOWAIT, 15-180 seconds
 Maximum controllers  . . . . . .   40            1-256
 Maximum frame size . . . . . . .   4105          265-4444
 Logging level  . . . . . . . . .   *OFF          *OFF, *ERRORS, *ALL
 Local manager mode . . . . . . .   *OBSERVING    *OBSERVING, *NONE
 Local adapter address  . . . . . > 400050010111  400000000000-7FFFFFFFFFFF...
 Exchange identifier  . . . . . .   *SYSGEN       05600000-056FFFFF, *SYSGEN
 SSAP list:                         _
   Source service access point  .   *SYSGEN       02-FE, *SYSGEN
   SSAP maximum frame . . . . . .   __________    265-4444, *MAXFRAME
   SSAP type  . . . . . . . . . .   _______       *CALC, *NONSNA, *SNA
              + for more values _

                                                                    More...
 F3=Exit   F4=Prompt   F5=Refresh   F12=Cancel   F13=How to use this display
 F24=More keys
```

```
                    Create Line Desc (DDI) (CRTLINDDI)

Type choices, press Enter.

Text 'description' . . . . . . . > 'Create DDI line 1'


                         Additional Parameters

Network controller . . . . . . .   __________   Name
Group address  . . . . . . . . .   *NONE        800000000000-FFFFFFFFFFFE...
               + for more values _
Token rotation time  . . . . . .   *CALC        4-167, *CALC
Link speed . . . . . . . . . . .   *MAX         *MIN, 1200, 2400, 4800...
Cost/connect time  . . . . . . .   0            0-255
Cost/byte  . . . . . . . . . . .   0            0-255
Security for line  . . . . . . .   *NONSECURE   *NONSECURE, *PKTSWTNET...
Propagation delay  . . . . . . .   *LAN         *PKTSWTNET, *LAN, *MIN...
User-defined 1 . . . . . . . . .   128          0-255
User-defined 2 . . . . . . . . .   128          0-255
                                                                   More...
F3=Exit   F4=Prompt   F5=Refresh   F12=Cancel   F13=How to use this display
F24=More keys
```

```
                    Create Line Desc (DDI) (CRTLINDDI)

Type choices, press Enter.

User-defined 3 . . . . . . . . .   128          0-255
Autocreate controller  . . . . .   *NO           *YES, *NO
Autodelete controller  . . . . .   1440         1-10000 (minutes), *NONE
Recovery limits:
  Count limit  . . . . . . . . .   2            0-99, *SYSVAL
  Time interval  . . . . . . . .   5            0-120 minutes
Authority  . . . . . . . . . . .   *LIBCRTAUT   Name, *LIBCRTAUT, *CHANGE...







                                                                    Bottom
F3=Exit   F4=Prompt   F5=Refresh   F12=Cancel   F13=How to use this display
F24=More keys
```

Figure 19-24: Create Line Description for DDI network (parts 1 through 3).

The Token Rotation Time parameter sets the amount of time in milliseconds that the token will take to circumvent the ring. The sending system will continue to send packets of data until this time limit is reached. One possible value for this parameter is *CALC, and that is the one most customers use. When the DDI circuit becomes active, the system will calculate the rotation time based on the equipment attached.

This command also has (on the third screen) Autocreate Controller and Autodelete Controller parameters, similar to Token-Ring and Ethernet lines.

Create Controller Description (CRTCTLAPPC)

Create the controller description with the Create Controller Description (CRTCTLAPPC) command. Figure 19-25 contains a sample of that command.

```
                     Create Ctl Desc (APPC) (CRTCTLAPPC)

Type choices, press Enter.

Controller description . . . . . > SYS01          Name
Link type  . . . . . . . . . . . > *LAN           *ANYNW, *FAX, *FR, *IDLC...
Online at IPL  . . . . . . . . .   *YES           *YES, *NO
APPN-capable . . . . . . . . . .   *YES           *YES, *NO
Switched line list . . . . . . . > DDILIN1        Name
              + for more values
Maximum frame size . . . . . . .   *LINKTYPE      265-16393, 256, 265, 512...
Remote network identifier  . . .   *NETATR        Name, *NETATR, *NONE, *ANY
Remote control point . . . . . . > SYS02          Name, *ANY
Exchange identifier  . . . . . .                  00000000-FFFFFFFF
Initial connection . . . . . . .   *DIAL          *DIAL, *ANS
Dial initiation  . . . . . . . .   *LINKTYPE      *LINKTYPE, *IMMED, *DELAY
LAN remote adapter address . . . > 400050010222   000000000001-FFFFFFFFFFFF
LAN DSAP . . . . . . . . . . . .   04             04, 08, 0C, 10, 14, 18, 1C...
LAN SSAP . . . . . . . . . . . .   04             04, 08, 0C, 10, 14, 18, 1C...
APPN CP session support  . . . .   *YES           *YES, *NO
```

Figure 19-25: Create Controller Description for DDI network.

Create the controller only if one doesn't exist and if Autocreate Controller was set to *NO on the Create Line Description command.

That's it for configuring a DDI network. There's no need to configure a device (the computer is the device). DDI is primarily for host-to-host communications.

FRAME RELAY (FR)

Frame relay (FR) is a *packet-switching protocol* that is similar to X.25, but much faster (up to two MBps). Frame relay uses established data-communications networks outside the organization, like phone and cable companies. Connection to such networks requires the customer to become a subscriber. Built-in reliability is such an accepted part of established data-communications networks that frame relay does not provide as much error-handling as the other protocols.

Frame relay is very expensive for in-house LANs or even across the same city. It is generally used to connect two LANs (or two AS/400s) across very large distances. It is the protocol of choice for WAN support.

A frame-relay LAN can be configured as direct or bridged. A *direct frame relay* is typically two or more AS/400s connected over a frame-relay network and running APPC or APPN. A direct frame relay can also connect to remote systems supporting the IP or IPX direct format.

A *bridged frame-relay network* is similar, except that the remote device is a remote bridge (such as the IBM 6611 Network Processor) to a LAN. Another AS/400 can be on the remote LAN, but it is not necessary. Through a bridged frame-relay network, an AS/400 can communicate with workstations on a remote LAN as efficiently as if they were locally attached. The AS/400 itself can act as a bridge on the frame-relay network.

The frame-relay physical pieces are more complex than those used by the other protocols. The AS/400 is referred to as *terminal equipment* (TE) on a frame-relay network. A network node on a frame-relay network (much like an intermediate node in APPN) is referred to as a *frame handler* (FH). TEs are connected to FHs through a device that is really two bundled devices. The bundled devices are a *data service unit* (DSU) and a *channel service unit* (CSU). Together, they are referred to as a DSU/CSU.

All together, frame relay will have an AS/400 (the TE) connected by some physical wiring into a DSU/CSU. The DSU/CSU connects to an FH, and the FH then connects to the frame-relay network. At other points on the frame-relay network, other FHs come off and connect to other TEs through DSU/CSUs.

Although you need at least the cabling and FH on both ends of the frame-relay network, each end also can be an *SNA direct connection* or bridged. An SNA-direct connection allows SNA systems to connect directly to the FH. Otherwise, Token-Ring, Ethernet, and DDI all connect to an FH by a bridge.

Two AS/400s can be connected together using frame relay without going through a frame-relay network. The result is much like connecting two PC communication ports by directly using a modem eliminator rather than a modem. In this case, the customer gets the high-speed benefits of a frame relay without the expense of joining the network. Just configure one AS/400's network interface description as LMIMODE(*FH) and the other's as LMIMODE(*TE).

Let us drill down into this physical stuff a little more. The AS/400 requires an adapter, which can be any of the following:

- 2666 High Speed Communications Input/Output Processor (IOP) (input–output processor).
- 2629-2699 High Speed Communications Input/Output Processor (IOP).
- 2809-2721 High Speed Communications Input/Output Processor (IOP).
- 2629-2699 LAN/WAN/Workstation IOP—Two-Line WAN IOA (input–output adapter).
- 2809-2721 PCI LAN/WAN/Workstation IOP—PCI Two-Line WAN IOA.

These adapters support any of four *physical interfaces* (or cable connectors). The possible physical interfaces, their cable connectors, and parameter values (see the following section on CRTNWIFR) are listed in Figure 19-26.

Physical Interface	Cable Connector Parameter Value	Interface
EIA RS-449	ISO4902 (37-pin)	*RS449V36
CCITT V.36	ISO4902 (37-pin)	*RS449V36
CCITT X.21	ISO4903 (15-pin)	*X21
CCITT V.35	ISO2593	*V35

Figure 19-26: Physical interfaces.

The cable types and adapter combinations dictate the cable lengths, clocking speed, and maximum speed available over the network. For more information on these relationships, refer to IBM manual *OS/400 LAN, Frame-Relay, and ATM Support V4R4*, section 5.1.1.

Frame-Relay Addressing

A single physical cable between nodes can support up to 256 virtual circuits. A virtual circuit between two nodes is referred to as a *permanent virtual circuit (PVC)* and is identified by a *data link connection identifier (DLCI)*. The DLCI number can be between one and 1,018 (although there can only be 256 of them on one physical cable). The frame-relay network provider assigns DLCI numbers at subscription time.

The operator must have the DLCI number when configuring either the line or network interface description. It can be specified on the line or the network interface description. If it is specified on the line, put it in on the NWIDLCI parameter. If specified on the network interface description, specify both the DLCI number and the line description name.

Unlike the other adapters in this chapter, frame-relay communications adapters do not come with preset addresses. This address is not required for SNA direct connections.

The Remote Adapter Address (ADPTADR) parameter on the controller description must match the adapter address of the remote system.

Frame-Relay Configuration

To set up a frame-relay connection, you must create these objects in sequence:

- CRTNWIFR (Create Network Interface Description).
- CRTLIND (Create Line Description).
- CRTCTLAPPC (Create Controller Description—APPC).
- CRTDEVAPPC (Create Device Description—APPC).

In the example that follows, we have included samples of setting up a two-AS/400 frame-relay network. With this example, one AS/400 is in Phoenix, as the local machine; and one is in New York, as the remote machine.

Create Network Interface Description (CRTNWIFR)

Use the Create Network Interface Description—Frame Relay (CRTNWIFR) command as shown in Figure 19-27.

```
                 Create Network Interface (FR) (CRTNWIFR)

 Type choices, press Enter.

 Network interface description  . > FRPHX        Name
 Resource name  . . . . . . . . . > LIN211       Name
 Online at IPL  . . . . . . . . .   *YES         *YES, *NO
 Vary on wait . . . . . . . . . .   *NOWAIT      *NOWAIT, 15-180 seconds
 Data link connection ID:           _
   DLCI number  . . . . . . . . . > 315          1-1018, *NONE
   Line description . . . . . . . > FR011AWS     Name
               + for more values _
 NRZI data encoding . . . . . . .   *NO           *NO, *YES
 Physical interface . . . . . . .   *RS449V36    *RS449V36, *V35, *X21
 Clocking . . . . . . . . . . . .   *MODEM       *MODEM, *LOOP, *INVERT
 Line speed . . . . . . . . . . .   1536000      56000-2048000, 56000...
 LMI mode . . . . . . . . . . . .   *TE          *TE, *FH, *NONE, *ANNEXA
 Polling interval . . . . . . . .   10           5-30
 Full inquiry interval  . . . . .   6            1-255
```

Figure 19-27: Create Network Interface Description for the frame-relay AS/400 located in Phoenix. The remote AS/400 is in New York.

Note that the frame-relay network provider (the phone company or cable company) supplies the Physical Interface and Line Speed parameters. When systems connect via frame relay, it is not like a direct connection. The frame-relay network allows a mismatch of things like line speeds between the nodes.

This example shows creating the local end (in this case, Phoenix). On the remote end (New York), change all instances of PHX to NEWYORK (or whatever your naming standards are).

Create Line Description (CRTLINFR)

Frame-relay lines can be created directly with the Create Line Description (Frame-Relay) (CRTLINFR) command, see Figure 19-28 for an example. Or, it can be created as a bridged line description for the following topologies:

- Token-Ring. Create Line Description (Token-Ring) (CRTLINTRN). For a bridged Token-Ring connection, you must connect to a controller created with the LINKTYPE(*LAN) parameter.
- Ethernet. Create Line Description (Ethernet) (CRTLINETH). For a bridged Ethernet connection, you must connect to a controller created with the LINKTYPE(*LAN) parameter.
- DDI. Create Line Description (DDI) (CRTLINDDI). For a bridged DDI connection, you must connect to a controller created with the LINKTYPE(*LAN) parameter.

Remember that the DLCI parameter comes from the frame-relay network provider. Also, refer to sections on Token-Ring Considerations and Ethernet Configuration for information on calculating the Maximum Frame Size (MAXFRAME). This example shows creating the local end (in this case, Phoenix). On the remote end (New York), change all instances of PHX to NEWYORK (or whatever the naming standards are). Also, change the DLC IDENTIFIER to the address assigned to the remote's line from the frame-relay service provider.

```
                 Create Line Desc (Frame Relay) (CRTLINFR)

Type choices, press Enter.

Line description . . . . . . . . > FRNEWYORK     Name
Attached NWI . . . . . . . . . . > FRPHX         Name, *NONE
DLC identifier . . . . . . . . . > 21            1-1018, *NONE
Online at IPL  . . . . . . . . .   *YES          *YES, *NO
Vary on wait . . . . . . . . . .   *NOWAIT       *NOWAIT, 15-180 seconds
Maximum controllers  . . . . . .   40            1-256
Maximum frame size . . . . . . .   1590          265-8182, 1590
Exchange identifier  . . . . . . > 05684452      05600000-056FFFFF, *SYSGEN
SSAP list:                         _
  Source service access point  .   *SYSGEN       02-FE, *SYSGEN
  SSAP maximum frame . . . . . .   __________    *MAXFRAME, 265-8182
  SSAP type  . . . . . . . . . .   _______       *CALC, *NONSNA, *SNA, *HPR
             + for more values _
Text 'description' . . . . . . . > 'Frame-relay from phx to new york'
____

                                                                    Bottom
F3=Exit   F4=Prompt   F5=Refresh   F10=Additional parameters   F12=Cancel
F13=How to use this display        F24=More keys
```

Figure 19-28: Create Line Description for frame-relay AS/400 located in Phoenix. The remote AS/400 is in New York.

Create Controller Description (CRTCTLAPPC)

Frame-relay controllers are created with the Create Controller Description (APPC) (CRTCTLAPPC) command, see Figure 19-29 for an example.

```
                    Create Ctl Desc (APPC) (CRTCTLAPPC)

Type choices, press Enter.

Controller description . . . . . > FRNEWYORK     Name
Link type  . . . . . . . . . . . > *FR           *ANYNW, *FAX, *FR, *IDLC...
Online at IPL  . . . . . . . . .   *YES          *YES, *NO
APPN-capable . . . . . . . . . .   *YES          *YES, *NO
Switched line list . . . . . . . > FRNEWYORK     Name
             + for more values _
Maximum frame size . . . . . . .   *LINKTYPE     265-16393, 256, 265, 512...
Remote network identifier  . . .   *NETATR       Name, *NETATR, *NONE, *ANY
Remote control point . . . . . . > NEWYORK       Name, *ANY
Exchange identifier  . . . . . . > 05622844      00000000-FFFFFFFF
Initial connection . . . . . . .   *DIAL         *DIAL, *ANS

                                                                    Bottom
F3=Exit   F4=Prompt   F5=Refresh   F10=Additional parameters   F12=Cancel
F13=How to use this display        F24=More keys
```

Figure 19-29: Create Controller Description for frame-relay AS/400 located in Phoenix. The remote AS/400 is in New York.

Specify APPN-CAPABLE(*YES). The Link Type parameter is set at *FR (Frame Relay). If this frame relay connects via a bridge to a Token-Ring, Ethernet, or DDI network, specify LINKTYPE(*LAN).

This example shows creating the local end (in this case, Phoenix). On the remote end (New York), change all instances of PHX to NEWYORK (or whatever the naming standards are).

Device Description

Use the Create Device Description (CRTDEVAPPC) command. See Figure 19-30.

```
                     Create Device Desc (APPC) (CRTDEVAPPC)

 Type choices, press Enter.

 Device description . . . . . . . > FRNEWYORK      Name
 Remote location  . . . . . . . . > NEWYORK        Name
 Online at IPL  . . . . . . . . .   *YES           *YES, *NO
 Local location . . . . . . . . .   *NETATR        Name, *NETATR
 Remote network identifier  . . .   *NETATR        Name, *NETATR, *NONE
 Attached controller  . . . . . . > FRNEWYORK      Name
 Mode . . . . . . . . . . . . . .   *NETATR        Name, *NETATR
               + for more values _
 Message queue  . . . . . . . . .   QSYSOPR        Name, QSYSOPR
   Library  . . . . . . . . . . .     *LIBL        Name, *LIBL, *CURLIB
 APPN-capable . . . . . . . . . .   *YES           *YES, *NO
 Single session:
   Single session capable . . . .   *NO            *NO, *YES
   Number of conversations  . . .   ___            1-512
 Text 'description' . . . . . . . > 'FR connection in Phoenix for remote in New
York'
                                                                        More...
 F3=Exit   F4=Prompt   F5=Refresh   F12=Cancel   F13=How to use this display
 F24=More keys
```

Figure 19-30: Create Device Description for frame-relay AS/400 located in Phoenix. The remote AS/400 is in New York.

The Device Description parameter is the name of the remote system (in this example, FRNEWYORK), the remote location name is the name of the remote system, and the attached controller is the name of the remote system's controller.

This example shows creating the local end (in this case, Phoenix). On the remote end (New York), change all instances of PHX to NEWYORK (or whatever your naming standards are).

When configuring objects for frame relay, be concerned with the maximum frame size. The frame-relay network provider provides a "frame size" referred to as the N203 number. The number can be between 262 and 8,192 bytes for everything except bridged DDI and Ethernet. Most commonly, the number is 1,600 bytes. Bridged DDI can be between 262 and 4,488; and bridged Ethernet can be between 262 and 1,522. When configuring the network, subtract routing information from this number to come up with a good number for the maximum frame size. The number to subtract depends on the connection type and protocol. Figure 19-31 provides guidelines, presuming you take the maximum frame size for each protocol.

	Size of Routing Data	Maximum Frame Size
Direct:		
SNA	10	8182
IP	2	8190
IPX	2	8190
HPR	6	8196
Bridged:		
Token-Ring	44	8148
DDI	44	4444
Ethernet IEEE 802.3	26	1496
Ethernet V2 SNA	22	1493
Ethernet V2 Non-SNA	26	1500

Figure 19-31: Guidelines for determining maximum frame size.

The maximum frame size can be specified in three places during configuration:

- Line description MAXFRAME parameter.
- Line description SSAP has a maximum frame-size parameter.
- Controller description MAXFRAME parameter.

AS/400 LAN CL COMMANDS

After a LAN is configured, no matter what its protocol is, there are several CLs common to all protocols to help. The overall most powerful one is the Work with Configuration Status (WRKCFGSTS) command. It allows the operator to work with adapters, lines, controllers, or devices. It will display their attributes, vary them on and off, display the mode or connection status, and hold or release a device. Figure 19-32 shows a sample of that command set up to work with the line, controller, and devices for all Token-Ring LANs (but it could be used for Ethernet, DDI, and frame relay).

```
                Work with Configuration Status (WRKCFGSTS)

 Type choices, press Enter.

 Type . . . . . . . . . . . . . . > *LIN          *NWS, *NWI, *LIN, *CTL, *DEV
 Configuration description  . . . > *TRLAN        Name, generic*, *ALL, *CMN...
 Output . . . . . . . . . . . . .   *             *, *PRINT
 Range  . . . . . . . . . . . . .   *NET          *NET, *OBJ
 Status . . . . . . . . . . . . .   *ALL          *ALL, *ACTIVE, *FAILED...
```

Figure 19-32: Prompted screen for WRKCFGSTS command.

After pressing Enter, the command displays all the objects related to the protocol requested (in this example, the Token-Ring LAN). Figure 19-33 shows the screen after you press Enter. Notice on this system that we have TCP/IP running over Token-Ring. That is reflected in the first three objects. From this screen, the operator can do a lot of work with the lines, controllers, and devices.

```
                    Work with Configuration Status                BIGBLUE
                                                        07/14/99  21:19:29
Position to  . . . . .  __________     Starting characters _______

Type options, press Enter.
  1=Vary on    2=Vary off    5=Work with job    8=Work with description
  9=Display mode status      13=Work with APPN status...

Opt  Description        Status                 -------Job-------
__   TCP_IP01           ACTIVE
__     TCP_INET         ACTIVE
__       TCP_ITCP       ACTIVE                 QTCPIP      QTCP        036772
__   TOKENRING1         ACTIVE
__     GE11S02          ACTIVE
__       WDRSE          ACTIVE
__         QPCSUPP      ACTIVE/TARGET          WDRSE       PCS         046630
__       WSMSE          ACTIVE
__         QPCSUPP      ACTIVE/TARGET          WSMSE       PCS         046749
                                                                       More . . .
Parameters or command
===>_______________________________________________________________________
F3=Exit   F4=Prompt   F12=Cancel   F23=More options   F24=More keys
```

Figure 19-33: Token-Ring lines, controllers, and devices from WRKCFGSTS.

Another CL command is the Work with Hardware Resource (WRKHDWRSC) command. Figure 19-34 shows its basic form. The example requests information about communication (*CMN) resources.

```
                 Work with Hardware Resources (WRKHDWRSC)

Type choices, press Enter.

Type . . . . . . . . . . . . . . > *CMN          *CMN, *CSA, *LAN, *LWS...
```

Figure 19-34: Formatted version of the WRKHDWRSC command.

Figure 19-35 shows the next screen after pressing the Enter key.

```
                  Work with Communication Resources
                                                            System:   BIGBLUE
 Type options, press Enter.
   5=Work with configuration descriptions   7=Display resource detail

 Opt  Resource          Type  Status                     Text
  _   CMB01             9164  Operational                Combined function IOP
  _     LIN01           2721  Operational                Comm Adapter
  _       CMN01         2721  Operational                V.24 Port
  _   CMB02             2809  Operational                MFIO Processor
  _     LIN02           2721  Operational                Comm Adapter
  _       CMN02         2721  Operational                Comm Port
  _       CMN03         2721  Operational                Comm Port
  _     LIN03           2838  Operational                LAN Adapter
  _       CMN04         2838  Operational                Ethernet Port
  _   CC01              2619  Operational                Combined function IOP
  _     LIN03           2619  Operational                LAN Adapter
  _       CMN04         2619  Operational                Token-Ring Port
  _     LIN10           605A  Operational                Virtual Controller
  _   CC03              2623  Operational                Comm Processor
  _     LIN07           2609  Operational                Comm Adaptor
  _       CMN05         2609  Operational                V.24 Port Enhanced

Bottom
 F3=Exit   F5=Refresh   F6=Print   F12=Cancel
```

Figure 19-35: IOPs, adapters, and lines displayed by the WRKHDWRSC command.

ASYNCHRONOUS TRANSFER MODE (ATM)

New with Version 4 is *Asynchronous Transfer Mode (ATM)* support on the AS/400. ATM provides data exchange between computers in the speed range of up to 155 Mbps, over a wide variety of cable types and connectors, and over distances formerly only possible with WANs.

ATM provides something new—*LAN Emulation (or LANE)*. It can run over Ethernet (IEEE 802.3 or Version 2) or Token-Ring lines. The AS/400 does not do LAN emulation; that must take place on some attached hardware such as:

- IBM 8260 Network Switch.
- IBM 2210 Multi-Protocol Switched Service (MSS).

When an ATM client station wants to transmit something to a server or another client, it does not have to know the ATM address of either device at transmission time. An ATM network is a *switched network*. That is, without a physical topology and layout scheme, every transmission must be dynamically routed or switched to its destination. APPN-based networks had predetermined nodes and lines. Even the network servers had directories of related nodes and lines.

A group of LAN workstations attached to a single LAN segment within an ATM network is referred to as a *LAN Emulation Domain* (*LED).*

A client on an ATM network is referred to as a *LAN Emulation Client* (*LEC).* This can be the AS/400 (which can service many of its own workstations, devices, or sessions, providing them a single access to the ATM network), PC, or UNIX computer. When an AS/400 is used as an LEC, only one client can be attached to an IOP (Input-Output Processor), but many IOPs supporting one client each can exist (each having its own adapter address).

The ATM interoperability standards that the AS/400 supports are UNI3.0 and UNI3.1. The piece of software that carries out these standards is the *interim local management interface* (*ILMI*). These standards are very important in ATM networks because, together, they determine how the end nodes and switches create and manage calls and addresses.

This is not that big of a deal as long as the operator remembers to configure the AS/400 to use the same UNI standard as the switch it is connecting to. Do this when the *ATM network interface* is created or changed.

In addition to the adapter cards on each node, an ATM LED has three components, all of them optional:

- LAN Emulation Configuration Server (LECS). A LECS is a server that provides configuration to clients. This configuration is not the same as the configuration one deals with when configuring a physical network; this is providing addresses and data-forwarding services. Only one can exist on an LED. It also provides some security because it can be told which stations to recognize. If the LECS is not used, all clients must know the ATM addresses of all other clients.

- LAN Emulation Server (LES). The LES provides ATM address resolution and control services. There is only one LES per LED.

- Broadcast and Unknown Server (BUS). Provides frame forwarding and broadcast-related services to clients.

The LECS is omitted where a customer has connected two AS/400s and only wants to use ATM to pump data very quickly between them. There is no ATM network per se, there are only the two machines. In that case, the two machines' IOP cards are connected together physically with a crossover cable and, on the line configuration (refer to section titled Line Description Parameters for ATM Lines), the Access Type parameter is set to *DIRECT.

ATM Addresses

An ATM address is a twenty-byte hexadecimal number. Each end node must have its own unique address. On the AS/400, this address is composed of a:

- 13-byte ATM address.
- 6-byte adapter MAC address.
- 1-byte selector byte.

We are used to dealing with MAC addresses on AS/400 LANs and on ATM networks—we still have to know the MAC addresses of the devices to which we are sending data. This address can be the manufacturer's preset address or one we assign the adapter (refer to section titled LAN Addresses for more information).

Receiving AS/400s use the selector byte to resolve which of several sessions attached to the adapter card is to receive the transmission.

ATM Transmission (Typical)

The ATM protocol is enabled when the line is varied on. It becomes active when the transmission starts. The client wishing to transmit data to another client must have the receiver's six-byte adapter address. It sends that address to the LECS for address resolution. If the LECS cannot determine the receiving client's ATM address, the request is passed to the BUS for address resolution. Either the LECS or the BUS calculates the receiver's 20-byte ATM address and returns it to the sending LEC.

The sending LEC then bundles the full ATM address with the data and begins the transmission to the LES. The LES forwards the data to the receiver LEC.

ATM Configuration

To configure an ATM network, create:

- ATM Network Interface.
- ATM Line Description parameters. These are parameters on the Ethernet (refer to Create Line Description [Ethernet] [CRTLINETH]) or Token-Ring (refer to Create Line Description [Token-Ring] [CRTLINTRN]) line descriptions.
- ATM Controller Description parameters. Ethernet (refer to Create Controller Description for APPC [CRTCTLAPPC] [Optional]) or Token-Ring (refer to Create Controller Description for APPC [CRTCTLAPPC] [Optional]) controller description.
- ATM Device Description parameters. Ethernet (refer to Create Device Description for APPC [CRTDEVAPPC] [Optional]) or Token-Ring (refer to Create Device Description for APPC [CRTDEVAPPC] [Optional]) device description.

Create ATM Network Interface

The ATM Network Interface defines all common attributes of the ATM interface. Each IOP has one network interface attached and one line attached. Work with network interfaces with these commands:

- CRTNWIATM (Create Network Interface).
- CHGNWIATM (Change Network Interface).
- DSPNWIATM (Display Network Interface).

All are similar. Figure 19-36 shows a prompted version of CRTNWIATM.

```
                        Create NWI ATM (CRTNWIATM)

 Type choices, press Enter.

 Network interface description  . > ATMINWI       Name
 Resource name  . . . . . . . . . > CMB01         Name
 Online at IPL  . . . . . . . . .   *YES          *YES, *NO
 Vary on wait . . . . . . . . . .   *NOWAIT       *NOWAIT, 15-180 seconds
 Network type . . . . . . . . . .   *AUTO         *AUTO, *UNI30, *UNI31...
 Text 'description' . . . . . . . > 'Network Interface for ATM'

                         Additional Parameters

 Maximum PMP end systems  . . . .   0             0-2048
 Switched virtual connections . .   516           16-2064
 Network switch timeout . . . . .   2             *NOMAX, 1-30 minutes
 Physical layer options . . . . .   *NONE         *NONE, 0000-FFFF
 Attached lines . . . . . . . . .   ETHLINE1      Name
                + for more values
                                                                  More...
 F3=Exit   F4=Prompt   F5=Refresh   F12=Cancel   F13=How to use this display
 F24=More keys
```

Figure 19-36: Prompted version of the CRTNWIATM command.

Name the interface on the Network Interface Description parameter. The resource name is the name of the IOP to which the interface is attached. If you do not know the name of the IOP, use the command:

```
WRKHDWRSC *CMN
```

This command will display a list of communications hardware.

The Network Type parameter indicates what interface standard the switch supports (so the AS/400 will be at the same support level). The valid values for this parameter are:

- UNI3.0.
- UNI3.1.
- *AUTO.
- *PVCONLY.

The most common value for this parameter is *AUTO. That one will have the system make the match.

*PVCONLY calls for a permanent virtual circuit and may be used when the Line Type (on the CRTLINATM command, discussed in the next section) is set to *PVC. If CRTLINEATM's Line Type is set to *DIRECT, *PVCONLY must be used here.

The Switched Virtual Connections (SVC) parameter is the maximum number of connections that may be active at one time for all devices associated with this interface.

The Network Switch Time-out value determines how many minutes the system will wait for the ATM switch to respond on initial contact. The default is two minutes, and that is fine most of the time.

Specify the name of the line that will be created in the next step on the Attached Lines parameter.

Two parameters, Maximum PMP End Systems and Physical Layer Options, are ignored at this time.

Line Description Parameters for ATM Lines

Line descriptions are not created just for ATM lines; they begin life as Ethernet or Token-Ring lines (refer to Create Line Description [Ethernet][CRTLINETH] and Create Line Description [Token-Ring] [CRTLINTRN] sections for more information). Only a few parameters on these descriptions make them ATM. The parameters specific to ATM lines and their possible values are:

- ACCTYPE (ATM Access Type). Determines the type of access the line will have. Possible values are:
  - *SVC (Switched Virtual Connections). Access through *SVC are connections that are created as needed, then deleted or dropped when no longer needed.
  - *PVC (Permanent Virtual Connections). Access through *PVC is through a connection that is always present. No call through the switch is required with *PVC. To use *PVC, configure all physical paths to other LECs in the ATM switch. This connection uses no LES or BUS to connect LECs.
  - *DIRECT (Direct). Access is between two AS/400s with their IOPs direct attached with a crossover cable. A crossover cable is like a modem eliminator cable, where the transmit from one end crosses over to become the receive on the other end, and vice versa for the receive/transmit pair.
- EMLLANNAME (Emulated LAN Name). THIS IS THE NAME OF THE EMULATED LAN THE CLIENT IS TO JOIN. USE THIS WHEN ACCTYPE is set to *SVC. This field is sort of case-sensitive—the resulting match to the LAN name certainly is—so be careful. Use upper-, lower-, or mixed upper-/lowercase characters to name the emulated LAN. However, lower- and mixed-case names are converted to uppercase before the match is made (and the match is definitely case-sensitive). For a match with unconverted characters, put this value in quotes.
- LECDSCTIMO (LEC Disconnect Time-Out). This value specifies the number of minutes (from one to thirty) that an LEC will stay connected to a virtual circuit after the circuit has become idle. If a circuit is expected to be idle and you want the connection to stay up, specify *NOMAX here.
- LECFRAME (LEC Frame Size).This parameter specifies the size of the frame of data that will be used. To set this, first determine the frame size of the LES, then add twenty bytes to it (for the ATM address).
- LESATMADR (LES ATM Address).If transmissions are not to be sent to a LECS to determine ATM addressing, this is the address of the server they should be sent to. The full 20-byte address must be specified, thirteen-byte network address of the switch, 6-byte switch adapter address, and one-byte selector byte address.
- ADPTADR (Local Adapter Address).This is the local computer's 6-byte MAC address.

- LCLATMADR (Local ATM Address).This is the full 20-byte address of the local LEC. It must contain the 13-byte network address, 6-byte adapter address and one-byte selector byte.
- MAXFRAME (Maximum Frame Size). This is the maximum frame size for this line. It must be at least twenty bytes less than the LEC frame size.
- NWITYPE (Network Interface Type). This must be set to *ATM.
- USELECS (Use LECS Address). If this is set to *YES, the LEC contacts the LECS to obtain the ATM address of the LES. If this is set to *NO, the LES ATM address must be supplied in the LES ATM Address parameter.

These are the ATM-specific parameters that may be supplied on the Create or Change Line Description (Ethernet and Token-Ring) commands. Other parameters specific for Ethernet and Token-Ring must also be supplied.

Also, controllers and devices must be created for those lines, although they have no ATM-specific parameters.

TCP/IP

While Ethernet, Token-Ring, DDI, and the other protocols are sufficient to connect many workstations into a single LAN, they are not enough to communicate outside of the LAN. The idea of communicating outside of the local LAN is to give many computers access to each other's networks to facilitate common marketing, commerce, messaging, or whatever. Extending the computing boundaries beyond the local LAN is referred to as *inter-networking*, or more popularly, the *Internet*.

A LAN (a rather large one, too) can exist with just the information presented in this and the previous chapter. But as soon as it is supposed to venture past its boundaries into public networks, TCP/IP will be the protocol.

TCP/IP runs over a physical network already in place, so we say that TCP/IP runs over any of the protocols discussed in the previous chapter.

Writing (and reading) about TCP/IP and the Internet takes some nonlinear thinking. This subject does not progress in nice A, B, and then C sequence. Some of the tasks are independent of each other. For example, bringing up TCP/IP requires you to know an *IP address, subnet mask*, and remote *domain name* server address—all of these are supplied by an Internet Service Provider (ISP). But you should know about TCP/IP before you try to arrange for Internet service.

TCP stands for *Transmission Control Protocol*. IP stands for *Internet Protocol*. They are almost always used together and we think of TCP/IP as a single protocol.

TCP/IP is a *packet-switching protocol*. Data is *encapsulated* into packets called *datagrams*.

Even though TCP/IP is almost always thought of as the *Internet protocol*, it is becoming a de facto communication standard. Years ago, computer hardware vendors would always offer their product with at least an asynchronous communication capability. That was the widest-used protocol there was. Today, the honor goes to TCP/IP—thanks to its wide acceptance and ubiquitousness, everyone can communicate TCP/IP—even those customers who have no intention of ever being on the Internet may find themselves bringing up TCP/IP to support some piece of hardware. The Internet application layer (above TCP/IP) is also very functional; some AS/400 customers look at that area for quick and reliable functionality. For example, Telnet provides cheap, simple remote AS/400 access. It's easy to throw together for someone away from home with a computer that does not have any terminal emulation loaded on it.

TCP/IP requires particular attention to system value QAUTOVRT, or the value that has the AS/400 autoconfigure remote devices. Check the value with the Display System Value (DSPSYSVAL) command, change it with the Change System Value (CHGSYSVAL) command. Do both at once with the Work with System Values (WRKSYSVAL) command. This system value determines how many virtual devices the AS/400 will be allowed to configure. Possible values are from zero through 32,500, and *NOMAX which says there is no limit.

IP Addressing

Like other protocols discussed in this chapter, we have to deal with addresses for TCP/IP nodes. Remember that TCP/IP runs over another LAN protocol, so the MAC addressing every adapter must have is still there.

But TCP/IP's purpose is to communicate with any computer network in the world, so it has to have another layer of addressing. That's right, every computer in the world, one way or the other, must have a unique address. If a mathematical genius takes a critical look at the Internet's addressing scheme, the mathematician would instantly see a problem. There aren't enough bits for every computer host in the world to have a unique address.

The solution has been a combination of straight addressing from a central authority and subnets, giving organizations the ability to concoct their own addressing scheme for hundreds of in-house hosts. This solution has also yielded an addressing scheme that gives most normal people nightmares.

IP's Basic Address

The basic TCP/IP address is a 32-bit integer expressed in terms of four hexadecimal numbers or four three-digit decimal numbers, each separated by a period. Here is how it works. A typical Internet address might be 204.145.193.104. The bits that make that up are listed in Figure 19-37.

```
Bit positions'
        values:  128  64  32  16 |  8   4   2   1
        Byte 0:    1   1   0   0 |  1   1   0   0  =  204 (Hex=X'CC')
        Byte 1:    1   0   0   1 |  0   0   0   1  =  145 (Hex=X'91')
        Byte 2:    1   1   0   0 |  0   0   0   1  =  193 (Hex=X'C1')
        Byte 3:    0   1   1   0 |  1   0   0   0  =  104 (Hex=X'68')
```

Figure 19-37: The bits making up a typical Internet address.

A TCP/IP network can be brought up between one or more AS/400(s) and other nodes and, if it is entirely local (never joining the actual Internet), the operator is free to make up these TCP/IP addresses. Be careful, though, TCP/IP brought up with made up IP addresses will have to be torn down and recreated if; at some later date, the company decides to join the Internet. With all the clients and servers that may be in place, this could be a daunting job.

The customer who really doesn't believe he or she will ever be on the Internet but wants to bring up TCP/IP locally should use one of the reserved private addresses mentioned below in this section.

Internet addresses come from an organization called the InterNIC. But the InterNIC no longer deals directly with individuals (including your company). IP addresses are issued from Internet Service Provider (ISP). There is a little more flexibility with your domain name. However, it, too, comes from the InterNIC, but the customer can deal with the organization directly without going through an ISP. If an operator is anticipating being on the Internet at any time in the future, contact InterNIC and find out if a domain name is available for your company. If it is, register it (for a small fee), so it will be ready when the company is. We discuss domain names later in this chapter.

If you are interested in contacting the InterNIC about either subject, it has two email addresses:

- For information about IP addresses: `hostmaster@internic.net`.
- For domain name information: `info@is.internet.net`.

Access into the Internet is through a local ISP. For a list of ISPs, contact InterNIC at the second address. IP addresses are made up of 32 bits, which are actually carved into two addresses:

```
<Network address><Host address>
```

The question is how many bytes for each piece? The division is a moving target. When more bytes are taken up by the network address, there are fewer bytes to hold individual host addresses. Conversely, fewer bytes for the network yield more bytes for host addressing.

This shifting demarcation determines the *class of network*. If the network address is low, the number of individual hosts that can be directly addressed is high, and this is a *class A network*. On the other hand, if the network address is high, the number of hosts that can be directly addressed is low, and this is a *class D network*. Figure 19-38 lists the classes of service and their network/host address divisions and possible values.

Class	Range of Left Byte	Bytes for Network	Bytes for Hosts	Max. # Hosts
A	0-126	1	3	16,777,214
B	128-191	2	2	65,534
C	192-223	3	1	254
D	224-239			Multicast

Figure 19-38: Classes of network, address divisions, and values.

A large network would be a class A network, and an example of its address would be 9.4.3.1, where 9 is the network address and 4.3.1 is the host address.

A small network would be a class C network, and an example of its address would be 221.5.6.233, where 221.5.6 is the network address and 233 is the host address.

Class D is a multicast network where the first 4 bits of the address determine that the address is multicast and the last 28 bits determine the multicast group address.

The Internet has a fifth class, E, reserved for future use. The AS/400 does not support that class at this time. As a quick clue to what class an address is, refer to its left three bits:

Class A	000
Class B	100
Class C	110
Class D	111

When a customer gets a unique Internet address from the ISP, the customer actually gets a unique network IP address and a range of addresses for host addressing. The customer has the option of assigning addresses in the host address part of the IP address.

IP Special Addresses

There are two forms of *special IP addressing*:

- Any 4-bit element of the address containing all zeros means "this" host.
- Any 4-bit element of the address containing all ones means "any" host.

Because 4-bit values of zero and 15 have special meaning, they are excluded from IP addressing. Therefore, any 4-bit element's maximum number of possible addresses is only 14.

Another special address is a network address of 127 in the left-most (network address) position, like 127.56.27.1. This indicates a loop-back address for testing and must not be used by devices or hosts on the network.

Finally, for those customers who really only want local TCP/IP and will never take their network out on the Internet, there are address ranges set aside for private use. They also have classes:

Class A	10.255.255.255
Class B	172.16.255.255 through 172.31.255.255
Class C	192.168.255.255 through 192.168.255.255

The decimal number 255 is special because it is an 8-bit field containing all 1s. It really means any address. So read the local addresses like this, "Class A private address has a 10 for its first address segment and can be followed by anything for its other three segments."

Masks

Masks are a way of referring to significant portions of the IP address through a mathematical filter. Let us apply a mask to what we know so far: The InterNIC supplies the network address; the customer, the host addresses. The boundary is variable, so the question is, "Which is which?"

The mathematical device is a *logical and* operation. Two-bit arrangements are stacked, and if either one of the operands is a 1, a 1 results. If both are zero, a zero results. Here is a sample:

1101 (13)
1001 (9)
1101 (13)

Another way to read that is 13 anded with 9 yields 13. Remember 255, our "any" address? Here is how that works:

1101 1001 (217)
1111 1111 (255)
1111 1111 (255)

Read this one that 217 (or any value) anded with 255 yields 255. Or read it this way, any 8-bit number anded with 255 yields 255. Or, again, 255 is your wildcard.

Once more, try anding with the other special IP address, zero or "this" address:

1101 1001 (217)
0000 0000 (0)
1111 1111 (217)

Read this one that 217 (or any value) anded with zero yields 217 (or the original value). Or, when a mask has a zero-bit, the original values come through.

Subnet Masks

When establishing a TCP/IP configuration, the ISP will supply both a host address and a *subnet mask*. This mask applies a series of ones and zeros to tell the Internet communications devices how to use addresses bound for your host. Start to build the subnet mask by assigning ones to all the network address bits. For an example, consider a Class B network (from the class table described above). Class B networks reserve 2 bytes or 16 bits for the network portion of the IP address.

A subnet mask for a Class B network would be 255.255. But we will not be finished until we have come up with the other 2 bytes of the mask. Here is a table of the network classes and the start of their subnet masks:

Class A	255
Class B	255.255
Class C	255.255.255

The problem of a finite number of addresses still exists within the host address, however. Many customers further divide the host address into two components:

```
<sub-network><host address>
```

There are no restrictions or rules on how to do this; you really do not need a subnetwork address at all. All addressable hosts could have a unique address, but what works for the Internet community at large also works for large companies.

One server can act as the "doorway" into the Internet, but many other servers can address their own local networks. A subnetwork, then, could be the designation of a router or host on the network. Then the host addresses could be a set of network end nodes each host supports. For example, an internal, secured network may have 100 AS/400 servers. The customer may anticipate some growth and allocate one full byte to identifying those servers as servers on the subnet. Then, if this were a Class B network, the remaining byte would be reserved for addressing the individual devices served by each AS/400. If another full byte were allocated to that, each AS/400 could service 254 devices directly.

When considering subnet and host addressing, there is no law that says you have to stick with even-byte boundaries. The IP host address portion is wide open. Typically, customers will designate the subnet portion of the host address with ones; the actual host addresses with zeros.

Consider our Class B example again. Remember, no matter what the customer decides, its subnet mask will start with 255.255. But a customer wants to describe a system as 254 servers each supporting 254 hosts. The customer will have a subnet mask of:

	255.255.255.1.1.1.1	Where each segment is:
255	network address byte 1	1111 1111
255	network address byte 2	1111 1111
255	Subnet Address—byte 3	1111.1111
0	Host addressing—byte 4	0000.0000

Another Class B customer has 10 AS/400s, each supporting thousands of end nodes. This customer doesn't have to stick with byte boundaries. It takes 4 bits to make a 10 (1010), so the customer may dedicate those 4 bits to the subnet address and the other 12 bits to host addresses. His subnet mask will look like this:

	255.255.240.1.1.1.1	Where each segment is:
255	IP network address byte 1	1111 1111
255	IP network address byte 2	1111.1111
240	Subnet address—first 4 bits of byte 3 (1111), plus Start of host addresses—second 4 bits of byte 3 (0000)	1111.0000
0	Remaining byte 4 for host Addressing	0000.0000

It is a common practice to set byte 4 of the subnet mask to either (00000000), 128 (10000000), or 240 (11110000). A subnet mask of 255.255.255.128 on a host with an IP address of 29.4.72.128 tells us two things:

- It will allow local host addresses of 29.4.72.129 through 29.4.72.254.
- If a packet came in with the address 29.4.72.132, it is destined for local host ID 4 (132 minus 128).

Internet addresses are not very intuitive. It is one thing to sweat through setting up one's own network; it is another to expect customers to remember them. To make accessing Internet addresses easy, use a *domain name*. This is usually the company name followed by .com (for example, ibm.com). Like addresses, domain names must be unique and are administered by InterNIC or ISP. If a company is planning to bring up an Internet site in the future, it can reserve a domain name now through InterNIC.

The Internet has name servers loaded with huge tables just to convert domain names into IP addresses. Internet-bound transmissions armed with only a domain name start by resolving the domain name to an absolute IP address before they even start.

TCP/IP Configuration

TCP/IP is a protocol that rides over other protocols as long as they are Ethernet, Token-Ring, DDI, or frame relay. The first things a shop needs, then, are the line, controller, and device supporting one of those protocols. Configure these the same way they were configured in the previous chapter.

The unusual TCP/IP addresses and domain names are a factor when adding the TCP/IP protocol. This protocol is added through an interface and a couple of address and name tables named after the non-TCP/IP lines are up.

For additional information about any of these commands or line types, refer to the appropriate section in this chapter:

- Create Line Description (Token-Ring).
- Create Line Description (Ethernet).
- Create Line Description (DDI).
- Create Line Description (Frame relay).

> **TIP:**
> System value QAUTOVRT has to have a value greater than zero or TCP/IP is not going to work.

Just make sure the SSAP parameter is filled in on the line description this way:

- If the line is Token-Ring, Ethernet IEEE 802.3, DDI, or wireless, X'AA' must be specified as an SSAP. This address can be added to the SSAP on an existing line.
- If the line is Ethernet V2, *ALL, or *SYSGEN, special SSAPs do not need to be configured—the system will include X'AA' automatically.

> **TIP:**
> You are going to have some users signing onto your system from the Internet through Telnet. For expected users, make sure their user IDs exist and are active on the system before you begin.

Configure a TCP/IP Interface

The AS/400 relies on the interface to identify its direct connection to TCP/IP. For other protocols, the line description is enough, but TCP/IP also works with host addressing so this interface connects the IP address and subnet mask with the line being used.

When TCP/IP is configured, the AS/400 automatically creates one interface record—the one that supports the loop-back. Use the Configure TCP/IP (CFGTCP) command and select option 1 (`Work with TCP/IP Interfaces`). This command will list all existing interfaces and, if this is tried immediately after the line is created with SSAP = "AA," you can see the single loop-back interface—its IP address will start with "127."

Configure other TCP/IP interfaces using the Add TCP/IP Interface (ADDTCPIFC) command or option 1 from the Configure TCP/IP (CFGTCP) command. Figure 19-39 shows a prompted version of the ADDTCPIFC command.

```
                     Add TCP/IP Interface (ADDTCPIFC)

Type choices, press Enter.

Internet address . . . . . . . . > '192.168.2.1'
Line description . . . . . . . . > ETHLINE       Name, *LOOPBACK, *VIRTUALIP
Subnet mask  . . . . . . . . . . > '255.255.255.0'
Associated local interface . . .   *NONE
Type of service  . . . . . . . .   *NORMAL       *MINDELAY, *MAXTHRPUT...
Maximum transmission unit  . . .   *LIND         576-16388, *LIND
Autostart  . . . . . . . . . . .   *YES          *YES, *NO
PVC logical channel identifier     ___           001-FFF
               + for more values   ___
X.25 idle circuit timeout  . . .   60            1-600
X.25 maximum virtual circuits  .   64            0-64
X.25 DDN interface . . . . . . .   *NO           *YES, *NO
TRLAN bit sequencing . . . . . .   *MSB          *MSB, *LSB



                                                                     Bottom
F3=Exit   F4=Prompt   F5=Refresh   F12=Cancel   F13=How to use this display
F24=More keys
```

Figure 19-39: Prompted version of command ADDTCPIFC.

Keep in mind what is going on: We are building an interface to other networks. This interface does not define all other hosts on the network. It should only define the address of the local AS/400.

Set TCP/IP Attributes

This step is optional and may be skipped when beginning to learn the AS/400 on the Internet. For the most part, the AS/400 defaults will work.

However, you may want to know that a TCP/IP connection can be tailored. It can be set to use Rapid Information Protocol (RIP) for faster packet routing or set up to allow forwarding of datagrams not addressed to the host. Do both of these with the Change TCP Attributes (CHGTCPA) command.

Add Routing Table Entries

Routing table entries can be optional but are considered required. They can be omitted only if the network is not going to attach to the Internet and the TCP/IP LAN being built will be a simple one. Otherwise, consider routing table entries required.

When connecting to the Internet, the actual connection from the AS/400's LAN out to the network is through a hardware device called an IP router, not the AS/400. Define at least a default route to this router.

Add routing table entries with the Add TCP Route (ADDTCPRTE) command. Figure 19-40 contains a prompted version of that command.

```
                        Add TCP/IP Route (ADDTCPRTE)

Type choices, press Enter.

Route destination . . . . . . . > *DFTROUTE
Subnet mask . . . . . . . . . . > *NONE
Type of service . . . . . . . .   *NORMAL      *MINDELAY, *MAXTHRPUT...
Next hop . . . . . . . . . . . . > '192.168.2.14'
Preferred binding interface . .   *NONE
Maximum transmission unit . . .   576          576-16388, *IFC
Route metric . . . . . . . . . .   1            1-16
Route redistribution . . . . . .   *NO          *NO, *YES
Duplicate route priority . . . .   5            1-10
```

Figure 19-40: Prompted version of the Add TCP/IP Route (ADDTCPRTE) command.

Note that, like the interface, the route table entry requires a subnet mask. The basic bits of information here are the route destination (the host address is the AS/400 to look for), the valid address range (determined by the subnet mask), and the destination (the next destination for the transmission). Next Hop may or may not be the final destination of the transmission.

Remote Domain Name Server

The typical way of communicating to stations on the Internet is by using domain names because they are a lot simpler to remember than IP addresses. Domain names are serviced by domain name servers, which support huge tables to convert domain names into IP addresses.

The AS/400 is more functional than most computers in that it has its own domain name server. But in reality, that server is not enough because it only holds the domain names for the local AS/400 hosts. Domain-to-address translation is fastest on this server, but most of the communications could be destined for hosts on the Internet and the AS/400 would have no knowledge of them.

Think of domain name servers, then, as two: A local one that resides on AS/400 and provides very fast address translation for the local LAN nodes. The other is a remote domain name server on the Internet that contains foreign domain names and IP addresses.

One of the services a good ISP provides is a remote domain name server. Subscribers to that ISP are provided with the server's IP address.

When configuring your AS/400 for Internet access, give it this address so it will know where to resolve remote domain names. Do so with the Configure TCP/IP (CFGTCP) command, and select option 13 (`Change Remote Name Server`) from its menu screen.

Enter the ISP-supplied IP address for its domain name server on the Server Address parameter.

Add Host Table Entries

Similar to the domain name servers and remote name servers that connect domains with IP addresses, the operator must specify an IP address-to-host name connection for the local AS/400 nodes. This is the *host name*, not the domain name. This connection is made through AS/400's Host Table Entry.

Add new entries with the Add TCP/IP Host Table Entry (ADDTCPHTE) command or option 10 from the Configure TCP/IP (CFGTCP) command. See Figure 19-41 for a prompted version of the ADDTCPHTE command.

```
                   Add TCP/IP Host Table Entry (ADDTCPHTE)

Type choices, press Enter.

Internet address . . . . . . . . > '192.168.2.1'
Host names:                        _
  Name . . . . . . . . . . . . . > TEST400.BIGCOMPANY.COM



  Name . . . . . . . . . . . . . > TEST400


               + for more values _
Text 'description' . . . . . . . > 'Two host names for one IP address'



                                                                  Bottom
F3=Exit   F4=Prompt   F5=Refresh   F12=Cancel   F13=How to use this display
F24=More keys
```

Figure 19-41: Add TCP/IP Host Table Entry (ADDTCPHTE).

Up to four local host names can be associated with each IP address. When a TCP/IP line description is created, it automatically creates a loop-back interface; it also automatically creates two local host names with that loop-back address. Those names are LOOPBACK and LOCALHOST.

Because the operator can define up to four local host names, it is common practice to give the host name in a couple of versions. If the host name is TEST400 and its domain is BIGCOMPANY.COM, define (as in Figure 19-41) two host names for its address:

- test400.bigcompany.com.
- test400.

After host table entries are added, they can be changed with the Change TCP/IP Host Table Entry (CHGTCPHTE) command. They can be removed with the Remove TCP/IP Host Table Entry (RMVTCPHTE) command.

Configure the Domain and Host Names

After the host name and IP address are associated as host table entries, associate the domain name with the host name. Use option 12 from the Configure TCP/IP (CFGTCP) menu or the Change TCP Domain (CHGTCPDMN) command. See Figure 19-42.

```
                    Change TCP/IP Domain (CHGTCPDMN)

Type choices, press Enter.

Host name . . . . . . . . . . . > TEST400

Domain name . . . . . . . . . . > TEST400.BIGCOMPANY.COM

Host name search priority . . . > *LOCAL      *REMOTE, *LOCAL, *SAME
Domain name server:
  Internet address . . . . . . . > '192.168.2.1'
                                  *SAME
                                  *SAME
```

Figure 19-42: Associate local domain name to local host name.

The example shown in Figure 19-42 uses the same host and domain name examples mentioned in the previous section.

If a datagram comes in with a domain name that does not match the one supplied, this table will help the system resolve the unknown name to a host. The Host Name Priority tells the system to look in the DNS first at a remote host or a local one. The Internet address parameter tells the system the Remote Internet Addresses of hosts that contain DNSs it can check.

TCP/IP CL COMMANDS

There are several CL commands to assist managing TCP/IP on the AS/400:

- TCP/IP must be started on the AS/400 before it will do anything. To start TCP/IP:
  - Type `GO TCPADM` on the command line and select option 3.
  - Issue the command STRTCP.
- To see if TCP/IP is even running, enter on a command line:
  - `WRKACTJOB SBS(QSYSWRK) JOB(QT*)`. Look for job QTCPIP being active.
- To end TCP/IP:
  - Type `GO TCPADM` on the command line and select option 4.
  - Issue the command ENDTCP.
- Messages from a TCP/IP session go to two queues:
  - The system operator queue (QSYSOPR). To display these messages, use the command:

    `DSPMSG QSYSOPR`
  - Its own queue (QTCP). To display these messages, use the command:

    `DSPMSG QTCP`
  - Sometimes messages can be hard to find or nondescriptive when they are found. In those cases, refer to the TCP/IP job log with the command:

    `WRKSPLF   QTCP`
- One function common to all TCP/IP sites is the PING function. It is used to verify that a connection exists between two TCP/IP nodes. Ping a remote system by system name or IP address with the commands:

```
PING RMTSYS(TEST400)
PING '192.168.2.1'
```

Check if the ping was successful (meaning the other nodes are connected) by checking messages in the job log. From the command line, use the Display Job Log (DSPJOBLOG) command.

- To perform many TCP/IP network functions, use the Work with TCP/IP Status (WRKTCPSTS) command and follow the menu.
- To perform many TCP/IP configuration functions, use the Configure TCP/IP (CFGTCP) command.

TCP/IP APPLICATIONS

TCP/IP is more than a communication protocol. It is that, but once the software is up on the computer, it provides a suite of functionality beyond communication protocol support. These additional applications are:

- Telnet (terminal emulation).
- FTP (file transfer).
- SMTP (mail interface).
- POP server (mail interface).
- REXEC server (command execution from a client).
- LPR/LPD (send and receive print files within a network).
- SNMP (network management).
- Workstation gateway (WSG) (automatic screen conversion into HTML).
- OS/400 TCP/IP functions (miscellaneous but neat TCP/IP stuff).

Note that there is not a standard for which functions other computers' TCP/IP offer. These are the AS/400's only; other computers may not offer all of them.

Telnet

Teletypewriter network (Telnet) is about as old and simple a protocol as you can get without getting into punched cards. But it is far from obsolete and, in some ways, it is far from simple. It is a great way to communicate to any computer from any computer. The AS/400 can be a client or server in a Telnet session.

With Telnet, a workstation could have equal access to an AS/400 or a UNIX machine without investing in and loading various terminal emulation packages. For quick remote access of computers on a heterogeneous network, Telnet cannot be beat. The terminal emulations Telnet provides are:

- 3270 (for mainframes).
- 5250.
- VT100.
- VT200.

5250 and VT100 in one program? That's right, and the downfall of Telnet (at least for a lot of serious work) is that things do not always flow very smoothly. VT100 is an asynchronous ASCII protocol, and 5250 is a bisynchronous EBCDIC. Every key pressed in a VT100 session sends a character to the host; where in a 5250 session, nothing goes to the host until the Enter key is pressed. Also, VT100s will not support any more than four function keys, while 5250 supports twenty-four.

Hats off to IBM for enhancing such a low-level application to the point that it supports the high- to low-end range of the terminals, but there must have been a lot of concessions that went into the emulation.

Configuring the AS/400 as a Telnet Client

With the AS/400 configured as a Telnet client, a user signed onto an AS/400 through TCP/IP can dial up another host (running TCP/IP and Telnet server) and act as a workstation on that computer.

Start a Telnet session with the Start TCP/IP Telnet (STRTCPTELN) command in one of these two formats:

- The easiest way to refer to the remote system is by its domain name:

```
STRTCPTELN <name of remote system>
```

- But the remote system's actual IP address can also be used:

```
STRTCPTELN *INTNETADR <IP address of remote system>
```

That is all there is to starting an AS/400 as a Telnet client. With the AS/400 as a server, as soon as the user signs off the remote system, Telnet ends.

Configuring the AS/400 as a Telnet Server

Ensure the AS/400 can support 5250 full-screen sessions by configuring Telnet with the Configure TCP/IP Telnet (CFGTCPTELN) command. It presents a menu, select option 1 (`Change Telnet Attributes`) from that menu. Or use the Change Telnet Attributes (CHGTELNA) command directly.

Telnet provides relatively free AS/400 access to the public—anyone with even an obsolete PC and modem can access the AS/400. Because of this free access, the wise system operator will think about security.

Carrying a Security Level 30 on an AS/400 (through the value of thirty on system value QSECURITY) restricts security officer access only through devices that have been specially allowed for that access.

Another security step to consider is to limit the security officer with the QLMTSECOFR system value. Set this to 1, and no security officer will be able to use the virtual devices configured by Telnet.

A final security issue to take care of is to set two time-out values within Telnet. Change these both with the Change Telnet Attributes (CHGTELNA) command. The parameters and what they do are:

- Telnet Inactivity Time-out Value. This value states how long a Telnet session can be inactive (the user presses no keys) before the system will sign the user off normally. "Normally" means taking the user off the system in the same way as it would if the user had requested to log off.

- Telnet Timemark Time-out Value: This value states how long a Telnet session can be active if it does not respond to the host's timemark. This is behind the scenes and does not affect the user. The AS/400 sends a timemark command to the Telnet workstation. If it does not receive an answer within that many seconds, it will assume the connection has broken and normally sign the user off.

Telnet devices must be known to an interactive subsystem. To check the workstations a subsystem will support, use the Display Subsystem Description (DSPSBSD) command and look at the Workstation Entries (WSE). To add Telnet workstations, use the Add Workstation Entries (ADDWSE) command:

```
ADDWSE SBSD(QINTER) WRKSTNTYPE(*ALL)
```

The QSYSWRK subsystem must be active. Use the Work with Active Jobs (WRKACTJOB) command and look for it. If it is not listed, enter on the command line:

```
STRSBS QSYSWRK
```

Be sure to create user profiles and passwords for the users who will be signing on through Telnet (if they do not already have AS/400 access).

To end the Telnet session on an AS/400 Telnet server, press the Attention (ATTN) key and take option 99 (End Telnet Session). The AS/400 Telnet server will not end automatically when a client signs off.

FTP

File transfer protocol (FTP) moves files and programs quickly from one system to another. It usually works well for moving large files between systems.

FTP features automatic data type conversion; from ASCII to EBCDIC or vice versa, as the need arises. It also treats files as a stream of bits, not as fields or records. For this reason, plan to unpack all packed numeric fields before using FTP.

FTP is often used to transfer data between AS/400s; just specify that no translation is to happen during the transfer, and numeric data will not have to be unpacked. Files can be sent with FTP interactively or scheduled to run in batch.

FTP sessions tend to be short, consisting of starting the session, moving a file or two, then ending the session. Once in the session, the work is done through FTP-specific commands referred to as *subcommands.* We will go over accessing the AS/400 as an FTP client and server, then present an overview of several of the subcommands.

In FTP, the difference between what is a client and what is a server is usually based on this simple rule: The computer making the request is the client; the other is the server. It makes no difference where the data is actually stored.

Only DB2/400 supports files with members, although files can be copied from another host into an AS/400 file member. When an attempt is made to copy a file member to a host other than the AS/400, FTP will create a new file consisting solely of that member.

FTP is built to move file data efficiently between hosts. The AS/400 can send or receive only a member of a file. Nobody can select (or omit) records from a file in any case; only all records within a file or member can be sent.

The AS/400 supports file-naming conventions beyond its traditional library/file. When referring to files in FTP, there is the option of using the traditional form or the UNIX form, with a path of subdirectories prefixing the name. We do not have to do anything special—either can be used at will. However, be aware that the AS/400 refers to library/file.member as NAMEFMT 0 and the other as NAMEFMT 1. Here are examples of each:

`library/file.member`	NAMEFMT 0
`/QSYS.LIB/libname.LIB/filename.FILE/mbrname.mbr`	NAMEFMT 1

In the text that follows, file name formats for source and target can be mixed. In other words, to copy an AS/400-based file to a non-AS/400-based file, use NAMEFMT 0 for the source, and NAMEFMT 1 for the target on the GET/PUT subcommand parameters.

Although the target parameter is optional on the GET and PUT commands, make it a point of using this to specify the target file names. If the target is not specified, the system will attempt to name the file, and when going from dissimilar hosts, this can get unpredictable.

When sending a file to an AS/400, precreate the file on the AS/400. Just make sure the file length is correct (use the Size parameter of the Create Physical File [(CRTPF)] command). Also, ensure the file can accommodate the records that are going to be sent to it. We prefer to use the MAXSTG(*NOMAX) parameter of the CRTPF command.

When accessing the AS/400 through an FTP session, the Initial Program (INLPGM) named in the user profile does not get invoked. One primary purpose of this program is to preset library lists, so be aware that the signing-on users' library lists may not be set correctly.

Configuring the AS/400 as an FTP Client

Start an FTP client session from an AS/400 workstation with either the Start TCP/IP File Transfer Protocol (STRTCPFTP) command or by entering FTP on the command line. There is only one command involved, STRTCPFTP; FTP is simply another way to invoke it. Figure 19-43 contains a prompted version of that command.

This command is similar to the STRTCPTELN that started a Telnet session in that the operator can either enter the remote system's name or its IP address. If the IP address is used, the operator does not have to enter the *INTNETADR parameter as on the other command

This command is significantly different, however (and different from most other AS/400 commands); we really have to watch the value we enter for the Coded Character Set Identifier (CCSID) parameter. You see, FTP moves files from one computer to the other. It is almost always translating ASCII to EBCDIC, or vice versa. The CCSID parameter on this command sets the default data type value when the FTP TYPE subcommand is used.

```
                     Start TCP/IP File Transfer (STRTCPFTP)

Type choices, press Enter.

Remote system  . . . . . . . . . > TEST400



Coded character set identifier     *DFT          1-65533, *DFT

                               Additional Parameters

Outgoing EBCDIC/ASCII table  . .   *CCSID        Name, *CCSID, *DFT
  Library  . . . . . . . . . . .     ________    Name, *LIBL, *CURLIB
Incoming ASCII/EBCDIC table  . .   *CCSID            Name, *LIBL, *CURLIB
  Library  . . . . . . . . . . .     ________    Name, *LIBL, *CURLIB



                                                                     Bottom
F3=Exit   F4=Prompt   F5=Refresh   F12=Cancel   F13=How to use this display
F24=More keys
```

Figure 19-43: Prompted version of the STRTCPFTP command.

Most normal ASCII data types will work when CCSID is set to 819—that will work most of the time on AS/400s. If it does not, try 850.

After typing the command and pressing the Enter key, the FTP session is started. The session will appear a little weird because the AS/400 workstation attempts to emulate the ASCII asynchronous mode that FTP would normally run on. That is, everything is a line at a time. The normal AS/400 full data screen will not appear. If the FTP application wants to know something, it will ask a simple question, and the user should answer it on the command line. Both question and answer will roll up to the first available line on the screen. If no question has been asked but the user wants to initiate something, the subcommand and its parameter(s) should be typed on the command line. The command will roll up into the upper part of the screen and the results of the command (successful or not) follow it.

Configuring the AS/400 as an FTP Server

The good news here is that the FTP server is normally automatically started when TCP is started. If, for some reason, TCP is up and the FTP server is not (FTP AUTOSTART may be set to *NO within TCP), it can be started on the command line with the Start FTP Server (STRFTPSVR) command.

The FTP server only runs in the QSYSWRK subsystem. The FTP server job names within the subsystem are *QTFTPnnnnn*, where *nnnnn* is the job number of the particular FTP server job.

The best thing about the AS/400 as an FTP server is that it can simultaneously support up to twenty FTP servers on the same AS/400. This is nice for a company that distributes free services along with pay-for software; it can have an FTP server that does not require logon for the free services. At the same time, it can have another FTP server that requires a logon for the pay-for materials.

To set the number of FTP servers the AS/400 will support, use the Change FTP Attributes (CHGFTPA) command and set the NBRSVR parameter to any number from 1 through 20.

Sample FTP Subcommands

There are approximately fifty FTP subcommands. We will only mention the more popular ones. Logically enough, both client and server do not share the same set of subcommands. Some of the subcommands they do share are slightly different for each.

Figure 19-44 lists the client and server versions of the subcommands. For more information, refer to sections titled FTP Subcommands and FTP Server Subcommands of the IBM manual *OS/400 TCP/IP Configuration and Reference V4R3*.

Client Subcommand	Description	Server Subcommand
?	Get general help	
	Add physical file member	ADDM
	Add physical file variable length member	ADDV
APPEND	Append a local file member to a remote file.	APPE
ASCII	Local file types become ASCII.	
BINARY	Local file types become BINARY.	
CD	Change Directory.	
	Create Library.	CRTL
	Create Physical File.	CRTP
	Create Source Physical File.	CRTS
DELETE	Delete a file on the remote system.	DELE
	Delete File.	DLTF
	Delete Library.	DLTL
EBCDIC	Local file types become EBCDIC.	
GET	Copy a file from the remote to the local system.	
HELP	Get specific help on an FTP command.	HELP
LTYPE	Local data type.	
MDELETE	Delete multiple files on the remote system.	
MGET	Copy multiple files from the remote to the local system.	
MKDIR	Make a directory.	MKD
MODE	Set transmission mode.	MODE

Figure 19-44: Client and server versions of the subcommands (part 1 of 2).

Client Subcommand	Description	Server Subcommand
MPUT	Copy multiple files from the local to the remote system.	
PASS	Enter your password.	PASS
PUT	Copy a file from the local to the remote system.	
PWD	Display current directory, folder, or library.	PWD
QUIT	Disconnect and end the FTP session.	QUIT
QUOTE	Pass a server subcommand to a server from a client.	
RMDIR	Remove a directory.	RMD
SUNIQUE	This is only in effect when the target computer is an AS/400. When the target file member is specified and it exists, this command toggles the option: <on> The existing member is replaced. <off> A new member is created with a sequential numeric suffix to make it unique.	
SYSCMD	Pass an AS/400 system command (not a server subcommand) to the remote AS/400.	
TYPE	Set the data transfer type.	TYPE
USER	Enter your user ID.	USER

Figure 19-44: Client and server versions of the subcommands (part 2 ov 2).

A Sample Interactive FTP Session

Start the session from a workstation with the commands mentioned in the section titled Configuring the AS/400 as an FTP Server. Sign on to the remote system with a user ID and password. If that system takes the lead and asks for each piece of the sign on, just follow along; if not, type in the subcommands:

```
===>  USER <your user id>
```

Wait for a response, then type:

```
===>  PASSWORD <your password>
```

Wait for a response indicating a successful login. It will look like this:

```
===>  <your user id> logged on
```

We will assume the user would know the name and type of file to transfer. ASCII is the default type for FTP files. For the file coming in to be converted to EBCDIC, type EBCDIC and press the Enter key to change the document. If the file is to be in binary or if no translation is required, type BINARY and press the Enter key.

Change to the directory you want on the remote computer with the subcommand:

```
CD <directory name>
```

To copy files, use the sunique subcommand to toggle how existing members are to be handled. When the session starts, the default is that SUNIQUE is off. Do not do anything if the existing file members are to be replaced when copied file members have the same name. If the file should have unique file members at all times, toggle this condition with the command:

```
SUNIQUE
```

On the other hand, the (REPLACE) option on the GET, PUT, MGET, and MPUT commands will dictate that similarly named file members are replaced.

To get a file from the remote system, type:

```
GET <file name> <file name> (replace)
  Remote      Local
  Optional     Optional
```

Either file (remote or local) can be qualified with the library and forward slashes, or with periods and extensions as suffixes. File names should follow the convention of the file system in which they reside. Here are two examples:

- `GET /QDLS/MYLIB/PROGRAM.EXE`

  This command is for files that do not reside in the AS/400 library file system.

- `GET MASTLIBR/MASTFILE.MEMBXX`

  This command is for files that do reside in the AS/400 library file system. In this example, the suffix set off with a period determines the file member to get.

The REPLACE parameter is optional and, if specified, causes the new data to write over the old.

Files can be moved from the local system to the remote system with the PUT subcommand. Here is its format:

```
PUT <file name> <file name>
  Local       Remote
              Optional
```

The file name rules that applied to GET, apply to PUT.

To GET or PUT several files using generic naming, use the MGET and MPUT subcommands. The structure of these subcommands is the same as GET and PUT.

End the session with the QUIT subcommand. There are no additional parameters.

A Sample Batch FTP Session

An FTP session in batch mode can be run unattended in the middle of the night to transfer large files. The key is a compiled CL program (CLP) that will schedule to run, and another CL source physical file member that contains the FTP session commands. (As system operator, you may or may not have access to the source editor, PDM, or the CLP compiler. CL programming is also beyond the scope of this book. The source codes are presented as helpful examples only.

Depending on your shop, you may have to give them to a programmer to have them compiled into a useful program.) Here is a sample of the first program:

```
PGM
OVRDBF INPUT TOFILE(<libr name>/QCLSRC) MBR(GOFTP)
OVRDBR OUTPUT TOFILE(<libr name>/QCLSRC) MBR(FTPERR)
  FTP    RMTSYS
ENDPGM
```

FTP is an application program with an input file named INPUT and an output file for session messages named OUTPUT. This simple CLP overrides file input, so it will take its subcommands from a source physical file member named GOFTP, located in <LIBR NAME>/QCLSRC. Also, all session messages, instead of going to a screen, will be directed into a file named FTPERR located in <LIBR NAME>/QCLSRC (as directed in the example override to the output file).

The input file, GOFTP, will contain all the commands to be used during an interactive session. Here is a sample of that file and what it could contain:

```
PGM
  USER <your user profile on the remote system>
  PASS <your password on the remote system>
  CD RMTMSTLIB
  GET MASTFILE LCLLIB/RMTMSTF
ENDPGM
```

After this has run in batch, display the contents of file FTPERR to see all messages that were issued during the session.

SMTP

Simple Mail Transfer Protocol (*SMTP*) is used to route email between different systems. The AS/400 uses SNADS (refer to chapter 18, SNA Distribution Services section) to route mail to and from SMTP; the AS/400 can be used as a gateway to other networks.

SMTP starts automatically when TCP/IP is started. If this is not to be used, disable the automatic starting with this command:

```
CHGSMTPA  AUTOSTART(*NO)
```

Change it back at any time with the same command but substitute *YES for *NO.

If TCP/IP is running with SMTP disabled and you want to bring it up, do so manually by typing on any command line:

```
STRTCPSVR *SMTP
```

Although SMTP is a routing protocol, it can send and receive SMTP individual mail through a client-based browser or OfficeVision/400. It will also send/receive SMTP mail by using the command line on the green-screen, but that is quite a chore.

If you are wondering if SMTP is up on your system, do a Work with Active Jobs (WRKACTJOB) command and look for four jobs that make up SMTP:

- QTSMTPSRVR (Server).
- QTSMTPCLNT (Client).
- QTSMTPBRSR (Bridge server).
- QTSMTPBRCL (Bridge client).

All four should be present if SMTP is up.

Configuring SMTP

If SMTP autostart in TCP is still in effect when TCP starts on the AS/400, SMTP will start with it. It will configure itself the first time.

This configuration's status can be checked by looking at the QSYSWRK subsystem. This is the only subsystem TCP/IP runs in. First, use the Display Subsystem Description (DSPSBSD) command, then select option 7 to display routing entries. Look for a routing entry with compare value of SMTPROUT.

Frankly, there is a way to manually configure SMTP, but it is unnecessary work. Change the TCP/IP command so SMTP will come up automatically with this command:

```
CHGSMTPA AUTOSTART(*YES)
```

Then start TCP/IP and it will configure SMTP. Turn off autostart afterward with the same command—just change *YES to *NO.

Whether SMTP was started automatically or not, the operator still has some things to do to configure an SMTP server. These are:

- Update the system distribution directory.
- Update SMTP aliases.
- Configure SMTP to use a domain name server.

Update the System Distribution Directory

The *system distribution directory* names the user to who mail will be sent and what system that user is located on, along with its address and name. To work with the system distribution directory, type the command:

```
WRKDIRE
```

Because SMTP routes mail between systems, its system directory entries pertain to system-to-system information. Individual users are not listed. We will add users in the section about POP3 Server.

From the WRKDIRE screen, place a 1 on the option line and press the Enter key. The command will present a screen similar to the one shown in Figure 19-45.

```
                         Add Directory Entry

 Type choices, press Enter.

   User ID/Address . . . .   *ANY      TEST400
   Description . . . . . .   TCP Remote System
   System name/Group . . .   TEST400   ________      F4 for list
   User profile  . . . . .   ________                F4 for list
   Network user ID . . . .   ______________________________________________

   Name:
     Last  . . . . . . . .   ______________________________________________
     First . . . . . . . .   __________________
     Middle  . . . . . . .   __________________
     Preferred . . . . . .   __________________
     Full  . . . . . . . .   ______________________________________________

   Department  . . . . . .   __________             F4 for list
   Job title . . . . . . .   ____________________________________
   Company . . . . . . . .   ______________________________________________
                                                                    More...
 F3=Exit   F4=Prompt   F5=Refresh   F12=Cancel   F18=Display location details
 F19=Add name for SMTP
```

Figure 19-45: Screen to add a directory entry.

Although the operator could name each user on each remote system, use *ANY for the user name, meaning all mail destined for the remote address will just be delivered to the system—that system can determine the deliverability of the user ID.

Optionally, use *ANY for one of the systems on the list. This creates a system that receives all unknown (destination system unknown) mail. Remember two things:

- When setting up a remote user on a non-IBM platform that supports upper- and lowercase letters for user profiles, this approach causes user profile names to fall under SNAD's rules which only passes uppercase letters.
- Never use user ID *ANY and a host name the same as your local host name. The system will try to work and the results will be unpredictable.

Be careful of using *ANY for the user profile and for the remote system address. It is a common way of providing routing for undeliverable mail, but this could set things up for a route-loop condition (messages go round and round the network forever). Here is what to do to avoid this problem (and still have *ANY *ANY for undeliverable mail):

- The system that is supposed to resolve undeliverable mail should not have an *ANY *ANY routing. (Remember, the System Distribution Directory entry will still have a system name and that will determine the system that gets this mail.)

Finally, there are two things to be wary about with the System Configuration Directory. One, this figure is of the System Distribution Directory on a local AS/400. It is nice that we can get by with just forwarding all users to the remote system (thanks to the *ANY user ID), but the System Distribution Directory on the remote system must identify all of its users. Two, the System Name/Group field shows the local name. This name must agree with the name on the system distribution routing entries. This system distribution routing entry is set up automatically the first time SMTP starts. To find out what the name is, use the Display Distribution Services (DSPDSTSRV) command with a parameter 2:

```
DSPDSTSRV 2
```

This command will produce a screen similar to the example shown in Figure 19-46.

```
                              Display Routing Table

Type options, press Enter.
  5=Display details

     ---System---
Opt  Name      Group    Description
 _   NOTHERE            Not Here
 _   RCHAS260           Gateway to RCHAS260
 _   TCPIP              TCP/IP Routing
```

Figure 19-46: System Distribution Routing Entries.

The correct name is the first one, with the Destination System Name/Group parameter. In this case, TCPIP (usually the generated name).

One thing that is new with the WRKDIRE entry is the Rename option, invoked with command key 7. Formerly, the only way to rename an existing entry was to delete it and re-add it. Now any directory entry can be renamed.

One of SMTP's strengths is mail routing, and we will see next how to describe a route for an individual. One thing that is kind of nice is that an alternate mail router can be defined to receive messages the AS/400 cannot figure out what to do with. To name this router, use the Change SMTP Attributes (CHGSMTPA) command and the MAILROUTER parameter. Here is a sample:

```
CHGSMPTA MAILROUTER(MAIL400.IBM.COM)
```

Update SMTP Name Table

The *SMTP name table* contains an AS/400 user ID and address (the system name) and an SMTP name and domain. Because the table makes a match between a very long SMTP and a "normal" AS/400 name, it is often called the "alias" table. This table is required whenever aliases are desired—this would be when:

- The AS/400 needs to distribute mail from non-AS/400 hosts where user profiles may be otherwise too long or contain embedded special characters. An SMTP name consists of two components:
  - User ID—up to 24 characters.
  - Domain—up to 255 characters.

  The user ID combined with the domain make up the SMTP name, which cannot be longer than 255 characters.

- A host's SMTP name is shorter than its SNADS host name. A typical SNADS host name may be MDAWSON RMTSYS while the SMTP name may be mike.
- If a specific routing (referred to as SMTP relay) needs to be specified, this is done on the alias.

Although those are the rules, the convention is to routinely set up aliases. To set up an alias table, use the Work with Names for SMTP (WRKNAMSMTP) command. From that screen, select option 1 to add a name, or 2 to change a name. Figure 19-47 contains a sample of the resulting screen.

```
                          Add Name for SMTP
                                                        System:   BIGBLUE
 Type choices, press Enter.

   User ID . . . . . . . . .   MIKE       Character value, *ANY, F4 for list
   Address . . . . . . . . .   TEST400    Character value, F4 for list



   SMTP user ID  . . . . . .   MDAWSON
   SMTP domain . . . . . . .   TEST400.BIGCOMPANY.COM



   SMTP route  . . . . . . .   @MINOT,@DENVER,MDAWSON@TEST400.BIGCOMPANY.COM
```

Figure 19-47: Adding a name for SMTP.

The screen in the figure does several things. The User ID and Address are those of the remote, not the local, host. These are shorter fields than the SMTP User ID and domain because they are SNADS names, not SMTP. As such, they must also be in capital letters. Both must be filled in. In mail distribution, they are combined to form a "TO" address. When SMTP receives mail from a remote host, this address is parsed into a local user ID and host name (which should match the local name or the mail will be forwarded).

The first two parameters make the SNADS name; the next two combined make the SMTP name. Notice how much larger the SMTP name can be than the SNADS name. If the user ID on a local host contains *ANY, then SMTP User ID must be left blank.

Although the SMTP domain name is just that, a domain name like COMPANY.COM, for AS/400s, the system name should be concatenated on the front. If the system name is TCPIP, the SMTP domain name becomes TCPIP.COMPANY.COM.

In either case, the SMTP name must also be defined in a host table or name server so the router can find an Internet address to associate with it.

We said our AS/400 name was MIKE and our address was TEST400. My SMTP ID is MDAWSON and my SMTP Domain is TCPIP.COMPANY.COM. The two of those concatenated together make the SMTP name:

```
MDAWSON@TCPIP.COMPANY.COM.
```

We also specified the route for our messages, although we did not have to. We may have wanted to skip the SMTP user and domain names and just specify our own route. In this case, maybe we are a part of a large network and want a specific route to be used when routing mail. In the figure, mail will come from a host named @MINOT, then a host named @DENVER, finally to the local host named @TEST400, and to user MDAWSON on domain COMPANY.COM. That is how remote stations with mail addressed to MIKE in PHOENIX will route the mail to a particular user. Note the construction: hosts are preceded with an at sign (@), hosts are separated from each other by a comma (,), finally, the destination name is preceded by a host name (and itself preceded with an at sign), followed by a colon (:) and the full, concatenated SMTP name.

By the way, it is a good idea to use the AS/400 user profile (refer to chapter 5) as the SMTP User ID.

This is another screen where *ANY is a valid entry for the User ID field. If *ANY is used, the SMTP User ID field should be left blank.

Configure SMTP to Use a Domain Name Server

When TCP/IP was configured on an AS/400, the operator may have included a domain name server on it. If he/she did, that is the local domain name server and the default where SMTP will go to resolve unknown names and IP addresses.

An AS/400 can only have a domain name server with local (to it and its LANs) names and IP addresses. It will not support an Internet-level domain name server. The ISP will offer that service. The domain name server on an AS/400 with its local names is referred to as the *local domain name server*. The one out on the ISP is the *remote domain name server*. The AS/400 can only be a local domain server, but it can access both.

To direct SMTP to a network-resident domain server, use the Change TCP/IP Domain (CHGTCPDMN) command. Figure 19-48 contains a sample of that screen.

```
                     Change TCP/IP Domain (CHGTCPDMN)

Type choices, press Enter.

Host name . . . . . . . . . . .   TEST400

Domain name . . . . . . . . . .   BIGCOMPANY.COM


Host name search priority . . .   *REMOTE       *REMOTE, *LOCAL, *SAME
Domain name server:
  Internet address . . . . . . .   '9.1.2.60'
                                   *SAME
                                   *SAME
```

Figure 19-48: Directing SMTP to use a remote (not local) domain name server.

The *host name search priority* tells the AS/400 which domain name server to use first when resolving domain names into IP addresses. *LOCAL (the default) will have the AS/400 access its own domain name server first; *REMOTE sends it to the ISPs first.

POP3 Server

The AS/400's TCP/IP support is for Version 3 of the *Post office protocol (POP)* standard. This allows the AS/400 to serve as a POP server for any client running POP mail on Windows, OS/2, AIX, and Macintosh.

While SMTP can receive users' mail, more typically you see SMTP routing mail, and POP providing electronic mailboxes on the local host from which users can retrieve mail.

The AS/400's POP support includes support for *Multipurpose Internet Mail Extension (MIME)*. This allows transmission of video, image, audio, binary, and text mail.

To support POP, the AS/400 has to have several things running but, for anyone serious about maintaining an Internet presence, SMTP and POP together make the mail standard.

POP itself does not have anything to do with SNADS or SMTP directly, but the AS/400 exchanges POP through the AnyMail/400 mail server framework. AnyMail/400 runs over SNADS and SMTP, so they must be up when POP is running. That means that to support POP mail, the AS/400 must have up:

- SNADS.
- AnyMail/400.
- TCP/IP.
- SMTP.
- POP.

Clients accessing POP can be local workstations with any flavor TCP/IP support or AS/400 Client Access Express for Windows with *messaging application program interface (MAPI)* on their client. The biggest difference between the two is that the standard TCP/IP client sends its mail to SMTP first, and SMTP routes it either away from the local host or to the POP server (for local mail). The AS/400 Client Access workstations send their mail directly to the POP server for either local delivery or routing to SMTP and external routing from there.

The key to all this working is our friend, the System Distribution Directory.

Bringing up the POP Server

The sequence to bringing up a POP server is:

- Ensure SNADS is up. It is its own subsystem so use Work with Active Jobs (WRKACTJOB) and look for subsystem QSNADS to be there. If it is not, start it with the Start Subsystem (STRSBS) command:

  ```
  STRSBS QSNADS
  ```

- Ensure the Mail Server Framework (MSF) is up. Use Work with Active Jobs (WRKACTJOB) and look for subsystem QSYSWRK to be active with job(s) named QMSF running under it. If there are no such jobs, start one with the Start Mail Framework (STRMSF) command:

  ```
  STRMSF
  ```

- If the clients connecting to the system are AS/400 Client Access and they are to connect to the POP server through IPX, make sure IPX is running.

- If the clients connecting to the system are AS/400 Client Access, issue the Start Host Server (STRHOSTSVR) command:

```
STRHOSTSVR *ALL
```

- Ensure SMTP is up. If it is not, start it. Refer to the section on Update the System Distribution Directory for more information.
- Ensure you have System Distribution Directories set up. Refer to the section on SMTP for basic information. For POP, though, we need a couple specific things:
  - An AS/400 system user profile for each local POP user.
  - The Mail Service Level parameter of each System Distribution Directory entry must be set to a 2 and the Preferred Address parameter set to:
    - 3 if you are using SMTP names.
    - 1 if you are using SNADS without a TCP/IP connection at all.
    - If you are using SMTP addressing (and have set the Preferred Address to 3), press F19 from the Work with Directory Entries (WRKDIRE) (Figure 19-6), and enter the SMTP name. Remember to name all local users but specify *ANY for remote systems' users. Also, for the local users, make their AS/400 User ID the SMTP User ID. For more information, refer to the section on SMTP.
- Ensure the connection is correctly specified in the POP application. Use the Change POP Attributes (CHGPOPA) command and check the Host Server Connection (HOSTSVRCNN) parameter. If any parameters are changed on the CHGPOPA command, the mail server should be ended and restarted (refer to the next bullet).
- Start the POP Server with the Start Mail Server Framework (STRMSF) command. End it with the End Mail Server Framework (ENDMSF) command.

POP Server Commands

POP clients have their own set of verbs to communicate with POP servers. Figure 19-49 lists them.

Verb <parameters>	Description
USER <user id>	Send the user ID.
PASS <password>	Send the password.
STAT	Check mailbox ("status").
LIST <msg # (optional)>	Check mail message statistics.
RETR <msg #>	Retrieve message.
DELE <msg #>	Delete message.
RSET	Reset message delete status.
TOP <msg #><lines>	Retrieve message header and data.
UIDL <msg # (optional)>	Get message unique ID listing.
NOOP	No operation.
QUIT	Quit client session.

Figure 19-49: Verbs for POP clients.

Bringing up the POP Client

Because a workstation can use any browser to bring up POP, the specifics of this will vary. If a workstation client is Client Access for Windows, the operator does not have to do anything. Otherwise, the operator will have to do the following:

- Give the client the User ID and Host Name of the person that will be the mail recipient. These probably will be entered separately through a GUI interface. If they are entered together as a string, put an @ sign between the two. Also:
  - The user ID will be the same as the AS/400 user ID.
  - The host name will be the system name concatenated with a period and the domain name. For example, if the domain name is COMPANY.COM and the system name is TEST400, the host name will be:

    ```
    TEST400.COMPANY.COM.
    ```
- On some clients, you will have to put in the host's IP address several times. Do not complain; just type away.
- The POP User (sometimes called the Account Name) should be the AS/400 user ID.
- The password must be the AS/400 password. (See why we have been using the AS/400 user ID?)

REXEC

The *Remote Executive (REXEC)* server allows any client to submit a system command to the AS/400. Embedded in that system command are the user's ID and password so the AS/400 can go through all its normal authorization approvals before executing the command.

Note that the commands that REXEC can submit must be capable of running in batch. Commands contain information on where they are allowed to run and one of these values must be *BATCH. To check, use the Display Object (DSPOBJ) command on any command.

Bringing up the REXEC Server

The REXEC server will start automatically when TCP is started unless you have disabled it. If you have disabled it or it is not running for any reason, you can start it with the Start TCP/IP Server (STRTCPSVR) command with the Server parameter set to *REXEC, as follows:

```
STRTCPSVR SERVER(*REXEC)
```

Start the REXEC server even if it is already started. This will cause the system to start another server. To find out if a REXEC server is running, its jobs will be in the QSYSWRK subsystem. Each server will be named *QTRXCnnnn*, where *nnnnn* is a unique five-digit number. To look at the subsystem, use the Work with Subsystem Jobs (WRKSBSJOB) with the subsystem specified or the Work with Active Jobs (WRKACTJOB) command:

```
WRKSBSJOB QSYSWRK
```

or

```
WRKACTJOB
```

To change the Autostart parameter (or others), use the Change REXEC Attributes (CHGRXCA) command.

Specify the End TCP/IP Server (ENDTCPSVR) command with the server attribute set to *REXEC, as follows:

```
ENDTCPSVR SERVER(*REXEC)
```

REXEC Client

REXEC clients use the Run Remote Command (RUNRMTCMD) command to send commands to the server. When connecting to an AS/400, the clients have one return connection; when connecting to UNIX, OS/2, Windows 95, or Windows NT, REXEC clients have two return connections.

What this means to you is that any printed output from the REXEC-submitted command will be sent back to the requesting client—that is one communication connection. Any error spool file will be sent back down the second connection if there is one; if there is only one, it will be sent over the first connection immediately after the command's output.

LPR/LPD

Line Printer Requester (*LPR*) and *Line Printer Daemon* (*LPD*) are used to send/receive print files around a network. LPR sends print files to remote systems including to LAN-attached printers. The AS/400 supports advanced printer graphics through Advanced Function Printer Definition System (AFPDS). These output files can be sent through LPR, however, some print transformation may lose some of the clever AFPDS effects.

LPD receives print files from remote systems. It will not convert ASCII print files, although it will receive them. The process that results from the combination LPR/LPD is referred to as *printer pass-through*.

LPR Configuration

LPR attempts to use the host and domain server names. It does not have to, but life would be better if these were configured when TCP/IP was configured on the AS/400. It also requires the names of remote systems to which it will be sending print files. Again, it can use the raw IP address, but the smart AS/400 person will have remote systems named in the host table so he/she can use either the host or domain name when sending spool files.

To configure printer pass-through using LPR, first configure a remote output queue. Do this with the Create Output Queue (CRTOUTQ) command. Figure 19-50 has a sample of that command.

In the figure, create the output queue with a name the same as the remote system (RMTSYS in this case). Name the specific print queue on the remote system. In this example, we named the remote print queue LCLSYS to show it is named after the system sending print files to it.

```
                        Create Output Queue (CRTOUTQ)

Type choices, press Enter.

Output queue . . . . . . . . . . > RMTSYS        Name
  Library . . . . . . . . . . .      *CURLIB     Name, *CURLIB
Maximum spooled file size:         _
  Number of pages . . . . . . .    *NONE         Number, *NONE
  Starting time . . . . . . . .    ________      Time
  Ending time . . . . . . . . .    ________      Time
             + for more values
Order of files on queue . . . .    *FIFO         *FIFO, *JOBNBR
Remote system . . . . . . . . .  > RMTSYS
______________________________________________________________________________

______________________________________________________________________________
Remote printer queue . . . . . . > LCLSYS
______________________________________________________________________________

______________________________________________________________________________
                                                                       More...
F3=Exit   F4=Prompt   F5=Refresh   F10=Additional parameters   F12=Cancel
F13=How to use this display        F24=More keys
```

Figure 19-50: Prompted version of the CRTOUTQ command—creating a remote output queue.

Connection and destination types are mutually dependent on each other. Possible values for destination type and what they mean are:

- *OS400. The destination is an AS/400 running OS/400 of version V2R3 or later.
- *OS400V2. The destination is an AS/400 running OS/400 of a version V3R1M0 and prior.
- *S390. The destination is an IBM mainframe.
- *NETWARE3. The destination is any computer running Version 3 of NetWare.
- *NDS. The destination is any computer running Version 4 of NetWare.
- *PSF2. The destination is a PC with PSF/2.
- *OTHER. The destination is something not defined. This can be UNIX machines, non-IBM machines, or System/36, System/38, or AS/400s running Version 1 of OS/400.

Possible values for connection type depend on the destination type. Here they are:

- If the destination type is *OS/400, the connection type must be either *IP or *USRDFN.
- If the destination type is *OS/400V2, the connection type must be *SNA.
- If the destination type is *S390, the connection type must be either *SNA or *USRDFN.
- If the destination type is *PSF2, the connection type must be *IP.
- If the destination type is *OTHER, the connection type must not be *IPX.
- If the destination type is *NETWARE3 or *NDS, the connection type must be either *IPX or *USRDFN.
- If the destination type is anything else, the connection type must be *IP.

Notice in the figure, we specified one writer job to autostart. Normally, only the remote writer will be up. To verify this, use the Work with Active Jobs (WRKACTJOB) command and look for subsystem QSPL to be active.

If we did not specify any autostart jobs or the job ended for some reason, start it with the Start Remote Writer (STRRMTWTR) command. Just name the remote printer as the first parameter:

```
STRRMTWTR RMTSYS
```

LPD Configuration

LPD receives spool files from LPR on remote systems (most typically non-AS/400 hosts) and routes their contents to output queues from which they are printed.

LPD AS/400 jobs run in the QSYSWRK subsystem. Check the jobs running in this subsystem with the Work with Active Jobs (WRKACTJOB) command. LPD jobs are named *QTLPDnnnnn*, where nnnnn represents a unique numerical suffix.

LPD servers are automatically configured when TCP/IP is started unless they have not been set to autostart. The only place that could have happened would be through the Change LPD Attributes (CHGLPDA) command, which also sets the number of servers to start. The system comes with autostart set to *YES (LPD servers will start automatically). The number of servers that will start is set to two. Two is the optimum number of servers to have up for normal operation. If the AS/400 is supporting a lot of printing from remote non-AS/400 hosts, feel free to raise this number to a maximum of 20.

If the LPD servers are not running, start them with the Start TCP Server (STRTCPSVR) command, which will bring up the number of servers specified on the LPD Attributes. If, for any reason, an LPD server is to be ended, use the End TCP/IP Server (ENDTCPSRV) command with the SERVER(*LPD) parameter specified.

Of the several LPD jobs running on an AS/400, only one is actively listening for incoming spool files at one time. When it gets a file, it sends the listening task to another LPD server while it starts translating and routing the spool file request. After it finishes, it starts another LPD server and terminates itself. The problem a busy AS/400 will have is that its remote hosts may have to wait until a fresh LPD is ready to receive it. That is when to increase the number of LPD servers with the CHGLPDA command.

Spool files have attributes like fonts, lines per inch, page widths, and number of copies. These attributes do not come in with the spool file—the receiving AS/400 must get the attributes from somewhere. The first place it looks for attributes is under the user ID.

If the receiving system does not recognize the file's "owner," the next area it looks for attributes is in the print file, QTMPLPD. This file is included in the AS/400 in library QTCP. Any customer can accept these defaults, change them, or copy file QTMPLPD to another user library and modify them there. Controlling the library lists is a way of supporting different remote printer attributes on the same system.

SNMP

Simple Network Management Protocol (SNMP) was designed specifically for TCP/IP networks.

SNMP is an odd group of *SNMP managers*, *SNMP agents*, and information objects called *Management Information Base* (*MIB*). *Managers* ask *agents* to do things for them, and agents do those things via the MIBs.

For example, a manager may want to know the contact person for a remote host. It asks the agent, who queries the remote's MIB that handles that (in this case, that MIB would be SYSCONTACT). Because the manager asked who it was, the agent "reads" the information and passes it back to the manager. If the manager had "write" authority, it could have asked the agent to change the same MIB.

There are some MIBs that the agents cannot directly access. In these cases, the agents use dedicated sub-agents. But they can be thought of as agents as far as we are concerned.

The set of managers and agents that work together is called the *community*. The community is defined by a table (within the agent) of the managers to which he will respond.

SNMP's two components, managers and agents, make a strange egalitarian community. Although the managers hold all the data, give users the information needed, and ask the agents to do the work, the agents determine which managers get to play and what access authorities each has.

In AS/400 terms, both SNMP managers and agents work through SNMP APIs, which you can reference in the IBM manual *System API Reference: UNIX-type APIs*.

SNMP Manager

An SNMP manager is a set of applications that collect data about the hosts and clients on the network. The SNMP manager is running when SNMP is started.

The manager contains a *trap manager* to handle *traps*. A trap is an event that causes an exception-type message. The trap manager receives traps, parses them out, then logs and/or forwards them. It can also forward traps to other managers. The commands to run the trap manager within the SNMP manager are:

- STRTRPMGR (Start Trap Manager). This command has a parameter, FWDTRP; valid values are *YES and *NO. This parameter determines if traps are to be forwarded to the trap manager specified on the agent. *Note*: Be careful of these parameters or you will have two or more nodes in a trap loop—each forwarding traps to the others.
- ENDTRPMGR (End Trap Manager).

SNMP Agents

The SNMP agent carries out valid requests from the managers and accesses or changes data about the network nodes through MIBs.

Configuring SNMP Agents

An AS/400 has one agent and one manager. They come with some defaults, and at least a couple of those defaults should probably be changed. Agents contain information that define:

- The community name.
- The table of valid managers.
- The access level of those managers.
- Logging level.

The command to add a community to the agent community list (yes, an agent can support multiple communities) is the Add Community for SNMP (ADDCOMSNMP) command. Change communities previously named with the Change Community for SNMP (CHGCOMSNMP) command. Remove communities from the list with the Remove Community for SNMP (RMVCOMSNMP) command.

Communities can also be added to agents via the Configure TCP/IP SNMP (CFGTCPSNMP) command—select option 2 (`Work with Communities`). That produces a list of all the communities and has the standard AS/400 menu options to manipulate them.

Valid managers are listed in the INTNETADR parameter. Be sure to use their IP addresses, not domain names. Each manager IP address is separated from its neighbor with a space. If the network is strictly local, use the generic *ANY as a single entry on this parameter and the agent will work with any manager on the network.

Name the access authority for attached managers with the OBJACC parameter. Possible values are *READ, *WRITE, *NONE, and *SNMPATR. The first two are logical enough; *NONE is used temporarily to logically remove a manager from its community without having to remove, rebuild, remove, and rebuild the whole community. *SNMPATR relies on the attributes of the SNMP for access rules.

The AS/400 comes with a default community name of *public*. If the TCP/IP network consists of only the local workstations, this will do. However, if it is going to support anything more than that, it should probably be changed.

Community names can consist of just about anything—even unreadable characters are permitted. But try to come up with names that mean something.

Two other parameters are LOGSET and LOGGET. Possible values for both are *YES, *NO, and *SNMPATR. These are nice for security logging.

That one command and those parameters will configure the agent. There are several attributes you can change within the agent. Change agent attributes with the Change SNMP Attributes (CHGSNMPA) command, or type the Configure TCP/IP SNMP (CFGTCPSNMP) command and select option 1. These agent attributes and their descriptions are listed in Figure 19-51.

Attribute	Description
SYSCONTACT	The contact person of the system. Generally enter a phone number here, too.
SYSLOC	Plain language description of the system location.
SNDAUTTRP	*YES or *NO, send failed authentication messages to an SNMP manager.
AUTOSTART	*YES or *NO, automatically start the snmp agent with TCP/IP. If this is set to *NO, STRTCPSVR must be used to start.
OBJACC	*SNMPATR, *READ, *WRITE, *NONE, these set the access the manager will have to MIBs.
LOGSET LOGGET	*YES, *NO, and *SNMP, sets whether set and get commands are logged.
LOGTRP	*YES and *NO, states whether traps are forwarded or not.
TRPMGR	Names the SNMP manager(s) to receive forwarded traps.

Figure 19-51: Attributes and descriptions for change agents.

Workstation Gateway (WSG)

WSG stands for Workstation Gateway. This automatically transforms AS/400 application screens into 5250/ HTML, so any workstation running through a browser can get a GUI-ed presentation of any AS/400 green-screen application.

Any browser connected to the AS/400 via TCP/IP (local or remote) can get slower, but prettier, application presentation through WSG. With WSG, you can mix and match workstations. Some, attached via a browser, view AS/400 applications through GUI-colored glasses, while others can connect with 5250 and see the same applications in green-screen.

Not all browsers are created equal, and some may interpret the embedded configuration commands in 5250/HTML differently. But only the appearance will change, the screens all work. Two things the customer should be aware of with WSG:

- Applications run through it much slower than they do on locally attached workstations.
- Without a firewall, transactions are not encrypted over the 'net. This includes sign-on passwords.

WSG Configuration

There is not much to do to configure the WSG server, but there are a couple of functions. Use the Configure TCP/IP WSG (CFGTCPWSG) command to do these steps:

- Change the Display Sign-on Panel to *YES.

That was hard, wasn't it? To enable users to sign on without seeing an AS/400 sign-on screen, refer to appendix I, section 10 in the IBM manual *OS/400 TCP/IP Configuration and Reference V4R3*. We will warn you, though: this technique is only for very advanced AS/400 professionals.

The WSG server uses virtual devices—if it needs a device, it just creates it. The system value QAUTOVRT enables and controls this virtual device creation. Check it with the Display System Value (DSPSYSVAL) command. If you need to change it, use the Change System Value (DSPSYSVAL) command. Do not let it be equal to zero. To start with, set it to about 50 or higher. To support some workstations, do this:

- Set QAUTOVRT to *NOMAX.
- Start the WSG server (refer to Starting WSG section).
- Allow users to sign on and check the number of devices WSG created. Use the Work with Device Descriptions (WRKDEVD) command to count the number of controllers (named QPACTLNNN) and devices (QPADEVNNNN), then add the numbers together. That is the minimum number of devices WSG requires to support those users. Then reset QAUTOVRT to that number plus 10 percent for error.

From time to time, the WSG server may require changes. Do so with the Change TCP WSG (CHGTCPWSG) command. Some that should be considered (not right away but soon after the network stabilizes) are:

- NBRCLT (Number of Clients per Server). The default is 20—change it to any number from 1 to 50, depending on how the network is configured.
- INACTTIMO (Inactivity Time-out). This is the value in minutes a WSG server can be inactive before the AS/400 shuts it down. The default is ten minutes.

- DTARQSTIMO (Data Request Time-out). This value is how many seconds the WSG server will wait for requested data from a client before taking the client offline. *Note*: This value does not account for network delays. If your network is very busy, increase this value or your users will get false error messages.

Starting WSG

While many other TCP/IP applications are shipped to start automatically, WSG is not. The customer must do some configuring first. The Change WSG Attributes (CHGWSGA) command sets WSG to automatically start. Here is a sample of it:

```
CHGWSGA AUTOSTART(*YES)
```

If WSG is not running but TCP/IP is, you can start it with the Start TCP Server (STRTCPSVR) command, specifying the *WSG value on the Server parameter:

```
STRTCPSVR SERVER(*WSG)
```

If the WSG server is already started when you issue the STRTCPSVR command, another will be started. Refer to the setting of NBRCLT in the section above. Adding another server will support that many more clients on your system.

End a WSG server with the End TCP Server (ENDTCPSVR) command. Like the start command, name the server with the *WSG value. Naming the parameter is optional—if you do not specify it, all TCP/IP servers will end.

Do not skim that paragraph too lightly. IBM does not ship WSG to start automatically for very good security reasons. Any customer should treat WSG as a potentially open door to the big, bad world. End WSG server during time periods you are not supporting browser-equipped workstations. Do not just leave it up.

The WSG Access Log

Remember what is going on with WSG. Most customers are allowing AS/400 access to people who could be strangers. WSG keeps a log of all accesses. The brave (or those really hurting for storage resources) can turn this log off, but such an action is extremely foolish from a security standpoint.

The name of the log is QATMTLOG and it is shipped with MAXMBRS(*NOMAX) and SIZE(*NOMAX). Change either or both of these, if desired, with the Change Physical File Description (CHGFD) command. If you fix the size of the file, be careful. If the file fills up, the AS/400 will rename it to a name based on the date (QCYYMMDD). If it fills up again on the same day, logging will stop (but TCP and the WSG will keep on going).

View the contents of the file with either the Display Physical File Member (DSPPFM) command or through the Programmer's Development Menu (PDM).

The View from the Browser

To access an AS/400 from a browser-equipped workstation, bring up the browser and type in:

```
http://host:port/WSG
```

where host is either:

- The host IP address in the form 999.999.999.999.
- The host domain name if the AS/400 has a domain name server or local host table.

and port is 5061 (the default). If you are thinking about changing the default port, refer to the Accessing the Workstation Gateway from a Web Browser section in the IBM manual *OS/400 TCP/IP Configuration and Reference V4R3*.

OS/400 TCP/IP Functions

The AS/400 also offers four miscellaneous functions for customers running its TCP/IP. They are:

- Bootstrap Protocol (BOOTP).
- RouteD server.
- Serial Line Internet Protocol (SLIP).
- Trivial File Transfer Protocol (TFTP).

BOOTP

BOOTP supports "thin clients," or client workstations with memory and logic but no media (hard or soft drives). When such a client connects to the AS/400, this service sends down a file to allow the client to boot up.

RouteD Server

Routing daemon (*RouteD*) supports the Routing Information Protocol (RIP). An Interior Gateway Protocol (IGP), RIP is the most popular routing protocol today. If the AS/400 is a TCP/IP server, it may have to route packets. If the network the AS/400 is on is an intranet (strictly local) and has redundant routes between nodes, try RIP for very fast dynamic routing of packets.

Remember, for security, the AS/400 cannot route packets out onto the Internet direct. RouteD support is strictly for intranet routing.

SLIP

Serial line Internet protocol (SLIP) gives the AS/400 dial-up TCP/IP support. SLIP is not an application as much as it is a protocol to enable the dial-up. Once the connection is made, the user will run applications like Telnet, FTP, and SMTP.

SLIP enables a personal computer, AS/400, or any other computer to dial into an AS/400 (or vice versa—an AS/400 to dial to any of those). SLIP must be installed and running on both computers when the connection is made.

SLIP communications is only asynchronous. As such, it will support popular modems (ZOOM, USRobotics, and Multitech), as well as IBM asynchronous modems.

On the AS/400, it is part of the base operating system starting with V3R2 and must work with a 2609 or 2612 communications adapter.

SLIP is driven with a *dialog script*. A dialog script is a source file member that specifies a series of prompts and responses—the handshake protocol between two computers. This handshake is not standard across all computers, so the dialog script gives the customer some latitude to customize it.

Because this handshake can vary from manufacturer to manufacturer, the system operator should work with the other vendor if connecting to a non-IBM host. For that reason, we will not attempt to show all the permutations of dialog scripts.

TFTP Server

Trivial file transfer protocol (*TFTP*) provides FTP support with no security checking. This protocol is usually used with BOOTP to provide thin-client support.

CONNECTING THE AS/400 TO THE INTERNET

After all this, the next logical step is to get the AS/400 connected to the Internet. Actually, that part is rather routine. One thing to be prepared for: When talking to ISPs, get used to people who have never heard of the AS/400.

Start with a phone call to a local ISP. If you do not know any, sign onto the InterNIC at `info@is.internet.net`. They have a list of local ISPs around the country.

When considering ISPs, IBM provides ISP services through IBM Global Network (IGN). Contact your IBM representative or local branch office for more information. An ISP will want to know what kind of support you want, and you will want to know what they offer.

We have covered a lot of ground in this chapter, so let us go back to some basics again. There are two primary ways you can connect to the Internet:

- LAN-to-LAN. The AS/400 is attached to a LAN. On the LAN is an IP router that provides the Internet connection, the AS/400 does not. There are two primary ways of connecting the IP Router to the ISP:
  - Leased line, usually an E1 or T1.
  - Dial-up through a high-speed modem attached to the IP router. This dial-up can be one-way or two-way. (The AS/400 can only dial out to the ISP, or either can dial the other.)
- Pure dial-up. Attach an asynchronous card and modem to your AS/400 and plan to dial into the ISP when you want Internet access. One common trick is to use the AS/400's existing Electronic Customer Support (ECS) modem (all AS/400s come with one).

An AS/400 cannot route messages to the Internet, so the LAN-to-LAN connection is made with a hardware device (another node) on your LAN called an IP router. IBM has a great router—model 2210. When considering any IP router, make sure it will support the LAN's protocol and the leased line or modem to the ISP.

For LAN-to-LAN dial-up, choose whether the preferred protocol will be SLIP or PPP. There may not be a choice here; many ISPs only offer PPP.

- SLIP. This is older and declining in popularity, yet it is very simple to use and ideal for simple two-node dial-up links. SLIP has received a bad reputation because it does not have much flow control or error-checking capability. That's not really a problem with the AS/400 as those functions are shifted to the host.

- Point-to-Point Protocol (PPP). This is quickly becoming the darling of the Internet community. It has strong flow control and error-checking features plus dynamic IP addressing, so support of a large, dynamic Internet environment is handled nicely.

In LAN-to-LAN, the leased line, the modem, and/or the IP router will probably be supplied by the ISP but make sure. Also ask what the charge is for: A monthly fee based on usage or a flat rate? If a modem, will it be purchased outright? Check if "usage" is minutes, messages, or flat rate combined with a per-minute or per-message charge.

Also, be prepared to tell the ISP how many hosts will be connecting to make sure there will be enough IP host address space from the ISP for everyone.

The other popular option for Internet connectivity is direct AS/400 dial-up. This uses an asynchronous adapter card, line, and modem (often the ECS modem). This method can only dial out to the Internet and it can only support SLIP.

You may ask yourself, "Why?" This method does seem limited; however, if you only want Internet access for limited reasons (file transfer and/or coast-to-coast communication without an expensive infrastructure, for two examples), this is a very cheap and fast way to get connected. Also, security is simplified greatly for basic on-and-off Internet connections.

Security on the Internet

Security is probably the hottest issue for most AS/400 Internet-bound customers. What is going to happen when the AS/400 opens its doors to the big, bad world?

The first thing the system operator must do is go back to basic AS/400 security as discussed in Chapter 11, Security and Security System Values. The AS/400 has more built-in security than any other computer, and it should be well used now. At least review the system's security to be sure it is in order. Some basic security measures to put in place are:

- Set *PUBLIC access to all objects to *EXCLUDE. It is amazing how many shops grant the public a lot of authorities.
- Think through and set the AS/400 system level security.
- Change the IBM-supplied default passwords to the following user IDs:
    - QSECOFR.
    - QSYSOPR.
    - IBM.
    - QSVR.
    - QSERV.
- Limit Internet user ID authorities as much as possible.
- Use the user environment of the user profile (refer to chapter 5 for more information).

- Use the Change System Value (CHGSYSVAL) or Work with System Value (WRKSYSVAL) commands to set QLMTSECOFR to one. This prohibits users with *ALLOBJ or *SERVICE authorities from Internet access.
- Use the password system values (refer to appendixes A and B in this book) so users are forced to use complex passwords. Better yet, consider having the system generate passwords for Internet users.
- When FTP users fail in a sign-on attempt, message CPF2234 is written to the QHST log. Consider having a monitor program that, when it detects too many failed sign-on attempts, ends FTP (and maybe all TCP/IP) servers.
- Tighten ASP thresholds and what action is taken when they are reached. An Internet user may be flooding your system.
- Do not start servers that are not needed.
- Restrict AS/400 command types like Restore, Start, and Power Down from Internet-based users.
- Remove compilers from the system or severely restrict access to them.
- Do not allow IP forwarding. Change this with the Change TCP/IP Attributes (CHGTCPA) command and set the IPDTGFWD parameter to *NO.
- Isolate the Internet AS/400 from any other network or segment in the following ways:
  - Do not allow AnyNet/400 to run. Turn it off with the Change Network Attributes (CHGNETA) command:

    ```
    CHGNETA ALWANYNET(*NO)
    ```

  - Take all authority to the Start Pass-Through (STRPASTHR) command from any outside user.

Be aware of several other security issues:

- User IDs and passwords are transmitted unencrypted—anyone can monitor a line for them.
- FTP users may only have *USE authority to your files, but they can still copy them to another computer's hard disk.
- Even though SMTP can route undeliverable mail by including an *ANY *ANY entry in the system directory, if you do this, someone can flood your system with computer-generated garbage messages. (Why? So they can delight in overflowing your DASD and crashing your system.)
- If you use POP and allow users who are not regular AS/400 users to send, store, and retrieve mail, set the following parameters on their user profile through the Work with User Profile (WRKUSRPRF) command:

  ```
  INLMNU(*SIGNOFF)
  INLPGM(*NONE)
  ```

- Most IP routers provide some simple security by *filtering packets*. That is, discarding those that are not destined for the hosts it supports before they get there. Remember, packets can be anything, not just messages or mail, so you are ahead of the game if incoming packets without valid addresses are discarded early.

Hesitate to provide Internet access to any production AS/400. Instead, opt for a smaller, separate AS/400 not normally connected to a production machine. Also, enforce strict one-way file transfers, from production to the Internet AS/400, never back again.

One solution to all that is to purchase Firewall/400. It is a superior firewall that will give superior protection.

Firewall/400 is a software package that runs on the Integrated PC Server (IPCS) and provides a *proxy-based firewall*. A proxy-based firewall is one that hides the secured part of the Internet from the unsecured. Like a gate guard, it will screen out unknown users, undeliverable mail, anything not approved. It will also protect individuals' true IP addresses from the riff-raff on the unsecured side. The unique thing about the AS/400 is that, with its firewall running on the IPCS, it is actually not running on the AS/400, so there is no way anyone can circumvent the firewall and find himself loose inside the system.

Finally, as we said, everything that goes over the Internet goes in the clear. Transmissions encryption allows protection of anything coming in and going out from the AS/400 but is done so with encryption technology installed on both the AS/400 and any browsers accessing it. This is becoming common as more corporations do business over the Internet. Two standards that are starting to emerge are:

- *Secure Sockets Layer (SSL)*. This protocol lies below HTTP, FTP, and Telnet but above TCP/IP. The handshake that starts an individual session sets the encryption algorithm, which is not reset and cannot be determined later by anyone outside that two-party handshake. Also, the server (and optionally the client) is authenticated. In other words, it ensures clients are connected to the server they thought they were.
- *Secure Hypertext Transfer Protocol (SHTTP)*. This is an extension to HTTP that provides built-in encryption of data and authentication of servers and clients. It also uses embedded signatures to detect any change to the data in transmission.

A firewall is a kind of gateway in the sense that it resides in front of and apart from the host (at least in the case of the AS/400; other firewalls are part of the host). Anyway, an emerging *gateway-based security* standard is *SOCKS*. SOCKS resides on the gateway (or Firewall/400) and enforces security issues more transparently to the users on either end. When discussing security, *transparency* is not a user-friendly issue, it is a security issue—hackers cannot hack what they cannot see going on.

END-OF-CHAPTER AIDS

CHAPTER SUMMARY

What many people do not realize is that the AS/400 is really a central location for all the major communications protocols available. And, it supports most, if not all, of these protocols in native mode. That is, they run as fast as any other protocol within the machine. The customer who can tap in and utilize these protocols free themselves from having to buy additional (and expensive) communication gear, live gateways, and servers.

In fact, any AS/400 can be a very powerful server in addition to being an equally powerful business computer. The task is up to the system operator to know these capabilities and how to enable them.

KEY TERMS

access point
acknowledged support
adapter address
agents
asynchronous transfer mode (ATM)
ATM network interface
BOOTP
bridged frame-relay environment
bridged frame-relay network
bridges
bus topology
carrier sense multiple access with collision detection (CSMA/CD) protocol
cell
channel service unit (CSU)
class A network
class D network
class of network
community
data link connection identifier (DLCI)
data service unit (DSU)
datagrams
device attachment (DA) cards
dialog script
direct frame relay
distributed data interface (DDI)
domain name
dropped (nodes)
DSU/CSU
duplex
Ethernet
extended commands
fast Ethernet
file transfer protocol (FTP)
filtering packets
firewall
frame
frame handler (FH)
frame relay (FR)
frame size
full-duplex Token-Ring
gateway
gateway-based security
half-duplex Token-Ring
host
host name
host name search priority
interim local management interface (ILMI)
Internet
Internet protocol
inter-networking
IP routers
LAN emulation (LANE)
LAN emulation client (LEC)
LAN emulation domain (LED)
layers
line printer daemon (LPD)
line printer requester (LPR)
local network
logical and
logical link control (LLC)
Management Information Base (MIB)
managers
masks
medium access control (MAC)
multistation access unit (MAU)
network segment
packets
packet-switching protocol
permanent virtual circuit (PVC)
physical interfaces
physical network layer
polling
polling parameters
port
portable transaction computer (PTC)
post office protocol (POP)
preset address
printer pass-through
proxy-based firewall
public
Remote Executive (REXEC)
remote network
repeating hubs
resource name
routers
routing daemon (RouteD)
routing table entries
Secure hypertext transfer Protocol (SHTTP)
Secure sockets layer (SSL)
serial line Internet protocol (SLIP)
service access points
Simple Mail Transfer Protocol (SMTP)
SMTP name table
SNA direct connection
SNMP agents
SNMP managers
SOCKS
special IP addressing
subcommands
subnet mask
switched
switched network
switching hub
symbols
system distribution directory
TCP/IP
teletypewriter network (Telnet)
terminal equipment (TE)
transceiver
transparency
trap manager
traps
trivial file transfer protocol (TFTP)
unacknowledged support
varying on a line and device
wireless communications

CHAPTER SELF-TEST

Solutions to these self-test questions are in appendix D.

True-False Questions

___ 1. SNA is always in effect when the AS/400 is supporting any communications protocol.

___ 2. SNA is an IBM proprietary network protocol.

___ 3. The AS/400 won't support any network protocol that is not acknowledged.

___ 4. Although each adapter comes with its own preset address, it is considered good practice to assign one's own address.

___ 5. Although one can use the IBM defaults for most other AS/400 work, using them for setting up networks does not work well.

___ 6. If a network has Token-Ring adapters that can handle a 16KBframe size and one that can only handle a 4KB size, the network must be created with the smaller size as the maximum frame size.

___ 7. An Ethernet LAN on an AS/400 can support two standard versions of Ethernet.

___ 8. A frame relay requires a attachment hardware known as a DSU/CSU.

___ 9. An ATM network uses an internal directory to route communication packets to remote hosts.

___ 10. The values used in TCP/IP's address mask determine its class of network.

Fill in the Blanks

1. A network physically connected to an AS/400 is a ________ network.
2. A concatenation of the adapter and port used on that adapter is the _________.
3. The MAC address, when used on an AS/400, is usually referred to as the _________ address.
4. A second set of addresses associated with adapters is the ________ ________ _______.
5. A hardware device that connects a Token-Ring to a controller is a ________ _________ __________.
6. A network on which communications is possible in two ways (send and receive) at the same time is _________.
7. The protocol on an Ethernet network is _______ _______ _______ _______ _______ _______ _______.
8. A DDI network ring requires _________ _________ cards to attach the devices to a concentrator.
9. A table of remote TCP/IP hosts, their common names, and their TCP/IP addresses is called a _______ _________ _________.

Chapter Review Questions

1. Networks can be linked together through:
   a. Routers.
   b. Gateways.
   c. Bridges.
   d. All of the above.
2. Describe the purpose of the medium access control (MAC) layer.
3. Discuss the term "switched" as it relates to attaching LAN devices to an AS/400.
4. Before a user works with LANs, what must be set in the user's profile?
5. What two decisions must be made about a Token-Ring LAN before starting to set one up? Discuss the criterion that goes into each.
6. Describe "symbols" as used by DDI rings.
7. How is a direct frame relay different from a bridged frame relay?
8. Discuss the TCP/IP protocol. Is it possible to configure an AS/400 as an Internet server without it?
9. Describe subnet masks.
10. What type of networking need would be best served with the FTP protocol?

20

Operations Navigator

Chapter Objectives

Upon completion of this chapter, you should be able to:

- Explore the main functions of Operations Navigator.
- Describe how to view a database file.
- Explore how to manage jobs.
- Explore how to manage printers and printouts.
- Describe how to send various types of messages.
- Display hardware and software inventory on your system.
- Explore various file systems.

Overview

The AS/400 is easy to use. Through clever design constructs such as F4 search and consistent language constructs, anyone—even the rawest rookie—can quickly navigate around the system.

If that isn't enough, there is another navigation tool, called *Operations Navigator*, available on the AS/400. Operations Navigator provides a GUI interface into most AS/400 operations. However,

Operations Navigator isn't the same as the other navigation devices. Because it's an optional part of *Client Access/400* (CA/400), it's not automatically part of the operating system.

CA/400 is something the customer pays extra for, and not all customers use it. Because Operations Navigator must be installed separately on each workstation, it might not be available on all stations.

Operations Navigator is installed during the CA/400 or *CA/Express* installation. A very important item to note is that to install any Operations Navigator components, the operator must select the `Selective Setup` installation. Even when Operations Navigator is installed on every workstation, what appears on it varies depending on four conditions:

- The operating system level of the AS/400.
- Optional features installed on the AS/400.
- The authority of the person using Operations Navigator.
- The individual items selected during installation.

For these reasons, the options available on Operations Navigator can vary greatly from those shown in this chapter.

Although Operations Navigator looks different from OS/400 both in its navigation method and in the GUI screen it puts over each command, it really invokes exactly the same commands as described earlier in this book. For that reason, this chapter doesn't dwell on commands or concepts of the AS/400. Instead, this chapter covers the Operations Navigator and how to use it.

STARTING OPERATIONS NAVIGATOR

To start Operations Navigator, connect your PC with the ISP (Internet Service Provider) or the internal TCP/IP line to which the AS/400 is connected. Then double-click on the Operations Navigator icon on the workstation screen. The first time starting the product, click on the `Add AS/400 Connection` option, and the setup wizard will walk you through setting up the AS/400 TCP/IP address, user profile, and password. After the first time, just clicking on the Operations Navigator icon will start the AS/400 session.

USING OPERATIONS NAVIGATOR

Figure 20-1 shows a sample of Operations Navigator's welcome screen.

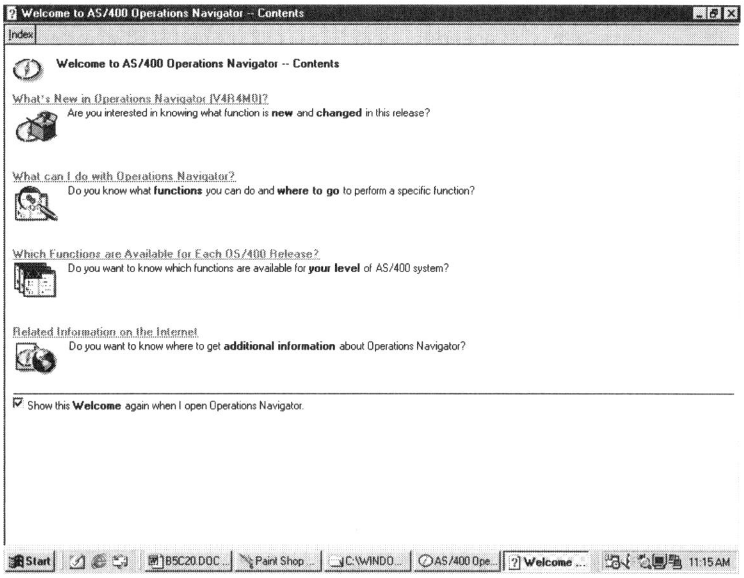

Figure 20-1: Operations Navigator's welcome screen.

The Welcome screen normally appears only the first time Operations Navigator is started. From this screen, the user can find reference material about aspects of Operations Navigator. After the first time the user starts Operations Navigator, another initial screen normally appears. Figure 20-2 contains a sample of that screen.

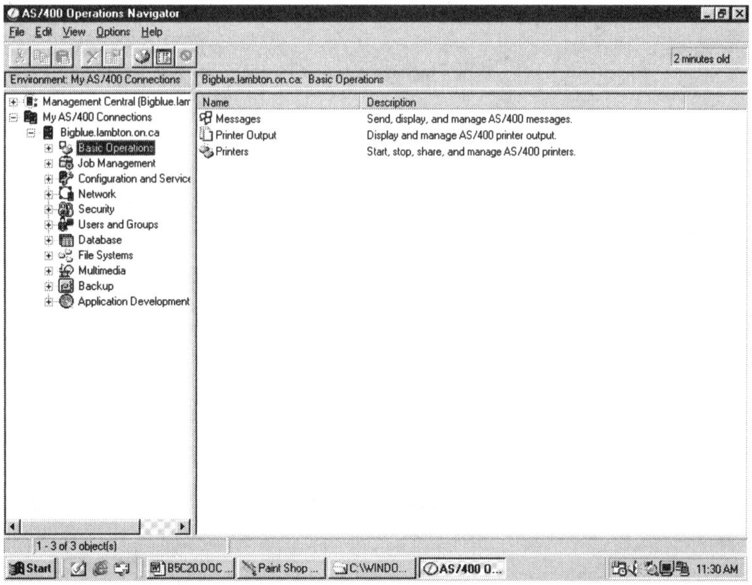

Figure 20-2: Operations Navigator initial screen.

Figure 20-2 shows the normal screen from which all Operations Navigator functions are accessed. Users who want to review Operations Navigator functions can do one of two things:

- Select `HELP` from the Operations Navigator menu, and then choose the `HELP TOPICS` option. Operations Navigator's `HELP` is interactive. When a user gets to the particular topic where assistance is needed, clicking on the subject will bring up the actual screen that will do the task.
- Click on the checkbox to show the `Welcome` window. Then, every time Operations Navigator is started, the window will appear.

On the initial screen, the first thing you probably will notice is the path called `My AS/400 Connection`. Immediately under that is the AS/400 connection currently in effect. As shown in Figure 20-2, the connection is an AS/400 named BIGBLUE at Lambton (College), in Ontario, Canada.

You might want to add a new session from time to time. Do so through Operations Navigator by right-clicking on `My AS/400 Connection` and selecting `Add AS/400 Connection` or `Environments` in the pop-up menu that appears.

Note (as in Figure 20-2) that the functions this user can do on this AS/400 are listed in a menu on the right half of the screen. Another option is to click on the plus sign, to the left of the connection, and the available options will appear under it. Because it's our preferred way of working with Operations Navigator's functions, this method is presented throughout this chapter.

By placing your cursor on the `My AS/400 Connection` branch and right-clicking, you get a drop-down menu like the one shown in Figure 20-3.

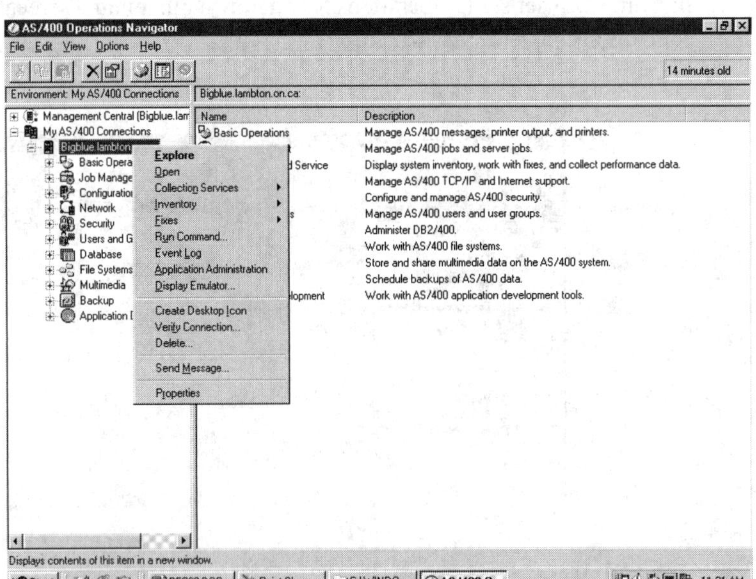

Figure 20-3: A drop-down main menu for working with the AS/400.

While the *EXPLORE option* (the top option) is the one you will primarily use to work with the AS/400, the following list provides brief descriptions of the other options on this menu:

- OPEN—Click on the OPEN option to replace the context menu with icons.Collection

- SERVICES—The COLLECTION SERVICES option allows users to start and end performance-data collection. COLLECTION SERVICES also allows users to specify collection intervals and to have some control over the database tables used to hold the data.
- INVENTORY—The INVENTORY option produces a report of all hardware, software, and *fixes* currently installed on the system. Any combination of the three items can be selected. INVENTORY is a nice feature because it isn't unusual for a *value added reseller (VAR)* to ask what is currently installed on the AS/400.
- FIXES (PTFs)—FIXES has a wizard attached, which means it has a lot of intelligence. With this option, a user can compare the update levels among two or more AS/400 models. FIXES can be used to install PTFs on one or more AS/400s and, after installations are complete, delete save files or cover letters from the systems.
- RUN COMMAND—Similar to the command line, the user can run a program, command, or utility from the RUN COMMAND screen. The user also can manage things like the job logging and message action.
- EVENT LOG—There may be many *triggers* based on *thresholds* on an AS/400. For example, the threshold in journaling or a CPU percentage in performance monitoring is a threshold. When these thresholds are reached, a trigger is released that results in an *event* occurring. This option reviews all events that have happened.
- DISPLAY EMULATOR—If an emulator hasn't already started, the DISPLAY EMULATOR option starts it. Most of the time when a session is started, an emulator also must be started, and the DISPLAY EMULATOR option won't appear.
- CREATE DESKTOP ICON—You can use this option to create a desktop icon for Operations Navigator. The icon's properties can be customized. Users can start Operations Navigator by double-clicking on the icon.
- VERIFY CONNECTION—If the connection from the workstation to the AS/400 is via TCP/IP, the VERIFY CONNECTION option allows the connection to be verified.
- DELETE—The DELETE option deletes the session currently connecting the workstation to the AS/400.
- SEND MESSAGE—The SEND MESSAGE option sends a message to another user. For additional information on this function, see the subheading Messages.
- PROPERTIES—The PROPERTIES option displays information about the AS/400 and the attached user. Properties displayed are:
  - GENERAL—Current release level of the AS/400.
  - CONNECTION—Sign-on information about the attached user.
  - LICENSES—Current status of the CA/400 on the attached user's workstation.
  - RESTART—Current settings (the user can change them) about the AS/400 restart capability.
  - DIRECTORY SERVICES—The user can specify the information to appear on a Lightweight Directory Access Protocol (LDAP) directory server.
- PLUG-INS—Shows the plug-ins currently on the workstation and identifies the plug-ins with which the AS/400 can work.

GENERAL FUNCTIONS OF OPERATIONS NAVIGATOR

Operations Navigator's general functions allow the user to control aspects of each specific function. Here are the general functions and how to access each:

- CREATING DESKTOP SHORTCUTS—Creates an icon on the workstation screen so that Operations Navigator does not have to be started each time. By double-clicking on this icon, the specific function can be invoked directly. Access this by highlighting the specific function and right-clicking your mouse. Select CREATING DESKTOP SHORTCUTS from the drop-down menu.
- PROPERTIES—The automatic refresh rate can be set for many commands. Access this by highlighting the specific function and right-clicking your mouse. Select PROPERTIES from the drop-down menu.
- OPTIONS MENU—Allows the resulting WORK WITH command to be sorted, limited in what it will report, or limited in the number of fields displayed. To access the OPTIONS MENU, highlight the specific function and use either OPTIONS from the application menu or click on the OPTIONS icon on the context sensitive toolbar.
  - SORT—Select the sort action from the OPTIONS MENU. A screen is displayed similar to Figure 20-4. This screen performs two functions. First, fields are selected for sorting. Just highlight each field and click on the box to add it to the sort key. Notice that there are two pushbuttons for adding fields to the key, one to add a field before the cursor position, and one to add it after the cursor position. If a key is added to the key list by mistake, press the REMOVE pushbutton after highlighting the field to remove it. Second, this screen does the actual sorting. Press the Sort pushbutton before leaving this screen to do that.

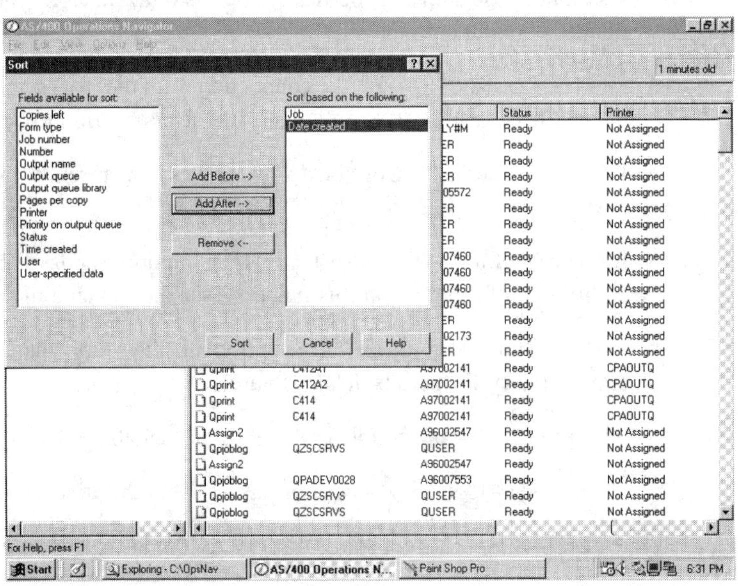

Figure 20-4: General function SORT setup screen.

  - INCLUDE—The Include function selects the records to be displayed. A screen will be displayed similar to that shown in Figure 20-5. The actual screen will vary depending on the function it is meant to support. The screen displayed in Figure 20-5 is context sensitive to the specific function of the Messages. Note that it allows messages to be filtered to show only those for the current user, the system operator, or another user (the name has to be specified).

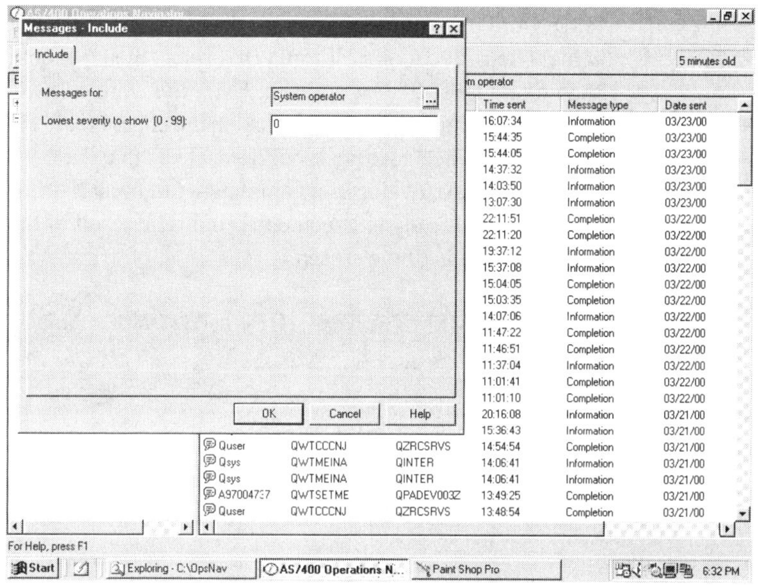

Figure 20-5: General function INCLUDE screen.

- COLUMNS—Sometimes the data that the AS/400 displays is a little overwhelming. The COLUMNS general function allows the user to display only those fields that are pertinent. Figure 20-6 shows a sample of the screen that selects those columns is shown in Figure 20-6. This screen is a lot like the sort screen. Highlight a column, and then press either the ADD BEFORE or ADD AFTER pushbutton to move it over. If a column is placed in the right-side screen by mistake, highlight it and press the REMOVE pushbutton. Notice that, through the use of the two add pushbuttons, columns are selected for output and their placement is also determined by the user.

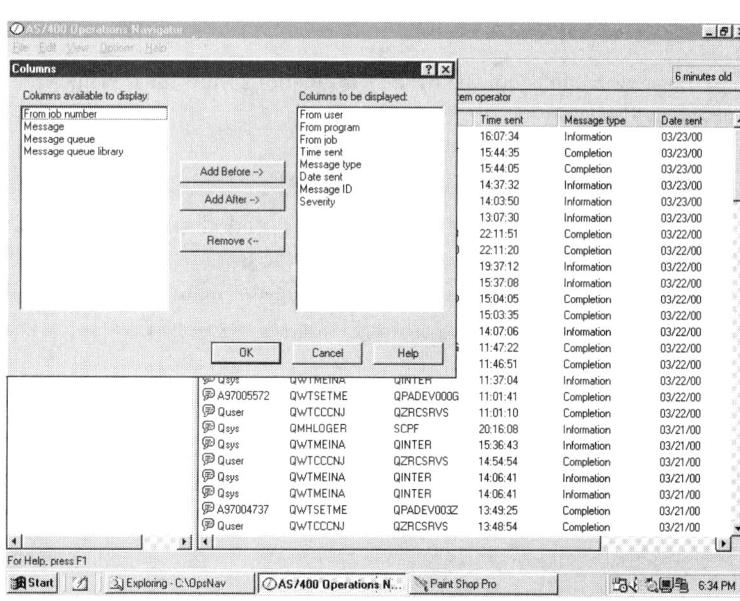

Figure 20-6: General function COLUMNS.

- FIND—Sometimes a WORK WITH command results in pages and pages of information. For example, jobs and printed output easily can become many pages. The FIND general function will help locate a particular entry from a long list. Access the general function FIND from the EDIT option on the APPLICATION menu or the EDIT icon on the context-sensitive toolbar. From EDIT, select the FIND action. A dialog box similar to that shown on Figure 20-7 will result. Enter the word or string that needs to be found on the SEARCH FOR box. Optionally, click on the checkbox to cause the search to go up or down from the current cursor position. Also, check that the FIND function is to matches the case or treat the search value as a complete word or as a string. Click on the FIND pushbutton when your are ready to execute the find. The result of the find will be a highlighted row on the right side of the screen.

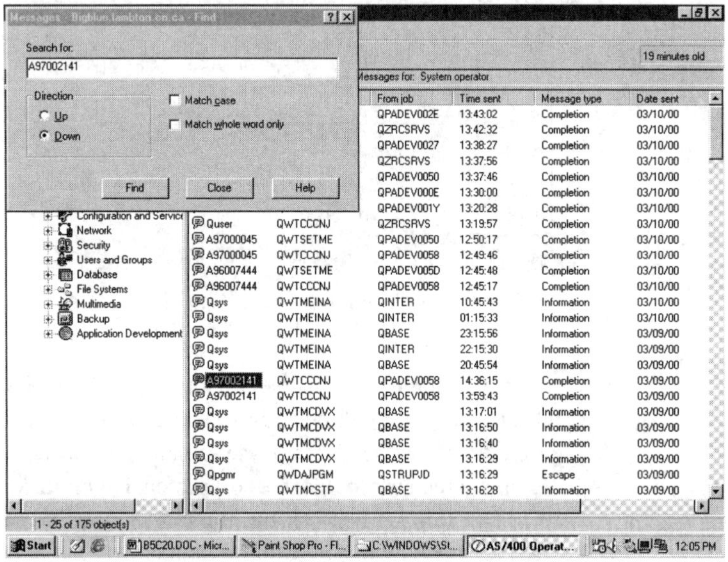

Figure 20-7: General function FIND.

BASIC OPERATIONS

Basic operations consist of the subfunctions Messages, Printer Output, and Printers.

Messages

Operations Navigator will help the user send, display, and manage AS/400 messages. To access this function, highlight MESSAGES on the BASIC OPERATIONS menu, right-click the mouse, and select the desired function from the pop-up menu. A sample of the SEND MESSAGE function is shown in Figure 20-8.

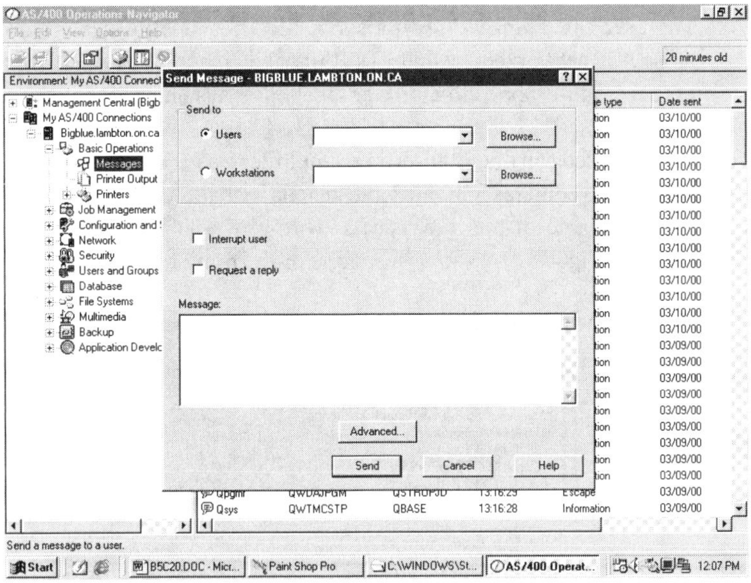

Figure 20-8: SEND MESSAGE dialog box.

The addressee can be selected by clicking on the appropriate radio button: USERS or WORKSTATIONS. Either USERS or WORKSTATIONS can be named. Within the name boxes, there are appropriate drop-down values for multiple addressees. One example is for USERS, where the message can be addressed to "All signed on users."

Under addressees, the user can (by clicking on checkboxes) select whether the message is to interrupt the addressee(s) and whether the addressee(s) should reply to the message. A large box under the heading MESSAGE is where the actual text of the message should be entered. Click on the SEND pushbutton to complete sending the message.

Printer Output

The Printer Output function allows the user to work with AS/400 spooled files. This includes information (unless the user limits the information displayed via the Columns general function) such as:

- *Output name*—The name of the spool file.
- *User*—The user who owns the spool file.
- *Status*—The status of the spool file.
- *Printer*—If any writer is assigned to the output queue, it will appear on this report.
- *Pages per copy*—The total number of pages to be printed.
- *Copies left*—Number of copies of the spool file to be printed.
- *Time created*—The time the spool file was created.
- *Date created*—The date the spool file was created.

When the desired spool file is located, double-click on it to display the contents on the workstation screen.

The user can *drag-and-drop* a spool file from one printer to another. If there are two or more AS/400s networked, using TCP/IP and having LPR/LPD running, spool files may be dragged-and-dropped to a printer on another system.

The user also can drag-and-drop a spool file to a PC printer. When this action is done, a copy of the spool file's contents is created and an icon to that file is created on the workstation. The user should note the name of this file, start a word-processing program, and open the file for editing and printing. Figure 20-9 shows a sample of the printer output subfunction.

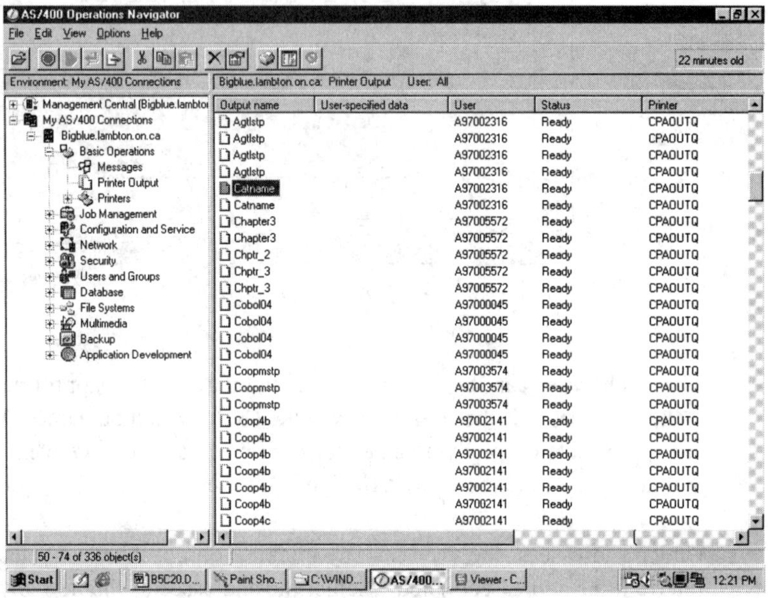

Figure 20-9: Working with printer output.

Printers

The user can work with printer queues, stop, start, hold, or release a printer through the printer's subfunction. Printers can be shared on the AS/400 through AS/400 NetServer. Shared printers are indicated on the printer subfunction with a hand icon near the bottom of the printer icon.

If AS/400 NetServer is up, non-shared printers can be made shareable by selecting the SHARING icon and the NEW SHARE activity from the context menu of a printer. Figure 20-10 shows a sample of the printer subfunction.

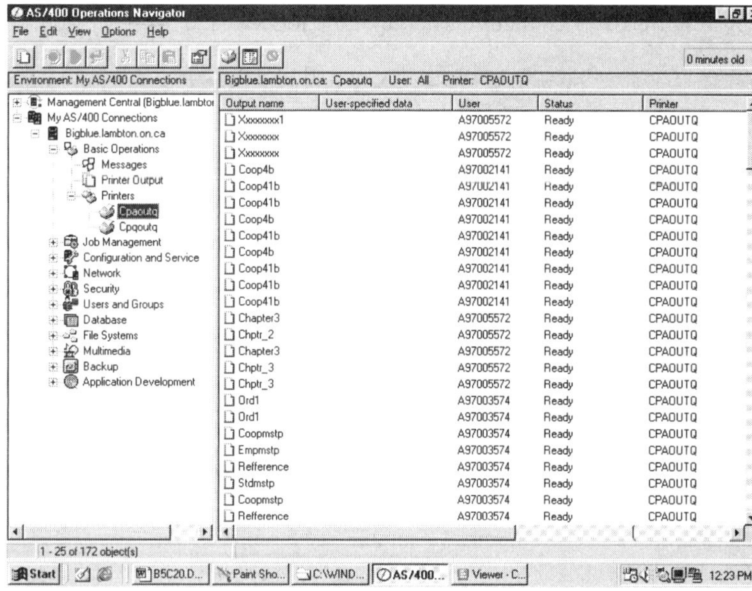

Figure 20-10: Working with printers.

JOB MANAGEMENT

Along with printer output and printers, job management is one of the functions you probably will use the most. The job management functions involve two types of jobs: jobs and *server jobs*. Most of what an operator will deal with are the plain, ordinary jobs. There are a few server jobs, such as AS/400 NetServer, and job management will help you work with them.

Working with jobs is one function that will almost always produce a lot of output. Be sure to make use of the general functions to limit or control this output. By highlighting and right-clicking on any job, the user can:

- Display the job's printed output (if any).
- Display the job's job log (if any).
- Reply to messages (if any).
- Hold the job.
- Release the job.
- Move the job to another job queue.
- Delete the job.
- Display the properties of the job.

Figure 20-11 contains a sample of the job-management function.

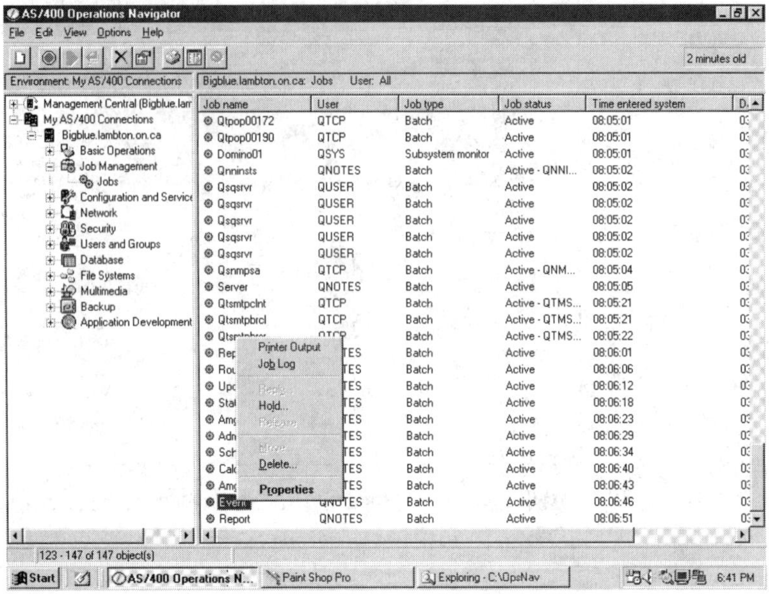

Figure 20-11: Working with jobs.

CONFIGURATION AND SERVICE

The Configuration and Service function will produce a screen of either hardware or software inventory of the system. Figure 20-12 contains a sample of the hardware inventory.

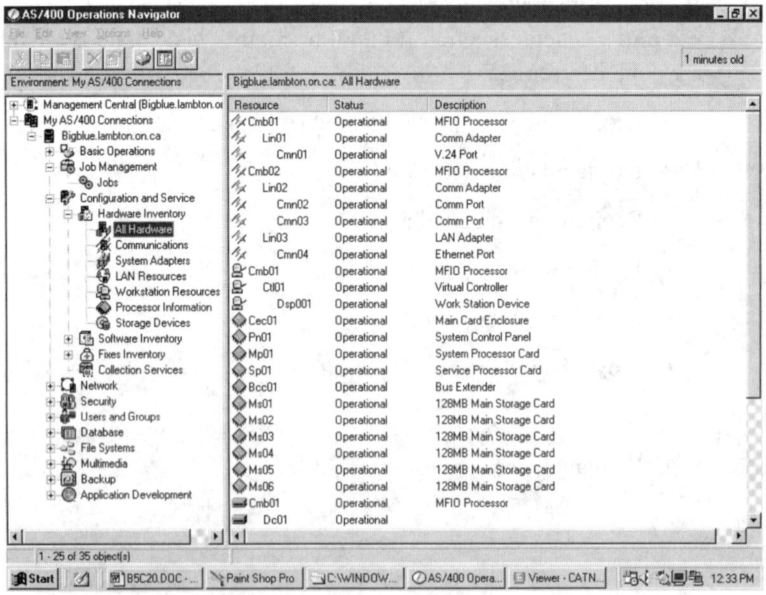

Figure 20-12: Hardware inventory.

All hardware can be selected or more focused displays can be requested based on just communication, system adapters, LAN resources, workstation resources, processor information, or storage devices.

By highlighting and double-clicking on any hardware device, the user can see a pop-up dialog box that shows detailed information about the device. Figure 20-13 shows a sample of this dialog box.

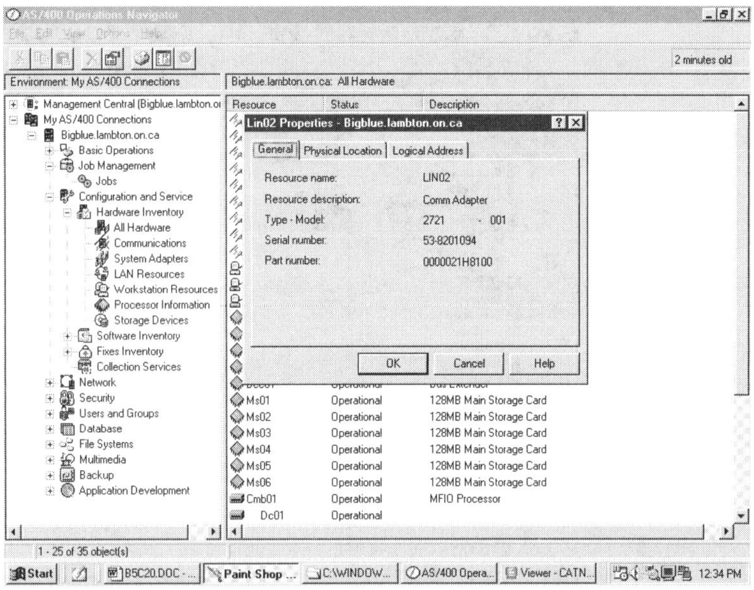

Figure 20-13: Hardware inventory with details in a dialog box.

Figure 20-14 contains a sample of the display of AS/400 software inventory.

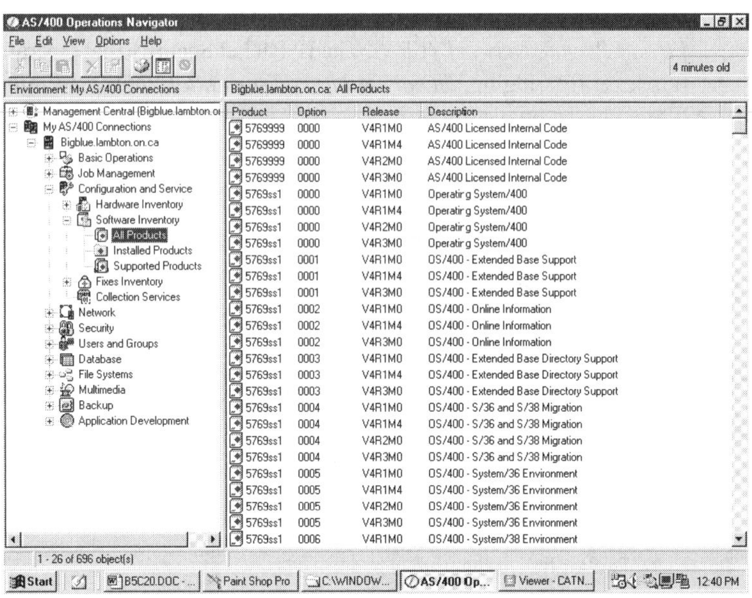

Figure 20-14: Software inventory.

NETWORK

The network function of Operations Navigator provides considerable support. These network functions include working with TCP/IP configuration, working with "wizards" for other protocols, setting up security, managing AS/400 network servers, and so on. Figure 20-15 indicates the capability of Operations Navigator's network subfunctions.

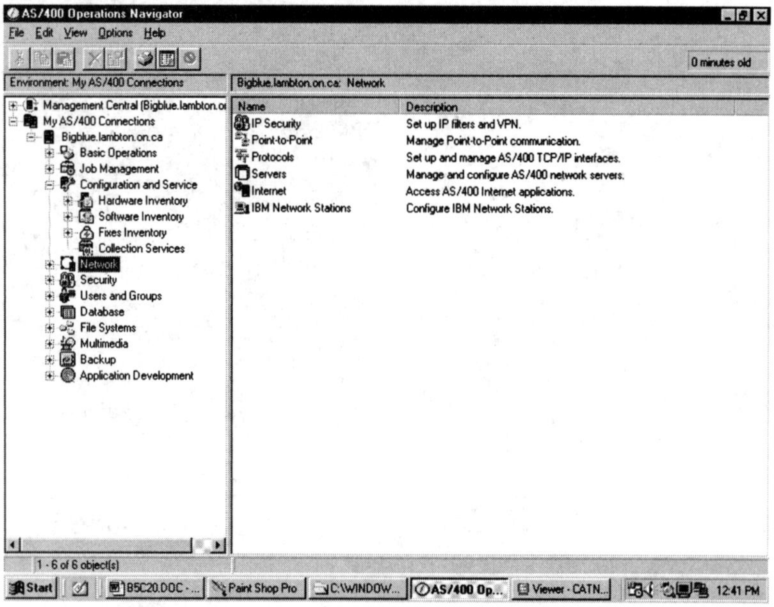

Figure 20-15: Network subfunctions of Operations Navigator.

Under the first subfunction (IP Security), Operations Navigator can set up *IP Packet Security* or *Virtual Private Network (VPN)*. The IP Packet Security that Operations Navigator sets up is either IP packet filtering or *Network Address Translation (NAT)*. Within the former, IP packets can be filtered based on:

- Source IP address.
- Destination IP address.
- Source port.
- Destination port.
- Protocol (TCP, TCP/Starting, UDP, ICMP).
- Direction (inbound, outbound, or both).
- System interface.
- Packet fragments.

NAT allows the public to use a public address, and that address is translated into the actual private address when messages are received. In this way, the public never knows the actual address of the AS/400.

Under the second subfunction, Point-to-Point, Operations Navigator creates and manages a *point-to-point protocol (PPP)* and *Serial Line Internet Protocol (SLIP)*, using PPP. Under PPP, Operations Navigator offers another subfunction (MODEMS) that provides the capability to work with modem settings. The modems can be standard modems or *Integrated Services Digital Network (ISDN)*.

The third Operations Navigator subfunction is Protocols. This subfunction allows the user to configure, start, ping, display status, and stop TCP/IP on the AS/400. Also, TCP/IP properties (such as addresses) can be displayed.

The fourth Operations Navigator subfunction, Servers, allows the user to configure and manage TCP/IP and Client Access servers. AS/400 NetServer can be started and stopped using this subfunction. Also, configuration wizards are in place to help the user configure TCP/IP *Domain Name Servers (DNS)* and *Dynamic Host Configuration Protocol (DHCP)*. Additionally, jobs associated with a server can be listed.

The fifth Operations Navigator subfunction, Internet, allows the user to configure and manage an Internet application server from the Web browser. It will configure the following three items:

- Firewall.
- IBM HTTP Server for AS/400.
- Digital ID.

The last subfunction, IBM Network Stations, allows the user to configure and manage any or all of the IBM Network Stations using the Web browser.

SECURITY

A wizard assists in managing AS/400 security. Highlight the Security function and right-click your mouse. This starts a security wizard that asks a series of questions. The answers to those questions are then analyzed and applied against the security actually in place on the AS/400. From that analysis, two reports—one for administrators and one for users—are generated. From these reports, showing the current security settings, and naming the desired security settings, the system operator may elect to make changes to the AS/400 security configuration.

In addition to the security wizard, the Security function provides the capability to work with authorization lists. The user can create new authorization lists or modify users and permissions on existing lists.

Finally, the Policies subfunction of Security allows the user to set system-level auditing control. By double-clicking on AUDIT POLICY, the system will activate auditing of specific actions such as object creating/deletion. Object auditing will track users who access one or more objects.

USERS AND GROUPS

The Users and Groups function allows you to work with all users and their groups on the system. User profiles can be dragged-and-dropped to create a duplicate on another networked system. Users also can be just as easily dropped into new groups.

DATABASE

Database helps the user create and maintain databases. There are three that Operations Navigator supports:

- Libraries.
- ODBC Data Sources.
- SQL Performance Monitors.

Probably, the one database that means the most to AS/400 people is Libraries. Figure 20-16 contains a sample of Operations Navigator displaying libraries.

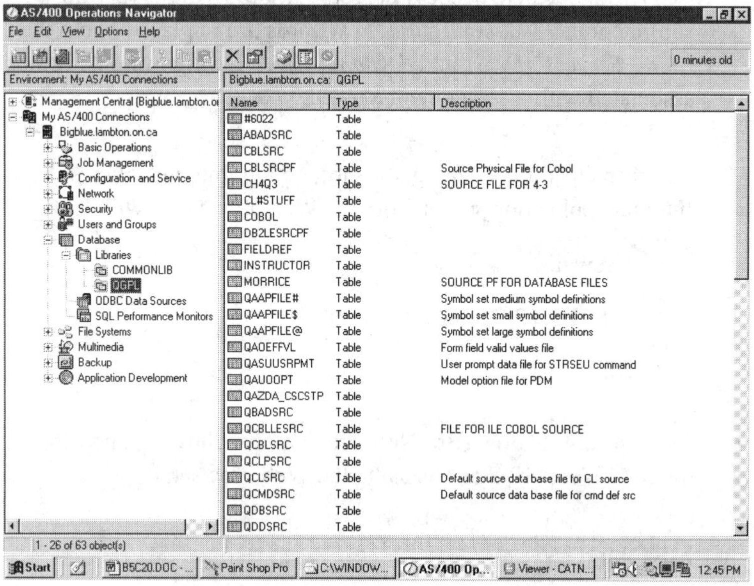

Figure 20-16: Displaying libraries with Operations Navigator.

With this subfunction, a user can display all libraries, create new libraries, and create new tables within libraries. A *QUICK VIEW option* allows the contents of tables to be easily viewed.

SQL statements can be created, run, debugged and saved with the SQL Performance Monitors subfunction.

FILE SYSTEMS

The File Systems function of Operations Navigator allows the user to perform many functions on the different file systems the AS/400 supports. The available file systems that are supported are:

- NFS—*Network File System*, which provides the user with access to data/objects stored on a remote NFS server.
- QDLS—Document library services provides access to documents and folders on the AS/400.
- QFileSvr.400—Provides access to other file systems that reside on remote but networked AS/400s.
- QLANSrv—OS/2 Warp server for AS/400 file server.

- QNetWare—Provides access to local or remote Novell Netware 4.10 or 4.11 data. It also provides access to PC servers running Novell Netware 3.12, 4.10, 4.11, or 5.0.
- QNTC—Windows NT Server file system. The user can access data residing on a Windows NT Server.
- QOpenSys—Access UNIX-based files such as POSIX and XPG.
- QOPT—Optical file system that supports optical devices.
- QSYS.LIB—Traditional AS/400 libraries.
- "root"—The most basic file system and similar to DOS or OS/2 files.
- UDFS—User Defined File System this resides on the user's Auxiliary Storage Pool (ASP).

The Operations Navigator file systems function allows the user to get to these file systems and:

- Create, rename, delete, and make folders sharable.
- Copy files into a folder.
- Drag-and-drop files and folders from one AS/400 to another or to a PC.
- Set up security to these file systems.

MULTIMEDIA

If *Ultimedia System Facilities (USF)* is installed on the AS/400, a user can use this function to create, copy, share, or delete multimedia objects.

BACKUP

The operator can schedule daily, weekly, or monthly backups on the AS/400 with this Operations Navigator function. Figure 20-17 shows a sample of the backup screen generated by double-clicking on "Monthly."

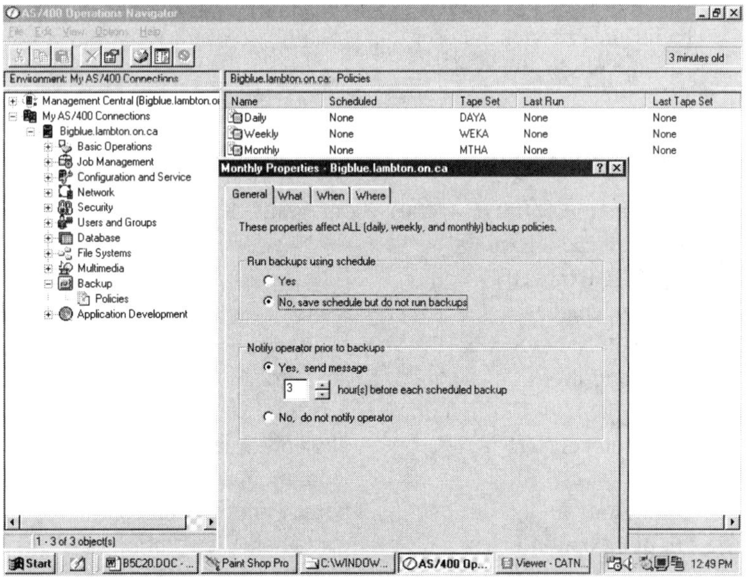

Figure 20-17: Backup properties in Operations Navigator.

APPLICATION DEVELOPMENT

The AS/400 provides Unix APIs for C/C++ programmers to use in their programming. The objects used for communication and sharing between programs are known as *Interprocess Communication (IPC)* objects. A user can use this function of Operations Navigator to display the states and properties of the IPC objects created by one of those programs. The function also can delete the states and properties if the programs fails to do so. There are three types of IPC objects supported by this function:

- Kernel Message Queues.
- Semaphore Sets.
- Shared Memory.

PLUG-IN SUPPORT

Plug-ins are custom tools and applications added to folders and objects. Plug-in support allows Operations Navigator users to work with these plug-ins.

FUNCTION AVAILABILITY

As is mentioned at the beginning of this chapter, some Operations Navigator functions might not be available. The function availability option displays the reasons functions are missing.

END-OF-CHAPTER AIDS

CHAPTER SUMMARY

Operations Navigator provides another easy path into the OS/400 command structure. It might not be for the experienced user, but it is a fine tool for those new to the AS/400 who quickly need to become productive.

KEY TERMS

Client Access/400 (CA/400)
Client Access Express (CA/Express)
display emulator
Domain Name Server (DNS)
drag-and-drop
Dynamic Host Configuration Protocol (DHCP)
event
event log
Explore option Fixes
Integrated Services Digital Network (ISDN)
Interprocess Communications (IPC)
IP Packet Security
Network Address Translation (NAT)
Network File System (NFS)
Operations Navigator
point-to-point protocol (PPP)
Quick View option
Serial Line Internet Protocol (SLIP)
server job
threshold
trigger
Ultimedia System Facilities (USF)
value added reseller (VAR)
Virtual Private Network (VPN)

CHAPTER SELF-TEST

Solutions to these self-test questions are in appendix D.

True-False Questions

___ 1. There is a separate set of commands used with Operations Navigator.

___ 2. Operations Navigator is a component of Client Access Express. It is installed on the local PC.

___ 3. PTFs can't be applied using Operations Navigator.

___ 4. When sending a message in the break mode using Operations Navigator, the user would select the check box to 'Interrupt user.'

___ 5. You use configuration and services to work with hardware and software on your system.

___ 6. You would use the configuration and services functions to work with the TCP/IP configuration.

___ 7. Security function allows you to work with authorization lists.

Fill in the Blanks

1. The _________ option of Operations Navigator is similar to the command line and can be used to issue commands.
2. Using the ______________ functions allows you to rearrange the order of the fields in the right window.
3. The Basic operations consist of the following: _________________, _______________, and ___________________.
4. To send an Inquiry message, a user would select the __________________ option on the Send message pop-up menu.
5. Through Operations Navigator job management you can work with two types of jobs: ____________ and ___________________.
6. _________________ is an example of a server job.
7. The ________________ subfunction of Security allows the user to set system-level auditing control.
8. __________________ allows the user to view the contents of a database file.

Chapter Review Questions

1. What must be active to share printers?
2. Identify some of the major functions you can perform using Operations Navigator?
3. What functions are allowed for user profiles?
4. How does Operation Navigator help to support databases?
5. What types of file system functions are available through Operations Navigator?

APPENDIX A

AS/400 KEYBOARD

When most of us think of the computers that we use today, we think of doing interactive movements: sitting at a keyboard, interacting with a program. Actually, this is a fairly new process that the personal computer made popular; before that, mainframes and other midrange computers specialized in batch processing. An AS/400 can have thousands of workstations connected to it at any time.

The IBM 3x line of computers has excelled in interactive programming support since the days of the System/34. That's another convenient quality about the line, but it also has produced a quirk. It took personal computers and LANs until about 1986 before they were able to serve as desktop workstations connected to a minicomputer. The terminals used before PCs came along were pretty much the same, but they did a couple things in a unique way.

The old terminals that the 3x line supported were known by their protocol (the rules they used to communicate to the host), which was 5250. Although the AS/400 today will connect to any industry standard protocol, you still see and hear of 5250. The keyboard of the 5250 dumb terminal had a layout similar to today's microcomputer keyboard, but it included some additional keys not found on the microcomputer keyboard.

Chief among these was the Field Exit key. When you see an AS/400 interactive screen, you'll see one or more areas in which to put data. You'll also see a cursor that lets you know where the next key you press will appear. If you are typing in the middle of a field and press the plain old Tab key, the cursor will go to the start of the next input field. The letters or numbers you keyed in the previous field will stay where you left them, probably with spaces to the right of where you pressed the Tab key. However, if you press the Field Exit key, the cursor would again advance to the next input field, but the data you had typed would automatically drag to the right of the field and either zero- or space-fill on the left—depending on whether the field is for numbers only or letters. This is a feature that is very nice for data entry. It also means that you should know which key on the PC keyboard is acting as the Field Exit key.

Another feature of the old 5250 terminal is the use of the F-keys (Function keys). These are on most PC keyboards; there are twelve across the top. Most of the time, their use is the same from program to program on the AS/400. The active F-keys are also usually documented at the bottom of the AS/400 screen. However, their use is not set in stone, and they do not have to be documented. Remember, applications programs, even very sophisticated ones, are written by humans and for one reason or another, F-key assignments may change, or they may not always be shown at the bottom of the screen. The lesson is: Know your application!

Figure A-1 contains the AS/400 keyboard template used when connecting a microcomputer to an AS/400. The first column lists the most common functions used with a 5250 terminal. The second column identifies the keystrokes necessary to emulate the original 5250 terminal when connecting a microcomputer to an AS/400.

Keyboard Mapping For 5250 Emulation	
Desired Function	5250 Emulation
Operational Assistant (ASSIST) Menu	Esc key
Backspace	
Delete	Delete key
Error Reset	Left Ctrl key
Field Backspace	Shift + Tab
Field Exit	Right Ctrl key
Field Minus	Pad Minus (-) key
Field Plus	Pad Plus (+) key
Help	F1
Hot Key Function	Alt + Esc
New Line	Shift + Enter
Print AS/400 Screen	Shift + Print Screen
System Request	Alt + Print Screen
F1 through F12	F1 through F12
F13	Shift + F1
F14	Shift + F2
F15	Shift + F3
F16	Shift + F4
F17	Shift + F5
F18	Shift + F6
F19	Shift + F7
F20	Shift + F8
F21	Shift + F9
F22	Shift + F10
F23	Shift + F11
F24	Shift + F12

Figure A-1: AS/400 5250 keyboard template.

COMMON ENGRAVED KEYS

Many of the engraved keys found on a microcomputer keyboard perform the same functions when the microcomputer is used in 5250 emulation mode. Generally, each of these keys performs a single function:

- The Caps Lock key is used to place the entire keyboard, except for the number keys, in an uppercase mode. To get out of uppercase mode, simply press the Caps Lock key again. A key that performs a function in this manner is called a toggle key; it allows you to turn a mode on and off.
- The Delete key is used to delete the character in the cursor position.
- The Insert key allows you to insert characters into a field on the screen. Each character that is inserted moves the characters following the inserted characters in the field one position to the right. Pressing the key a second time takes you out of the insert mode and back to overtype. The Insert key is a toggle key similar to the Caps Lock key.
- The Page Up and Page Down keys are called the Roll keys and are used to move the display up or down to show additional information on the display screen. When `More...` is shown in the lower-right corner of the display, you can use the Page Down key (Roll Up key) to move toward the end of the information. When `Bottom` is shown, you have reached the end of the information. Similarly, use the Page Up key (Roll Down key) to move toward the top of the information.
- The Shift key is used to put the alphabetic keys into uppercase (capital) letters. It has two other special functions as well that will be discussed in the next section.

DISTINCT AS/400 KEYS

The following keys have special meaning when used in the 5250 emulation mode on the AS/400:

- The Field Advance key (Tab) moves the cursor to the start of the next field. If the cursor is located in the first position of a field when the Field Advance key (Tab) is pressed, the cursor will "jump" over the field and move to the first position of the next field. If the next field is not shown on the screen, the display rolls forward to the next field, and the cursor moves to the first position of that field.
- The Field Back-Tab key (Shift + Tab keys) moves the cursor back one field to the previous field on the screen. If the previous field is not shown on the screen when the Field Back-Tab key is pressed, the display rolls backward to the previous field, and the cursor moves to the first position of that field.
- The Field Exit key (Right Ctrl key) moves the cursor to the next field on the screen. This key is different from the Field Advance key (Tab key) in that any characters at and to the right of the cursor in the field where you were keying are deleted, and the ones to the left are right-adjusted and zero- or space-filled on the left. When the Field Exit key is used after entering data into a numeric field, the data is right-justified and zero-filled. When pressed after entering data into an alphanumeric field, the data is left-justified and padded with blanks.
- The Enter key is used to transmit the data on the screen to the AS/400 CPU. The Enter key is not used to move from one field to the next while entering data on the screen. Instead, either the Field Exit key or the Field Advance key (Tab key) is used for this function. It is important that you do not press the Enter key until you are sure all the values for fields on the screen

have been entered. Pressing the Enter key instead of the Field Exit key may prematurely submit the data you are entering.

- The Error Reset key (Left Ctrl key) is used to reset or correct a keyboard error. An example of a keyboard error is when you try to key into a protected area of the screen. When an error such as this occurs, a message will appear on the last line of the screen, and the keyboard will lock. The Error Reset key must be pressed to unlock the keyboard before the error can be corrected.
- The Help key (F1) will show you additional information about the display you are using, about messages you have received, or about other problems that might happen. For example, if you receive a message from the operating system that you do not understand, place the cursor on the message and press F1 (Help) for help information about the message.
- The Hot key (Alt + Esc keys) allows you to toggle between the AS/400 screen and the DOS prompt.
- The New Line key (Shift + Enter keys) allows you to move down the display screen one line at a time, rather than moving from field to field.
- The End key moves the cursor to the end of the data on the line where the cursor is located.
- The Print key (Shift + Print Screen) is used to print the information currently shown on the screen. Normally, when you press the Print key, the screen information is put on an output queue and printed at a later time. A message is shown and the Error Reset key must be pressed to unlock the keyboard.

USING FUNCTION KEYS ON THE AS/400

The Function keys are the top row of keys that are labeled F1 through F12 and are normally referred to as F keys. There are twenty-four function keys that can be used with the AS/400 computer system. To use F1 through F12, press the Function key that corresponds to the number you want to use. To use F13 through F24:

1. Press and hold the Shift key.
2. Press the Function key that corresponds to the number you want to use. For example, to press F13, hold down the Shift key and press the F1 key. For F14, hold down the Shift key and press the F2 key. F24 is used by holding down the Shift key and pressing F12.

Normally, not all Function keys are active at the same time. Active or not active means that the program may or may not be set up to respond to them. The Function keys that are active are usually shown at the bottom of the display screen along with a brief description of their functions.

Function keys could have different meanings depending on the program running at the time. Although different Function keys are shown on the different displays and menus, there are a few standard keys:

- The F1 (Help) key provides online help information. The AS/400 provides context-sensitive help information that is related to the field or area where the cursor is located on the screen. When displaying help, the F2 key allows you to display extended help.
- The F3 (Exit) key is used to end the current function and return you to the screen from which the current function was started.

- The F4 (Prompt) key provides assistance when entering data. When the cursor is on a field and F4 is pressed, a prompt screen appears from which the user can select a particular value for a field. It also is used to display a fill-in-the-blanks screen when entering a line containing several fields of data.
- The F5 (Refresh) key removes any data you have keyed into the display screen since the last time the Enter key was pressed. It not only removes changes you made, but it also displays all of the original values that appeared on the display screen.
- The F9 (Retrieve) key displays, on the command line, the last command that was entered on the command line. It also displays any parameters that were entered with the command. By repeatedly pressing F9, the system retrieves previously entered commands, going back one command with each press of F9.
- The F12 (Cancel) key cancels the current screen and returns to the previous menu or display. It can be easily confused with the Exit key (F3), which is used to end the current function.
- The F16 (System Main Menu) key returns to the AS/400 Main Menu.
- The Home key displays the menu that was shown after you signed on the system.
- The F24 (More) key is shown when a screen has more active Function keys than can be shown in the space provided at the bottom of the screen. In such cases, you will see that one of the active Function keys is F24 (More). A list of additional active Function keys will replace the current list of active Function keys when you press the F24 key (Shift + F12). The F24 key may have to be pressed more than once to display all the active Function keys available.

APPENDIX **B**

SYSTEM VALUES (ALPHABETICAL ORDER)

System Value	Description	Parameters: Values
QABNORMSW	Previous end-of-system indicator	0=Normal
		1=Abnormal
QACGLVL	Accounting level	*JOB Job resource use is written to a journal.
		*NONE Accounting information is not written to a journal.
		*PRINT Spooled and printer file resource use is written to a journal.
QACTJOB	Initial number of active jobs	1-32,767
QADLACTJ	Additional number of active jobs	1-32,767
QADLSPLA	Spooling control block additional storage	1,024-32,767
QADLTOTJ	Additional number of total jobs	1-32,767

System Value	Description	Parameters: Values
QALWOBJRST	Allow object restore option	*ALL All objects are restored regardless of security-sensitive attributes.
		*NONE Objects with security-sensitive attributes are not restored.
		*ALWYSSTT Programs with the system state attribute are restored.
		*ALWPGMADP Programs with the adopt authority attribute are restored.
QALWUSRDMN	Allow user domain objects in libraries	Name of libraries that can contain user domain user objects.
QASTLVL	User assistance level	*BASIC
		*INTERMED
		*ADVANCED
QATNPGM	Attention program	*NONE
		*ASSIST
		Library/program name
QAUDCTL	Auditing control	*AUDLVL
		*OBJAUD
QAUDENDACN	Auditing end action	*NOTIFY
		*PWRDWNSYS
QAUDFRCLVL	Force auditing data	*SYS
		1-100
QAUDLVL	Security auditing level	*SECURITY
		*AUTFAIL
		*DELETE
		*OBJMGT
		*CREATE
		*SAVRST
		*SPLFDTA
		*SYSMGT
		*SERVICE
		*PGMADP
		*JOBDTA
QAUTOCFG	Autoconfigure devices	0=Off
		1=On

System Value	Description	Parameters: Values
QAUTORMT	Autoconfigure of remote controllers	0=Off
		1=On
QAUTOSPRPT	Automatic system disabled reporting	0=Off
		1=On
QAUTOVRT	Autoconfigure virtual devices	0-32,500 or *NOMAX
QBASACTLVL	Base storage pool activity level	1-32,767
QBASPOOL	Base storage pool minimum size (sizes in KB)	256-2,147,483,647
QBOOKPATH	Book and bookshelf search path for books. Default: /QDLS/QBKBOOKS/BOOKS	Directories to be searched.
QCCSID	Coded character set identifier	1-65,535
QCHRID	Graphic character set and code page	Character ID: 1-32,767
		Code page: 1-32,767
QCHRIDCTL	Character identifier control	Character ID: 1-32,767
		*DEVD
		*JOBCCSID
QCMNRCYLMT	Communications recovery limits	Recovery limit attempts: 0-99
		Time interval in minutes: 0-120
QCNTRYID	Country identifier	Country abbreviation
QCONSOLE	Console name	Device description
QCRTAUT	Create default public authority	*CHANGE
		*ALL
		*USE
		*EXCLUDE
QCRTOBJAUD	Create object auditing	*NONE
		*USRPRF
		*CHANGE
		*ALL
QCTLSBSD	Controlling subsystem	Library/subsystem name
QCURSYM	Currency symbol	Character
QDATE	System date	Date (refer to QDATFMT, next, for format)

System Value	Description	Parameters: Values
QDATFMT	Date format	YMD
		MDY
		DMY
		JUL
QDATSEP	Date separator	Numeric code:
		1=/
		2=-
		3=.
		4=,
		5=Blank
QDAY	Day	1-31
QDBRCVYWT	Database recovery wait indicator	0=Do not wait
		1=Wait
QDECFMT	Decimal format	1=Blank (Period for decimal, zero suppression)
		2=J (Comma for decimal, one leading zero)
		3=I (Comma for decimal, zero suppression)
QDEVNAMING	Device naming conventions	*NORMAL
		*S36
		*DEVADR
QDEVRCYACN	Device I/O error action	*MSG
		*DSCMSG
		*DSCENDRQS
		*ENDJOB
		*ENDJOBNOLIST
QDSCJOBITV	Time interval in minutes before disconnected jobs end	*NONE
		5-1,440
QDSPSGNINF	Sign-on display information control	0=Do not display
		1=Display

System Value	Description	Parameters: Values
QDYNPTRADJ	Dynamic priority adjustment. Only in effect for AS/400e models with QSYNPTRSCD set to "1."	0=Interactive jobs' priorities will not be changed. 1=Interactive jobs' priorities will be changed.
QDYNPTYSCD	Dynamic priority scheduler. Automatically adjusts job priorities.	0=Off
		1=On
QFRCCVNRST	Force conversion on restore	0=Off
		1=On
QHOUR	Current hour of the day	Hour (0-23)
QHSTLOGSIZ	Maximum history log records	1-32.767
QIGC	DBCS version installed indicator	0=Not installed
		1=Installed
QIGCCDEFNT	Double byte code font	Library/font name
QIGCFNTSIZ	Double byte coded font point size	
QINACTITV	Inactive job timeout (minutes)	*NONE
		5-300
QINACTMSGQ	Inactive job message queue	*ENDJOB
		*DSCJOB
		Library/message queue name
QIPLDATTIM	Date and time to automatically IPL	*NONE
		IPL date: MM/DD/YY
		IPL time: HH:MM:SS
QIPLSTS	IPL status indicator	0=Operator panel IPL
		1=Auto-IPL after power is restored
		2=Restart IPL
		3=Time of day IPL
		4=Remote IPL
QIPLTYPE	Type of IPL to perform	0=Unattended IPL
		1=Attended IPL with dedicated service tools
		2=Attended IPL, console in debug mode

System Value	Description	Parameters: Values
QJOBMSGQFL	Job message queue full action	*NOWRAP
		*WRAP
		*PRTWRAP
QJOBMSGQMX	Maximum size in MB of job message queue	8-64
QJOBMSGQSZ	Job message queue initial size (in KB)	1-16,384
QJOBMSGQTL	Job message queue maximum initial size (in KB)	1-16,384
QJOBSPLA	Spooling control block initial size(in bytes)	3,516-32,767
QKBDBUF	Type ahead and/or attention key option	*TYPEAHEAD
		*YES
		*NO
QKBDTYPE	Keyboard language character set	Language/country abbreviation
QLANGID	Language identifier	Language abbreviation
QLEAPADJ	Leap year adjustment	0-3
QLMTDEVSSN	Limit device sessions	0=Do not limit
		1=Limit
QLMTSECOFR	Limit security officer device access	0=Do not limit
		1=Limit
QLOCALE	Locale path name	*NONE
		Locale path name
QMAXACTLVL	Maximum activity level of system	*NOMAX
		2-32,767
QMAXSGNACN	Action to take for failed sign-on attempts	Numeric code:
		1=Disable device
		2=Disable profile
		3=Disable device and profile
QMAXSIGN	Maximum sign-on attempts allowed	*NOMAX
		1-25
QMCHPOOL	Machine storage pool size(in KB)	256-2,147,483,647
QMINUTE	Current minute of the hour	Minute (00-59)
QMODEL	Current system model number	System model number

System Value	Description	Parameters: Values
QMONTH	Current month of the year	Month (1-12)
QPFRADJ	Automatic performance adjustment	0=No adjustment
		1=Adjustment at IPL
		2=Adjustment at IPL and automatic adjustment
		3=Automatic adjustment
QPRBFTR	Problem log filter	Library/name of problem log filter
QPRBHLDITV	Problem log hold interval	0-999
QPRCFEAT	Processor feature	Four-character processor feature code
QPRCMLTTSK	Processor multitasking	0=Multitasking is off
		1=Multitasking is on
QPRTDEV	Printer device description	Name
QPRTKEYFMT	Print header and/or border information	*PRTHDR
		*PRTBDR
		*PRTALL
		*NONE
QPRTTXT	Print text	Text
QPWDEXPITV	Password expiration interval in days	*NOMAX (passwords don't expire)
		1-366
QPWDLMTAJC	Limit adjacent digits in password	0=Adjacent digits OK
		1=Adjacent digits not OK
QPWDLMTCHR	Limit characters in password	*NONE
		Characters not allowed
QPWDLMTREP	Limit repeating characters in password	0=Can be repeated
		1=Cannot be repeated
		2=Cannot be repeated consecutively
QPWDMAXLEN	Maximum password length	1-10
QPWDMINLEN	Minimum password length	1-10
QPWDPOSDIF	Limit password character positions	0=Can be the same
		1=Cannot be the same
QPWDRQDDGT	Require digit in password	0=Not required
		1=Required

System Value	Description	Parameters: Values
QPWDRQDDIF	Duplicate password control	Numeric code:
		0=Duplicates allowed - or - cannot be the same as any in the last
		1=32 passwords
		2=24 passwords
		3=18 passwords
		4=12 passwords
		5=10 passwords
		6=8 passwords
		7=6 passwords
		8=4 passwords
QPWDVLDPGM	Password validation program	*NONE
		Library/program name
QPWRDWNLMT	Maximum time in seconds for PWRDWNSYS *IMMED	0-32,767
QPWRRSTIPL	Automatic IPL after power restored	0=Not allowed
QRCLSPLSTG	Days to reclaim spool storage	*NONE
		*NOMAX
		1-366
QRMTIPL	Remote power on and IPL	0=Not allowed
		1=Allowed
QRMTSIGN	Remote sign-on control	*FRCSIGNON
		*SAMEPRF
		*REJECT
		*VERIFY - or - library/remote session sign-on program
QRMTSRVATR	Remote service attribute	0=Off
		1=On
QSCPFCONS	IPL action with console problem	0=End IPL
		1=Unattended IPL
QSECOND	Current second of the minute	Second (0-59)

System Value	Description	Parameters: Values
QSECURITY	System security level	10=Physical security only
		20=Password security only
		30=Password and object security
		40=Password, object, and operating system integrity
		50=Password, object, and enhanced operating system integrity (C2)
QSETJOBATR	Set job attributes from locale	*NONE - or - job attributes option
QSFWERRLOG	Software error logging	*LOG
		*NOLOG
QSPCENV	Special environment	*NONE
		*S36
QSRLNBR	System serial number	System serial number
QSRTSEQ	Sort sequence	Library/name
		*HEX
		*LANGIDUNQ
		*LANGIDSHR
QSRVDMP	Service dump control	*DMPUSRJOB
		*DMPSYSJOB
		*DMPALLJOB
		*NONE
QSTRPRTWTR	Start print writers at IPL	0=Do not start
		1=Start
QSTRUPPGM	Startup program	*NONE
		Library/name
QSTSMSG	Display status messages	*NONE
		*NORMAL
QSVRAUTITV	Server authentication interval in minutes	1-108,000
QSYSLIBL	System part of the library list (can be many entries)	Sequence/library name
QTIME	Current time of day	Time in HH:MM:SS format

System Value	Description	Parameters: Values
QTIMSEP	Time separator	Numeric code:
		1=:
		2=.
		3=,
		4=Blank
QTOTJOB	Initial total number of jobs	1-32,767
QTSEPOOL	Time slice end pool	*NONE
		*BASE
QUPSDLYTIM	Uninterruptible power supply delay time in seconds	*CALC
		*BASIC
		*NOMAX
		0-99,999
QUPSMSGQ	Uninterruptible power supply message queue	Library/message queue name
QUSRLIBL	Default user part of the library list	Sequence/library (may be many)
QUTCOFFSET	Coordinated universal time offset	-24:00 to +24:00
QYEAR	Current year	Year (0-99)

APPENDIX C

SYSTEM VALUES (FUNCTIONAL ORDER)

TABLE C-1: CHARACTER SETS/LANGUAGES

System Value	Description	Parameters
QCCSID	Coded character set identifier	1-65,535
QCHRID	Graphic character set and code page	Character ID: 1-32,767
		Code page: 1-32,767
QCHRIDCTL	Graphic character set/code page control	*DEVD *JOBCCID Code page: 1-32,767
QCNTRYID	Country identifier	Country abbreviation
QCURSYM	Currency symbol	Character
QDECFMT	Decimal format	1=Blank (Period for decimal, zero suppression)
		2=J (Comma for decimal, one leading zero)
		3=I (Comma for decimal, zero suppression)

TABLE C-1: CHARACTER SETS/LANGUAGES (*continued*)

System Value	Description	Parameters
QIGC	DBCS version installed indicator	0=Not installed
		1=Installed
QIGCCDEFNT	Double byte code font	Library/font name
QIGCFNTSIZ	Double byte code font size (in points)	*NONE 000.1 – 999.9
QKBDBUF	Type ahead and/or attention key option	*TYPEAHEAD
		*YES
		*NO
QKBDTYPE	Keyboard language character set abbreviation	Language/country
QLANGID	Language identifier	Language abbreviation

TABLE C-2: DATE/TIME

System Value	Description	Parameters
QDATE	System date	Date (refer to QDATFMT, next, for format)
QDATFMT	Date format	YMD
		MDY
		DMY
		JUL
QDATSEP	Date separator	Numeric code:
		1=/
		2=-
		3=.
		4=,
		5=Blank
QDAY	Day	1-31
QHOUR	Current hour of the day	Hour (0-23)
QLEAPADJ	Leap year adjustment	0-3
QMINUTE	Current minute of the hour	Minute (00-59)
QMONTH	Current month of the year	Month (1-12)
QSECOND	Current second of the minute	Second (0-59)
QTIME	Current time of day	Time in HH:MM:SS format
QTIMSEP	Time separator	Numeric code:
		1=:
		2=.
		3=,
		4=Blank
QUTCOFFSET	Coordinated universal time offset	-24:00 to +24:00
QYEAR	Current year	Year (0-99)

TABLE C-3: DISASTER

System Value	Description	Parameters
QABNORMSW	Previous end-of-system indicator	0=Normal
		1=Abnormal
QAUTOSPRPT	Automatic system Disabled reporting	0=Off
		1=On
QCMNRCYLMT	Communications recovery limits	Recovery limit attempts: 0-99
		Time interval in minutes:
		0-120
QDBRCVYWT	Database recovery wait indicator	0=Do not wait
		1=Wait
QDEVRCYACN	Device I/O error action	*MSG
		*DSCMSG
		*DSCENDRQS
		*ENDJOB
		*ENDJOBNOLIST

TABLE C-4: IPL

System Value	Description	Parameters
QIPLDATTIM	Date and time to automatically IPL	*NONE or IPL date: MM/DD/YY
		IPL time: HH:MM:SS
QIPLSTS	IPL status indicator	0=Operator panel IPL
		1=Auto-IPL after power is restored
		2=Restart IPL
		3=Time of day IPL
		4=Remote IPL
QIPLTYPE	Type of IPL to perform	0=Unattended IPL
		1=Attended IPL with dedicated service tools
		2=Attended IPL, console in debug mode
QPWRDWNLMT	Maximum time in seconds for PWRDWNSYS *IMMED	0-32,767
QPWRRSTIPL	Automatic IPL after power restored	0=Not allowed
QRMTIPL	Remote power on and IPL	0=Not allowed
		1=Allowed
QSCPFCONS	IPL action with console problem	0=End IPL
		1=Unattended IPL
QSTRPRTWTR	Start print writers at IPL	0=Do not start
		1=Start
QSTRUPPGM	Startup program	*NONE
		Library/name

TABLE C-5: MISCELLANEOUS

System Value	Description	Parameters
QACGLVL	Accounting level	*JOB Job resource use is written to a journal.
		*NONE No accounting information is written to a journal.
		*PRINT Spooled and printer file resource use is written to a journal.
QBOOKPATH	Book and bookshelf search path	Directories to be searched for books. Default: /QDLS/QBKBOOKS/BOOKS
QLOCALE	Locale path name	*NONE
		Locale path name
QMODEL	Current system model number	System model number
QPRCFEAT	Processor feature	System processor feature
QRMTSRVATR	Remote service attribute	0=Off
		1=On
QSETJOBATR	Set job attributes from locale	*NONE - or -job attributes option
QSPCENV	Special environment	*NONE
		*S36
QSRLNBR	System serial number	System serial number
QSRTSEQ	Sort sequence	Library/name
		*HEX
		*LANGIDUNQ
		*LANGIDSHR
QSRVDMP	Service dump control	*DMPUSRJOB
		*DMPSYSJOB
		*DMPALLJOB
		*NONE
QSTSMSG	Display status messages	*NONE
		*NORMAL
QUPSDLYTIM	Uninterruptible	*CALC
	power supply delay	*BASIC
	time in seconds	*NOMAX
		0-99,999
QUPSMSGQ	Uninterruptible power supply message queue	Library/message queue name

TABLE C-6: PROBLEM REPORTING

System Value	Description	Parameters
QPRBFTR	Problem log filter	Library/name of problem log filter
QPRBHLDITV	Problem log hold interval	0-999
QSFWERRLOG	Software error logging	*LOG

TABLE C-7: SECURITY

System Value	Description	Parameters
QALWOBJRST	Allow object restore option	*ALL All objects are restored regardless of security-sensitive attributes.
		*NONE No objects with security- sensitive attributes are restored.
		*ALWYSSTT Programs with the system state attribute are restored.
		*ALWPGMADP Programs with the adopt authority attribute are restored.
QAUDCTL	Auditing control	*AUDLVL
		*OBJAUD
QAUDENDACN	Auditing end action	*NOTIFY
		*PWRDWNSYS
QAUDFRCLVL	Force auditing data	*SYS
		1-100
QAUDLVL	Security auditing level	*SECURITY
		*AUTFAIL
		*DELETE
		*OBJMGT
		*CREATE
		*SAVRST
		*SPLFDTA
		*SYSMGT
		*SERVICE
		*PGMADP
		*JOBDTA
QALWOBJRST	Allow object restore option	*ALL All objects are restored regardless of security-sensitive attributes.
		*NONE No objects with security- sensitive attributes are restored.
		*ALWYSSTT Programs with the system state attribute are restored.
		*ALWPGMADP Programs with the adopt authority attribute are restored.
QCRTAUT	Create default public authority	*CHANGE
		*ALL
		*USE
		*EXCLUDE

TABLE C-7: SECURITY (*continued*)

System Value	Description	Parameters
QCRTOBJAUD	Create object auditing	*NONE
		*USRPRF
		*CHANGE
		*ALL
QDSCJOBITV	Time interval in minutes before disconnected jobs end	*NONE
		5-1,440
QDSPSGNINF	Sign-on display information control	0=Do not display
		1=Display
QFRCCVNRST	Force conversion on restore	0=Off
		1=On
QINACTITV	Inactive job timeout (minutes)	*NONE
		5-300
QINACTMSGQ	Inactive job message queue	*ENDJOB
		*DSCJOB
		Library/message queue name
QLMTDEVSSN	Limit device sessions	0=Do not limit
		1=Limit
QLMTSECOFR	Limit security officer device access	0=Do not limit
		1=Limit
QMAXSGNACN	Action to take for failed sign-on attempts	Numeric code:
		1=Disable device
		2=Disable profile
		3=Disable device and profile
QMAXSIGN	Maximum sign-on attempts allowed	*NOMAX
		1-25
QPWDEXPITV	Password expiration interval in days	*NOMAX (passwords don't expire)
		1-366

TABLE C-7: SECURITY (*continued*)

System Value	Description	Parameters
QPWDLMTCHR	Limit characters in password	*NONE
		Characters not allowed
QPWDLMTREP	Limit repeating characters in password	0=Can be repeated
		1=Cannot be repeated
		2=Cannot be repeated consecutively
QPWDMAXLEN	Maximum password length	1-10
QPWDMINLEN	Minimum password length	1-10
QPWDPOSDIF	Limit password character positions	0=Can be the same
		1=Cannot be the same
QPWDRQDDGT	Require digit in password	0=Not required
		1=Required
QPWDRQDDIF	Duplicate password control	Numeric code:
		0=Duplicates allowed - or - cannot be the same as any in the last 1=32 passwords
		2=24 passwords
		3=18 passwords
		4=12 passwords
		5=10 passwords
		6=8 passwords
		7=6 passwords
		8=4 passwords
QPWDVLDPGM	Password validation program	*NONE
		Library/program name
QRMTSIGN	Remote sign-on control	*FRCSIGNON
		*SAMEPRF
		*REJECT
		*VERIFY - or - library/remote session
		sign-on program

TABLE C-7: SECURITY (*continued*)

System Value	Description	Parameters
QSECURITY	System security level	10=Physical security only
		20=Password security only
		30=Password and object security
		40=Password, object, and operating system integrity
		50=Password, object, and enhanced operating system integrity (C2)
QSVRAUTITV	Server authentication interval in minutes	1-108,000

TABLE C-8: SPOOL FILE CONTROL

System Value	Description	Parameters
QADLSPLA	Spooling control block additional storage	1,024-32,767
QJOBSPLA	Spooling control block initial size (in bytes)	3,516-32,767
QRCLSPLSTG	Days to reclaim spool storage	*NONE
		*NOMAX
		1-366

TABLE C-9: SYSTEM CONFIGURATION

System Value	Description	Parameters
QALWUSRDMN	Allow user domain objects in libraries	Name of libraries that can contain user domain user objects
QASTLVL	User assistance level	*BASIC
		*INTERMED
		*ADVANCED
QATNPGM	Attention program	*NONE
		*ASSIST
		Library/program name
QAUTOCFG	Autoconfigure devices	0=Off
		1=On
QAUTORMT	Autoconfigure of remote controllers	0=Off
		1=On

TABLE C-9: SYSTEM CONFIGURATION (*continued*)

System Value	Description	Parameters
QAUTOVRT	Autoconfigure virtual devices	0-32,500 or *NOMAX
QCONSOLE	Console name	Device description
QCTLSBSD	Controlling subsystem	Library/subsystem name
QDEVNAMING	Device naming conventions	*NORMAL
		*S36
		*DEVADR
QHSTLOGSIZ	Maximum history log records	1-32,767
QJOBMSGQFL	Job message queue full action	*NOWRAP
		*WRAP
		*PRTWRAP
QJOBMSGQMX	Maximum size in MB of job message queue	8-64
QJOBMSGQSZ	Job message queue initial size (in KB)	1-16,384
QJOBMSGQTL	Job message queue maximum initial size (in KB)	1-16,384
QPRTDEV	Printer device description	Name
QPRTKEYFMT	Print header and/or border information	*PRTHDR
		*PRTBDR
		*PRTALL
		*NONE
QPRTTXT	Print text	Text
QSYSLIBL	System part of the library list (can be many entries)	Sequence/library name
QUSRLIBL	Default user part of the library list	Sequence/library (may be many)

TABLE C-10: PERFORMANCE

System Value	Description	Parameters
QBASACTLVL	Base storage pool activity level	1-32,767
QBASPOOL	Base storage pool minimum size (sizes in KB)	256-2,147,483,647
QDYNPTYADJ	AS/400e only, if QDYNPTYSCD is on. Determines if interactive jobs will have their priorities adjusted	0=No Adjustment 1=Adjusted
QDYNPTYSCD	Enables dynamic priority scheduling	0=Dynamic priority scheduling off 1=Dynamic priority scheduling on.
QMAXACTLVL	Maximum activity level of system	*NOMAX
		2-32,767
QMCHPOOL	Machine storage pool size (in KB)	256-2,147,483,647
QPFRADJ	Automatic performance adjustment	0=No adjustment 1=Adjustment at IPL 2=Adjustment at IPL and continuously thereafter 3=Continuously after IPL
QTOTJOB	Initial total number of jobs	1-32,767
QTSEPOOL	Time slice end pool	*NONE
		*BASE
		*NOLOG

TABLE C-11: WORK MANAGEMENT

System Value	Description	Parameters
QACTJOB	Initial number of active jobs	1-32,767
QADLACTJ	Additional number of active jobs	1-32,767
QADLTOTJ	Additional number of total jobs	1-32,767
QBASACTLVL	Base storage pool activity level	1-32,767
QBASPOOL	Base storage pool minimum size (sizes in KB)	256-2,147,483,647
QMAXACTLVL	Maximum activity level of system	*NOMAX
		2-32,767
QMCHPOOL	Machine storage pool size (in KB)	256-2,147,483,647
QTOTJOB	Initial total number of jobs	1-32,767
QTSEPOOL	Time slice end pool	*NONE
		*BASE
		*NOLOG

APPENDIX D

ANSWERS TO CHAPTER SELF-TEST QUESTIONS

CHAPTER 1: BACKGROUND OF THE AS/400

TRUE-FALSE QUESTIONS

1. T
2. F
3. F
4. F
5. F
6. T
7. T
8. T

Fill in the Blanks

1. Application system
2. Multiuser
3. Multitasking
4. RISC

5. Above
6. EDCDIC
7. operating system

CHAPTER 2: NAVIGATING AROUND THE AS/400

True-False Questions

1. T
2. F
3. T
4. T
5. F
6. T
7. T

Fill in the Blanks

1. F11
2. entry panel
3. help
4. System Request
5. InfoSeeker
6. put cursor on message and press F1

CHAPTER 3: OS/400 COMMAND STRUCTURE AND CONTROL LANGUAGE

True-False Questions

1. T
2. T
3. F
4. F
5. T
6. F
7. T

Fill in the Blanks

1. F4
2. Call QCMD
3. Control Language
4. positional notation (positional parameters)
5. special values
6. keyword

CHAPTER 4: OBJECTS, LIBRARIES, AND LIBRARY LISTS

True-False Questions

1. T
2. F
3. F
4. F
5. T
6. F
7. F
8. T
9. T

Fill in the Blanks

1. QSYS
2. Lock enforcement
3. QUSRLIB
4. QTEMP
5. libraries in the library list
6. ADDLIBLE, RMVLIBLE

CHAPTER 5: MESSAGE HANDLING

True-False Questions

1. F
2. F
3. T
4. T
5. T
6. T
7. F

Fill in the Blanks

1. break
2. impromptu
3. system
4. inquiry
5. DSPMSG *SYSOPR
6. informational
7. message file
8. 60 or greater

CHAPTER 6: HANDLING SPOOLED FILES AND PRINTING FUNCTIONS

True-False Questions

1. F
2. T
3. F
4. T
5. F
6. F
7. T

Fill in the Blanks

1. output queue
2. will not
3. released
4. +15
5. B
6. F16
7. CHGSPLFA
8. STRPRTWTR

CHAPTER 7: MANAGING DEVICES

True-False Questions

1. F
2. T
3. F
4. T
5. F
6. T
7. T

Fill in the Blanks

1. device description
2. *ACTIVE
3. ASP
4. QAUTOCFG
5. MOVOBJ and CRTDUPOBJ
6. CRTDEVPRT

CHAPTER 8: STARTING AND STOPPING THE AS/400

True-False Questions

1. T
2. T
3. F
4. F
5. T
6. F

Fill in the Blanks

1. unattended
2. manual
3. QIPLTYPE
4. license key or license authorization code
5. WRKSYSSTS
6. PWRDWNSYS *IMMED

CHAPTER 9: OPERATING SYSTEM, LICENSED PROGRAM PRODUCTS, AND PTFs

True-False Questions

1. T
2. T
3. F
4. F
5. T
6. F
7. F

Fill in the Blanks

1. multitasking
2. QSECOFR and QLPINSTL
3. GO LICPGM
4. loaded, applied
5. HIPERs
6. SF98410, SF99410
7. DSPPTF *ALL

CHAPTER 10: BACKUP AND RECOVERY

True-False Questions

1. F
2. F
3. T
4. T
5. F
6. T
7. T
8. F

Fill in the Blanks

1. SAVLIB, Target Release
2. Checkpoint, Checkpoint image
3. system configuration, security objects
4. RSTOBJ
5. RSTOBJ
6. Logical files

CHAPTER 11: SECURITY AND SECURITY SYSTEM VALUES

True-False Questions

1. F
2. F
3. T
4. F
5. T
6. T
7. T

Fill in the Blanks

1. user-based
2. *SAVSYS, *JOBCTL
3. *IOSYSCFG
4. user, group
5. object
6. Public, *USE
7. *USE
8. QLMTDEVSSN, 0
9. QINACTITV, 30
10. QMAXSGNACN

CHAPTER 12: WORKING WITH JOBS

True-False Questions

1. T
2. T
3. F
4. T
5. F
6. F
7. T

Fill in the Blanks

1. workstation
2. 123456/Alincoln/Payroll
3. job class
4. job description
5. priority
6. hold
7. job scheduler

CHAPTER 13: SUBSYSTEMS

True-False Questions

1. T
2. F
3. T
4. F
5. T
6. F
7. T
8. T
9. F

Fill in the Blanks

1. 256KB
2. QMCHPOOL, QBASPOOL
3. MAXACTLVL
4. routing entry
5. job description, routing table/entry, job class
6. QSYS/QCMD

CHAPTER 14: WORK MANAGEMENT AND PERFORMANCE

True-False Questions

1. F
2. T
3. T
4. T
5. T
6. F
7. F
8. T
9. F
10. T
11. T

Fill in the Blanks

1. workstation, job queue
2. ADDJOBQE
3. communication
4. ADDCMNE
5. QBASE, QCTL
6. WRKACTJOB
7. F16
8. 50, 20
9. user, system
10. base
11. MAX ACT
12. pool size
13. base

CHAPTER 15: LOGS AND CLEANUP

True-False Questions

1. F
2. F
3. T
4. F
5. F
6. T
7. T
8. T
9. F
10. T

Fill in the Blanks

1. messages
2. workstation
3. second
4. QSYSOPR or System operator
5. QSYSMSG, QSYS
6. QHSTLOGSIZ
7. DSPLOG
8. job description
9. receiver, journal, QACGLVL
10. system operator, security officer

CHAPTER 16: BASIC TROUBLESHOOTING, PROBLEM SOLVING, AND USING ELECTRONIC CUSTOMER SUPPORT

True-False Questions

1. F
2. T
3. T
4. T
5. F
6. T
7. T
8. F
9. F

Fill in the Blanks

1. UPS
2. varied on
3. WRKWTR
4. WRKCFGSTS
5. QSYSOPR, history
6. ANZPRB

CHAPTER 17: JOURNALING

True-False Questions

1. F
2. T
3. F
4. T
5. F
6. F
7. T
8. T
9. F
10. F
11. T
12. F

Fill in the Blanks

1. Journal, journal receiver (either order)
2. threshold
3. SAVLIB, SAVOBJ, SAVCHGOBJ
4. Journal receiver, journal
5. MNGRCV, *SYSTEM
6. Omit journal entries (OMTJRNE), record image (IMAGES) (either order)
7. Physical files, access paths
8. WRKJRNA
9. Receiver chain
10. V4R2

CHAPTER 18: COMMUNICATIONS: SNA, APPC, AND APPN

True-False Questions

1. F
2. T
3. F
4. T
5. T
6. F
7. T
8. T
9. T
10. F

Fill in the Blanks

1. 5250 or Twin-ax
2. end node or peripheral node
3. System Network Architecture (SNA)
4. Distributed Data Management (DDM)
5. CA/400
6. propagation delay
7. device description
8. DSPNETA
9. vary it on
10. Opticonnect/400

CHAPTER 19: COMMUNICATIONS: LANS AND TCP/IP

True-False Questions

1. T
2. F
3. F
4. T
5. F
6. T
7. T
8. T
9. F
10. T

Fill in the Blanks

1. local
2. resource name
3. adapter
4. Service Access Points (SAP)
5. Multistation Access Unit (MAU)
6. duplex
7. Carrier Sense Multiple Access with Collision Detection (CSMA/CD)
8. Device Attachment (DA)
9. Domain Name Server (DNS)

CHAPTER 20: OPERATION NAVIGATOR

True-False Questions

1. F
2. T
3. F
4. T
5. T
6. F
7. T

Fill in the Blanks

1. Run
2. Columns
3. messages, printer output, printers
4. request a reply
5. jobs, server jobs
6. Netserver
7. policies
8. Quick view

GLOSSARY

activity level

The number of jobs in a subsystem that the system will allow to be active at one time.

adopted authority

A security feature where a running program takes on the authority of the program creator instead of the program user.

advanced peer-to-peer communications (APPC)

The protocol for communicating between two AS/400s.

advanced peer-to-peer networking (APPN)

The protocol for most AS/400 network computing. LAN communication runs under APPN.

automatic mode

When an AS/400 is IPLed, it will come up automatically, without operator intervention (unless there is a problem).

authorities

In security, authorities are "permissions" for a person to access an AS/400 object.

authorization lists

A list of authorized users and their authorization level. This is a fast method of granting the same authorities to many objects.

base memory pool

Special shared memory pool that contains all unallocated memory available to all subsystems.

batch job

A program or set of commands that runs in the background in intervals and segments. It does not tie up a workstation while it runs. *See* interactive job; job.

bridged frame relay

A frame-relay network where the remote attachment is a bridge into a LAN.

broken chain

Journal receivers are sequentially numbered and should be accessed that way. A broken chain occurs when one or more receivers are missing.

Carrier Sense Multiple Access with Collision Detection (CSMA/CD)

The protocol used by Ethernet networks. Transmissions are made when the network thinks the line is not busy. If it detects another transmission made at the same time (a collision occurs), it will attempt to resend both after waiting a random amount of time.

channel service unit (CSU)

Half of the attachment device into a frame-relay network. *See* data service unit (DSU); CSU/DSU.

class-of-service

User-defined preferences for each link and node on a network. The AS/400 will take these preferences into consideration when routing network transmissions. The result should be transmission routing that the user prefers.

concentrator

A communication device that allows multiple devices to be used where one would normally be used. For example, a single wire may support one workstation. If a concentrator is attached to that wire, it may support up to seven workstations.

control points

Information kept on network node servers about the adjacent links and nodes. Used to calculate optimum routing of transmissions.

controller

A device to control sending and receiving information to DASD or workstations. Controllers are connected to IOPs.

data link connection identifier (DLCI)

A unique number to identify each permanent virtual circuit (PVC) on a frame-relay physical connection.

data service unit

Half of the attachment hardware into a frame-relay network. *See* data service unit (DSU); CSU/DSU.

data striping

AS/400's method of writing data to disk.

DDI network

Direct Data Interchange network protocol. Uses two counter-rotating rings.

destination service access points (DSAP)

The SAP of the remote (the receiving) computer. *See* service access points (SAP*)*; source service access points (SSAP).

device

Any apparatus connected to an AS/400 (printer, workstation, tape drive, etc.).

device attachment (DA) card

Used to connect remote workstations to a DDI network.

device configuration

The description and simple operating characteristics of a device.

direct frame relay

Frame relay consisting of two or more AS/400s running APPC/APPN.

domain name

In Internet addressing, the easy way of addressing a node.

DSU/CSU

The device used to attach into a frame-relay network. Think of the DSU/CSU as a modem.

end nodes

Nodes on a network that do not participate in routing transmissions beyond themselves. They can only send and receive their own transmissions.

Ethernet

A LAN that supports one of two standards: Ethernet Version 2 or the IEEE 802.3 standard. *See* Carrier Sense Multiple Access with Collision Detection CSMA/CD).

faulting

When the AS/400 is running a job and it unexpectedly finds a page missing from memory, it finds the page on disk and restores it. Usually a symptom of an out-of-capacity AS/400 or a poorly tuned one.

file A collection of records. *See* physical file; logical file.

frame handler (FH)

An intermediate (not end) node on a frame-relay network.

frame relay

A packet-switching protocol that is similar to X.25 that uses established data communications networks.

frame size

In frame relay, the size of each frame or packet that the network can handle.

general shared pools

A memory pool shareable among subsystems.

initial program load (IPL)

The AS/400 way of referring to bootstrapping the system.

interactive

AS/400 terminology for on-line.

Internet

A collection of networks for the public to use for business, recreation, reference, and other purposes.

interoperable

An IBM term referring to how shareable data between operating system releases are. If two releases are interoperable, saved data from one can be restored on another.

IOP (input-output processor)

The last piece of AS/400 communications equipment before the controller. Disk data being written goes through an IOP and then a DASD controller. Outgoing screen data goes through an IOP then a workstation controller.

job On an AS/400, a job is a program or set of programs run as a unit. When a user signs onto the system, he or she starts an interactive job that doesn't end until her or she signs off. *See* interactive jobs; batch jobs.

job queue

A queue—like a bank teller line—where jobs wait their turn to run.

journal identifier

A label put on a file that it is currently being journaled.

journal receiver

The repository for data being journaled (records before-images and after-images, file open and close, etc.).

journaling

A feature you turn on that records every operation against one or more files and many system operations. Great security and disaster-recovery tool.

list management rights

The capability to create, change, and delete authorization lists.

logical file

A file with no data; just a key index.

low-entry nodes

See end nodes.

machine pool

The memory pool reserved for machine tasks.

manual mode

When an AS/400 is IPLed, it will stop to give the operator a chance to do something before it is fully operational.

members

An AS/400 file can consist of one or more members, each one of which can be processed as a complete file. All AS/400 files contain at least one member.

memory pools

An amount of memory set aside for use by one or more subsystems.

native support

An indication that IBM supports something used by the AS/400, such as a communications protocol, without using emulation.

network node server

A network node capable of administering its own traffic, other traffic on the network, and transmissions to and from end nodes or low-entry nodes. Network nodes become network node servers through the Change Network Attributes (CHGNETA) command. Up to five network node servers are allowed per APPN application.

network nodes

Intelligent nodes on a network that not only send and receive their own transmissions, they can receive and reroute transmissions for other nodes. Network nodes build control-point information about the links and nodes attached to them.

network topology database

The aggregate knowledge about the network accumulated by all network nodes' control-point information. If a link or node goes down, adjacent network nodes will reconfigure this network topology database.

nodes

Devices that can send into and receive from the network.

normal mode

See automatic mode.

object

Everything on the AS/400 is an object. The object type determines what the object really is (for example, a file or a device).

object type

See object.

OS/400

The name of the AS/400 operating system.

out file

Many informational commands can send their output to physical files referred to as out files.

output queue

Output scheduled for a printer will wait in an output queue until it has a chance to be printed.

paging

Efficient use of memory by keeping seldom-used sections, or pages, on a disk until they are needed.

permanent virtual circuit (PVC)

In frame relay, a single physical cable can support up to 256 virtual circuits, each one of which is referred to as a permanent virtual circuit (PVC) and is identified by a data-link connection identifier (DLCI).

physical file

A file that actually contains records. *See* file; logical file.

physical interfaces

The connector used on network cabling.

pool

See memory pools.

pool identifier

In a subsystem, the relative number of the memory pools it will use.

preset address

The unique address assigned by the manufacturer to LAN adapter cards.

private pool

A memory pool dedicated to one subsystem that cannot be shared by other subsystems.

Program Temporary Fix (PTF)

An added feature or a solution to an operating-system problem. PTFs are released sporadically.

public authority

Permission for any user without specific authorization to access an object.

resource name

Used in the AS/400 for all LAN connections merely as an addressing method. A concatenation of the adapter and port of that adapter the object will use.

restricted state

An AS/400 with only the controlling subsystem (QCTL) active.

route addition resistance

A user can indicate a preference that the network should or should not use a particular route for transmissions.

route congestion

A way of indicating user preference of transmission routing. When APPN determines that a route is congested, it will start to route transmissions away from the congestion. APPN concludes that congestion happens when the link is 90 percent full. Users can lower the percentage-full number and can start routing away from the link sooner.

save file

A special file that contains the output from a save operation. You cannot use this file directly like others, but you can copy it to tape or restore it.

save-while-active

A special AS/400 feature that allows files to be saved while users are accessing them.

server node

See network server node.

service access points (SAP)

Simple, two-digit addressing used at the adapter level on an AS/400. These addresses can be assigned by the user, or the user can allow the AS/400 to assign them. *See* source service access points (SSAP); destination service access points (DSAP).

service providers

For Internet and frame-relay networks, companies provide access into the public-use networks. You will be a subscriber to them.

session

When an interactive user signs onto the system, he or she has created a session. Many terminals allow multiple sessions where the user can acquire another sign-on display and sign on again, creating a second session.

shared pool

Memory pools are shareable among subsystems.

SNA-direct connection

In frame relay, the SNA systems can connect directly to the frame handler.

source service access points (SSAP)

The SAP of the source (the sending) computer. *See* service access points (SAP); destination service access points (DSAP).

special authorities

Associated with a user profile to allow users—such as system operators—who don't have any access to some objects to work with objects and do routine system functions such as save and restore.

special IP addressing

In TCP/IP, some addresses (all bit ones or all bit zeros) take on special meaning.

special shared pools

Machine pools and base pools are set up by IBM. Customers have limited control over the pools.

specific authorities

The user profiles grant some authority to each object. Specific authorities reside with the objects.

spooled output file

Printed output from jobs or programs does not usually go directly to a printer on the AS/400. They are held as spooled output files until directed to an output queue to which a printer is attached.

storage pool

See memory pool.

subsystem

A runtime environment for specific types of jobs. All interactive jobs run in an interactive subsystem. All batch jobs run in a batch subsystem.

switched

Theoretically, a line is switched if devices attach by dialing up. However, with the AS/400's automatic configuration, any line or device unknown to the AS/400 can be configured as soon as its presence is detected. These lines/devices are referred to as switched.

symbols

In DDI networks, frame sizes are often referred to in double-byte or symbols.

TCP/IP

See transmission control protocol/Internet protocol.

terminal equipment (TE)

On frame-relay networks, the end AS/400s.

thrashing

The point where an AS/400 spends more time faulting and paging than it does working on jobs or programs. Usually, a symptom of a very out-of-capacity AS/400 or one that is very poorly adjusted.

Token-Ring

A LAN protocol that supports the IEEE 802.5 standard. A token—an object or message—passes data over a ring topology.

transceiver

On an Ethernet network, a device that connects any nodes into the cable.

transmission control protocol/Internet protocol (TCP/IP)

The standards allowing computers to exchange information. AS/400s and workstations can be connected with the TCP/IP protocol.

user Generally, the person working on a workstation attached to the AS/400 or receiving reports from the AS/400. However, in the AS/400, some tasks have their own pseudo user. For example, ODBC jobs typically are represented by their own user (who is not the person making the ODBC request).

user profile

A user is made known to the AS/400 through an object, called a user profile, which contains basic information about who the person is and what they are authorized to do on the system.

vary on/vary off

Essentially, you can turn devices on and off from any workstation attached to an AS/400. This is a soft turn on or off that is similar to, but not really the same as, switching mechanical switches on and off.

workstation

AS/400 terminology for a display station.

writer

AS/400 terminology for a printer.

INDEX

Note: boldface numbers indicate illustrations; (t) indicates a table.

Note: boldface numbers indicate illustrations; (t) indicates a table.

D

Note: boldface numbers indicate illustrations; (t) indicates a table.

J

K

L

Note: boldface numbers indicate illustrations; (t) indicates a table.

P

T

U

V

W

X